THE TIMES
Good University Guide 2011

John O'Leary

with
Patrick Kennedy
Dr Nicki Horseman

TIMES BOOKS

Published in 2010 by Times Books

HarperCollins Publishers
77–85 Fulham Palace Road
Hammersmith
London W6 8JB

www.harpercollins.co.uk

First published in 1993 by Times Books. Seventeenth edition 2010

© Times Newspapers Ltd 2010

The Times is a registered trademark of Times Newspapers Ltd

ISBN 978-0-00-735614-0

Patrick Kennedy and Dr Nicki Horseman have been lead consultants for Exeter Enterprises Limited, which has compiled the main university league table and the individual subject tables for this guide on behalf of *The Times* and HarperCollins.

Please see chapters 4 and 5 for a full explanation of the sources of data used in the ranking tables. The data providers do not necessarily agree with the data aggregations or manipulations appearing in this book and are also not responsible for any inference or conclusions thereby derived.

Project editor: Christopher Riches
Design, editorial and additional research: Edenside Computing Services Ltd

All rights reserved. No part of this publication may be reproduced, stored in a retrieval system or transmitted, in any form or by any means electronic, mechanical, photographing, recording or otherwise without the prior written permission of the publisher and copyright owners.

Printed and bound in Great Britain by Clays Ltd, St Ives plc.

FSC is a non-profit international organisation established to promote the responsible management of the world's forests. Products carrying the FSC label are independently certified to assure consumers that they come from forests that are managed to meet the social, economic and ecological needs of present and future generations.

Find out more about HarperCollins and the environment at
www.harpercollins.co.uk/green

Contents

About the Author   4

Acknowledgements   4

How to Use this Book   5

Introduction   7

1. What and Where to Study   15
2. Graduate Employment Prospects   32
3. Going Abroad to University   40
4. The Top Universities   47
5. The Top Universities by Subject   58
6. Making Your Application   187
7. The Cost of Studying   198
8. Finding Somewhere to Live   220
9. Sporting Opportunities   231
10. What Parents Should Do   244
11. Coming to the UK to Study   248
12. Oxbridge   259
13. University Profiles   294

   Colleges of Higher Education   536

   Index   538

About the Author

John O'Leary is a freelance journalist and education consultant. He was the Editor of *The Times Higher Education Supplement* from 2002 to 2007 and was previously Education Editor of *The Times*, having joined the paper in 1990 as Higher Education Correspondent. He has been writing on higher education for more than 30 years and was co-founder of what are now the QS World University Rankings. He now edits *Policy Review* and is the author of *Higher Education in England*, published in 2009 by the Higher Education Funding Council for England. He has a degree in politics from the University of Sheffield.

Acknowledgements

We would like to thank the many individuals who have helped with this edition of *The Times Good University Guide,* particularly Greg Hurst, Education Editor of *The Times*, and Patrick Kennedy and Dr Nicki Horseman, the lead consultants for Exeter Enterprises Limited, which has compiled the main university league table and the individual subject tables for this *Guide* on behalf of *The Times* and HarperCollins Publishers; to the members of *The Times Good University Guide* Advisory Group for their time and expertise: Josie Lewis-Gibbs, Planning Officer, Imperial College, London; Rona Smith, Senior Strategic Planner, University of Edinburgh; Sue Hybart, Director of Planning, Cardiff University; Fidelma Hannah, Director of Planning, Loughborough University; Christine Couper, Head of Planning and Statistics, University of Greenwich; and Janet Isaac, Head of Corporate Information, University of Plymouth; Simon Kemp and Jonathan Waller of HESA for their technical advice; Martin Ince, Laura Dixon, Laura Pitel and Adam O'Leary for their contributions to the book.

We also wish to thank the publishers of the QS World University Rankings and the Academic Ranking of World Universities for permission to reproduce some of their main league tables; Sodexo for permission to use material taken from the *Sodexo University Lifestyle Survey 2008* (a summary of the survey can be found on their website: **www.sodexo.co.uk**), the NatWest Bank for material taken from the *NatWest Student Living Survey 2009*, the Lloyds Banking Group for material taken from the *2009 Halifax Student Cost of Living Survey* and all the university staff who assisted in providing information for this edition.

How to Use this Book

The Times Good University Guide 2011 will help you to select the subject and university of your choice and to guide you through the whole process of getting to university. The answers to the questions below will help you to get the most out of the information we offer.

How do I choose a course?
- » The first half of chapter 1 provides advice on what you should consider when choosing a subject area and relevant courses within that subject.
- » The tables near the beginning of chapter 2 give details of the employment prospects for all major subjects.
- » Chapter 5 provides details for 62 different subject areas (as listed on page 60).
- » For each subject there is a league table that provides our assessment of the ranking of all universities offering courses in the particular subject area.
- » For each subject we also provide some background information, details of employment prospects and selected websites where you can find out more about the subject.
- » Specific advice for international students is given in chapter 11.

How do I choose a university?
- » The second half of chapter 1 provides advice on choosing a university.
- » If you are considering studying abroad, chapter 3 provides guidance and practical information.
- » Central is the main *Times* league table on pages 52–56. This ranks the universities by assessing their quality not just according to student satisfaction (drawn from the National Student Survey) but also through seven other factors, including research quality, the spending on services and facilities, and graduate employment prospects. This table gives an indication of the overall performance of each university.
- » The second half of the book contains two pages on each university, giving a general overview of the institution as well as data on student numbers, how to contact the university, the accommodation provided by the university, and the fees payable and the bursaries available.
- » In addition, chapter 9 provides information on sport and sporting facilities across all the universities.
- » For those considering Oxford or Cambridge, details of admission processes and of all the colleges can be found in chapter 12.
- » Specific advice for international students is given in chapter 11.

How do I apply?
- » Chapter 6 outlines the application procedure for university entry.
- » It starts by advising you on how to complete the UCAS application, and then takes you step-by-step through the process that we hope will lead to your university place for autumn 2011.
- » Specific information about applying to Oxford and Cambridge is given in chapter 12.

Can I afford it?
» Chapter 7 outlines the costs of studying at university (including the payment of fees) as well as sources of funds (including student loans, grants and bursaries).
» Chapter 8 provides advice on where to live while you are there.
» Accommodation charges for each university are given in the university profiles in chapter 13.

How will university enhance my career?
» The employment prospects and average starting salaries for the main subject groups are given in chapter 2.
» Universities are now doing more to increase the employability of their graduates. Some examples are given in chapter 2 – and check whether your chosen universities provide similar services.

How do I find out more?
» In each university profile (chapter 13) contact details are given (including e-mail addresses and websites), so you can obtain more information on any university you are interested in.
» At the end of each chapter, a selection of useful websites is given.
» A further listing (pages 536–37) provides contact details for Higher Education Institutes and Colleges that are not covered elsewhere within the book.
» *The Times Good University Guide* website **www.thetimes.co.uk/gug** will keep you up to date with developments throughout the year and contains further information and online tables.

Introduction

Higher education has never been so popular. Fuelled by the economic downturn and swollen by tens of thousands of repeat candidates who had failed to find places in the previous year, the pool of applicants to UK universities in 2010 is much larger than ever before. Universities have become used to coping with growth in the demand for places of 10 or even 20 per cent, but some had 50 per cent more applications. While this may have been the high-water mark in the demand for full-time degree places, there is no reason to think that the level of competition in 2011 will be significantly lower.

No one can predict the eventual impact of the downturn on the jobs market, but few good judges expect the outcome to be an economy in which a degree is less of an advantage than it has been in recent years. International surveys continue to show the salary premium enjoyed by UK graduates over those who choose not to go to university as among the highest in the world, and, with more and more jobs requiring a degree, the financial case for going to university remains compelling, in addition to the wider benefits of an undergraduate education.

Before long, this may have to be balanced against higher fees for UK and EU students. But it is unlikely that any increase beyond inflation will affect students beginning courses in 2011. The current review of fees and higher education funding in England will have reported before the deadline for applications for 2011–12, and it would be possible for the new Government to rush through legislation well before the start of the academic year. Any change will have to be agreed by both Houses of Parliament, however, and the further lead time needed to include new rates in university prospectuses makes an above-inflation increase unlikely before 2012, even if the political will exists to sanction one. Previous increases have never applied to those already enrolled on courses.

The spectre of higher fees in England, Wales and Northern Ireland may add to the pressure on places in 2011, however. Those who might otherwise take a year out after A levels, or postpone their re-entry into the education system, will not want to risk adding to the eventual cost. The same trend was evident in the year before top-up fees were introduced. This is yet another reason why choosing the right course at the right university will be vitally important this year.

The outlook for applicants

Previous editions of this *Guide* have asserted confidently that there would be a place somewhere in higher education for every qualified applicant who wanted one. Tens of thousands of candidates fail to secure a place each year, most either do not achieve the necessary entrance qualifications or change their mind about going to university. Last year was different and 2010 promises to be the same. The fact that 45,000 of last year's candidates reapplied in 2010 demonstrates that the shortage of places was real and that – despite the promise of more places this summer – even more prospective students will be disappointed this year.

There are reasons why the squeeze might not be quite so severe in 2011. The 18–20 age group, which still produces the largest numbers of applicants, will be in decline; there might be more alternative opportunities for young people if the economy continues to recover; and the experience of those who waited for a place after failing to win one in 2009 may discourage others from taking the same route this year. But these effects are likely to be marginal and the chances are that there will be fewer places available in 2011. Cuts in the higher education budget and the threat of fines for universities that over-recruit may produce even stiffer competition for places.

The good news from the bumper application figures in 2010 is that the demand for places is spread a little more evenly. Some of the universities at the top of the league tables had no more applicants than in 2009 and most saw only modest increases. The really big rises have been at universities in the lower reaches of our table, partly because the most substantial growth has been in nursing and art and design, which tend to be concentrated in the post-1992 institutions. The other factor has been the 45,000 "second-timers", many of whom have lowered their sights to ensure that they are not rejected again.

Of course, competition for places in universities at the top of the table was already intense. It will not be any easier to win a place at any of them in 2011, but at least the lesson of this year is that it should not be more difficult. The real change in 2010 was that many universities had to be selective for the first time – not, perhaps in every subject, but certainly in the popular areas. Those hoping to enter in 2011 will need to be aware of this new pattern of applications and to target their own accordingly.

One consequence may be that candidates give more serious consideration to an "insurance choice". Over recent years, the fashion has been for those aiming for the top universities to use up all five of their choices on courses with similar entry requirements, relying on UCAS Extra or Clearing for an alternative, if they ended up with a full set of rejections. In 2010, however – and quite possibly 2011 – the pressure on places is such that Clearing is likely to be much reduced. It would be unwise to rely on the availability of vacancies in the next tier of universities; much better to have a place in the bag at your insurance choice.

Many of those who are reapplying from the 2009 cohort undoubtedly had results that were good enough to have secured a place somewhere in the higher education system. They opted for a second run, rather than accept a place that was not all that they hoped for. Some will end up at universities that could have been their insurance choice in the first place. Applicants for courses beginning in 2011 do not need to lower their sights for their top choices, but they would do well to recognise that the world has changed and to be realistic about their other options.

Nor should applicants pin their hopes on the Adjustment Period, introduced last year to give those with better grades than their highest offer the chance to "trade up" to a more selective university. This opportunity exists for five days immediately after A-level results are published, but there is no obligation on universities to hold back places and many are full by then. Only 382 students out of 481,854 secured their place that way in 2009 and the figure could well be lower in 2010, given the squeeze on places and the pressure on universities not to over-recruit.

The other new factor for those who take A levels in 2010, which will almost certainly assume growing importance in 2011, is the A* grade. Only Cambridge chose to use the new grade for selection purposes in 2010, but many more universities have been considering it for the following year. Most are doing so reluctantly, having opposed its introduction by the Labour Government, but they feel that they cannot continue to ignore an opportunity to distinguish between the growing numbers achieving A grades. Some may follow Cambridge and require at least one A*, without nominating a particular subject. Candidates should look carefully at university prospectuses and websites to see exactly what the policy is because there will be no uniformity, even among the leading universities, in 2011.

Universities and league tables

League tables are seldom popular with those being measured. But the rankings at the heart of this *Guide* have stood the test of time, after 17 years of publication, and are quoted frequently by universities themselves and by those with an interest in higher education, both at home and abroad.

Indeed, favourable results invariably appear prominently on universities' websites. Professor David Eastwood, now the Vice-Chancellor of Birmingham University and chief executive of the Higher Education Funding Council for England at the time of its review of university rankings, reminded universities at a conference to discuss its findings that they often "deplore league tables one day and deploy them the next". He said the tables had become part of the higher education landscape and one of the sources to which prospective students would refer when choosing where and what to study.

Five universities have refused to release information for any newspaper league tables this year, although one (London Metropolitan) has since decided to end its boycott. Wolverhampton, the latest to join this group, says on its website that measures of its quality are available elsewhere – as they are, if you know where to look. But the way in which it quotes existing measures may help to explain why readers value the independent nature of guides such as this. Wolverhampton says, quite accurately, that it is among the top universities in the National Student Survey for the quality of its learning resources and access to specialist equipment, but it neglects to mention that it was 85th in the 2009 survey for overall satisfaction.

In any case, this *Guide* contains far more than league tables. There are chapters on choosing a course and a university, the application process, managing your money as a student, where to live and what to expect in terms of sport. There are two new chapters in this edition, on employment and on going abroad to study. There are also special sections for overseas applicants and for parents, as well as profiles of every university and Oxbridge college.

This year's trends

The applications boom of 2010 makes it hard to predict with any certainty where the peaks and troughs of demand will be in the coming year. At the time of writing, the volume of applications had levelled off somewhat as the deadline for courses in art and design passed, but it had still reached an unprecedented level, almost 17 per cent up on April 2009. Most universities and most subjects have enjoyed increased demand for places, but not all. Many vocational courses have seen a surge in popularity, but applicants were making their own judgments about the prospects for different areas of employment. Building courses were still struggling, for example, while computer science was enjoying a new lease of life.

Not surprisingly, given the economic picture, one discernible pattern appears to be continued growth in home-based study. The longstanding British preference for studying away from home had begun to reassert itself among those who can afford it, after a move in the opposite direction when top-up fees were introduced in 2006. Now, it may be that a change of culture will become established. Several of the big city post-1992 universities have seen the biggest growth in applications both in 2009 and 2010.

There is no consistent pattern of subject choices, however. For several years, students have been more conscious of the need for a marketable qualification to service growing levels of debt among graduates. But the initial rush away from pure academic subjects towards the vocational has not persisted. While some job-related degrees, including most branches of engineering, continue to prove attractive, subjects such as politics, with no direct link to employment, have again increased their popularity in 2010. Some subjects obviously have been affected by the recession, but prospective students seem to recognise that the majority of graduate jobs are open to any discipline.

What has not changed in 2010 is the growing tendency for UK students to remain within national borders. More Scots have applied to Scottish universities, where they no longer pay the graduate endowment; more Welsh are applying to study in Wales, although they no longer enjoy the advantage of reduced fees; and more English are chasing places at universities in England, with fewer looking further afield.

So far, top-up fees have seen a gradual increase in working-class participation in higher education, although far less than the Government was seeking. Indeed, the fee changes have not all been bad news for students: the requirement to pay fees of £1,000-plus upfront has gone and grants, bursaries and scholarships made available to bring down the cost for those from poor backgrounds. The institutional profiles in this year's *Guide* include a section detailing the (sometimes complex) arrangements at each university.

Finding a place

Despite the growing popularity of higher education, there will be a place somewhere in the UK higher education system in 2011 for the vast majority of candidates with the basic qualifications for a course at this level, whether those are A levels, Highers or relevant vocational qualifications. There were 1.3 applications per place in full-time higher education in every year of the 21st century until 2010, when it may reach 1.5 to the place. This is a significant change, but still far from impossible odds. More than 90 per cent of those with two A-level passes go on to higher education each year, and almost all of the remainder choose a different career path, rather than being rejected.

Commentators on higher education distinguish between "selecting universities" and "recruiting universities", but these labels underestimate the complexity of the choices facing today's applicants. Even now, there are very few universities where all the courses are heavily selective – there are simply not enough well-qualified candidates to go around in some subjects – and most so-called recruiting universities have areas in which they excel and can attract a strong field of applicants. This *Guide* uses the ratings of academics and students, plus entry standards and graduate employment rates, to differentiate between universities in 62 different subject areas.

When *The Times Good University Guide* first appeared almost 17 years ago, it helped to explode the myth that any British degree was as good as any other. Since then, the statistics behind the tables have confirmed significant variations in performance within British higher education. Employers distinguish between universities as well as individuals. The need to know the standing of a university, both as an institution and in the various subjects it offers, can only become more important as time goes on.

This year's tables

Unlike most of the rankings that have sprung up in recent years, *The Times Good University Guide* has maintained as much consistency as possible in the methods used to compare universities. The indicators and weightings used in the overall ranking of universities are the same as last year. One change in the main table is a reweighting of the grades awarded in the 2008 Research Assessment Exercise to give universities extra credit for work considered to be world-leading. The previous scores mirrored the official system used to allocate research funds and the new ones follow a change in that procedure.

The other change in the main table sees a widening of the qualifications used to compile entry scores. Rather than simply taking account of the grades from A levels and Highers, the UCAS tariff has been used to take account of other qualifications, including the International Baccalaureate.

In addition, there is a change this year to three of the subject tables – medicine, dentistry and veterinary medicine – where employment scores have been removed. In all three subjects graduate employment levels are so high that the expert group, which meets every year to review the methodology, felt that small differences could distort the overall subject ranking. Employment rates are still shown, but not included in the calculations.

There are no new universities in this year's edition of the *Guide*. Indeed, there is one fewer in the tables, following Wolverhampton's refusal to release data on its performance. It joins Swansea Metropolitan, London Metropolitan, Liverpool Hope and the West of Scotland in a boycott of league tables, although London Metropolitan will release data for next year's exercise. Other published statistics suggest that all five would have been in the lower reaches of *The Times* League Table, but prospective applicants can only guess at their actual standing.

The first *Times* ranking, 17 years ago, effectively produced a dead heat between Oxford and Cambridge, with the light blues a fraction of a point ahead. After several years of Cambridge domination, changes in methodology saw the roles reversed in the 2003 edition and Oxford subsequently extended its lead. The current table sees Oxford maintain its leadership, despite playing second fiddle to Cambridge in most of the subject tables. Cambridge has the better record on research, entry standards and completion rates, but Oxford's lead in staffing levels, degree classifications, graduate destinations and particularly in spending on libraries and other student facilities makes the difference. Accurate comparisons of the two are difficult because of the mix of college and central university responsibilities, but Oxford appears to include more college spending in its submission. Cambridge remains well ahead of Imperial College and St Andrews, the top university in Scotland. Cardiff is well clear in Wales.

For most readers, however, the scramble over a handful of points at the top of the overall ranking of universities will be literally academic. The key information is contained in the subject tables, which now cover every area of higher education. One of the strengths of this *Guide*, and others like it, has been to highlight the quality of previously underestimated universities such as York and Bath, and to celebrate the achievements of centres of excellence such as the social sciences at Essex.

Universities' own research suggests that well over half of all applicants use newspaper guides, and this year's review predicts that league tables will become increasingly influential as fees rise further. Candidates have already become more selective about the courses they choose, as top-up fees have been introduced and the financial pressures on students and their families have grown.

The benefits of information

Higher education has seen other important changes with the introduction of incentives to extend access to a wider share of the population, and much more selective allocation of research funds. All the main political parties support moves to widen participation in higher education, although there will soon be less funding available to encourage that trend. But alongside the huge expansion in student numbers that has taken place over the last two decades there has been a gradual return to the hierarchical system that seemed to have been abandoned when the polytechnics acquired university status; only this time there are more than two tiers. Although a handful of post-1992 universities appear above one or two older foundations in this year's table, the divisions remain stark.

At the top of the pile, in terms of funding and prestige, is a group of little more than 20 universities, which attract 90 per cent of the resources available for research and also take the lion's share of money for teaching, partly because they offer expensive subjects such as medicine and engineering. A middle group, composed mainly of traditional universities, has been recruiting more undergraduates – especially overseas – while trying to compete on research. The remainder have remained buoyant mainly by expanding, or at least maintaining student numbers, while interacting with local companies.

There always was a pecking order of sorts. Oxford and Cambridge were world leaders long before most British universities were established, and parts of the University of London have always enjoyed a high status in particular fields. But few outside the higher-education world could discriminate between Keele and Kent, for example.

Employers, careers advisers, even academics, had their own ideas of which were the leading universities, but there was little hard evidence to back their conclusions. Often they were based on outdated, inaccurate impressions of distant institutions. The expanded higher education system has made such judgements more scientific as well as more necessary. Employers of graduates and those who commit their money to student sponsorship or funding research are comparing institutions department by department.

This has become possible because of a new transparency in what a former Higher Education Minister described as the "secret garden of academe". Official demands for more and more published information may have taxed the patience of university administrators, but they have also given outsiders the opportunity to make more meaningful comparisons. The **www.unistats.com** website represents the latest attempt to bring together the statistics relevant to applicants and there are promises of further transparency from the incoming Government. Universities will be required to publish the employment rates of individual courses and the average salaries of their graduates. But many readers value the more concise nature of guides such as this one, which distil the information displayed on such sites into a more manageable form.

Why university?

Particularly in an economic downturn, some will be tempted, once the cost of living has been added to the fees burden and the attractions of university life balanced against loss of potential earnings, to write off higher education. There are plenty of self-made millionaires who still swear by the University of Life as the only training ground for success. Yet even by narrow financial criteria it would be rash to dismiss higher education. With so many more competing for jobs, a degree will never again be an automatic passport to a fast-track career. But graduates' financial prospects remain much brighter than school leavers', as are their prospects in other important areas, such as health.

Even for those who cannot or do not wish to afford three or more years of full-time education after leaving school, university remains a possibility. The modular courses adopted by most universities enable students to work through a degree at their own pace, dropping out for a time if necessary, or switching to part-time attendance. Distance learning is another option, and advances in information technology now mean that some nominally full-time courses are delivered mainly via computers.

For many – perhaps most – students, therefore, the university experience is not what it was in their parents' day. There is more assessment, more crowding, more pressure to get the best possible degree while also finding gainful employment for at least part of the year. The proportion of students achieving first-class degrees has risen significantly, while an upper second (rather than the previously ubiquitous 2:2) has become the norm. Research shows that the classification has a real impact in the labour market.

An uncertain future

Universities are already facing serious cuts to their budgets, and there will be more to come as the new Government gets to grips with the national deficit. Already, some campuses are closing where universities are facing financial difficulties and it is even possible that some institutions will close or merge with stronger neighbours. However, every government has shown a marked reluctance to close universities and there is no reason to believe that the new administration will be any different. Universities are often the biggest employers in their area, as well as a source of local pride, and a closure would be a big step politically, as well as educationally.

What almost certainly will change is the system of student finance, following the Browne Review in England. Its decisions, which will have to be considered by the Government and, where fees are concerned, ratified by both Houses of Parliament, will have knock-on effects for students in Wales and Northern Ireland. They may even encourage a rethink in Scotland, where the graduate contribution has been abolished and universities' funding levels are falling behind those in England. Higher fees and less favourable repayment terms for student loans seem certain to follow, in England at least, although entrants in 2011 may escape the full effects.

None of the changes seem unlikely to alter the long-term direction of travel for higher education, however. Overall competition for places should ease over the coming decade, as the population of 18-year-olds begins to decline, as long as further restrictions are not placed on universities' ability to recruit. But numbers will remain more buoyant among the socio-economic groups that provide the bulk of university students than in the population as a whole, so the effects of demographic change may be less dramatic than many commentators have predicted. In the future it is likely that more students will begin their degrees at further education colleges, more will opt initially for two-year courses and the range both of subjects and teaching methods will grow still further. Some predict the rise of the "virtual university" or the demise of the conventional higher-education institution, as companies customise their own courses. However, universities have demonstrated enduring popularity and show every sign of weathering the current turbulence.

1 What and Where to Study

Choosing what and where to study are life-shaping decisions. The outcome will help determine your career and personal life far beyond the next three or four years (and they are important enough). Many graduates end up living and working near their university; they may make their closest friends in their student days and may even meet their future partner there. So finding the right university demands serious thought and research, and this *Guide* may play an important part.

The current outlook
Career prospects have always been uppermost in the mind of most people considering a higher education course. But, with graduate unemployment rising rapidly and the cost of going to university continuing to grow, economic considerations have become even more dominant. Yet there are good reasons not to let fear of the future squeeze out all other considerations.

No one knows which subjects will be in demand when the downturn ends, but graduates will almost undoubtedly be in a stronger position than those who choose not to invest in better qualifications. In any case, the majority of graduate jobs are not subject-specific – employers value the transferable skills that higher education confers. Rightly or wrongly, however, most employers are influenced by which university a graduate attended, so the choice of institution remains as important as ever.

Some students may cut their costs by taking a part-time course; others by enrolling on a two-year Foundation degree, which can be converted into an honours degree later. But, at a time of low employment generally, logic suggests that it would be a false economy to dismiss higher education entirely.

Those who want to add value to their degree in the jobs market will find that growing numbers of universities are offering employment-related schemes that are considered in more detail in Chapter 2. In many cases, this will involve work experience or extra activities organised by the careers service. Some universities, such as Leicester, now run certificated employability programmes, while others, such as Liverpool John Moores, have built such skills into degree programmes. Such programmes are also highlighted in chapter 2, the institutional profiles in chapter 13 and should be described in detail on university websites.

Is higher education for you?

Before you start, there is one important question to ask yourself: what do you want out of higher education? The answer will make it easier to choose where (and whether) to be a student. With more than a third of school-leavers going on to university, it is easy to drift that way without much thought, opting for the subject in which you expect the best grades and looking for a university with a reasonable reputation and a good social life. Your career will look after itself – you hope.

With graduate debt soaring, however, and job prospects varying widely between subjects, now is the time to look at your own motivation. Love of a subject is perhaps the best reason for taking a degree, and one that allows you to focus almost exclusively on the search for a course that corresponds with your passions. If, on the other hand, higher education is a means to an end, you need to think about career ambitions and look carefully at employment rates for any courses you might consider.

Many graduates look back on their student days as the best years of their lives, and there is nothing wrong with wanting to have a good time. Remember, though, that you will be paying for it later (literally) and there will be more studying than partying. If you have not enjoyed sixth-form or college courses, you may be better off in a job and possibly becoming one of the hundreds of thousands each year who return to education later in life.

Key reasons for going to university

To improve job opportunities	74%
To improve salary prospects	60%
To improve knowledge in an area of interest	58%
To specialise in a certain subject / area	47%
To obtain an additional qualification	46%
Essential to my chosen profession	43%
To experience a different way of life	41%
It's the obvious next step	40%
To have a good social life	31%
My parents expected me to	24%
I didn't want to get a job straightaway	23%
I didn't know what else to do	18%
All my friends were going	14%
Can live at home and still go to university	9%

Sodexo University Lifestyle Survey 2008

Narrowing down the choices

Once you have decided that higher education is for you, the good news is that, as long as you start early enough, finding the right university need not be stressful. Media attention focuses on the scramble for places on a relatively small proportion of courses where competition is intense, but there are plenty of places at good universities for candidates with the basic qualifications – it's just a matter of finding the one that suits you best. For older applicants, relevant work experience and demonstrable interest in a subject may be enough to win a place.

If anything, the problem is that of too much choice. Students prepared to move away from home will have more than 100 universities and numerous specialist colleges to consider, most with hundreds – even thousands – of course combinations on offer. Institutions come in all shapes and sizes, so there is work to do at the outset narrowing down your options.

Deciding what you want to study may reduce the field considerably – only seven institutions offer veterinary medicine for example, although the total is closer to 100 in subjects such as law and English. By the time you have factored in personal preferences about the type or location of your ideal university, the list of possibilities may already be reduced to manageable proportions.

After that, you can take a closer look at what the courses contain and what life is really like for students. Prospectuses and university websites will give you an accurate account of course combinations, and important facts like the accommodation available to new students, but it is their job to sell the university. To get a true picture, you need more – preferably a visit not just to the university, but to the department where you would be studying. If that is not possible, there are plenty of other sources of objective information, such as the National Student Survey (which is available online, with a range of additional data about each institution, at **www.unistats.direct.gov.uk**).

Many students' unions publish alternative prospectuses, giving a "warts and all" view of the university, and those that do not provide this service may be able to arrange a brief discussion with a current student, either by phone or email. Your school or college may put you in contact with someone who went to a university that you are considering. Guides and collections of statistics may give you valuable information about a course or a university, but there is no substitute for personal experience.

What to study?

Most people seeking a place in higher education start by choosing a subject and a course, rather than a university. If you take a degree, you are going to spend at least three years immersed in your subject. It has to be one you will enjoy and can master – not to mention one that you are qualified to study. Many economics degrees require maths, for example, while some medical schools demand chemistry or biology. The UCAS website (**www.ucas.com**) contains course profiles, including entrance requirements, which is a good starting point, while universities' own sites contain more detailed information. In Chapter 5, we describe 62 subject areas and provide league tables for each of them.

Your school subjects and the UCAS tariff

The official yardstick by which your results will be judged is the UCAS tariff (see page 18), which gives a score for each grade of every type of UK qualification considered relevant for university entrance, as well as for the International Baccalaureate (IB). This tariff has become more controversial as more subjects and types of qualifications have been included in it. Top scores in the new vocational diplomas, for example, will attract more points than a full set of A grades at A level, while the most successful IB students already earn considerably more points. If this process continues, it is likely that more of the leading universities will abandon the tariff, as some have done already.

A recent change increased the points awarded for high grades in Scottish qualifications. A review raised the number of points awarded for grade A Highers from 72 to 80 points, while an A in Advanced Highers has risen from 120 to 130 points – ten points more than a grade A at A level. Grades B and C are also worth more, although a D in an Advanced Higher has stayed at 72 points and a Higher grade D actually dropped from 42 to 36 points.

"Soft subjects"

There is a separate issue for some of the top universities about the subjects studied at A level. The variety of A-level courses now available includes many subjects that they do not consider on a par with traditional academic subjects. For many years, a minority of universities have refused to accept General Studies as a full A level for entrance purposes (although even some top universities do). The growth of supposedly "soft" subjects, such as media studies and photography, has prompted a few to produce lists of subjects that will only be accepted as a third, or fourth, A level. Cambridge would prefer to see only one subject from the list shown below in your mix of A levels subjects.

The UCAS Tariff

GCE/VCE Qualifications					Points	Scottish Qualifications	
GCE AS/AS VCE	GCE AS Double Award	GCE A level/A VCE	A level with additional AS (9 units)	GCE/AVCE Double Award		Advanced Higher	Higher
				A*A*	280		
				A*A	260		
				AA	240		
				AB	220		
			A*A	BB	200		
			AA	BC	180		
			AB		170		
				CC	160		
			BB		150		
		A*	BC	CD	140		
					130	A	
	AA	A	CC	DD	120		
	AB		CD		110	B	
	BB	B		DE	100		
	BC		DD		90	C	
	CC	C	DE	EE	80		A
					72	D	
	CD				70		
					65		B
A	DD	D	EE		60		
B	DE				50		C
C	EE	E			40		
					36		D
D					30		
E					20		

UCAS Tariff for International Baccalaureate

Points for the International Baccalaureate (IB) are awarded to candidates who achieve the IB Dip. The scores have been reduced for 2010 entry.

IB Dip	Points	IB Dip	Points	IB Dip	Points	IB Dip	Points	IB Dip	Points
45	720	40	611	35	501	30	392	25	282
44	698	39	589	34	479	29	370	24	260
43	676	38	567	33	457	28	348		
42	654	37	545	32	435	27	326		
41	632	36	523	31	413	26	304		

For most courses at most universities, there are no such restrictions, although those choosing A levels would be wise to bear the list in mind in case more of the leading universities move in this direction. At the very least, it is an indication of the subjects that admissions tutors may take less seriously than the rest. Although only Cambridge and the London School of Economics identify those subjects publicly, others may adopt less formal weightings.

Diplomas

This concern about "soft subjects" also applies to the new diplomas, just as it has to vocational qualifications down the years. Although there has been university involvement in designing the diplomas, there remains confusion about which will be accepted by leading universities – especially for admission to degree courses outside the direct scope of the diploma. The engineering diploma has now won near-universal approval (for admission to engineering courses and possibly some science degrees), but some of the other diplomas are in fields that are not on the curriculum of the most selective universities. Regardless of the points awarded under the tariff, it is essential to contact universities direct to ensure that a diploma will be an acceptable qualification for your chosen degree.

Use of tariffs and admission tests

While the majority of universities use the tariff to make offers of places, those that are heavily oversubscribed will tend to demand particular grades even at A level, often naming the subjects in which the highest grades are required. There are no set rules about using the tariff. Some universities will give credit for qualifications in key skills, for example, while others exclude them from candidates' points totals. In certain universities, some departments, but not others, will use the tariff to set offers. The university's prospectus or website should show which does what. In addition, some universities now require applicants to take an entrance test. The details are listed on page 20.

Making a choice

Choosing a subject to study at university is not always as straightforward as it sounds. Your A

A-level subjects only acceptable as a third or fourth subject at Cambridge (Camb) and London School of Economics (LSE)

- » Accounting (Camb, LSE)
- » Art and Design (Camb, LSE)
- » Business Studies (Camb, LSE)
- » Communication Studies (Camb, LSE)
- » Dance (Camb)
- » Design and Technology (Camb, LSE)
- » Drama/Theatre Studies (Camb, LSE–some departments)
- » Film Studies (Camb)
- » Health and Social Care (Camb)
- » Home Economics (Camb, LSE)
- » Information and Communication Technology (Camb, LSE)
- » Law (LSE)
- » Leisure Studies (Camb)
- » Media Studies (Camb, LSE)
- » Music Technology (Camb, LSE)
- » Performance Studies (Camb)
- » Performing Arts (Camb)
- » Photography (Camb)
- » Physical Education (Camb)
- » Sports Studies (Camb, LSE)
- » Travel and Tourism (Camb, LSE)

General Studies and Critical Thinking A levels will only be considered as fourth A level subjects and will not therefore be accepted as part of a conditional offer.

Admissions Tests

Some courses now have additional entrance tests. The most significant are listed below. A few other courses may also require tests, so check the course details on the UCAS website.

BioMedical Admissions Test (BMAT): for entry to medicine and veterinary medicine at Cambridge, Imperial College London, Oxford, Royal Veterinary College, University College London.
Standard closing date for 2011 admissions is 30 September 2010.
www.admissionstests.cambridgeassessment.org.uk/adt/bmat

English Literature Admissions Test (ELAT): for entry to English at Oxford.
Closing date for 2011 entry is 15 October 2010.
www.admissionstests.cambridgeassessment.org.uk/adt/elat

Graduate Medical School Admissions Test (GAMSAT): for graduate entry to medicine and dentistry at Keele, Nottingham, Peninsula College of Medicine and Dentistry, St. George's, University of London, Swansea.
Closing date for registration is 13 August 2010. **www.gamsatuk.org**

Health Professions Admissions Test (HPAT): for certain medical courses at Ulster.
Closing date for 2011 registration not confirmed. For 2010 admissions it was 15 January 2010.
www.hpat.org.uk

History Aptitude Test (HAT): for entry to history or a joint honours degree involving history at Oxford.
Test taken on 3 November 2010, usually at candidate's educational institution.
www.history.ox.ac.uk/prosundergrad/applying/hat_introduction.htm

Modern and Medieval Languages Test (MML): for entry to modern and medieval languages at Cambridge, taken at Cambridge during interview process.
www.cam.ac.uk/admissions/undergraduate/courses/mml/tests.html

National Admissions Test for Law (LNAT): for entry to law courses at Birmingham, Bristol, Durham, Glasgow, King's College London, Leeds, Nottingham, Oxford, University College, London.
Registration opens 1 August 2010. **www.lnat.ac.uk**

Sixth Term Examination Papers (STEP): for entry to mathematics at Cambridge and Warwick.
Standard closing date for 2010 entry is 30 April 2010. Date for 2011 entry to be announced in September 2010.
www.admissionstests.cambridgeassessment.org.uk/adt/step

Thinking Skills Assessment (TSA) Cambridge: mainly for computer science, economics, engineering, land economy, natural sciences and politics, psychology and sociology at most Cambridge colleges, taken at Cambridge during interview process.
www.admissionstests.cambridgeassessment.org.uk/adt/tsacambridge

Thinking Skills Assessment (TSA) Oxford: for economics and management, experimental psychology, philosophy, politics and economics (PPE), and psychology and philosophy.
Last date for entry is 15 October 2010 and test taken 3 November 2010.
www.admissionstests.cambridgeassessment.org.uk/adt/tsaoxford

Thinking Skills Assessment (TSA) UCL: for entry to European social and political studies at University College London; the test is arranged in the interview process.
www.admissionstests.cambridgeassessment.org.uk/adt/tsaucl

UK Clinical Aptitude Test (UKCAT): for entry to medical and dental schools at Aberdeen, Brighton and Sussex Medical School, Barts and the London School of Medicine and Dentistry, Cardiff, Dundee, Durham, East Anglia, Edinburgh, Glasgow, Hull York Medical School, Keele, King's College London, Imperial College London (graduate entry), Leeds, Leicester, Manchester, Newcastle, Nottingham, Oxford (graduate entry), Peninsula College of Medicine and Dentistry, Queen's University, Belfast, Sheffield, Southampton, St Andrews, St George's, University of London, Warwick (graduate entry).
Registration deadline for candidates for 2011 entry is 27 September 2010.
www.ukcat.ac.uk

levels, or Scottish Highers, may have chosen themselves, but the range of subjects across the whole university system is vast. Even subjects that you have studied at school may be quite different at degree level – some academic economists actually prefer their undergraduates not to have taken economics A level because they approach the subject so differently. Other students are disappointed because they appear to be going over old ground when they continue with a subject that they enjoyed at school. Universities now publish quite detailed syllabuses, and it is a matter of going through the fine print.

The greater difficulty comes in judging your suitability for the many subjects that are not on the school or college curriculum. Philosophy and psychology sound fascinating (and are), but you may have no idea what degrees in either subject entail – for example, the level of statistics that may be required. Forensic science may look exciting on television – more glamorous than plain chemistry – but it may open fewer doors if the type of work portrayed in "Silent Witness" or "Raising the Dead" is not available.

Vocational subjects

The introduction of top-up fees has encouraged more students into job-related subjects, rather than traditional academic disciplines, in the hope of improving their employment prospects. This is understandable and, if you are sure of your future career path, possibly also sensible. But much depends on what that career is – and whether you are ready to make such a long-term commitment. Some of the programmes that have attracted public ridicule, such as surf science or golf course management, may narrow graduates' options to a worrying extent, but there is nothing wrong with their employment records. Jibes about so-called "Mickey Mouse" courses have become less frequent, although there are some who are yet to accept that the higher education curriculum has moved into new areas since they were students.

Many vocational courses are tailored to particular professions. If you choose one of these, make sure that the degree is recognised by the relevant professional body (such as the Engineering Council or one of the institutes) or you may not be able to use the skills that you acquire. Most universities are only too keen to make such recognition clear in their prospectus; if no such guarantee is published, contact the university department running the course and seek assurances.

Even where a course has professional recognition, bear in mind that a further qualification may be required to practise. Both law and medicine, for example, demand additional training

The ten most popular subject groups by applications

1	Nursing	94,644
2	Psychology	87,590
3	Law	83,567
4	Design studies	82,521
5	Pre-clinical medicine	80,894
6	English studies	58,232
7	Management studies	57,580
8	Business and administration	53,003
9	Social work	52,238
10	Sports science	49,207

UCAS number of applicants to 22 January 2010

The ten most popular subject groups by acceptances

1	Business and administrative studies	58,545
2	Creative arts and design	52,382
3	Subjects allied to medicine	48,171
4	Biological sciences	37,049
5	Social Studies	36,977
6	Mathematical and computer sciences	28,538
7	Engineering	25,452
8	Law	22,059
9	Sciences combined with social sciences or arts	21,016
10	Physical sciences	17,328

UCAS acceptances in 2009

to become a fully qualified solicitor, barrister or doctor. Nor is either degree an automatic passport to a job: only about half of all law graduates go into the profession and the UK is now training more medical students than the National Health Service can afford. Both law and medicine also provide a route into the profession for graduates who have taken other subjects. Law conversion courses, though not cheap, are increasingly popular, and there is a growing number of graduate-entry medical degrees.

One way to ensure that a degree is job-related is to take a "sandwich" course, which involves up to a year in business or industry. Students often end up working for the organisation which provided the placement, while others gain valuable insights into a field of employment – even if only to discount it. The drawback with such courses is that, like the year abroad that is part of most language degrees, the period away from university inevitably disrupts living arrangements and friendship groups. But most of those who take this route find that the career benefits make this a worthwhile sacrifice.

Academic or vocational courses?

Employers' organisations calculate that more than half of all graduate jobs are open to applicants from any subject, and recruiters for the most competitive graduate training schemes often prefer traditional academic subjects to apparently relevant vocational degrees. Newspapers, for example, often prefer a history graduate to one with a media studies degree; computing firms take a disproportionate number of classicists. A good degree classification and the right work experience are more important than the subject for most non-technical jobs. But it is hard to achieve a good result on a course that you do not enjoy, so scour prospectuses, and email or phone university departments to ensure that you know what you are letting yourself in for. Their reaction to your approach will also give you an idea of how responsive they are to their students.

If you are not sure whether you will be suited to a particular subject, you can take an online aptitude test through the UCAS website. The "What to study" section gives you access to the Stamford Test, which uses an online questionnaire to match your interests and strengths to possible courses and careers (**www.ucas.com/students/beforeyouapply/whattostudy/stamfordtest**).

Studying more than one subject

You may find that more than one subject appeals, in which case you could consider Joint Honours – degrees that combine two subjects – or even Combined Honours, which will cover several related subjects. Such courses obviously allow you to extend the scope of your studies, but they should be approached with caution. Even if the number of credits suggests a similar workload to Single Honours, covering more than one subject inevitably involves extra reading and often more essays or project work.

However, there are advantages. Many students choose a "dual" to add a vocational element to make themselves more employable – business studies with languages or engineering, for example, or media studies with English. Others want to take their studies in a particular direction, perhaps by combining history with politics, or statistics with maths. Some simply want to add a completely unrelated interest to their main subject, such as environmental science and music, or archaeology and event management – both combinations that are available at UK universities.

At most universities, however, it is not necessary to take a degree in more than one subject in order to broaden your studies. The spread of modular programmes ensures that you can take courses in related subjects without changing the basic structure of your degree. You may not be able to take an event management module in a single-honours archaeology degree, but it should be possible to study some history, or a language. The number and scope of the combinations offered at many of the larger universities is extraordinary. Indeed, it has been criticised by academics who believe that "mix-and-match" degrees can leave a graduate without a rounded view of a subject. But for those who seek breadth and variety, close scrutiny of university prospectuses (whether online or on paper) is a vital part of the selection process.

What type of course?
Once you have a subject, you must decide on the level and type of course. Most readers of this *Guide* will be looking for full-time degree courses, but higher education is much broader than that. You may not be able to afford the time or the money needed for a full-time commitment of three or four years at this point in your life.

Part-time courses
Tens of thousands of people each year opt for a part-time course – usually while holding down a job – to continue learning and improve their career prospects. It can be exhausting, unless your employer gives you time off to study, and any financial support you receive from the Government will not be the same as that provided for full-time students. However, if you have the stamina for a course that will usually take twice as long as the full-time equivalent, this route may make a degree more affordable. Part-time students tend to be highly committed to their subject, and many claim that the quality of the social life associated with their course makes up for the quantity of leisure time enjoyed by full-timers.

Distance learning
Another option, if you are confident that you can manage without regular face-to-face contact with teachers and fellow students, is distance learning. Courses are delivered mainly or entirely online or through correspondence, although some programmes offer a certain amount of local tuition. The process might sound daunting and impersonal, but students of the Open University (OU), all of whom are educated in this way, are the most satisfied in the country, according to the results of the annual National Student Survey. Attending lectures or oversized seminars at a conventional university can be less personal than regular contact with your tutor at a distance. Of course, not all universities are as good at communicating with their distance-learning students as the OU, or offer such high-quality course materials, but this mode of study does give students ultimate flexibility to determine when and where they work. Distance learning is becoming increasingly popular for the delivery of professional courses, which are often needed to supplement degrees. The OU now takes students of all ages, not just mature students.

Foundation degrees
Even if you are set on a full-time course, you might not want to commit yourself for three or more years. Growing numbers are taking two-year Foundation degrees – vocational courses which the Government would like to be the main source of expansion in universities and colleges. Even more students take longer-established two-year courses, such as Higher National Diplomas or other diplomas tailored to the needs of industry or parts of the health service. Those who do well on such courses usually have the option of converting their qualification into a degree with further study, although many achieve their goal without immediately

staying on for a further two or more years that completing a full degree will require.

Other short courses

A number of universities have experimented with two-year degrees, squeezing more work into an extended academic year. The so-called "third semester" makes use of the summer vacation for extra teaching, so that mature students, in particular, can reduce the length of their career break. Several universities are experimenting with accelerated degrees as part of a pilot project encouraged by the Government. But the pattern has really only caught on at the University of Buckingham, the UK's only established private university, where it has had a small but enthusiastic following for more than 30 years.

Other short courses – usually lasting a year – are designed for students who do not have the necessary qualifications for a degree in their chosen subject. Foundation courses in art and design have been common for many years, and are the chosen preparation for a degree at leading departments, even for many students whose A levels would win them a degree place elsewhere. Access courses perform the same function in a wider range of subjects for students without A levels, or for those whose grades are either too low or in the wrong subjects to gain admission to a particular course. Entry requirements are modest, but students have to reach the same standard as regular entrants if they are to progress to a degree.

Yet more choice

No single guide can allow for personal preferences in choosing a course. You may want one of the many degrees that incorporate a year at a partner university abroad, or to try a six-month exchange on the Continent through the European Union's Erasmus Programme. Either might prove a valuable experience and add to your employability. You might prefer a January or February start to the traditional autumn start – there are plenty of opportunities for this, mainly at new universities. In some subjects – particularly engineering and the sciences – the leading degrees may be Masters courses, taking four years rather than the norm (in England) of three.

Job prospects

Even before the recession, job prospects were the key element in choosing a subject for many (probably most) students. Chapter 2 examines this topic in detail, providing information on employment prospects by subject and initial starting salaries by subject as well as giving advice on how to enhance your chances in the jobs market.

Where to study

Once you have decided what to study, there are still several factors that might influence your choice of university or college. Obviously, you need to have a reasonable chance of getting in, you may want reassurance about the university's reputation, and its location will probably also be important to you. On top of that, most applicants have views about the type of institution they are looking for – big or small, old or new, urban or rural, specialist or comprehensive. You may surprise yourself by choosing somewhere that does not conform to your initial criteria, but working through your preferences is another way of narrowing down your options.

Entry standards

Unless you are a mature student or have taken a gap year, your passport to your chosen university will be a conditional offer based on your predicted grades, previous exam performance, personal statement and school or college reference. A lucky few may get an offer that is so low that success is a foregone conclusion – because the university considers them outstanding and needs no further evidence of their potential. But only those who already have their grades receive unconditional offers.

Supply and demand dictate whether you will receive an offer – particularly in the new climate of much larger numbers applying – and that is influenced both by the university and the subject. A few universities (but not many) at the top of the league tables are heavily oversubscribed in every subject; others will have areas in which they excel, but may make relatively modest demands for entry to other courses. Even in many of the leading universities, the number of applicants for each place in languages or engineering is still not high. Conversely, three As at A level will not guarantee a place on one of the top English or law degrees, but there are enough universities running courses to ensure that three Cs will put you in with a chance somewhere. The difference now is that the pressure on places in popular subjects is greater than before at the more lowly ranked universities.

University prospectuses and the UCAS website will give you the "standard offer" for each course, but in some cases this is pitched deliberately low in order to leave admissions staff extra flexibility. The standard A-level offer for medicine, for example, is often two As and a B, but nearly all successful applicants have three As or more.

The average entry scores in our subject tables give the actual points obtained by successful applicants – many of which are far above the offer made by the university, but which give an indication of the pecking order at entry. The subject tables (in chapter 5) are, naturally, a better guide than the main table (in chapter 4), where average entry scores are influenced by the range of subjects available at each university.

Non-academic factors considered when choosing a university

Good impression from open days	**51%**
Friendly atmosphere	**46%**
Attractive university environment	**42%**
Active social life and good social facilities	**31%**
Campus university	**31%**
Close to transport links	**28%**
Living away from home, but sufficiently close if support needed	**27%**
City centre university	**26%**
Recommendation from friends	**23%**
Quality of accommodation	**22%**
Close to home/able to live at home	**21%**
Internet research favourable to university	**18%**
Advice from teachers	**16%**
Low cost of living	**14%**
Cost of accommodation	**13%**
Advice from parents	**11%**
Good sporting facilities	**10%**
Opportunities for part-time jobs	**8%**

Sodexo University Lifestyle Survey 2008

Location

The most obvious starting point is the country you study in. Most degrees in Scotland take four years, rather than the UK norm of three. It is possible, but not normal, for A-level candidates to go straight into the second year of a Scottish degree course. Otherwise, four years obviously cost more than three, especially given the loss of the year's salary you might have been earning after graduation. A later chapter will go into the details of the system, but suffice to say that students from Scotland pay no fees, while those from the rest of the UK do. Nevertheless, Edinburgh and St Andrews remain particularly popular with English students and more than 1,000 students from Northern Ireland entered Scottish universities in 2009.

Close to home

Far from crossing national boundaries, however, growing numbers of students choose to study near home, whether or not they continue to live with their family. This may be to cut costs or for personal reasons, such as family circumstances, a girlfriend or boyfriend, continuing employment, or religion. Some simply want to stick with what they know. But the trend for full-time students who do go away to study, is to choose a university within about two hours' travelling time. The assumption is that this is far enough to discourage parents from making unannounced visits, but close enough to allow for occasional trips home to get the washing done and have a decent meal. The leading universities recruit from all over the world, but most still have a regional core.

City universities

The most popular universities, in terms of total applications, are nearly all in big cities – generally with other major centres of population within that two-hour travelling window. For those looking for the best nightclubs, top sporting events, high-quality shopping or a varied cultural life – in other words, most young people, and especially those who live in cities already – city universities are a magnet. The big universities also, by definition, offer the widest range of subjects, although that does not mean that they necessarily have the particular course that is right for you. Nor does it mean that you will actually use the array of nightlife and shopping that looks so alluring in the prospectus, either because you cannot afford to, because student life is focused on the university, or even because you are too busy working.

Campus universities

City universities are the right choice for many young people, but it is worth bearing in mind that the National Student Survey shows that the highest satisfaction levels tend to be at smaller universities, often those with their own self-contained campuses. It seems that students identify more closely with institutions where there is a close-knit community and the social life is based around the students' union rather than the local nightclubs.

Few UK universities are in genuinely rural locations, but some – particularly among the newly promoted – are in relatively small towns. Several longer-established institutions in Wales and Scotland also share this type of setting, where the university dominates the town.

Top increases in applications 2010 over 2009

1	University of the Arts London	112%
2	University for the Creative Arts	94%
3	Thames Valley	86%
4	Edinburgh Napier	78%
5	Middlesex	56%
6	West of Scotland	55%
7	De Montfort	53%
8	Robert Gordon	52%
9	East London	50%
10	Anglia Ruskin	49%

UCAS applications to 22 January 2010

Decreases and smallest increases in applications 2010 over 2009

1	Brunel	−8.8%
2	Lancaster	−4.3%
3	Bristol	−3.9%
4	London School of Economics	−0.4%
5	Cardiff	−0.3%
6	Edinburgh	0.4%
7	Warwick	0.9%
8	Bath	1.0%
9	Roehampton	1.1%
10	Reading	1.2%

UCAS applications to 22 January 2010

Importance of Open Days

The only way to be certain if this, or any other type of university, is for you is to visit. Schools often restrict the number of open days that sixth-formers can attend in term-time, but some universities offer a weekend alternative. The full calendar of events is available at **www.opendays.com** and on universities' own websites. Bear in mind, if you only attend one or two, that the event has to be badly mismanaged for a university not to seem an exciting place to someone who spends his or her days at school, or even college. Try to get a flavour of several institutions before you make your choice.

How many universities to pick?

When that time comes, of course, you will not be making one choice but five; four if you are applying for medicine, dentistry or veterinary science. (Full details of the application process are given in chapter 6.) Tens of thousands of students each year eventually go to a university that did not start out as their first choice, either because they did not get the right offer or because they changed their mind along the way. UCAS rules are such that applicants do not list universities in order of preference anyway – indeed, universities are not allowed to know where else you have applied. So do not pin all your hopes on one course; take just as much care choosing the other universities on your list.

Until recently, it was normal for applicants to include at least one "insurance" choice on that list – a university or college where entry grades were significantly lower than at their preferred institutions. This practice has been in decline, presumably because candidates expecting high grades think they can pick up a lower offer either in Clearing or through UCAS Extra, the service that allows applicants rejected by their original choices to apply to courses that still have vacancies after the first round of offers.

The recent switch from being able to choose six courses to only being able to apply for five seems to have cemented this change but, if you are at all uncertain about your grades, including an insurance choice remains a sensible course of action – especially when entry requirements are rising in response to increased demand for places. The main proviso, as with all your choices, is that you must be prepared to take up that place. If not, you might as well go for broke with courses with higher standard offers and take your chances in Clearing, or even retake exams if you drop grades.

The ten most popular universities for living at home

1	Wolverhampton	8,900
2	Glasgow Caledonian	7,845
3	Ulster	7,210
4	London Metropolitan	6,800
5	Westminster	6,635
6	Manchester Metropolitan	6,505
7	Glasgow	6,170
8	Northumbria	6,080
9	Kent	6,040
10	Glamorgan	5,905

HESA 2008

The ten most popular universities by applications

1	Manchester	49,961
2	Leeds	48,642
3	Manchester Metropolitan	46,067
4	Edinburgh	45,010
5	Nottingham	41,514
6	Birmingham	39,759
7	Sheffield Hallam	38,111
8	Bristol	37,668
9	Sheffield	36,724
10	Nottingham Trent	36,099

UCAS applications to 22 January 2010

Reputation

The reputation of a university is something intangible, usually built up over a long period and sometimes outlasting reality. Before universities were subject to external assessment and the publication of copious statistics, reputation was rooted in the distant past. League tables are partly responsible for changing that, although employers are often influenced by what they remember as the pecking order of higher education when they were students.

The fragmentation of the British university system into groups of institutions is another factor: the Russell Group (**www.russellgroup.ac.uk**) represents 20 research-intensive universities, nearly all with medical schools; the 1994 Group (**www.1994group.ac.uk**) a similar number of smaller research universities; and the Million Plus Group (**www.millionplus.ac.uk**) containing many of the former polytechnics and newer universities. To these have been added the University Alliance (**www.university-alliance.ac.uk**), which provides a home for 22 universities, both old and new, that did not fit into the other categories. In addition there is Guild HE (**www.guildhe.ac.uk**), an organisation mainly for specialist colleges, but including five of the newest universities.

Many of you will barely have heard of a polytechnic, let alone be able to identify which of today's universities had that heritage, but you will know which of two universities in the same city has the higher status. While that should matter far less than the quality of a course, it would be naïve to ignore institutional reputation entirely if that is going to carry weight with a future employer. Some big firms restrict their recruitment efforts to a small group of leading universities, for example (see chapter 2), and, however shortsighted that might be, it is something to bear in mind if a career in the City or a big law firm is your ultimate aim.

Cost

Critics of top-up fees feared that the fees, introduced in 2006, would add cost to the list of factors driving students' choice of university. But only Leeds Metropolitan University pitched its fees significantly below the original £3,000 maximum, opting for £2,000 and leaving them at that level until 2009–10. Now all universities in England charge the maximum, which stood at £3,290 a year in 2010. Other than in Oxford and Cambridge, where there is an additional college fee (not paid by those paying the standard UK tuition fee), cost differences are restricted to rents and the general cost of living in different parts of the country. Some cities – notably London – are notoriously expensive for students and non-students alike. But even

The ten universities that scored highest in the 2011 *Times* table for student satisfaction

1	Cambridge	85%
2	Leicester	85%
3	Loughborough	85%
4	Oxford	85%
5	Exeter	84%
6	St Andrews	84%
7	Aberystwyth	83%
8	East Anglia	83%
9	Aberdeen	82%
10	Chichester	82%

The ten universities that scored highest in the 2011 *Times* table for graduate prospects

1	Imperial College	88.9%
2	Robert Gordon	83.4%
3	Oxford	82.8%
4	Cambridge	82.3%
5	London School of Economics	81.9%
6	Bath	80.9%
7	University College London	80.8%
8	King's College London	80.5%
9	Surrey	79.6%
10	City	79.4%

these comparisons can be complicated by the availability of part-time employment – an important factor for a growing number of students today. One survey rated London as one of the cheapest places in the UK to study once earning opportunities were taken into account. If you intend to take part-time employment while studying, check that your chosen university has a "job shop", or some other organisation to help students find reasonably paid work.

Accommodation costs listed alongside the university profiles in this *Guide* are probably the nearest proxy for a cost-of-living indicator. The *Guide* also includes a summary of the bursaries available at each university. The size of bursaries varies enormously, as do the rules governing eligibility. Most bursaries are available only to students who qualify for at least some Government support, but scholarships are awarded for other achievements, regardless of family income.

Facilities

Universities compete for the best students not only through their courses but, increasingly, also through non-academic facilities. Accommodation is the main selling point for those living away from home, but sports facilities, libraries and computing equipment also play an important part. Even campus nightclubs have become part of the facilities race that has coincided with the introduction of top-up fees.

Many universities guarantee first-year students accommodation in halls of residence or university-owned flats. But it is as well to know what happens after that. Are there enough places for second or third-year students who want them, and if not, what is the private market like? Rents for student houses vary quite widely across the country and there have been tensions with local residents in some cities. All universities offer specialist accommodation for disabled students – and are better at providing other facilities than most public institutions. Their websites give basic information on what is provided, as well as contact points for more detailed inquiries.

Special-interest clubs and recreational facilities, as well as political activity, tend to be based in the students' union – sometimes knows as the guild of students, especially in Scotland. In some universities, the union is the focal point of social activity, while in others the attractions of the city seem to overshadow the union to the point where facilities are underused. Students' union websites are included with the information found in the university profiles (chapter 13).

Sources of information

With nearly 120 universities to choose from, the Unistats and UCAS websites, as well as guides such as this one, are the obvious places to start your search for the right course. But once you have narrowed down the list of candidates, you will want to go through undergraduate prospectuses. Most are available online, where you can select the relevant sections rather than waiting for an account of every course to arrive in the post. Beware of generalised claims about the standing of the university, the quality of courses, friendly atmosphere and legendary social life. Stick, if you can, to the factual information, which is generally accurate.

If the material that the universities publish about their own qualities is less than objective, much of what you will find on the internet is equally unreliable, for different reasons. A simple search on the name of a university will turn up spurious comparisons of everything from the standard of lecturing to the attractiveness of the students. These can be seriously misleading and are usually based on anecdotal evidence, at best. Make sure that any information you may take into account comes from a reputable source and, if it conflicts with your impression of a university, try to cross-check it with this *Guide* and the institution's own material.

Checklist

Choosing a subject and a place to study is a major decision. Make sure you can answer these questions:

Choosing a course:
» What do I want out of higher education?
» Which subjects do I enjoy studying at school?
» Which subject or subjects do I want to study?
» Do I have the right qualifications?
» What are my career plans and does the subject and course fit these?

Choosing a university:
» What type of university do I wish to go to: campus, city or smaller town?
» How far is the university from home?
» Is it large or small?
» Is it specialist or general?
» Does it offer the right course?
» How much will it cost?
» Have I arranged to visit the university?

Useful websites

The following websites will help you find out more about the topics discussed in this chapter. The best starting point is the UCAS website. On the site there's lots of information on courses, universities and the whole process of applying to university.

www.ucas.com
Within the UCAS site, useful but not immediately obvious pages include:
The Stamford Test
www.ucas.com/students/beforeyouapply/whattostudy/stamfordtest
The UCAS tariff (and especially its use with vocational qualifications)
www.ucas.com/students/ucas_tariff/tarifftables

As a source of statistical information which allows limited comparison between universities (and for full details of the National Student Survey), visit:
www.unistats.direct.gov.uk

For information on Foundation degrees: Foundation Degree Forward
www.findfoundationdegree.co.uk

For an official listing of recognised degrees and recognised higher education institutions:
www.dcsf.gov.uk/recognisedukdegrees

UK Course Finder:
www.ukcoursefinder.co.uk

Unofficial Guides to universities:
www.unofficial-guides.com

For a full calendar of university and college open days:
www.opendays.com

Students with disabilities: SKILL, the National Bureau for Students with Disabilities:
www.skill.org.uk

University groupings
1994 Group, a group of medium and small research-intensive universities:
www.1994group.ac.uk
GuildHE, a group of higher education colleges, specialist institutions and some universities:
www.guildhe.ac.uk
Million + Group, a group of newer universities:
www.millionplus.ac.uk
Russell Group: a group of large research-intensive universities:
www.russellgroup.ac.uk
The University Alliance, a group of old and new universities:
www.university-alliance.ac.uk

2 Graduate Employment Prospects

The graduate labour market has taken a dive since the figures in this *Guide* were compiled, as the banking crisis and worldwide recession depressed recruitment. No one can predict the changes that may take place over the three or four years before those starting a degree in 2011 begin their careers. But those choosing a course now will want to know what, if anything, they can do to insulate themselves against the possibility of eventually joining the growing band of unemployed (or underemployed) graduates.

The good news is that, in the private sector at least, the worst may be over. Leading employers had increased their recruitment targets by almost 12 per cent coming into 2010, according to the annual *Graduate Market* survey by High Fliers. The bad news is that vacancies had dropped by nearly 18 per cent in 2009 and the public sector – a huge employer of graduates – is only just starting to feel the pinch.

As a result, the UK may never return to the days of plentiful, well-paid graduate jobs that it enjoyed only a few years ago. Certainly, that era is not going to return in the immediate future and graduates will need to do all they can to make themselves attractive to employers. They will still be in a much better position than young people without higher education qualifications, but there are going to be a lot of them chasing a more limited number of opportunities.

Subject choice and career opportunities

The tables on pages 34–37 are the obvious starting point in assessing whether your prospective course will pay off in career terms. Although they date from before the downturn in graduate employment, there is no reason to believe that the pattern of success rates will have changed.

The Higher Education Statistics Agency (HESA) collects data both on what graduates do straight after graduation (sometimes called graduate destinations) and their average salaries. But the results are to be treated with caution because they represent only the first six months of a graduate's career – not even that if he or she has gone on to postgraduate study – and they make no allowances for the variety of entry routes into different areas of employment. Dentists, for example, have been virtually guaranteed a job if they complete a degree successfully, whereas those going into art and design know that periods of freelance and/or casual work may be an occupational hazard at the start of their career.

This type of table can mislead. We use classifications developed at the universities of Warwick and the West of England to distinguish between "graduate-level" work and jobs that do not normally require a degree. Subjects are ranked on "positive destinations", which include postgraduate study and other forms of training, whether or not they are combined with a job. Some similar tables do not make a distinction between different types of job – thus giving universities and subjects uniformly high employment rates.

The second table, on pages 36–37, gives average earnings six months after graduation. It contains interesting – and in some cases surprising – information about early career pay levels. Few would have placed social work and nursing among the top dozen fields for graduate pay, for example, while business studies and accounting do not make the top 20. Those positions underline the differences between starting salaries and long-term prospects in different jobs.

By three years after graduation, the figures are significantly different, according to recent research. HESA found that by then, overall unemployment had dropped from 5 per cent, six months after graduation, to 2 per cent, while 80 per cent were in graduate occupations, compared with 71 per cent in the initial survey of the same group. Corresponding differences emerged when the sample was broken down by subject.

Enhancing your employability

Universities are well aware of the difficulties in the graduate employment market and have been introducing all manner of schemes to try to give their graduates an advantage in the labour market. Many have incorporated specially designed employability modules into degree courses; some are certificating extra-curricular activities to improve their graduates' CVs; others are stepping up their efforts to provide work experience to complement degrees.

Universities targeted by the largest number of top employers in 2009–10

1	(1)	Manchester
2	(2)	London
3	(3)	Warwick
4	(4)	Cambridge
5	(5)	Oxford
6	(8)	Nottingham
7	(9)	Bath
8	6)	Bristol
9	(10)	Leeds
10	(11)	Birmingham
11	(7)	Durham
12	(13)	Sheffield
13	(14)	Loughborough
14	(12)	Edinburgh
15	(15)	Southampton
16	(18)	Newcastle
17	(16)	Cardiff
18	(19)	York
19	(-)	Liverpool
20	(-)	Lancaster

Last year's position in brackets
Source: *Graduate Market in 2010*

Opinion is divided on the value of such schemes. After all, some of the biggest employers restrict their recruitment activities to a small number of universities, believing that these institutions attract the brightest minds and that trawling more widely is not cost-effective. These companies, often big payers from the City of London and including some of the top law firms, are not likely to change their ways at a time when they are more anxious than ever to control costs. As before, they will expect to pick up outstanding candidates who went to other universities later in their careers.

The best advice, therefore, for those looking to maximise their employment opportunities (and who isn't?) must be to go for the best university you can. But most graduates do not work in the City and most students do not go to universities at the top of the league tables.

What graduates do by subject studied

Times Subject (ranked by the total of the first three columns on the right)	Employed in graduate job	Employed in graduate job and studying	Studying and not employed	Employed in non-graduate job and studying	Employed in non-graduate job	Unemployed
1 Medicine	90%	5%	5%	0%	0%	0%
2 Dentistry	83%	16%	0%	0%	0%	0%
3 Nursing	90%	5%	1%	0%	2%	1%
4 Pharmacology and Pharmacy	63%	16%	12%	1%	5%	3%
5 Veterinary Medicine	84%	3%	4%	0%	5%	3%
6 Civil Engineering	68%	8%	9%	1%	7%	8%
7 Other Subjects Allied to Medicine	70%	6%	7%	1%	11%	5%
8 Chemical Engineering	59%	4%	19%	1%	7%	10%
9 Social Work	71%	5%	5%	2%	12%	5%
10 Education	62%	6%	10%	2%	17%	3%
11 Physics and Astronomy	31%	8%	40%	1%	11%	9%
12 Mechanical Engineering	58%	7%	13%	1%	10%	11%
13 Chemistry	33%	5%	39%	1%	13%	9%
14 Building	65%	9%	4%	0%	11%	11%
15 Architecture	50%	16%	11%	1%	11%	11%
16 General Engineering	57%	6%	13%	2%	15%	8%
17 Land and Property Management	63%	9%	4%	0%	12%	12%
18 Law	19%	5%	45%	6%	19%	6%
19 Celtic Studies	28%	3%	42%	2%	18%	6%
20 Mathematics	34%	14%	25%	2%	17%	8%
21 Town and Country Planning and Landscape	43%	8%	21%	2%	16%	9%
22 Electrical and Electronic Engineering	55%	4%	12%	2%	16%	11%
23 Food Science	54%	4%	12%	2%	22%	5%
24 Middle Eastern and African Studies	43%	8%	20%	2%	18%	9%
25 Anatomy and Physiology	26%	4%	40%	3%	22%	6%
26 Economics	41%	13%	16%	2%	20%	9%
27 Aeronautical and Manufacturing Engineering	51%	5%	13%	1%	17%	11%
28 Theology and Religious Studies	31%	5%	31%	5%	23%	6%
29 German	44%	5%	19%	3%	22%	8%
30 French	42%	4%	21%	2%	24%	7%
31 Geology	37%	2%	28%	2%	20%	10%
32 Russian	37%	6%	23%	1%	25%	8%
33 Music	34%	6%	24%	3%	25%	8%
34 Iberian Languages	39%	5%	19%	3%	26%	7%

Times Subject
(ranked by the total of the first three columns on the right)

	Employed in graduate job	Employed in graduate job and studying	Studying and not employed	Employed in non-graduate job and studying	Employed in non-graduate job	Unemployed
35 Biological Sciences	29%	4%	30%	3%	24%	9%
36 Italian	43%	4%	16%	3%	25%	10%
37 Accounting and Finance	30%	21%	9%	5%	24%	10%
38 Computer Science	49%	3%	11%	2%	21%	14%
39 East and South Asian Studies	42%	5%	17%	0%	23%	13%
40 Materials Technology	47%	3%	12%	2%	29%	7%
41 Politics	34%	4%	22%	3%	28%	9%
42 Sports Science	36%	5%	18%	3%	31%	5%
43 Geography and Environmental Sciences	33%	4%	22%	3%	30%	8%
44 Business Studies	45%	6%	8%	3%	29%	10%
45 Philosophy	29%	4%	24%	4%	28%	10%
46 Classics and Ancient History	28%	4%	27%	3%	30%	9%
47 Anthropology	29%	4%	24%	4%	32%	8%
48 English	28%	3%	24%	5%	32%	8%
49 History of Art, Architecture and Design	31%	2%	20%	6%	33%	8%
50 Linguistics	29%	3%	23%	2%	33%	8%
51 History	26%	4%	25%	4%	32%	10%
52 Archaeology	29%	3%	21%	5%	31%	11%
53 Librarianship and Information Management	41%	5%	11%	0%	30%	13%
54 Psychology	30%	5%	16%	5%	37%	7%
55 Agriculture and Forestry	37%	8%	8%	2%	36%	8%
56 Drama, Dance and Cinematics	38%	3%	9%	4%	37%	9%
57 Art and Design	40%	2%	7%	3%	34%	13%
58 Social Policy	30%	3%	14%	4%	38%	10%
59 Sociology	29%	3%	15%	4%	40%	8%
60 American Studies	28%	2%	17%	4%	38%	11%
61 Communication and Media Studies	40%	2%	6%	2%	37%	12%
62 Hospitality, Leisure, Recreation, and Tourism	36%	3%	8%	3%	41%	9%
Overall	**44%**	**5%**	**16%**	**3%**	**24%**	**8%**

Source: HESA 2007–08 DLHE return

What graduates earn by subject studied

	Subject	Graduate employment or self employment	Non-graduate employment or self employment
1	Dentistry	£29,805	..
2	Medicine	£28,913	..
3	Chemical Engineering	£28,415	£14,785
4	Economics	£25,726	£16,539
5	General Engineering	£25,455	£16,655
6	Veterinary Medicine	£25,206	£19,861
7	East and South Asian Studies	£24,769	£16,498
8	Building	£24,755	£15,078
9	Civil Engineering	£24,473	£14,614
10	Mechanical Engineering	£24,446	£16,168
11	Social Work	£23,834	£15,236
12	Mathematics	£23,654	£15,835
13	Aeronautical and Manufacturing Engineering	£23,464	£16,181
14	Electrical and Electronic Engineering	£23,276	£17,926
15	Physics and Astronomy	£23,275	£16,203
16	Librarianship and Information Management	£22,935	£16,784
17	Russian	£22,568	£15,534
18	Geology	£22,282	£13,425
19	Computer Science	£22,276	£16,240
20	Land and Property Management	£21,758	..
21	Nursing	£21,459	£16,714
22	Business Studies	£21,452	£16,226
23	Politics	£21,446	£15,279
24	Chemistry	£21,224	£15,550
25	Accounting and Finance	£21,154	£16,294
26	German	£20,938	£16,361
27	Middle Eastern and African Studies	£20,875	..
28	Education	£20,652	£14,227
29	French	£20,454	£15,399
30	Food Science	£20,298	£14,992
31	Other Subjects Allied to Medicine	£20,260	£15,477
32	Town and Country Planning and Landscape	£20,233	£15,016
33	Italian	£20,193	£15,389
34	Philosophy	£19,968	£15,052
35	Geography and Environmental Sciences	£19,962	£14,606
36	Classics and Ancient History	£19,947	£15,413
37	Iberian Languages	£19,939	£15,615
38	Materials Technology	£19,883	£15,176
39	Social Policy	£19,659	£14,697
40	History	£19,656	£14,654
41	Pharmacology and Pharmacy	£19,453	£16,411
42	Anatomy and Physiology	£19,443	£14,347

Subject	Graduate employment or self employment	Non-graduate employment or self employment
43 American Studies	£19,376	£14,685
44 Law	£19,322	£15,228
45 Biological Sciences	£19,148	£14,303
46 Architecture	£19,136	£14,294
47 Agriculture and Forestry	£18,976	£15,461
48 Sociology	£18,887	£14,918
49 Anthropology	£18,665	£16,245
50 History of Art, Architecture and Design	£18,477	£15,658
51 Archaeology	£18,392	£14,440
52 Psychology	£18,384	£14,328
53 English	£18,350	£14,523
54 Sports Science	£18,217	£14,520
55 Theology and Religious Studies	£18,170	£15,185
56 Music	£18,111	£14,516
57 Hospitality, Leisure, Recreation and Tourism	£18,000	£15,483
58 Art and Design	£17,774	£14,062
59 Communication and Media Studies	£17,649	£14,637
60 Linguistics	£17,437	£14,948
61 Drama, Dance and Cinematics	£17,145	£14,355
62 Celtic Studies	£16,820	£14,551
Overall	**£21,311**	**£15,040**

NOTE: .. indicates a suppressed mean salary based on 7 or less graduates
Source: HESA 2007–08 DLHE return

University schemes

If a university that offers extra help towards employment, it is worth considering whether its scheme is likely to work for you. Some are too new to show results in the labour market, but they may have been endorsed by big employers or introduced at an institution whose graduates already have a record of success in the jobs market.

At Liverpool John Moores University, for example, the World of Work (WoW) programme was devised with the help of the CBI, Shell, Sony and Marks and Spencer. Taken by students in all subjects, it offers classes in finance, entrepreneurship and negotiation skills, among many other topics. There are guest lectures and demonstrations related to the eight employment-related skills that WoW is intended to develop and employers carry out mock interviews to assess students' strengths and weaknesses.

Hertfordshire is another university to have demonstrated a sustained focus on its students' job prospects. It was arguably the first of many universities to describe itself as "business facing". Employer groups are consulted on the curriculum and often supply guest lecturers on degree courses. Like some other universities, such as Derby, it offers career development support to graduates throughout their working life.

Other universities, like Exeter, have taken a different tack and are helping students make the most of their voluntary and extra-curricular activities by certificating them. The Exeter Award gives credit for attendance at skills sessions and training courses, active participation in sporting and musical activities, engagement in work experience and voluntary work. The university already claimed to have more students than any other involved in voluntary activities. It believes that the award will encourage employers to take more notice of them.

The York Award is another well-established example of this type of scheme that has the involvement of organisations from the public, private and voluntary sectors. The university has found that employers value a combination of academic study, work experience and leisure interests. The scheme offers York students a framework to gain recognition for activities that are not formally recognised through the degree programme. Among the subjects on an extensive list of courses are networking, time management, counselling and understanding different cultures.

The value of work experience

As the table earlier in this chapter showed, there are also big differences in the average employment prospects in different subjects, but the majority of graduate jobs are open to applicants from any discipline. For those general positions, employers tend to be more impressed by a good degree from what they consider a prestigious university than by an apparently relevant qualification.

Specialist jobs – for example in engineering or design – are a different matter. Employers may be much more knowledgeable about the quality of individual courses and less influenced by a university's overall position in league tables when the job relies directly on knowledge and skills acquired as a student. That goes for the likes of medicine and architecture as well as the new vocational areas such as computer games design or environmental management.

In either case, however, work experience has become increasingly important. Sandwich degrees, which are extended programmes that include up to a year at work, have always boosted employment prospects – graduates are often end up working where they undertook their placement. But many conventional degrees now include shorter work placements that should offer some advantages in the labour market. Not all are arranged by the university so, unless you have an opening that you would like to pursue, that is something to establish and weigh in the balance when choosing a course.

If your chosen course does not include a work placement, you may still want to consider the possibilities for arranging your own part-time or temporary employment. The majority of supposedly full-time students now take jobs during term time, as well as in vacations, to make ends meet. But such jobs can also boost your CV – even working in a bar or a shop shows some experience of dealing with the public and coping with the disciplines of the workplace. Inevitably, the more prosperous cities are likely to offer more employment opportunities than rural areas or conurbations that have been hard hit in the recession.

Of course, the ultimate work-related degree is one sponsored by an employer or even taken in the workplace – something that ministers have encouraged recently. Middlesex University, for example, provides tailored programmes for Dell and Marks and Spencer, among other organisations, and has more than 1,000 students taking courses run by its Institute of Work Based Learning. Most such courses are provided for people already employed by the companies concerned, rather than as a route into the company. But they may come to be considered as an alternative to entering full-time higher education straight from school or college.

Consider part-time degrees

Another option, also favoured by ministers, is part-time study. Although the low level of financial support has deterred many prospective students, the numbers taking part-time degrees has been rising recently. Of the extra 20,000 university and college places announced by Lord Mandelson before the 2010 general election, 5,000 were earmarked for part-timers and the brief for Lord Browne's review of higher education funding specifically included part-time students.

Part-time study requires a high degree of commitment – knuckling down to an essay or an assignment after a hard day at work is not easy – but it does reduce the cost of higher education for those in work. Bear in mind, however, that most part-time courses take twice as long to complete as the full-time equivalent so, if your earning power is linked to the qualification, it will take that much longer for you to enjoy the benefits.

Plan early for your career

Whatever type of course you choose, it is sensible to start thinking about your future career early in your time at university. There has been a growing tendency in recent years for students to convince themselves that there would be plenty of time to apply for jobs after graduation and they were better off on focusing entirely on their degree while at university. In the current depressed employment market, all but the most obviously brilliant graduates need to offer more than just a degree, whether it be work experience, leadership qualities demonstrated through clubs and societies, or commitment to voluntary activities. Many students finish a degree without knowing what they want to do, but a blank CV will not impress any prospective employer.

The recession had the effect of reducing the number of vacancies for graduate-level jobs while simultaneously increasing the number of applications, intensifying the level of competition yet more. Almost three in ten students in the High Fliers survey had made more applications than they originally intended to, including to firms that did not really interest them. It is reasonable to assume that, despite the apparent rise in vacancies in 2010, this process will continue for some time as graduates who failed to secure jobs or traineeships in their chosen field apply again. Two-fifths of applications to firms in the High Fliers survey in 2009 came from people who had already left university.

The survey showed that final-year undergraduates were more pessimistic than their predecessors about their employment prospects and more willing to take a relatively low salary and a less-than-ideal job as a result. Nearly 40 per cent wished that they had started for a graduate job sooner. Everyone hopes the economy will be in better shape by the time this year's university entrants are looking for work, but it is better to be safe than sorry.

Useful websites

Prospects, the UK's official graduate careers website:
prospects.ac.uk

For information on internships, graduate schemes and career advice:
www.milkround.com

3 Going Abroad to University

There are many reasons for a British student to think about studying abroad, but let's dismiss one of them immediately. The UK has 133 universities and higher education colleges. Between them, they provide courses in Asian art, astronautics, tropical agriculture, and just about any other subject you can think of. There is no branch of science or culture, no language however arcane, that you cannot study somewhere in the UK. More importantly, UK universities are strong in the mainstream subjects that attract most students.

Where students go to

Even so, thousands of British people see the attraction of study abroad. The statistics are dubious, but it seems from figures gathered by the Organisation for Economic Cooperation and Development that 2,595 UK students were studying in France in 2007, 1,854 in Germany, 1,687 in Australia and 2,181 in Canada. The highest total was 8,625 in the USA. But 400 had found their way to Japan, 22 to Korea, and 26 to Slovakia. The total seems to be about 23,000, modest by comparison with the 450,000 non-UK citizens studying in Britain.

Many of these students have an abiding interest in some foreign culture that means they want to immerse themselves in it instead of studying it in the UK and making occasional visits. But the figures suggest that British students are more attracted to countries that are familiar or close at hand, and where they can speak English, than they are to the exotic. Many are doubtless planning to stay in, say, Canada, the USA or Australia after they graduate. Often they are already in the country where they will study – perhaps because their parents live and/or work there – and they may well have been to school there.

Financial implications

One key consideration in favour of study abroad is the introduction of fees for UK students. You may be able to save money by studying abroad, especially in another EU nation. You are entitled to study there for the same fees as a local, which can be lower than in the UK or even zero for some courses. In the EU, you will also be able get a job while studying. Farther afield your student visa might not allow you to take on paid work. In the USA, you may not be allowed to work off-campus.

This potential saving has to be considered with care. Despite the Bologna process, an inter-governmental agreement which means that degrees across Europe are becoming more similar in content and duration, many continental courses are longer than their UK equivalents, adding to the cost and to your lost earnings from university attendance. And, of course, you will have higher travel costs. It is harder to generalise about the cost of living. It can be lower than the UK in southern Europe or in small-town USA, but eyewateringly high in Scandinavia or Manhattan.

You can cut down the cost of an international experience and hedge your bets about committing yourself to a full course overseas by opting instead for an exchange scheme. UK universities have exchange partners all over the world, providing opportunities for everything from a summer school of less than a month to a full year abroad.

The most common offering is the EU's Erasmus scheme, which funds exchanges of between three months and a year, the work counting towards your degree. More than 2 million students throughout Europe have used the scheme, and there are 2,000 universities to choose from in 30 countries. Applications, which are made through universities' international offices, must be approved by the UK university as well as by the Erasmus administrators. Erasmus students do not pay any extra fees and they are eligible for grants to cover the extra expense of travelling and living in another country.

For those who opt for more than an exchange, there is still the chance of financial support. Many universities in the developed world offer their own grants or loans to selected international students, especially postgraduates, as some countries do on a national scale. The best way to find out what is available is to decide what course you want to take and where, and then investigate possible fees, scholarships and subsistence packages. You may have a good experience here. But bear in mind that for most universities in any country, foreign students are a source of big fees. You must assume that you will be seen in this light.

Which countries are best?
Anyone going abroad to study will be in search of a good experience. In early 2010 the British Council completed a detailed analysis of how well countries around the world work to attract foreign students, as well as how well-regarded the degrees they award are internationally.

The report has not been published in full, but it shows that, relative to their student population, smaller countries send the most people abroad to study. Almost 11 per cent of Moroccan students are outside Morocco, and 10 per cent of Irish students are outside Ireland. The equivalent for the UK would be about 0.5 per cent. However, the figure is not available for China, which is both the world's most populous country and its most energetic exporter of students.

The British Council report, prepared by the Economist Intelligence Unit, went on to look in detail at which countries have the most developed approach to welcoming international students. It began by looking at which countries have a proper strategy in place to internationalise their universities, at their policies on migration and at their international presence, including their ability to negotiate student exchange agreements with other nations. The authors then looked at the international acceptability of degrees from a range of countries, and finally at access, the steps which countries take to make their university systems open to students and academics from around the world.

The UK itself scores highly on these measures, no doubt to the British Council's relief. Britain comes third in the world as a destination for international students. The top place goes to Germany, with Australia second. China is in fourth place, while Malaysia, the USA, Japan, Russia, Nigeria, Brazil and India (these two in joint tenth place) complete the top eleven.

The report says that Germany is one of the few nations that does not allow public universities to increase fees for foreign students, and a German student visa lasts until a year after graduation, to help you look for a permanent job there. In Australia, universities can charge foreign students big fees, but other aspects of its system are highly rated. The quality of Australian degrees is generally regarded as high, and despite the high cost of getting there, life in Australia costs less than in the UK once you arrive.

This top eleven contains some surprising entries. The authors of the report admit that although Nigeria's university system is an open one, it is also "woefully inadequate for Africa's largest country". Unless you are already comfortable in Nigeria, perhaps by family background, it would be a bold decision to attend university there. And Russia, despite having one of the world's great cultures and having been a scientific powerhouse in the past, is now struggling to rebuild its university system as an important world player.

More interesting is Japan. The sheer cost of living in Japan may put off many potential students, as may the unfamiliarity of its language. But the collapsing number of young people there means that the country's universities are looking abroad to fill the gap. This means more support for more overseas students and more courses in English. However, as with any non-English speaking country, the language of instruction is only part of the story. You will need to know enough of the local language to manage the shops and the transport system, and of course to make friends and get the most out of being there.

Whatever its ranking, however, the USA will always be the top overseas destination. Its high-prestige universities, its use of English and its massive economy, make the USA a magnet for footloose British students. The Ivy League and other world-famous universities dominate global league tables, and many students hope to stay on the other side of the Atlantic to work after graduation, rather than coming straight home.

The individual systems of each state and the importance of private universities means that practices in relation to international students vary from university to university in the USA. There are only a few thousand state-funded places for overseas students in the whole country. On the other hand, many US universities have some sort of student support package on offer, and big institutions spend millions on supporting students. The sheer depth of the US university system means that if you are thinking of studying abroad, the USA is almost bound to be on the list of possibilities.

Another option of growing interest is China. While you may not believe the whole of the story that China is about to take over the world, it has already grown massively in importance. Its university system is growing in quality, especially at the C9 group of international institutions, which have become known as the Chinese Ivy League. Familiarity with China is unlikely to be a career disadvantage for anyone in the 21st century.

Will my degree be recognised?
Even in the era of globalisation, you need to bear in mind that not all degrees are equal. At one extreme is the MBA, which has an international system for accrediting courses, and a global admissions standard. But with many professional courses, study abroad is a potential hazard. To work as a doctor, engineer or lawyer in the UK, you need a qualification which the relevant professional body will recognise. It is understandable that to practise law in England, you need to have studied the English legal system. For other subjects, the issues are more to do with the quality and content of courses outside UK control.

There are ways of researching this issue in advance. One is to contact Naric, the National Recognition Centre for the UK (**www.naric.org.uk**). Naric exists to examine the compatibility and acceptability of qualifications from around the world. The other approach is to ask the UK professional body in question – maybe an engineering institution, the Law Society or the General Teaching, Medical or Dental Council – about the qualification you propose to study for.

The British Council report suggests that Australian and German degrees are the most internationally acceptable from its Top 11 countries, with Brazil at the bottom. The USA comes fifth. While it is home to the world's top universities, the USA also has many less prestigious institutions whose qualifications are less likely to be welcomed around the world.

Which are the best universities?

Going abroad to study is a big and expensive decision, and you want to get it right. But a 2009 survey of UK students who were studying abroad or planning to do so suggested that excitement, adventure and glamour were more important in their choice than career positioning. Many have family money and have been privately educated. Their approach contrasts with that of overseas students coming to the UK, most of whom are highly tactical and career-minded about the choice they are making.

But let's assume that you are more thoughtful in your approach than this survey suggests. Especially if you plan to study abroad to establish yourself as an internationally mobile high-flyer, you will want to know that the university you are going to is taken seriously around the world. Systems for global university ranking offer one avenue for researching this problem.

At the moment there are two main systems for ranking universities on a world scale. One is run by QS Quacquarelli Symonds, an educational research company based in London (**www.topuniversities.com**). The other is by Shanghai Ranking Consultancy, a company set up by Shanghai Jiao Tong University in China and is called the Academic Ranking of World Universities (ARWU) (**www.arwu.org**). The QS system uses a number of measures including academic opinion, employer opinion, international orientation, research impact and staff/student ratio to create its listing, while the ARWU uses measures such as Nobel Prizes and highly cited papers which are more related to excellence in scientific research. Despite these different approaches, many universities appear on both. If you go to a university that features highly on either table, you will be at a place that is well-regarded around the world. Even the 500th university on either of these rankings is an elite institution, after all, in a world with 4000 universities. The top 50 universities in both rankings are listed here.

These systems tend to favour universities which are good at science and medicine. Places that specialise in the humanities and the social sciences, such as the London School of Economics, can appear in deceptively modest positions. In addition, the rankings tend to look at universities in the round, and contain only limited information on specific subjects.

One advantage of the QS ranking system is that 10 per cent of a university's possible score comes from a global survey of recruiters. So you can look at this column of the table for an idea about where the major employers like to hire. Note that the author of this *Guide* has a role in developing the QS Rankings.

Other options for overseas studies

If you decide that studying abroad for a complete degree is too much, other options remain open. A language degree will typically involve a year abroad, but a look at the UCAS web site will show many options for studying another subject alongside your language of choice. UK universities offer degrees in information technology, science, business and even journalism with a major language such as Chinese.

Another possibility is a joint degree awarded by more than one university. Here you would

The top 50 universities in the world in 2009 according to QS World University Ranking (QS) and the Academic Ranking of World Universities (ARWU)

QS Rank	Institution Name	Country	ARWU Rank	Institution Name	Country
1	Harvard University	USA	1	Harvard University	USA
2	University of Cambridge	UK	2	Stanford University	USA
3	Yale University	USA	3	University of California, Berkeley	USA
4	University College London	UK	4	University of Cambridge	UK
=5	Imperial College London	UK	5	Massachusetts Institute of Technology	USA
=5	University of Oxford	UK	6	California Institute of Technology	USA
7	University of Chicago	USA	7	Columbia University	USA
8	Princeton University	USA	8	Princeton University	USA
9	Massachusetts Institute of Technology	USA	9	University of Chicago	USA
10	California Institute of Technology	USA	10	University of Oxford	UK
11	Columbia University	USA	11	Yale University	USA
12	University of Pennsylvania	USA	12	Cornell University	USA
13	Johns Hopkins University	USA	13	University of California, Los Angeles	USA
14	Duke University	USA	14	University of California, San Diego	USA
15	Cornell University	USA	15	University of Pennsylvania	USA
16	Stanford University	USA	16	University of Washington	USA
17	Australian National University	Australia	17	University of Wisconsin, Madison	USA
18	McGill University	Canada	18	University of California, San Francisco	USA
19	University of Michigan, Ann Arbor	USA	19	Johns Hopkins University	USA
=20	University of Edinburgh	UK	20	University of Tokyo	Japan
=20	ETH Zurich (Swiss Federal Institute of Technology)	Switzerland	21	University College London	UK
22	University of Tokyo	Japan	22	University of Michigan, Ann Arbor	USA
23	King's College London	UK	23	ETH Zurich (Swiss Federal Institute of Technology)	Switzerland
24	University of Hong Kong	Hong Kong	24	Kyoto University	Japan
25	Kyoto University	Japan	25	University of Illinois, Urbana-Champaign	USA
26	University of Manchester	UK	26	Imperial College London	UK
27	Carnegie Mellon University	USA	27	University of Toronto	Canada

QS Rank	Institution Name	Country	ARWU Rank	Institution Name	Country
28	Ecole Normale Supérieure, Paris	France	28	University of Minnesota, Twin Cities	USA
29	University of Toronto	Canada	29	Washington University, St Louis	USA
30	National University of Singapore	Singapore	30	Northwestern University	USA
31	Brown University	USA	31	Duke University	USA
=32	University of California, Los Angeles	USA	32	New York University	USA
=32	Northwestern University	USA	33	Rockefeller University	USA
34	University of Bristol	UK	34	University of Colorado, Boulder	USA
35	Hong Kong University of Science and Technology	Hong Kong	35	University of California, Santa Barbara	USA
=36	École Polytechnique	France	36	University of British Columbia	Canada
=36	University of Melbourne	Australia	37	University of Maryland, College Park	USA
=36	University of Sydney	Australia	38	University of Texas at Austin	USA
39	University of California, Berkeley	USA	39	University of North Carolina at Chapel Hill	USA
40	University of British Columbia	Canada	40	Pierre and Marie Curie University - Paris 6	France
41	University of Queensland	Australia	41	University of Manchester	UK
42	École Polytechnique Fédérale de Lausanne	Switzerland	42	Vanderbilt University	USA
=43	Osaka University	Japan	43	University of Copenhagen	Denmark
=43	Trinity College Dublin	Ireland	44	University of Paris Sud (Paris 11)	France
45	Monash University	Australia	45	Pennsylvania State University, University Park	USA
46	Chinese University of Hong Kong	Hong Kong	46	University of California, Irvine	USA
=47	University of New South Wales	Australia	47	University of Southern California	USA
=47	Seoul National University	Korea, South	48	University of Texas Southwestern Medical Center, Dallas	USA
=49	University of Amsterdam	Netherlands	49	University of California, Davis	USA
=49	Tsinghua University	China	50	Karolinska Institute	Sweden

We gratefully acknowledge permission to reproduce these two rankings. The full QS World University Rankings 2009 can be consulted at www.topuniversities.com and the full Academic Ranking of World Universities 2009 at www.arwu.org

be admitted to a UK institution but would spend about half of your time at the partner organisation, and be awarded a degree from both. Many British universities now work this way and the Bologna process means that it is becoming simpler for European universities to offer them.

The best approach is to decide what you want to study and then see if there is a UK university that offers it as a joint degree. Then you should ask some searching questions. Employers and academics alike sometimes look askance at these degrees. In principle they should match the quality control systems of both the nations involved – or all, as some have up to five awarding universities. In practice, some have been criticised for inadequate standards. They are also an unfamiliar concept for employers. At least make sure that all the universities involved are well-regarded, for example by looking at their rankings on one or other of the web sites mentioned above.

Useful websites

The following websites will help you find out more about the topics discussed in this chapter.

Association of Commonwealth Universities: **www.acu.ac.uk**
College Board (USA): **www.collegeboard.com**
Education Ireland: **www.educationireland.ie**
Erasmus Programme (EU): **www.britishcouncil.org/erasmus**
Finaid (USA): **www.finaid.org**
Fulbright Commission: **www.fulbright.co.uk**
Study in Australia: **www.studyinaustralia.gov.au**
Study in Canada: **www.studyincanada.com**

Recognition of international degrees

National Recognition Centre for the UK (Naric): **www.naric.org.uk**

Global university ranking tables

QS World University Rankings: **www.topuniversities.com**
Academic Ranking of World Universities: **www.arwu.org**

4 The Top Universities

What distinguishes a top university? And who is to say that one course is better than another – especially when the university system is so reluctant to make any such comparison?

Higher education now publishes copious statistics, but resists combining them in a way that might answer applicants' questions. Critics of league tables insist that this is because every university has different priorities, and every course different ways of approaching a subject. Students must choose the one that suits them best.

So they must. However, the sheer range of universities and courses in the UK is such that most applicants need some help paring down the options to create a shortlist for their five application choices. For 17 years, *The Times Good University Guide* has been assisting students and their parents with that process, using the statistics that universities themselves employ to measure their own performance.

Every element of the table in this chapter has been chosen for the light it shines on the undergraduate experience and a student's future prospects. The selection of these eight measures and the way in which they are combined give a particular view of universities' overall strengths, but it is one that has stood the test of time. Unlike some others, *The Times Good University Guide* has placed a premium on consistency, confident that the measures are the best available for the task.

Some changes have been forced upon us. Universities stopped assessing teaching quality subject by subject, when this was the most heavily weighted measure in the table. Spending on libraries, which was a measure in virtually all university league tables, is no longer collected separately from that relating to museums, galleries and observatories. There have been developments, too, such as the National Student Survey, which was first used in the table four years ago.

The basic information that applicants need, however, in order to judge universities and their courses does not change. A university's entry standards, staffing levels, completion rates, degree classifications and graduate employment rates are all vital pieces of intelligence for anyone deciding where to study. Research grades, while not directly involving undergraduates, bring with them considerable funds and enable a university to attract top academics. Leading researchers in any subject may deliver the most inspiring lectures.

Most of the measures in *The Times Good University Guide*'s table have been used since it was first published and, while any element can be discounted by the individual, the package has struck a chord with readers. The ranking is the most-quoted of its type both in Britain and overseas, and has built a reputation as the most authoritative arbiter of changing fortunes in higher education.

The measures used in the ranking are kept under review by a group of university administrators and statisticians, which meets annually. The raw data that go into the table in this chapter and the subject tables in chapter 5 are all in the public domain and are sent to universities for checking before any scores are calculated.

Indeed, while the various official bodies concerned with higher education do not publish league tables, several produce system-wide statistics in a format that encourages comparison. The Higher Education Funding Councils' Research Assessment Exercise was one early example of this, with universities trumpeting their successes almost as soon as the grades had been announced. The Higher Education Statistics Agency (HESA), which supplies most of the figures used in our tables, also publishes annual "performance indicators" on everything from completion rates and research output to the proportion of under-represented social groups at each university.

Any scrutiny of league table positions is best carried out in conjunction with an examination of the relevant subject table – it is the course, after all, that will dominate your undergraduate years and influence your subsequent career.

How *The Times* League Table works

The table is presented in a format that displays the raw data, wherever possible. In building the table, scores for Student Satisfaction and Research Quality were weighted by 1.5; all other measures were weighted by 1. The indicators were combined using a common statistical technique known as Z-scores, to ensure that no indicator has a disproportionate effect on the overall total for each university, and the totals were transformed to a scale with 1000 for the top score.

For Entry Standards, Good Honours and Graduate Prospects, the score was adjusted for subject mix. It is accepted that engineering, law and medicine graduates will tend to have better graduate prospects than their peers from English, psychology and sociology courses. Comparing results in the main subject groupings helps to iron out differences attributable simply to the range of degrees on offer. This subject-mix adjustment means that it is not possible to replicate the scores in the table from the published indicators because the calculation requires access to the entire dataset.

The Z-score technique makes it impossible to compare universities' total scores from one year to the next, although their relative positions in the table are comparable. Individual scores are dependent on the top performer, so a university might drop from 60 per cent of the top score to 58 per cent but still have improved, if the leading university had done better still.

Only where data are not available from HESA are figures sourced directly from universities. Where this is not possible – for example, in the case of those Scottish universities that are not part of the National Student Survey – scores are generated according to a university's average performance on other indicators.

The organisations providing the raw data for the tables are not involved in the process of aggregation, so are not responsible for any inferences or conclusions we have made. Every care has been taken to ensure the accuracy of the tables and accompanying information, but no responsibility can be taken for errors or omissions.

The Times league table uses eight important measures of university activity, based on the most recent data available at the time of compilation:

- » Student satisfaction
- » Research quality
- » Entry standards
- » Student–staff ratio
- » Services and facilities spend
- » Completion
- » Good honours
- » Graduate prospects

Student satisfaction

This is a measure of students' views of the quality of their courses. The National Student Survey (NSS) was the source of this data. The NSS is an initiative undertaken by the Funding Councils for England, Northern Ireland and Wales. It is designed, as an element of the quality assurance for higher education, to inform prospective students and their advisers in choosing what and where to study. The survey encompasses the views of final-year students on the quality of their courses. Data from the surveys published in 2008 and 2009 were used.

- » The National Student Survey covers six aspects of a course: teaching, assessment and feedback, academic support, organisation and management, learning resources and personal development, with an additional question gauging overall satisfaction. Students answer on a scale from 1 (bottom) to 5 (top) and the measure is the percentage of positive responses (4 and 5) in each section, averaged to produce the final score.
- » The survey is based on the opinion of final-year students rather than directly assessing teaching quality. Most undergraduates have no experience of other universities, or different courses, to inform their judgements. Although all the questions relate to courses, rather than the broader student experience, some types of university – notably medium-sized campus universities – tend to do better than others.
- » Scottish universities were not automatically included in the survey, although 11 out of 14 have so far opted in.
- » Where a university did not have sufficiently high response rates to publish results for one of the two years used to compile this measure, a single year's data have been used.

Research quality

This is a measure of the quality of the research undertaken in each university. The information was sourced from the 2008 Research Assessment Exercise (RAE), a peer-review exercise used to evaluate the quality of research in UK higher education institutions undertaken by the UK Higher Education funding bodies. Additionally, academic staffing data for 2007–08 from the Higher Education Statistics Agency have been used.

- » A research quality profile was given to every university department that took part. This profile used the following categories: 4* world-leading; 3* internationally excellent; 2* internationally recognised; 1* nationally recognised; and unclassified. The Funding Bodies decided to direct more funds to the very best research by applying weightings. The English, Scottish and Welsh funding councils have slightly different weightings. Those adopted by HEFCE (the funding council for England) for funding in 2010–11 are used in the tables: 4* receiving nine times the weight of 2*, and 3* receiving three times the weight of 2*.
- » Universities could choose which staff to include in the RAE, so, to factor in the depth of the research quality, each quality profile score has been multiplied by the number of staff returned in the RAE as a proportion of all eligible staff.

» Estimations of the eligible staff for each university were made drawing from publicly available data that have been quality assured by universities themselves. The eligible staff data include all staff directly responsible for teaching and research (excluding those on part-time contracts of less than 20 per cent of a full-time position as they were not eligible), with an adjustment made to remove more junior staff on research-only contracts. An adjustment has also been made to reflect patterns of staffing in those institutions which carry out further education as well as higher education. The calculations were checked against the figures published by a number of universities that declared the proportion of eligible staff entered for assessment.

Estimation was necessary because, as you will see from the note on page 51, HESA decided not to publish data on numbers of staff in university departments who were eligible to be submitted in the RAE. The proportion of staff entered by each university was considered sufficiently important to be included in the grades used in every previous RAE to give an indication of the ethos and overall quality of departments. The methodology used in *The Times* league table attempts to replicate that process as accurately as possible, given the restrictions imposed by HESA.

Entry standards

This is the average score, using the UCAS tariff (see page 16), of new students under the age of 21 who took A and AS Levels, Highers and Advanced Highers and other equivalent qualifications (e.g. International Baccalaureate). It measures what new students actually achieved rather than the entry requirements suggested by the universities. The data comes from HESA for 2008–09. The original sources of data for this measure are data returns made by the universities themselves to HESA.

» Using the UCAS tariff, each student's examination results were converted to a numerical score. HESA then calculated an average for all students at the university. The results have then been adjusted to take account of the subject mix at the university.
» A score of 360 represents three As at A level. Although all of the top 30 universities in the table have entry standards of at least 360, it does not mean that everyone achieved such results – let alone that this was the standard offer. Courses will not demand more than three subjects at A level and offers are pitched accordingly. You will need to reach the entry requirements set by the university, rather than the scores represented here.

Student–staff ratio

This is a measure of the average number of students to each member of the academic staff, apart from those purely engaged in research. In this measure a low score is better than a high score. The data comes from HESA for 2008–09. The original sources of data for this measure are data returns made by the universities themselves to HESA.

» The figures, as calculated by HESA, allow for variation in employment patterns at different universities. A low value means that there are a small number of students for each academic member of staff, but this does not, of course, ensure good teaching quality or contact time with academics.
» Student–staff ratios are usually low for medicine and this will influence the scores of universities with medical schools.

Services and facilities spend

The expenditure per student on staff and student facilities, including library and computing

facilities. The data comes from HESA for 2007–08 and 2008–09. The original data sources for this measure are data returns made by the universities to HESA.
» This is a measure calculated by taking the expenditure on student facilities (sports, grants to student societies, careers services, health services, counselling, etc.) and library and computing facilities (books, journals, staff, central computers and computer networks, but not buildings) and dividing this by the number of full-time-equivalent students. Expenditure is averaged over two years to even out the figures (for example, a computer upgrade undertaken in a single year).

Completion

This measure gives the percentage of students expected to complete their studies (or transfer to another institution) for each university. The data comes from the HESA performance indicators, based on data for 2008–09 and earlier years.
» This measure is a projection, liable to statistical fluctuations.

Good honours

This measure is the percentage of graduates achieving a first or upper second class degree. The results have been adjusted to take account of the subject mix at the university. The data comes from HESA for 2008–09. The original sources of data for this measure are data returns made by the universities themselves to HESA.
» Four-year first degrees, such as an MChem, are treated as equivalent to a first or upper second.
» Scottish Ordinary degrees (awarded after three years of study) in Scotland are excluded.
» Universities control degree classification, with some oversight from external examiners. There have been suggestions that since universities have increased the numbers of good honours degrees they award, this measure may not be as objective as it should be. However, it remains the key measure of a student's success and employability.

Graduate prospects

This measure is the percentage of the total number of graduates who take up graduate-level employment or further study. The results have been adjusted for subject mix. The data come from HESA for 2008 graduates.
» HESA surveys graduates six months after graduation to find out what they are doing and the data are based on this survey.

Statement from the Higher Education Statistics Agency (HESA) regarding the use of staffing data in looking at Research Assessment Exercise performance:

This analysis of the results of the Research Assessment Exercise 2008 makes use of contextual data supplied under contract by the Higher Education Statistics Agency (HESA). It is a contractual condition that this statement should be published in conjunction with the analysis.

HESA holds no data specifying which or how many staff have been regarded by each institution as eligible for inclusion in RAE 2008, and no data on the assignment to Units of Assessment of those eligible staff not included. Further, the data that HESA does hold is not an adequate alternative basis on which to estimate eligible staff numbers, whether for an institution as a whole, or disaggregated by Units of Assessment, or by some broader subject-based grouping.

	Student satisfaction (%)	Research quality	Entry standards	Student–staff ratio	Services and facilities spend per student (£)	Completion (%)	Good honours (%)	Graduate prospects (%)	Total
	100	9.0	n/a	n/a	n/a	100.0	100.0	100.0	1000
1 Oxford	85	4.2	532	10.8	3168	98.5	91.8	82.8	1000
2 Cambridge	85	4.3	547	11.6	2635	98.6	87.3	82.3	965
3 Imperial College	76	3.1	504	10.4	4090	95.1	72.7	88.9	851
4 St Andrews	84	2.8	455	13.4	1856	94.9	85.6	74.4	798
5 London School of Economics	72	3.7	494	13.2	2232	95.2	76.5	81.9	789
6 Durham	81	3.0	468	15.4	2084	97.8	79.0	77.8	788
7 University College London	78	3.2	458	8.9	2124	94.8	81.0	80.8	784
8 Warwick	79	2.8	464	13.0	1927	95.4	79.9	77.9	766
9 York	81	2.9	423	13.7	1920	94.9	75.3	71.5	748
10 Lancaster	80	2.8	393	13.4	1746	94.1	68.3	77.6	737
11 Edinburgh	74	3.2	439	13.3	2572	92.0	80.2	76.2	733
12 Exeter	84	2.8	408	18.4	1732	95.8	79.6	66.8	723
13 Bath	80	2.3	451	15.7	1610	94.8	74.2	80.9	714
14 Bristol	74	3.0	448	13.6	2015	95.1	78.6	78.3	706
15 Leicester	85	2.2	372	14.4	1618	92.6	71.6	74.2	691
=16 Loughborough	85	2.5	370	18.0	1288	93.8	69.9	71.3	687
=16 King's College London	76	2.3	421	11.1	2060	94.1	75.6	80.5	687
18 Sheffield	80	2.7	411	13.8	1488	92.1	72.8	72.3	686
19 Southampton	79	2.3	407	13.4	1854	92.6	74.4	76.3	682
20 Nottingham	78	2.4	412	13.6	1574	94.5	75.0	75.7	679

21	Sussex	78	2.6	371	15.2	1428	90.8	80.0	72.6	674
22	Birmingham	79	2.4	404	15.1	1893	93.3	72.2	69.9	661
=23	East Anglia	83	2.1	366	15.3	1617	90.3	71.2	69.1	658
=23	Glasgow	81	2.4	399	14.0	1888	84.3	70.3	72.1	658
25	Newcastle	79	2.2	399	15.0	1624	92.9	72.0	72.4	651
26	Leeds	78	2.3	397	14.1	1484	92.6	74.2	70.5	648
27	School of Oriental and African Studies	73	2.2	387	11.2	2016	87.9	73.1	73.1	643
28	Liverpool	77	2.1	403	12.5	1994	89.6	71.1	70.6	641
29	Aston	80	1.4	364	17.8	1718	91.6	70.1	75.2	630
30	Manchester	73	2.8	416	13.5	1777	92.3	70.3	71.1	629
31	Royal Holloway	76	2.8	366	14.8	1495	93.1	70.9	62.7	623
32	Surrey	78	2.1	372	18.0	1515	83.5	68.1	79.6	606
33	Aberdeen	82	2.1	357	14.9	1344	80.0	67.6	76.8	605
34	Cardiff	77	2.1	392	14.9	1348	93.4	69.0	72.8	604
35	Reading	79	2.4	350	16.7	1152	91.8	69.8	66.0	595
=36	Strathclyde	77	1.8	388	17.7	1558	84.6	71.7	75.5	592
=36	Queen Mary, London	77	2.3	354	12.9	1531	89.6	64.6	76.0	592
38	Queen's Belfast	77	2.0	368	15.2	1745	85.3	68.5	74.7	588
39	Kent	80	1.7	319	14.8	1245	86.8	63.9	68.6	580
40	Aberystwyth	83	2.1	292	16.0	1320	85.8	60.1	61.5	568
41	Essex	77	2.2	311	13.8	1672	86.5	58.3	60.2	565
42	Keele	79	1.3	302	13.0	1141	88.5	65.6	68.3	555
43	Heriot-Watt	74	1.9	338	16.8	1726	82.6	68.6	74.7	551
44	Dundee	80	1.6	344	14.0	1333	79.5	68.4	68.6	549
45	Stirling	78	1.5	314	17.0	1205	82.9	65.5	67.6	513
46	Robert Gordon	78	0.6	314	18.7	1305	83.6	56.9	83.4	509
47	City	72	1.5	340	18.6	1381	82.8	68.2	79.4	506

		Student satisfaction (%)	Research quality	Entry standards	Student–staff ratio	Services and facilities spend per student (£)	Completion (%)	Good honours (%)	Graduate prospects (%)	Total
		100	9.0	n/a	n/a	n/a	100.0	100.0	100.0	1000
48	Hull	81	1.2	290	19.5	1216	82.4	58.0	70.0	504
49	Swansea	79	1.7	299	14.9	1227	88.1	56.0	58.4	501
50	Brunel	73	1.9	315	19.7	1531	86.2	66.8	66.1	493
51	Oxford Brookes	78	0.6	309	17.7	1206	85.6	66.8	67.0	489
52	Goldsmiths College	73	2.5	318	16.8	911	82.5	66.0	56.7	479
53	Chichester	82	0.2	270	15.3	1105	87.0	50.2	59.9	478
54	Bangor	78	1.7	284	17.1	1082	86.4	56.9	57.8	469
55	Nottingham Trent	76	0.5	274	18.2	1361	85.5	55.1	71.0	467
56	Ulster	77	1.2	269	15.9	1480	77.8	61.2	58.9	452
=57	De Montfort	79	0.6	247	16.3	1078	82.0	51.5	69.4	451
=57	Bradford	76	1.1	275	15.8	1170	79.8	62.2	71.1	451
=59	Bournemouth	75	0.5	297	23.8	1282	85.3	61.5	70.8	447
=59	Northumbria	78	0.3	299	21.3	1160	85.8	56.2	70.5	447
61	Plymouth	75	0.8	279	15.3	1222	83.8	61.8	57.7	435
62	Lincoln	78	0.6	273	20.3	1073	83.5	56.2	60.6	434
63	Hertfordshire	75	0.4	241	15.6	1644	81.3	59.5	62.9	429
64	Gloucestershire	75	0.3	255	18.1	1397	81.8	60.9	60.3	424
65	Glasgow Caledonian	77	0.4	328	20.7	1158	79.7	66.0	62.6	423
66	Edinburgh Napier	76	0.4	264	19.2	1162	75.6	63.9	72.0	421
=67	UWIC, Cardiff	76	0.4	260	20.0	1432	82.5	54.5	61.1	418

=67	Queen Margaret Edinburgh	::		299	19.7	1105	79.6	63.4	66.3	418
=69	West of England	77	0.5	273	19.5	1184	81.1	62.9	60.0	416
=69	Central Lancashire	77	0.4	263	17.0	1606	73.9	49.7	61.0	416
71	Brighton	75	1.0	281	19.7	931	83.5	58.9	61.6	415
72	Sheffield Hallam	73	0.4	274	18.3	1050	85.2	63.0	63.0	413
73	Huddersfield	75	0.2	272	15.9	1409	77.7	57.3	61.1	410
=74	Portsmouth	80	0.6	273	20.2	1242	82.9	51.3	54.6	405
=74	Winchester	77	0.5	270	17.4	936	85.4	57.5	51.6	405
76	Edge Hill	78	0.1	259	18.0	1425	79.0	47.6	63.9	402
77	Staffordshire	76	0.1	241	19.1	1274	79.8	50.8	67.4	399
78	Cumbria	73	0.1	274	15.2	1148	82.6	50.6	67.2	398
79	Sunderland	79	0.6	232	15.6	932	76.1	48.6	58.6	396
80	Bath Spa	78	0.4	283	24.2	653	90.3	65.9	55.1	394
=81	York St John	76	0.2	280	19.9	1259	85.6	56.2	57.1	391
=81	Birmingham City	73	0.3	254	18.0	1554	77.4	56.2	69.1	391
83	Chester	75	0.2	268	17.5	854	79.0	56.7	65.6	390
84	Coventry	74	0.3	274	17.9	1155	76.4	64.9	64.2	388
85	Lampeter (Trinity Saint David)*	77	1.1	262	17.8	1029	73.0	53.6	57.2	377
86	University of the Arts London	63	2.0	280	19.6	1008	85.7	60.5	56.2	375
87	Roehampton	72	0.9	245	18.3	1292	82.1	52.2	57.7	363
88	Salford	74	1.0	266	18.5	1133	74.6	52.3	59.8	358
89	Northampton	77	0.2	240	20.9	1123	80.6	57.6	54.9	356
=90	Teesside	79	0.2	258	19.5	1043	71.2	53.5	60.0	355
=90	Worcester	76	0.1	260	20.7	930	79.9	52.1	62.4	355
92	Kingston	74	0.4	235	20.0	1134	81.5	60.7	57.7	353
93	Glyndŵr	75	0.2	232	21.0	1561	77.2	52.8	62.6	348
94	Glamorgan	74	0.5	271	18.1	1244	69.8	56.0	56.1	344

		Student satisfaction (%)	Research quality	Entry standards	Student–staff ratio	Services and facilities spend per student (£)	Completion (%)	Good honours (%)	Graduate prospects (%)	Total
		100	9.0				100.0	100.0	100.0	1000
95	Manchester Metropolitan	72	0.5	268	19.8	1127	78.8	57.2	57.5	341
96	UWCN, Newport	75	0.3	249	22.6	987	79.3	52.5	58.7	331
97	Canterbury Christ Church	74	0.2	247	20.3	919	80.5	49.2	64.7	329
98	Liverpool John Moores	74	0.4	246	19.7	1150	77.2	53.6	54.2	328
99	Leeds Metropolitan	68	0.2	263	21.2	941	81.3	53.4	67.2	323
100	Westminster	69	0.5	267	16.3	1032	79.3	52.7	53.2	322
101	Bedfordshire	75	0.2	200	19.3	728	82.7	44.5	60.2	321
102	Abertay	..	0.4	256	20.8	1361	70.1	54.0	56.6	314
103	Greenwich	78	0.4	241	25.1	1023	75.7	47.4	59.7	309
=104	Middlesex	70	0.6	184	22.8	2128	75.8	50.3	56.5	307
=104	Derby	74	0.1	237	19.6	1367	74.2	46.2	56.8	307
106	Thames Valley	72	0.2	201	20.6	1421	67.2	49.2	59.6	278
107	Anglia Ruskin	67	0.2	254	19.6	1049	75.8	55.4	58.5	272
108	Bolton	73	0.3	209	18.0	734	62.6	48.5	56.5	264
109	University for Creative Arts	67	0.6	264	24.3	1672	83.8	50.0	45.3	251
110	Southampton Solent	70	0.1	241	22.1	1085	75.0	42.3	49.2	244
111	East London	69	0.5	187	22.3	1117	79.4	46.4	52.9	234
112	Buckinghamshire New	69	0.1	207	20.5	1283	77.9	43.8	45.7	232
113	London South Bank	72	0.3	192	23.4	976	66.4	45.8	58.5	195

Liverpool Hope, Swansea Metropolitan, the University of the West of Scotland and Wolverhampton have refused to allow the release of data, and so do not appear in this year's league table.

The decision of London Metropolitan to release data again for use in league tables unfortunately came too late to allow for their inclusion in this year's table.

*Lampeter and Trinity University College Carmarthen are merging in 2010 to form Trinity Saint David. The data in this table relate solely to Lampeter as they predate the merger.

Useful websites

For more information on the data collected by HESA and a detailed explanation of the HEFCE performance indicators, visit the HESA site:
www.hesa.ac.uk

Information on the 2008 Research Assessment Exercise can be found at:
www.rae.ac.uk

5 The Top Universities by Subject

Knowing where a university stands in the pecking order of higher education is a vital piece of information for any prospective student, but the quality of the course is what matters most. As the latest Research Assessment Exercise (RAE) confirmed, the most modest institution may have a centre of specialist excellence, and even famous universities have mediocre departments. This section offers some pointers to the leading universities in a wide range of subjects.

The subject tables in this *Guide* also include scores from the National Student Survey (NSS). These distil the views of final-year undergraduates on several aspects of their course, including teaching quality, assessment and feedback, and the quality of learning resources. The three other measures used are research quality, students' entry qualifications and graduate employment prospects. None of the measures are weighted.

The tables include the research grades drawn from the deliberations of expert assessors in the 2008 RAE. No data have been released on the proportion of academics entered for assessment, for example, so it has not been possible to mirror the approach adopted in the main institutional ranking (see pages 49–50). Data supplied by the Higher Education Statistics Agency (HESA) are used to calculate average entry qualifications and the employment prospects of graduates. The prospects information draws a distinction between different types of employment: graduate employment, where a degree is normally required, and non-graduate employment. The tables give the percentage of "positive destinations" by adding those undertaking further study to the total in graduate employment.

Many subjects, such as dentistry or sociology, have their own table, but others are grouped together in broader categories, such as subjects allied to medicine, which includes such specialisms as physiotherapy and radiology. Not all universities in Scotland participate in the National Student Survey, so to qualify for inclusion in the table a university has to have data for at least two of the other measures. Scores are not published where the number of students is too small for the outcome to be statistically reliable. In the NSS, a 50 per cent response rate is required from a minimum of 30 students.

Cambridge is again by far the most successful university. It tops 31 of the 62 tables. Oxford has the next highest number of top places with 12.

The subject rankings demonstrate that there are "horses for courses" in higher education. Thus the London School of Economics is more than a match for its rivals in social science, while Imperial College remains a force in engineering. In their own fields, table-toppers such as Loughborough in librarianship and sports science, Warwick in American studies and Reading and Nottingham in agriculture, are equally well-known. But the tables contain less obvious success stories, such as Queen's, Belfast in social work, York in nursing, and Exeter in accounting and finance.

Research quality
This is a measure of the quality of the research undertaken in the subject area. The information was sourced from the 2008 Research Assessment Exercise (RAE), a peer-review exercise used to evaluate the quality of research in UK higher education institutions, undertaken by the UK Higher Education Funding Bodies.

For each subject, a research quality profile was given to those university departments that took part, showing how much of their research was in various quality categories. These categories were: 4* world-leading; 3* internationally excellent; 2* internationally recognised; 1* nationally recognised; and unclassified. The funding bodies decided to direct more funds to the very best research by applying weightings. The English, Scottish and Welsh funding councils have slightly different weightings. Those adopted by HEFCE (the funding council for England) for funding in 2010–11 are used in the tables: 4* receiving 9 times the weight of 2*, and 3* receiving 3 times the weight of 2*.

Staffing data to show how many of a department's academics were submitted in the RAE are not currently available. Some research ratings shown could relate to a relatively low proportion of the academic staff in the department.

Entry standards
This is the average UCAS tariff score for new students under the age of 21, taken from HESA data for 2008–09. Each student's examination grades were converted to a numerical score using the UCAS tariff (see page 18 for details) and added up to give a total score. HESA then calculated an average score for each university. The full qualifications range (e.g. including the International Baccalaureate) are included in deriving the average tariff.

Student satisfaction
This measure is taken from the National Student Survey results published in 2008 and 2009. A single year's figures are used when that is all that is available, but an average of the two years' results is used in all other cases. The score for each university represents the percentage of final-year undergraduates declaring themselves satisfied or very satisfied with their course, averaged over the seven sections of the survey.

Graduate prospects
This is the percentage of graduates undertaking further study or in a graduate job, in the annual survey by HESA six months after graduation. Two years of data (2007 and 2008 graduates) are aggregated to make the data more reliable. A low score on this measure does not necessarily indicate unemployment – some graduates may have taken jobs that are not categorised as graduate work. The averages for each subject are given at the bottom of the relevant subject table in this chapter and in a table in chapter 2 (see pages 34–35).

The Education table uses a fifth measure: teaching quality, as measured by the outcomes of Ofsted inspections of teacher training courses.

The subjects listed below are covered in the tables in this chapter:

- Accounting and Finance
- Aeronautical and Manufacturing Engineering
- Agriculture and Forestry
- American Studies
- Anatomy and Physiology
- Anthropology
- Archaeology
- Architecture
- Art and Design
- Biological Sciences
- Building
- Business Studies
- Celtic Studies
- Chemical Engineering
- Chemistry
- Civil Engineering
- Classics and Ancient History
- Communication and Media Studies
- Computer Science
- Dentistry
- Drama, Dance and Cinematics
- East and South Asian Studies
- Economics
- Education
- Electrical and Electronic Engineering
- English
- Food Science
- French
- General Engineering
- Geography and Environmental Sciences
- Geology
- German
- History
- History of Art, Architecture and Design
- Hospitality, Leisure, Recreation and Tourism
- Iberian Languages
- Italian
- Land and Property Management
- Law
- Librarianship and Information Management
- Linguistics
- Materials Technology
- Mathematics
- Mechanical Engineering
- Medicine
- Middle Eastern and African Studies
- Music
- Nursing
- Other Subjects Allied to Medicine (see page 156 for included subjects)
- Pharmacology and Pharmacy
- Philosophy
- Physics and Astronomy
- Politics
- Psychology
- Russian and East European Languages
- Social Policy
- Social Work
- Sociology
- Sports Science
- Theology and Religious Studies
- Town and Country Planning and Landscape
- Veterinary Medicine

Accounting and Finance

Surprisingly, even before the recession, accounting and finance were in the bottom half of the table of subjects for employment and not much further up for initial earnings, averaging little more than £21,000 for graduate jobs. Nevertheless, the demand for places was holding up well at the start of 2010, when applications were up by 12 per cent.

Bath's one-year reign at the top of the table for accounting and finance has come to an abrupt halt because of a low level of student satisfaction. Exeter and Warwick jointly take over at the top, with a very different pattern of scores. Exeter has a low research score, but has the most satisfied students; Warwick is in the top four for entry standards, research and graduate prospects. Strathclyde moves up to third place and clear of its rivals in Scotland through a consistent set of scores, without being right at the top on any individual measure.

Cardiff had the best grade in the 2008 assessments, but is restricted to seventh place because more than a third of its graduates were without a graduate-level job or a training place six months after completing their degrees. Fourth-placed London School of Economics had the highest entry standards and, for the third year in a row, Robert Gordon (the top post-1992 university) had the best graduate employment record. Like last year, only Lincoln, in 42nd place, comes anywhere near Exeter's 93 per cent satisfaction level.

As in many of the subject tables, higher entry scores and research grades make the difference for the old universities. Entry grades have risen since the last edition of the *Guide*: 16 universities (rather than 12) averaged more than 400 points at A level, while six had averages below 200 points, two fewer than last year.

In the latest survey, more than one graduate in five was continuing to study while in a graduate job six months after leaving university – by far the highest proportion for any subject. This reflects the professional structure of accountancy and shows that a high proportion of graduates are going on to practise accountancy. However, a quarter of all leavers start work in a non-graduate job and the 10 per cent unemployment rate is well above average for all subjects.

Employed in graduate job:	30%	Employed in non-graduate job and studying:	5%
Employed in graduate job and studying:	21%	Employed in non-graduate job:	24%
Studying:	9%	Unemployed:	10%
Average starting graduate salary:	£21,154	Average starting non-graduate salary:	£16,294

Accounting and Finance	Research quality/9	Entry standards	Student satisfaction %	Graduate prospects %	Overall rating
=1 Exeter	2.7	405	93	81	100.0
=1 Warwick	4.0	473	79	87	100.0
3 Strathclyde	3.8	438	82	81	98.6
4 London School of Economics	4.2	482	74	87	98.4
5 Loughborough	3.1	412	84	84	97.2
6 Lancaster	4.0	385	80	83	96.3
=7 Cardiff	4.5	399	81	65	95.5
=7 Bath	4.2	452	74		95.5
9 Glasgow	2.3	440	84	82	94.9

Accounting and Finance cont.

		Research quality/9	Entry standards	Student satisfaction %	Graduate prospects %	Overall rating
10	City	2.9	414	84	78	94.7
11	Reading	2.5	386	80	93	93.6
12	Leeds	3.6	426	74	84	93.4
=13	Newcastle	2.5	413	82	79	92.5
=13	Manchester	3.8	439	75	72	92.5
15	Nottingham	3.6	406	78	74	92.4
=16	Southampton	2.9	425	78	81	92.3
=16	Edinburgh	2.5	423	77	90	92.3
18	Queen's, Belfast	3.0	401	77	84	91.9
=19	Robert Gordon	1.4	329	85	96	91.3
=19	Kent	2.8	328	82	82	91.3
21	Durham	3.0	384	78	77	90.0
22	Liverpool	2.5	377	81	74	89.6
23	Birmingham	3.2	391	76	73	89.2
=24	Bangor	3.2	269	85	66	88.3
=24	East Anglia	2.4	329	82	77	88.3
26	Bristol	2.6	430	71	85	88.2
27	Northumbria	1.1	300	88	83	87.8
28	Sheffield	3.1	357	77	72	87.7
29	Aberdeen	2.2	324	81	76	87.0
30	Portsmouth	1.7	284	89	61	85.1
31	Heriot-Watt	2.4	328	78	73	84.8
32	Ulster	1.9	301	82	73	84.6
33	De Montfort	2.1	259	84	70	84.5
34	Stirling	1.8	335	80	72	84.4
35	Queen Mary, London	2.9	340	75	64	83.9
36	Hull	2.1	268	80	78	83.7
37	Dundee	1.9	336	77	72	82.7
38	Bournemouth	1.6	301	81	70	82.4
39	Surrey	2.5	353	74		82.3
40	West of England	2.2	259	80	70	82.2
41	Oxford Brookes		306	89	71	82.0
=42	Nottingham Trent	1.7	248	78	83	81.6
=42	Lincoln		258	92	68	81.6
44	Sheffield Hallam	1.5	263	80	70	79.6
=45	Essex	2.7	293	72	67	79.5
=45	Keele	2.3	272	73	72	79.5
47	Bradford	2.7	306	74	58	79.4
48	Salford	1.6	283	85	47	78.9
49	Glasgow Caledonian	1.0	327	79	63	78.5
50	Brighton	2.8	253	76	54	78.4
51	Aberystwyth	1.6	284	80	57	78.0
52	Glamorgan	1.3	270	82	57	77.5

53 Huddersfield	1.4	270	84	47	77.3
54 Manchester Metropolitan	1.8	263	76	62	77.0
55 Greenwich	1.3	249	84	45	75.6
56 Central Lancashire	1.6	271	75	57	74.9
57 Birmingham City	1.3	212	77	68	74.7
58 Leeds Metropolitan		251	86	54	74.6
59 Plymouth	1.7	273	75	47	73.0
60 Hertfordshire	1.8	221	76	49	72.6
61 Gloucestershire		274	73	77	72.4
=62 Kingston		253	81	57	72.3
=62 Edinburgh Napier	0.9	251	72	69	72.3
64 Northampton		203	83	60	72.1
65 Thames Valley		209	85	45	70.3
66 Derby		219	76	62	68.7
67 Liverpool John Moores	0.6	239	79	42	68.6
68 UWIC, Cardiff		255	78	48	68.3
=69 Staffordshire		178	73	68	66.7
=69 Coventry		260	70	62	66.7
71 East London		188	86	29	66.5
72 Middlesex		172	75	57	65.1
73 Anglia Ruskin		199	66	68	63.1
74 Bedfordshire		135	82	34	62.8
75 London South Bank	1.2	171	73	29	61.8
76 Southampton Solent		220	69	47	60.9

» Actuarial Profession: **www.actuaries.org.uk**
» Association of Chartered Certified Accountants: **www.accaglobal.com**
» Careers in accounting: **www.careers-in-accounting.com**
» Chartered Institute of Public Finance and Accountancy: **www.cipfa.org.uk**
» Institute of Chartered Accountants: **www.icaew.co.uk/students**
» Institute of Chartered Accountants of Scotland: **www.icas.org.uk**
» Institute of Financial Services: **www.ifslearning.ac.uk**

Aeronautical and Manufacturing Engineering

Most of the courses in this table focus on aeronautical or manufacturing engineering, but it includes some with a mechanical title. To add to the confusion, manufacturing degrees often go under the rubric of production engineering (*see* General Engineering *and* Mechanical Engineering). The number of institutions in the ranking had stabilised after a period of decline, but two more have dropped out of this edition of the *Guide*.

Cambridge has stretched its lead still further over the other 36 universities. It has by far the highest entry grades and easily the best performance in the latest Research Assessment Exercise (RAE), when some of the university's work in this field was submitted in other engineering categories. Only third-placed Surrey has more satisfied students, while second-placed Bristol and Newcastle, in fifth, pip Cambridge on graduate prospects.

Aeronautical and Manufacturing Engineering cont.

Bristol and Surrey have swapped places within the top three, but there is little change elsewhere in the top 10. Surrey has the most satisfied students, while Bristol has the top employment score. Imperial was second only to Cambridge in the RAE but was let down by an unusually low student satisfaction rate. De Montfort is the only new university in the top half of the table, while Swansea remains the leader in Wales but Glasgow has overtaken Strathclyde in Scotland.

Applications for aerospace engineering at the start of 2010 had grown by more than 20 per cent for the second successive year, with big increases both for Honours and Foundation degrees. The smaller area of manufacturing and production engineering saw more modest growth of nearly 10 per cent. Many graduates go on to further study or training to meet professional requirements and – particularly for aeronautical engineering graduates – employment prospects have been bright in recent years. The subjects are just outside the top 10 for graduate salaries, with an average of almost £23,500 for those in graduate jobs. Surprisingly, even though more than half go straight into graduate jobs, the unemployment rate of 11 per cent is among the highest for any subject area.

Entry grades have been rising, with Cambridge posting a particularly high average and Imperial also averaging more than 500 points, but three Cs at A level (and another at AS level) has been enough secure a place at most universities outside the top 20.

Employed in graduate job:	51%	Employed in non-graduate job and studying:	1%
Employed in graduate job and studying:	5%	Employed in non-graduate job:	17%
Studying:	13%	Unemployed:	11%
Average starting graduate salary:	£23,464	Average starting non-graduate salary:	£16,181

Aeronautical and Manufacturing Engineering	Research quality/9	Entry standards	Student satisfaction %	Graduate prospects %	Overall rating
1 Cambridge	5.5	567	85	94	100.0
2 Bristol	4.1	466	77	95	88.5
3 Surrey	3.4	370	90	91	88.0
4 Sheffield	4.3	394	82	91	87.9
5 Newcastle	3.2		83	97	87.4
6 Bath	2.7	468	83	88	84.7
7 Southampton	3.1	447	84	81	84.4
8 Imperial College	4.4	505	68	86	84.3
9 Loughborough	3.6	391	79	84	82.5
10 Nottingham	4.0	352	79	77	81.1
11 Swansea	2.5	305	78	94	77.5
12 Leeds	3.7	380	73	71	76.8
13 Queen's, Belfast	3.2	350	78	68	75.7
14 Queen Mary, London	2.3	309	81	79	75.2
=15 Liverpool	3.5	377	68	74	74.3
=15 Aston	2.2	326	85	66	74.3
17 De Montfort	2.2		77	79	73.7
18 Manchester	3.6	429	63	73	73.6

19	Glasgow	2.4	385	74	71	72.7
20	Strathclyde	2.7	370	73	69	72.4
21	Hertfordshire	2.7	237	79	66	70.1
22	Brunel	2.5	343	68	76	70.0
23	West of England	2.6	291	72	70	69.6
24	Glamorgan	2.5		61	89	68.5
25	Portsmouth	2.1	227	82	64	68.4
26	Sussex		346	75	77	65.8
27	Salford	2.5	251	73	61	65.7
28	Liverpool John Moores	3.3	234	69	57	65.0
29	Sheffield Hallam	1.8	274	73	59	63.7
=30	City	2.4	315	70	48	63.3
=30	Plymouth	1.3		81	50	63.3
32	Coventry	1.0	243	71	71	62.2
33	Kingston	1.5	235	71	65	62.1
34	UWIC, Cardiff		304	76	59	60.6
35	Manchester Metropolitan	1.5	209	68	66	60.0
36	Ulster		224	70	81	59.9
37	London South Bank	2.5	183	66	45	56.6

» Manufacturing Institute: **www.makeit.org.uk**
» Royal Aeronautical Society: **www.aerosociety.com**
» Why Aeronautical engineering?:
   www.science-engineering.net/aeronautical_engineering.htm

Agriculture and Forestry

Nottingham and Reading – two of the big names in agriculture and forestry – tie for the leadership for the first time. There are generally low scores on all measures in these subjects – Nottingham averages only just over 350 points but still has the highest entry standards, while only two universities (led by Harper Adams) had satisfaction levels of more than 85 per cent.

Aberdeen, the only university in Scotland to offer the subjects, registered the top research grades, while Harper Adams University College, in Shropshire, was the only institution to see more than 80 per cent of leavers go straight into graduate jobs or further training. But for a low research score, Harper Adams would have challenged the top two.

Aberystwyth remains just ahead of Bangor in Wales, while Greenwich and the West of England are the leading new universities. The number of institutions in the ranking has crept back up to 18, after dropping to 16 last year. The demand for places both on Honours and Foundation degrees in agriculture had grown enormously at the start of 2010, topping 4,500. The 35 per cent increase at degree level, in particular, may mean higher entry requirements. Forestry is a much smaller area, with only 115 degree applications by the official deadline for courses starting in 2010.

A quarter of those enrolling for degrees in agriculture and more than a third in forestry do so without A levels, often coming with relevant work experience. About one in seven has been arriving through the Clearing system, although this may be reduced this year. Entry grades have been rising from a low base: for the first time no university averages less than 200 points.

Agriculture and Forestry cont.

The definition of a graduate job does no favours to agriculture or forestry in the employment statistics, but the figures are still low in several universities. Half of the institutions in the table saw no more than 50 per cent of leavers go straight into graduate jobs or training courses. More than a third of graduates start in lower-level jobs, although the unemployment rate is not high. The subjects are never going to lead to big starting salaries, but they are above psychology and English, and not in the bottom ten again this year.

Employed in graduate job:	37%
Employed in graduate job and studying:	8%
Studying:	8%
Average starting graduate salary:	£18,976

Employed in non-graduate job and studying:	2%
Employed in non-graduate job:	36%
Unemployed:	8%
Average starting non-graduate salary:	£15,461

Agriculture and Forestry	Research quality/9	Entry standards	Student satisfaction %	Graduate prospects %	Overall rating
=1 Nottingham	3.1	351	80	60	100.0
=1 Reading	2.4	334	83	74	100.0
3 Harper Adams	1.2	294	89	81	96.3
4 Newcastle	2.1	306	82	62	93.2
5 Queen's, Belfast	1.8	304	78	69	91.1
6 Aberystwyth	2.5	262	86	43	88.8
7 Aberdeen	3.3			29	87.3
8 Bangor	2.1	290		44	86.5
9 Greenwich	1.7	243		58	82.6
10 West of England	2.1	262		33	79.8
11 Plymouth	0.9	293	77	39	79.6
12 Royal Agricultural College	0.7	253	80	50	79.1
13 Nottingham Trent		279	78	51	78.0
14 Bristol	1.7		67	50	75.8
15 Bournemouth		208		70	74.8
16 Cumbria	0.4	276			73.8
17 Lincoln	1.1	220	67	56	72.1
18 Sheffield Hallam		254	78	29	70.8

» Institute of Chartered Foresters: **www.charteredforesters.org**
» Royal Agricultural Society of England: **www.rase.org.uk**
» Royal Forestry Society: **www.rfs.org.uk**
» Royal Scottish Forestry Society: **www.rsfs.org**
» Sector Skills Council for the Environmental and Land-Based Sector (LANTRA): **www.lantra.co.uk**

American Studies

American studies was never going to repeat the surge in popularity that it experienced last year, with the huge interest in the election of Barack Obama. The 22 per cent increase was one of the biggest in any subject then, although there were still only 2,500 applications. Another 8 per cent rise in applications at the start of 2010 will make the competition for places marginally stiffer. About 550 students started degree courses in 2008.

Warwick remains well clear of the field, sharing the lead for research quality and student satisfaction, while boasting the highest entry standards and the best graduate employment record. Manchester was the other research star in the 2008 assessments, while Hull matched Warwick's score in the National Student Survey.

Warwick was the only university to see three quarters of leavers go straight into graduate-level jobs or continue their studies. Just second-placed Leicester and Sussex, of the other 19 universities in the ranking, recorded a success rate of 70 per cent or over on this measure. Leicester has moved up two places, having also improved its student satisfaction score, but the table is otherwise similar to last year's. King's College, a notable riser, moves into the top 10.

American Studies	Research quality/9	Entry standards	Student satisfaction %	Graduate prospects %	Overall rating
1 Warwick	4.3	428	90	75	100.0
2 Leicester	3.1	355	88	70	90.1
3 Lancaster	4.2	393	80	65	90.0
4 Sussex	4.0	377	78	71	88.5
5 Manchester	4.3	389	79	51	87.4
6 East Anglia	3.1	349	83	57	85.0
7 King's College London	2.6	412	78	66	84.8
8 Birmingham	3.0	394	77	60	83.3
9 Hull	2.6	276	90	51	83.0
10 Nottingham	3.2	357	77	62	82.9
11 Kent	4.0	266	82	46	81.6
12 Essex	2.7	328	79	62	81.2
=13 Liverpool	2.3	329	79	52	78.1
=13 Keele	2.6	284	82	49	78.1
15 Portsmouth	2.6	270	85	36	76.9
16 Swansea	1.9	295	81	47	75.2
17 Goldsmiths College		315	74	68	69.8
18 Winchester		262	85	27	65.5
19 Liverpool John Moores		249	78	33	62.2
20 Canterbury Christ Church		218	77	35	60.5

» British Association for American Studies: **www.baas.ac.uk**

Portsmouth is the top-rated new university and the only one to enter the latest Research Assessment Exercise. Swansea is the only university from outside England.

Entry scores are more bunched than in many subjects, with only Warwick and King's

American Studies cont.

averaging more than 400 points and no university slipping below 200. Nine out of ten students taking American Studies have A levels or equivalent qualifications and there is an impressive level of firsts and 2:1s. The downside is in the employment statistics, with four universities reporting success rates in the graduate jobs market of less than 40 per cent and one less than 30 per cent. The subject is in the bottom three for graduate employment, although it only just in the bottom 20 in the salaries table.

Employed in graduate job:	28%	Employed in non-graduate job and studying:	4%
Employed in graduate job and studying:	2%	Employed in non-graduate job:	38%
Studying:	17%	Unemployed:	11%
Average starting graduate salary:	£19,376	Average starting non-graduate salary:	£14,685

Anatomy and Physiology

Over the past two years, anatomy, physiology and pathology have recovered their popularity after a big drop in applications in 2008. It was already a competitive field, with more than six applications for every place, although average entry scores at some of the universities towards the bottom of the table remain below 300 points. At Oxford – and probably at Cambridge, which does not collect separate entry scores for these subjects – the average is more than 500 points. Grades are boosted by the fact that the subjects are often a fall-back for candidates whose real target was medical school.

Oxford has slipped back two places this year, after a big rise in the previous *Guide*, because of an unusually poor employment score. It achieved much the best grades in the 2008 Research Assessment Exercise, but has been overtaken by Loughborough, which is one of two universities with the most satisfied students, and University College London, which did especially well on employment. Cambridge retains the leadership with good scores across the board. Keele, in 25th place, has the other top student satisfaction score, while Reading, in 17th, had the best record for graduate destinations. Dundee has overtaken Edinburgh to become the top university in Scotland, while Cardiff is the only provider of these subjects in Wales. Huddersfield is the best-placed of six post-1992 universities in the ranking.

Scores in the National Student Survey were generally high, with only two universities registering less than 75 per cent satisfaction among final-year undergraduates. Anatomy and physiology are in the top 25 for employment prospects, with one of the lowest unemployment rates, at 6 per cent. Four out of ten students go on to full-time postgraduate training – one of the highest proportions for any group of subjects. Average earnings in graduate jobs are below average, at close to £19,500 in the latest statistics.

This ranking covers degrees in cell biology, neurosciences and pathology, as well as anatomy and physiology. Universities often demand at least two science subjects at A level – usually biology and chemistry, although some new universities will accept just one science qualification.

Employed in graduate job:	26%	Employed in non-graduate job and studying:	3%
Employed in graduate job and studying:	4%	Employed in non-graduate job:	22%
Studying:	40%	Unemployed:	6%
Average starting graduate salary:	£19,443	Average starting non-graduate salary:	£14,347

Anatomy and Physiology	Research quality/9	Entry standards	Student satisfaction %	Graduate prospects %	Overall rating
1 Cambridge	3.3		85	82	100.0
2 Loughborough	3.2	384	92	71	99.2
3 University College London	3.4	447	78	83	98.2
4 Oxford	4.4	515	74	67	98.1
5 Cardiff	2.9		84	80	96.8
6 Manchester	3.5	425	84	65	96.0
7 Dundee	3.7	368	85	68	95.6
8 Edinburgh	2.8		90	66	95.4
9 Bristol	2.9	418	80	80	95.0
10 Newcastle	3.0	380	87	69	94.8
11 Sussex	3.2	365	84	72	94.0
12 Leeds	3.1	391	87	62	93.6
13 Aberdeen	1.9	369	88	80	93.4
14 Queen's, Belfast	3.0	354	83	72	92.3
15 Liverpool	2.6	413	85	63	92.1
16 King's College London	3.2	388	79	71	91.9
17 Reading	1.8	346	81	90	90.9
18 Nottingham	2.0	387	83	73	90.4
19 Glasgow	2.9	393	80	64	89.8
20 Leicester		418		79	87.3
21 Huddersfield		331	86	89	86.1
22 Nottingham Trent	3.1		76	62	85.1
23 Bradford	1.9		82	62	83.7
24 Salford	1.8		83	52	80.5
25 Keele		287	92	61	80.1
26 Ulster		307	75	83	77.4
27 Plymouth	1.0	252	85		76.8
28 Manchester Metropolitan	1.9		74	42	70.4
29 Northampton		234	72	76	70.2
30 Westminster		267	77	52	68.1

» Anatomical Society of Great Britain and Ireland: **www.anatsoc.org.uk**
» British Association of Clinical Anatomists: **www.liv.ac.uk/HumanAnatomy/BACA.html**
» Physiological Society: **www.physoc.org**

Anthropology

The relatively small numbers taking anthropology – fewer than 700 started degrees in 2009 – make for substantial swings in average performance. The subject had the highest unemployment rate in last year's *Guide*, for example, but is back down to the average of 5 per cent in this edition. Nearly a quarter of all graduates go on to take a higher degree or some form of postgraduate training and the proportion in non-graduate jobs has improved considerably.

Anthropology cont.

Cambridge has retained the top position that it lost to second-placed Oxford two years ago. It has slightly higher entry standards and ties with Oxford and St Andrews for the top score on student satisfaction. It is on graduate destinations that Cambridge really pulls ahead, registering easily the best score in a subject in which only four universities saw more than 70 per cent of leavers go straight into graduate-level jobs or onto postgraduate courses.

St Andrews is the biggest riser at the top of the table, moving up three places to third. The London School of Economics (LSE), in fourth, eclipsed both of the ancient universities in the 2008 Research Assessment Exercise, with 40 per cent of its work judged to be world-leading. The LSE would have finished higher but for (jointly with Manchester) the lowest student satisfaction rating in the table.

Anthropology tends to be the preserve of old universities, but Roehampton is the highest-placed of three post-1992 universities in this year's table. St Andrews is the top university in Scotland; Lampeter (now Trinity Saint David) the only representative of Wales.

Entry standards are high: seven of the 20 universities in the table averaged more than 400 points and none slipped below 200. There was a 17 per cent rise in applications at the beginning of 2010, continuing a positive trend that has continued for most of the decade. Clearing usually accounts for a significant share of the places in anthropology. There are no subject-specific requirements at most universities.

Employed in graduate job:	29%	Employed in non-graduate job and studying:	4%
Employed in graduate job and studying:	4%	Employed in non-graduate job:	32%
Studying:	24%	Unemployed:	8%
Average starting graduate salary:	£18,665	Average starting non-graduate salary:	£16,245

Anthropology	Research quality/9	Entry standards	Student satisfaction %	Graduate prospects %	Overall rating
1 Cambridge	4.3	499	88	78	100.0
2 Oxford	3.5	496	88	69	93.5
3 St Andrews	3.5	449	88	68	91.2
4 London School of Economics	4.7	438	65	74	87.9
5 School of Oriental and African Studies	4.2	401	74	72	87.6
6 University College London	3.9	425	76	62	85.4
7 Durham	3.1	391	78	69	83.3
8 Sussex	3.5	377	74	68	82.5
9 Lampeter (Trinity Saint David)	2.8			70	81.4
10 Edinburgh	3.6	440	67	64	80.7
11 Queen's, Belfast	4.0	356	78	50	80.2
12 Kent	2.8	320	86	56	79.0
13 Goldsmiths College	3.5	321	79	52	77.8
14 Aberdeen	3.7	307	83	42	77.3
15 Brunel	3.1	309	74	59	75.5
16 Manchester	3.1	396	65	59	75.1
17 Glasgow	2.2	387	76	50	73.0
18 Roehampton	3.5	210	71	46	68.4

19 Oxford Brookes	1.7	312	78	42	66.8
20 Liverpool John Moores	2.3	200	73		64.0

» Royal Anthropological Institute: **www.therai.org.uk**

Archaeology

Cambridge holds on to first place in archaeology, with the highest entry standards. Second-placed Durham has the best record for research, with three quarters of its work rated as world-leading or internationally excellent in 2008. York, in fifth place, has the most satisfied students. And, for the second year in a row, Robert Gordon has the best graduate employment record, making it the leading post-1992 university, despite dropping out of the top 20.

The top four universities for archaeology remain unchanged for the third successive year (although University College London and Oxford swap places), with York moving up to fifth. Glasgow remains the top university in Scotland; Cardiff the leader in Wales.

The number of universities in the ranking continues to grow by leaps and bounds – the 2005 *Guide* contained only 25 institutions, compared with this year's 47. New universities are mainly responsible, their numbers growing from three to 18 over the same period. The change has had the effect of spreading out entry scores, which now range from less than 200 points to almost 500.

Archaeology has produced consistently high levels of satisfaction. Only two universities in the ranking failed to satisfy at least two thirds of their final-year undergraduates in the results published in 2009. The subject appeared to be one of the victims of top-up fees – perhaps because of the uncertain employment prospects and relatively low salaries for those who make a career in the subject – with applications dropping for two years after the change was introduced. But there was a recovery in 2009 and a further 12 per cent increase at the start of 2010, which took total applications over the 2,000 mark. The broader category of forensic and archaeological science was up even more.

Unemployment six months after graduation remains higher than average, at 11 per cent,

Archaeology	Research quality/9	Entry standards	Student satisfaction %	Graduate prospects %	Overall rating
1 Cambridge	4.0	499	88	78	100.0
2 Durham	4.6	411	88	75	97.8
3 University College London	3.9	416	90	71	95.1
4 Oxford	4.3	493	85	60	94.3
5 York	3.6	367	92	61	89.7
6 Sheffield	3.6	365	84	64	86.8
7 Reading	4.6	307	87	54	86.2
8 Exeter	3.2	356	85	64	85.4
9 Leicester	3.7	355	84	58	84.8
10 Southampton	3.7	335	84	57	83.9
11 Glasgow	2.5	379	88	58	83.7
12 Queen's, Belfast	3.6	335	82	59	82.9

Archaeology cont.

	Research quality/9	Entry standards	Student satisfaction %	Graduate prospects %	Overall rating
13 Liverpool	3.8	383	76	57	82.4
14 Cardiff	2.9	334	80	66	81.9
15 Nottingham	3.3	339	78	63	81.6
16 Edinburgh	3.3	413	77	51	80.4
17 Birmingham	2.6	387	77	60	79.7
18 Warwick		445	80	72	78.7
19 Aberdeen	2.5	293	84		78.4
20 Manchester	3.0	337	78	49	76.5
21 Newcastle	2.8	313	78	53	75.5
22 Bradford	3.1	245	73	64	74.9
23 Dundee		374	85	60	74.4
=24 Kent	1.3	283	82	62	73.7
=24 Bristol	2.8	399	61	60	73.7
=24 Robert Gordon		389	68	82	73.7
27 Hull		278	88	66	73.4
28 Central Lancashire	1.4	267	81	62	73.2
29 Nottingham Trent	1.7	265	73	70	72.6
30 Lampeter (Trinity Saint David)	2.8	246	76	52	71.5
31 West of England		279	84	65	71.3
32 Staffordshire		241	84	67	69.9
33 Bournemouth	2.1	246	76	52	69.2
34 Lincoln		291	82	58	68.5
35 Keele		282	81	60	68.4
36 Glamorgan		296	73	65	66.7
37 Chester		239	80	56	64.7
38 Glasgow Caledonian		316	73	52	63.5
39 Derby		219	79	55	63.2
40 Swansea		315	82	36	62.9
41 De Montfort		214	64	70	60.4
42 Teesside		243	75	48	59.9
43 Liverpool John Moores		245	68	56	59.5
44 Winchester	1.2	249	73	30	57.8
45 Worcester		196	75	42	56.4
46 London South Bank		193	67	53	55.6
47 Canterbury Christ Church		231	73	33	53.9

» Council for British Archaeology: **www.britarch.ac.uk**
» TORC (Training Online Resource Centre for Archaeology): **www.torc.org.uk**

but the average starting salary for graduate-level jobs had improved sufficiently in the latest survey to take archaeology out of the bottom ten subjects. Nevertheless, at six universities, fewer than half of the graduates found graduate-level work or went on to further study within six months of completing their course.

Employed in graduate job:	29%	Employed in non-graduate job and studying:	5%
Employed in graduate job and studying:	3%	Employed in non-graduate job:	31%
Studying:	21%	Unemployed:	11%
Average starting graduate salary:	£18,392	Average starting non-graduate salary:	£14,440

Architecture

With more than six applications for every place, architecture is one of the most competitive of the major subjects. Entry grades at the leading universities reflect this, with almost a dozen averaging over 400 points. Some universities ask candidates to produce a portfolio of work if they have not taken an art- or design-based A level. Cambridge averages more than 500, but still only moves up to second in this year's table.

Bath remains at the head of the ranking, with the most satisfied students and good scores on the other indicators. University College London, which had the best research grades in the latest assessments, slips one place to third position, which it shares with Sheffield.

Training in architecture is a long haul – usually seven years, in which the first degree is but one step on the way. Until now, the graduate employment rate has been some compensation, but the recession saw unemployment shoot up from 2 per cent to 11 per cent in the latest survey. The subject has dropped from 4th to 15th in the employment table as a result. Robert Gordon still saw 96 per cent of its architects go straight into graduate jobs or continue their training, but only 13 universities reached the 90 per cent mark, compared with 30 in last year's *Guide*. Glasgow Caledonian even dropped below 30 per cent positive destinations, although nearly all the other universities reached at least 70 per cent.

Edinburgh is the top university in Scotland, while fifth-placed Cardiff remains the leader in Wales and Ulster outperforms Queen's, Belfast, in Northern Ireland. New universities take up more than half the places in the ranking, with Sheffield Hallam the highest-placed of seven in the top 20.

A third of all undergraduates enter architecture degrees with qualifications other than A level or Advanced Highers. A series of increases in applications continued at the start of 2010, when there was another rise of almost 9 per cent, making a total more than 26,000. Satisfaction rates are high at undergraduate level and beyond – three years into their careers, architects were among the least likely of all graduates to say that they wished they had taken a different degree or chosen a different profession.

This cannot be a matter of money: architecture is in the bottom 20 subjects for graduate starting salaries, averaging little more than £19,000. The growing numbers in lower-level jobs are among the lowest paid of any subject.

Employed in graduate job:	50%	Employed in non-graduate job and studying:	1%
Employed in graduate job and studying:	16%	Employed in non-graduate job:	11%
Studying:	11%	Unemployed:	11%
Average starting graduate salary:	£19,136	Average starting non-graduate salary:	£14,294

Architecture cont.

	Research quality/9	Entry standards	Student satisfaction %	Graduate prospects %	Overall rating
1 Bath	3.9	478	86	93	100.0
2 Cambridge	4.4	523	80	90	98.9
=3 University College London	4.6	459	78	81	94.0
=3 Sheffield	4.2	451	78	89	94.0
5 Cardiff	3.4	473	76	93	92.7
6 Newcastle	3.6	431	71	93	88.7
7 Liverpool	4.3	449	69	84	88.3
8 Edinburgh	3.9	425	67	89	86.3
9 Manchester School of Architecture	2.5	442	70	93	85.6
=10 Nottingham	2.3	434		86	84.8
=10 Brighton	4.3	368	73	74	84.8
12 Strathclyde	1.9	402		95	84.7
13 Northumbria	2.2	346	77	93	84.5
14 Ulster	3.2	286	77	91	84.4
15 Sheffield Hallam	2.0	331	84	81	84.2
16 Dundee	1.8	365	73	94	82.2
17 Liverpool John Moores	3.1	263	81	76	82.0
18 Westminster	3.3	340	70	71	78.3
19 West of England	2.1	283	73	85	77.6
20 Robert Gordon	1.9	356	64	96	77.5
=21 Nottingham Trent	1.3	319	71	92	77.2
=21 Oxford Brookes		387	75	88	77.2
23 Kent		347	74	94	76.8
24 Greenwich	2.2	257	76	75	76.2
=25 De Montfort	3.1	249	65	88	75.6
=25 Portsmouth	0.8	315	75	84	75.6
27 Plymouth	2.5	345	61	84	74.4
28 Salford	3.7	237	65		73.7
29 University for Creative Arts		272	75	90	73.4
30 Huddersfield		291	76	84	73.3
31 Lincoln	1.7	273	71	76	72.9
32 Queen's, Belfast		373	67	89	72.5
33 Central Lancashire	1.9	264	67		69.9
34 UWIC, Cardiff		267		84	68.8
35 Leeds Metropolitan		295	68	81	68.1
36 East London		205	72	80	66.6
37 London South Bank		225	69	76	64.5
38 Birmingham City		286	70	58	63.3
39 Glasgow Caledonian	3.0		70	29	62.8
40 Kingston		307	59	75	62.5
41 Arts University College, Bournemouth	0.4	262			60.5
42 Southampton Solent		214	63	66	58.3
43 Derby		203		44	50.6

- » Commission for Architecture and the Built Environment: **www.cabe.org.uk**
- » Royal Institute of British Architects: **www.architecture.com**
- » Royal Incorporation of Architects in Scotland: **www.rias.org.uk**

Art and Design

Comparisons of the demand for places in art and design between this year and last cannot be entirely accurate because of a change of application deadlines. But far more applications had been made by the end of January 2010 than after the March deadline in 2009 – more than 82,000 for design degrees against 66,000 in 2009. The trend was the same in fine art, where there were 22,000 applications compared with 17,000 in 2009.

Increases have continued despite employment rates and average starting salaries that are both in the bottom ten for all subjects. Artists and designers accept that they are likely to have a period of self-employment early in their career while they find a way to pursue their vocation, but two thirds of those surveyed three years after graduation said they would make the same choice again.

Only computer science had a higher unemployment rate than the 13 per cent for art and design in the latest survey. More than 40 per cent of all leavers went straight into graduate-level jobs, but only 7 per cent went on to take another course – one of the lowest proportions for any subject.

Most courses in art and design are at new universities – often in former art colleges – but the top 15 places in this year's ranking are all filled by older institutions. University College London, where students attend the Slade School of Fine Art, is back in first place, sharing the best research score with Kent. The two universities have benefited from the revaluation of grades in the 2008 Research Assessment Exercise to reward world-leading submissions, mirroring the system used to allocate research grants.

Oxford, where fine art is taught at the Ruskin School of Drawing, has the highest entry standards and the most satisfied students in the UK, but is relegated to second place by an unusually low graduate destinations score. Only 45 per cent of leavers found graduate jobs or continued their studies within six months of graduating.

For the third year in a row, the best employment prospects were at Bangor, the top university in Wales, where an impressive 92 per cent enjoyed "positive destinations". Only Edge Hill, Heriot-Watt and Roehampton, of the remaining 77 institutions in the ranking, reached 80 per cent on this measure.

Edinburgh, in third place, has overtaken Glasgow to resume its position as the top university in Scotland. University College Falmouth, in 16th place, finishes higher than any of the former polytechnics. However, Oxford Brookes, Brighton, Bournemouth and Nottingham Trent also made the top 20. Low entry grades and research scores count against many of the new universities and colleges, although most artists would argue that these are of less significance than in other subjects.

Employed in graduate job:	40%	Employed in non-graduate job and studying:	3%
Employed in graduate job and studying:	2%	Employed in non-graduate job:	34%
Studying:	7%	Unemployed:	13%
Average starting graduate salary:	£17,774	Average starting non-graduate salary:	£14,062

Art and Design cont.

	Research quality/9	Entry standards	Student satisfaction %	Graduate prospects %	Overall rating
1 University College London	4.4	405		79	100.0
2 Oxford	4.0	441	92	45	94.8
3 Edinburgh	3.1	439		64	92.5
4 Loughborough	4.1	354	81	61	89.2
5 Lancaster	4.1	374	75	66	88.9
6 Brunel	1.5	365	85	74	87.9
7 Glasgow	3.5		78	67	86.8
8 Kent	4.4	315	68	77	85.5
9 Leeds	3.5	386	72	61	85.0
10 Heriot-Watt	2.6	331	69	85	84.3
11 Dundee	4.0	317	82	51	84.0
12 Newcastle	4.2	382	68	58	83.8
13 Goldsmiths College	3.7	361	72	60	83.7
14 Bangor		277	79	92	80.1
15 Reading	4.3	344	60	61	79.3
16 Falmouth	1.8	311	80	60	78.9
17 Oxford Brookes	2.5	279	82	56	78.8
18 Bournemouth	3.3	283	69	69	78.7
19 Nottingham Trent	1.7	313	75	68	78.4
20 Brighton	4.3	297	72	47	77.8
=21 Northumbria	2.5	302	72	61	77.2
=21 Edge Hill		262	76	89	77.2
23 Robert Gordon	1.9	289	74	67	77.1
24 UWIC, Cardiff	3.0	288	77	45	75.4
25 Arts University College, Bournemouth	0.4	331	80	56	75.3
26 Norwich University College of the Arts	1.9	334	75	46	74.4
=27 Teesside		297	88	51	74.1
=27 Aberystwyth		334	82	51	74.1
29 University of the Arts London	3.3	292	62	61	74.0
30 Birmingham City	3.8	280	69	47	73.9
31 Coventry	1.9	306	66	64	73.4
32 Roehampton		258	70	86	73.3
=33 De Montfort	1.9	269	71	61	73.0
=33 Kingston	1.4	290	72	60	73.0
35 Lincoln	1.2	283	74	58	72.3
=36 West of England	2.7	261	74	44	71.1
=36 Manchester		356	77	45	71.1
38 Westminster	3.7	293	65	41	70.7
39 Bath Spa	1.6	275	72	52	70.1
40 Southampton	1.6	353	62	50	69.8
41 Edinburgh Napier	1.1	269	62	73	69.6
=42 Ulster	2.9	260	69	45	69.4
=42 Newport	3.0	284	65	45	69.4

44 Portsmouth	0.8	276	78	47	69.3
=45 Chester	0.2	278	74	58	69.0
=45 Manchester Metropolitan	2.3	281	68	46	69.0
47 Canterbury Christ Church		285	80	46	68.3
48 Staffordshire	0.5	246	75	57	67.9
=49 Sheffield Hallam	2.9	290	66	38	67.8
=49 Greenwich		256	70	67	67.8
51 Plymouth	2.5	272	66	45	67.7
52 Derby	1.5	269	72	45	67.5
53 Cumbria	0.6	243	76	51	67.1
=54 Central Lancashire	0.7	240	72	55	66.5
=54 Hertfordshire	2.7	259	61	50	66.5
56 Middlesex	1.6	208	71	54	66.3
57 Salford	1.5	234	73	46	65.9
58 Glamorgan		287	68	54	65.3
=59 Anglia Ruskin	1.6	268	66	46	65.1
=59 Sunderland	1.9	199	74	44	65.1
61 University for Creative Arts	1.6	247	66	51	65.0
62 Leeds Metropolitan	1.2	242	68	50	64.7
63 Southampton Solent	1.4	275	62	50	64.6
64 Buckinghamshire New	1.6	241	67	47	64.4
65 Northampton	0.4	247	73	46	64.1
66 Gloucestershire	1.2	262	65	48	64.0
67 Huddersfield		273	70	49	63.5
68 Worcester		315	64	48	63.1
69 Glasgow Caledonian		345	70	26	61.9
70 East London	2.3	202	63	46	61.6
71 Liverpool John Moores	1.5	195	67	47	61.3
72 Bolton	0.3	258	63	47	59.9
73 Essex		154	73	54	59.2
74 York St John		283	57	48	57.9
75 Chichester		261	71	28	57.5
76 Glyndŵr	0.6	227	56	53	57.0
77 Thames Valley	0.9	150	62	52	55.5
78 Bedfordshire		219	49	53	51.5

» Design Council: **www.designcouncil.org.uk**
» National Society for Education in Art and Design: **www.nsead.org**
» Sector Skills Council for Creative Media: **www.skillset.org**

Biological Sciences

While other science subjects have struggled to attract applicants in recent years, biological subjects have thrived. The various combinations all registered increases at the start of 2010, when the main subject of biology remained well ahead of chemistry and physics after

Biological Sciences cont.

21 per cent growth in the demand for places. Two thirds of all entrants arrive with A levels or their equivalent, and more than half of the undergraduates are awarded firsts or 2:1s. Well over a third go on to take postgraduate courses, either full or part-time.

Cambridge has maintained its lead over its rivals, with some of the highest entry grades in any subject – the equivalent of four As at A level and another at AS level. Only Oxford comes close, although Manchester achieved the best grades in the 2008 Research Assessment Exercise and Dundee, jointly in eighth place, has the most satisfied students. Surrey, which shares eighth place, is in a tie with Hertfordshire (just outside the top 40) for the best graduate employment record.

Sheffield has moved up to third, while Dundee is the new leader in Scotland and Cardiff remains well clear of the competition in Wales. Nottingham Trent is the highest-placed post-1992 university, just outside the top 30.

Entry standards have been rising: in addition to Oxford and Cambridge, where successful candidates average more than 500 points, another 13 universities average 400 or more. Like last year, only four universities have an average below 200 points, even though a relatively high proportion of the entrants (11 per cent) win places through Clearing.

Graduate employment prospects nationally are slightly below average for all subjects. Starting salaries are in the bottom 20 and are among the lowest for any subject for those who fail to find a graduate-level job.

Employed in graduate job:	29%	Employed in non-graduate job and studying:	3%
Employed in graduate job and studying:	4%	Employed in non-graduate job:	24%
Studying:	30%	Unemployed:	9%
Average starting graduate salary:	£19,148	Average starting non-graduate salary:	£14,303

Biological Sciences	Research quality/9	Entry standards	Student satisfaction %	Graduate prospects %	Overall rating
1 Cambridge	3.3	576	85	82	100.0
2 Oxford	3.7	516	83	80	97.4
3 Sheffield	3.6	434	87	71	93.6
4 York	3.6	436	87	70	93.5
5 Manchester	3.8	435	85	70	92.9
6 Imperial College	3.4	469	77	78	91.2
7 Bristol	3.0	444	84	72	90.4
=8 Dundee	3.7	351	90	61	89.8
=8 Surrey	3.4	360	79	84	89.8
10 Lancaster	3.3	380	84	73	89.4
11 Leicester	2.4	405	85	76	88.8
12 St Andrews	2.6	428	85	70	88.5
13 University College London	3.4	423	78	72	88.1
14 Sussex	2.6	370	84	76	87.9
15 Durham	2.5	468	77	77	87.7
16 Bath	2.5	450	79	74	87.5
17 East Anglia	2.5	349	88	70	87.1

18	Glasgow	2.9	372	88	62	87.0
=19	Edinburgh	3.0	432	78	67	86.0
=19	King's College London	3.4	384	79	68	86.0
21	Warwick	2.5	422	82	68	85.9
22	Aston	2.8	316	84	73	85.6
=23	Leeds	3.1	357	82	66	84.8
=23	Birmingham	2.5	387	83	66	84.8
25	Nottingham	2.9	375	80	67	84.5
=26	Newcastle	3.0	365	80	65	83.8
=26	Exeter	2.5	377	80	69	83.8
28	Cardiff	2.9	385	79	65	83.4
29	Liverpool	2.3	400	78	69	83.0
30	Brunel	1.6	308	80	82	81.9
31	Aberdeen	2.9	337	80	61	81.3
32	Queen's, Belfast	1.7	324	82	72	81.1
33	Nottingham Trent	3.1	193	82	71	81.0
34	Kent	1.8	295	85	68	80.8
=35	Southampton	2.5	384	77	63	80.6
=35	Strathclyde	2.9	344	73	72	80.6
37	West of England	2.8	235	87	57	80.1
38	Essex	2.0	270	79	76	80.0
39	Royal Holloway	3.3	312	73	67	79.9
40	Reading	1.8	334	80	66	79.3
41	Hertfordshire	1.8	249	76	84	79.2
42	Abertay	2.4	252		71	78.7
=43	Heriot-Watt	1.9	291	83	63	78.4
=43	Portsmouth	2.6	268	84	55	78.4
=43	Glasgow Caledonian	1.7	318	84	60	78.4
=43	Keele	0.9	267	84	74	78.4
47	Queen Mary, London	2.0	349	76	67	78.2
48	Salford	1.8	232	79	76	77.6
49	Ulster		248	87	79	77.3
50	Sheffield Hallam	1.2	261	80	72	76.1
51	Hull	1.3	281	81	65	75.9
=52	Brighton	2.1	273	77	63	75.6
=52	Manchester Metropolitan	1.9	259	82	60	75.6
54	Edinburgh Napier	1.1	244	81	71	75.3
55	UWIC, Cardiff	1.1	252	81	69	75.1
56	Coventry		256	79	83	74.7
57	Northumbria	1.6	293	70	74	73.7
58	Plymouth	1.8	294	78	55	73.2
59	Staffordshire		211	86	71	73.1
60	Liverpool John Moores	1.6	248	79	59	72.7
61	Swansea	1.2	306	76	61	72.6
62	Huddersfield	1.3	230	81	60	72.3
63	Bradford	1.9	262	74	62	72.2
64	Greenwich		221	85	66	71.8

Biological Sciences cont.

	Research quality/9	Entry standards	Student satisfaction %	Graduate prospects %	Overall rating
65 Robert Gordon		322	72	76	71.7
66 Stirling	2.1	329	77	41	71.2
67 Bangor	1.6	311	72	57	70.8
68 Teesside		272	82	60	70.3
69 Edge Hill		225	74	78	69.8
70 Derby	0.8	240	84	47	69.0
71 Bournemouth		231	79	65	68.9
72 Chester	0.8	268	79	51	68.7
73 Oxford Brookes	1.4	300	69	58	68.3
74 Aberystwyth		286	83	48	67.6
75 Glamorgan	0.6	307	76	49	67.2
76 Worcester		213	75	68	66.8
=77 Sunderland		258	76	52	64.4
=77 Bolton		174	71	72	64.4
79 Central Lancashire		275	62	72	63.2
80 Leeds Metropolitan		264	68	62	63.1
81 Roehampton	0.5	182	69	63	63.0
82 Westminster		242	72	54	62.0
83 Bath Spa	0.2	272	80	32	61.8
84 Anglia Ruskin		252	77	39	61.0
85 Kingston	1.5	201	68	44	60.9
86 East London		163	63	65	58.0

» Biochemical Society: **www.biochemistry.org**
» British Society for Cell Biology: **www.bscb.org**
» Society of Biology: **www.societyofbiology.org**
» Society for Experimental Biology: **www.sebiology.org**

Building

The recession had done less damage than might have been expected to the employment prospects of graduates with building degrees when the latest survey was conducted. The subject had dropped out of the top 10, but only as far as 14th, and it was still in the top 10 for graduate starting salaries, which averaged more than £24,750. This is also reflected in individual universities' employment scores: while one university slipped below 70 per cent last year, only two, Bolton and Northampton, did so this year.

The unemployment rate for building graduates had shot up from 4 per cent to 11 per cent and by the start of 2010 it had become more difficult to attract students. While other subjects were up by 20 per cent or more, building experienced a small drop in applications, following a much more serious decline in 2009.

Entry grades have always been comparatively modest. No university averages 400 points,

Building	Research quality/9	Entry standards	Student satisfaction %	Graduate prospects %	Overall rating
1 Loughborough	4.0	341	87	93	100.0
2 University College London	4.6	393	75	80	95.7
3 Manchester	3.3		76	93	92.4
4 Reading	3.9	338	75	86	92.2
5 Nottingham	2.3	364			89.4
6 Heriot-Watt	2.7	367	62	91	86.6
7 Westminster	3.3	284	70	88	86.3
8 Northumbria	2.2	298	78	86	85.6
9 Glasgow Caledonian	3.0	333	70	80	85.0
10 Salford	3.7	279	64	83	83.1
11 Robert Gordon	1.9	270	70	95	82.7
12 West of England	2.1	276	77	83	82.0
13 Aston	2.2	293		86	81.9
14 Ulster	3.2	262	67	83	81.4
15 Brighton	1.7	258	79	84	81.2
16 Sheffield Hallam	2.0	269	71	88	81.0
17 Edinburgh Napier	1.8	251	73	90	80.7
18 Nottingham Trent	1.3	251	69	94	79.0
=19 Coventry		268	84	88	78.9
=19 Plymouth	2.5	260	72	78	78.9
21 Greenwich	2.2	208	69	88	77.4
22 Liverpool John Moores	3.1	256	64	76	76.9
23 Bolton	2.1		79	67	75.5
24 Central Lancashire	1.9	254	65	76	73.5
=25 Oxford Brookes		283	74	78	72.6
=25 Leeds Metropolitan		259	62	95	72.6
27 Birmingham City		222	69	89	71.0
28 Glamorgan	2.5	218	54	82	70.9
29 Kingston		276	66	82	70.2
30 Anglia Ruskin		273	60	74	65.3
31 Southampton Solent		187	62	75	61.4
32 London South Bank		186	61	74	60.5
33 Northampton		238		60	56.9

» Chartered Institute of Building: **www.ciob.org.uk**

although second-placed University College London (UCL) comes close. Only six of the 33 universities in the table reach 300 points and two average less than 200.

Loughborough has stretched its lead, with the most satisfied students and good scores on the other indicators. UCL registered the best grades in the 2008 Research Assessment Exercise, while Robert Gordon, in 11th place, and Leeds Metropolitan, in equal 25th, shared the best employment score. Westminster is the leading post-1992 university and is joined in the top 10 by Northumbria and Glasgow Caledonian. Heriot-Watt is the top university in Scotland,

Building cont.

while Glamorgan is the only representative of Wales in the ranking.

Despite the recruitment difficulties, there is one more university in the table than in last year's *Guide*. The subject has been one of the best prospects for a place in Clearing and may be so again if places in other subjects are restricted. Almost half of all building students come with qualifications other than A level.

Employed in graduate job:	65%	Employed in non-graduate job and studying:	0%
Employed in graduate job and studying:	9%	Employed in non-graduate job:	11%
Studying:	4%	Unemployed:	11%
Average starting graduate salary:	£24,755	Average starting non-graduate salary:	£15,078

Business Studies

Taken together, the various branches of business and management represent by far the most popular area of higher education. Even without the many dual or combined honours degrees that are common for both of the main areas, there were nearly 106,000 applications by the official deadline for courses beginning in 2010. That represented an increase of almost 10 per cent on the previous year for management and more than 13 per cent growth in business studies. The subjects are the biggest recruiters in many of the new universities, although some of the most famous business schools are absent from this ranking because they do not offer undergraduate courses.

There is no change in the top four in this year's table. Oxford has stretched its lead over Cambridge, although the two universities can only be compared on two measures. Neither Cambridge's Judge School of Management, nor Oxford's Said Business School qualify for the table as exclusively postgraduate institutions, so both universities are assessed on courses offered by other colleges. Oxford has the best employment score and the highest entry standards in the ranking. Third-placed Imperial produced the best research score in the 2008 assessments, while Loughborough, in fifth place, has the most satisfied students.

Even before the recession, employment scores were surprisingly varied. Overall, the subjects are in the bottom half of the employment table, even though more than half of those completing courses go straight into graduate-level jobs. Three years after graduation, this proportion rises to nearly three-quarters. Those who do find graduate-level work enjoy average starting salaries of almost £21,500 that are only just outside the top 20 for all subjects.

St Andrews has maintained its position as the top university in Scotland, while Cardiff remains the clear leader in Wales. More than half of the institutions in one of the biggest tables in the *Guide* are new universities, of which Bournemouth is the highest-placed, just outside the top 30. Robert Gordon, Oxford Brookes and De Montfort are also in the top 40.

Up to now, about 10 per cent of those securing places in business and management have done so through Clearing. Entrance qualifications vary widely, with 16 universities averaging more than 400 points and nine less than 200. Satisfaction levels have been improving in the National Student Survey, but only nine universities managed to satisfy more than 80 per cent of final-year undergraduates.

Employed in graduate job:	45%	Employed in non-graduate job and studying:	3%		
Employed in graduate job and studying:	6%	Employed in non-graduate job:	29%		
Studying:	8%	Unemployed:	10%		
Average starting graduate salary:	£21,452	Average starting non-graduate salary:	£16,226		

Business Studies	Research quality/9	Entry standards	Student satisfaction %	Graduate prospects %	Overall rating
1 Oxford	4.2	533		91	100.0
2 Cambridge	4.6			79	93.4
3 Imperial College	4.8	442		70	91.8
4 Bath	4.2	448	79	89	91.6
5 Loughborough	3.1	401	90	80	90.9
6 Warwick	4.0	455	80	83	90.7
7 St Andrews	2.8	426	85	80	88.5
8 Lancaster	4.0	411	81	77	88.2
9 Exeter	3.0	394	89	69	87.8
10 London School of Economics	4.2	465	71	86	87.4
11 City	2.9	422	81	83	87.1
12 Nottingham	3.6	407	76	80	84.8
13 Strathclyde	3.8	398	80	67	84.6
14 Aston	3.1	390	80	76	84.4
15 Leicester	2.9	318	86	74	84.1
16 King's College London	4.2	434	71	75	83.5
17 Leeds	3.6	413	75	73	83.2
18 Sussex	3.0	335	79	81	82.6
19 Birmingham	3.2	395	78	71	82.2
20 Cardiff	4.5	386	74	65	82.0
21 Durham	3.0	393	76	75	81.7
22 Sheffield	3.1	377	78	70	81.4
23 Manchester	3.8	412	72	69	81.0
24 Reading	2.5	374	80	68	80.6
=25 Kent	2.6	310	79	78	80.0
=25 Southampton	2.9	407	73	74	80.0
27 Newcastle	2.5	368	74	80	79.6
28 Glasgow	2.6	388	78	65	79.4
29 Aberdeen	2.2	341	79	72	78.7
30 East Anglia	2.4	323	80	68	78.3
31 Surrey	2.5	363	72	78	77.8
32 Edinburgh	2.5	409	73	66	77.2
33 Liverpool	2.5	379	74	66	76.8
34 Bournemouth	1.6	310	79	77	76.5
35 Robert Gordon	1.8	281	78	79	76.3
36 Royal Holloway	3.0	348	69	75	76.0
37 Oxford Brookes	1.5	319	80	69	75.8
38 York	2.5	346	71	73	75.5

Business Studies cont.

		Research quality/9	Entry standards	Student satisfaction %	Graduate prospects %	Overall rating
39	De Montfort	2.1	227	85	62	75.4
40	Hull	2.1	256	80	69	75.0
41	Heriot-Watt	2.4	331	72	72	74.6
42	Queen's, Belfast	3.0	361	70	64	74.5
43	Brighton	2.8	269	76	66	74.4
=44	Keele	2.3	273	75	70	73.8
=44	Bangor	3.2	241	78	58	73.8
46	School of Oriental and African Studies	2.0	326			73.7
=47	Northumbria	1.1	312	75	76	73.1
=47	Nottingham Trent	1.7	262	74	80	73.1
49	Stirling	2.2	318	75	60	72.7
50	Sheffield Hallam	1.5	274	78	68	72.6
=51	Central Lancashire	1.6	269	77	68	72.1
=51	Lincoln	1.0	271	80	66	72.1
=53	Queen Mary, London	2.9	333	69	60	71.8
=53	Swansea	2.3	300	74	60	71.8
55	University College London		411	74	69	71.7
56	Plymouth	1.7	252	79	62	71.4
57	Portsmouth	1.7	265	78	59	71.2
58	Aberystwyth	1.6	264	80	54	70.5
=59	Salford	2.4	263	74	55	70.1
=59	West of England	1.5	262	75	66	70.1
=59	Bradford	2.7	258	74	55	70.1
62	Bath Spa		286	84	57	70.0
63	Ulster	1.9	262	78	52	69.7
64	Brunel	2.3	312	67	64	69.6
65	Edinburgh Napier	0.9	254	74	74	69.5
66	Harper Adams		259		76	69.3
67	Kingston	2.4	219	78	49	68.9
68	Glamorgan	1.3	254	79	53	68.6
69	Staffordshire	1.6	220	72	67	67.7
=70	Hertfordshire	1.8	217	75	58	67.3
=70	York St John		319	76	59	67.3
72	Manchester Metropolitan	1.8	255	69	63	66.9
=73	Essex	2.7	291	66	54	66.7
=73	Teesside	1.4	234	79	47	66.7
75	Winchester		259	79	58	66.5
76	Northampton	1.1	217	80	50	66.3
77	Worcester		261	76	63	66.2
78	Huddersfield	1.4	254	72	56	66.0
79	Greenwich	1.3	227	78	49	65.9
80	Glasgow Caledonian	1.3	309	72	47	65.5
=81	Dundee		295	75	56	65.0

=81	Gloucestershire	0.7	233	72	65	65.0
83	Royal Agricultural College		253	75	61	64.6
84	Westminster	1.6	256	71	48	64.3
85	St Mary's College		198	80	52	63.5
86	Birmingham City	1.3	223	71	54	63.4
87	Sunderland		205	78	55	63.2
=88	Coventry	1.0	265	71	50	63.1
=88	Southampton Solent		231	76	56	63.1
90	University College Birmingham		241	77	51	62.9
91	Chester		263	70	64	62.7
=92	Canterbury Christ Church		214	77	52	62.2
=92	Bedfordshire	0.9	148	78	49	62.2
94	London South Bank	1.2	151	78	41	61.6
95	Chichester		227	83	33	61.5
96	Liverpool John Moores	0.6	231	71	52	61.2
97	UWIC, Cardiff	0.6	234	68	57	60.9
98	Leeds Metropolitan	1.1	263	62	61	60.7
99	Edge Hill		230	75	44	59.9
100	Abertay	0.8	263		39	59.1
=101	Derby		241	73	41	58.9
=101	Cumbria		262	71	44	58.9
103	Roehampton		195	74	46	58.7
104	Anglia Ruskin		247	68	52	58.4
105	Buckinghamshire New	1.0	197	70	42	58.2
106	Middlesex	1.7	158	70	38	58.0
107	Bolton	0.6	218	70	41	57.9
108	Glyndŵr		189		52	57.2
109	Thames Valley		151	75	41	56.2
110	Queen Margaret Edinburgh	0.4	246		37	55.9
111	East London		168	62	46	51.2
112	University of the Arts London		237	56	42	49.5

» Chartered Management Institute: **www.managers.org.uk**
» Confederation of British Industry: **www.cbi.org.uk**
» Institute of Business Consulting: **www.ibconsulting.org.uk**

Celtic Studies

Applications for places on Celtic studies degrees were up by more than a third at the start of 2010, but there were still fewer than 700 in total. Most of the successful candidates have good A levels, or equivalent qualifications: only one of the nine universities in the table averaged less than 300 points. And students seem to enjoy their courses: all but three universities had satisfaction scores of more than 80 per cent.

Cardiff is the new leader of the table, leapfrogging Cambridge and Aberystwyth, with by far the best employment score. It also has the highest entry standards, since Cambridge did not have enough entrants to compile a reliable score. Second-placed Cambridge has the most

Celtic Studies cont.

satisfied students and also produced extremely good results in the 2008 Research Assessment Exercise, when almost half of its submission was judged to be world-leading.

The ranking is split between the four universities from the Principality, which naturally major in Welsh, and the remaining five, which focus on Irish or Gaelic studies. Queen's, Belfast has overtaken Ulster this year as the top university in Northern Ireland. Glasgow is the only Scottish university in the ranking.

Only 137 students started degrees in 2009 and the small numbers play havoc with the employment data. Celtic studies appears in this year's top 20 for graduate employment, with nearly half of the leavers going on to take postgraduate courses. Only 6 per cent are unemployed, although 20 per cent start their career in lower-level employment. However, Celtic studies remains rock bottom of the earnings league, as the only subject with average starting salaries below £17,000 in graduate jobs. That figure was only £2,300 better than the average for graduates in lower-level jobs.

Employed in graduate job:	28%	Employed in non-graduate job and studying:	2%
Employed in graduate job and studying:	3%	Employed in non-graduate job:	18%
Studying:	42%	Unemployed:	6%
Average starting graduate salary:	£16,820	Average starting non-graduate salary:	£14,551

Celtic Studies	Research quality/9	Entry standards	Student satisfaction %	Graduate prospects %	Overall rating
1 Cardiff	2.9	377	83	91	100.0
2 Cambridge	5.2		89	59	99.4
3 Aberystwyth	3.7	325	88	81	97.5
4 Bangor	2.6	360	83	83	95.5
5 Glasgow	2.7		85	71	90.7
6 Queen's, Belfast	1.9	346	79	78	89.1
7 Ulster	4.6		60	74	87.0
8 Swansea	3.5	277	81	71	86.6
9 Liverpool	2.8	308	79	48	80.8

» Celtic studies within Intute modern languages and area studies: **www.intute.ac.uk/mlas**

Chemical Engineering

Only medicine and dentistry produce higher starting salaries than chemical engineering. The £28,400 average in graduate-level jobs is almost twice the average for lower-level work. This may help to explain the continuing popularity of the subject, which has been growing for several years. Although still one of the smaller branches of engineering, an 18 per cent surge in applications in 2009 was followed by a further rise of 8 per cent at the start of 2010, taking the applications total to more than 9,000.

Cambridge tops the chemical engineering table for the ninth year in a row, with much the highest entry standards and one of the two top research scores. Second-placed Imperial

College London matched Cambridge's rating for research, both universities having 30 per cent of their work rated as world-leading.

The most satisfied students were at Loughborough and Aston, which repeated its success of last year but is now only three places off the bottom of the table, while fourth-placed Sheffield had the best employment record. Loughborough is the other big riser in this year's table, moving up four places to third. All but five of the 20 universities in the table registered "positive destinations" for at least 80 per cent of those graduating.

Edinburgh remains the highest-placed Scottish institution. Swansea is the only representative of Wales and London South Bank the only post-1992 university left in the ranking.

Four out of five students have A levels or equivalent qualifications, and average entry grades are the highest for any engineering subject. This helps produce engineering's largest proportion of firsts and 2:1s. Most courses offer industrial placements in the final year and leading to Chartered Engineer status. Almost two thirds of students go straight into graduate jobs, although the 10 per cent unemployment rate is above average for all subjects.

Employed in graduate job:	59%	Employed in non-graduate job and studying:	1%
Employed in graduate job and studying:	4%	Employed in non-graduate job:	7%
Studying:	19%	Unemployed:	10%
Average starting graduate salary:	£28,415	Average starting non-graduate salary:	£14,785

Chemical Engineering	Research quality/9	Entry standards	Student satisfaction %	Graduate prospects %	Overall rating
1 Cambridge	4.5	571	85	92	100.0
2 Imperial College	4.5	504	81	93	95.6
3 Loughborough	3.6	396	86	84	88.8
4 Sheffield	3.0	407	84	94	88.4
5 Manchester	4.2	440	74	88	87.6
6 Birmingham	3.5	434	79	85	86.4
7 Surrey	3.4	354	85	84	85.8
8 Edinburgh	3.0	445	76	91	85.7
9 University College London	3.4	402	81	83	85.4
10 Newcastle	2.8	373	83	89	84.5
11 Nottingham	4.0	366	75	86	84.4
12 Bath	2.7	475	74	76	81.3
13 Queen's, Belfast	2.2	369	78	93	81.2
14 Heriot-Watt	3.1	353	77	83	80.9
15 Leeds	3.8	374	72	79	80.6
16 Strathclyde	1.9	405	78	89	80.3
17 Aberdeen	3.2	379	74		79.7
18 Aston	2.2	323	86	72	78.1
19 Swansea	3.5	298	73	71	75.3
20 London South Bank	2.5		66	46	61.4

» Institution of Chemical Engineers: **http://cms.icheme.org**
» Royal Society of Chemistry: **www.rsc.org**

Chemistry

Applications for chemistry degrees were up by almost 20 per cent at the start of 2010, the latest in a series of increases. But Government policy is ensuring that there are more places available in science subjects, so the level of competition may not be significantly stiffer. The number of universities in the ranking is back up to 50 for the first time in three years, following a much-publicised series of departmental closures. Forensic science has become an attractive alternative to the pure subject but, for many, chemistry remains the classic science. There are now five applications for every place.

Cambridge remains well clear of Oxford at the top of the table, with the highest entry standards and the best research grades. Both universities had average entry scores of more than four As at A level, and 40 per cent of Cambridge's research was rated world-leading. The most satisfied students are at Southampton and Loughborough, the latter not even in the top 20 overall.

The most impressive achievement in this year's table, however, was at Nottingham Trent, where every chemist had found a graduate-level job or were continuing their studies six months after completing a degree. Although not unusual in previous years, very few departments achieved this feat as the recession began to take hold.

There were good employment scores throughout the ranking. Chemistry is in the top 20 subjects for graduate destinations, with almost half of all graduates continuing their studies, either full or part-time. Starting salaries have improved since last year's *Guide*, but chemistry is still only just in the top half of the table for all subjects.

Chemistry is old university territory, with Nottingham Trent the only former polytechnic in the top 20. There are only 11 post-1992 universities in the table, with Plymouth nearly making the top 30. Almost nine out of ten undergraduates have A levels or their equivalent, but entry requirements are not far above the average for all subjects.

Employed in graduate job:	33%	Employed in non-graduate job and studying:	1%
Employed in graduate job and studying:	5%	Employed in non-graduate job:	13%
Studying:	39%	Unemployed:	9%
Average starting graduate salary:	£21,224	Average starting non-graduate salary:	£15,550

Chemistry	Research quality/9	Entry standards	Student satisfaction %	Graduate prospects %	Overall rating
1 Cambridge	5.0	578	85	82	100.0
2 Oxford	4.3	546	84	89	98.1
3 Durham	3.5	530	85	84	94.6
4 York	3.4	449	88	83	92.6
5 St Andrews	4.2	440	82	84	92.5
6 Southampton	2.8	412	91	85	92.1
7 Bristol	4.0	448	82	78	90.4
8 Nottingham	4.5	397	84	74	90.1
9 Sheffield	3.3	402	87	80	89.7
10 Warwick	3.4	425	82	85	89.6

11	Strathclyde	3.0	387	88	82	89.4
12	Edinburgh	4.2	436	78	80	89.0
=13	Imperial College	3.7	493	73	85	87.9
=13	Hull	2.3	274	89	95	87.9
15	Glasgow	3.0	389	83	83	87.0
16	Sussex	2.6	420	83	84	86.9
17	Liverpool	3.6	395	81	78	86.7
=18	Leeds	3.6	363	78	84	86.2
=18	Nottingham Trent	3.0	203	83	100	86.2
20	University College London	3.2	442	82	72	85.8
21	Leicester	2.1	344	86	86	85.6
=22	Manchester	3.5	416	78	76	85.2
=22	Bath	2.5	416	81	82	85.2
=24	Loughborough	1.5	315	91	84	84.7
=24	Aberdeen	2.1	372	81	89	84.7
26	Heriot-Watt	2.6	314	83	84	84.0
27	Surrey	3.4	325	78	84	83.7
28	Keele	2.5	307	82	84	83.0
29	Queen's, Belfast	2.2	365	80	85	82.8
30	Cardiff	2.8	362	78	80	82.5
31	East Anglia	2.4	366	84	71	81.9
32	Plymouth	1.8	231	81	95	81.1
33	Birmingham	2.8	371	75	74	79.2
34	Newcastle	2.2	367	75	78	78.5
35	Queen Mary, London	2.3	303	81	69	77.7
36	Sheffield Hallam	1.2	234	82	81	75.5
37	Reading	1.4	314	74	82	74.7
=38	Northumbria	1.6	297	78	64	72.2
=38	Bradford	2.9	212	73		72.2
40	Aston	2.2			65	71.7
41	Brighton	2.1	253	79	52	69.9
42	Huddersfield	1.3	250	77	64	69.1
43	Manchester Metropolitan	1.3	215	74	72	68.9
44	Bangor	2.4	281	67	63	68.1
45	Abertay		365		61	67.7
46	Kent		290	77	63	66.5
47	Liverpool John Moores		227	72	77	65.8
48	Glamorgan		235	72	69	63.9
49	Kingston		248	70	63	61.6
50	University of the Arts London		196		50	55.7

» European Association for Chemical and Molecular Sciences: **www.euchems.org**
» Royal Society of Chemistry: **www.rsc.org**
» Society of Dyers and Colourists: **www.sdc.org.uk**

Civil Engineering

Civil engineering is in the top 10 subjects both for employment levels and graduate starting salaries, although both the unemployment rate of 8 per cent and the proportion in non-graduate jobs have crept up since last year. Those in graduate-level employment were paid average starting salaries of almost £24,500. Graduate destinations scores are good throughout the table, but only two universities – Imperial College London and Dundee – achieved full employment at graduate level, compared with four universities last year.

Cambridge maintains its lead in civil engineering after three years at the top. The university enjoys a predictably enormous lead over the rest on entry standards and has the top research grades. Imperial College London closes the gap slightly in second place, while Bath has moved up five places to third. Greenwich, although not in the top 30, has the highest satisfaction levels, but Nottingham Trent remains the top-placed new university. Dundee is again the top university in Scotland and Cardiff the leader in Wales.

Entry scores have been rising, with three universities averaging more than 500 points this year. Fewer than half of all undergraduates are admitted with A levels or equivalent qualifications, reflecting the large numbers of mature students who are upgrading their qualifications. Applications were up by nearly 9 per cent at the start of 2010, a good increase in any other year but lower than in other branches of engineering – perhaps due to pessimism over the construction market.

Some of the top courses in civil engineering are four-year courses leading to an MEng degree; others are sandwich courses incorporating a period at work. The leading departments will expect physics and maths A levels, or their equivalent.

Employed in graduate job:	68%
Employed in graduate job and studying:	8%
Studying:	9%
Average starting graduate salary:	£24,473
Employed in non-graduate job and studying:	1%
Employed in non-graduate job:	7%
Unemployed:	8%
Average starting non-graduate salary:	£14,614

Civil Engineering	Research quality/9	Entry standards	Student satisfaction %	Graduate prospects %	Overall rating
1 Cambridge	5.5	567	85	94	100.0
2 Imperial College	5.3	507	72	100	93.6
3 Bath	3.9	437	86	95	91.7
4 Sheffield	3.9	466	84	91	91.0
5 Bristol	4.1	448	82	94	90.6
6 Dundee	3.6	344	85	100	89.2
=7 Durham	2.7	513	78	98	88.5
=7 Cardiff	4.3	374	83	92	88.5
9 Loughborough	3.1	378	89	91	87.6
10 Surrey	3.4	355	83	96	86.7
11 Nottingham	4.2	368	82	88	86.6
12 Southampton	4.1	432	76	90	86.3
13 Newcastle	4.0	358	83	87	85.8
14 Queen's, Belfast	3.7	374	77	95	85.5

15	Manchester	3.6	413	75	93	84.9
16	Swansea	5.0	308	75	91	84.8
17	Edinburgh	3.0	421	75	94	83.8
18	University College London	3.0	441	75	89	83.1
19	Warwick	3.6	386	75	89	82.5
20	City	2.4	299	82	97	82.0
21	Birmingham	2.9	385	72	91	80.0
22	Leeds	2.7	369	75	89	79.6
23	Exeter	2.7	353	81	82	79.4
24	Aberdeen	3.2	294	74	93	79.3
25	Liverpool	3.2	376	70	86	78.1
26	Heriot-Watt	2.3	347	76	86	77.4
27	Nottingham Trent	1.3	245	82	96	76.5
28	Glasgow	2.8	365	65	91	75.6
29	Plymouth	2.7	257	81	80	75.5
30	Strathclyde	1.8	396	66	89	74.0
31	Portsmouth		251	82	95	73.0
32	Edinburgh Napier	1.7	245	73	94	72.9
33	Greenwich	1.7	251	90	64	71.9
34	Salford	3.7	243	76	65	71.4
35	Kingston	1.5	192	83	81	71.3
36	Brighton	1.7	210	78		69.5
37	Glamorgan	2.5		61	88	69.2
38	Bradford	2.3	274	68	78	69.1
39	Northumbria	2.2	253	63	82	67.0
40	Ulster		249	70	88	65.6
41	Coventry	1.0	260	71	76	65.5
42	Abertay		256		77	62.6
43	Liverpool John Moores		265	69	77	62.3
44	Teesside		246	76	61	60.0
45	Leeds Metropolitan		251	67	57	55.2

» EngineeringUK: **www.engineeringuk.com**
» Institution of Civil Engineers: **www.ice.org.uk**
» Institution of Structural Engineers: **www.istructe.org**

Classics and Ancient History

Oxford and Cambridge have been locked together at the top of the classics table since it was first published seven years ago, when their scores were identical. They could not be any closer this year, when only the revaluation of grades in the 2008 Research Assessment Exercise keeps Cambridge ahead. The new scoring system, mirroring the one used to distribute research grants, gives extra credit for world-leading research, of which Cambridge had slightly more than Oxford. Balancing that, Oxford again has the highest entry standards in the table.

Swansea, only five places off the bottom of the table, tied with the top two for the most satisfied students in a subject of generally high satisfaction levels. Employment prospects are

Classics and Ancient History cont.

much more mixed, with tenth-placed Bristol registering the best score. St Andrews remains the clear leader in Scotland, while Roehampton is the only post-1992 university in the ranking, rooted to the bottom with a particularly low employment score.

Several universities teach the subjects as part of a modular degree scheme, but not as a degree in its own right. A-level grades in classics are among the highest for any group of subjects, but most universities offering classics teach the subject from scratch, as well as to more practised students.

The subjects' reputation for attracting analytical high-fliers helps in the jobs market, but relatively few (32 per cent) go directly into graduate jobs. Almost as many opt for postgraduate courses. The 9 per cent unemployment rate six months after graduation is only just above average for all subjects, but the proportion in non-graduate work is relatively high. The subjects are in the bottom half of the salaries table, but the average starting salary was close to £20,000 when the latest survey was conducted. There had been a relatively modest increase in applications for classics at the start of 2009, but ancient history continued to grow in popularity. There are more than five applications for every place in both areas.

Employed in graduate job:	28%	Employed in non-graduate job and studying:	3%
Employed in graduate job and studying:	4%	Employed in non-graduate job:	30%
Studying:	27%	Unemployed:	9%
Average starting graduate salary:	£19,947	Average starting non-graduate salary:	£15,413

Classics and Ancient History	Research quality/9	Entry standards	Student satisfaction %	Graduate prospects %	Overall rating
1 Cambridge	5.1	526	88	78	100.0
2 Oxford	4.8	539	88	80	99.9
3 Durham	3.8	477	83	78	91.5
4 University College London	4.1	443	81	78	90.5
5 St Andrews	3.1	466	87	72	90.3
6 King's College London	4.0	429	86	66	89.3
7 Exeter	3.9	439	84	62	87.5
8 Warwick	3.8	443	83	62	86.4
9 Manchester	3.5	412	83	53	82.6
10 Bristol	3.3	439	70	81	82.5
11 Edinburgh	2.4	456	75	71	81.3
12 Birmingham	3.1	373	85	51	80.7
13 Glasgow	1.9	425	87	50	80.1
14 Royal Holloway	2.1	353	83	61	78.5
15 Nottingham	2.6	376	78	53	76.3
16 Leeds	1.7	381	79	60	75.9
17 Newcastle	2.4	382	76	55	75.4
18 Liverpool	2.5	343	82	47	75.1
19 Swansea	1.6	299	88	47	74.7
20 Reading	2.5	327	80	52	74.6
21 Lampeter (Trinity Saint David)	1.3		78	59	73.0

22 Kent		1.3	266	79	50	68.2
23 Roehampton			233	69	38	55.3

» Classical Association: **www.classicalassociation.org**
» Society for the Promotion of Roman Studies: **www.romansociety.org**

Communication and Media Studies

Students continue to flock to degrees in this area, despite continued carping in newspapers and other branches of the media about their currency in the employment market. Applications for journalism were up by 25 per cent at the start of 2010, to add to 24 per cent growth in the previous year. Media studies and mass communications degrees could not match this level of popularity, but still posted respectable increases. Together, they attracted more applications than mathematics.

The division of jobs into graduate and non-graduate fields of employment hits communication and media studies harder than any other group of subjects. Only one set of subjects has a lower proportion of "positive destinations". Academics in the field argue that it is normal for students completing media courses to take "entry level" work that is not classified as a graduate job. Nevertheless, the 12 per cent unemployment rate is well above average and the subjects are in the bottom four for graduate starting salaries.

Communication and media studies are mainly the preserve of the new universities, but older universities have been moving in and now fill the top 10 places. Warwick remains at the top after an outstanding performance in the 2008 Research Assessment Exercise. The university, which also has the highest entry standards, achieved one of the highest grades in any subject for its film and television studies. Westminster matched Warwick's 60 per cent of world-leading research in media studies, but is restricted to 18th place for the second successive year by low scores for student satisfaction and graduate employment.

Leicester takes second place with the most satisfied students, while third-placed Sheffield has the best record in the graduate jobs market. No university saw three-quarters of their leavers go straight into graduate-level jobs or continue their studies within six months of graduation and the proportion dropped below 50 per cent at nearly half of the universities in the table.

Bournemouth is the highest-placed new university this year, only just outside the top 10 and only a point ahead of Nottingham Trent. Cardiff has dropped five places to eighth, but remains the top university in Wales, while Strathclyde maintains its advantage over Stirling as the leader in Scotland. Entry grades have not risen as much as in other subjects: only two universities (compared with last year's four) average more than 400 points, while three average less than 200 points.

Employed in graduate job:	40%	Employed in non-graduate job and studying:	2%
Employed in graduate job and studying:	2%	Employed in non-graduate job:	37%
Studying:	6%	Unemployed:	12%
Average starting graduate salary:	£17,649	Average starting non-graduate salary:	£14,637

Communication and Media Studies cont.

		Research quality/9	Entry standards	Student satisfaction %	Graduate prospects %	Overall rating
1	Warwick	6.4	428	83	59	100.0
2	Leicester	4.4	317	92	66	94.2
3	Sheffield	2.1	393	88	74	93.6
4	Loughborough	3.2	382	83	72	93.1
5	Southampton	3.8	375	86	64	92.8
6	King's College London	5.1	408	71	68	92.6
7	Queen Mary, London	3.9	368	90	54	91.3
8	Cardiff	5.2	380	73	59	89.3
9	Goldsmiths College	5.3	345	72	66	88.7
10	East Anglia	5.8	337	80	46	87.1
=11	Leeds	2.9	377	71	69	85.6
=11	Bournemouth	2.8	353	75	70	85.6
=13	Nottingham Trent	3.8	293	79	65	84.6
=13	Lancaster	4.2	346	79	51	84.6
=13	Sussex	3.4	356	75	62	84.6
16	Strathclyde		400		61	83.6
17	Birmingham City	3.8	317	80	51	82.6
18	Westminster	6.4	325	67	47	82.0
19	Stirling	3.0	337		55	81.6
20	Central Lancashire	2.3	305	77	65	81.0
21	Lincoln	3.3	293	77	58	80.4
22	Royal Holloway	3.7	344	73	48	79.3
23	De Montfort	3.6	247	80	55	78.7
24	Brunel	2.3	304	72	65	78.2
25	Glasgow Caledonian	2.1	351	74	50	77.2
26	Liverpool		357	81	48	75.2
27	Staffordshire	1.4	253	76	64	74.6
=28	West of England	3.1	283	79	39	74.2
=28	Keele		286	80	61	74.2
30	Hull	2.6	269	75	50	73.9
31	Surrey	1.7	344	61	63	73.7
32	Hertfordshire	1.8	246	79	53	73.0
33	Brighton	1.8	285	74	51	72.6
34	Oxford Brookes		314	79	51	72.4
35	Robert Gordon		269	79	59	72.1
36	Salford	2.8	290	66	51	71.9
37	Sunderland	3.2	229	75	47	71.8
38	Northumbria	2.5	292	66	53	71.7
=39	Birmingham		386	74	42	71.6
=39	Bangor		271		62	71.6
=41	Leeds Metropolitan	2.9	279	63	56	71.3
=41	Portsmouth	2.0	278	79	40	71.3
43	Kingston	1.3	259	73	58	71.2

44 Ulster	3.1	257	74	40	70.5
45 Edinburgh Napier		284	70	63	70.2
46 Bath Spa	1.5	269	75	47	70.1
47 Queen Margaret Edinburgh	2.4	284		42	69.8
48 Teesside		237	89	43	69.6
49 City		331	58	70	69.5
50 Derby	3.2	214	69	51	69.4
=51 Roehampton	2.0	249	82	34	69.1
=51 Bedfordshire	2.6	206	86	31	69.1
53 Greenwich	0.8	238	83	42	68.8
=54 Winchester	1.9	268	74	41	68.6
=54 Swansea	1.9	270	74	40	68.6
56 Aberystwyth		261	73	58	68.4
57 Queen's, Belfast		335	76	39	68.2
58 St Mary's College		236	75	59	67.9
59 Manchester		394	68	37	67.8
60 University of the Arts London		279	62	68	67.3
61 Falmouth		302	69	51	66.7
62 Worcester		249	74	53	66.6
63 Bradford	1.1	245	69	52	66.5
64 Coventry	2.3	263	61	51	66.2
65 East London	3.8	199	67	41	65.9
66 York St John		255	76	46	65.7
67 Sheffield Hallam	2.1	281	60	48	65.6
68 Chichester		239	81	40	65.2
69 Chester		250	66	60	65.0
70 Southampton Solent		255	71	51	64.8
71 Essex		286		43	64.4
=72 Lampeter (Trinity Saint David)	0.9	246		48	64.3
=72 UWIC, Cardiff		243	76	44	64.3
74 Liverpool John Moores		265	71	47	64.0
=75 Marjon, Plymouth		233	76	41	62.5
=75 Middlesex	1.6	193	65	53	62.5
77 Anglia Ruskin		230	76	41	62.4
78 Huddersfield	0.2	275	63	45	61.1
79 London South Bank	2.6	210	67	33	61.0
80 Canterbury Christ Church		224	74	39	60.4
81 Northampton		220	75	36	60.1
82 Glamorgan	2.0	282	57	31	58.9
83 Gloucestershire	0.2	251	60	44	58.2
84 Edge Hill		272	71	25	58.0
85 Thames Valley	0.9	201	62	45	57.9
86 Cumbria		262	66	33	57.4
87 Buckinghamshire New		196	67	44	57.2
88 Glyndŵr		276		30	57.1
89 Manchester Metropolitan	1.8	204	67	24	55.8

» Broadcast Journalism Training Council: **www.bjtc.org.uk**
» Chartered Institute of Journalists: **www.cioj.co.uk**
» National Union of Journalists: **www.nuj.org.uk**
» Sector Skills Council for Creative Media: **www.skillset.org**

Computer Science

Computer science, once seen as the guarantee of a lucrative career, again has the highest unemployment rate of any subject in this year's *Guide*, at a worrying 14 per cent. However, it is not all bad news in the computing world: the subject is still among the top 20 for graduate salaries and more than half of those completing degrees do go straight into graduate-level jobs.

Applications for degree places were up by 19 per cent at the start of 2010 – by far the best figure since a prolonged decline set in the last decade. With more than 50,000 applications, including 2,000 for Foundation degrees, computer science remains among the 20 most popular subjects.

The top four are unchanged since last year, with Cambridge still clear of Oxford in first place, thanks to the best research grades and by far the highest entry scores. Cambridge's computer scientists average nearly five As at A level, one of the highest scores in any subject, while 45 per cent of the university's research was considered world-leading in the 2008 assessments.

Oxford has the best employment record, with an impressive 97 per cent of graduates in graduate-level jobs or further study six months after completing a degree. Sheffield, in 11th place, and Loughborough, in 18th place, had the most satisfied undergraduates in the 2009 National Student Survey, with Dundee and Glasgow close behind. Three years after graduation, more than a quarter of computing students said they would be "very likely" to choose a different course if they had their time again – the second-highest total among 19 groups of subjects.

Edinburgh has reclaimed top position in Scotland from Glasgow, while Cardiff remains the leader in Wales. Only five post-1992 universities, headed by Plymouth, feature in the top 50. The others are Bournemouth, De Montfort, Lincoln and Robert Gordon. Entry standards are spread more widely than in any other subject, average scores on the UCAS tariff ranging from 575 points to only 143, the equivalent of a D and an E at A level. Ten universities average more than 400 points, while 15 have an average of less than 200, six fewer than last year.

Employed in graduate job:	49%	Employed in non-graduate job and studying:	2%
Employed in graduate job and studying:	3%	Employed in non-graduate job:	21%
Studying:	11%	Unemployed:	14%
Average starting graduate salary:	£22,276	Average starting non-graduate salary:	£16,240

Computer Science	Research quality/9	Entry standards	Student satisfaction %	Graduate prospects %	Overall rating
1 Cambridge	5.5	575	83	96	100.0
2 Oxford	4.7	526		97	98.8
3 Imperial College	4.8	507	83	94	95.4

4	Southampton	4.8	411	85	87	91.7
5	Edinburgh	4.8	440	79	86	89.1
6	University College London	4.7	409	80	85	88.3
7	Bristol	4.2	455	77	92	88.0
8	Glasgow	4.4	358	86	79	87.5
9	Warwick	3.2	467	83	82	87.1
10	York	4.0	425	80	86	86.8
11	Sheffield	3.2	389	87	82	86.5
12	Bath	4.0	435	77	86	85.9
13	Dundee	3.2	378	86	79	85.1
14	Newcastle	3.6	315	84	86	84.5
=15	Leeds	4.1	369	79	82	84.3
=15	Royal Holloway	3.7	275	83	90	84.3
17	Birmingham	4.3	374	83	70	84.2
18	Loughborough	2.9	318	87	85	84.0
19	Surrey	2.4	352	82	89	82.4
=20	Manchester	4.5	390	74	77	82.1
=20	Aberdeen	3.6	366	78	82	82.1
22	Lancaster	4.1	369	75	81	81.8
=23	Cardiff	3.6	343	82	74	81.7
=23	Nottingham	4.4	372	73	82	81.7
25	St Andrews	3.1	392		79	81.6
26	Durham	3.5	400	71	85	79.6
=27	Sussex	3.6	321	78	77	79.4
=27	Strathclyde	2.8	365	78	80	79.4
29	Leicester	3.5	266	84	72	79.3
30	Liverpool	4.3	363	75	68	79.2
31	East Anglia	3.5	293	79	78	78.8
32	Essex	3.2	288	82	72	78.3
33	Kent	3.2	310	75	84	78.2
34	Aberystwyth	3.9	264	78	73	77.3
35	Swansea	3.9	299	76	73	77.2
36	King's College London	3.1	369	72	81	77.1
37	Queen's, Belfast	3.0	328	76	77	76.9
38	Heriot-Watt	3.0	282	79	72	76.2
39	Exeter	3.1	356	74	72	75.8
40	Reading	1.7	329	76	82	75.0
41	Plymouth	4.0	251	77	65	74.9
42	Hull	1.8	229	83	78	74.5
43	City	2.9	285	71	80	73.6
44	Bournemouth	1.9	248	76	85	73.4
45	De Montfort	2.4	188	84	67	72.6
46	Queen Mary, London	4.0	277	69	67	72.1
47	Aston	2.2	305	76	67	72.0
48	Brunel	3.1	298	73	63	71.3
49	Lincoln	2.8	266	74	66	70.8
50	Robert Gordon	2.1	278	72	77	70.6

Computer Science cont.

	Research quality/9	Entry standards	Student satisfaction %	Graduate prospects %	Overall rating
51 Glyndŵr	2.0	220		79	70.3
52 Oxford Brookes	2.8	212	73	73	69.9
=53 West of England	2.4	232	73	73	69.8
=53 Brighton	2.9	270	69	70	69.8
55 Stirling	2.1	269		69	69.7
56 Bangor	2.8	241		64	69.3
57 Ulster	2.6	234	77	58	69.0
58 Northumbria		240	79	78	67.9
59 Staffordshire	1.4	258	73	72	67.5
=60 Hertfordshire	2.7	185	74	63	67.3
=60 Greenwich	1.1	203	85	55	67.3
=60 Liverpool John Moores	2.3	193	75	65	67.3
63 Portsmouth	1.5	229	78	61	67.1
=64 Nottingham Trent	1.5	234	68	83	66.9
=64 Salford	3.2	240	68	61	66.9
=66 Glasgow Caledonian	1.0	300	78	53	66.6
=66 Huddersfield	1.6	259	71	69	66.6
68 Goldsmiths College	3.3	187	71	60	66.5
69 Teesside	2.6	260	73	51	66.0
70 Edinburgh Napier	1.4	242		68	65.9
71 Middlesex	2.1	152	77	62	65.8
=72 Keele		235	81	64	65.6
=72 Glamorgan	1.9	248	74	56	65.6
74 Newman		202		80	65.2
75 Chester		239	73	74	64.1
76 Manchester Metropolitan	1.8	241	71	58	63.8
77 Central Lancashire		225	75	71	63.7
78 Sheffield Hallam	1.4	229	69	67	63.3
=79 Kingston	1.8	192	72	58	62.8
=79 Gloucestershire		229	74	69	62.8
81 Sunderland	1.4	207	72	59	62.6
82 Northampton		223	74	66	61.9
83 Coventry	1.7	235	66	61	61.7
84 Abertay		281		57	61.1
85 London South Bank	1.7		76	40	60.7
86 Bradford	2.1	217	66	56	60.4
87 Worcester		215	73	60	59.8
88 Edge Hill		227	69	67	59.7
89 Derby		233	68	68	59.6
90 Bedfordshire	1.4	143	75	48	59.5
91 Southampton Solent		196	71	61	58.6
92 Newport		262	73	46	57.9
93 Westminster	1.6	198	66	50	57.3

94 Canterbury Christ Church		162	74	52	56.6
95 Roehampton		182	73	50	56.2
96 Anglia Ruskin		220	66	59	56.1
97 UWIC, Cardiff		201		52	55.5
98 Buckinghamshire New		178	72	46	54.8
=99 Birmingham City		178	67	56	54.6
=99 East London		143	72	50	54.6
101 Thames Valley	0.9	165	67	47	54.5
102 Leeds Metropolitan		204	65	57	54.4

» British Computer Society: **www.bcs.org**

Dentistry

The average starting salary of nearly £30,000 for dentists is the highest in any subject. Only medicine has a fractionally better graduate employment rate than dentistry. At nearly half of the 13 undergraduate dental schools, every leaver was in a graduate job or studying six months after finishing the course when the latest survey was carried out. As a result, not even medicine can match the level of competition for places in dentistry: almost nine applications to the place in 2009. The demand for places is still growing, with another increase in applications of 12.5 per cent at the start of 2010 taking the total to more than 13,000.

Most degrees last five years, although several universities offer a six-year option for those without the necessary scientific qualifications. The number of places has been increased in recent years to tackle shortages in the profession, but entry standards are still high: none of the schools averages less than 428 points on the UCAS tariff. Most demand chemistry and may give preference to candidates who also have biology A level.

Scores in the subject are so close that the ranking changes frequently. This year we have dropped employment scores as a measure (although they are included for guidance) to avoid very small differences distorting positions. Glasgow took over the leadership last year, but is down to third in this edition of the *Guide*. Manchester is the new leader, thanks to the best research grades and good scores on the other indicators. Sheffield moves up two places to second, while fourth-placed Birmingham has the most satisfied students. Dundee has the highest entry standards.

Cardiff offers the only dentistry degree in Wales and there are no new universities in the ranking. However, that will change when there are data for Central Lancashire, which opened a purpose-built dental school in 2007. The Peninsula Dental School, a partnership of Exeter and Plymouth, also had its first intake in 2007.

Employed in graduate job:	83%	Employed in non-graduate job and studying:	0%
Employed in graduate job and studying:	16%	Employed in non-graduate job:	0%
Studying:	0%	Unemployed:	0%
Average starting graduate salary:	£29,805	Average starting non-graduate salary:	*

Dentistry cont.

	Research quality/9	Entry standards	Student satisfaction %	Graduate prospects %	Overall rating
1 Manchester	4.3	444	90	100	100.0
2 Sheffield	3.3	467	89	100	98.8
3 Glasgow	3.0	477	87	99	98.7
4 Birmingham	2.7	468	92	100	98.1
5 Newcastle	3.1	458	89	100	97.1
6 Dundee	2.5	489	79	99	96.3
7 King's College London	4.2	459	70	98	95.5
8 Queen Mary, London	4.0	451	72	98	94.6
9 Queen's, Belfast	2.6	450	87	99	93.8
10 Liverpool	2.4	476	76	100	92.9
=11 Leeds	3.3	439	78	98	92.2
=11 Bristol	3.4	428	82	100	92.2
13 Cardiff	3.2	446	73	99	91.2

» British Dental Association: **www.bda.org**
» Dental Professionals Association: **www.uk-dentistry.org**

Drama, Dance and Cinematics

Warwick retakes top position for drama, dance and cinematics after surrendering it to equal third-placed Glasgow last year. It has the highest entry standards and is among the leaders on the other measures. Queen Mary, University of London, is up to second, with a good student satisfaction score and the best results in the 2008 Research Assessment Exercise, when half of its submission was rated world-leading. Roehampton's research in dance achieved an even higher score, but it was not sustained over the whole group of subjects in this category.

The most satisfied students are at Teesside, which also has the lowest entry standards. Teesside shares 36th place with Nottingham, which has the lowest employment rate, a surprising 29 per cent. For the second year in a row, by far the best graduate destinations score (eight percentage points ahead of its nearest rival) is at the Central School of Speech and Drama, also part of the University of London. Other employment scores remain low: even at some top-20 universities more than half of the leavers were unemployed or in low-level work six months after graduation.

There are no post-1992 universities in the top 20, although De Montfort is only a whisker away. This is another table where the gulf in qualifications between entrants to new and old universities is evident, although for drama and dance in particular, this is unlikely to be the main criterion for selection. Recent rises in entry standards seem to have stalled in the latest survey: five universities, compared with only one last year, average less than 200 points and just four have averages of more than 400 points, compared with six a year ago. The overall tariff score remains the lowest in any of the subject tables.

Drama, dance and cinematics is out of the bottom five in the employment table this year. The subjects are in an even lower position in the salaries league, but freelancing and periods of temporary employment are common throughout the performing arts. This does not seem to put off prospective students: drama is in the top 20 subjects in terms of applications, while cinematics and photography registered the biggest increase in any subject apart from design and nursing (where technical issues cloud comparisons this year) with a 47 per cent rise. The smaller area of dance also enjoyed a 24 per cent increase in applications.

Employed in graduate job:	38%
Employed in graduate job and studying:	3%
Studying:	9%
Average starting graduate salary:	£17,145

Employed in non-graduate job and studying:	4%
Employed in non-graduate job:	37%
Unemployed:	9%
Average starting non-graduate salary:	£14,355

Drama, Dance and Cinematics	Research quality/9	Entry standards	Student satisfaction %	Graduate prospects %	Overall rating
1 Warwick	4.5	444	83	66	100.0
2 Queen Mary, London	5.8	367	86	60	98.0
=3 Glasgow	5.0	387	83	55	94.3
=3 Exeter	4.6	412	86	51	94.3
5 Central School of Speech and Drama	2.9	341	78	85	93.2
6 Lancaster	4.1	367	79	66	92.3
7 Royal Holloway	4.6	387	76	63	92.2
8 Manchester	5.4	417	67	59	91.1
9 Birmingham	3.1	384	77	69	90.7
10 Kent	4.4	347	79	56	88.5
11 Loughborough	2.5	397	78	56	86.0
12 Surrey	3.2	360	67	72	85.8
13 East Anglia		381	84	67	85.1
14 Hull	2.8	310	84	59	84.8
15 Bristol	5.2	436	52	58	84.6
16 Goldsmiths College	3.4	366	68	61	83.9
17 Leeds	3.5	372	66	58	82.8
18 Aberdeen	3.3	326	83	39	80.4
19 Reading	3.8	315	77	44	80.0
20 Queen's Belfast	2.9	362	74	46	79.9
=21 De Montfort	3.0	266	76	56	78.0
=21 Essex	2.7	325	72	53	78.0
23 Aberystwyth	3.8	270	79	44	77.9
24 UWIC, Cardiff		304	78	68	77.4
25 Coventry	2.3	299	74	55	77.3
26 Arts University College, Bournemouth	0.4	320	79	60	77.0
=27 Queen Margaret Edinburgh	0.2	329		66	76.2
=27 Roehampton	4.4	281	71	43	76.2
29 Brighton	4.3	279	68	47	75.7
30 Nottingham Trent		305	67	77	75.6
31 Oxford Brookes		326	73	63	74.9
32 Brunel	2.6	287	73	49	74.6
33 Bishop Grosseteste		223		76	74.0
34 Sussex		380	56	73	73.7

Drama, Dance and Cinematics cont.

		Research quality/9	Entry standards	Student satisfaction %	Graduate prospects %	Overall rating
35	Chichester	1.7	301	75	47	73.6
=36	Teesside		168	88	69	73.4
=36	Nottingham	3.2	332	74	29	73.4
38	Staffordshire	1.4	229	83	51	73.0
39	Glamorgan	1.7	294	69	54	72.7
40	Middlesex	3.1	189	69	63	72.6
41	Liverpool John Moores		281	80	55	72.4
42	Bath Spa		283	73	62	71.9
43	Chester	1.9	269	67	56	71.7
44	Plymouth	2.2	277	74	43	71.4
45	Huddersfield		285	75	58	71.3
46	Gloucestershire		275	78	52	70.5
47	Winchester	1.9	268	72	45	69.9
48	Birmingham City		238	77	58	69.8
49	Falmouth		305	71	53	69.5
50	Salford	1.5	312	66	46	69.0
=51	Hertfordshire	1.2	261	66	58	68.9
=51	Manchester Metropolitan	1.8	250	73	45	68.9
53	Kingston	1.7	242	79	38	68.5
54	University of the Arts London		298	63	61	67.9
55	St Mary's College		270	75	50	67.7
56	West of England		285	80	40	67.6
=57	Northumbria		260	70	57	67.2
=57	Edge Hill		276	75	47	67.2
59	Cumbria		266	68	57	66.9
60	London South Bank		235	73	52	65.3
61	Westminster		301	65	49	64.9
62	Portsmouth	0.8	271	77	32	64.8
63	Bedfordshire	2.6	201	72	37	64.7
64	Anglia Ruskin		266	72	44	64.4
65	Sunderland	1.2	215	78	36	64.2
=66	Sheffield Hallam		281	76	35	64.1
=66	Northampton	1.2	256	63	48	64.1
=68	Worcester		243	79	38	63.8
=68	York St John	1.8	273	59	44	63.8
70	Bolton		289	68	42	63.5
71	University for Creative Arts		260	67	49	63.4
72	Canterbury Christ Church		289	74	32	62.7
73	Ulster		266	68	43	62.2
74	Greenwich		245	73	39	61.7
75	Newport		261	64	46	61.2
76	Lincoln	1.2	257	61	42	61.1
=77	Southampton Solent		247	64	49	61.0

=77 Newman			188	57	61.0
79 Central Lancashire			260	64	45	60.6
80 Marjon, Plymouth			190	71	44	59.3
81 East London		1.9	213	57	42	58.9
82 Derby			248	65	38	58.1
83 Thames Valley			239	53	53	57.0
84 Leeds Metropolitan			278	42	56	55.4
85 Buckinghamshire New			187	64	32	51.8

» The Stage: **www.thestage.co.uk**
» UKP-Arts: **www.ukperformingarts.co.uk**

East and South Asian Studies

One additional university has joined the East and South Asian studies ranking since last year, making four more than the total three years ago, when these subjects were identified as officially "vulnerable". Universities come in and out of the table because small numbers of students mean that reliable averages cannot always be compiled, even though courses are still running.

Numbers may well grow in future years, with the clamour for more interaction with China and India. However, as yet fewer than 4,000 students take the languages at any level of higher education. Yet around half those completing degrees go straight into graduate jobs. The small numbers make for exaggerated swings in some of the data: this year's *Guide* shows a huge rise in starting salaries, for example. An average of more than £24,750 propelled the subjects into the top 10 on this measure.

Japanese is still the biggest draw, with another near 30 per cent increase bringing the number of applications to more than 1,600 by the official deadline for courses beginning in 2010. A total of 221 students started degrees in the language in 2009. Surprisingly, in view of the number of schools now teaching Mandarin, applications for Chinese had dropped a little at the start of 2010.

Cambridge remains clear of Oxford at the top of the table, with the highest entry standards and the most satisfied students. Cardiff, which overtakes Oxford to take second place, has the best research score. Edinburgh is the only Scottish university in the ranking and Westminster the only post-1992 institution.

Four out of five students enter with tariff scores that are above average for all subjects, so degree classifications are also high. Most undergraduates learn their chosen language from scratch, although universities expect to see evidence of potential in other modern language qualifications.

Employed in graduate job:	42%	Employed in non-graduate job and studying:	0%
Employed in graduate job and studying:	5%	Employed in non-graduate job:	23%
Studying:	17%	Unemployed:	13%
Average starting graduate salary:	£24,769	Average starting non-graduate salary:	£16,498

East and South Asian Studies cont.

	Research quality/9	Entry standards	Student satisfaction %	Graduate prospects %	Overall rating
1 Cambridge	2.7	515	89	82	100.0
2 Cardiff	4.5	358	83		95.3
3 Oxford	3.5	514	80	69	94.5
4 School of Oriental and African Studies	4.0	397	74	74	90.3
5 Nottingham	1.9	390	66	83	81.4
6 Sheffield	1.6	411	77	66	79.9
7 Manchester	2.1	378	72		77.9
8 Leeds	2.1	399	74	51	74.9
9 Edinburgh	1.9	490	55	58	73.4
10 Westminster	1.9	230	63		62.5

» Association of South-East Asian Studies (UK): **http://aseasuk.org.uk**
» British Association for Chinese Studies: **www.bacsuk.org.uk**
» British Association for Japanese Studies: **www.bajs.org.uk**
» British Association for Korean Studies: **www.baks.org.uk**
» British Association for South Asian Studies: **www.basas.org.uk**
» Royal Asiatic Society: **http://royalasiaticsociety.org**
» Royal Society for Asian Affairs: **www.rsaa.org.uk**

Economics

Economics was one of the few major subjects to see a drop in applications at the start of 2010, but competition for places remains stiff, with more than six applications for every degree place. This year's fractional decline follows a 15 per cent increase in applications in 2009, so the subject remains in the top 20 in terms of popularity. Economics is also in the top four for graduate starting salaries, reflecting the value that employers place on a subject that they see combining the skills of the sciences and the arts.

Indeed, many prospective students underestimate the mathematical skills required for an economics degree. Many universities demand maths at A level, or its equivalent, as part of offers that are consistently high. Entry standards in this year's table reflect that, with the top three universities all averaging over 540 points – the equivalent of more than four As at A level and another at AS level. Another seven universities have averages of at least 450 points, while only two of the 67 institutions in the ranking average less than 200 points.

Oxford tops the table for the second successive year, having been out of the top 10 only six years ago. A much-improved performance in the 2008 Research Assessment Exercise, when 40 per cent of its submission was rated world-leading, is partly responsible. However, the third-placed London School of Economics (LSE) and University College London, in fourth, won even higher research grades.

Cambridge, which remains in second place, has the highest entry standards, while the LSE has the best employment score. Surrey, just outside the top 10, had the most satisfied undergraduates in the 2009 National Student Survey, with Oxford and Greenwich close behind, despite Greenwich failing to make the top 50 overall. St Andrews is the leading university in Scotland, retaining its place in the top 10, while Cardiff remains the leader in Wales. Brighton is the only post-1992 university in the top 40.

Economics is not the sure-fire bet for a good job that many assume it to be: more than three graduates in ten are in non-graduate jobs or unemployed after six months, leaving the subject outside the top 25 in the employment table. But starting salaries in the latest survey averaged more than £25,700 for graduate-level jobs and the £16,500 average for other types of employment is also among the highest for any subject.

Employed in graduate job:	41%
Employed in graduate job and studying:	13%
Studying:	16%
Average starting graduate salary:	£25,726
Employed in non-graduate job and studying:	2%
Employed in non-graduate job:	20%
Unemployed:	9%
Average starting non-graduate salary:	£16,539

Economics	Research quality/9	Entry standards	Student satisfaction %	Graduate prospects %	Overall rating
1 Oxford	5.3	542	87	87	100.0
2 Cambridge	4.3	561		88	97.8
3 London School of Economics	6.5	556	72	91	95.8
4 University College London	6.2	495	75	87	93.6
5 Warwick	5.3	518	75	88	93.1
6 Durham	3.0	505	79	90	89.6
7 Nottingham	4.5	478	76	85	89.3
8 St Andrews	3.0	462	81	88	89.0
=9 Exeter	3.7	426	86	74	88.4
=9 Bath	4.2	483	74	89	88.4
11 Surrey	3.2	363	89	75	86.8
12 Glasgow	4.0	418	79	74	85.2
=13 Birmingham	3.2	412	82	74	84.7
=13 York	3.7	440	80	71	84.7
=15 Bristol	4.5	451	69	83	84.1
=15 Southampton	3.8	425	75	79	84.1
17 Kent	3.4	318	86	73	84.0
18 Essex	5.3	319	77	74	83.8
=19 Sheffield	3.3	379	83	71	83.5
=19 Lancaster	4.0	417	76	75	83.5
=21 Leeds	3.6	427	74	79	82.9
=21 Leicester	3.6	352	83	69	82.9
=23 Edinburgh	3.9	446	71	79	82.8
=23 East Anglia	3.2	368	85	67	82.8
25 Newcastle	2.5	410	78	81	82.3
26 Cardiff	4.5	401	77	65	82.2
27 Aberdeen	3.5	338	84	66	81.8
28 Royal Holloway	3.8	386	72	80	81.4
29 Sussex	2.8	359	79	77	81.3
=30 Loughborough	2.2	395	80	75	80.5

Economics cont.

	Research quality/9	Entry standards	Student satisfaction %	Graduate prospects %	Overall rating
=30 Liverpool	2.5	389	80	73	80.5
32 Swansea	3.1	271	83	73	80.2
33 Manchester	4.1	419	70	70	79.2
34 Brighton	2.8	259	83		77.8
35 Stirling	3.1	312	75	71	76.6
=36 School of Oriental and African Studies	2.2	421	70	75	76.0
=36 Hull	2.1	266	78	77	76.0
38 Heriot-Watt	2.4	307	74	79	75.9
39 Queen Mary, London	4.5	364	69	61	75.7
40 Aberystwyth	1.6	270	86	63	75.5
41 West of England	1.5	265	83	68	75.0
42 Nottingham Trent	1.7	251	83	67	74.8
43 Queen's, Belfast	3.0	354	74	62	74.5
44 Strathclyde		407	81	66	74.3
45 Reading	2.5	358	73	64	73.9
46 Coventry		262	86	72	73.5
47 Oxford Brookes		300	84	69	73.4
48 Portsmouth	1.7	265	78	68	72.7
49 City	2.7	355	67	71	72.4
50 Northumbria	1.1		75	73	71.8
51 Plymouth	1.7	275	79	61	71.6
52 Central Lancashire	1.6	291	77		71.4
53 Greenwich	1.3	295	87	43	71.2
54 Ulster		254	78	76	70.1
=55 Keele	2.3	287	68	71	69.9
=55 Bradford	2.5	231	78	54	69.9
57 Brunel	2.8	308	69	59	69.1
58 Dundee	2.2	317	73	51	68.2
59 Salford	1.6	263	77	52	67.9
60 Hertfordshire	1.8	203	74	54	65.0
61 Kingston	1.5	195	73	51	62.5
62 Manchester Metropolitan	0.8	256	70	54	62.1
63 Middlesex		201	75	56	61.9
64 Liverpool John Moores	0.6	243	73	41	59.9
65 Leeds Metropolitan		270	67	57	59.7
66 East London		180	78	39	58.6

» Economics and Business Education Association: **www.ebea.org.uk**
» Royal Economic Society: **www.res.org.uk**
» Why Study? Economics: **www.whystudyeconomics.ac.uk**

Education

Education is the only ranking that still contains teaching scores – because teacher training assessments by Ofsted at English universities remain current. Table-topping Cambridge ties with East Anglia, in second place, and Northumbria, in equal 17th place, for the best performance in those assessments. Cambridge also has entry standards that are almost 80 points ahead of its nearest challenger, the top research grades and the most satisfied students, so its lead at the top is considerable.

Huddersfield is again the only university to register 100 per cent positive destinations, although Glasgow comes within a single percentage point of matching this feat and ten others reach the 90 per cent mark. Education is high up the employment table, with 80 per cent of graduates going straight into schools or continuing to study and only 3 per cent unemployed. However, the average starting salary of £20,650 is only just in the top 30 for all subjects.

Employment scores at different universities reflect to some extent the variations in demand for new staff between primary and secondary schools and between different parts of the UK. But even in the bottom ten, there are universities where at least eight out of ten leavers went straight into graduate jobs or further study.

Outside Cambridge, the most satisfied students are at Aberystwyth and Derby – neither of them in the top 25 overall. Satisfaction levels are high generally, not only among the final-year undergraduates who complete the National Student Survey, but also in the early stage of careers. Three years after graduation, those with education degrees were among the most satisfied at work and least inclined to wish they had taken a different subject.

Some of the leading universities are absent from the education table because they offer only the postgraduate courses that have become the normal route into secondary teaching and an increasingly popular choice for those wanting a career in primary schools. As such, they are not included in the National Student Survey for the subject and neither entry scores nor graduate destinations are comparable. The University of London's Institute of Education, which achieved the top grades in the 2008 research assessments, is one example; Oxford and King's College London, which ran it close, are others.

Low entry scores have been a concern in the past, but only one university averages less than 200 points in the latest table, while most score more than 250. Teacher training courses have become more selective of late and there are now more than five applications to the place – more than the average for all subjects. The economic downturn stimulated the demand for places still further and a 16 per cent increase took total applications beyond 50,000 at the start of 2010, when education remained among the ten most popular subjects.

Employed in graduate job:	62%	Employed in non-graduate job and studying:	2%
Employed in graduate job and studying:	6%	Employed in non-graduate job:	17%
Studying:	10%	Unemployed:	3%
Average starting graduate salary:	£20,652	Average starting non-graduate salary:	£14,227

Education cont.

		Research quality/9	Teaching quality/5	Entry standards	Student satisfaction %	Graduate prospects %	Overall rating
1	Cambridge	4.0	3.8	463	89	88	100.0
2	East Anglia	2.8	3.8	327			90.9
3	Stirling	2.9		332	84	93	89.4
4	Durham	3.2	3.0	384	82	90	87.1
5	Brighton	2.0	3.7	298	82	88	85.1
6	Reading	1.9	3.7	288	85	87	85.0
7	Glasgow	1.9		325	75	99	84.2
8	Dundee	1.3		306	85	91	83.6
9	Edinburgh	2.6		356	68	93	83.5
=10	Brunel	1.1	3.3	344		96	83.4
=10	Leeds	3.4	3.0	367	81	72	83.4
12	Aberdeen	1.5		328	76	98	83.1
13	Sussex	3.2	3.0			88	82.7
14	Manchester	3.2	3.7	329	78	59	82.6
15	Warwick	3.3	3.7	357	66	69	82.2
16	Canterbury Christ Church	2.0	3.7	306	68	91	81.5
=17	Northumbria		3.8	303	84	82	81.3
=17	York	3.0	3.7	347	70	63	81.3
19	Huddersfield	1.3	3.0	288	85	100	81.2
20	Strathclyde	1.6		353	72	86	81.0
=21	Birmingham City	1.5	3.7	256	79	88	80.7
=21	Oxford Brookes	1.6	3.5	303	81	78	80.7
23	Manchester Metropolitan	3.2	3.5	272	70	79	79.7
24	Northampton	1.2	3.7	273	81	76	79.4
25	Sunderland	1.1	3.3	283	82	86	79.3
26	Keele	3.2	3.3	300	78	63	79.2
27	Plymouth	1.9	3.7	285	77	66	78.7
28	Cardiff	3.5		324	73	58	78.6
29	Bangor	1.7		270	81	73	77.1
30	Aberystwyth			285	87	73	76.8
31	Chichester		3.0	288	85	88	76.5
=32	UWIC, Cardiff	0.3		249	83	91	76.4
=32	West of England	1.3	3.3	280	80	72	76.4
=32	Gloucestershire	1.8	3.0	268	79	82	76.4
=32	York St John	0.2	3.3	311	81	75	76.4
36	Edge Hill	0.4	3.3	287	77	87	76.3
37	Birmingham	2.3	3.3	335	72	57	76.2
38	Ulster	1.9		238	80		75.9
39	Hull	1.5	3.2	254	75	83	75.4
40	Roehampton	1.7	3.2	270	74	75	74.9
41	Newman	1.1	3.2	250	78	80	74.7
42	Cumbria	0.4	3.5	283	69	83	74.5
43	Bishop Grosseteste	0.5	2.7	265	82	93	74.3

44 Kingston	1.0	3.0	258	81	79	74.2
45 Goldsmiths College	1.8	3.0	231	78	81	74.1
46 St Mary's College	0.5	3.0	276	75	89	74.0
47 Worcester		3.3	287	77	76	73.8
48 Wolverhampton	1.3	3.5		75		73.7
49 Newport	0.3		279	74	86	73.5
50 Winchester	1.8	2.7	281	76	76	73.1
51 Hertfordshire	1.0	3.0	261	79	73	72.7
=52 Central Lancashire	0.4		242	80	78	72.6
=52 Derby		3.0	249	87	73	72.6
54 Bath Spa	0.8	2.8	269	81	75	72.3
=55 De Montfort			247	84	68	72.0
=55 Sheffield Hallam	1.4	2.7	284	71	83	72.0
=55 Leeds Metropolitan	1.0	3.0	283	69	81	72.0
58 Chester	0.9	3.0	271	73	77	71.5
59 Glyndŵr	0.4		244	83	67	71.4
60 Liverpool John Moores	1.0	3.3	233	73	71	71.2
61 Marjon, Plymouth	0.3	3.2	238	72	84	71.0
62 Bedfordshire		3.3	236	69	86	70.4
63 Greenwich	1.1	3.0	252	68	80	70.2
64 Nottingham Trent		2.7	274	78	76	69.5
65 Middlesex		3.3	223	59	90	67.5
66 Anglia Ruskin		3.0	264	56	81	64.8
67 East London	1.4	3.2	177	61	57	62.5
68 University College Birmingham		3.0	222	73	37	60.6

» Graduate Teacher Training Registry (GTTR): **www.gttr.ac.uk**
» TeacherNet: **www.teachernet.gov.uk**
» Training and Development Agency for Schools: **www.tda.gov.uk**

Electrical and Electronic Engineering

Cambridge retains its lead over Southampton in electrical and electronic engineering, with by far the best research grades and a lead of 110 points on entry standards. Southampton has the best employment record, while the most satisfied students are at York, in joint seventh place.

Applications were in decline nationally for much of the decade, but a recovery that started in 2009 had gathered pace at the start of 2010, when there had been 16 per cent growth in the demand for degree places. Three universities have joined the table since last year. In its heyday at the start of the decade, electronic and electrical engineering used to attract far more applications than civil or mechanical engineering, but it is now the least popular of the three.

Glasgow has overtaken Edinburgh this year to become the top university in Scotland, while Cardiff again takes the honours in Wales. Portsmouth is the leading post-1992 institution, at equal 30th, in a table where old universities predominate.

Employment rates vary considerably among the 64 universities in the ranking. Most of the top 30 see at least 80 per cent of leavers go straight into graduate jobs or further training, but the proportion drops below 60 per cent at seven institutions in the bottom half.

About half of the students – more in electrical engineering – come with qualifications other than A levels. Yet it is electrical engineering which has the higher proportion of firsts and 2:1s. Almost three quarters of the graduates nationally go straight into graduate jobs or continue their studies, but the unemployment rate is above average, at 11 per cent. For those who do find graduate work, the average starting salary of nearly £23,300 is in the top 15 of all subjects. Those in lower-level jobs are the second-best paid of any subject's graduates, averaging nearly £18,000.

Employed in graduate job:	55%	Employed in non-graduate job and studying:		2%
Employed in graduate job and studying:	4%	Employed in non-graduate job:		16%
Studying:	12%	Unemployed:		11%
Average starting graduate salary:	£23,276	Average starting non-graduate salary:		£17,926

Electrical and Electronic Engineering	Research quality/9	Entry standards	Student satisfaction %	Graduate prospects %	Overall rating
1 Cambridge	5.5	567	85	94	100.0
2 Southampton	3.8	457	83	97	90.2
3 Surrey	4.2	436	87	87	90.0
4 Imperial College	3.7	491	82	87	88.2
5 Sheffield	3.3	377	85	89	84.8
6 Glasgow	3.5	411	83	84	84.2
=7 York	2.6	387	90	78	82.7
=7 Loughborough	3.1	340	85	91	82.7
9 Bristol	2.9	443	76	94	82.6
10 Queen's Belfast	3.3	372	82	86	82.5
11 Bath	3.6	397	80	82	82.3
12 Edinburgh	3.0	384	82	88	82.1
13 University College London	3.7	454	76	77	82.0
14 Newcastle	3.0	342	83	91	81.8
15 Essex	3.3			83	80.7
=16 Nottingham	2.9	353	79	90	79.8
=16 Leeds	4.4	399	70	80	79.8
18 Strathclyde	2.8	414	77	84	79.6
19 Birmingham	2.7	372	79	88	79.4
20 Cardiff	2.6	364	78	87	78.1
21 Exeter	2.7	353	81	82	78.0
22 Manchester	3.9	378	71	74	76.7
23 Kent	2.6	255	81	88	75.8
24 Aberdeen	3.2	292	75	81	74.5
25 Heriot-Watt	2.7	308	77	80	74.1
26 Bangor	4.2	238		69	74.0
27 Lancaster	2.6		70	90	73.6
28 King's College London	1.9	364	77	77	73.2
29 Salford	3.2	295	75	72	72.9

=30 Portsmouth	1.5	233	88	80	72.4
=30 Brunel	2.3	306	78	74	72.4
32 Reading	1.9	329	76	81	72.2
33 Liverpool	2.9	335	72	69	71.1
34 Sussex	2.8		75	67	70.4
35 Staffordshire	2.2		69	85	69.6
36 Queen Mary, London	2.8	265	78	61	69.4
37 Aston	2.2	270	77	69	68.9
38 West of England	2.6	243	72	75	68.1
39 Liverpool John Moores	3.3	229	72	65	67.9
40 Northumbria	2.2	240	74	75	67.7
41 Swansea	1.9	330	73	67	67.6
42 Plymouth	1.4	268	84	61	67.4
43 Hertfordshire	2.7	202	76	61	65.9
44 Robert Gordon		302	74	89	65.5
=45 Hull	1.8	219	73	75	64.9
=45 Central Lancashire	1.4	262	78	63	64.9
47 Huddersfield	1.9	279	73	59	64.2
48 City	2.4	263	64	73	64.0
49 Coventry	2.1	237	71	66	63.6
50 Westminster	0.9	302	73	64	62.5
51 Manchester Metropolitan	1.5	226	69	71	61.5
52 Bradford	0.8		74	66	61.1
53 Glasgow Caledonian		302	68	76	59.9
54 Sheffield Hallam	1.8	186	67	65	58.7
55 London South Bank	2.5		65	51	58.2
56 Teesside		251	79	52	58.0
57 De Montfort	1.8	207	77	37	57.9
58 Derby		248	74	62	57.6
59 Southampton Solent		259	72	64	57.5
60 Ulster		224	70	66	55.7
61 Birmingham City		242	67	64	54.5
62 Glamorgan	2.1	256	61	33	52.5
63 Oxford Brookes		234	66	55	51.7
64 Bolton		199	61	50	47.3

» Institute of Electrical and Electronic Engineers, UK section: **www.ieee.org.uk**
» Institution of Engineering and Technology: **www.theiet.org**

English

Nothing, it seems, can dent the popularity of English among undergraduates: more than 10,000 of them began degrees in 2009. The subject is only just in the top 50 for employment levels and lower still for starting salaries, but it remains among the top six choices by applicants. The number of applications had risen again, by more than 8 per cent at the start of 2010. High entry grades reflect this, with 24 universities averaging more than 400 points in the latest data and

English cont.

only three dropping below 200. Only 14 of the 99 institutions in the ranking average less than 250 points on the UCAS tariff.

Top place in English has changed for the third year in a row, with Oxford overtaking Cambridge to reclaim the leadership it last enjoyed in the 2006 *Guide*.

Oxford has the highest entry standards, while sixth-placed York produced the best results in the 2008 Research Assessment Exercise, with three quarters of its work judged to be world-leading or internationally excellent.

Loughborough, in 15th place, has the most satisfied students, while Bishop Grosseteste University College, in Lincoln, in 35th, registered much the best of a generally mediocre set of employment scores. Only University College London, in third place overall, came within ten percentage points of its record of 91 per cent of graduates in graduate-level work or continuing their studies within six months of completing a degree.

Durham, the leader for three years, has now slipped to fifth, behind Exeter. St Andrews remains the top university in Scotland, while Cardiff has the same status in Wales. De Montfort is easily the top post-1992 university, breaking into the top 30 for the first time and finishing above the likes of Birmingham and Manchester in the table.

Almost a third of English graduates continue their studies, either full or part-time – more than go into graduate-level jobs. Starting salaries in graduate jobs have fallen since last year's *Guide*, averaging £18,350. However, English has produced consistently good scores in the National Student Survey. In the results published in 2009, only two universities out of 99 failed to satisfy at least 70 per cent of the final-year undergraduates.

Employed in graduate job:	28%	Employed in non-graduate job and studying:	5%
Employed in graduate job and studying:	3%	Employed in non-graduate job:	32%
Studying:	24%	Unemployed:	8%
Average starting graduate salary:	£18,350	Average starting non-graduate salary:	£14,523

English	Research quality/9	Entry standards	Student satisfaction %	Graduate prospects %	Overall rating
1 Oxford	4.7	521	87	69	100.0
2 Cambridge	4.6	513	87	69	99.1
3 University College London	4.0	486	84	82	98.8
4 Exeter	4.9	429	87	66	96.4
5 Durham	3.9	509	83	73	96.3
6 York	5.2	472	80	72	96.1
7 Warwick	4.4	471	81	76	95.6
8 St Andrews	4.4	469	84	64	93.9
9 Queen Mary, London	4.8	374	86	66	92.9
10 Leeds	4.4	442	83	64	92.5
11 Edinburgh	4.8	446	80	64	91.7
12 Sheffield	3.9	438	81	68	91.1
13 Southampton	3.7	418	85	61	90.4
14 Leicester	3.1	383	87	68	90.3
15 Loughborough	2.5	370	90	66	90.0

16	Liverpool	4.1	433	81	61	89.7
=17	Glasgow	4.4	400	82	61	89.5
=17	Nottingham	4.5	446	77	65	89.5
19	Lancaster	3.3	405	82	65	88.5
20	Kent	4.0	337	83	65	88.3
21	Aberdeen	4.1	346	86	58	88.2
22	Bristol	3.6	463	72	76	88.1
23	Cardiff	4.2	423	79	60	88.0
24	East Anglia	3.5	406	82	61	87.8
25	Royal Holloway	4.0	417	76	64	86.6
26	De Montfort	4.6	262	83	63	86.2
27	King's College London	3.3	448	72	72	85.9
28	Newcastle	3.9	444	74	62	85.8
29	Hull	2.6	332	83	68	85.5
=30	Queen's, Belfast	4.3	371	79	56	85.0
=30	Reading	3.7	365	83	54	85.0
=32	Birmingham	3.7	421	74	63	84.5
=32	Sussex	3.3	403	73	70	84.5
34	Manchester	4.3	428	71	60	84.1
35	Bishop Grosseteste	0.8	241		91	82.7
36	Strathclyde	2.7	369	78	62	82.5
37	Brunel	2.7	303	82	62	82.1
=38	Stirling	2.6	319	82	60	81.9
=38	Dundee	2.4	352	85	49	81.9
40	Keele	2.6	316	79	62	81.0
41	Sunderland	2.3	237	89	53	80.9
42	Essex	2.7	320	79	61	80.8
43	Nottingham Trent	2.6	280	82	61	80.7
44	Goldsmiths College	3.1	360	75	58	80.6
45	Oxford Brookes	2.1	333	81	59	80.2
46	Aberystwyth	2.4	312	83	54	79.8
47	Chester	1.4	298	86	57	79.7
48	Northumbria	1.6	319	82	57	79.0
49	Portsmouth	2.6	295	85	44	78.5
50	Aston	1.4	341	81		78.4
51	Cumbria	0.7	276		75	78.1
52	Hertfordshire	2.4	271	80	57	78.0
53	Swansea	2.7	310	81	46	77.7
54	Anglia Ruskin	3.1	273	75	60	77.6
55	Bath Spa	1.7	305	78	60	77.5
=56	Bangor	2.8	301	79	46	76.3
=56	Roehampton	2.2	291	77	57	76.3
58	Huddersfield	1.4	307	79	56	76.1
59	Kingston	2.3	258	80	52	76.0
60	Salford	2.2	282	82	46	75.8
61	Bedfordshire	2.4	187	82	54	75.2
62	West of England	1.8	290	82	46	75.0

English cont.

	Research quality/9	Entry standards	Student satisfaction %	Graduate prospects %	Overall rating
63 Sheffield Hallam	1.8	311	78	50	74.6
64 Birmingham City	1.5	261	74	66	74.3
65 St Mary's College	1.6	236	82	51	74.2
=66 Central Lancashire	1.1	275	78	58	74.1
=66 Winchester		277	84	54	74.1
=66 Lincoln		290	79	63	74.1
69 Edge Hill	0.9	254	80	56	73.8
70 Ulster	1.9	257	83	41	73.6
71 Middlesex	1.9	196	77	62	73.4
72 Worcester	1.4	276	79	50	73.3
=73 Staffordshire	1.4	243	75	61	72.2
=73 Gloucestershire	1.8	257	80	44	72.2
75 Newman		251	71	78	72.0
76 Teesside		241	84	52	71.8
=77 York St John	0.6	281	77	54	71.6
=77 Edinburgh Napier	1.5	283			71.6
=79 Manchester Metropolitan	2.5	303	74	42	71.1
=79 Newport		214	83	54	71.1
=81 Plymouth	1.9	300	74	46	71.0
=81 Westminster	1.0	265	75	56	71.0
=81 Chichester	1.2	298	86	26	71.0
84 Marjon, Plymouth	0.4	241	80	52	70.8
85 Lampeter (Trinity Saint David)	0.9	284	74	55	70.7
86 Bradford	1.6	246	76		70.3
=87 Liverpool John Moores	1.7	256	82	34	70.2
=87 Glamorgan	2.6	255	79	33	70.2
89 Greenwich	1.0	249	74	55	69.8
90 Falmouth		298	77	50	69.7
91 Bolton	0.6	236		58	69.6
92 Brighton	1.8	299	70	47	68.9
93 Leeds Metropolitan		268	71	63	68.5
94 Northampton	1.0	258	77	43	68.4
95 Canterbury Christ Church	0.9	268	74	45	67.2
96 East London		182	78	42	63.3
97 Derby		214	74	44	63.0
98 Coventry	1.0	280	64		61.3
99 UWIC, Cardiff		273	59	38	54.7

» Poetry Society: www.poetrysociety.org.uk
» Royal Society of Literature: www.rslit.org
» Society of Authors: www.societyofauthors.org
» Society for Editors and Proofreaders: www.sfep.org.uk
» Teaching English as a Foreign Language: www.eflweb.com

Food Science

King's College London stretches its lead at the head of the food science table, with the best grades in the 2008 Research Assessment Exercise, when two thirds of its submission in nutritional sciences was considered world-leading or internationally excellent. Third-placed Surrey has the highest entry standards – the only university in the table where entrants average more than 400 points on the UCAS tariff.

Newcastle, with the most satisfied students, jumps seven places into second position. Coventry, which shares seventh place with Ulster, has the best employment record and becomes the leading post-1992 university as a result. The majority of the 29 institutions in the ranking are new universities, although higher entry standards and research grades ensure that their older counterparts fill the top six places. Both of Northern Ireland's universities are in the top 10, with Ulster the highest-placed institution outside England. Heriot-Watt is the top university in Scotland, while UWIC is the only representative of Wales.

Entry standards have been rising – no university in this year's ranking averages less than 200 points – but there were still only three applications per place in 2009. Almost a third of entrants to food science courses arrive with alternative qualifications to A levels. The subjects attracted big increases in the number of applications earlier in the decade, but had been in the doldrums for two years before recovering in 2009. There had been a further increase of more than 17 per cent at the start of 2010.

Career prospects are good, with almost three quarters of graduates going straight into graduate-level work or further study. The unemployment rate of 5 per cent was among the best in any subject at the time of the latest survey. Food science is just in the top half of the graduate salaries league, with an average starting rate of more than £20,000.

Employed in graduate job:	54%	Employed in non-graduate job and studying:	2%
Employed in graduate job and studying:	4%	Employed in non-graduate job:	22%
Studying:	12%	Unemployed:	5%
Average starting graduate salary:	£20,298	Average starting non-graduate salary:	£14,992

Food Science	Research quality/9	Entry standards	Student satisfaction %	Graduate prospects %	Overall rating
1 King's College London	4.0	398	84	91	100.0
2 Newcastle	2.1	378	87	77	90.9
3 Surrey	3.4	407	73	82	90.8
4 Nottingham	3.1	337	78	89	89.6
5 Reading	2.4	320	82	83	87.3
6 Leeds	3.2	345	82	59	85.3
=7 Ulster	1.6	305	86	69	82.5
=7 Coventry		340	80	93	82.5
9 Heriot-Watt	1.9	312			80.4
=10 Queen's, Belfast	1.8	326	79	66	80.1
=10 Plymouth	0.9	328	73	89	80.1
12 Brighton	2.0		77	70	79.0
13 Liverpool John Moores	1.5	252	84	64	76.8

Food Science cont.

	Research quality/9	Entry standards	Student satisfaction %	Graduate prospects %	Overall rating
14 Glasgow Caledonian		329	77	76	76.1
15 Leeds Metropolitan		283	79	82	75.9
16 Robert Gordon		357	69	83	75.8
17 Northumbria	1.5	288	75	67	75.4
18 Bath Spa		270	84	71	74.9
19 Queen Margaret Edinburgh		321		69	74.4
20 Sheffield Hallam		273	80	75	74.3
21 Manchester Metropolitan	1.3	290	70	74	73.8
22 UWIC, Cardiff	1.1	247	76	65	71.6
23 Bournemouth		261	77	68	70.2
=24 Oxford Brookes		282	72	70	69.3
=24 Chester	0.8	285	62	80	69.3
26 Central Lancashire		235	80	62	68.7
27 University College Birmingham		255	84	45	67.6
28 Kingston		243	77	53	65.7
29 St Mary's College		219	71	51	60.4

» Institute of Food Science and Technology: **www.ifst.org**
» Society of Food Hygiene and Technology: **www.sofht.co.uk**

French

French at degree level has weathered the problems that have afflicted the teaching of modern languages in secondary schools: there are more applications and more places than there were five years ago. But a rise in applications of only 1 per cent at the start of 2010, when the average increase was over 20 per cent, showed that languages still have their problems. Nevertheless, a ratio of five applications for every place is well above average for all subjects and is reflected in the usual high entry grades. Entrants to one of the bottom ten universities in this year's table averaged more than 400 points, as did all but five of the top 20.

Oxford retains the slim lead over Cambridge that it established last year, thanks to the best performance in the 2008 Research Assessment Exercise, when 30 per cent of its submission was rated world-leading. Cambridge is ahead on all the other indicators and has the highest entry grades in the table. Leicester, in 27th place, again has the most satisfied students, while the employment score at 10th-placed Lancaster is more than ten percentage points ahead of any other. Ninety-four per cent of Lancaster graduates in French were in graduate-level jobs or continuing their studies six months after completing a degree.

Sheffield has made the most progress in the upper reaches of the table, moving up five places to share fourth place with Durham. St Andrews remains easily the top university in Scotland for French, while Cardiff has retaken top position from Swansea in Wales. Portsmouth is the leading post-1992 university and one of only two in the top 40, the other being Nottingham Trent.

French still attracts nearly twice as many degree applications as any other language, although there were still fewer than 4,000 at the start of 2010. Nine out of ten undergraduates enter with A levels or their equivalents, almost 10 per cent securing their place in Clearing.

Seven out of ten of those completing a degree in French go on to graduate jobs or further study within six months and the 7 per cent unemployment rate is better than average for all subjects. Only two universities dipped below the 50 per cent success mark for graduate destinations. Graduate starting salaries improved in the latest survey, bur remain under the average for all subjects.

Employed in graduate job:	42%	Employed in non-graduate job and studying:	2%
Employed in graduate job and studying:	4%	Employed in non-graduate job:	24%
Studying:	21%	Unemployed:	7%
Average starting graduate salary:	£20,454	Average starting non-graduate salary:	£15,399

French	Research quality/9	Entry standards	Student satisfaction %	Graduate prospects %	Overall rating
1 Oxford	4.0	522	85	81	100.0
2 Cambridge	3.2	538	88	82	99.3
3 Southampton	3.8	420	89	65	92.7
=4 Durham	2.8	491	81	76	90.8
=4 Sheffield	3.4	417	83	75	90.8
6 St Andrews	2.8	443	85	76	90.7
=7 Leeds	2.9	415	85	75	90.4
=7 Warwick	3.5	443	84	67	90.4
9 King's College London	3.7	458	78	70	89.5
10 Lancaster	1.9	381	83	94	89.4
11 Bath	2.4	446	84	77	89.3
12 Exeter	2.8	437	83	70	88.2
13 Nottingham	3.2	400	79	73	87.1
14 Aberdeen	3.2	366	84	68	86.9
15 Glasgow	2.7	404	82	72	86.5
16 Hull	2.6	331	87	73	86.2
17 Kent	2.9	321	87	69	85.5
18 Newcastle	2.8	427	80	66	85.1
19 Birmingham	2.3	378	86	67	85.0
20 University College London	2.6	446	75	71	84.1
21 Aston	1.4	387	85	76	83.8
22 Queen's, Belfast	2.1	386	81	73	83.6
23 Edinburgh	2.6	481	68	76	83.1
24 Manchester	2.8	427	75	67	82.8
25 Cardiff	2.6	398	84	56	82.6
26 Portsmouth	2.6	270	86		82.1
27 Leicester	1.4	350	92	61	81.9
28 Royal Holloway	2.6	367	80	63	81.4
29 Queen Mary, London	2.6	329	76	74	81.0

French cont.

	Research quality/9	Entry standards	Student satisfaction %	Graduate prospects %	Overall rating
30 Bristol	1.8	444	71	77	80.6
31 Liverpool	2.6	364	78	64	80.5
32 Heriot-Watt	1.9	367	82	63	80.0
33 East Anglia		356	86	80	79.3
34 Reading	3.0	342	80	47	77.3
35 Salford	1.6	341	78	68	77.2
36 Stirling	1.7	312	79	69	77.0
37 Ulster	1.4	280	90	52	76.1
38 Aberystwyth		336	86	68	75.4
39 Strathclyde		361	82	67	73.9
40 Nottingham Trent	1.4	244	84	60	73.4
41 Swansea	1.9	295	80	52	72.9
42 Oxford Brookes	1.8	312	75	57	72.2
43 Sussex		392	73	72	71.7
44 Northumbria		287	83	61	70.3
45 Manchester Metropolitan	1.1	257	79	54	69.1
46 York		410	77	49	68.2
47 Chester		298	78	61	68.1
=48 Liverpool John Moores		246	76	66	66.4
=48 Bangor		307	77	55	66.4
50 West of England		272	77	57	65.7
51 Westminster	1.0	230	67		59.7

» Alliance Française: **www.alliancefrancaise.org.uk**
» Chartered Institute of Linguists: **www.iol.org.uk**
» National Centre for Languages (CILT): **www.cilt.org.uk**
» Society for French Studies: **www.sfs.ac.uk**

General Engineering

Cambridge again extends its lead over Oxford in general engineering, with the highest entry standards and the top grades in the 2008 Research Assessment Exercise (RAE), when 45 per cent of the university's work was classified as world-leading. Leicester has the most satisfied students in the 2009 National Student Survey, while Oxford has the best employment record.

Nottingham enters the ranking in third place, eclipsing its neighbour Nottingham Trent, which drops to ninth this year but remains the leading post-1992 university. Cardiff remains the top university in Wales, while Aberdeen is the top university in Scotland.

As in the specialist branches of engineering, there is an enormous spread of entry grades, from well over 500 points at Oxford and Cambridge to less than 200 at Birmingham City, Sheffield Hallam, Oxford Brookes and some of the universities which have too few students to publish a reliable score.

Applications were up by more than 22 per cent to over 11,000 by the official deadline for entry in 2010. But there were only 3.5 applications per place in the previous year, making admissions the least competitive of any of the main branches of engineering.

Nationally, the subject is in the top 20 for employment, with almost 80 per cent of all those completing a degree going straight into graduate jobs or further study. Only two universities in this year's ranking registered "positive destinations" for fewer than half of its general engineering graduates. The subject is also among the most rewarding financially. Average starting salaries close to £25,500 for graduate-level jobs place general engineering fifth on this measure.

Employed in graduate job:	57%
Employed in graduate job and studying:	6%
Studying:	13%
Average starting graduate salary:	£25,455
Employed in non-graduate job and studying:	2%
Employed in non-graduate job:	15%
Unemployed:	8%
Average starting non-graduate salary:	£16,655

General Engineering	Research quality/9	Entry standards	Student satisfaction %	Graduate prospects %	Overall rating
1 Cambridge	5.5	567	84	91	100.0
2 Oxford	4.2	543	82	92	94.2
3 Nottingham	4.0	393	79		86.7
4 Durham	2.7	499	78	89	85.3
5 Cardiff	3.5	281	83	91	84.8
6 Leicester	2.7	345	85	79	82.7
7 Warwick	3.6	420	69	91	81.3
8 Exeter	2.7	353	81	82	81.2
9 Nottingham Trent	3.0	277	82	83	80.7
10 Queen Mary, London	2.3	267	81	85	78.3
11 Aberdeen	3.2	305	74		75.9
12 Central Lancashire	1.4		80	73	73.3
13 Swansea	3.5	228	73		73.2
14 Edinburgh Napier	1.7	248	79	76	73.0
15 West of England	2.6	273	84	45	72.9
16 De Montfort	1.8		77	73	72.4
=17 Strathclyde	3.0		73	63	71.5
=17 Bournemouth	1.8	274	76	71	71.5
19 Sheffield Hallam	1.8	199	73	80	69.1
20 Liverpool John Moores	3.3	213	69	57	67.3
21 London South Bank	2.5		72	56	67.2
22 Glasgow Caledonian	1.1	293	77	55	67.0
23 Hertfordshire	2.7		73	38	64.2
24 Oxford Brookes	1.9	195	68		61.8
25 Ulster		223	69	78	61.7
=26 Glamorgan	2.5		65	51	60.5
=26 Coventry	1.0		71	58	60.5
28 Birmingham City		166	67	74	58.2

General Engineering cont.

» Engineering Council: **www.engc.org.uk**
» Engineering and Technology Board: **www.etechb.co.uk**
» Institution of Engineering and Technology: **www.theiet.org**

Geography and Environmental Sciences

Geography and environmental sciences have been benefiting from growing interest in "green" issues among potential students. Physical geography and environmental sciences are slightly more popular than human and social geography, but both had more than 16,000 applicants early in 2010. Both also had more than five applications to the place in 2009 and had little resort to Clearing.

Cambridge has maintained its lead in this year's ranking, with Bristol overtaking Oxford in the race for second place. Cambridge has the highest entry standards and one of the best research scores. The top four all had 30 per cent of their research rated as world-leading in the 2008 assessments.

The seventh-placed London School of Economics again has by far the best employment score, while Brighton, which does not even make the top 40, has the most satisfied students. Westminster is the leading post-1992 university and the only one in the top 30. St Andrews has opened up a big lead as the top Scottish university, while Aberystwyth remains just ahead of Cardiff in Wales.

Entry grades are not as high as they are in some other popular subjects. Although a dozen universities average more than 400 points at entry, only Cambridge and Oxford top 500 and even some old universities have averages of less than 300 points. The subjects are also in the bottom half of the employment and salaries tables. In the latest survey, a third of graduates were in low-level jobs six months after completing their courses, although the unemployment rate was no worse than average for all subjects. There are some low scores for employment in the ranking for geography and environmental science, including at three universities where the proportion of "positive destinations" dropped below 40 per cent.

Employed in graduate job:	33%	Employed in non-graduate job and studying:	3%
Employed in graduate job and studying:	4%	Employed in non-graduate job:	30%
Studying:	22%	Unemployed:	8%
Average starting graduate salary:	£19,962	Average starting non-graduate salary:	£14,606

Geography and Environmental Sciences	Research quality/9	Entry standards	Student satisfaction %	Graduate prospects %	Overall rating
1 Cambridge	4.2	510	87	82	100.0
2 Bristol	4.2	473	82	79	95.3
3 Oxford	4.2	509	80	75	94.4
4 Durham	4.2	456	83	70	93.1
5 St Andrews	3.4	433	83	79	92.0
6 Southampton	3.4	406	83	73	89.9

7	London School of Economics	3.6	480	70	88	89.4
8	Lancaster	3.3	384	84	72	89.3
9	Leeds	3.9	398	81	67	88.3
10	East Anglia	3.8	401	82	63	87.8
11	University College London	3.8	424	75	76	87.5
=12	Exeter	3.4	385	84	64	87.4
=12	Aberystwyth	3.5	312	88	64	87.4
14	Loughborough	2.5	362	87	68	87.3
=15	Cardiff	3.7	322	83	71	87.2
=15	Birmingham	3.0	384	83	69	87.2
17	King's College London	3.6	391	78	73	86.8
18	Leicester	2.3	343	88	68	86.6
19	Reading	3.6	356	81	67	86.0
20	Nottingham	3.4	411	80	64	85.5
21	Royal Holloway	3.5	366	85	56	85.4
22	Edinburgh	3.2	426	76	71	85.2
23	Sheffield	3.6	405	78	63	85.0
24	Glasgow	2.4	368	85	63	84.6
25	Sussex	3.2	366	80	66	84.5
26	Queen Mary, London	4.0	320	79	64	83.6
27	Hull	2.9	301	85	62	83.4
28	Newcastle	2.6	374	80	67	83.2
29	Dundee	3.1	317	83	61	82.7
30	Westminster	2.5			65	82.4
31	Aberdeen	2.5	334	82	64	82.2
32	Queen's Belfast	2.6	320	82	65	82.0
33	Manchester	3.2	392	76	61	81.8
34	Liverpool	2.6	356	81	59	81.5
35	Sheffield Hallam	3.1	279	81	64	81.0
36	Strathclyde	1.2	336	82	67	79.7
37	Coventry	0.9	279	84	72	79.5
38	Swansea	3.1	296	82	51	78.7
39	Chester	0.8	280	84	68	78.1
40	Bradford	3.1	244		58	78.0
41	Brighton	1.7	249	90	49	77.9
42	Keele		283	84	72	77.5
43	Plymouth	2.4	267	83	52	76.9
44	York	2.8	372	72	56	76.4
45	Nottingham Trent	0.7	260	84	65	76.1
46	Stirling	2.0	298	80	50	75.0
=47	Portsmouth	1.8	282	85	44	74.7
=47	Gloucestershire	0.9	234	82	64	74.7
=47	Northampton	1.1	218	87	53	74.7
50	Ulster	2.0	239	82	52	74.5
51	Bath Spa	0.8	283	85	51	74.3
52	Staffordshire		243	79	75	74.0
53	Northumbria		274	85	58	73.9

Geography and Environmental Sciences cont.	Research quality/9	Entry standards	Student satisfaction %	Graduate prospects %	Overall rating
54 West of England	1.1	278	84	46	73.5
55 Manchester Metropolitan	1.9	264	79	52	73.2
56 Central Lancashire		252	85	53	72.0
57 Oxford Brookes		294	81	56	71.8
58 Hertfordshire		258	77	68	71.6
59 Cumbria		256	82	56	70.9
60 Sunderland	0.8	221		62	70.6
61 Worcester	0.8	248	76	61	70.4
=62 Bangor		278	78	54	69.0
=62 Greenwich		272		54	69.0
64 St Mary's College		253		56	68.9
65 Edge Hill	0.5	257		56	68.8
=66 Liverpool John Moores		221	79	57	68.6
=66 Canterbury Christ Church		236	87	38	68.6
68 Kingston	1.8	234	71	57	68.3
69 Leeds Metropolitan		258		54	68.2
70 Glamorgan		249	80	48	67.1
71 Brunel	1.7			44	67.0
72 Salford	1.7	242		36	65.4
73 Derby		219		50	64.5
74 Southampton Solent		186		50	63.0
75 Bournemouth	2.3	235	61	53	62.9
76 Marjon, Plymouth	0.9			33	57.6

» British Cartographic Society: **www.cartography.org.uk**
» Royal Geographical Society (with the Institute of British Geographers): **www.rgs.org**
» Royal Scottish Geographical Society: **www.rsgs.org**

Geology

Cambridge has stretched its lead over Oxford in geology again, with better scores than its ancient rival on all four indicators. Cambridge registered the best performance in the 2008 Research Assessment Exercise and has the highest entry standards in the table. Third-placed St Andrews has by far the best employment score – ten percentage points ahead of any other university – with all of its geologists finding graduate-level work or continuing their studies within six months of graduation.

Leicester, which tied for the best score in the last two National Student Surveys, has that distinction to itself this year. Glasgow, the previous joint leader on this measure, is the only other university to satisfy more than 90 per cent of final-year undergraduates.

All but six of the 29 institutions in this year's ranking are pre-1992 universities. Plymouth is again the highest-placed of the new universities. Scotland has two of this year's top 10, while Cardiff is the leading university in Wales but only just in the top 20.

Geology	Research quality/9	Entry standards	Student satisfaction %	Graduate prospects %	Overall rating
1 Cambridge	5.2	578	85	82	100.0
2 Oxford	4.8	538	82	78	94.5
3 St Andrews	3.4	437	84	100	91.7
4 Imperial College	3.9	496	78	87	90.0
5 Bristol	4.0	440	78	84	87.7
6 Southampton	3.6	372	88	76	87.2
7 Leicester	2.9	383	94	66	86.2
8 Durham	3.3	390	86	77	86.1
9 Glasgow	2.3	335	91	90	86.0
10 East Anglia	3.9	364	84	76	85.8
11 Royal Holloway	3.6	320	85	74	83.6
12 Liverpool	3.4	385	82	72	83.3
13 University College London	4.1		71	88	82.8
14 Edinburgh	3.3	434	77	78	82.7
15 Exeter	1.7	373	87	84	81.9
16 Leeds	3.3	363	78	80	81.7
17 Birmingham	3.2	359	84	68	81.5
18 Cardiff	3.3	355	82	68	80.8
19 Manchester	3.6	365	80	64	80.1
20 Aberdeen	2.8	322	80	83	80.0
21 Plymouth	2.4	241	87	68	76.5
22 Brighton	1.7		79	64	69.9
23 Keele		276	85	75	69.8
24 Aberystwyth		304	87	63	69.2
25 Portsmouth	2.1	264	79	51	68.4
26 Bangor	2.7		74	30	62.0
27 Kingston		233	70	74	60.1
28 Liverpool John Moores		251	72	62	59.3
29 Derby		239	75	41	55.8

» Geological Society of London: **www.geolsoc.org.uk**

Applications to study geology have fluctuated in recent years, but the subject has been booming over the past two years. A 15 per cent increase in applications in 2009 was followed by a similar rise by the official deadline for degrees starting in 2010. However, a 10 per cent increase in places ensured that entry standards were not raised significantly in 2009, and the policy of expanding science places in England should ensure that this continues.

Outside Cambridge, Oxford and Imperial, there is less contrast in entry standards in geology than in many other subjects. The average is above 230 points at every university in the ranking, and only six average less than 300. Relatively few places are filled in Clearing.

Seven geology students in ten go on to graduate jobs or further study within six months of graduation, although the unemployment level is above the average for all subjects, at 10 per cent. Average salaries for graduate-level jobs were in the top 20 for all subjects, at more than

Geology cont.

£22,000, when the latest survey was compiled. By contrast, the 20 per cent of geologists who go into lower-level jobs are the worst-paid of all new graduates and the only group to average less than £14,000 a year.

Some of the leading universities expect candidates to have two, or even three, scientific or mathematical subjects at A level.

Employed in graduate job:	37%	Employed in non-graduate job and studying:	2%
Employed in graduate job and studying:	2%	Employed in non-graduate job:	20%
Studying:	28%	Unemployed:	10%
Average starting graduate salary:	£22,282	Average starting non-graduate salary:	£13,425

German

The number of universities in the German ranking has stabilised after six dropped out last year and ten the year before that. This reflected a worldwide decline in the language that has been worrying the German government, as well as academic linguists. Applications continued to drop at the start of 2010, but only by 0.7 per cent.

Cambridge makes it five years in a row as the leader in German. Indeed, the top four are the same as last year, with Oxford close to all Cambridge's scores and ahead on research. There is more movement further down the ranking, with Southampton moving up five places to fifth and Newcastle making a 17-place leap to tenth. Cambridge has the highest entry standards and Southampton the best results in the 2008 Research Assessment Exercise, when grades were lower than in many other subjects.

There were high levels of satisfaction in the 2009 National Student Survey, however, with Swansea recording the best score. All 36 universities in the ranking satisfied at least 70 per cent of final-year undergraduates. Queen's, Belfast has the best graduate employment record, despite only just making the top 20 after a low research score.

Third-placed St Andrews is the leading university in Scotland, while Swansea remains the leader in Wales. Portsmouth is one of just three post-1992 universities left in the ranking and the only one in the top 30.

Despite the drop in demand for degrees in German, there are still more than five applications for every place. Nine out of ten undergraduates enter with A levels or equivalent qualifications, and entry standards are relatively high, especially at the leading universities. At nearly half of the universities in the table, entrants average more than 400 points.

As in other modern languages, career prospects are reasonable: 68 per cent of leavers go straight into graduate jobs or further study, and the unemployment rate is on the average for all subjects. German has dropped out of the top 20 for starting salaries, but the average was still almost £21,000 in graduate-level jobs at the time of the latest survey. Most universities in the table offer German *ab initio* as part of a languages package.

Employed in graduate job:	44%	Employed in non-graduate job and studying:	3%
Employed in graduate job and studying:	5%	Employed in non-graduate job:	22%
Studying:	19%	Unemployed:	8%
Average starting graduate salary:	£20,938	Average starting non-graduate salary:	£16,361

German

		Research quality/9	Entry standards	Student satisfaction %	Graduate prospects %	Overall rating
1	Cambridge	3.5	538	88	82	100.0
2	Oxford	3.6	523	85	81	98.0
3	St Andrews	3.3	445	85	78	93.4
4	Durham	3.3	491	81	75	92.2
5	Southampton	3.8	427	87	60	90.2
6	King's College London	3.5	416	79	78	89.7
7	Warwick	2.6	430	89	66	89.4
8	Leeds	3.4	388	83	74	89.3
9	Bath	2.4	443	85	73	89.2
10	Newcastle	3.0	411	82	75	89.1
11	Manchester	3.2	410	79	77	88.2
12	University College London	3.5	475	73	74	87.6
13	Swansea	2.5	295	90	75	87.4
14	Nottingham	2.3	401	86	70	86.8
15	Birmingham	3.0	393	85	63	86.4
16	Exeter	2.9	434	84	59	85.6
=17	Glasgow	1.8	429	82	75	85.4
=17	Cardiff	2.6	383	82	71	85.4
19	Bristol	2.8	444	77	69	85.0
20	Queen's, Belfast	1.3	398	80	86	84.8
21	Lancaster	1.9	393	80	78	84.6
22	Edinburgh	3.3	472	70	65	82.7
23	Sheffield	2.0	398	78	72	82.1
24	Royal Holloway	3.2	372	71	73	81.9
25	Aberdeen	1.3	362	85	69	81.3
26	Portsmouth	2.6	273	86	61	80.6
=27	Kent	1.4	330	82	73	80.5
=27	Heriot-Watt	1.9	367	82	63	80.5
=29	Liverpool	2.4	365	79	63	79.7
=29	Aston	1.4	365	80	71	79.7
31	Reading	1.8	329	80		77.5
32	Queen Mary, London	1.9	313	77		75.5
33	East Anglia		355	86	50	72.0
34	Nottingham Trent		244	84	60	70.1
35	Manchester Metropolitan	1.1	254	79	53	69.5
36	Bangor		299	77	59	68.5

» Chartered Institute of Linguists: **www.iol.org.uk**
» Goethe-Institut: **www.goethe.de/enindex.htm**
» National Centre for Languages (CILT): **www.cilt.org.uk**

History

History's currency in the graduate jobs market has been a matter of debate. Surveys have shown a strong representation of historians among business leaders, celebrities and senior politicians, but more are in non-graduate jobs than those categorised as graduate occupations six months after completing a degree. Only law has a lower proportion of leavers going straight into graduate jobs.

Nevertheless, history remains only just outside the top 10 subjects as a degree choice, despite not quite sharing in the applications boom of 2010. An increase of almost 8 per cent (a cause for celebration in any other year) pushed the number of applicants past 48,000 at the official deadline for courses starting in 2010. The subject was already among the most competitive at entry, and the latest increase is likely to produce almost six applications to every place.

Cambridge remains the leading university for history, with the highest entry standards and one of the two top scores for research, a distinction it shares with University College London. Three other universities – Oxford, Liverpool and Essex – matched the top research score last year, but have lost out in the revaluation of grades in the 2008 Research Assessment Exercise, which gives extra credit to submissions judged to be world-leading. In fact, Imperial College London's work on the history of science won the top research grade, but history is not an undergraduate subject at Imperial so it does not appear in the table.

Oxford loses second place in the overall ranking to Durham, which has among the most satisfied students. The London School of Economics, in fourth place, has by far the best employment score, a full 16 points ahead of its nearest rival. While the LSE saw 94 per cent of historians go straight into graduate jobs or onto postgraduate courses, at 28 of the 89 universities in the table the proportion was below 50 per cent.

Average entry scores at the top three universities are all over 500 points, the equivalent of more than four As at A level. Other leading universities' entry standards are closer to the top three than in many other subjects: all the top 10 – and another ten universities further down the ranking – average at least 400 points.

Satisfaction levels are high at most of the universities in the ranking, but most of the top scores are to be found outside the top 20. Teesside has the most satisfied students of all, but Derby, Chichester, Portsmouth and St Mary's University College, Twickenham, also satisfied more than 90 per cent of their final-year undergraduates. However, none of them is the top post-1992 university. That distinction goes to Oxford Brookes, in 26th place. St Andrews remains the top university in Scotland, while Cardiff does the same in Wales.

Employed in graduate job:	26%	Employed in non-graduate job and studying:	4%
Employed in graduate job and studying:	4%	Employed in non-graduate job:	32%
Studying:	25%	Unemployed:	10%
Average starting graduate salary:	£19,656	Average starting non-graduate salary:	£14,654

History	Research quality/9	Entry standards	Student satisfaction %	Graduate prospects %	Overall rating
1 Cambridge	4.6	522	88	73	100.0
2 Durham	3.3	510	91	78	98.4
3 Oxford	4.5	512	85	74	98.0

4	London School of Economics	4.3	470	76	94	95.6
=5	Warwick	4.3	479	81	72	92.9
=5	University College London	4.6	444	80	74	92.9
7	St Andrews	3.4	458	88	65	91.8
8	York	3.6	460	85	69	91.7
9	King's College London	3.6	465	82	72	91.5
10	Sheffield	4.3	432	82	66	90.6
11	Exeter	3.4	437	86	66	89.8
12	Queen Mary, London	3.9	366	83	74	89.0
13	Southampton	4.2	391	83	63	88.5
14	Liverpool	4.5	391	85	56	88.3
15	Leeds	3.2	440	83	65	87.5
16	Kent	4.5	339	84	62	87.4
=17	Glasgow	3.6	401	88	50	86.7
=17	Aberdeen	4.0	349	84	63	86.7
=17	East Anglia	3.3	372	89	56	86.7
20	Sussex	3.7	372	80	70	86.2
=21	Lancaster	3.0	400	84	63	85.5
=21	Leicester	3.1	360	87	59	85.5
=23	Nottingham	2.9	425	79	68	84.9
=23	Royal Holloway	3.3	383	82	63	84.9
25	Hull	3.1	329	88	59	84.6
26	Oxford Brookes	3.7	314	84	63	84.3
27	Essex	4.5	322	84	49	83.6
28	Birmingham	3.3	398	80	60	83.5
29	Teesside	2.4	258	93	63	83.4
30	School of Oriental and African Studies	3.9	361	78	60	83.1
31	Edinburgh	3.6	441	73	64	83.0
32	Bristol	2.9	454	68	76	82.1
=33	Newcastle	2.6	410	78	61	81.3
=33	Manchester	3.6	412	71	64	81.3
35	Huddersfield	2.1	282	89	62	81.2
36	Keele	3.2	300	82	61	80.6
37	Cardiff	2.4	402	80	53	79.1
38	Portsmouth	2.6	282	91	44	78.9
39	Dundee	3.1	333	85	42	78.8
40	Stirling	2.8	309	83	53	78.6
=41	Queen's, Belfast	3.1	363	78	51	78.2
=41	Strathclyde	2.0	363	80	59	78.2
43	Hertfordshire	3.9	257	84	43	77.8
=44	Reading	2.5	345	81	51	77.4
=44	Chester	2.6	279	79	63	77.4
46	Winchester	2.9	269	86	45	76.8
47	Chichester	1.4	257	91	50	76.0
48	Aberystwyth	2.3	287	81	54	75.6
49	Swansea	2.8	292	82	46	75.5
50	St Mary's College		226	92	67	75.4

History cont.

	Research quality/9	Entry standards	Student satisfaction %	Graduate prospects %	Overall rating
51 Nottingham Trent	1.7	254	85	54	74.3
52 De Montfort	1.8	259	88	45	74.2
53 Bangor	2.8	284	83	40	74.0
=54 Central Lancashire	2.1	237	83	53	73.7
=54 Sunderland	2.5	226	79	59	73.7
=56 Bath Spa	2.0	283	82	47	73.4
=56 Glamorgan	2.6	249	84	43	73.4
58 Goldsmiths College	2.0	308	77	55	73.1
=59 Lincoln	1.7	272	79	58	72.7
=59 Newman	0.9	240	83	63	72.7
61 West of England	2.0	261	83	47	72.6
62 Lampeter (Trinity Saint David)	1.9	245	79	58	72.5
63 Derby		221	92	55	72.3
64 Greenwich	2.1	221	83	49	72.1
65 Northumbria	1.1	298	79	57	71.9
66 Cumbria	1.3	278		59	71.7
67 Ulster	2.9	253	79	41	71.3
68 Anglia Ruskin	3.3	242	74	48	71.2
69 Kingston	1.7	236	76	62	71.0
70 Northampton	2.0	234	87	33	70.1
71 Brighton	4.3	257	74	24	68.8
72 Coventry		289		55	68.4
73 Gloucestershire	1.5	268	74	53	68.1
74 Canterbury Christ Church	1.4	260	82	36	67.7
75 Bradford	1.6	260	80	36	67.2
76 Plymouth	1.4	264	79	40	67.0
77 Sheffield Hallam	1.9	261	77	36	66.4
78 Roehampton	2.2	284	69	45	66.2
79 Salford	1.6	259	75	43	65.9
80 Newport	1.0	238	78	42	65.2
81 Brunel		313	71	56	64.7
=82 Manchester Metropolitan	1.1	288	74	38	64.0
=82 York St John		258	85	32	64.0
=84 Worcester	0.5	237	74	53	63.8
=84 Bishop Grosseteste		218		54	63.8
86 Liverpool John Moores	1.1	247	79	29	62.9
87 Edge Hill	1.7	243	61	59	62.0
=88 Westminster	1.2	246		30	59.8
=88 Leeds Metropolitan		245	74	42	59.8

» Historical Association: **www.history.org.uk**
» Institute of Historical Research: **www.history.ac.uk**
» Royal Historical Society: **www.royalhistoricalsociety.org**

History of Art, Architecture and Design

Cambridge has stretched its lead at the top of the table for history of art, where London's Courtauld Institute, the one-time leader, has again become its nearest challenger. Cambridge has by far the highest entry standards and is a dozen percentage points ahead of the next most successful university in the graduate jobs market. Nowhere else did three-quarters of the leavers find graduate jobs or start new courses within six months of completing a degree. The 10 per cent employment rate at Aberystwyth was among the lowest figures in any subject in the latest survey.

Cambridge's lead would have been bigger, were it not for an unusually low research score by its own standards. Glasgow did best in the 2008 Research Assessment Exercise, which classified 85 per cent of its work as world-leading or internationally excellent.

History of Art, Architecture and Design	Research quality/9	Entry standards	Student satisfaction %	Graduate prospects %	Overall rating
1 Cambridge	2.8	521	88	86	100.0
2 Courtauld	5.0	442	85	67	97.4
3 Glasgow	5.4	404	88	60	96.7
4 York	5.1	401	86	71	96.6
5 St Andrews	3.3	447	88	71	94.9
6 East Anglia	5.4	392	89	50	94.8
7 Sussex	5.1	383	80	74	93.1
8 University College London	4.3	427	80	67	91.6
9 Aberdeen	3.3	338	84	74	87.7
10 Warwick	3.3	412	80	64	87.2
11 Birmingham	4.2	409	79	51	87.0
12 Leeds	3.3	401	82	59	86.6
13 Edinburgh	3.1	470	73	68	86.5
14 Nottingham	3.7	372	79	62	85.0
15 Reading	3.1	336	83	58	82.9
16 Leicester	2.3	356	86		82.4
17 School of Oriental and African Studies	3.7	336	78	56	82.0
18 Southampton	2.8		84	48	81.9
19 Manchester	5.0	352	72	49	81.7
20 Goldsmiths College	3.2	354	77	48	79.1
21 Oxford Brookes	2.9	324	84	41	78.8
22 Bristol	2.7	425	66	59	77.4
23 Brighton	4.3	263	73	44	75.0
24 Kingston	2.5	267	76	54	73.5
25 Sheffield Hallam	2.9		77	33	73.2
26 Plymouth	2.4	288	79	22	69.3
27 Aberystwyth	1.5		81	10	64.8
28 Roehampton		264	69	52	61.1

» Association of Art Historians: **www.aah.org.uk**
» Society of Architectural Historians of Great Britain: **www.sahgb.org.uk**

History of Art, Architecture and Design cont.

There were good scores in art history for most universities in the National Student Survey published in 2009. All 28 institutions in the ranking satisfied at least two-thirds of their final-year undergraduates. The most satisfied of all were at sixth-placed East Anglia.

However, employment scores are low: the subject is in the bottom 15 for "positive destinations", but the 8 per cent unemployment rate is about average. The specialised nature of the jobs market has always made for uncertain prospects immediately after graduation. Starting salaries are in the bottom 20 for all subjects and had dropped to less than £18,500 since the previous survey was conducted.

Glasgow remains just ahead of St Andrews as the top university in Scotland, while Aberystwyth is the only representative of Wales in this year's table. Only six post-1992 universities are left in the ranking, with Oxford Brookes the highest-placed, just outside the top 20.

Fewer than 4,000 undergraduates take full-time degrees in the history of art, although another 1,000 are registered on part-time courses. The majority of students are female. Entry standards are high, with more than a third of the table averaging over 400 points and no university less than 250.

Employed in graduate job:	31%	Employed in non-graduate job and studying:	6%
Employed in graduate job and studying:	2%	Employed in non-graduate job:	33%
Studying:	20%	Unemployed:	8%
Average starting graduate salary:	£18,477	Average starting non-graduate salary:	£15,658

Hospitality, Leisure, Recreation and Tourism

Sports courses were removed from this still wide-ranging category in order to give a fast-growing set of courses a ranking of their own. What remains is a much more coherent table that should be of more use in choosing a university. A 28 per cent increase in applications, making a total of more than 33,000, ensures that it will be well used.

Most of the 47 institutions in the ranking are post-1992 universities, although the top three are older foundations. Surrey, with its 40-year reputation in hotel and tourism management, is almost ten points ahead of second-placed Southampton, which has moved up two places with by far the best graduate destinations record. Surrey is one of only four universities with average entry grades of more than 300 points and it achieved the best of an extremely modest set of results in the 2008 Research Assessment Exercise.

The most satisfied students are at Ulster, which is at 23rd place because it did not enter the RAE and had a low employment score. The Arts University College at Bournemouth, which shares ninth place in this year's table, is the only institution (apart from Southampton) to manage "positive destinations" for more than 70 per cent of graduates. The 7 per cent employment score at Chichester was probably the lowest in any subject in the last survey. Nationally, the proportion in graduate-level jobs or further study six months after completing a degree is the lowest of any subject: more than half of all graduates were in lower-level work or unemployed at that point. The subjects fare a little better in terms of starting salaries, although the average of £18,000 for graduate-level jobs had dropped since the previous survey was carried out. Central Lancashire, in fourth place, is the highest-placed post-1992 university and is joined in the top 10 by Bournemouth, Brighton, Sheffield Hallam, Plymouth and

Hertfordshire. Stirling, in third place, is the top university in Scotland, while UWIC has that distinction in Wales.

The category covers a variety of courses, most directed towards management in the leisure and tourism industries. The subjects are among the top 20 degree choices, with Foundation degrees showing even stronger growth. The number of places for new entrants grew by 8 per cent in 2009, helping to keep pace with demand.

Employed in graduate job:	36%	Employed in non-graduate job and studying:	3%
Employed in graduate job and studying:	3%	Employed in non-graduate job:	41%
Studying:	8%	Unemployed:	9%
Average starting graduate salary:	£18,000	Average starting non-graduate salary:	£15,483

Hospitality, Leisure, Recreation and Tourism	Research quality/9	Entry standards	Student satisfaction %	Graduate prospects %	Overall rating
1 Surrey	2.5	348	85	70	100.0
2 Southampton	2.1		75	87	91.6
3 Stirling	2.3	324	75	63	90.5
4 Central Lancashire	2.3	216	82	66	86.9
5 Bournemouth	1.6	287	77	67	84.1
6 Brighton	2.0	240	83	52	83.5
7 Sheffield Hallam	2.1	248	79	49	82.6
8 Plymouth	1.7	229	82	40	77.8
=9 Hertfordshire	1.8	222	75	54	77.6
=9 Arts University College, Bournemouth		293		73	77.6
=11 Strathclyde		325	83	53	74.5
=11 Sunderland	1.6	231	78	36	74.5
13 West of England	1.1	243	81	42	74.2
14 Chester	1.5	239	71	50	73.4
15 UWIC, Cardiff	1.5	220	78	38	73.1
16 Manchester Metropolitan	1.8	233	65	51	72.9
17 Salford	1.6	178	81	41	72.8
18 Oxford Brookes		297	78	59	71.7
19 Robert Gordon		256	79	69	71.5
20 Queen Margaret Edinburgh		252		63	70.0
21 Manchester		312	73	55	69.4
22 Winchester		250	79	49	66.9
23 Ulster		225	89	34	66.6
24 Gloucestershire		228	75	64	66.5
25 Edinburgh Napier		265	75	52	66.2
=26 Portsmouth		248	78	44	65.1
=26 Bedfordshire	1.3	165	78	25	65.1
28 Glasgow Caledonian		299	72	39	64.9
29 Hull		184	80	56	64.1
30 Lincoln		242	74	48	63.8
31 University College Birmingham		222	80	40	63.4

Hospitality, Leisure, Recreation and Tourism cont.

	Research quality/9	Entry standards	Student satisfaction %	Graduate prospects %	Overall rating
32 Leeds Metropolitan		252	68	57	63.1
33 Thames Valley		194	78	51	62.8
34 Canterbury Christ Church		212	74	51	62.2
35 Glamorgan		225	77	32	60.7
36 Coventry		252	70	39	60.6
=37 Derby		214	73	44	60.2
=37 Greenwich		249	67	47	60.2
39 Southampton Solent		210	70	46	59.2
40 Huddersfield		235	66	45	58.5
41 Buckinghamshire New		239	67	34	57.1
42 Liverpool John Moores		189	71	41	57.0
43 Chichester		237	78	7	56.4
44 University of the Arts London		268	57	45	56.2
45 London South Bank		153	75	24	52.8
46 Middlesex		139	67	44	51.9
47 Anglia Ruskin		190	66	28	51.6

» Association for Tourism in Higher Education: **www.athe.org.uk**
» Council for Hospitality Management Education: **www.chme.org.uk**
» Institute of Hospitality: **www.instituteofhospitality.org**
» Leisure Studies Association: **www.leisure-studies-association.info**

Iberian Languages

Spanish has been growing in popularity as an alternative to French in schools, and is a common choice as an element of a broader modern languages degree. The positive trend was continuing at the start of 2010, when an increase in applications of more than 17 per cent contrasted favourably with a decline in German and only a small rise in French. However, total applications were still not far above 2,000, well behind the figure for French. The table also includes Portuguese, which had only a dozen applications at degree level at the start of 2010, although it is still offered at 17 universities, at least as part of a broader languages programme.

Cambridge has stretched its lead at the top of the table, with the highest entry standards and (jointly with Leicester) the most satisfied students. Nottingham, in fifth position, and Manchester, seven places lower, tie for the best performance in the 2008 Research Assessment Exercise. Lancaster has easily the best employment record and would have been much higher than eighth if it had had better research grades. Durham remains in second place, with Oxford moving up to third.

The 2009 National Student Survey showed high levels of satisfaction in most universities. Only three failed to satisfy at least 70 per cent of the final-year undergraduates. All but seven of the 45 institutions in the ranking are pre-1992 universities. Portsmouth is the by far highest-placed of the newer foundations and, for the third year in a row, the only one in the top 30.

Entry standards have levelled off since last year, but are still high: 15 universities average over 400 points and only two slip below 250. The languages are around the middle of the employment table, but the 7 per cent unemployment rate is among the lowest in any subject. Average starting salaries, at a fraction under £20,000, are slightly below the level in last year's survey. Employment prospects appear to be more evenly spread than in many subjects: only two universities in the table saw fewer than half of their leavers go into graduate jobs or further training in 2008.

Employed in graduate job:	39%
Employed in graduate job and studying:	5%
Studying:	19%
Average starting graduate salary:	£19,939
Employed in non-graduate job and studying:	3%
Employed in non-graduate job:	26%
Unemployed:	7%
Average starting non-graduate salary:	£15,615

Iberian Languages	Research quality/9	Entry standards	Student satisfaction %	Graduate prospects %	Overall rating
1 Cambridge	4.1	538	88	82	100.0
2 Durham	3.4	491	81	75	90.7
3 Oxford	3.0	516	87	64	89.9
4 Bath	2.4	445	87	78	89.0
5 Nottingham	4.3	375	76	80	87.4
=6 St Andrews	2.8	434	84	70	86.6
=6 Sheffield	3.4	407	81	73	86.6
8 Lancaster	1.9	420	80	88	85.7
9 King's College London	3.7	410	77	74	85.5
10 Southampton	3.8	398	84	58	84.8
11 Leeds	3.3	407	79	70	84.3
12 Manchester	4.3	400	71	69	82.9
13 Newcastle	2.9	439	78	65	82.5
14 Aberdeen	2.4	359	85	68	81.8
15 Bristol	2.0	430	77	75	81.4
16 Leicester	2.1	350	88	64	81.1
17 Queen's, Belfast	2.9	385	74	69	79.7
18 Queen Mary, London	3.6	330	76	66	79.5
19 University College London	2.4	421	79	56	78.2
20 Heriot-Watt	1.9	367	82	63	78.0
21 Exeter	2.6	412	74	63	77.9
22 Royal Holloway	2.6	343	81	60	77.7
23 Aston	1.4	390	82		77.5
24 Portsmouth	2.6	273	86	60	77.4
=25 Kent	1.6	285	81	78	76.7
=25 Cardiff	2.6	366	78	58	76.7
27 Stirling	1.7	328	79	72	76.4
28 Edinburgh	2.8	468	60	71	76.2
29 Birmingham	2.3	390	76	57	75.2
30 Swansea	2.4	303	81	58	75.1

Iberian Languages cont.

	Research quality/9	Entry standards	Student satisfaction %	Graduate prospects %	Overall rating
31 Sussex		372	75	85	74.5
32 Liverpool	2.8	363	71	59	74.3
33 Strathclyde	1.2	349	78	64	73.1
34 Salford	1.6	353	77	56	72.2
35 Hull		280	82	77	71.8
36 Glasgow	1.5	393	62	75	70.7
37 Ulster	0.8		80	59	70.2
38 Northumbria		290	80	72	70.0
39 Chester		263	78	78	69.6
40 East Anglia		355	86	50	69.5
41 Manchester Metropolitan	1.1	267	79	53	67.1
42 Nottingham Trent		244	84	60	66.7
43 Roehampton	1.6		80	35	65.2
44 Westminster		266	69	73	63.8
45 Liverpool John Moores		233	73	40	55.7

» Association for Contemporary Iberian Studies: **www.iberianstudies.net**
» Association of Hispanists of Great Britain and Ireland: **www.dur.ac.uk/hispanists**
» Instituto Cervantes: **http://londres.cervantes.es/en/default.shtm**
» National Centre for Languages (CILT): **www.cilt.org.uk**

Italian

Cambridge continues to lead a group of 22 universities qualifying for the ranking in Italian – 12 fewer than four years ago. It has the top score on all four measures, making this one of the few tables where there is a clean sweep. Under the circumstances, it is surprising that Cambridge's lead is not bigger, but Oxford comes second on three of the four measures and has actually closed the gap since the last edition of the *Guide*. Both of the ancient universities average more than 500 points at entry and there is only one percentage point between them on student satisfaction.

At Cambridge, 80 per cent of research was judged to be world-leading or internationally excellent in the latest assessments. This is the only measure on which any other universities – third-placed Leeds and ninth-placed Warwick – managed to split the leaders. University College London makes the most progress this year, jumping nine places into sixth position. St Andrews, a new entrant to the ranking, is the top university in Scotland, while Cardiff has overtaken Swansea in Wales. There are only three post-1992 universities left in the table, with Portsmouth much the best-placed, in 14th position.

As in previous years, student satisfaction was generally high in the 2009 National Student Survey. No university failed to satisfy at least 70 per cent of final-year undergraduates. But employment scores are more variable: Cambridge was the only university to see over 80 per cent of leavers go straight into graduate-level jobs or postgraduate courses. At two universities, the proportion slipped below 50 per cent.

There were only 254 applications to study Italian as a separate subject at the start of 2010, although many students include the language in combined degree programmes. Only 78 started degrees in 2009, but the language remains widely available at degree level, with 37 universities offering courses involving Italian. A high proportion – up to 15 per cent – secure places in Clearing. Most students have no previous knowledge of the language, but there is a high completion rate.

The low numbers can make for big swings in the annual statistics: three years ago, for example, starting salaries were in the bottom six, whereas in this year's *Guide* they are only just outside the top 30, averaging more than £20,000.

Employed in graduate job: 43%	Employed in non-graduate job and studying: 3%
Employed in graduate job and studying: 4%	Employed in non-graduate job: 25%
Studying: 16%	Unemployed: 10%
Average starting graduate salary: £20,193	Average starting non-graduate salary: £15,389

Italian	Research quality/9	Entry standards	Student satisfaction %	Graduate prospects %	Overall rating
1 Cambridge	5.3	538	88	82	100.0
2 Oxford	3.8	501	87	78	94.1
3 Leeds	4.0	371	85	60	85.7
4 Durham	1.7	491	81	75	85.4
5 Bristol	3.3	457	79	71	85.3
6 University College London	3.0	429	79	75	84.4
=7 Bath	2.4	430	81	69	83.4
=7 Birmingham	2.8		83	62	83.4
9 Warwick	4.0	418	77	64	83.1
10 Manchester	3.3	380	81	63	82.7
11 St Andrews	1.7	443	85	56	82.0
12 Glasgow	1.5	456	82		81.2
13 Exeter	2.1	424	79	68	81.1
14 Portsmouth	2.6	273	86	60	80.6
15 Cardiff	2.6	306	84	58	80.0
16 Reading	3.7	333	80	47	77.9
17 Royal Holloway	1.8	368	81	56	77.2
18 Edinburgh	1.1	462	70	78	76.5
19 Swansea	1.6	291	80		74.4
20 Nottingham Trent		244	84	60	72.8
21 Manchester Metropolitan	1.1	254	79	53	71.0
22 Strathclyde	1.2		80	39	69.4

» Chartered Institute of Linguists: **www.iol.org.uk**
» National Centre for Languages (CILT): **www.cilt.org.uk**
» Society for Italian Studies: **www.sis.ac.uk**

Land and Property Management

Two universities have rejoined the land and property management table, reversing the trend of recent years. But there are still only seven in the ranking, compared with 23 in 2005 edition. The subject tends to have small intakes, making it impossible to compile reliable scores for some universities, even though they are still offering one or more of the subjects. More than 25 universities and one college are advertising degrees in this field starting in 2011.

Cambridge maintains the lead, with entry standards that are almost 100 points higher than at second-placed Reading and nearly 200 points above the other universities in the table. Cambridge also shares the highest employment score and registered the best performance in the 2008 Research Assessment Exercise. Birmingham City, in fourth place, has the other top employment score.

The response to the 2009 National Student Survey was too low to produce a score for Cambridge. Second-placed Reading has the most satisfied students, with Ulster close behind.

Land and property management has been enjoying considerable success in the graduate jobs market, although it has dropped out of the top 10 for "positive destinations" this year. The unemployment rate was below 3 per cent in last year's table, but had shot up to 12 per cent this time. Graduates' prospects inevitably depend to some extent on the state of the property market, which had gone into decline when these statistics were collected.

Only about 2,000 students are taking the subject at degree or diploma level, although the subjects are often included in wider environmental programmes. Starting salaries in graduate-level jobs were in the top 20 for all subjects at the end of 2008, but the average of less than £22,000 was over £1,000 down on the previous year.

Employed in graduate job:	63%	Employed in non-graduate job and studying:	0%
Employed in graduate job and studying:	9%	Employed in non-graduate job:	12%
Studying:	4%	Unemployed:	12%
Average starting graduate salary:	£21,758	Average starting non-graduate salary:	*

Land and Property Management	Research quality/9	Entry standards	Student satisfaction %	Graduate prospects %	Overall rating
1 Cambridge	4.3	483		93	100.0
2 Reading	3.6	394	81	89	94.5
3 Queen's, Belfast	2.0	283	76		82.0
4 Birmingham City	1.7	258	71	93	80.5
5 Ulster		284	80	73	79.4
6 Westminster	1.5	265	71	83	78.1
7 Greenwich		193	77	59	71.

» Chartered Institute of Housing: **www.cih.org**
» Institute of Residential Property Management: **www.irpm.org.uk**
» Royal Institution of Chartered Surveyors: **www.rics.org**

Law

Law is in the top three subjects for applications – more than 83,000 at the start of 2010, after a 6 per cent rise in the demand for places. Entry standards reflect its popularity: nine subjects have higher average entry scores, but only in medicine do so many universities make such testing demands. Almost a third of the 91 universities have average entry scores of more than 400 points. However, it is still possible to secure a place at a handful of new universities with less than 200 points. Nationally, there were only just over five applications to the place in 2009.

Oxford has taken over the leadership from Cambridge, despite not leading the table on any of the measures. Cambridge has the highest entry standards, and seventh-placed Aberdeen the best record for graduate destinations. Law is only just in the top 20 subjects for employment because of some low scores at the bottom of the ranking, but most of the leading universities saw at least 80 per cent of graduates go straight into graduate-level jobs or continue studying.

Aspiring solicitors go on to take the Legal Practice Course, while those aiming to be barristers take the Bar Vocational Course, so it is no surprise that law has by far the highest proportion engaged in postgraduate study. Many law graduates opt for careers in other areas, but the 6 per cent unemployment rate shows that they are still in demand.

Once more, the most satisfied students are not at one of the top universities. That distinction goes to Sunderland, in 41st place, with Teesside, not even in the top 50, sharing the next-best score with Cambridge. Sunderland achieved the same feat last year, but there were good scores in law throughout the 2009 National Student Survey. Only five universities – and only one of the top 50 – failed to satisfy at least 70 per cent of the undergraduates.

The London School of Economics, in fourth place, achieved the best grades in the 2008 Research Assessment Exercise, when three-quarters of its submission was rated world-leading or internationally excellent. Aberdeen remains the top university in Scotland, while Cardiff is now well clear of the rest in Wales. Buckingham again holds the highest position outside the traditional universities, but has to share that distinction this year with Oxford Brookes. Robert Gordon is the other post-1992 university in the top 40.

Average starting salaries are not as high as tales might suggest. At less than £20,000, the average for graduate-level jobs is in the bottom half of the earnings league.

Employed in graduate job:	19%	Employed in non-graduate job and studying:	6%
Employed in graduate job and studying:	5%	Employed in non-graduate job:	19%
Studying:	45%	Unemployed:	6%
Average starting graduate salary:	£19,322	Average starting non-graduate salary:	£15,228

Law	Research quality/9	Entry standards	Student satisfaction %	Graduate prospects %	Overall rating
1 Oxford	4.5	530		87	100.0
2 Cambridge	3.7	542	90	89	99.6
3 University College London	4.6	498	78	92	95.2
4 London School of Economics	5.1	488	75	88	93.6
5 Nottingham	4.1	474	82	84	92.9
6 Queen Mary, London	3.3	423	85	85	90.9

Law cont.

		Research quality/9	Entry standards	Student satisfaction %	Graduate prospects %	Overall rating
7	Aberdeen	1.8	404	88	93	89.9
8	Durham	4.1	496	74	82	88.7
9	Birmingham	3.0	428	85	79	88.5
10	King's College London	2.8	462	81	82	88.2
11	Newcastle	1.7	446	88	81	88.0
12	Glasgow	2.9	456	77	87	87.6
13	Bristol	2.9	483	77	84	87.4
=14	Reading	3.3	395	83	78	86.8
=14	Edinburgh	3.8	456	71	88	86.8
=14	Strathclyde	3.3	434	76	87	86.8
=17	Exeter	2.3	426	85	80	86.7
=17	Southampton	2.3	438	84	79	86.7
=17	Leicester	1.9	402	85	86	86.7
20	Dundee	2.3	386	85	82	86.3
21	Warwick	2.4	469	80	80	85.8
22	Kent	4.0	340	80	79	85.3
23	Lancaster	2.1	415	80	87	85.2
24	Sussex	2.4	368	82	84	84.9
25	East Anglia	1.9	393	85	79	84.6
26	Manchester	2.5	455	75	83	84.1
=27	Cardiff	3.7	411	77	72	83.5
=27	Liverpool	2.5	422	79	77	83.5
29	Hull	2.1	351	81	87	83.4
30	Leeds	2.9	431	76	78	83.0
31	Queen's, Belfast	3.7	418	72	78	82.7
32	Sheffield	2.8	418	74	81	82.5
33	School of Oriental and African Studies	2.1	413	76	82	81.6
34	Brunel	2.2	365	74	84	80.1
35	Swansea	2.2	321	81	72	79.0
=36	Oxford Brookes	2.4	335	75	80	78.9
=36	Buckingham		302	89	81	78.9
38	Aberystwyth	1.7	294	81	79	78.3
39	Keele	2.5	316	74	82	78.2
40	Robert Gordon	0.7	315	77	92	78.0
=41	Nottingham Trent	0.8	309	81	83	77.4
=41	Sunderland	0.4	244	96	65	77.4
=43	Stirling	1.8	333	84	60	76.5
=43	Abertay	1.2	228		92	76.5
45	Loughborough		329		84	76.4
=46	Portsmouth	1.7	292	81	72	76.3
=46	Surrey	1.7	378	68	86	76.3
48	Essex	2.2	340	75	72	76.2
49	Northumbria		349	79	83	76.1

Rank	University				
50	De Montfort	1.1	237	83	78	75.8
51	Greenwich	0.6	271	87	72	75.7
52	West of England	1.3	302	80	73	75.4
53	Teesside		290	90	67	75.1
54	Central Lancashire	0.8	272	79	81	75.0
55	Manchester Metropolitan	1.8	312	73	78	74.9
56	Hertfordshire	1.8	241	83	67	74.8
=57	Brighton	2.8	278		63	73.9
=57	Lincoln	0.7	273	83	70	73.9
=57	City	1.7	358	69	78	73.9
60	Salford	1.0	352			73.6
61	Ulster	3.2	307	75	53	72.6
62	Huddersfield		284	78	79	71.9
63	Derby		250	89	61	71.7
=64	Glasgow Caledonian	0.8	373	74	65	71.5
=64	Glamorgan	0.8	270	76	76	71.5
66	Bournemouth	0.3	309	78	70	71.4
67	Edinburgh Napier	0.4	308	73	79	71.1
68	East London	1.8	171	77	72	70.7
69	Buckinghamshire New		229	80	77	70.5
=70	Chester		295	75	77	70.4
=70	Gloucestershire		259	79	73	70.4
72	Staffordshire		240	78	78	70.2
73	Kingston	0.7	269	74	70	69.1
74	Plymouth	1.8	271	74	60	68.8
75	Coventry	0.3	281	76	68	68.6
76	Westminster	1.6	305	64	72	67.6
=77	Sheffield Hallam	0.5	278	73	67	67.4
=77	Bradford	2.7	250	80	38	67.4
79	Liverpool John Moores		256	81	58	67.0
80	Birmingham City		250	71	76	66.5
81	Bangor		258	76	66	66.4
82	Edge Hill		237	84	51	65.9
83	Middlesex	0.8	194	72	70	65.2
84	Anglia Ruskin		265	72	65	64.5
=85	Leeds Metropolitan		277	69	68	64.1
=85	Southampton Solent	0.1	239	71	68	64.1
87	Bedfordshire		200	78	55	62.4
88	Northampton		231	77	47	60.8
89	Thames Valley		173	71	59	59.3
90	London South Bank		199	67	63	58.8
91	Canterbury Christ Church		237	73	41	57.5

» Law Society of England and Wales: **www.lawsociety.org.uk**
» Law Society of Northern Ireland: **www.lawsoc-ni.org**
» Law Society of Scotland: **www.lawscot.org.uk**

Librarianship and Information Management

The top four universities for librarianship and information are unchanged for the third year in a row. Sheffield might have regained first place from Loughborough since it has the best scores for research and entry standards, but Loughborough's strengths in graduate employment and student satisfaction gave it a reduced lead. King's College London produced the top results in the 2008 Research Assessment Exercise but does not have undergraduate courses in this field. Sheffield was close behind, with two thirds of its work classed as world-leading or internationally excellent, followed by third-placed University College London.

Employment prospects, even among such a small group of universities, are extremely variable. While more than 80 per cent of Loughborough graduates found graduate–level work or further courses within six months of competing a degree, the rate at the bottom of the table was well below 50 per cent. This contributes to a high unemployment rate of 13 per cent and leaves the subjects in this year's bottom ten overall.

Student numbers are low – almost half the universities in the table did not recruit enough undergraduates for entry grades to be published. Only 630 candidates had applied to study information sciences at the start of 2010, but this still represented a 12 per cent increase on the previous year. Another university has dropped out of the table this year, making five fewer than there were in the 2006 edition of the *Guide*. There is no representative of Scotland and only Aberystwyth from Wales. Northumbria has overtaken Brighton as the highest-placed post-1992 university.

Librarianship and information management are not the poor payers that their reputation might suggest, however. Average starting salaries in graduate-level jobs had shot up to almost £23,000, placing them in the top 20 for the first time in the listing of subject areas.

Employed in graduate job:	41%	Employed in non-graduate job and studying:	0%
Employed in graduate job and studying:	5%	Employed in non-graduate job:	30%
Studying:	11%	Unemployed:	13%
Average starting graduate salary:	£22,935	Average starting non-graduate salary:	£16,784

Librarianship and Information Management	Research quality/9	Entry standards	Student satisfaction %	Graduate prospects %	Overall rating
1 Loughborough	2.9	325	87	81	100.0
2 Sheffield	4.0	333	79	79	98.0
3 University College London	3.8		74	58	87.0
4 Aberystwyth	2.5		73	59	81.5
5 Northumbria	1.1	238	80	61	81.1
6 Brighton	2.2		71	59	78.8
7 Manchester Metropolitan	1.1	240	74	43	72.9
8 London South Bank	0.8		75	39	70.7
9 Liverpool John Moores	1.4	207	70		70.2

» Association for Information Management: **www.aslib.com**
» Chartered Institute of Library and Information Professionals: **www.cilip.org.uk**

Linguistics

There was a big drop in applications for linguistics – almost 15 per cent – in 2009, when most subjects were seeing healthy increases. But the subject had bounced back at the beginning of 2010, when a 24 per cent increase took total applications over 2,500. However, entry standards remain comparatively high: only one university averages less than 250 points and nearly a third of the universities in the ranking have an average of more than 400 points. Eight out of ten students arrive with A levels or their equivalent.

Oxford has narrowed the gap on Cambridge at the top of the table and might have taken the lead but for a surprisingly low set of grades in the 2008 Research Assessment Exercise. The two ancient universities tie for the most satisfied students, while Cambridge leads the table on entry standards.

For the second successive year, the School of Oriental and African Studies, in London, has the best employment score. Oxford and University College London, in fourth place, were the only other institutions to see three-quarters of their linguists go straight into graduate-level work or further study. Although only two universities dropped below 50 per cent on this measure, the rate was below 60 per cent in more than half of the table.

Cardiff, in sixth place, produced the best grades in the 2008 Research Assessment Exercise, while Queen Mary, London, was close behind, holding on to third place as a result.

Edinburgh is Scotland's only representative in the table, while Cardiff is well ahead of Bangor in Wales. Portsmouth is the highest-placed post-1992 university, only just outside the top 10 in a ranking that is dominated by the older foundations. Hertfordshire is the only other former polytechnic in the top 20.

Linguistics is close to the bottom ten subjects for immediate employment prospects, although the unemployment rate is no more than average, at 8 per cent. Average starting salaries for graduate jobs are in the bottom three, however, at less than £17,500.

Employed in graduate job:	29%	Employed in non-graduate job and studying:	2%
Employed in graduate job and studying:	3%	Employed in non-graduate job:	33%
Studying:	23%	Unemployed:	8%
Average starting graduate salary:	£17,437	Average starting non-graduate salary:	£14,948

Linguistics	Research quality/9	Entry standards	Student satisfaction %	Graduate prospects %	Overall rating
1 Cambridge	3.1	519	87	72	100.0
2 Oxford	2.2	517	87	79	99.5
3 Queen Mary, London	4.1	353	86		95.5
4 University College London	3.1	402	83	75	94.3
5 Edinburgh	3.9	451	76	69	93.4
6 Cardiff	4.2	380	83	61	92.7
7 Sheffield	3.3	432	79	62	90.0
=8 Lancaster	3.0	402	80	59	87.0
=8 Essex	3.6	316	75	71	87.0
10 School of Oriental and African Studies	2.0	383	73	81	86.3

Linguistics cont.

	Research quality/9	Entry standards	Student satisfaction %	Graduate prospects %	Overall rating
11 York	3.5	406	74	59	86.1
12 Portsmouth	2.6	266	85	67	85.7
13 Reading	2.2		83	58	83.8
14 Leeds	2.1	389	78	62	83.6
15 Salford	1.8	292	82	64	81.1
16 Manchester	2.6	385	74	56	80.9
17 Newcastle	2.5	423	74	51	80.8
18 Sussex	1.2	396	74	66	79.7
19 Hertfordshire	2.4	263	78	55	77.1
20 King's College London		379	79	57	74.9
=21 West of England	2.4	281	74	49	73.5
=21 York St John		304	82	56	73.5
23 Bangor	1.8	299	79	42	73.0
24 Westminster	1.0	241	75		68.0
25 Ulster	2.5	269	60	50	66.9
26 Brighton	0.7	300	70		66.4

» British Association for Applied Linguistics: **www.baal.org.uk**
» Linguistics Association of Great Britain: **www.lagb.org.uk**

Materials Technology

There had been only 751 applications to study materials technology by the official deadline for courses beginning in 2010, but this represented a rise of 32 per cent. Courses in this category cover three distinct areas: materials science, mining and engineering; textiles technology and printing; and marine technology. The leading universities demand chemistry and sometimes also physics or maths at A level or its equivalent.

The top four in the table are unchanged, with Cambridge retaining the leadership it won from Oxford two years ago. Cambridge achieved the best grades in the 2008 Research Assessment Exercise. Only 5 per cent of the university's research was considered less than world-leading or internationally excellent.

Neither Oxford nor Cambridge had enough students taking materials technology to compile reliable entry scores, so third-placed Imperial College is well ahead of the field on this measure. Other entry scores are tightly bunched, with only three universities averaging more than 350 points and none below 250 points.

Oxford had seen a huge improvement in the employment prospects of its graduates at the end of 2008, when the latest survey was carried out. Every leaver was in a graduate-level job or on a more advanced course six months after completing a degree. Cambridge also did well on this measure but there were mixed scores elsewhere in the table.

The most satisfied students are at Sheffield Hallam, the leading post-1992 university but still not a member of the top ten. Swansea is the only Welsh university in the table and there is no representative from Scotland.

Employment prospects are slightly below average for all subjects: almost two thirds of those completing a degree go straight into graduate-level work or further study and the unemployment rate remained at 7 per cent – now less than the norm for all subjects. Average starting salaries for those who find graduate jobs are also below average, at less than £20,000.

Employed in graduate job:	47%	Employed in non-graduate job and studying:	2%
Employed in graduate job and studying:	3%	Employed in non-graduate job:	29%
Studying:	12%	Unemployed:	7%
Average starting graduate salary:	£19,883	Average starting non-graduate salary:	£15,176

Materials Technology	Research quality/9	Entry standards	Student satisfaction %	Graduate prospects %	Overall rating
1 Cambridge	5.3		85	96	100.0
2 Oxford	4.1		82	100	94.3
3 Imperial College	3.3	460	85	82	93.8
4 Nottingham	4.0		85	81	89.4
5 Sheffield	3.2	344	82	89	86.8
6 Birmingham	3.4	381	77	80	85.5
7 Loughborough	3.6	278	87	75	82.2
8 Exeter	1.7	357	81	88	81.8
9 Queen Mary, London	2.9	324	84	70	80.7
10 Leeds	3.8	346	72	70	80.2
11 Swansea	3.1	254	76	88	77.5
12 Sheffield Hallam	1.8	288	89		77.3
13 Manchester	3.8	368	67	59	76.7
14 De Montfort	1.7	266	79	71	70.9
15 Manchester Metropolitan	1.3	287	68	67	65.7
16 Bolton	1.7		62	55	58.7
17 Huddersfield		290	70	46	57.6
18 University of the Arts London		268	57	57	53.4

» Institute of Materials, Minerals and Mining: **www.iom3.org**
» UK Centre for Materials Education (materials science): **www.materials.ac.uk**

Mathematics

Maths has been enjoying a renaissance as a degree subject since sixth-form numbers began to recover earlier in the decade. Another 10 per cent increase in applications at the start of 2010 brought the total back within sight of 40,000 – about 15,000 more than there were five years ago. The number of places has grown as well – more than 6,900 started degrees in 2009, a rise of 8 per cent on the previous year – but the ratio of applications to places is still well over 5:1.

This shows in the high entry grades. Seven universities had average entry grades of more than 500 points, a number exceeded only in medicine, while another 20 averaged more than 400 points. The totals are boosted by the fact that many candidates for the leading universities

Mathematics cont.

take two A levels in the subject, as well as two or three others.

Oxford remains in first place, but its lead over Cambridge is even slimmer this year. Oxford has the best grades in two of the three of the subjects grouped together as mathematics in the 2008 Research Assessment Exercise, sharing that distinction with Cambridge in applied maths. Ninety per cent of Oxford's work in statistics and operational research was considered world-leading or internationally excellent. Imperial was top for pure mathematics, with Warwick managing the next-best grades, helping the university to stay in third place.

Cambridge still has the highest entry standards, but the most satisfied students are at Plymouth, which only just makes the top 50. Maths attracted high satisfaction levels in most universities in the 2008 National Student Survey, but no other university satisfied over 90 per cent of its undergraduates.

The top employment score was at Kent, in 29th place, where almost nine out of ten of those completing degrees went straight into graduate-level jobs or continued their studies. Nowhere did the proportion of "positive destinations" fall below 50 per cent. Often cited as one of the subjects most likely to lead to a lucrative career, maths is among the top 20 subjects for

Mathematics	Research quality/9 Pure Mathematics	Research quality/9 Applied Mathematics	Research quality/9 Statistics	Entry standards	Student satisfaction %	Graduate prospects %	Overall rating
1 Oxford	4.6	4.3	5.2	568	83	83	100.0
2 Cambridge	4.3	4.3	4.3	576	83	83	98.8
3 Warwick	4.7	4.0	3.9	542	78	85	96.1
4 Bath	3.7	3.6	3.4	498	77	84	91.7
5 St Andrews	1.9	3.9	2.8	489	81	81	91.3
6 Imperial College	5.1	3.5	4.0	532	72	80	90.7
7 Durham	3.4	3.4	2.3	533	78	79	90.6
8 Aberdeen	3.5			356		80	89.0
9 Lancaster	2.5		3.1	442	84	73	88.8
10 University College London	3.4	2.5	2.5	489	77	80	88.3
11 Glasgow	2.9	2.5	2.8	403	86	74	88.2
=12 Loughborough	2.7	2.5		398	84	78	88.0
=12 Bristol	4.2	3.9	3.9	516	70	77	88.0
=14 East Anglia	3.1	2.1		403	88	70	87.8
=14 Nottingham	2.9	3.5	3.6	461	79	73	87.8
=14 Surrey		3.3		441	79	76	87.8
=17 Northumbria		2.2		317	87	83	87.5
=17 Edinburgh	3.9	3.2	2.4	458	76	77	87.5
19 Sheffield	3.0	2.5	2.7	407	81	79	87.4
=20 Leicester	2.6	2.2		387	88	69	86.8
=20 London School of Economics	2.2		2.9	519	72	84	86.8
22 Southampton	2.2	3.3	3.2	460	77	77	86.6
23 Exeter	2.7	2.8		430	83	69	86.4
24 Sussex		2.5		379	78	83	85.9
25 Aston	2.2	2.2	2.2	331	82	83	85.3

26	Heriot-Watt	3.9	3.2	2.4	386	73	83	85.0
=27	Birmingham	2.9	2.3		423	83	67	84.7
=27	King's College London	3.6	3.1		446	75	71	84.7
29	Kent	1.6	2.5	3.5	297	76	88	84.4
30	Strathclyde		2.6	2.3	399	78	76	83.8
31	Newcastle	2.0	3.1	2.7	413	76	75	83.5
32	York	2.5	2.6		451	77	69	83.2
=33	Greenwich			1.6	237	86	82	83.0
=33	Sheffield Hallam	1.4	1.4	1.4	269	87	80	83.0
35	Manchester	3.4	3.7	3.2	451	73	68	82.9
36	Dundee		2.4		384		72	82.7
=37	Cardiff	2.0			418	79	73	82.6
=37	Stirling		2.0		327		81	82.6
39	Leeds	2.7	3.0	3.8	432	73	70	81.7
40	Hertfordshire	2.9			233	80	77	81.6
=41	Portsmouth		3.4		283	85	58	81.4
=41	Keele		3.1		296	80	68	81.4
43	Reading		2.0	1.9	354	83	67	81.3
44	Queen's, Belfast	2.2			365	77	73	80.9
=45	Liverpool	2.4	3.1	1.6	411	76	65	80.5
=45	Royal Holloway	1.1			379	81	73	80.5
=47	Plymouth		1.3	1.5	307	91	56	78.8
=47	Cumbria				324		84	78.8
49	Aberystwyth	2.0			337	78	69	78.7
50	Glamorgan		1.1		275		85	78.4
51	West of England		0.8		298	82	69	76.0
52	Queen Mary, London	2.8	2.5	2.3	328	71	66	75.5
53	City		1.6		319	75	68	75.2
54	Brunel		2.4	2.8	281	74	64	75.0
55	Manchester Metropolitan	2.1			260	77	62	73.9
56	Swansea	2.0			300	77	59	73.8
57	Central Lancashire				280		76	73.3
58	Essex				323		71	72.8
59	Oxford Brookes		0.9		328		67	72.2
60	Brighton		0.9		276		70	72.0
61	Chester		0.9		263	78	65	71.8
62	Coventry	1.0	1.3		286		64	70.6
63	Edge Hill				319		66	70.0
64	Bolton				273		69	69.7
65	Nottingham Trent	1.7	1.7	1.7	262	70	60	68.6
66	Derby				273		62	66.5
67	Kingston				233	81	53	66.4
68	Liverpool John Moores				243		50	59.6

» London Mathematical Society: **www.lms.ac.uk**
» Maths Careers: **www.mathscareers.org.uk**
» Royal Statistical Society: **www.rss.org.uk**

Mathematics cont.

employment. It does better still in the earnings league, with average starting salaries in graduate jobs of more than £23,500.

St Andrews is the top university in Scotland, despite dropping one place this year, while Cardiff, in equal 37th place, has regained the lead in Wales. Northumbria is the highest-placed post-1992 university, at equal 17th, and is joined in the top 40 by Greenwich, Sheffield Hallam and Hertfordshire.

Employed in graduate job:	34%	Employed in non-graduate job and studying:	2%
Employed in graduate job and studying:	14%	Employed in non-graduate job:	17%
Studying:	25%	Unemployed:	8%
Average starting graduate salary:	£23,654	Average starting non-graduate salary:	£15,835

Mechanical Engineering

Cambridge's lead in mechanical engineering is the largest in any subject – and even bigger than last year. Sheffield has moved up to second, but is nearly 12 points behind. Cambridge has by far the highest entry standards and the best research grades. Like last year, only one university has a better employment record and only two outscore it on student satisfaction.

Nottingham Trent, which finishes in a creditable seventh position, had a 100 per cent employment record in the 2008 survey, while Loughborough, in fourth place, has the most satisfied students. Imperial College London hangs on to third place, as the nearest challenger to Cambridge on entry standards and research.

Mechanical Engineering	Research quality/9	Entry standards	Student satisfaction %	Graduate prospects %	Overall rating
1 Cambridge	5.5	567	84	94	100.0
2 Sheffield	4.3	403	81	94	88.3
3 Imperial College	4.4	511	75	87	87.9
4 Loughborough	3.6	376	89	89	87.3
5 Bristol	3.8	468	81	85	87.1
6 Southampton	3.1	431	82	89	84.7
7 Nottingham Trent	3.0		79	100	84.1
8 Nottingham	4.0	391	82	77	83.5
=9 Surrey	3.4	362	83	88	83.4
=9 Cardiff	3.5	385	83	84	83.4
11 Newcastle	3.2	384	80	93	83.3
12 Bath	2.7	464	85	76	82.8
13 Strathclyde	2.7	439	77	90	81.5
14 Birmingham	3.5	392	76	81	80.0
15 Exeter	2.7	353	84	82	79.7
16 Liverpool	3.5	401	72	84	79.4
17 Leeds	3.7	368	74	82	78.9
18 Queen's, Belfast	3.2	364	74	82	77.1
19 University College London	3.2	410	76	68	76.7

20	Aberdeen	3.2	312	77	81	76.6
21	Glasgow	2.4	355	82	76	76.5
22	Edinburgh	3.0	410	69	80	75.7
23	King's College London	2.4	354	79	76	74.9
24	Manchester	3.6	418	64	77	74.7
25	West of England	2.6	315	76	82	74.5
26	Sussex	2.8	311	76		73.7
27	Greenwich	4.2	224	83	54	73.3
28	Lancaster	2.6	363	70	80	72.9
29	Liverpool John Moores	3.3	288	69	79	72.0
30	Northumbria	2.2	249	77	86	71.8
31	Queen Mary, London	2.3	328	83	60	71.5
32	Portsmouth	2.1	251	79	80	71.2
33	Heriot-Watt	2.7	356	68	77	71.1
34	Robert Gordon		304	83	94	71.0
35	Brunel	2.5	343	66	81	70.4
36	Dundee		332	81	90	70.2
37	Harper Adams		294	84	89	70.1
38	Swansea	2.5	279	72	78	70.0
39	Durham		485	78	72	69.9
40	Brighton	2.7	271	78	65	69.8
41	Aston	2.2	329	68	83	69.7
42	Bradford	2.3	246	77	69	68.4
43	Warwick		390	78	80	68.3
44	Hull	1.8	217	73	89	68.2
45	Hertfordshire	2.7	251	69	73	67.1
46	City	2.4	245	73	68	66.7
47	Plymouth	1.3	289	80	61	65.9
48	De Montfort	2.2	183	77		65.6
49	Staffordshire	2.2	222	71	74	65.4
50	Manchester Metropolitan	1.5	215	68	86	64.5
51	Central Lancashire		245	84	69	63.6
52	Sheffield Hallam	1.8	204	69	79	63.5
53	Teesside		262	77	79	63.3
54	Birmingham City		245	74	83	62.2
55	Coventry	1.0	258	72	65	60.8
56	Kingston	1.5	189	71	70	60.6
57	Huddersfield	1.9	245	56	81	60.2
58	Oxford Brookes		283	69	78	59.9
59	Ulster		234	68	71	56.3
60	Sunderland	1.1	210			54.6
61	London South Bank	2.5	211	56	44	52.4
62	Bolton	1.7	159	67	30	49.4
63	Glyndŵr	1.7			35	46.5

» Engineering UK: **www.engineeringuk.com**
» Institution of Mechanical Engineers: **www.imeche.org**

Mechanical Engineering cont.

Cardiff remains the top university in Wales and Strathclyde does the same in Scotland.

The large numbers of mature students upgrading their qualifications in mechanical engineering mean that more than a third of the entrants at post-1992 universities are admitted without A levels or their equivalent. However, only three universities in the table have average entry scores of less than 200 points.

Mechanical engineering now attracts more applicants than any other branch of the wider discipline. Indeed, it was among the 20 most popular subjects at the start of 2010, following a second successive rise in applications of almost 20 per cent. There was a 12 per cent rise in the number of places in 2009, allowing more than 6,000 students to start degrees. Most universities demand maths and another science subject (usually physics) at A level or its equivalent.

The recession did not hit graduate employment prospects as it did other branches of engineering. The subject is among the top dozen for graduate destinations, despite an above-average unemployment rate of 11 per cent in the latest survey. Almost 80 per cent of graduates go straight into graduate-level work or continue their studies. Mechanical engineering is also in the top 10 in the earnings league: starting salaries in graduate jobs averaged almost £24,500 at the end of 2008.

Employed in graduate job:	58%	Employed in non-graduate job and studying:	1%
Employed in graduate job and studying:	7%	Employed in non-graduate job:	10%
Studying:	13%	Unemployed:	11%
Average starting graduate salary:	£24,446	Average starting non-graduate salary:	£16,168

Medicine

The number of universities in the ranking has been growing year by year, as graduates emerge from the medical schools established earlier in the decade, but there are no newcomers this year. No subject has such high entry standards – eight schools average more than 500 points. Cambridge has the highest, its entrants averaging close to five As at A level.

The three leaders remain the same as last year, with Oxford ahead of Cambridge at the top of the table, but there are changes in almost every other position. Edinburgh is still third, but the two London giants move above Aberdeen, while Leeds, which was bottom only four years ago, enters the top 10. Oxford has the highest levels of satisfaction, but Cambridge has the best-qualified entrants and the best results in the RAE. At least 80 per cent of its research was considered world-leading or internationally excellent in all but one of the eight specialisms it submitted work in. In the 2008 RAE universities were able to submit research in up to 12 areas (called units of assessment, UoA). Full details can be seen for UoA 1–9, 12, 14 and 15 at **www.rae.ac.uk/results**.

Only dentistry had more applications for each place than the 9.1 in medicine, and a 13 per cent increase by the deadline for courses beginning in 2010 ensured that this ratio would go higher still. Even though candidates are restricted to four medical schools, the subject was once more among the top five in terms of total applications at the start of 2010.

The designation of new medical schools was expected to ease this pressure, but entry standards have risen again this year, with only two medical schools averaging (marginally) less than 450 points. Most schools demand chemistry and either biology or physics, as well as evidence of commitment to the subject through work experience or voluntary work. Nearly all

Medicine	Research quality/9	Entry standards	Student satisfaction %	Graduate prospects %	Overall rating
1 Oxford	4.5	557	89	100	100.0
2 Cambridge	4.8	577	81	98	99.8
3 Edinburgh	4.2	532	83	100	94.5
4 University College London	4.1	502	78	99	89.5
5 Imperial College	3.9	514	77	100	89.3
6 Aberdeen	3.5	481	83	100	87.6
7 Newcastle	2.8	504	82	100	86.8
8 St Andrews	2.5	491	87	100	86.5
9 Hull-York	3.3	483	80	100	85.7
10 Leeds	2.9	475	81	100	84.0
11 Glasgow	2.9	493	75	100	83.4
12 Southampton	2.9	457	81	99	82.4
13 Leicester	2.3	477	81	100	82.2
14 Dundee	2.4	470	80	100	81.6
15 Birmingham	3.0	503	68	100	81.5
16 Peninsula Medical School	2.4	463	81	100	81.2
17 Brighton & Sussex Medical School	1.8	475	83	100	81.1
=18 Manchester	3.3	482	66	100	80.2
=18 Queen Mary, London	3.5	454	70	99	80.2
20 Liverpool	2.7	504	66	100	80.1
=21 Nottingham	1.9	498	74	99	79.9
=21 King's College London	3.0	473	70	100	79.9
23 Queen's, Belfast	2.4	469	75	100	79.5
24 Sheffield	2.5	478	72	100	79.4
25 East Anglia	2.1	453	81	99	79.2
26 Bristol	3.0	466	65	100	77.2
27 Warwick	2.4		70	100	76.6
28 Keele	1.8	448	77	98	76.4
29 St George's	2.1	440	74	100	75.3
30 Cardiff	2.4	468	62	100	74.3

» British Medical Association: **www.bma.org.uk**
» NHS Careers: **www.nhscareers.nhs.uk**
» Student BMJ: **http://student.bmj.com**

schools interview candidates and several use one of the two specialist aptitude tests (*see* chapter 1).

Employment scores have been dropped as a measure in this year's table (although they are still shown for guidance) to avoid small differences distorting positions in a subject where virtually all graduates become junior doctors or researchers.

Undergraduates have to be prepared to work long hours, particularly towards the end of the course. But student satisfaction is generally high, although it does not reach the levels seen in some subjects. No medical school managed to satisfy 90 per cent of undergraduates, but

Medicine cont.

none dropped below 60 per cent on this measure. Medicine is also second in the earnings league, with average starting salaries of almost £29,000 in 2008.

Employed in graduate job:	90%	Employed in non-graduate job and studying:	0%
Employed in graduate job and studying:	5%	Employed in non-graduate job:	0%
Studying:	5%	Unemployed:	0%
Average starting graduate salary:	£28,913	Average starting non-graduate salary:	*

Middle Eastern and African Studies

Durham has narrowed the gap on Oxford at the head of the table for Middle Eastern and African Studies, but Oxford's research grades and entry standards – both by far the best in the ranking – ensure that it is not toppled. St Andrews enters the table in third place, as one of three universities tying for the best student satisfaction rating. Durham and sixth-placed Exeter are the others.

Like last year, the School of Oriental and African Studies, in London, has the best employment record, as the only institution to have seen over three-quarters of those completing a degree go straight into graduate-level work or continue their studies in 2008. There are no universities in the ranking from Wales or Northern Ireland, and the last post-1992 university has dropped out this year.

The small numbers make for big swings even in the national statistics. Middle Eastern and African studies had by far the highest unemployment rate two years ago, but that figure had dropped to just 4 per cent in last year's *Guide*. Now it is just above average, at 9 per cent, and subject is not far outside the top 20 for "positive destinations". However, while the subjects appeared in the top 10 of the earnings league last year, with average graduate starting salaries close to £23,500, they are back down to the mid-table this time, with an average of less than £21,000.

Middle Eastern and African Studies	Research quality/9	Entry standards	Student satisfaction %	Graduate prospects %	Overall rating
1 Oxford	4.7	514	80	70	100.0
2 Durham	3.4	491	84	75	97.3
3 St Andrews	3.4		84	65	90.0
4 School of Oriental and African Studies	3.6	358	70	77	88.7
5 Edinburgh	3.9	459	63	70	88.2
6 Exeter	2.5	389	84	71	87.9
7 Manchester	2.9	367	72	71	84.1
8 Birmingham	3.3	319	79	58	81.1
9 Leeds		360	75	58	66.8

» African Studies Association of the UK: **www.asauk.net/**
» British Society for Middle Eastern Studies: **www.brismes.ac.uk**
» Egypt Exploration Society: **www.ees.ac.uk**
» Society for the Promotion of Byzantine Studies: **www.byzantium.ac.uk**

Middle Eastern Studies is the larger of the two subjects, in terms of student numbers. Little more than 100 applications had been made for African studies at the start of 2010, but Middle Eastern subjects have been growing in popularity: a 27 per cent increase saw them pass 600 at the same date. The vast majority – all, in the case of African studies – come with A levels or their equivalent. Completion rates are good, and a high proportion graduate with a first or 2:1.

Employed in graduate job:	43%	Employed in non-graduate job and studying:	2%
Employed in graduate job and studying:	8%	Employed in non-graduate job:	18%
Studying:	20%	Unemployed:	9%
Average starting graduate salary:	£20,875	Average starting non-graduate salary:	..

Music

Music has been growing in popularity as a degree subject. A 20 per cent increase in applications at the start of 2010 took the total past 25,000 for the first time, including a growing number seeking places on Foundation degrees. Nine out of ten degree applicants come with A levels and most university departments expect music to be among them, although they may accept a distinction or merit in Grade 8 music exams.

There is considerable variation in the character of courses, from the practical and vocational programmes in conservatoires to the more theoretical degrees in some of the older universities. But entry standards tend to be high throughout: nearly a dozen of the 66 universities in this year's ranking average at least 400 points, while only two slip below 200.

Oxford maintains its lead in the music ranking with the most satisfied students and good scores on the other measures. Manchester has taken second place from Cambridge, but the real progress has been made by Royal Holloway, which leaps from 17th place to fourth, with much-improved scores on three of the four indicators. It already had the best grades in a high-scoring set of research assessments, with no less than 90 per cent of its research considered world-leading or internationally excellent.

Employment scores varied enormously, with a specialist institution again leading the way. The Royal College of Music tops the pile with 97 per cent of graduates going straight into graduate-level work or continuing their studies. The Royal Academy of Music and Middlesex also registered at least 90 per cent "positive destinations", whereas seven universities (compared with only three last year) fell below 50 per cent on this measure.

Birmingham City, where Sir Simon Rattle was the first president of the conservatoire, is the top post-1992 university and the only one in the top 30. As in most subjects, the new universities suffer for their lower entry grades, although selection is more a matter of musical ability as academic achievement.

The 8 per cent unemployment rate in the latest survey remains no worse than the average for all subjects, despite the fact that career prospects for musicians are notoriously uncertain. Music is only just in the bottom half of the top half of the employment table, although nearly 30 per cent of leavers were in non-graduate jobs six months after graduation. Starting salaries are in the bottom ten, averaging little more than £18,000 in graduate jobs.

Employed in graduate job:	34%	Employed in non-graduate job and studying:	3%
Employed in graduate job and studying:	6%	Employed in non-graduate job:	25%
Studying:	24%	Unemployed:	8%
Average starting graduate salary:	£18,111	Average starting non-graduate salary:	£14,516

Music cont.

	Research quality/9	Entry standards	Student satisfaction %	Graduate prospects %	Overall rating
1 Oxford	5.5	463	90	80	100.0
2 Manchester	5.7	427	88	79	97.7
3 Cambridge	5.4	467	80	86	96.6
4 King's College London	5.4	458	81	75	93.5
5 Royal Holloway	6.4	390	82	75	93.2
6 York	5.5	416	79	76	91.4
7 Royal Academy of Music	3.9		81	91	91.1
8 Sheffield	5.3	357	84	72	89.4
9 Southampton	5.6	378	80	73	89.2
10 Birmingham	5.7	420	80	63	89.1
11 Newcastle	4.7	346	83	77	88.3
12 Bristol	3.3	386	82	81	87.9
13 Durham	3.9	427	75	82	87.8
14 Nottingham	4.2	426	81	68	87.6
15 Bangor	3.8	329	81	78	85.1
=16 School of Oriental and African Studies	4.6			69	84.1
=16 Royal Scottish Academy of Music and Drama	2.6			87	84.1
18 Queen's, Belfast	4.4	331	76	75	83.2
19 Cardiff	3.2	388	82	63	82.7
20 Leeds	3.5	365	83	62	82.4
21 Edinburgh	3.4	400		65	81.9
22 Royal College of Music	2.8	329	69	97	81.5
23 Goldsmiths College	4.1	339	72	78	81.4
24 Keele	3.5	277	82	75	81.2
25 Surrey	3.4	400	74	67	80.8
26 Sussex	3.5	331	75	75	80.6
27 Birmingham City	2.6	318	74	86	80.3
28 Aberdeen	2.2	328	83		79.7
=29 Lancaster	4.1	343	71	72	79.5
=29 Royal Northern College of Music	1.9	328	76	84	79.5
31 Huddersfield	3.7	286	80	69	79.4
32 Glasgow	4.3	407	66	63	78.2
33 Hull	1.9	261	82	80	77.9
34 Strathclyde		370		74	76.0
35 Liverpool	2.7	336	77	57	75.3
36 Bath Spa	2.0	302	81	59	74.5
37 City	4.1	292	63	76	74.1
38 East Anglia	1.6	285	81	64	73.7
39 De Montfort	2.9	199	81	67	73.5
40 Coventry	2.3	285	73	67	72.2
41 Glamorgan		293	75	73	70.1
42 Oxford Brookes	2.4	254	72	64	69.9

43	Ulster	1.4	275	70	71	69.2
44	Canterbury Christ Church	2.0	251	75	57	68.0
=45	Hertfordshire	1.2	276	78	51	67.2
=45	Westminster	1.8	285	65	68	67.2
=45	Cumbria		306	67	75	67.2
48	Central Lancashire		275	78	59	66.7
49	Salford	1.3	236	75	58	66.2
50	Plymouth	2.5	231	74	50	66.1
51	Chichester		260	75	62	65.6
52	Brunel	2.7	318	59	59	65.5
53	Brighton	4.3	305	65	33	65.0
54	Edinburgh Napier	0.4	338	63	64	64.9
55	Anglia Ruskin	1.4	266	75	46	64.8
56	Middlesex		150	65	91	63.1
57	Kingston	0.6	224	71	58	62.2
58	Derby		217	74	52	60.3
59	Thames Valley	0.6	204	66	59	59.2
60	Falmouth		229	71	51	59.1
61	Essex		209	74	48	58.5
62	Bournemouth		239	69	46	57.2
63	East London		221	57	65	55.9
64	Buckinghamshire New		211	66	49	55.3
65	York St John		218	68	39	54.0
66	Southampton Solent		237	59	41	50.8

» Incorporated Society of Musicians: **www.ism.org**
» Royal Musical Association: **www.rma.ac.uk**

Nursing

Nursing has been one of the main growth points of higher education since moving towards becoming a graduate profession, and the impending withdrawal of the diploma option has produced another surge in applications. Almost 95,000 applications at the start of 2010 represented growth of no less than 73 per cent, making nursing the most popular degree choice of all. There were another 64,000 applications for the last diplomas and 5,000 for Foundation degrees – by far the largest number in any subject at that level, too. It is all a far cry from 2008, when well-publicised stories of nurses finishing their training to face the dole led to a decline in the demand for places.

The number of places has expanded significantly in recent years, with a 20 per cent increase in 2009. But there is no prospect of universities keeping pace with such massive growth in demand in 2010, so an already competitive selection process – there were well over five applications to the place in 2009 – is certain to tighten further. However, only York, Edinburgh, Southampton and Nottingham average more than 350 points for A levels and Highers. Entry scores are more closely bunched than in many tables, so just three have averages below 200 points.

York tops this year's table, perhaps benefiting in the scoring system for not having enough

Nursing cont.

students to compile reliable scores for student satisfaction or graduate destinations. Second-placed Edinburgh, last year's leader, has much the highest entry grades and the most satisfied students. Southampton stays third.

Fourth place is shared by Manchester, which produced the best grades in the 2008 Research Assessment Exercise, with 85 per cent of its submission considered world-leading or internationally excellent, and Sheffield, which is one of four universities with 100 per cent employment records. The others are Surrey, Manchester Metropolitan and the joint school at Kingston and St George's, in south London. The subject is in the top three for employment, with only 1 per cent of 2008 graduates unemployed at the end of the year. However, it is not in the top 20 for starting salaries, which average less than £21,500 in graduate-level jobs.

Glasgow Caledonian is the highest-placed new university in a ranking where less than a third of the institutions are pre-1992 foundations. Worcester, Cumbria, Thames Valley and Central Lancashire join it in the top 20. Cardiff is the top university in Wales, Edinburgh is top in Scotland, while Ulster outperforms Queen's, Belfast in Northern Ireland.

Almost two-thirds of the students arrive without A levels, many of them upgrading other health-related qualifications. A quarter of those who join pre-registration programmes drop out, but the wastage rate is nearer 10 per cent thereafter.

Employed in graduate job:	90%	Employed in non-graduate job and studying:		0%
Employed in graduate job and studying:	5%	Employed in non-graduate job:		2%
Studying:	1%	Unemployed:		1%
Average starting graduate salary:	£21,459	Average starting non-graduate salary:		£16,714

Nursing	Research quality/9	Entry standards	Student satisfaction %	Graduate prospects %	Overall rating
1 York	4.5	366			100.0
2 Edinburgh	4.0	418	90	98	99.6
3 Southampton	5.4	365	76	98	95.9
=4 Manchester	5.7	339	75	94	93.4
=4 Sheffield	2.8		84	100	93.4
=6 Glasgow	3.0	335	85	97	93.3
=6 Ulster	5.0	255	82	98	93.3
8 Nottingham	3.2	359	77	96	91.7
9 Leeds	3.6	330	74	98	91.4
10 Liverpool	2.2	323	88	94	90.8
11 Surrey	0.7	336	84	100	90.6
12 East Anglia	2.1	301	81	98	89.8
13 Glasgow Caledonian	3.0	303	87	91	89.5
14 Cardiff	2.6	294	77	99	89.4
15 Bradford	2.1	312	78	98	89.0
16 Worcester		349	82	98	88.4
17 Cumbria		339	84	97	88.2
18 Thames Valley	2.2		77	98	88.0
19 King's College London	2.5	321	71	97	87.7

20	Central Lancashire	2.5	281	77	96	87.6
21	Queen's, Belfast	2.1	265	78	98	87.3
22	Glamorgan	2.1	254	83	95	87.0
23	Kingston/St George's	2.5	271	69	100	86.9
=24	Salford	2.3	264	81	95	86.8
=24	Swansea	2.0	278	77	97	86.8
26	Northumbria	2.8	317	85	87	86.6
27	De Montfort	1.9	309	72	97	86.4
28	Teesside		285	85	97	86.2
=29	Oxford Brookes		312	78	97	85.4
=29	Queen Margaret Edinburgh		314		96	85.4
31	Hull		305	74	99	85.2
32	Brighton	0.9	259	78	98	85.1
33	Manchester Metropolitan	1.3	238	74	100	85.0
=34	Bangor		266	79	99	84.9
=34	Hertfordshire	3.5	244	74	93	84.9
36	Edinburgh Napier	1.9	243	77	96	84.6
37	Edge Hill	1.6	237	83	93	84.3
38	Anglia Ruskin		260	81	96	83.9
=39	West of England	1.9	236	70	98	83.7
=39	Greenwich	1.6	223	86	91	83.7
41	Robert Gordon		289	78	95	83.6
42	Canterbury Christ Church		268	75	99	83.5
43	Plymouth	1.9	285	69	95	83.4
44	Keele		249	87	93	83.3
=45	Staffordshire		266	79	95	83.1
=45	Bedfordshire		244	78	98	83.1
47	Stirling	3.1	126	76	98	83.0
48	Bournemouth	2.2	280	72	91	82.8
49	Birmingham		334	81	89	82.7
=50	Dundee	2.5	174	74	97	82.6
=50	Chester	0.9	276	67	98	82.6
52	Birmingham City		256	78	96	82.5
53	Sheffield Hallam	1.9	281	60	98	82.3
54	City	4.1	269	57	93	81.9
55	Glyndŵr	1.1	247		95	81.8
=56	Coventry		295	77	92	81.6
=56	London South Bank	1.8	186	77	94	81.6
58	Middlesex	1.8		80	85	79.6
59	Liverpool John Moores	1.9	228	76	87	79.3
60	Leeds Metropolitan		261	74	90	78.3
61	Abertay		224		90	75.4
62	Northampton		235	66	88	73.9

» NHS Careers: **www.nhscareers.nhs.uk**
» The Royal British Nurses' Association: **www.r-bna.com**
» Royal College of Nursing: **www.rcn.org.uk**

Other Subjects Allied to Medicine

The "allied to medicine" category covers audiology, complementary therapies, counselling, health services management, health sciences, nutrition, occupational therapy, optometry, ophthalmology, orthoptics, osteopathy, physiotherapy, podiatry, radiography and speech therapy. Traditional universities dominate the top 10, but big names such as Bristol and Birmingham find themselves outside the top 30.

Aston remains at the top of the table, while Cardiff has overtaken Leeds to become the nearest challenger. Cambridge, in sixth place, has by far the highest entry grades – nearly 100 points ahead of Imperial College – but, like a number of universities in the ranking, did not enter the 2008 Research Assessment Exercise in this category. Third-placed Leeds and University College London, which is in a tie for tenth place, share the best of a mediocre set of research grades. Leeds also has the best employment score, having seen all its leavers go straight into graduate-level work or further study in 2008.

Stiff competition for places in subjects such as optometry and physiotherapy has been pushing up entry grades, with nine universities averaging at least 400 points on the UCAS tariff, while only one (compared with four last year) dropped below 200 in the latest survey. The choice of specialism also affects graduate employment rates, which range from full employment in graduate-level jobs to less than half that rate at some universities around the bottom of the table.

The table is more mixed than most in terms of the performance of new and old universities. Glasgow Caledonian is the highest-placed post-1992 institution, while Robert Gordon, Oxford Brookes, Portsmouth and the West of England all join it in the top 20. Across the whole range of subjects, almost half of the students arrive without A levels.

Applications were up by almost a quarter at the start of 2010, approaching 33,000. The subjects are now among the top 20 most popular degree choices. They have also shot up the employment table this year, with more than 80 per cent going straight into graduate jobs or continuing their studies and only 5 per cent unemployed. This represents seventh place for "positive destinations", although the subjects are still not in the top 30 for starting salaries.

Employed in graduate job:	70%	Employed in non-graduate job and studying:	1%
Employed in graduate job and studying:	6%	Employed in non-graduate job:	11%
Studying:	7%	Unemployed:	5%
Average starting graduate salary:	£20,260	Average starting non-graduate salary:	£15,477

Other Subjects Allied to Medicine	Research quality/9	Entry standards	Student satisfaction %	Graduate prospects %	Overall rating
1 Aston	2.8	401	86	98	100.0
2 Cardiff	3.2	386	85	93	98.9
3 Leeds	3.6	342	81	100	97.2
4 Lancaster	3.4	396	82	84	95.9
5 Newcastle	3.0	393	88	75	95.7
6 Cambridge		578	85	82	95.3
=7 Manchester	3.1	408	74	93	93.7
=7 Sheffield	3.0	414	84	72	93.7

9	Exeter	3.1	314	80	93	92.1
=10	Nottingham	2.2	400	78	88	91.4
=10	King's College London	1.8	381	84	84	91.4
=10	University College London	3.6	403	73	80	91.4
13	Glasgow Caledonian	3.0	377	76	85	91.3
=14	Bradford	1.9	370	81	91	91.2
=14	Keele	2.6	314	88	79	91.2
16	Robert Gordon	1.4	366	82	96	90.7
17	West of England	3.1	283	83	86	90.1
18	Oxford Brookes	1.9	325	87	83	89.9
=19	Liverpool	2.2	346	76	95	89.4
=19	Portsmouth	2.9	306	75	97	89.4
21	Strathclyde	3.0	407	72	79	89.1
22	Hull	3.3	310	78	76	87.2
23	Glamorgan	0.1	348	83	99	86.9
24	Imperial College		482	75	88	86.7
25	Durham		395	87	79	86.1
=26	East Anglia	0.8	363	81	87	86.0
=26	City	2.0	324	73	96	86.0
28	Nottingham Trent	3.1	280	74	88	85.9
29	Southampton	1.1	372	77	87	85.7
30	Swansea	3.2	327	77	70	85.5
31	Bournemouth		323	84	96	85.1
32	Anglia Ruskin	1.2	309	82	86	84.5
33	Ulster	3.1	332	70	78	84.2
34	Kent	1.8	282	87	70	83.8
35	Reading		367	84	80	83.7
36	Northumbria	1.6	330	76	83	83.2
37	Hertfordshire	2.7	265	75	82	83.1
38	Birmingham		420	81	75	83.0
39	Coventry	0.9	292	79	84	80.8
=40	Cumbria	0.1	292	81	89	80.6
=40	Teesside	1.0	274	81	81	80.6
=40	Bangor		271	81	94	80.6
43	Central Lancashire	1.7	296	82	66	80.4
44	Brighton	0.9	306	77	85	80.3
45	Salford	1.8	276	76	80	80.2
46	Sheffield Hallam	1.2	320	73	85	80.1
47	Manchester Metropolitan	1.6	340	74	69	79.2
48	Brunel	1.6	325	70	78	78.7
49	Queen Margaret Edinburgh	0.5	335		80	78.5
50	De Montfort	1.5	255	77	79	78.4
51	York St John	0.3	282	80	80	77.9
52	Kingston	1.5		79	64	77.8
53	Birmingham City		285	77	89	77.7
=54	London South Bank		234	79	94	77.3
=54	St George's		315	73	90	77.3

Other Subjects Allied to Medicine cont.

	Research quality/9	Entry standards	Student satisfaction %	Graduate prospects %	Overall rating
56 Bedfordshire		228	78	91	75.9
57 Essex		282	78	78	75.2
58 Canterbury Christ Church	0.4	240	73	90	75.1
59 Plymouth	0.5	316	68	85	75.0
60 Huddersfield		275	81	71	74.9
61 Westminster	2.1	249	64	84	74.8
62 Greenwich		288	87	53	74.1
63 Northampton	0.9	270	63	93	73.8
64 Lincoln	0.5	268	75	75	73.7
65 UWIC, Cardiff	1.1	308	64	80	73.3
66 Leeds Metropolitan	0.6	289	68	81	73.2
67 Marjon, Plymouth		338	70	72	72.5
68 Edinburgh Napier	1.0		77	60	72.4
69 St Mary's College		291	79	59	71.8
70 Middlesex	1.6	215	64	85	71.3
=71 Derby		255	69	81	70.2
=71 East London	1.9	223	65	73	70.2
73 Chester	0.8	229	77	57	69.4
74 Bristol		316	57	89	69.2
75 Liverpool John Moores	1.5	257	73	49	69.0
76 Abertay	0.7	254		58	66.3
77 Sunderland	0.7	192	81	40	65.1
78 University College Birmingham		209	76	56	64.8
79 Roehampton	1.0	202	77	32	61.9

» Association of Health Professions in Ophthalmology: www.ahpo.org
» British Association and College of Occupational Therapy: www.cot.org.uk
» British Society of Audiology: www.thebsa.org.uk
» Chartered Society of Physiotherapy: www.csp.org.uk
» General Chiropractic Council: www.gcc-uk.org
» General Osteopathic Council: www.osteopathy.org.uk
» General Optical Council: www.optical.org
» Health Professions Council: www.hpc-uk.org
» NHS Careers: www.nhscareers.nhs.uk
» Royal College of Radiologists: www.rcr.ac.uk
» Royal College of Speech and Language Therapists: www.rcslt.org
» Society of Chiropodists and Podiatrists: www.feetforlife.org
» Society of Radiographers: www.sor.org

Pharmacology and Pharmacy

Pharmacology and pharmacy have been among the big successes of higher education in recent years. The numbers of applications and places have grown significantly and the subjects are in the top four for "positive destinations". There were still six applications for every place in 2009, despite an increase of more than 5 per cent in places for first-year students, and the start of 2010 saw further growth of 15 per cent in the demand for places. Only 3 per cent of graduates were unemployed at the end of 2008, when 91 per cent were already in graduate-level jobs or continuing their studies.

Nottingham has taken over top position from Edinburgh this year, as one of eight universities with 100 per cent employment records. The others are East Anglia, Queen's, Belfast, Aston, Kent, Robert Gordon, Brighton and the University of London's School of Pharmacy. The recession seems to have had no impact on graduates' employment prospects since these were better figures than in 2007. No university saw fewer than 70 per cent of leavers go on to "positive destinations".

Second-placed Edinburgh boasts the top research score, while East Anglia, one place lower, has the most satisfied students. University College London, in ninth place, has the highest-qualified entrants. Even without separate scores for Edinburgh and Cambridge, a third of the universities in the table average more than 400 points and none less than 200.

Cardiff, in seventh place, is again the only representative of Wales in a table that contains six more institutions than there were three years ago. Robert Gordon is the highest-placed post-1992 university and is joined by Huddersfield in the top 20.

Departments in England are evenly split between those specialising in pharmacy and pharmacology. Only four cover both. Since 1997, pharmacy degrees have been converted to the four-year MPharm, whereas pharmacology is available either as a three-year BSc or as an extended course. Surprisingly, given graduates' success in the labour market, the subjects are not high in the earnings league: average starting salaries below £19,500 for graduate-level jobs place them 41st out of the 62 subjects.

Employed in graduate job:	63%	Employed in non-graduate job and studying:	1%
Employed in graduate job and studying:	16%	Employed in non-graduate job:	5%
Studying:	12%	Unemployed:	3%
Average starting graduate salary:	£19,453	Average starting non-graduate salary:	£16,411

Pharmacology and Pharmacy	Research quality/9	Entry standards	Student satisfaction %	Graduate prospects %	Overall rating
1 Nottingham	4.7	441	79	100	100.0
2 Edinburgh	5.0		90	77	99.7
3 East Anglia	2.9	383	92	100	99.4
4 Queen's, Belfast	3.0	418	87	100	99.0
=5 Manchester	4.2	421	79	95	96.3
=5 Bath	3.3	408	83	97	96.3
7 Cardiff	2.9	403	85	98	96.1
8 Aston	2.8	418	82	100	95.3
9 University College London	3.4	444	80	85	93.5
10 Kent	1.8	343	89	100	93.2
11 Strathclyde	2.9	426	79	91	92.3
12 Cambridge	3.3		85	82	92.0
13 School of Pharmacy	3.7	382	72	100	90.9

Pharmacology and Pharmacy cont.

	Research quality/9	Entry standards	Student satisfaction %	Graduate prospects %	Overall rating
14 Glasgow	2.9	385	83	82	90.5
15 Robert Gordon		423	85	100	90.0
16 King's College London	2.9	396	78	90	89.8
17 Leeds	3.1	362	87	75	89.7
18 Bradford	2.9	338	78	90	87.9
19 Liverpool	3.0	379	83	72	87.8
20 Huddersfield	1.3	354	86		87.7
21 Reading	2.3	349	81		87.3
22 Brighton	2.1	359	74	100	87.0
23 Bristol	2.9	401	78	75	86.5
=24 De Montfort	2.1	290	80	95	85.8
=24 Liverpool John Moores	1.5	332	79	97	85.8
26 Newcastle		419	83	88	85.6
27 Portsmouth	2.9	281	78	92	85.5
28 Aberdeen		366	86	89	85.0
29 Sunderland	0.9	320	81	96	84.7
30 Hertfordshire	1.8	299	88	74	84.3
31 Greenwich	1.4	253	90	77	83.0
32 Nottingham Trent	3.1	219	76		78.9
33 Kingston	1.5	249	80	74	77.0

» Association of Pharmacy Technicians UK: **www.aptuk.org**
» British Pharmacological Society: **www.bps.ac.uk**
» Royal Pharmaceutical Society of Great Britain: **www.rpsgb.org.uk**

Philosophy

Many expected philosophy to struggle in the era of top-up fees, with perceptions of employability dominating subject choices. But there were still approaching six applications to the place in 2009 – one of the highest ratios in the arts and social sciences – and the demand for places had grown by another 9 per cent at the start of 2010, building on 16 per cent growth a year earlier. Entry standards are correspondingly high, with a third of the 47 universities in the ranking averaging at least 400 points on the UCAS tariff.

Oxford and Cambridge have swapped places at the top of the philosophy table. Like the third-placed London School of Economics, which has the best employment record in the table, both have averages that are the equivalent of four As at A level and another at AS level. Employment scores are noticeably lower than in last year's *Guide*, when 96 per cent of philosophers at the LSE went straight into graduate-level jobs or postgraduate courses, compared with 86 per cent in the latest survey.

The best of a generally high set of scores in the 2009 National Student Survey came at Aberdeen, the only university where more than nine out of ten undergraduates were satisfied with their course. Only Manchester failed to satisfy at least 70 per cent of its students.

University College London, in fifth place, produced the best results in the 2008 Research Assessment Exercise, when three-quarters of its submission was rated world-leading or internationally excellent. St Andrews was close behind on research and remains the top university in Scotland, a place above UCL in the UK. Cardiff remains top in Wales, while University College Plymouth (Marjon) records the highest finish among post-1992 institutions.

Philosophy is among the bottom 20 subjects in the employment table, with nearly a third of leavers starting their working life in non-graduate jobs. The subject has dropped out of the top 20 for starting salaries, but is only just in the bottom half of the table, with an average of nearly £20,000 for graduate-level work.

Relatively few philosophy undergraduates studied the subject at A level – indeed, Bristol warns that even an A in the subject is "not necessarily evidence of aptitude for philosophy at university". Degrees can require more mathematical skills than many candidates expect, especially when there is an emphasis on logic in the syllabus.

Employed in graduate job:	29%
Employed in graduate job and studying:	4%
Studying:	24%
Average starting graduate salary:	£19,968
Employed in non-graduate job and studying:	4%
Employed in non-graduate job:	28%
Unemployed:	10%
Average starting non-graduate salary:	£15,052

Philosophy	Research quality/9	Entry standards	Student satisfaction %	Graduate prospects %	Overall rating
1 Oxford	4.4	547	87	83	100.0
2 Cambridge	4.1	530	83	64	92.0
3 London School of Economics	4.4	530	70	86	90.8
4 St Andrews	4.9	461	85	58	90.6
5 University College London	5.2	479	79	63	90.1
6 King's College London	4.6	435	82	66	89.3
7 Durham	2.9	467	79	78	88.3
8 Newcastle	2.8	359	87	76	88.0
9 Sheffield	4.5	422	82	63	87.9
10 Bristol	4.1	479	75	70	86.7
11 York	3.0	438	81	67	85.5
12 Exeter	3.3	409	85	57	84.8
=13 Essex	3.7	324	87	58	84.2
=13 Warwick	3.0	474	77	66	84.2
15 Stirling	3.9	304	88	53	83.2
16 Dundee	2.5	341	84	67	82.7
17 Sussex	2.8	389	84	57	82.1
18 Aberdeen	1.5	329	91	56	80.7
19 Glasgow	2.4	391	83	56	80.6
=20 Nottingham	3.7	402	72	65	80.4
=20 Leeds	3.5	400	77	57	80.4
22 Southampton	2.1	412	81	56	79.5
23 Edinburgh	3.5	456	70	57	78.7

Philosophy cont.

	Research quality/9	Entry standards	Student satisfaction %	Graduate prospects %	Overall rating
24 East Anglia	1.9	360	81	61	78.6
25 Marjon, Plymouth	1.1		79	71	78.2
=26 Cardiff	1.8	382	84	50	77.6
=26 Reading	4.3	340	77	47	77.6
28 Lancaster	2.4	375	80	51	76.7
29 Hull	1.8	302	85	50	76.0
30 Liverpool	1.4	377	76	63	75.5
31 Kent	2.2	314	76	62	75.3
32 Birmingham	2.1	373	75	54	74.1
33 West of England	0.8	295	83	57	73.3
34 Heythrop College	0.7	363	74	66	72.9
35 Manchester	2.5	428	65	58	72.7
36 Brighton	4.3	250	78	36	72.2
37 Greenwich		281	87	50	72.1
38 Hertfordshire	1.6	236	82	51	71.5
39 Staffordshire	1.2	249	83	50	71.1
40 Queen's, Belfast	2.5	350	74	42	70.8
41 Keele	2.0	278	74	55	70.5
42 Manchester Metropolitan	2.1	266	81	41	70.3
43 Central Lancashire		255	84	55	70.2
44 Oxford Brookes	0.8	310	78	48	69.1
45 Lampeter (Trinity Saint David)	0.9		78	38	65.0
46 Roehampton		252	76	40	62.2
47 Newport		232	78	30	60.0

» British Philosophical Association: **www.bpa.ac.uk**
» Philosophical Society of England:
   http://atschool.eduweb.co.uk/cite/staff/philosopher/philsocindex.htm
» Royal Institute of Philosophy: **www.royalinstitutephilosophy.org**

Physics and Astronomy

There has been constant concern about the state of physics in recent years, with sixth-form numbers dropping and university departments closing. One more university has dropped out of the ranking this year. But 7 per cent more undergraduates started courses in 2009 than in the previous year and applications were up by almost 20 per cent at the start of 2010. Approaching 20,000 candidates were seeking places then and with at least five (generally well-qualified) candidates for every place, competition was bound to be stiff.

Indeed, physics is one of the most competitive tables, with high scores on all the indicators among the leading universities. Oxford, for example, improved its scores on two measures and only declined marginally on one, yet dropped three places to sixth. Cambridge retained its lead at the top, but there were substantial changes throughout the rest of the table. Birmingham jumped five places to become Cambridge's nearest challenger, and St Andrews did the same to take third place. Further down the table, Kent and Surrey moved into the top 20 with rises of 18 and 14 places respectively.

Cambridge has the highest entry standards but, once again, the other top scores are spread around the table. Surrey and Hull share the best employment record in a subject where almost half of all graduates continue their studies, either full or part-time. Physics has moved up the employment table this year and is only just outside the top ten – all but three of the universities in the ranking saw at least 70 per cent of those completing degrees go straight into graduate-level jobs or further study.

Physics has also produced consistently high scores in the National Student Survey, with every university satisfying at least 70 per cent of undergraduates – and most more than 80 per cent – in the 2009 results. Kent achieved one of the best satisfaction scores in any subject. By contrast, physics was one of the lowest-scoring subjects in the 2008 Research Assessment Exercise, when only Lancaster had more than 20 per cent of its work rated world-leading.

Both physics and astronomy command high entry grades: five of the top ten average at least 500 points for A levels and Highers. Only one university outside the bottom seven averages less than 300 points, leaving the rest tightly bunched. Most universities demand both physics and maths at A level, as well as good grades overall.

Cardiff is the leading university in Wales. Nottingham Trent and Hertfordshire are the only post-1992 universities left in the table, both moving out of the bottom five this year. The profile of undergraduates is among the most traditional: only one in five is female and a similar proportion arrives without A levels or their equivalent. About 5 per cent transfer to other courses or drop out, usually at the end of the first year, but over half of those who remain get firsts or 2:1s. The subjects are in the top 20 for starting salaries, averaging more than £23,000 in graduate-level jobs.

Employed in graduate job:	31%	Employed in non-graduate job and studying:	1%
Employed in graduate job and studying:	8%	Employed in non-graduate job:	11%
Studying:	40%	Unemployed:	9%
Average starting graduate salary:	£23,275	Average starting non-graduate salary:	£16,203

Physics and Astronomy	Research quality/9	Entry standards	Student satisfaction %	Graduate prospects %	Overall rating
1 Cambridge	3.8	578	85	82	100.0
2 Birmingham	3.3	452	92	79	97.1
3 St Andrews	3.8	500	83	81	96.6
=4 Durham	3.4	542	83	82	96.1
=4 Glasgow	3.4	402	88	86	96.1
6 Oxford	3.2	573	80	84	95.4
7 Sheffield	3.4	392	89	79	94.2
8 Manchester	3.2	483	88	75	94.0
9 Imperial College	3.4	531	76	86	93.6
10 Lancaster	3.9	394	81	82	93.4
11 Nottingham	3.8	436	81	77	92.6
12 Southampton	3.0	414	85	81	92.0

Physics and Astronomy cont.

	Research quality/9	Entry standards	Student satisfaction %	Graduate prospects %	Overall rating
13 Warwick	2.9	494	83	78	91.6
14 Exeter	3.1	404	88	74	91.5
15 Sussex	3.1	384	85	77	90.4
16 Kent	2.8	280	95	72	90.2
17 Surrey	2.6	360	83	88	90.1
18 Edinburgh	3.5	454	78	76	89.6
19 Queen's, Belfast	2.5	405	85	81	89.4
=20 York	2.9	387	87	71	89.3
=20 Bath	3.6	419	78	76	89.3
22 Bristol	3.2	482	78	75	89.2
23 Royal Holloway	2.6	384	88	73	88.7
24 Leeds	2.8	424	82	77	88.6
25 Liverpool	3.2	409	81	73	88.5
26 Hull	2.3	259	89	88	88.4
27 University College London	3.4	455	74	77	87.9
28 Aberdeen	3.2	368	81	71	86.7
29 Loughborough	2.8	319	86	72	86.4
30 Leicester	2.9	371	79	77	86.0
31 Heriot-Watt	3.0	362	81	71	85.5
32 Strathclyde	2.0	329	86	77	84.4
33 Cardiff	2.1	383	82	76	83.8
34 King's College London	2.6	405	77	73	83.1
35 Nottingham Trent	3.0	232	76	80	82.2
36 Hertfordshire	2.9	258		72	82.0
37 Salford	2.5	194	81	76	80.3
38 Swansea	2.6	299	76	72	79.7
39 Keele	1.9	256	83	62	76.1
40 Aberystwyth	1.4	295	81	65	74.6
41 Queen Mary, London	2.8	288	81	37	73.1

» British Astronomical Association: **http://britastro.org**
» Institute of Physics: **www.iop.org**

Politics

Politics has been enjoying a boom as a degree subject. Having grown substantially earlier in the decade, applications rose by more than double the average for all subjects in 2009 and saw another 18 per cent increase at the start of 2010. With more than five applications for every place, entry scores have been rising. Eighteen universities, almost twice as many as three years ago, average over 400 points and only one less than 200 points.

Oxford holds onto top place with the highest entry grades and – jointly with University College London – the best graduate employment prospects. Sheffield moves up to second, overtaking St Andrews, as one of the two universities with the best results in the 2008 Research Assessment Exercise. The other was fifth-placed Essex, which also had three-quarters of its research rated world-leading or internationally excellent.

The most satisfied students are at Leicester, which has moved into the top 20 as a result. Scores in politics were generally high in the 2009 National Student Survey: only six of the 70 universities failed to satisfy at least 70 per cent of their final-year undergraduates. Aberystwyth is the top university in Wales, while Brighton is the highest-placed post-1992 university, followed closely by Portsmouth. Neither makes the top 30 this year.

Employment scores are variable. At almost a dozen universities, fewer than half of the politics graduates went straight into graduate-level jobs or continued their studies. Yet the subject has climbed out of the bottom 20 for job prospects this year with an unemployment rate that is only just above average, at 9 per cent. Politics is comfortably in the top half of the earnings league, however, with starting salaries close to £21,500 for those who do find graduate-level employment.

Employed in graduate job:	34%	Employed in non-graduate job and studying:	3%
Employed in graduate job and studying:	4%	Employed in non-graduate job:	28%
Studying:	77%	Unemployed:	9%
Average starting graduate salary:	£21,446	Average starting non-graduate salary:	£15,279

Politics	Research quality/9	Entry standards	Student satisfaction %	Graduate prospects %	Overall rating
1 Oxford	4.2	538	85	86	100.0
2 Sheffield	5.2	437	82	72	94.4
3 Cambridge	3.0	502	86	75	93.1
4 St Andrews	2.3	456	82	81	88.9
5 Essex	5.2	338	82	64	88.5
=6 University College London	3.4	423	75	86	88.4
=6 London School of Economics	3.9	490	71	80	88.4
8 Warwick	3.3	476	79	72	88.3
9 Exeter	3.2	412	84	68	87.7
10 King's College London	2.6	433	78	80	86.5
11 School of Oriental and African Studies	3.0	421	75	82	86.2
12 Durham	2.7	459	75	76	85.0
13 York	2.6	461	78	70	84.8
14 Bath	2.4	438	76	75	83.9
15 Aberystwyth	4.6	318	81	56	83.8
16 Sussex	3.0	367	79	67	82.7
17 Hull	2.1	335	83	73	82.4
18 Cardiff	2.6	398	78	68	82.1
19 Nottingham	2.8	416	73	72	81.8
20 Leicester	1.3	346	88	66	81.5
21 Queen Mary, London	2.1	370	79	73	81.4
22 Newcastle	2.5	386	79	66	81.2
23 Glasgow	2.6	407	80	56	80.4

Politics cont.

	Research quality/9	Entry standards	Student satisfaction %	Graduate prospects %	Overall rating
=24 Loughborough	2.2	326	86	56	80.0
=24 Bradford	2.7	291	78	73	80.0
26 Birmingham	2.1	390	81	60	79.9
27 East Anglia	1.9	337	83	58	78.4
28 Surrey	1.7	326	72	85	78.3
29 Dundee	1.9	330	87	49	78.1
30 Edinburgh	2.5	436	68	68	77.7
31 Southampton	1.6	399	76	65	77.5
32 Brighton	4.3	273	71		76.9
33 Lancaster	1.4	378	78	62	76.6
34 Portsmouth	2.6	268	85	49	76.5
=35 Manchester	3.0	422	64	66	76.3
=35 Aberdeen	1.6	337	80	59	76.3
37 Bristol	2.2	427	64	74	75.7
38 Leeds	1.3	397	74	65	75.5
39 Liverpool	1.0	368	76	68	75.4
=40 Kent	1.5	295	77	68	75.1
=40 Reading	2.0	316	75	63	75.1
42 Keele	2.0	299	76	63	74.5
43 Queen's, Belfast	2.4	377	71	57	74.4
44 Strathclyde	1.4	359	79	53	74.3
45 Northumbria	1.8	272	78	58	73.2
=46 Royal Holloway	1.7	366	68	68	73.0
=46 Aston	1.4	357	75	57	73.0
48 Swansea	1.5	293	78	55	72.1
49 Brunel	1.6	307	73	62	71.9
50 De Montfort	1.4	182	83	58	71.5
51 Plymouth	2.2	250	79	48	71.4
52 Oxford Brookes	1.2	319	73	61	71.1
53 Stirling	1.2	306	77	52	70.6
54 Nottingham Trent		234	81	62	69.2
55 Coventry	1.1	303	78	46	69.1
56 Goldsmiths College	2.0	308	67	58	69.0
57 Ulster	2.0	248	76	48	68.8
58 West of England	0.8	250	78	50	67.6
59 Leeds Metropolitan		223	77	63	67.1
60 Salford	1.6	249	74	48	67.0
61 Huddersfield	0.3	272	76	55	66.7
62 Birmingham City	1.6	251	73	47	66.1
63 Kingston	1.3	215	73	56	66.0
64 Lincoln	1.2	250	75	47	65.8
65 City		277	68	67	65.0
66 Manchester Metropolitan	1.1	254	73	47	64.9

67 Westminster	1.3	236	73	43	63.5
68 UWIC, Cardiff		243	75	50	63.3
69 Liverpool John Moores		228	73	50	61.8
70 Greenwich	0.4	241	71	40	59.6

» Political Studies Association: **www.psa.ac.uk**
» Study Politics: **www.studypolitics.org**

Psychology

Only nursing attracted more applications than psychology at the start of 2010. Another increase of almost 20 per cent in the demand for places took the number of applications over 87,000. The subject's popularity has continued to rise in spite of its relatively poor record in the graduate employment market: it is in the bottom ten for the proportion of graduates with "positive destinations" and only two places higher for average starting salaries in graduate-level jobs.

Most undergraduate programmes are accredited by the British Psychological Society, which ensures that key topics are covered, but the clinical and biological content of courses still varies considerably. Some universities require maths and/or biology A levels among an average of at least three Bs, but others are much less demanding. The contrast is obvious in the ranking, with 22 universities averaging more than 400 points at entry and several not much more than 200 points. There was only a small increase in the number of first-year places for psychology in 2009, which accounts for the higher entry standards then. But the subject has since been reclassified for funding purposes as a science, making it likely that there will be more places at least in 2010.

Cambridge still leads Oxford at the top of the table, although the gap has narrowed since last year. Having tied for the highest entry scores then, the two ancient rivals are within a point of each other this year. Cambridge leads the table on all the other measures. It was the only university to see eight out of ten psychologists go straight into graduate-level work or further study in 2008 and the only one to satisfy more than 85 per cent of undergraduates. Cambridge also registered the top performance in the 2008 Research Assessment Exercise, when 80 per cent of its work was considered world-leading or internationally excellent.

Elsewhere in the table, Sheffield, Royal Holloway and Durham have all made considerable progress to break into the top ten. Glasgow remains the top university in Scotland and Cardiff the same in Wales. Northumbria is again the only post-1992 university in the top 30.

A majority of graduates at no fewer than 34 universities were in low-level employment or unemployed six months after completing their degrees in 2008, but even this was one fewer than in the previous year. Psychology is one of the biggest tables in the *Guide*, but this still represented a third of the ranking.

Employed in graduate job:	30%	Employed in non-graduate job and studying:	5%
Employed in graduate job and studying:	5%	Employed in non-graduate job:	37%
Studying:	16%	Unemployed:	7%
Average starting graduate salary:	£18,384	Average starting non-graduate salary:	£14,328

Psychology

	Research quality/9	Entry standards	Student satisfaction %	Graduate prospects %	Overall rating
1 Cambridge	4.8	502	86	81	100.0
2 Oxford	4.7	503	82	78	96.8
3 University College London	4.3	487	83	75	94.9
4 Bath	4.6	480	76	68	89.8
5 York	3.5	439	83	65	87.4
6 Sheffield	3.1	412	80	74	87.0
7 Royal Holloway	3.3	398	84	65	86.2
8 Durham	3.1	423	81	67	85.4
=9 Glasgow	3.4	387	85	61	85.3
=9 Bristol	2.7	454	78	70	85.3
11 Loughborough	3.6	404	81	62	84.7
12 St Andrews	3.5	444	83	53	84.6
=13 Exeter	2.9	431	83	58	83.9
=13 Sussex	3.1	387	80	69	83.9
=15 Cardiff	3.9	425	76	60	83.1
=15 Birmingham	4.1	406	76	60	83.1
=15 Aston	2.8	378	82	66	83.1
18 Leeds	2.6	432	78	65	82.5
19 Lancaster	2.3	404	79	69	82.3
20 Warwick	2.6	438	77	65	82.2
21 Edinburgh	3.1	427	74	65	81.4
22 Kent	2.2	371	78	73	81.2
23 Southampton	3.1	421	77	56	80.5
24 Nottingham	2.8	430	75	60	80.0
25 Newcastle	2.3	430	76	60	79.3
26 Leicester	1.3	367	80	70	78.8
27 Northumbria	1.4	332	84	64	78.6
28 Hull	1.8	320	82	66	78.5
29 Bangor	3.4	301	79	55	77.6
30 Aberdeen	2.2	322	84	54	77.1
31 Essex	2.7	334	80	55	76.9
32 Strathclyde	1.4	369	79	61	76.0
=33 Surrey	2.3	403	67	68	75.7
=33 Brunel	1.9	338	80	58	75.7
35 City	2.2	347	69	70	75.3
36 Lincoln	1.5	299	84	56	75.1
37 Bournemouth	1.9	268	81	60	74.2
38 Portsmouth	1.3	344	82	52	73.9
39 Liverpool	1.7	392	77	50	73.8
=40 Nottingham Trent	0.8	284	82	63	73.7
=40 Central Lancashire	1.4	292	79	61	73.7
42 Swansea	1.8	333	78	54	73.2
=43 East Anglia	0.9	348	82	52	72.8

=43 Stirling	1.3	322	80	54	72.8
=43 Goldsmiths College	2.5	309	73	57	72.8
46 Reading	2.8	383	71	49	72.7
47 Manchester	2.5	418	66	54	72.3
48 Oxford Brookes	1.3	354	81	46	72.2
49 Dundee	1.9	323	82	43	71.8
50 Staffordshire	1.2	243	78	65	71.5
51 Queen's, Belfast	1.7	368	76	46	71.0
52 Keele	1.2	303	78	55	70.7
53 Plymouth	1.8	307	77	49	70.4
54 Hertfordshire	1.8	268	77	53	70.1
55 Chester	0.8	274	80	56	69.9
=56 West of England	1.9	308	80	40	69.5
=56 Bath Spa	0.8	287	80	53	69.5
58 Manchester Metropolitan	2.0	332	72	48	69.3
59 Glasgow Caledonian	0.7	327	78	48	68.6
60 Bradford	2.6	230	76	47	68.3
61 Teesside		258	84	51	68.0
62 Greenwich	0.9	276	74	58	67.9
63 Coventry	0.8	296	79	46	67.6
64 Edinburgh Napier	0.5	254	79	55	67.5
65 Sunderland	0.5	256	85	41	66.6
66 St Mary's College		233	83	51	66.3
67 York St John	0.3	283	75	54	66.0
=68 Ulster	1.5	232	81	39	65.6
=68 UWIC, Cardiff	1.1	268	74	50	65.6
=70 Leeds Metropolitan		317	68	63	65.3
=70 Sheffield Hallam	0.7	308	75	44	65.3
72 De Montfort		244	82	46	65.0
=73 Anglia Ruskin	2.0	251	70	47	64.7
=73 Queen Margaret Edinburgh		297		51	64.7
75 Thames Valley	0.3	233	73	59	64.3
76 Bolton	0.5	242	67	66	64.1
77 Liverpool John Moores	1.5	270	73	41	63.8
=78 East London	1.3	182	71	57	63.7
=78 Winchester		277	79	43	63.7
=80 Brighton	1.6	303	72	37	63.5
=80 Heriot-Watt	0.5	320	73	43	63.5
=82 Salford	1.8	314	66	43	63.3
=82 Westminster	0.9	259	73	47	63.3
84 Glamorgan	0.6	241	76	45	62.8
85 Northampton		256	80	39	62.4
=86 Huddersfield		266	80	38	62.2
=86 Abertay	0.9	232		49	62.2
88 Bedfordshire		214	76	50	61.8
89 Middlesex	0.6	204	65	64	61.4
90 Roehampton	1.1	222	67	53	61.3

Psychology cont.

	Research quality/9	Entry standards	Student satisfaction %	Graduate prospects %	Overall rating
=91 Derby	0.8	240	70	46	60.8
=91 Gloucestershire	0.6	264	70	44	60.8
93 Canterbury Christ Church		259	75	42	60.7
94 Buckinghamshire New		200	71	57	60.6
95 Kingston	1.0	224	73	41	60.3
96 Newman		232	77	39	59.9
97 Newport		207	74	48	59.7
98 Worcester		237	67	55	59.5
99 Southampton Solent		259	72	42	59.0
100 Cumbria		258	51	73	57.7
101 Edge Hill		278	67	42	57.2
102 London South Bank	1.1	224	64	39	55.8

» British Psychological Society: www.bps.org.uk

Russian and Eastern European Languages

Oxford and Cambridge have swapped places at the top of the ranking for Russian and Eastern European languages but, as in the previous two editions of the *Guide*, there is little to separate them. Cambridge still leads the table for entry standards and student satisfaction, but Oxford's improved score in the 2008 National Student Survey makes the difference.

Durham enters the table in third position, but Bristol, two places lower, had the best employment record among those who graduated in 2008. Portsmouth re-enters the ranking in 13th place and is the representative of the post-1992 universities. Glasgow is the only Scottish university and there is none from Wales or Northern Ireland.

Entry standards are high throughout the table. Although three of the 14 universities do not have enough undergraduates taking Russian to calculate reliable entry scores, only one of the remainder averages less than 350 points on the UCAS tariff. Although there were fewer than 500 applications in 2008, that still represented five for each place.

Apart from three universities that had too few students studying the language to compile reliable scores, all other universities satisfied more than 70 per cent of the undergraduates in the 2009 results. Russian has been growing in popularity in schools, although most students learn the language from scratch. The 514 applications received by February 2010 represented an increase of 22 per cent on the previous year.

The small numbers make for exaggerated swings in institutional and national statistics, but Russian has been around the middle of the table for employment prospects in last two editions of the *Guide*. Starting salaries for graduate-level jobs are in the top 20, at more than £22,500.

Employed in graduate job:	37%	Employed in non-graduate job and studying:	1%
Employed in graduate job and studying:	6%	Employed in non-graduate job:	25%
Studying:	23%	Unemployed:	8%
Average starting graduate salary:	£22,568	Average starting non-graduate salary:	£15,534

Russian

	Research quality/9	Entry standards	Student satisfaction %	Graduate prospects %	Overall rating
1 Oxford	4.4	516	87	83	100.0
2 Cambridge	3.6	538	88	82	99.5
3 Durham	1.8	491	81	75	88.0
4 Bath	2.4		85	69	87.5
5 Bristol	3.0	434	74	85	86.6
6 Exeter	2.5	382	81	79	86.5
7 University College London	2.4	449	77	78	85.7
8 Sheffield	3.8	411	80	61	85.4
9 Birmingham	2.9		81	62	84.0
10 Manchester	4.5	357	74		83.1
11 Nottingham	3.3	357	75	74	82.4
12 Glasgow	0.4		82	65	77.4
13 Portsmouth		273	86	64	76.1
14 Leeds	1.2	387	81	45	75.1

» British Association for Slavonic and East European Studies: **www.basees.org.uk**
» National Centre for Languages (CILT): **www.cilt.org.uk**

Social Policy

The London School of Economics has retained its accustomed position at the head of the social policy ranking, stretching its lead still further with much the highest scores for research and entry qualifications, as well as the best of a generally mediocre set of employment statistics. The 94 per cent of LSE graduates finding graduate-level work or continuing their studies within six months of completing a degree was 20 or 30 percentage points ahead of all but one other university in the ranking. That university was Bolton, which makes an unexpected appearance in second place for social policy. A lack of reliable entry scores means that, with among the best results for both employment and student satisfaction, Bolton is in second place.

In the 2008 assessments, 80 per cent of the LSE's research in the wider category of social work and policy and administration was rated world-leading or internationally excellent. Its only blemish is in student satisfaction, a frequent concern for the school. The best record in the 2009 National Student Survey was at fifth-placed Loughborough. There were good scores for most universities, only two failing to satisfy at least 70 per cent of their final-year undergraduates.

Entry standards are comparatively modest – the LSE is the only university to average 400 points this year. This reflects the fact that there were fewer than three applications to the place in 2009, one of the lowest ratios for any subject. Although two thirds of entrants come with A levels or their equivalent, some courses cater very largely for mature students.

Social policy is also among the bottom five subjects for graduate employment, although it does better in the earnings league, with starting salaries averaging more than £19,500 in graduate-level jobs.

Social Policy cont.

Glasgow has widened the gap on Edinburgh as the top university in Scotland, while Cardiff leads Swansea in Wales. There are 11 post-1992 universities in the table – three fewer than last year. Bolton is by far the highest-placed, but Lincoln also makes the top 20, in 15th place.

Demand for places in social policy has fluctuated in recent years, but there was an increase in applications of more than 13 per cent early in 2010. A significant proportion of the places have been filled in Clearing in recent years.

Employed in graduate job:	30%
Employed in graduate job and studying:	3%
Studying:	14%
Average starting graduate salary:	£19,659
Employed in non-graduate job and studying:	4%
Employed in non-graduate job:	38%
Unemployed:	10%
Average starting non-graduate salary:	£14,697

Social Policy	Research quality/9	Entry standards	Student satisfaction %	Graduate prospects %	Overall rating
1 London School of Economics	5.6	418	70	94	100.0
2 Bolton	2.0		85	83	90.4
3 Southampton	4.5		79	60	90.3
4 Glasgow	2.8	390	85	53	89.1
5 Loughborough	3.2	356	88	49	88.7
6 Bath	4.6	356	76	50	87.7
7 Edinburgh	4.0		71	75	86.8
8 Leeds	4.4	308	75	66	86.4
9 Hull	2.3	324	86	62	86.1
=10 Bristol	3.3	348	75	63	85.0
=10 Sheffield	3.5	343	75	62	85.0
12 Kent	4.2	272	78	56	83.7
13 York	3.8	301	76	58	83.2
14 Stirling	2.7	293	79	65	82.4
15 Lincoln	1.9		83	58	81.8
16 Keele	3.2	295	77	58	81.4
17 Queen's, Belfast	3.2		75	55	80.6
18 Birmingham	3.1	312	76	54	80.5
19 Leicester	1.8	327	81	54	79.9
20 Cardiff	3.5	294	76	48	79.8
21 Nottingham	2.5	341	70	60	78.7
22 Central Lancashire	2.2		76	57	77.5
23 Aston	1.4	368	75		77.4
24 Swansea	2.7	270	77	51	77.2
25 Bangor	1.8		75	60	75.7
26 Nottingham Trent	3.1	229	71	62	74.6
27 Sheffield Hallam	3.1	270	73	45	74.5
28 Salford	2.2	215	74	66	73.9
29 Birmingham City	1.6	246	80		72.7
30 Brighton	1.6	288	71	47	70.0

31 Ulster	2.8	240	72	24	66.9
32 London South Bank	3.1	181	72	34	66.5
33 Plymouth	2.4		72	25	65.9
34 Anglia Ruskin	1.8	248	66	40	64.5
35 Manchester	2.8		56	49	63.2
36 Manchester Metropolitan	1.4		74	12	60.2

» National Institute for Economic and Social Research: **www.niesr.ac.uk**
» UK Social Policy Association: **www.social-policy.org**

Social Work

Despite all the bad publicity endured by social work in recent years, the subject is now among the ten most popular choices for higher education candidates. That may be partly because it is also in the top dozen for employment prospects and – even more surprisingly – only just outside the top ten for starting salaries, which averaged nearly £24,000 in 2008.

Social work used to be unusual for having more students taking certificate or diploma courses than degrees, but the diploma was withdrawn in the move to a graduate profession. Extra places at undergraduate level brought 42 more universities into the table in the last two years and another four have been added for this edition of the *Guide*. A 42 per cent increase in applications for degree courses at the start of 2010 meant there would be at least six applications for every place. However, entry grades are still the lowest in the *Guide*.

The ranking had a new top three in each of the last two years and only second-placed Bath, which had the best results in the 2008 Research Assessment Exercise, remains among the leading trio in this edition of the *Guide*. Queen's, Belfast, which, with Birmingham, has the highest entry standards in the table, has moved up from fifth place to be the new leader. York is third and Sussex, which has the second most satisfied students, has come from outside the top ten to be fourth this year.

Four universities have 100 per cent employment records, compared with only one last year. They are Glamorgan, Chester, Dundee and Swansea. However, employment scores for social work are surprisingly variable, with more than half of the graduates at two universities in low-level work or unemployed six months after completing their degrees.

Edinburgh remains the top university in Scotland, while Glamorgan is the leader in Wales, as well as being the only post-1992 university to appear in the top 20. The majority of the institutions in the table are new universities, but most are in the bottom half. Entry grades are largely responsible: most of the older universities in the table have average entry scores of more than 300 points, whereas only Glasgow Caledonian, of the post-1992 universities, reaches that threshold. Seven average less than 200 points, although there were almost twice as many last year.

Employed in graduate job:	71%	Employed in non-graduate job and studying:	2%
Employed in graduate job and studying:	5%	Employed in non-graduate job:	12%
Studying:	5%	Unemployed:	5%
Average starting graduate salary:	£23,834	Average starting non-graduate salary:	£15,236

Social Work cont.

	Research quality/9	Entry standards	Student satisfaction %	Graduate prospects %	Overall rating
1 Queen's, Belfast	3.2	386	80	94	100.0
2 Bath	4.6		75	95	99.7
3 York	3.8	354	79	91	98.6
4 Sussex	3.1		87	93	97.8
5 Sheffield	3.5	353	80	90	97.6
6 Lancaster	3.4	333	79	96	97.0
7 Kent	4.2	243	88	90	96.8
8 Edinburgh	4.0	358	69	91	95.2
9 Leeds	4.4	347	78	73	95.1
10 Keele	3.2	316	75	93	92.4
11 Birmingham	3.1	386	74	74	90.7
12 East Anglia	2.6	279	81		90.1
13 Reading	2.3	294	77	96	89.0
14 Stirling	2.7		77	89	88.3
15 Glamorgan	2.2	285	74	100	87.8
16 Bristol	3.3	364	68	71	87.2
17 Strathclyde	2.0	341	73	89	87.1
18 Manchester	2.8	344	66		87.0
19 Goldsmiths College	2.1		79	87	85.8
20 Bradford	2.6	283	71	91	85.6
21 Chester	0.9	284	78	100	84.6
22 Hull	2.3	269	72	92	84.0
23 Glasgow Caledonian		319	84	92	83.4
24 Dundee	1.9	293	65	100	83.1
25 Northumbria	1.8	264	78	86	82.9
26 Middlesex	2.2		72	88	82.5
27 Ulster	2.8	269	67	84	82.1
28 West of England	1.3	252	76	95	81.7
29 Robert Gordon		288	85	89	81.3
30 London South Bank	3.1		67	80	81.1
31 Nottingham Trent	3.1	210	67	90	80.9
32 Lincoln	1.9	234	76	86	80.8
33 De Montfort	1.7	232	71	97	80.5
34 Coventry	1.7	244	77	84	80.2
35 Huddersfield	2.4	249	75	75	80.0
36 Swansea	2.7		54	100	78.8
37 Oxford Brookes		288	83	82	78.6
38 UWIC, Cardiff		224	84	94	78.0
39 Anglia Ruskin	1.8	251	69	82	77.2
40 Central Lancashire	2.2	221	66	89	77.1
41 Bournemouth		300	71	93	76.8
42 Newport	2.0	183	75	84	76.6
43 Kingston		265	77	86	75.7

44	Plymouth	2.4	237	65	79	75.6
45	Gloucestershire	0.7	276	71	84	75.4
46	Staffordshire		290	69	93	75.3
47	Bedfordshire	2.3	132	79	80	75.2
48	Southampton Solent		220	77	95	75.1
49	Teesside		273	84	69	74.4
50	Salford	2.2	250	61	79	74.1
51	Hertfordshire	1.0	209	67	95	73.8
52	Sheffield Hallam	1.9	229	63	80	73.1
53	Portsmouth		270	66	88	71.5
54	Birmingham City	1.6	236	56	89	71.4
55	Marjon, Plymouth		192	82	80	71.2
56	Greenwich		261	70	82	70.8
57	Buckinghamshire New		154	73	97	69.5
58	Manchester Metropolitan	1.4	196	66	77	69.1
59	Chichester		252	77	63	68.4
60	Sunderland		203	78	72	68.1
61	Glyndŵr	1.0	212	68	70	67.4
62	Northampton		209	66	86	66.9
63	Royal Holloway	2.4		44	87	66.5
64	Leeds Metropolitan		234	69	73	66.0
65	East London	1.5	143	64	77	65.0
66	Bangor	1.8	220	59	59	63.9
67	Canterbury Christ Church		244	67	66	63.7
68	Brunel	1.8		51	76	63.2
69	Cumbria		216	70	61	62.3
70	Winchester		274		54	61.4
71	Liverpool John Moores		202	71	59	61.2
72	Edge Hill	0.8	208	77	32	59.7
73	Derby		186	67	63	59.4
74	Roehampton		206	74	47	59.3

» British Association of Social Workers: **www.basw.co.uk**
» General Social Care Council: **www.gscc.org.uk**
» Social Care Association: **http://socialcareassociation.co.uk**

Sociology

The popular image of sociology may be stuck in the 1960s, but it remains one of the largest of the social sciences. Applications were up by nearly 20 per cent early in 2010, following a series of increases earlier in the decade. Numbers have remained buoyant despite an employment record that is in the bottom four for all subjects. More than half of those graduating in 2008 were in low-level jobs or unemployed at the end of the year.

Cambridge is well clear in first place, despite uncharacteristically low grades for research. The sociology panel for the 2008 assessments was no respecter of reputations: neither Cambridge nor the London School of Economics is among the top dozen universities on this measure. Bath, which is up four places to third this year, did best for research, with three-quarters of the university's work judged to be world-leading or internationally excellent. Grades in sociology were not as high as in many subjects, but fifth-placed Southampton also did well, with 70 per cent of research in the top two categories.

Cambridge has the most satisfied students, however, and by far the highest entry standards, nearly 80 points ahead of the field. Aberdeen and St Mary's University College, in Twickenham, were only one percentage point behind in the 2009 National Student Survey, which showed generally high levels of satisfaction.

Sociology's low standing in the employment table is naturally reflected in the performance of individual universities. It is one of the few subjects in which not a single university saw 80 per cent of leavers to straight into graduate-level jobs or continue their studies. Royal Holloway came closest to that mark, but at University of Wales Institute, Cardiff, Cumbria, Gloucestershire, Derby and the West of England, there were "positive destinations" for fewer than one student in three.

Edinburgh has overtaken Aberdeen to resume its position as the leading university in Scotland, while Cardiff is best-placed in Wales. Portsmouth is the top post-1992 university and is joined in the top 30 by Northumbria.

Other subjects such as criminology, urban studies, women's studies and some communication studies are included in the category of sociology and a large number of institutions teach the subject as part of a combined studies or modular programme.

Employed in graduate job:	29%	Employed in non-graduate job and studying:	4%
Employed in graduate job and studying:	3%	Employed in non-graduate job:	40%
Studying:	15%	Unemployed:	8%
Average starting graduate salary:	£18,887	Average starting non-graduate salary:	£14,918

Sociology	Research quality/9	Entry standards	Student satisfaction %	Graduate prospects %	Overall rating
1 Cambridge	3.2	502	86	75	100.0
2 Warwick	3.8	389	80	72	92.4
3 Bath	4.6	375	77	70	91.7
4 Surrey	3.8	350	82	60	88.8
5 Southampton	4.5	373	82	51	88.7
=6 Leeds	4.4	363	79	56	88.1

=6	Loughborough	3.2	338	83	66	88.1
8	Essex	4.2	317	82	60	88.0
9	Durham	3.0	406	77	65	87.5
10	London School of Economics	2.9	426	70	75	87.3
11	Lancaster	4.2	355	79	54	86.5
12	Edinburgh	3.8	406	76	56	86.4
13	York	4.0	334	79	56	85.7
14	Sussex	3.4	348	77	63	85.3
15	Exeter	3.3	359	80	54	84.5
16	Leicester	2.0	321	80	70	83.8
=17	Stirling	2.7	305	79	61	81.9
=17	Cardiff	3.5	350	76	51	81.9
19	Aberdeen	2.9	327	85	43	81.7
20	Kent	4.2	277	76	54	81.1
=21	Sheffield	3.5	344	75	52	81.0
=21	Goldsmiths College	4.2	265	75	58	81.0
=23	Birmingham	1.6	358	78	60	80.4
=23	Glasgow	2.2	372	79	49	80.4
25	Bristol	2.4	372	67	69	79.9
26	Portsmouth	2.6	285	82	49	79.1
27	Queen's, Belfast	3.2	340	74	49	78.6
28	Keele	3.2	305	73	55	78.5
=29	Northumbria	1.8	280	81	57	78.4
=29	Newcastle	2.8	348	75	49	78.4
31	Brunel	2.5	295	77	56	78.2
32	Nottingham	2.5	337	70	60	77.9
33	Strathclyde	1.2	352	76	59	77.7
34	Manchester	4.5	377	65	42	76.9
=35	East Anglia		319	84	55	76.6
=35	Liverpool	1.6	346	79	45	76.6
37	Edinburgh Napier	0.7	260	82	63	76.5
38	Hull	2.3	260	81	47	76.1
39	Aston	1.4	325	75	57	76.0
=40	Glasgow Caledonian	1.4	305	83	43	75.4
=40	Salford	2.4	261	76	54	75.4
42	Robert Gordon	0.7	245	81	62	74.8
43	Lincoln		255	84	55	73.5
44	Teesside	1.5	241	80	50	73.0
45	Birmingham City	1.6	228	80	49	72.6
46	Bedfordshire	2.3	182	80	50	72.2
=47	Oxford Brookes		324	80	47	71.8
=47	Royal Holloway		295	66	79	71.8
49	Staffordshire	1.4	222	76	56	71.6
50	Chester	0.9	249	74	61	71.4
51	Nottingham Trent		246	76	64	70.7
52	City	2.6	284	65	53	70.6
53	East London	2.2	171	78	49	70.4

Sociology cont.

	Research quality/9	Entry standards	Student satisfaction %	Graduate prospects %	Overall rating
54 Central Lancashire		235	78	58	70.1
55 Worcester		229	76	64	70.0
=56 Bradford	2.6	213	77	38	69.8
=56 Manchester Metropolitan	1.8	244	76	43	69.8
58 St Mary's College		204	85	48	69.6
59 Brighton	1.7	290	69	46	69.3
60 Plymouth	1.8	265	72	46	69.2
61 Bath Spa		244	81	45	68.5
62 Huddersfield	1.0	207	78		67.6
=63 Southampton Solent		242	83	34	66.4
=63 Bangor		263	74	48	66.4
=65 Glamorgan		233	70	60	65.9
=65 Coventry		267	76	43	65.9
=67 West of England	0.9	264	76	32	65.7
=67 Northampton		252	78	41	65.7
=67 Canterbury Christ Church		212	76	51	65.7
=70 Kingston	1.3	218	71	46	65.3
=70 Sheffield Hallam		245	74	48	65.3
72 Greenwich		222	73	49	64.2
73 Derby		242	79	32	63.8
74 Westminster		226	75	41	63.5
75 Gloucestershire		254	78	30	62.9
76 Ulster		243	75	35	62.4
77 Buckinghamshire New		216	73	43	61.9
78 Roehampton	1.7	218	67	37	61.8
=79 Middlesex		176	73	48	61.6
=79 Anglia Ruskin		246	70	42	61.6
=79 Abertay		225		43	61.6
82 London South Bank		194	70	49	61.3
83 Leeds Metropolitan		243	72	36	61.2
84 Sunderland		199	72	40	60.0
85 Liverpool John Moores		207	73	34	59.5
86 Cumbria		228	71	32	58.5
87 UWIC, Cardiff		241	50	23	44.9

» The British Sociological Association: www.britsoc.co.uk

Sports Science

This is the second appearance of a separate table for the growing range of courses listed under the category of sports science. In earlier editions of the *Guide*, they appeared in the broader ranking that covers hospitality, leisure, recreation and tourism, but the popularity of sport as a degree subject demands more detailed scrutiny. The 49,000 applications by February 2010 – 19 per cent up on the previous year – took sports science into the top ten subjects for the first time.

The subject covers more than 40 specialisms at degree level, from sports therapy to equestrian sport studies and marine sport technology. Many contain more science and less physical activity than candidates may expect. Brunel, for example, requires at least an AS level in one of the sciences. Many universities now offer sports scholarships for elite performers, but most are not tied to a particular course and, officially at least, do not mean that the normal entry requirements are waived.

Loughborough, the most famous name in university sport, tops the ranking, as it did last year and when the broader classification was used. It is one of only two universities where entrants average more than 400 points on the UCAS tariff. The other is Bath, which has jumped five places this year to take second position. Loughborough also shares with fifth-placed Birmingham the best record in the 2008 Research Assessment Exercise. Both had 60 per cent of their research rated world-leading or internationally excellent.

The most satisfied students are at Aberystwyth, just outside the top 20. Third-placed Exeter, another university with an illustrious sporting pedigree, through the former St Luke's College, and the new university of Glyndŵr, in Wrexham, also satisfied more than 90 per cent of their undergraduates in the 2009 National Student Survey.

Edinburgh and Glasgow tie for title of the top university in Scotland, sharing sixth place overall, while Bangor is the leader in Wales. Brighton, which has the best graduate employment record in the table, is the leading post-1992 university, with a place in the top ten. Liverpool John Moores, Portsmouth, Chichester, Sheffield Hallam, Leeds Metropolitan and UWIC are all in the top 20.

Entry standards are modest, but still higher than last year: ten universities, compared with 15 then, average less than 200 points and one is below 150, the equivalent of less than two Cs at A level.

Sports science is in the bottom ten subjects for starting salaries. Although the unemployment rate among graduates is low, at only 5 per cent, more than a third begin their working life in low-level jobs. Apart from Brighton, the only institution to see more than 80 per cent of its leavers go straight into graduate jobs or continue their studies in 2008 was Newman University College, in Birmingham.

Employed in graduate job:	36%	Employed in non-graduate job and studying:	3%
Employed in graduate job and studying:	5%	Employed in non-graduate job:	31%
Studying:	18%	Unemployed:	5%
Average starting graduate salary:	£18,217	Average starting non-graduate salary:	£14,520

Sports Science	Research quality/9	Entry standards	Student satisfaction %	Graduate prospects %	Overall rating
1 Loughborough	3.6	417	86	67	100.0
2 Bath	2.4	416	85	74	96.9
3 Exeter	2.1	394	92	70	96.3
4 Durham	3.0	358	81	75	93.9
5 Birmingham	3.6	379	84	59	93.7

Sports Science cont.

	Research quality/9	Entry standards	Student satisfaction %	Graduate prospects %	Overall rating
=6 Edinburgh	2.6	368	77	77	91.8
=6 Glasgow	3.2	357	83	63	91.8
8 Brighton	2.0	245	85	84	88.7
9 Stirling	2.6	336	79		88.4
10 Leeds	2.0	372	82	63	88.0
11 Bangor	2.1	262	87	71	86.9
12 Brunel	2.4	317	77	70	85.8
13 Liverpool John Moores	3.4	272	83	57	85.5
14 Portsmouth	2.9	256	86	57	84.4
15 Chichester	1.3	266	88	67	83.1
16 Essex	2.0	290	82	61	82.4
17 Ulster	1.7	268	85	63	82.2
=18 Sheffield Hallam	2.1	291	79	62	81.7
=18 Leeds Metropolitan	2.5	270	71	73	81.7
20 UWIC, Cardiff	1.5	293	83	61	81.0
21 Aberystwyth	1.0	243	94	58	80.8
22 Chester	1.5	253	80	70	80.4
23 Heriot-Watt	1.7	294	80	60	80.1
24 Newman	0.4	240	79	83	79.4
25 Swansea	0.4	284	85	67	79.1
26 Bournemouth		283	81	76	79.0
27 Nottingham Trent	0.6	272	82	69	78.8
=28 Northumbria	1.3	278	78	64	78.2
=28 Strathclyde	2.9		77	50	78.2
30 Hertfordshire	1.8	266	75	60	76.6
31 Manchester Metropolitan	1.6	243	68	75	76.5
32 Aberdeen	1.6	282	81	48	76.1
33 Glyndŵr		217	92	62	75.7
=34 Kent	2.6	236	69	61	75.5
=34 Dundee		327	83	55	75.5
36 Hull	0.7	227	77	73	75.4
37 Staffordshire	1.0	185	85	64	75.3
38 Central Lancashire		221	88	62	74.3
39 Lincoln		227	89	59	74.0
40 Coventry	0.9	262	79	58	73.9
41 Teesside		275	82	59	73.4
42 Salford	1.8	257	82	41	73.2
43 St Mary's College	0.6	219	79	65	73.0
44 Worcester		269	80	62	72.9
45 Greenwich		207	78	69	71.2
46 Edinburgh Napier		267	81	54	71.1
47 Sunderland	1.6	166	76	60	70.7
48 Robert Gordon		300	72	59	70.4

49	Winchester		231	82	55	69.7
50	Gloucestershire	0.6	250	78	49	69.0
51	York St John	0.5	240	77	53	68.9
52	West of England		247	80	51	68.6
53	Glamorgan	1.2	210	76	50	68.5
54	Abertay		235		58	68.2
55	Edge Hill		241	76	54	67.0
56	Marjon, Plymouth	0.2	206	79	53	66.7
57	Bedfordshire	1.3	199	64	62	66.5
58	East London		195	71	67	66.4
59	Canterbury Christ Church	1.0	177	76	52	66.3
60	Southampton Solent		237	74	54	66.0
61	Derby		198	71	64	65.7
62	Roehampton	0.3	208	74	54	65.5
63	Middlesex		173	69	71	65.4
64	Northampton		208	79	48	64.9
65	Cumbria		273	51	76	64.6
66	Kingston		209	67	60	63.1
67	Huddersfield		285	63	51	62.7
68	Plymouth		246	79	35	62.6
69	Newport		134	74	57	60.7
70	London South Bank	1.5		70	35	60.1
71	Buckinghamshire New	0.7	177	64	50	58.9
72	Bolton		172	69	26	51.1

» British Association of Sport and Exercise Sciences: **www.bases.org.uk**
» English Institute of Sport: **www.eis2win.co.uk**
» London 2012: **www.london2012.com**
» Scottish Institute of Sport: **www.sisport.com**
» Welsh Institute of Sport: **www.welsh-institute-sport.co.uk**

Theology and Religious Studies

Theology and religious studies have been growing in popularity in recent years and registered an increase in applications of almost 15 per cent at the start of 2010. However, it is still one of the least competitive subjects in the arts and social sciences: there were little more than four applications to the place in 2009, despite a cut of almost 10 per cent in the number of first-year degree places.

Cambridge stays top of the table, despite losing the lead on three of the four measures. It has the highest graduate employment score, but second-placed Oxford has the top entry standards this year and Chichester, in 16th place, has the most satisfied students. Durham, which has dropped to third place, produced the best results in the 2008 Research Assessment Exercise, when two-thirds of its work was considered world-leading or internationally excellent.

Theology and religious studies are in the top half of the graduate destinations table, with an unemployment rate of only 6 per cent. By no means all graduates go into the church, but the vocation helps to maintain this record. The table has none of the extremes that are evident in

Theology and Religious Studies cont.

other subjects: more than half of the leavers at every university had graduate jobs or were continuing their studies at the end of 2008, but nowhere did this proportion exceed 85 per cent.

Half of the top eight places are filled by Scottish universities, with St Andrews overtaking Edinburgh to be the highest-placed this year. Lampeter (Trinity Saint David) has enjoyed the biggest rise up the table, overtaking Cardiff in the process, to become easily the top university in Wales. St Mary's College, Twickenham, again records the highest finish outside the pre-1992 universities and is joined in the top 20 by Chichester.

Entry qualifications are more tightly bunched than in many of the subject tables. Only seven of the 37 institutions average more than 400 points and just four slip below 250 points. Starting salaries had slipped since the survey used in last year's *Guide* was compiled. The average rate in graduate jobs at the end of 2008 was little more than £18,000, taking theology and religious studies from outside the bottom 20 to within eight places of the foot of the earnings table.

Employed in graduate job:	31%	Employed in non-graduate job and studying:	5%
Employed in graduate job and studying:	5%	Employed in non-graduate job:	23%
Studying:	31%	Unemployed:	6%
Average starting graduate salary:	£18,170	Average starting non-graduate salary:	£15,185

Theology and Religious Studies	Research quality/9	Entry standards	Student satisfaction %	Graduate prospects %	Overall rating
1 Cambridge	4.3	507	86	85	100.0
2 Oxford	4.1	523	83	82	97.6
3 Durham	4.7	445	86	80	97.0
4 St Andrews	3.2	426	86	78	91.7
5 Edinburgh	3.9	459	80	75	91.0
6 Aberdeen	3.5	327	89	73	88.4
7 Glasgow	2.3	363	82	80	85.9
8 Exeter	2.5	392	87	67	85.6
9 Sheffield	3.5	353	91	53	84.8
10 Nottingham	3.4	381	77	72	84.1
11 Lampeter (Trinity Saint David)	1.9	292	83	84	83.3
12 Manchester	3.8	367	76	69	82.8
13 Stirling	1.7	300	87	75	82.6
14 Lancaster	2.9	363	77	69	81.8
15 St Mary's College	2.2	268	83	79	81.4
16 Chichester	1.1	283	92		81.2
17 King's College London	2.9	423	75	64	81.0
18 Birmingham	3.0	356	72	72	80.0
19 Kent	2.1	302	74	82	79.5
20 Bristol	2.7	403	67	72	78.2
21 Chester	1.5	246	80	80	77.4
22 Cardiff	1.9	339	82	59	77.2
23 School of Oriental and African Studies	3.1	340	71	66	77.1

24	Leeds	2.8	367	76	57	76.8
25	Roehampton	1.5	267	80	74	76.6
26	Hull		288	83	74	75.4
27	Bangor	1.7	288	78	66	74.5
28	Queen's, Belfast		338	79	72	74.4
=29	Newman		222	82	81	74.3
=29	Cumbria	1.2	254		74	74.3
31	Heythrop College	0.7	324	84	56	73.5
32	York St John	0.6	275	88	53	72.5
33	Gloucestershire	1.7	242	78		71.6
34	Oxford Brookes		289	81	62	70.7
35	Bath Spa	0.4	293	83	53	70.3
36	Winchester	0.8	274	71	57	65.6
37	Canterbury Christ Church	0.9	230	71	52	62.4

» British Association for the Study of Religions: **http://basr.open.ac.uk**
» Society for the Study of Theology: **www.theologysociety.org.uk**

Town and Country Planning and Landscape

Cambridge remains at the head of the ranking for town and country planning and landscape studies, with the best research grades and entry standards that are nearly 80 points higher than the nearest challenger. Cambridge's average grades are 30 points lower than last year, but third-placed Reading is the only other university to top 400 points at entry. Competition was much closer in the 2008 Research Assessment Exercise: Cambridge had the most work placed in the top two categories, but Sheffield – up to second this year – had a higher proportion judged to be world-leading.

There are high employment scores throughout the table: Reading (for the second year in a row) and Birmingham City, which is 21st out of the 25 universities, both saw all their graduates find graduate-level work or continue their studies within six months of completing a degree. Only Birmingham and the bottom two in the table, Liverpool John Moores and Ulster, recorded such "positive destinations" for less than 70 per cent of those graduating in 2008.

Loughborough, which has slipped a place to fourth after a big rise last year, has the most satisfied students. Cardiff, in sixth place, is the top university outside England, while Dundee has overtaken Heriot-Watt to become the leader in Scotland. Sheffield Hallam, in eighth place, is by some way the leading new university, but Nottingham Trent is also close to the top 10.

Planning courses were among the few to see a decline in applications at the start of 2010. It was the second successive year in which there had been a big fall in demand for the subjects – a 17 per cent drop following a similar decline in 2009 – although the much smaller area of landscape design saw an increase in both years. About 12 per cent of places across the whole category tend to be filled through Clearing. The size of university departments varies from more than 500 students to less than 150, with about a third of the total being postgraduates.

Job prospects have been good in recent years, although the subjects have dropped from inside the top 10 to just outside the top 20 in the latest employment table. Despite this, more than 70 per cent of graduates were in graduate-level jobs or still studying at the end of 2008. Average starting salaries in graduate-level jobs were about average for all subjects, at £20,200.

Town and Country Planning and Landscape cont.

Employed in graduate job:	43%
Employed in graduate job and studying:	8%
Studying:	21%
Average starting graduate salary:	£20,233

Employed in non-graduate job and studying:	2%
Employed in non-graduate job:	16%
Unemployed:	9%
Average starting non-graduate salary:	£15,016

	Town and Country Planning and Landscape	Research quality/9	Entry standards	Student satisfaction %	Graduate prospects %	Overall rating
1	Cambridge	4.3	483	77	93	100.0
2	Sheffield	4.1	364	82	94	96.0
3	Reading	3.6	406	75	100	94.9
4	Loughborough	4.0	316	88	77	91.6
5	Newcastle	3.7	328	79	90	90.6
6	Cardiff	4.0	351	75	86	89.5
7	University College London	3.3	382	75	80	87.0
8	Sheffield Hallam	3.1	281	83	72	83.6
9	Queen's, Belfast	2.0	328	75	90	83.3
10	Manchester	3.3	337	74	72	82.2
11	Dundee	1.8	279	76	89	80.9
12	Liverpool	2.5	315	70	86	80.6
13	Nottingham Trent	1.3	297	78	86	80.4
14	Gloucestershire	2.0	326		82	79.9
15	Heriot-Watt	3.1	334	63	85	79.8
16	Oxford Brookes	1.9	329	74	74	78.7
17	Manchester Metropolitan	1.8	283	69	91	78.1
18	Aberdeen	3.3	342	59	81	78.0
19	Birmingham	2.4	346		68	77.6
20	West of England	2.1	284	74	75	77.0
21	Birmingham City	1.7	196	69	100	75.9
22	Leeds Metropolitan		273	69	86	70.9
23	Kingston	0.6	219	73	75	68.9
24	Liverpool John Moores	1.4	204	68	67	65.4
25	Ulster		228	69	54	59.8

» Royal Town Planning Institute: **www.rtpi.org.uk**
» Planning Officers Society: **www.planningofficers.org.uk**
» Landscape Institute: **www.landscapeinstitute.org**

Veterinary Medicine

Only medicine itself compares with veterinary medicine for high entry standards. Although there was a small drop in the demand for places in 2009, upward progress was soon resumed. There was an increase of nearly 14 per cent in applications for veterinary degrees starting in 2010. The number of places has been rising, but there are still more than seven applications for each one.

Veterinary medicine is another of the rankings from which employment scores have been removed from the calculations this year. The scores are still shown in the table below, but the review group of academic planners consulted on *The Times Good University Guide* each year agreed that employment rates in the subject were so tightly bunched that small differences could distort the overall ranking.

Cambridge has jumped three places on the basis of the three remaining measures to take over the leadership from Liverpool. Ironically, Cambridge had the lowest employment score at the time of the last survey and Liverpool the best, but Cambridge has by far the highest entry standards and the most satisfied students.

Nottingham, in third place, does not yet have a full set of statistics because it only opened in 2006, so its first students are yet to graduate. However, it shared with fourth-placed Edinburgh the best grades in the 2008 Research Assessment Exercise. There are no degrees in veterinary medicine in Wales or Northern Ireland, but Edinburgh remains fractionally ahead of Glasgow in Scotland.

The subject has slipped out of the top three for employment this year, but only to fifth place. More than nine out of ten vets were in graduate jobs or still studying six months after graduating. Starting salaries are high, at more than £25,000, but the subject is one place lower in the earnings table.

Most courses demand high grades in chemistry and biology, with some accepting physics or maths as one alternative subject. Cambridge and the Royal Veterinary College also set

Veterinary Medicine	Research quality/9	Entry standards	Student satisfaction %	Graduate prospects %	Overall rating
1 Cambridge	2.1	548	82	93	100.0
2 Liverpool	2.1	507	79	97	94.8
3 Nottingham	3.1	453			94.1
4 Edinburgh	3.1	486	67	94	93.0
5 Glasgow	2.3	473	78	96	92.7
6 Royal Veterinary College	2.6	466	66	96	88.3
7 Bristol	1.7	450	76	93	86.1

» Royal College of Veterinary Surgeons: **www.rcvs.org.uk**

Veterinary Medicine cont.

applicants a specialist aptitude test also used by a number of medical schools. Few candidates win places without evidence of commitment to the subject through work experience, either in veterinary practices or laboratories.

Vets' final qualifications are not classified, but between 5 and 15 per cent are awarded a commendation. The five-year courses have to meet the requirements of the Royal College of Veterinary Surgeons, and they vary in size from 65 to 155 students.

Employed in graduate job:	84%	Employed in non-graduate job and studying:	0%
Employed in graduate job and studying:	3%	Employed in non-graduate job:	5%
Studying:	4%	Unemployed:	3%
Average starting graduate salary:	£25,206	Average starting non-graduate salary:	£19,861

6 Making Your Application

Once the nerve-wracking business of choosing courses is over, you may feel you can sit back and concentrate on getting the right results. Don't be fooled – there is another vital stage to go through if you are to attract the right offers and win that coveted place in higher education. Too many people take their eye off the ball in actually making the application. Surprising numbers of applicants each year spell their own name wrongly, or enter an inaccurate date of birth, or the wrong course code. And that is to say nothing of the damage that can be done in the personal statement and teachers' references.

In an era when there are relatively few interviews and more candidates each year achieve high A-level grades, what goes on your UCAS form is becoming more and more important – too important, many would say. The art of conveying knowledge of and enthusiasm for your chosen subject – preferably with supporting evidence from your school or college – can make all the difference. While UCAS will decode misspelt names, other errors in grammar or spelling present admissions officers with an easy starting point in cutting applications down to a more manageable number.

The applications process has come under increased scrutiny in recent years, as the fairness of university admissions has become a political issue, as well as an educational one. There are no changes planned for entry in 2011, but there have been plenty in recent years, including a reduction in the number of choices per applicant and, most recently, the introduction of an "adjustment period" of a week in which those whose results are better than expected can seek an alternative course.

The application process
Most applications for full-time higher education courses go through UCAS, although specialist admissions bodies still handle applications to the music conservatoires (Conservatoires UK Admissions Service: **www.cukas.ac.uk**) and some postgraduate courses, including teacher training (Graduate Teacher Training Registry: **www.gttr.ac.uk**). The trend is towards the UCAS model even among specialist providers, however: recruitment to nursing and midwifery diploma and degree courses in Scotland switched to the UCAS system in 2010 and the art and design courses that used to recruit using the separate "Route B" scheme also reverted to the main system in 2010.

Universities that have not filled all their places, even during Clearing, will accept direct applications up to and after the start of the academic year, but UCAS is both the official route and the only way into the most popular courses.

Since 2006, all UCAS applications have been made online. The Apply electronic system is accessed via the UCAS website and is straightforward to use. For those who do not have the internet at home and prefer not to use school or college computers, the UCAS website lists 900 libraries, all over the UK, where you can make your application. Apply is available 24 hours a day, and, when the time comes, information on the progress of your application may arrive at any time.

Registering with Apply

The first step in the process is to register. If you are at a school or college, you will need to obtain a "buzzword" from your tutor or careers adviser – it is used when you log on to register. It links your application to the school or college so that the application can be sent electronically to your referee (usually one of your teachers) for your reference to be attached. If you are no longer at a school or college, you do not need a "buzzword", but you will need details of your referee. More information is given on the UCAS website.

To register, go to the UCAS website and click on "Apply". The system will guide you through the business of providing your personal details and generating a username and password, as well as reminding you of basic points, such as amending your details in case of a change of address. You can register separate term-time and holiday addresses – a useful option for boarders, who could find offers and, particularly, the confirmation of a place, going to their school when they are miles away at home. Remember to keep a note of your username and password in a safe place.

Throughout the process, you will be in sole control of communications with UCAS and your chosen universities. Only if you nominate a representative and give them your unique nine-digit application number (sent automatically by UCAS when your application is submitted), can a parent or anyone else give or receive information on your behalf, perhaps because you are ill or out of the country.

Once you are registered, you can start to complete the Apply screens. The details required cover the following areas:

» Personal details and some addition non-educational details for UK applicants.
» Your university choices.
» Details of your education so far including examination results and examinations still to be taken.
» Details of any jobs you have done.
» Your personal statement.
» A reference from one of your teachers.
» A declaration that you confirm that the information is correct and that you will be bound by the UCAS rules.
» Payment details (in 2010 applications cost £19, or £9 to apply to just one course).

The sections that follow cover the most important sections.

Personal details

This information is taken from your initial registration, and you will be asked for additional information, for example, on ethnic origin and national identity, used to monitor equal opportunities in the application process.

Choices

Since 2007–08, you have been restricted to a maximum of five, rather than six, courses on your UCAS form. The switch met remarkably little resistance – perhaps because most applicants, having set their heart on one or two courses with genuine appeal, were going through the motions by the time it came to choosing a sixth. Applicants in medicine, dentistry and veterinary science were already restricted to four choices, so they now have the option of only one additional choice in another subject.

The other important restriction is that if you are considering applying to Oxford or Cambridge, you can only apply to one or the other; you cannot apply to both Oxford and Cambridge. For both Oxford and Cambridge you may need to take a written test and submit examples of your work (depending on the course selected) and, in addition, for Cambridge, you will be asked to complete a Supplementary Application Questionnaire once Cambridge has received your application from UCAS. The deadline for Oxbridge applications – and for all medicine, dentistry and veterinary science courses – is 15 October. For all other applications the deadline is 15 January (or 24 March for some specified art and design courses).

Applicants do not have to use up all five choices, although obviously you may reduce your chances of success by narrowing your options. If you do choose fewer than five courses, you can still add another to your form up to June 30, as long as you have not accepted or declined any offers. Nor do you have to choose five different universities if more than one course at the same institution attracts you – perhaps because the institution itself is the real draw and one course has lower entrance requirements than the other. Universities are not allowed to see where else you have applied, or whether you have chosen the same subject elsewhere. But they will be aware of multiple applications within their own institution. It is, in any case, more difficult to write a convincing personal statement if it has to cover more than one subject.

For each course you select, you will need to put the UCAS code on the form – and you should check carefully that you have the correct code and understand any special requirements that may be detailed on the UCAS description of the course. You will also need to indicate whether you are applying for a deferred entry (for example, if you are taking a gap year – see page 197).

Education

In this section you will need to give details of the schools and colleges you have attended, and the qualifications you have obtained or are preparing for. The UCAS website gives plenty of advice on the ways in which you should enter this information, to ensure that all your relevant qualifications are included with their grades. While UCAS does not need to see qualification certificates, it can double-check results with the examination boards to ensure that no-one is tempted to modify their results.

Personal statements

As the competition for places on popular courses has become more intense, so the value attached to the personal statement has increased. Admissions officers look for a sign of potential beyond the high grades that growing numbers of applicants offer. Many (but not all) value success in extracurricular activities such as drama, sport or the Duke of Edinburgh's

Award scheme. But your first priority should be to demonstrate an interest in and understanding of your chosen subject beyond the confines of the exam syllabus.

This is not easy in a relatively short statement that can readily sound trite or pretentious. You should resist any temptation to lie, particularly if there is any chance of an interview. A claim to have been inspired by a book that you have not read will backfire instantly under questioning and, even without an interview, experienced academics are likely to see through grandiose statements that appear at odds with a teacher's reference. Genuine experiences of after-hours clubs, lectures or visits – better still, work experience or actual reading around the syllabus – are much more likely to strike the right note. Take advice from teachers and, if there is still time before you make your application, look for some subject-related activities that will help fill out your statement.

Admissions officers are also looking for evidence of character that will make you a productive member of their university and, eventually, a successful graduate. Taking responsibility in any area of school or college life suggests this, while evidence of initiative and self-discipline is also valuable, since higher education involves much more independent study than sixth-formers are used to.

Your overall aim in writing your personal statement is to persuade the admissions officer to pick you out of the piles of applications on his or her desk. That means trying to stand out from an often rather dull and uniform set of statements based around the curriculum and the more predictable sixth-form activities. Everyone is going to say they love reading, for example; narrow your interest down to an area of (real) interest. Don't be afraid to include the unusual, but bear in mind that an academic's sense of humour may not be the same as yours.

Give particular thought to why you want to study your chosen subject – especially if it is not one you have taken at school or college. You need to show that your interests and skills are well-suited to the course and, if it is a vocational degree, that you know how you envisage using the qualification. Admissions officers want to feel that you will be committed to their subject for the length of the course, which could be three, four or even five years, and capable of achieving good results.

Your school or college should be the best source of advice, since they see personal statements every year, but there are others. The UCAS website has a useful checklist of themes that you may wish to address, while sites such as **www.studential.com** also provide tips. But do not fall into the trap of cutting and pasting from the model statements included on such sites – both UCAS and individual universities have software that will spot plagiarism immediately. In one year, no fewer than one in twenty applicants came to grief in this way, and more than 200 applicants claimed to trace a passion for science back to setting their pyjamas on fire when experimenting with a chemistry set that they received as a birthday present. Plagiarists of this type are unlikely to be disqualified, but they destroy the credibility of their application.

Try not to cram in more than the limited space will allow – admissions officers will have many statements to go through, and judicious editing may be rewarded. As long as you write clearly – preferably in paragraphs and possibly with sub-headings – it will be up to you what to include. It is a personal statement. But consider these points:

» What attracts you to this subject (or subjects, in the case of dual or combined honours)?
» Have you undertaken relevant work experience or voluntary activities, either through school or elsewhere?
» Have you taken part in other extra-curricular activities that demonstrate character – perhaps as a prefect, on the sports field or in the arts?

- » Have you been involved in other academic pursuits, such as Gifted and Talented programmes, widening participation schemes, or courses in other subjects?
- » Which aspects of your current courses have you found particularly stimulating?
- » Are you planning a gap year? If so, explain what you intend to do and how it will affect your studies. Some subjects – notably maths – actively discourage a break in studies.
- » What other outside interests might you include that show that you are well rounded?

The Apply system allows 4,000 characters, or 47 lines for your statement. While there is no requirement to fill all the space, it should not look embarrassingly short. UCAS recommends using a word-processing package to compile the statement before pasting it into the application system. This is because Apply will time-out after 35 minutes of inactivity, so there is a danger of losing valuable material. Working offline also has the advantage of leaving you with a copy and making it easier to show it to others.

References

Hand in hand with your personal statement goes the reference from your school, college or, in the case of mature students, someone who knows you well but is not a friend or family member. The reference has to be independent – you are specifically forbidden to change any part of it if you send off your own application – but that does not mean you should not try to influence what it contains. Most schools and colleges conduct informal interviews before compiling a reference, but it does no harm to draw up a list of the achievements that you would like to see included. Referees cannot know every detail of a candidate's interests and most welcome an aide memoire.

The UCAS guidelines skirt around the candidate's right to see his or her reference, but it does exist. Schools' practices vary, but most now show the applicant the completed reference. Where this is not the case, the candidate can pay UCAS £10 for a copy, although at this stage it is obviously too late to influence the contents. Better, if you can, to see it before it goes off, in case there are factual inaccuracies that can be corrected.

Timing

The general deadline for applications through UCAS is 15 January but even those received up to 30 June will be considered if the relevant courses still have vacancies. After that, you will be limited to Clearing, or an application for the following year. In theory – and usually in practice – all applications submitted by the January deadline are given equal consideration. But the best advice is to get your application in early: before Christmas, or earlier if possible. Applications are accepted from September onwards, so the autumn half-term is a sensible target date for completing the process. While no offers are made before the deadline, many admissions officers look through applications as they come in and may make a mental note of promising candidates. If your form arrives with the deadline looming, you may appear less organised than those who submitted in good time; and your application may be one of a large batch that receives a more cursory first reading than the early arrivals. Under UCAS rules, last-minute applicants should not be at a disadvantage, but why take the risk?

Next steps

Once your application has been processed by UCAS, you will receive a welcome letter confirming your choices and summarising what will happen next. The letter will contain a reminder of your identification number and the username and password that you used to

Timetable for applications (based on 2009-10 dates)

May onwards	Find out about courses and universities. Attend university open days.
September	Registration starts for UCAS Apply.
15 October	Final day for applications to Oxford and Cambridge and for all courses in medicine, dentistry and veterinary science.
15 January	Final day for all other applications from UK and EU students to ensure that your application given equal consideration with all other applicants. Now also the deadline for all art and design courses except those which have a 24 March deadline (specified in UCAS Course Search).
16 January-30 June	New applications continue to be accepted by UCAS, but only considered by universities if the relevant courses have vacancies.
25 February	Start of applications through UCAS Extra.
24 March	Final day for applications for those art and design courses that specify this date.
31 March	Universities should have sent decisions on all applications received by 15 January, but decisions may be later than this.
5 May	Final day by which applicants have to decide on their choices if application submitted by 15 January and all decisions received by 31 March (exact date for each applicant will be confirmed by UCAS). If you do not reply to UCAS, they will decline your offers.
7 May	UCAS must receive all decisions from universities if you applied by 15 January.
8 June	Final day by which applicants have to decide on their choices if application submitted by 15 January and all decisions received by 7 May (exact date for each applicant will be confirmed by UCAS).
1 July	Any application received from this date held until Clearing starts.
6 July	Final day for applications through UCAS Extra.
20 July	Universities must give decisions on all applications submitted by 30 June. You must make a decision on these offers by 27 July.
mid August	Clearing and Adjustment start after publication of exam results. Scottish results issued earlier than for the rest of the UK.
31 August	Adjustment closes.
20 September	Last day UCAS will accept applications for courses about to start.
25 October	Last date by which a university can accept you through Clearing. Last day to add a Clearing choice.

apply. These will also give you access to Track, the online system that allows you to follow the progress of your application. Check all the details carefully: you have 14 days to contact UCAS to correct any errors. From 2010 universities can make direct contact with you through Track, including arranging interviews.

After that, it is just a matter of waiting for universities to make their decisions, which can take days, weeks or even months, depending on the university and the course. Some obviously see an advantage in being the first to make an offer – it is a memorable moment to be reassured that at least one of your chosen institutions wants you – and may send their response almost immediately. Others take much longer, perhaps because they have so many good applications to consider, or maybe because they are waiting to see which of their applicants withdraw when Oxford and Cambridge make their offers. Universities are asked to make all their decisions by the end of March, and most have done so long before that.

Interviews

Unless you are applying for a course in health or education that brings you into direct contact with the public, the chances are you will not have a selection interview. For prospective medics, vets, dentists or teachers, a face-to-face assessment of your suitability will be crucial to your chances of success. Likewise in the performing arts, the interview may be as important as your exam grades. Oxford and Cambridge still interview applicants in all subjects, and a few of the top universities see a significant proportion. But the expansion of higher education has made it impractical to interview everyone, and many admissions experts are sceptical about interviews.

What has become more common, however, is the "sales" interview, where the university is really selling itself to the candidate. There may still be testing questions, but the admissions staff have already made their minds up and are actually trying to persuade you to accept an offer. Indeed, you will probably be given a clear indication at the end of the interview that one is on its way. The technique seems to work, perhaps because you have invested time and nervous energy in a sometimes lengthy trip, as well as acquiring a more detailed impression of both the department and the university.

The difficulty can come in spotting which type of interview is which. The "real" ones require lengthy preparation, revisiting your personal statement and reading beyond the exam syllabus. Dress smartly and make sure that you are on time. Impressions count for a lot at interviews, so have a question of your own ready, as well as being prepared to give answers.

While you would not want to appear ignorant at a "sales" interview, lengthy preparation might be a waste of valuable time during a period of revision. Naturally, you should err on the side of caution, but if your predicted grades are well above the standard offer and the subject is not one that normally requires an interview, it is likely that the invitation is a sales pitch. It is still worth going, unless you have changed your mind about the application.

Offers

When your chosen universities respond to your application, there will be one of three answers:
- » Unconditional Offer (U): This is a possibility only if you applied after satisfying the entrance requirements – usually if you are applying as a mature student, while on a gap year, after resitting exams or, in Scotland, after completing Highers.
- » Conditional Offer (C): The university offers a place subject to you achieving set grades or points on the UCAS tariff.
- » Rejection (R): You do not have the right qualifications, or have lost out to stronger competition.

If you have chosen wisely, you should have more than one offer to choose from, so you will be required to pick your favourite as your firm acceptance – known as UF if it was an unconditional offer and CF if it was conditional. Candidates with conditional offers can also accept a second offer, with lower grades, as an Insurance choice (CI). You must then decline any other offers that you have.

You do not have to make an Insurance choice – indeed, you may decline all your offers if you have changed your mind about your career path or regret your course decisions. But most people prefer the security of a back-up route into higher education if their grades fall short. You must be sure that your firm acceptance is definitely your first choice because you will be allocated a place automatically if you meet the university's conditions. It is no good at this stage deciding that you prefer your Insurance choice because UCAS rules will not allow a switch.

The only way round those rules – if your personal circumstances have changed, or you do much better than expected and are determined to "trade up" to another university – is through direct contact with the universities concerned. Your firm acceptance institution has to be prepared to release you so that your new choice can award you a place in Clearing. Neither is under any obligation to do so but, in practice, it is rare for a university to insist that a student joins against his or her wishes. Admissions staff will do all they can to persuade you that your original choice was the right one – as it may well have been, if your research was thorough – but it will almost certainly be your decision in the end.

UCAS Extra

If things do go wrong and you receive five rejections, that need not be the end of your higher education ambitions. From the end of February until the end of June, you have another chance through UCAS Extra, a listing of courses that still have vacancies after the initial round of offers. Extra is sometimes dismissed (wrongly) as a repository of second-rate courses. In fact, even in the boom year for applications of 2010, even most Russell Group universities had hundreds of courses listed in a wide variety of subjects.

You will be notified if you are eligible for Extra and can then select courses marked as available on the UCAS website. Applications are made, one at a time, through UCAS Track. If you do not receive an offer, or you choose to decline one, you can continue applying for other courses until you are successful. About half of those applying through Extra normally find a place.

Results Day

Rule Number One on results day is to be at home, or at least in communication. Places are filled extremely rapidly with the newest electronic admissions systems, and you cannot afford to be on some remote beach if there are complications. If you get the grades stipulated in your conditional offer, the process should work smoothly and you can begin celebrating. You don't need to do anything – Track will let you know as soon as your place is confirmed and the paperwork will arrive in a day or two. You can phone the university to make quite sure, but it should not be necessary and you will be joining a long queue of people doing the same thing.

If the results are not what you hoped – and particularly if you just miss your grades – you need to be on the phone and taking advice from your school or college. In a year when results are better than expected, some universities will stick to the letter of their offers, perhaps refusing to accept your AAC grades when they had demanded ABB. Others will forgive a dropped grade to take a candidate who is regarded as promising, rather than go into Clearing to recruit an unknown quantity. Admissions staff may be persuadable – particularly if there are extenuating personal circumstances, or the dropped grade is in a subject that is not relevant to your chosen course. Try to get a teacher to support your case, and be persistent if there is any prospect of flexibility.

One option, if your results are lower than predicted, is to ask for papers to be re-marked, as growing numbers do each year. The school may ask for a whole batch to be re-marked, and you should ensure that your chosen universities know this if it may make the difference to whether or not you satisfy your offer. If your grades improve, the university will review its decision, but if by then it has filled all its places, you may have to wait until next year to start the course.

Results Day is bound to be stressful, unless you are absolutely confident that you achieved the required grades – more of a possibility in an era of modular courses with marks along the way. But for thousands of students Track has removed the agony of opening the envelope or scanning a results noticeboard. From midnight on the eve of A-level results day, the system informs those who have already won a place on their chosen course. You will not learn your grades until later, but at least your immediate future is clear.

If you took Scottish Highers, you will have had your results for more than a week by the time the A-level grades are published. If you missed your grades, there is no need to wait for A levels before you begin approaching universities. Admissions staff at English universities may not wish to commit themselves before they see results from south of the border, but Scottish universities will be filling places immediately and all should be prepared to give you an idea of your prospects.

Adjustment

If your grades are better than those demanded by your first-choice university, there is now an opportunity to "trade up". Introduced in 2009, the Adjustment Period runs for only five days after you have received your results, so there is no time to waste. First, go into the Track system and click on "Register for Adjustment" and then contact your preferred institutions to find another place. If none is available, or you decide not to move, your initial offer will remain open.

Only 382 students switched places in the first year of adjustment. UCAS is yet to publish a breakdown of which universities were involved, but it is known that many students successfully went back to institutions that had rejected them at the initial application stage. The numbers using the system may well rise as it becomes better known, particularly if students become more cautious with their applications in response to the increased demand for places.

Clearing

If you have the opposite problem and do not have a place on Results Day, there will still be plenty of options through the UCAS Clearing scheme. Over 47,000 people – very nearly 10 per cent of all applicants – found a place through this route in 2009. There may well be fewer places filled through Clearing in 2011, but thousands of applications will still be successful. Although the most popular courses fill up quickly, many remain open up to and beyond the start of the academic year. And, at least at the start of the process, the range of courses with vacancies is much wider than in Extra. You will not find Oxford or Cambridge, but most universities will list some courses, and most subjects will be available somewhere.

Clearing runs from Results Day until late September, matching students without places to full-time courses with vacancies. As long as you are not holding any offers and you have not withdrawn your application, you are eligible automatically. Indeed, you will go straight into

Clearing if you apply after 30 June. You will be sent a Clearing number via Track to quote to universities.

After that, it is just a matter of trawling through the lists on the UCAS website, and elsewhere, before making a direct approach to the university offering the course that appeals most, and where you have a realistic chance of a place. Tens of thousands of hopefuls will be doing the same thing, so do not waste time on courses where the standard offer is far above your grades. Universities run Clearing hotlines and have become adept at dealing with a large number of calls in a short period, but you can still spend a long time on the phone at a time when the most desirable places are beginning to disappear. If you can't get through – or even if you can – send an email setting out your grades and detailing the course that interests you.

The best advice is to plan ahead and not to wait for Results Day to draw up a list of possible Clearing targets. Many universities publish lists of courses that are likely to be in Clearing on their websites from the start of August. Think again about some of the courses that you considered when making your original application, or others at your chosen universities that had lower entrance requirements – perhaps dual honours, rather than single honours. But beware of switching to another subject simply because you have the right grades – you still have to sustain your interest and be capable of succeeding over three or more years. Many of the students who drop out of degrees are those who chose the wrong course in a rush during Clearing.

In short, you should start your search straight away if you do find yourself in Clearing, and act decisively, but do not panic. Apply the same criteria that you used in choosing courses initially: look at the syllabus and satisfy yourself that you will enjoy the course, that the university is one which you are happy to attend, and that the qualification will take you where you want to go in your career. You can make as many approaches as you like, until you are accepted on the course of your choice.

Most of the available vacancies will appear in Clearing lists, but some of the universities towards the top of the league tables may have a limited number of openings that they choose not to advertise – either for reasons of status or because they do not want the administrative burden of fielding large numbers of calls to fill a handful of courses. If there is a course that you find particularly attractive – especially if you have good grades and are applying late – it may be worth making a speculative call. Sometimes a number of candidates holding offers drop grades and you may be on the spot at the right moment.

What are the alternatives?

If your results are lower than expected and there is nothing you want in Clearing, there are several things you can do. The first is to resit one or more subjects. The modular nature of most courses means that you will have a clear idea of what you need to do to get better grades. You can go back to school or college, try a "crammer" or take a job and revise in the evenings. Although some colleges have a good success rate with re-takes, you have to be highly focused and realistic about the likely improvements. Some of the most competitive courses, such as medicine, may demand higher grades for a second application, so be sure you know the details before you commit yourself to a year's delay.

Other options are to get a job and study part-time, or to take a break from studying and return later in your career. The part-time route can be arduous – many young people find a job enough to handle without the extra burden of academic work. But others find it just the combination they need for a fulfilling life. It all depends on your job, your social life and your commitment to the subject you will study. It may be that a relatively short break is all that you need to rekindle your enthusiasm for studying. Many universities now have a majority of mature students, so you need not be out of place if this is your chosen route.

Taking a gap year

The other increasingly popular option – despite the economic downturn – is to take a gap year. About 7 per cent of applicants now defer their entry until the following year while they travel, or do voluntary or paid work. A whole industry has grown up around tailor-made activities, many of them in Asia, Africa or Latin America. Some have been criticised for doing more for the organisers than the underprivileged communities that they purport to assist, but there are programmes that are useful and character-building, as well as safe. Most of the overseas programmes are not cheap, but raising the money can be part of the experience. The alternative is to stay closer to home and make your contribution through organisations like Community Service Volunteers (**www.csv.org.uk**) or to take a job that will make higher education more affordable when the time comes.

Many admissions staff are happy to facilitate gap years because they think it makes for more mature, rounded students than those who come straight from school. The right programme may even increase your chances of winning a place, if it is relevant to your course. But there are subjects – maths in particular – that discourage a break because it takes too long to pick up study skills where you left off. From the student's point of view, you should also bear in mind that a gap year postpones the moment at which you embark on a career. This may be important if your course is a long one, such as medicine or architecture.

If you are considering a gap year, it makes sense to apply for a deferred place, rather than waiting for your results before applying. The application form has a section for deferments. That allows you to sort out your immediate future before you start travelling or working, and leaves you the option of changing your mind if circumstances change.

Useful websites

The following websites will help you find out more about the topics discussed in this chapter. The essential website for making an application is, of course, that of UCAS:
www.ucas.com/students/applying/
For applications to music conservatoires: **www.cukas.ac.uk**
For applications for graduate teacher training: **www.gttr.ac.uk**
For advice on your personal statement:
www.ucas.com/students/applying/howtoapply/personalstatement
www.studential.com

Gap years

To help you consider options and start planning: **www.gapadvice.org**
For links to volunteering opportunities in the UK: **www.do-it.org.uk**
For links to many not-for-profit gap year organisations: **www.yearoutgroup.org**
For work placements relevant to university courses: **www.yini.org.uk**
Also consult: Community Service Volunteers: **www.csv.org.uk**
v (the national young volunteers service): **www.vinspired.com**
Worldwide Volunteering: **http://wwv.org.uk**
Lattitude Global Volunteering: **www.lattitude.org.uk**
Volunteer Africa: **www.volunteerafrica.org**

7 The Cost of Studying

Students have been notoriously lax about money in the past, but the mountain of debt that many now accumulate has made even the most casual applicant think twice about how they will afford higher education. There is no denying that going to university has become an expensive business, but funding is available – especially for those from less affluent backgrounds – to make it affordable.

No one knows what the long-term effects of the recession will be, but most independent research continues to show that it is worth investing in a degree – as long as you pick the right course and work hard enough to ensure that you at least gain your qualification. The extra amount you earn during a lifetime, over and above what you would have got without a degree, should far outstrip the cost of your higher education in most subjects at most universities.

Funding help

Fortunately, there are still enough sources of funding to enable most students to meet the costs of higher education and live reasonably – albeit building up considerable debts in the process. But, once again, it takes perseverance to put together the best possible package. Depending on your family income and where you live in the UK, you may be entitled to a range of grants, bursaries or scholarships. And then there are further calculations to do on fee levels, the length of courses and the cost of living at different universities. With many families feeling the pinch, it has never been more important to get it right.

Getting into debt is now a fact of life for almost all students – the Student Loans Company is paying out almost £3 billion a year in maintenance loans, on top of the £2 billion in tuition fees that it administers. Most research now puts average graduate debt at around £20,000. The good news is that most of it is in the form of student loans, which are pegged to inflation and repayable only when a graduate is earning at least £15,000 a year – although many students also have bank overdrafts and owe money on credit cards.

Forewarned is forearmed, and a little bit of careful financial planning and research into help that is available can go a long way to helping you emerge from your university education with a level of debt that is not going to become a millstone for life. As well as student loans, which are still provided at generous rates and under very favourable terms and conditions, you can shop around for university bursaries and scholarships and other sponsorship packages, and seek out any supplementary support to which you may be entitled. The latter may include a maintenance grant: despite recent changes in eligibility, these are available to a much larger slice of the population than was the case in the early years of tuition fees.

However, even with a grant, you will need to gather together all the resources you can to survive. Analysis by the National Union of Students (NUS) suggests that it is not possible to get by on student loans and grants alone. Savings, earnings, and help from family and friends generally have to be added to the pot. The information provided below should at least help you understand how big your pot needs to be, and what you can expect to be added and taken away from it.

University tuition fees

A new student funding system was introduced in England and Northern Ireland in 2006 that also had a major impact on the systems in Scotland and Wales. A review of higher education funding in England was under way as the *Guide* went to press, under the chairmanship of Lord Browne. It will consider the position of postgraduates and part-time students, as well as the full-time undergraduates who pay top-up fees. Student finance has become a recurring problem for governments, as well as for the students themselves, and the new administration will have to decide which of the review's recommendations to adopt.

With changes, large or small, becoming almost an annual occurrence, it is essential to consult the latest information provided by Government agencies. It is worth checking the following websites for the latest information:

» England: **www.direct.gov.uk/studentfinance**
» Wales: **www.studentfinancewales.co.uk**
» Scotland: **www.saas.gov.uk**
» Northern Ireland: **www.studentfinanceni.co.uk**

What follows is a summary of the position for British students at the start of 2010. While there are substantial differences across the four countries of the UK, there is one important piece of common ground. Up-front payment of fees is no longer compulsory, as students can take out a fee loan (see below) to cover them. This is repayable in instalments after graduation, when your earnings reach the threshold set by the Government.

Fees in England and Northern Ireland

In England and Northern Ireland the maximum tuition fee for full-time undergraduates will be £3,290 in 2010-11, rising again in line with inflation in 2011-12. Lord Browne's review of tuition fees might allow universities to charge significantly more, but any rise above inflation

Tuition fees within the UK for 2010-11

Country	Level
England	**£3,290**
Northern Ireland	**£3,290**
Wales	**£3,290** (new students no longer receive a tuition fee grant)
Scotland	**£1,820** (no fees paid by students whose homes are in Scotland)
Scotland (Medicine)	**£2,895** (no fees paid by students whose homes are in Scotland)

» Universities in England, Northern Ireland and Wales can charge reduced fees, but no institution is taking up this option for courses starting in 2010.
» The Scottish fees are fixed.

would be difficult to implement before 2012 and is unlikely to apply to students beginning courses in 2011. Such a decision would be a political hot potato for an incoming government – particularly in the current economic circumstances – but the worsening state of university budgets has shortened the odds on some increase for new students flowing from the review. It would be unprecedented for this to apply to those who have already started courses.

Individual universities can, theoretically, charge less than the maximum, including setting different fees for different subjects. Some do charge less for foundation degrees and Higher National Diplomas, two-year courses that can be a cost-effective stepping stone to a full degree. But so far almost every university has been charging the top rate for full-time degree courses, and has been trying instead to lure students with a range of bursaries, scholarships and other offers, such as free laptops. Only two universities, Leeds Metropolitan University and the University of Greenwich, charged less than the maximum tuition fee for degrees in 2009–10, and both have now come into line with the rest and are planning to charge £3,290 in 2010–11.

Fees in Scotland
In Scotland, the fee for 2010–11 has been held at £1,820 (£2,895 for medical students), but only students coming to study in Scotland from other UK countries have to pay it. These students can also avoid having to pay up front by applying for a student loan administered by their funding agency. Students whose home is in Scotland and are studying at a Scottish university apply to the Student Awards Agency for Scotland (SAAS) to have their fees paid for them. Scottish students no longer have to contribute to a graduate endowment to cover this cost, following a decision by the Scottish Parliament to abolish graduate endowments.

Fees in Wales
The Welsh Assembly Government has agreed a similar fee policy to England, with universities allowed to charge variable fees of up to £3,290 in 2010–11. Students who normally live in Wales and choose to study there have been eligible for a tuition fee grant of up to £1,980 a year to offset this cost, but this has now been withdrawn in order to provide more bursaries for students from low-income families. The only exceptions will be continuing students and new entrants who deferred their place from 2009-10 to take a gap year.

Student loans
Around 80 per cent of students take out a student loan, and it is not difficult to work out why. First of all, as noted earlier, it is very difficult to get by financially without one. If you don't take out a loan to cover your fees, then you will have to pay for them up front, and with living costs estimated to average more than £9,000 a year (over £11,000 in London), most students find it impossible to cover everything on savings and earnings alone. The only reasons to consider paying your fees up front might be if your parents are offering to meet the costs, or if a university is offering a discount if you do so. The University of Gloucestershire, for instance, has been offering a 10 per cent discount to those who pay the full fee in advance. There are two types of student loan – one to cover the cost of tuition fees and another to help you cover the cost of living.

Tuition fees loan
In the case of fees loans, everyone can borrow up to the full amount needed to cover the cost of their tuition fees. Scots studying in Scotland are even better off, as there are no tuition fees to pay so no need for a loan.

Maintenance loan

The second type of student loan, a maintenance loan, is means-tested. The amount you can borrow therefore depends on a number of factors, including your family income, where you intend to study, and whether you expect to be living at home. Final-year students also receive less than those in earlier years. The maximum maintenance loan available in 2010–11 is £4,950 (£6,928 in London) for a full academic year. Three quarters of the maintenance loan is available to you regardless of your family circumstances, while the remaining quarter is means-tested. If your parents are separated, divorced or widowed, then only the parent with whom you normally live will be assessed. However, if that parent has married again, entered into a civil partnership, or has a partner of the opposite sex, then both their incomes will be taken into account.

Maintenance loans in Scotland

In Scotland, the rules and regulations for maintenance loans are different. The loans available are lower than the rest of the UK, particularly in the case of students going to study in London, and the proportion that is means-tested is higher. In 2010–11 the maximum loan available is £5,710. All the latest details can be found at **www.saas.gov.uk**.

Loans for mature students

Mature students (those who are over the age of 25, married, or have supported themselves for at least three years before entering university) are assessed for loan and grant entitlements on their own income plus that of their spouse or partner. Grants are also available for those with children, for single parents, and for students with adult dependants. Further support is available for students with children through the Parents' Learning Allowance and Child Tax Credit system.

Payment of loans

Maintenance loans are usually paid in three instalments into your bank or building society account. English students should apply for grants and loans through Student Finance England,

Maintenance grants and loan amounts for a new first-year English student 2010

Household income	Maintenance grant	Maintenance loan living away from home but not in London	Maintenance loan living away from in London	Maintenance loan living at parents' home
£25,000	£2,906	£3,497	£5,475	£2,385
£30,000	£1,906	£3,997	£5,975	£2,885
£40,000	£711	£4,595	£6,573	£3,483
£50,000	£52	£4,924	£6,902	£3,812
£50,778	£0	£4,950	£6,928	£3,838

» No maintenance grants are paid when the household income exceed £50,020.
» The size of the maintenance loan is reduced by £1 for every £5 of the total income over £50,778, until the loan is 72 per cent of the value of the full loan. Every eligible student, regardless of household income, is eligible to a loan equivalent to 72 per cent of the full loan.
» Total funding available is the maintenance grant plus the relevant maintenance loan.
» Schemes are different in Northern Ireland, Wales and Scotland and the relevant funding organisations should be consulted.

Welsh students through Student Finance Wales, Scottish students through the Student Awards Agency for Scotland, and those in Northern Ireland through Student Finance NI or their Education and Library Board. You should make your application as soon as you have received an offer of a place at university. European Union students from outside the UK will usually be sent an application form by the university that has offered them a place.

Repaying loans

Any money you borrow via the Student Loans Company that administers the scheme, is lent at a "nominal" interest rate. This fell in 2009–10 to just 1.5 per cent, which was very attractive compared with any loans available from high-street banks or credit card companies. Some students try to make their loan money for living costs go further by putting it into a high interest bank account or an ISA. Whatever you do with it, you won't have to start making repayments until you graduate and begin earning at least £15,000 a year. Even then, under new rules introduced in 2008–09, you will be able to take a "repayment holiday" of up to five years after graduation, so you don't have to repay a penny in that time.

Remember, however, that interest on your loan continues to accrue from the time you take it out to until you have paid it off. The good news is that the amount you repay each month is linked to your income, rather than the amount you owe. Repayments are deducted through the tax system at a rate of 9 per cent on anything you are earning above £15,000 a year: for example monthly repayments for a graduate earning £20,000 a year would work out at £37.50 a month. If your income falls below the £15,000 threshold, then your repayments stop until you start earning more again.

Grants

In the good old days, most students didn't have to pay fees and many received relatively generous maintenance grants to help them cover day-to-day costs. After a brief disappearance, these non-repayable grants have made a comeback, and are particularly significant if you come from a low-income family. The size and type of grants available, and the rules and regulations governing their distribution, are different for each country of the UK. To receive a grant, students whose home is in England must apply through Student Finance England, in Wales to Student Finance Wales, those from Scotland must apply to the Student Awards Agency for Scotland, and those from Northern Ireland to Student Finance NI or their Education and Library Board. In addition, there are various types of bursaries and scholarships you can apply for, and other types of grants or support in each country to help students in particular circumstances, such as those that have a disability. What follows is a description of the maintenance grant arrangements country-by-country.

England

Students from England can apply for a maintenance grant from the Government and a bursary from their university. Maintenance grants in England are worth up to £2,906 in 2010–11, but the amount you actually get (paid in three instalments) depends on your family or "household residual" income. If you come from a household with an income of £25,000 a year or less, then you can get a full grant. A partial grant is available for all of those from households earning between £25,000 and £50,020 a year. The actual amount you will get in this case is subject to a fairly complicated calculation to work out how much your family should theoretically contribute to your upkeep. There is no obligation on your family to provide their share, but you will certainly receive some kind of grant from the state. However, those whose family income is calculated to be higher than £50,020 will not receive a grant. Another important rule is that for every £1 you receive in maintenance grant, the amount you can borrow in student loans falls by £1. Thus, it is not possible to have both a full grant and a maximum student loan.

The almost bewildering array of bursaries and scholarships on offer from universities is discussed in a separate section below.

Northern Ireland

Arrangements for applying for and receiving means-tested maintenance grants and university bursaries and scholarships are very similar in Northern Ireland to those in England. The main difference is that there is a more generous upper limit (£3,475 for 2010–11) on grants in Northern Ireland. Up to £1,887 of the maintenance grant will be paid in substitution for an element of the student loan for maintenance. There is also a Special Support Grant of the same value for full-time students who may be eligible to receive benefits such as Income Support or Housing Benefit while they are studying. However, you cannot receive both the maintenance grant and the Special Support Grant.

Wales

Students from Wales can apply for a means-tested Assembly Learning Grant which was frozen at a maximum of £2,906 for 2010–11. In addition, every full-time higher education student, regardless of where they come from in the UK, will be considered for a means-tested Welsh Bursary worth a maximum of £329 a year. This comes on top of whatever scholarships and

---

Funding timetable

It is vital that you sort out your funding arrangements before you start at university. Note that each funding agency has its own arrangements, and it is very important that you find out the exact details from them. The dates below give general indications of key dates.

March/April
» Online and paper application forms become available from funding agencies.
» You must contact the appropriate funding agency to make an application. For funding in England contact **www.studentfinanceengland.co.uk** rather than your LEA, as was the case before 2009.
» Complete application form as soon as possible. At this stage select the university offer that will be your first choice.
» Check details of bursaries and scholarships available from your selected universities.

May/June
» Funding agencies will give you details of the financial support they can offer.
» Last date for making an application to ensure funding is ready for you at the start of term (exact date varies significantly between agencies).

August
» Tell your funding agency if the university or course you have been accepted for is different from that originally given them.

September
» Take letter confirming funding to your university for registration.
» After registration, the first part of funds will be released to you.

bursaries Welsh institutions may offer.

Scotland

In Scotland, the maintenance grant is known as a Young Students' Bursary (YSB), and is also means-tested and does not have to be repaid. For 2010–11, the maximum bursary is £2,640 if you come from a family with an annual income of £19,310 or less. If your family income is between this amount and £34,195 you will be entitled to a partial bursary, but if it is higher than £34,195 you will receive nothing. You can get an additional student loan if your family income is £21,760 or less. If you qualify for the YSB then you may also qualify for an additional loan of up to £605.

Bursaries and scholarships

Bursaries and scholarships offered by universities and colleges are an important part of the student financial support system ushered in by the Government to try to ensure people could still afford to go to university. All English universities and colleges charging more than £2,835 a year for a course are required to provide a non-repayable bursary or scholarship to students on these courses from low-income families who are receiving the full maintenance grant. What this means is that students who receive a full grant and are being charged the maximum tuition fee of £3,290 are entitled to a bursary or scholarship of at least £329. However, most universities are offering far more than this – and have also extended the principle to cover students in receipt of a partial grant. Some have been offering bursaries of £1,000 a year, or more, on the basis of household income, examination results and/or a home in the region.

Finding out about bursaries

There is now such a variety of bursaries and scholarships on offer that while, on the one hand, it is worth shopping around to see what you can get, on the other, you could well feel bewildered by the experience of doing so. The Universities and Colleges Admissions Service (UCAS) has done its best to help by getting institutions to provide information about what's on offer to students applying for particular courses on its course search pages at **www.ucas.com**. The websites of individual institutions also carry details of scholarships, bursaries and other financial support available. Details are given in the table at the end of this chapter.

The whole system of bursaries and scholarships is overseen for England and Wales by the Office for Fair Access. It requires all universities to submit what are called "Access Agreements" that contain details of what fees they intend to charge and what scholarships and bursaries they are offering. Access Agreements also describe other kinds of financial support, such as "hardship funds". Some awards are guaranteed depending on your personal circumstances, while others are available through open competition. St Mary's University College, Twickenham, for instance, has been offering 75 "entry scholarships" worth up to £1,000 each for students who can demonstrate a high level of commitment and ability in sport, creativity or work for the community. Copies of access agreements can be found at **www.offa.org.uk**.

Applying for bursaries

Do take note of the application procedures for scholarships and bursaries, as these vary from institution to institution, and even from course to course within individual institutions. There may be a particular deadline you have to meet to apply for an award, or in some cases the university will work out for you whether you are entitled to an award by referring to your funding agency's financial assessment. Remember, too, that if your personal circumstances change part way through a course then your entitlement to a scholarship or bursary may be reviewed.

Where the money comes from
Percentage of UK students receiving the following types of funding:

Student loans	**79%**
Parents	**50%**
Bank overdrafts	**37%**
Part-time job in term time	**34%**
Savings	**32%**
Student grants	**29%**
Part-time holiday work	**26%**
University bursaries	**26%**
Full-time holiday work	**23%**
Relatives (other than parents)	**8%**
Credit cards	**8%**
Bank loans	**5%**
Sponsorship	**3%**
Full-time job in term time	**2%**

Sodexo University Lifestyle Survey 2008

If you feel you still need more help or advice on scholarships or bursaries, you can get this in most cases by referring to a university's website or prospectus. Some institutions also maintain a helpline. Some questions you will need answered include whether the bursary or scholarship is automatic or conditional and, if the latter, when you will find out whether your application has been successful. For some awards, you won't know whether you have qualified until you get your exam results.

Another obvious question is how the scholarship or bursary on offer compares with awards made by another university you might consider applying to. Watch out for institutions that list entitlements that others don't mention but you would get anyway.

Some institutions offer "fee remission" (a lower tuition fee) rather than scholarships or bursaries, which means you may have less cash in hand during your course, but will owe less after you have graduated.

Living in one country, studying in another
As each of the countries of the UK develop their own distinctive systems of student finance, they have been keen to address the question of how students leaving home in one country to go and study in another are affected. For instance, both the Scottish Parliament and the Welsh Assembly have put arrangements in place to try to ensure that Scottish and Welsh students accepting places at English universities are not financially disadvantaged.

UK students who cross borders to study pay the tuition fees of their chosen university and are eligible for a fees loan to cover these. They are also entitled to apply for the scholarships or bursaries on offer from that institution. Any maintenance loan or grant will still come from the awarding bodies of their home country.

The fees loan for Scottish students going to study in Northern Ireland, England or Wales is not dependent on family income, but students from low-income families can get relief from a means-tested non-repayable Students Outside Scotland Bursary. The income thresholds used to decide who qualifies for this are the same as those for the Young Students' Bursary (for Scottish students studying in Scotland, see above) but the maximum award is lower, at £2,150 (cf. £2,640) for 2010–11.

For students studying in Wales from September 2008, every eligible full-time higher education student, regardless of where they come from in the UK, is considered for a means-tested Welsh Bursary of a maximum of £329 a year.

European Union laws stipulate that EU students from outside the UK must be charged the same tuition fees as those paid by UK students who are studying in their home country, rather than the higher fees paid by students from outside the EU. They can also apply for a fee loan and may be considered for some of the scholarships and bursaries offered by individual institutions. Only students who have been living and studying in the UK for at least three years can apply for a maintenance loan or grant.

If you haven't, then you will need to apply for such assistance from the authorities in your own country. Tuition fee rules for non UK European Union students are the same in Scotland as for Scottish students – that is, you do not have to pay a tuition fee. There are also no fees to pay for exchange students coming to the UK, including those on the Socrates Programme.

Further sources of income
If you are feeling daunted by the potential costs, you can take some comfort from this section outlining just some of the ways you can raise additional money to help you cover your expenses.

Taking a gap year
You can begin the process of earning money to help pay for your higher education even before you enter university, by taking a gap year. Many students are attracted to the idea of taking a year out because it offers them a chance to travel, gain new experiences, grow up a little – and maybe earn some money. Indeed, necessity seems to have recently shifted the reasons for taking a gap year from an emphasis on personal development to one more focused on boosting the bank balance in preparation for beginning life as a student. Of course, there is still potentially much more to taking a gap year than financial gain, and while short-term considerations may be focusing your mind in that direction, the longer-term benefits of taking part in cultural exchanges and courses, expeditions, volunteering or structured work placements are considerable for most people. Such benefits include gaining a place at university and embarking on a worthwhile career after graduation. Both university admissions officers and employers look for evidence in candidates that they have more about them than academic ability. The experience you gain on a gap year can help you develop many of the attributes they are looking for, such as interpersonal, organisational and teamwork skills, leadership, creativity, experience of new cultures or work environments, and enterprise.

Various organisations can help you find voluntary work, if this is the way you prefer to spend at least some of your year out. Some examples include v (**www.vinspired.com**), Lattitude Global Volunteering (**www.lattitude.org.uk**) and Volunteer Africa (**www.volunteerafrica.org**).

Work placements can be structured or casual. An example of the structured variety is the Year in Industry Scheme (**www.yini.org.uk**). Sponsorship is also available mainly to those wishing to study engineering or business. To find out more, visit **www.everythingyouwantedto-know.com**.

Further Government support
There are various types of support available from Government sources for students in particular circumstances, other than the main loans, grants and bursaries.
» Undergraduates in financial difficulties can apply for help from the Access to Learning Fund (Financial Contingency Fund in Wales, Hardship Fund in Scotland, Support Funds in Northern Ireland). These are allocated by universities to provide support for anything from

day-to-day study and living costs to unexpected or exceptional expense. The university decides which students need help and how much money to award them. These funds are often targeted at older or disadvantaged students and finalists.

» Students with children can apply for a childcare grant, worth £148.75 a week if you have one child and £225 a week if you have two or more children; and a parents' learning allowance, for help with course-related costs, of between £50 and £1,508.
» Students with disabilities can apply for a disabled students' allowance, worth up to £20,520 for full-time students.
» Any students with a partner, or another adult such as a family member who is financially dependent on them, can apply for an adult dependants' grant of up to £2,642.

If you do not qualify for any of this kind of financial support you may still be able to apply for a Professional and Career Development Loan available from Barclays, the Cooperative Bank and the Royal Bank of Scotland, in partnership with the Young People's Learning Agency. Students on a wide range of vocational courses can borrow from £300 to £8,000 at a fixed rate of interest to fund up to two years of learning.

Part-time work

The need to hold down a part-time job during term time is now a fact of life for more than half of students. Unsurprisingly, students from a working-class background are more likely to need to earn while they learn. A report by UNITE showed that 51 per cent of students from low-income families worked during term time, compared with just over a third of those from higher-income families. If you need or want to earn during term time, it is important to try to ensure that you do not work so many hours that it starts to affect your studies. A survey by the NUS found that 59 per cent of students who worked felt it had an impact on their studies, with 38 per cent missing lectures and over a fifth failing to submit coursework because of their part-time jobs.

Student employment agencies, which can now be found on many university campuses, can help you get the balance right. These introduce employers with work to students seeking work, sometimes even offering jobs within the university itself. But they also abide by codes of practice that regulate both minimum wages and the maximum number of hours worked in term time (typically 15 hours a week).

According to the Halifax bank, the average working student puts in about 18 hours a week, and makes around £6,000 a year out of this. Some firms, such as the big supermarkets, offer continuing part-time employment to their school part-time employees when they go to university. Some students show some enterprise by making use of their expertise in areas like web design to earn some extra money. But most take on casual work in retail stores, restaurants, bars and call centres.

Most students, including those who don't work during term time, get a job during vacations. A Government survey found that 86 per cent of students in their second year of study or above worked during their summer vacation. Most of this kind of work is casual, but some is formalised in a scheme like STEP (Shell Technology Enterprise Programme, www.step.org.uk) or may be part of a sponsorship programme. Many vacation jobs are fairly mundane, but with a bit of imagination and get-up-and-go, it is possible to find more interesting work. Some students broaden their experience by working abroad, others work as film extras earning up to £140 a day, or do a variety of jobs at big events such as the Farnborough Air Show. It is also a good idea to try to use the summer holidays to get some work experience in a field that has some relevance to your career aspirations. Even if you don't get paid, this can significantly enhance your chances of finding employment after graduation.

Banks

You can be certain that once you become a student you will be inundated with special offers from banks, all keen to win you as a customer in the hope that you will remain so after graduation and well into your life as a highly paid professional. Make sure you shop around and try to think beyond the introductory offers of cash, discounted driving lessons, railcards, etc., and consider which account has the best long-term benefits. Banks are more sympathetic to your financial situation as a student than they have been for other customers in the recession, and will generally be ready to offer modest free overdraft facilities.

What you will need to spend money on
Living costs

The NUS estimated that in 2007–08 the average student living outside London would spend £9,176 a year on regular living costs, including rent, food, personal items, travel and leisure. For those living in the capital, the estimated average expenditure was £11,142. Costs will have risen since then, despite low inflation. Little surprise, then, that a growing number of students are choosing to live at home and study at a local university. However, even this option is not necessarily low cost, once travel to and from the university is taken into account.

Certain costs are unavoidable. You have to have a roof over your head, eat enough, clothe yourself, and probably do a certain amount of travelling. But the cost of even these essential items can be cut down significantly through a mixture of shopping around and careful budgeting. If you set aside a certain amount of money a week for food, you will find it goes much further if you keep takeaways and ready-meals to a minimum, and stick to a shopping list when you go to a supermarket (shop at one of the cheaper supermarkets if possible). Some catering outlets at your university or in the students' union may well offer good value meals. If so, making use of these facilities can be a good way to ensure you eat reasonably healthily without blowing your budget. But probably the most economical way to eat is to cook and share meals with fellow students with whom you may be living in a shared house. Charity shops and markets are good places to hunt out bargain clothes, especially basic items such as jeans and tee shirts. Make sure you make full use of student travel cards and other offers and facilities available locally to help you cut the cost of travel. In certain locations, a bicycle is a very worthwhile investment (though not buying a lock for it may well prove a false economy).

If you can keep your essential costs down without starving yourself, then this will leave more money for what you would probably prefer to spend your money on – going out and personal items. Most students spend a good proportion of their budget on socialising, and this

Total average weekly term time costs by region

London	£247.90
South East England	£207.10
Eastern England	£206.50
South West England	£203.10
Scotland	£191.50
West Midlands	£186.20
North West England	£176.30
Wales	£175.50
Yorkshire and Humberside	£167.80
East Midlands	£166.50
Northern Ireland	£159.80
North East England	£157.50
UK Average	**£193.50**

Information from the 2009 *Halifax Student Cost of Living Survey* is certainly an important part of the university experience. You can have plenty of fun and keep your leisure costs down by making the most of the facilities, clubs and events provided by your students' union.

Studying costs

An NUS survey in 2008 estimated that the average student spent £471 a year on costs associated with course work and studying, but the amount you spend will be determined largely by the nature of your course and what you study. For some, the costs could amount to significantly more than £471. Additional financial support may be available for certain expenditure, but this is unlikely to cover you fully for spending on books, stationery, equipment, fieldwork or electives. A long reading list could prove very expensive if you tried to buy all of the required books brand new. Find out as soon as possible which books are available either in your university library or local libraries (you may need to be quick off the mark to get your hands on any books that are the first ones to be covered on your course). Another standard approach is to buy books second hand from students who no longer need them. Your students' union or your university may run second-hand book sales or offer a service helping students to buy and sell books. Another possible tactic is to share books with a fellow student: the only drawback being that you may both need to be working from a particular book at the same time!

What is the money spent on every week?

Accommodation	**£77.20**
Total food spend	**£41.10**
Total alcohol spend	**£21.60**
Transport	**£14.50**
Utility bills	**£14.60**
Leisure and social activities	**£12.40**
Materials, books and equipment for your course	**£10.50**
Cigarettes	**£1.60**

Information from the 2009 *Halifax Student Cost of Living Survey*.

There was a 5 per cent increase over 2008 (only expenditure on cigarettes recorded a decline).

Other costs

The first thing to say about any other costs you may incur is that you should do everything you can to keep them as low as possible. This may sound trite, but it is easy to let "other costs" get out of hand to the extent that they start to eat into your budget for day-to-day living. Mobile phone bills are a case in point. Look at your previous bills, or think carefully about your usage, and then shop around for the best deal to cover this. Remember that extras like downloading games or music, or sending pictures, can add significantly to your bill. Most of all, try to avoid getting tied up with an expensive and inflexible contract.

Overdrafts and credit cards

Another cost it is best to avoid is the cost of debt. Many banks offer free overdraft facilities for students, but if you go over that limit without prior arrangement, you can end up paying over the odds for your borrowing. Credits cards can be useful if managed properly. The best deals offer zero per cent interest on both balance transfers and purchases for a limited period – but if you don't pay off your debt before the offer period expires, you will start to incur hefty interest charges. Aside from these offers, the best way to manage a credit card is to set up a direct debit to pay off your balance in full every month, which means you will avoid paying any interest. One of the worst ways is just paying the minimum charge each month, which can cost you a small fortune over a long period. If you are the kind of person that spends impulsively and doesn't keep track of that spending, then you are probably better off without a credit card.

Insurance
One kind of additional spending that can actually end up saving you money is getting insurance cover for your possessions. Most students arrive at university with a number of items, such as digital cameras, mobile phones, laptops, CD players, MP3 players, and portable TVs, that are tempting and offer all-too-easy pickings for petty thieves. It is estimated that around a third of students fall victim to crime at some point during their time at university. If you shop around, you should be able to get a reasonable amount of cover for these kinds of items without it costing you an arm and a leg. It may be possible to add cover cheaply to your parents' policy.

Planning your budget
University websites and many other sites offer guidance on preparing a budget, usually with the basic headings provided for you to complete. First, list out your likely income (grants, bursaries, loans, part-time work, savings, parental support) and then see how this compares with what you will spend. Try to be realistic and not too optimistic about both sides of the equation. Hopefully, you will end up either only slightly in the red, or preferably far enough in the black for you to be able to afford things you would really like to spend your money on.

Above all, remember to keep track of your finances so that your university experience isn't ruined by money worries or finding you can't go to the ball because the cash machine has eaten your card.

Useful websites
The following websites will help you find out more about the topics discussed in this chapter.

As a starting point, the Student Finance section within the direct.gov website covers the basics: **www.direct.gov.uk/studentfinance**. There is a useful Student Finance Calculator that you can reach from a link on the Student Finance home page.

UCAS also provides helpful advice: **www.ucas.com/students/studentfinance**
For England, visit Student Finance England through : **www.direct.gov.uk/studentfinance**
Office for Fair Access: **www.offa.org.uk**
For Wales, visit Student Finance Wales: **www.studentfinancewales.co.uk**
For Scotland, visit the Student Awards Agency for Scotland: **www.saas.gov.uk**
For Northern Ireland, visit the Department for Employment and Learning:
www.delni.gov.uk/index.cfm/area/information/page/StudentFinance
Online applications are made through Student Finance Northern Ireland:
www.studentfinanceni.co.uk
All UK student loans are administered by the Student Loan Company:
www.slc.co.uk

Bursaries
Each university in England, Wales and Northern Ireland has its own bursary scheme. Website details are given in the University Profiles in this book (chapter 13).

Scholarships
Each university in the United Kingdom has its own selection of scholarships. Consult university websites. Course-related scholarships are included on the UCAS site in the description of a course.

Further help can be obtained from the following sites:
Professional and Career Development Loans: **www.ypla.gov.uk/learnersupport/pcdl**
Educational Grants Advisory Service (EGAS):
www.family-action.org.uk/section.aspx?id=1924
HM Revenue and Customs: **www.hmrc.gov.uk/students**
Need 2 Know, a student advice site: **www.need2know.co.uk/money/students**
NHS Student Bursaries for students on pre-registration health professional training courses:
www.nhsstudentgrants.co.uk

Fees and bursaries at universities in England, Northern Ireland, Scotland and Wales
The table on the next eight pages provides information on the fees charged to UK, EU and other international (non-EU) students. It also gives information on the bursary schemes offered by each university to UK students.
» Wherever possible the information relates to 2010–11.
» In the headings, "those on full grant" refers to those receiving a full maintenance grant from their funding body; "those on partial grant" refers to those receiving any grant other than a full grant.
» HI refers to "Household Income". For young students this is usually the income of their parents. In England in 2010–11, a household income of £25,000 or less qualified a student for a full grant. See page 202 for further details.
» Note that Scotland has no fees for Scottish students and also that universities do not have to provide a scheme of bursaries (although many do have their own bursaries and scholarships) and Wales has its own system of fees and bursaries.

ENGLAND

	Undergraduate fees UK / EU students	Undergraduate fees International students	University bursary for those on full grant. HI (Household Income) up to £25,000	University bursary for those on partial grant. HI (Household Income) above £25,000
Anglia Ruskin	£3,290	£9,500–£10,500	£329	n/a
Aston	£3,290	£10,700–£12,250	HI up to £28K: sliding scale £800–£480	HI up to £39,333: sliding scale £320–£160
Bath	£3,290	£11,000–£14,000	£1,200[1]	HI up to £50K: sliding scale £900–£300
Bath Spa	£3,290	£9,000–£9,580[1]	HI up to £25K: sliding scale £1,200–£350	HI up to £39K: sliding scale £200–£100
Bedfordshire	£3,290	£8,950	£329	£329
Birmingham	£3,290	£10,800–£13,950 £25,685 (clinical)	£877	HI up to £36,170: £877
Birmingham City	£3,290	£9,250–£13,770	£525	HI up to £50K: sliding scale £525–£300
Bolton	£3,290	£7,900[1]	HI up to £39,333: £350	HI up to £60K: £120
Bournemouth	£3,290	£9,000–£14,000	£329	n/a
Bradford	£3,290	£9,000–£11,400	Year 1 £500 Year 2 £700 Year 3 £900	HI up to £40K: Year 1 £500 Year 2 £700 Year 3 £900 HI up to £60K: Year 1 £400 Year 2 £500 Year 3 £600
Brighton	£3,290	£9,600–£11,160 £23,678 (medicine)	£1,080	HI up to £40.3K: sliding scale £860–£540
Bristol	£3,290	£11,900–£14,950 £27,600 (medicine)	£1,230 + £1,100 (local students)	HI up to £40K: £790 HI up to £50K: £320 All plus £1,100 (local students)
Brunel	£3,290	£9,750–£11,765	£1,000	HI up to £33K: £500
Buckingham	£8,640[2]	£19,677[2]	n/a	(subject and academic scholarships available)
Buckinghamshire New	£3,290	£8,100–£8,850	£500	£500
Cambridge	£3,290[3]	£10,752–£14,073	£3,400	HI up to £50K: sliding scale £3,150–£50

		£26,028 (medicine)[4]	
Canterbury Christ Church	£3,290	£8,880–£9,130	£880	HI up to £50K: partial award on a sliding scale
Central Lancashire (UCLan)	£3,290	£8,950–£9,500	£500 (£329 from Year 2)	HI up to £60K: £500 (£329 from Year 2)
Chester	£3,290	£7,614–£8,892	£1,000	n/a
Chichester	£3,290	£8,500–£9,700	£1,077[1]	HI up to £50K: sliding scale £1,026–£256[1]
City	£3,290	£8,900–£11,500	£770	HI up to £30K: £360
Coventry	£3,290	£8,560–£9,100	£329	£329
Cumbria	£3,290	£8,325	£1,100	HI up to £50K: £500
De Montfort	£3,290	£8,750–£9,250	HI up to $40K: £600	HI up to £50K: £300
Derby	£3,290	£8,500–£8,800	£850 + £300 (local address) or £850 + £400 (partner school)	HI £26.1K–£36.5K: £530 HI £36.5K–£52.5K: £215 All + £300 or £400 local bursary
Durham	£3,290	£12,400–£14,865	£1,000	n/a
East Anglia	£3,290	£10,400–£13,000 £20,225 (clinical medicine)	£600	HI up to £50K: £300
East London	£3,290	£9,990–£13,800	£319[1]	n/a
Edge Hill	£3,290	£8,600	£500 + £200 learning support bursary	£200 learning support bursary
Essex	£3,290	£9,250–£11,990[1]	£384	£25.5K: £484; increasing to max. £2,184 at £34K; decreasing to £52 at £50K
Exeter	£3,290	£11,100–£13,200 £13,200–£21,500 (medicine)	£1,500	HI up to £35K: £750
Gloucestershire	£3,290	£8,615	£385	n/a
Goldsmiths	£3,290	£10,170–£13,680	HI up to £19K: £1,000 then £500	HI up to £40K: £329
Greenwich	£3,290	£8,950	£400; £550 for mature students	HI up to £34K: sliding scale £375–£350; for mature students, sliding scale £535–£500
Hertfordshire	£3,290	£8,000	£1,000	n/a
Huddersfield	£3,290	£10,500–£11,500	£500	n/a

ENGLAND	Undergraduate fees UK/EU students	Undergraduate fees International students	University bursary for those on full grant. HI (Household Income) up to £25,000	University bursary for those on partial grant. HI (Household Income) above £25,000
Hull	£3,290	£9,800–£11,900 £22,700 (medicine)	£1,000	HI up to £40k: £500
Imperial	£3,290	£19,800–£21,850 £26,250–£39,150 (medicine)	£3,500	HI up to £50K: sliding scale £2,500–£500
Keele	£3,290	£9,500–£11,800 £19,000–£22,250 (medicine)	£800	n/a
Kent	£3,290	£10,850–12,950	£1,000	HI up to £40K sliding scale: £750–£250
King's College London	£3,290	£12,500–£15,850 £29,400 (medicine)	£1,350	HI up to £50K: sliding scale: £1,050–£100
Kingston	£3,290	£9,600–£10,650	HI up to £1K: £1,000 then £600	HI up to £39.7K: £384
Lancaster	£3,290	£10,500–£13,060	£1,000	HI up to £34K: £1,000
Leeds	£3,290	£10,900–£14,200 £25,970 (medicine)	£1,540	HI up to £36.6K: sliding scale £1,540–£335
Leeds Metropolitan	£3,290	£8,250–£9,500	Year 1: £500; Year 2: £800; Year 3 or above: £1,000	n/a
Leicester	£3,290	£9,825–£13,150 £23,820 (medicine)	HI up to £20K: £1,384 HI up to £25K: £1,084	HI up to £40K: sliding scale £400–£100
Lincoln	£3,290	£10,292–£10,914	£600[1]	HI up to £50K: sliding scale £370–£20[1]
Liverpool	£3,290	£9,870–£12,000 £19,530 (medicine)	£1,400	n/a
Liverpool Hope	£3,290	£6,980	£500	HI up to £39.3K: £500
Liverpool John Moores	£3,290	£9,950–£10,600	£1,075	HI £25–£50K: £430
London Metropolitan	£3,290	£9,600	Sliding scale: £1,000–£325[1]	n/a[1]
London School of Economics	£3,290	£13,680	HI up to £25K: sliding scale £2,500–£1,000	HI up to £50K: sliding scale £1,000–£100
London South Bank	£3,290	£8,360–£8,600	Year 1 £500	Year 1 £500

University			Year 2 £750 / Year 3 £750 (+ £250 graduation bonus for Hons graduates)[1]	Year 2 £750 / Year 3 £750 (+ £250 graduation bonus for Hons graduates)[1]
Loughborough	£3,290	£10,990–£14,400	HI up to £24.6k: sliding scale £1,420–£800 (doubled for mature students)	HI up to £36.3k: sliding scale £660–£220 (doubled for mature students)
Manchester	£3,290	£11,300–£14,200 £25,900 (medicine)	£1,250	n/a
Manchester Metropolitan	£3,290	£8,555–£14,200	HI up to £21K: £1,025 HI up to £25k: £475	HI £25K–£40K: £475
Middlesex	£3,290	£9,900	£329	n/a
Newcastle	£3,290	£10,525–£13,765 £25,480 (medicine)	£1,500	HI £25K–£32.2K: £750
Northampton	£3,290	£8,750	£2,906	HI £30K–£50K: sliding scale £1,906–£50
Northumbria	£3,290	£9,000–£10,200	£329 plus additional amount depending on course: sliding scale £250–£1,000	n/a
Nottingham	£3,290	£10,880–£14,260 £15,030–£19,450 £14,660–£25,480 (medicine)	£1,100	HI £25K–£45.5K: sliding scale £1,100–£275
Nottingham Trent	£3,290	£9,600–£10,700	£1,095	HI up to £35K: sliding scale £675–£525
Oxford	£3,290[3]	£12,200–£14,000[4] £25,500 (medicine)[4]	£3,225	HI up to £50K: sliding scale £3,290–£200
Oxford Brookes	£3,290	£10,200–£11,740	HI up to £25K: sliding scale £1,800–£1,050	HI up to £36K: sliding scale £1,050–£150
Plymouth	£3,290	£8,925 £14,000–£21,500 (medicine)	£900	HI £25K–£40K: £300
Portsmouth	£3,290	£9,200–£10,500	£900	HI up to £32K: £600
Queen Mary	£3,290	£10,250–£12,500 £15,350–£24,480 (medicine)[1]	£1,100	HI up to £34.6k: £878

ENGLAND	Undergraduate fees UK/EU students	Undergraduate fees International students	University bursary for those on full grant. HI (Household Income) up to £25,000	University bursary for those on partial grant. HI (Household Income) above £25,000
Reading	£3,290	£10,200–£12,300	£1,385[1]	HI up to £35k: £923 HI up to £45k: £462[1]
Roehampton	£3,290	£9,599	£1,500	n/a
Royal Holloway	£3,290	£11,555–£13,120[1]	£750	HI up to £39.3k: £750
Salford	£3,290	£9,050–£11,250	£384	(subject and academic bursaries available)
Sheffield	£3,290	£10,940–£14,380 £25,990 (medicine)	HI up to £17.5k: £715 HI up to £25k: £440	HI up to £36.2k: £440 (subject and academic bursaries available)
Sheffield Hallam	£3,290	£9,480–£11,280	£700	n/a
SOAS	£3,290	£12,600	£860	HI £25k–£39.3k: £420
Southampton	£3,290	£10,400–£13,300 £23,800 (medicine)	£1,200[1]	HI up to £35k: £600[1]
Southampton Solent	£3,290	£8,600	£750	n/a
Staffordshire	£3,290	£9,385[1]	HI up to £20.8k: £1,000 HI up to £25.5k: £850[1]	HI up to £30.8k: £500[1]
Sunderland	£3,290	£8,550	£525	HI up to £39.3k: £525
Surrey	£3,290	£10,000–£12,500	HI up to £10k: £2,100 HI up to £25k: sliding scale	HI up to £35k: sliding scale
Sussex	£3,290	£10,475–£14,050 £23,678 (medicine)	£1,000	(subject and academic bursaries available)
Teesside	£3,290	£8,950	£750	HI up to £31k: £750
Thames Valley	£3,290	£7,830–£9,170[1]	£1,060[1]	HI £25k–£40k: £530[1]
University of the Arts London	£3,290	£12,250	£319[1]	Considered for £1,000 University Access Bursary[1]
University College London	£3,290	£12,770–£16,725 £24,940 (medicine)	HI up to £11.9k: £2,775 HI up to £14.1k: £2,220 HI up to £16.2k: £1,650 then	At least 50% of maintenance grant

			at least 50% of maintenance grant	(subject and academic bursaries available)
University for the Creative Arts	£3,290	£7,855–£10,500	£450	
Warwick	£3,290	£11,500–£15,000	£1,500	HI up to £36K: £1,500
West of England	£3,290	£9,250–£9,700	£1,000	n/a
Westminster	£3,290	£10,125	£400	£400
Winchester	£3,290	£8,370	£820	HI up to £39.3K: £410
Wolverhampton	£3,290	£9,150	£500	HI up to £35K: £300
Worcester	£3,290	£8,500	£750	£625; if not eligible for maintenance grant: £500
York	£3,290	£11,300–£14,850 £22,700 (medicine)	£1,436	HI up to £35.9K: £718; HI up to £41K: £360
York St John	£3,290	£8,250–£11,250	HI up to £18,360: £1,610 HI up to £20,970: £1,075	n/a

1 Figures for 2009–10
2 Duration of degree course is two years
3 UK & EU students eligible for tuition fee support not liable for College fees (Cambridge and Oxford)
4 Plus College fees (£5,692, Oxford; £4,000–£5,000, Cambridge)

THE COST OF STUDYING 217

NORTHERN IRELAND

	Undergraduate fees UK / EU students	Undergraduate fees International students	University bursary for those on full grant. HI (Household Income) up to £25,000	University bursary for those on partial grant. HI (Household Income) above £25,000
Queen's, Belfast	£3,290	£9,889–£12,115 £13,395–£25,270 (medicine)	HI up to £19,203: £1,100 HI up to £24.2K: £550	n/a
Ulster	£3,290	£9,020	HI up to £18.8: £1,095 HI up to £21.5k: £640	HI up to £40.2K: £320

SCOTLAND

	Fees for Scottish students and eligible non-UK EU students	Fees for students from elsewhere in the UK	International fees
Aberdeen	Tuition fee paid by SAAS	£1,820 £2,895 (medicine)	£9,500–£11,800 £23,625 (medicine)
Abertay	Tuition fee paid by SAAS	£1,820	£9,250
Dundee	Tuition fee paid by SAAS	£1,820 £2,895 (medicine)	£8,925–£11,025 £16,000–£23,000 (medicine)
Edinburgh	Tuition fee paid by SAAS	£1,820 £2,895 (medicine)	£11,600–£15,250 £15,250–£31,900 (medicine)
Edinburgh Napier	Tuition fee paid by SAAS	£1,820	£9,120–£10,600
Glasgow	Tuition fee paid by SAAS	£1,820 £2,895 (medicine)	£10,750–14,000 £20,000 (veterinary medicine) £25,750 (dentistry) £24,750 (medicine)
Glasgow Caledonian	Tuition fee paid by SAAS	£1,820	£9,500–£10,500
Heriot-Watt	Tuition fee paid by SAAS	£1,820	£9,730–£12,270
Queen Margaret	Tuition fee paid by SAAS	£1,820	£9,250–£10,200¹
Robert Gordon	Tuition fee paid by SAAS	£1,820	£8,950–£10,400

	Undergraduate fees UK / EU students	Undergraduate fees International students	University bursary for those on full grant with HI up to £18,370. All UK nationals eligible for Welsh National Bursary of £329 which is included in the figures below.	University bursary for those on partial grant with HI over £18,370. Not eligible for Welsh National Bursary.
St Andrews	Tuition fee paid by SAAS		£1,820	£12,600
			£2,895 (medicine)	£19,200 (medical science)
Stirling	Tuition fee paid by SAAS		£1,820	£9,900–£11,950
Strathclyde	Tuition fee paid by SAAS		£1,820	£11,000–£12,600
West of Scotland	Tuition fee paid by SAAS		£1,820	£9,300–£10,050
WALES				
Aberystwyth	£3,290	£8,870–£11,250	£1,000[1]	HI from £18.3K to £39.3K: sliding scale £800–£200[1]
Bangor	£3,290	£8,800–£9,900[1]	£1,000	HI up to £39.7K: either £500 or £1,000
Cardiff	£3,290	£10,100–£12,950	£1,000	HI up to £50K: sliding scale £500–£350
		£23,500 (medicine)		
Cardiff (UWIC)	£3,290	£8,000–£9,200	HI up to £18.3K: £500	HI up to £39.3K: £300
		£11,200 (podiatry)		
Glamorgan	£3,290	£9,500	£329	n/a
Glyndŵr		£3,290	£6,950[1]	£500 HI up to £22K: £450; HI up to £95K: £350
Newport	£3,290	£7,950–£8,950	£329 plus £1,000 (limited)[1]	HI up to £30K: £600 (limited); HI up to £40K: £300 (limited)[1]
Swansea	£3,290	£9,500–£12,200	£329	n/a
Swansea Metropolitan	£3,290	£7,500[1]	£329 plus £500 if living more than 45 miles from University	£500 if living more than 45 miles from University (UK & EU students)
Trinity Saint David	£3,290	£9,348	£329	n/a

1 Figures for 2009–10

8 Finding Somewhere to Live

Other than for the growing band of home-based students, finding somewhere to live will be the first challenge of your university years – and one that is likely to shape your experience of student life. For the lucky majority, the challenge may not be so great because the university can offer a place in one of its halls of residence or self-catering flats. The choice (for those who can afford it) may come down to the type of accommodation and whether or not to do your own cooking. For others, however, the offer of a place will be the start of an anxious search for a room in a strange city.

The pattern of applications for 2010–11 suggests that the trend towards studying from home is accelerating, and there is no reason to think that will change while the downturn continues. Indeed, it may be a permanent shift, given the rising cost of taking a degree and the willingness of many young people to live with their parents well into their twenties. More than one student in five now lives at home – a figure that is inflated by the large number of mature students, but still a sign of the times.

Yet most of those who can afford it still see moving away to study as integral to the rite of passage that student life represents. Some have little option because, in spite of the expansion of higher education, the course they want is not available locally. Others are happy to travel to secure their ideal place and widen their experience.

For most of those who take the "away" option, going to university will be the first time that have given any thought to the practicalities of living away from home. This can make the decision about where to live – both in terms of location and the type of accommodation – doubly difficult, but vital to get right. It may even influence your choice of university, since there are big differences across the sector in the cost and standard of accommodation – and your choice can have a significant impact on the quality of your life as a student.

How much will it cost?

Students in the UK are estimated to spend almost twice as much on rent as their combined spending on food, going out, books and music. A recent survey the National Union of Students (NUS) suggested that the average student is paying a weekly rent of nearly £100, with those living in London paying more than £150 a week and those at the cheaper end of the spectrum in Belfast and Lancaster paying around £70 a week. The survey, which represents the costs for the 2009–10 academic year, found that the cost of accommodation for students had risen 22 per cent in the last three years. One can point to the sheer increase in demand as university numbers rise, as well as the increase in en suite accommodation, which is up roughly 5 per cent in those three years. However, the NUS blames the private sector for pushing up the price of housing.

Generally speaking, the cost of student accommodation is highest in London and the southeast of England and lowest in the Midlands and North of England, Wales, Scotland and Northern Ireland. But the NatWest Student Living Index shows considerable variations within those regions. Renting in new blocks of flats and especially those that are en suite, is often more expensive than sharing a house with friends, but the latter is a lot more common after the first year.

It is important to remember that both your living costs and your potential earnings should be factored into your calculations when deciding where to live. While living costs in London are, unsurprisingly, the highest – an estimated average of £131 a week excluding rent – your earnings potential is nearly double what it might be in other parts of the country. Students in London were earning over £100 a week on average in 2008, according to the NatWest survey, compared with less than £60 in Southampton. Of course, those earnings figures may be significantly lower this year, whereas student rents undoubtedly have risen.

The choices you have

No longer are you faced with a straightforward choice between a university hall of residence and a poor quality rented house. A report from the NUS puts accommodation into 16 categories, ranging from luxurious university halls to a bedsit in a shared house. The choices include:

» University hall of residence, with individual study bedrooms and a full catering service; many will have en-suite accommodation.

NatWest Student Living Index 2009

The NatWest Student Living Index was calculated as follows: for each town listed, average local weekly student expenditure on living and accommodation costs was divided by average local weekly income for working students. This provided a value, by which the 20 university towns were ranked. At the top is Brighton, where an average student spends £220 per week but earns £128 from part-time work during terms. At the bottom was York, where an average student earns only £64 from part-time work during terms. The figures in brackets are for 2008; NE indicates a new entry.

1	(4)	Brighton	11	(22)	Birmingham
2	(8)	Liverpool	12	(7)	Leeds
3	(13)	Glasgow	13	(1)	Plymouth
4	(NE)	Reading	14	(17)	Cardiff
5	(24)	Manchester	15	(5)	Portsmouth
6	(6)	Bristol	16	(11)	Newcastle
7	(20)	Leicester	17	(3)	Dundee
8	(2)	Cambridge	18	(NE)	Norwich
9	(21)	Oxford	19	(15)	Nottingham
10	(18)	Edinburgh	20	(19)	York

- » University halls, flats or houses where you have to provide your own food.
- » Private, purpose-built student accommodation.
- » Rented houses or flats, shared with fellow students.
- » Living at home.
- » Living as a lodger in a private house.

This chapter will provide you with more information to help you decide where you would like to live and whether you can afford it.

Making your choice

Financial considerations are not the only factor you should consider when deciding where to live. Feeling comfortable and happy in your student home is of crucial importance to your success at university and to the quality of your experience. It is therefore worth investing some time to find the right place, and to avoid the false economy of choosing somewhere cheap where you may end up feeling depressed and isolated. Most students who drop out of university do so in the first few months, when homesickness and loneliness can be felt most acutely. Being warm and well fed is likely to have a positive effect on your studies.

Perhaps for these reasons, most undergraduates in their first year plump for living in university halls, which offer a convenient, safe and reliable standard of accommodation, along with a supportive community environment. If meals are included, then this adds further peace of mind both for students and their parents. The sheer number of students – especially first years – in halls also makes this form of accommodation an easy way of meeting people from a wide range of courses and making friends.

Wherever you chose to live, there are some general points you will need to consider, such as how safe the neighbourhood seems to be, and how long it might take you to travel to and from the university – especially during rush hour. A recent survey of travel time between term-time accommodation and the university found that most students in London can expect a commute of at least 30 minutes and often over an hour, while those living in Wales are usually much less than 30 minutes away from their university. Be sure to make use of any local or national Student Travel Card and any university or students' union transport system that may be provided to help you get back to your accommodation cheaply and safely.

Information to help you

In the university profiles (which are in the second half of this book), we provide details of what accommodation each university offers. You will be able to find the following:

- » The number of university-provided places. A quick check against the number of undergraduates will show you how well provided for the university is.
- » The percentage of places that are catered.
- » The percentage of places that are self-catered.
- » The weekly cost of catered and self-catered accommodation.
- » A summary of the offer of accommodation that can be made to first years.
- » A summary of the offer of accommodation that can be made to international students.
- » The web address for details of the university's accommodation provision.

Continuing to live at home

The first decision must be whether to move at all. If the course you want is within reasonable travelling time and you are happy in the family home, you may decide to stay there – particularly if money is tight. You can always move out later, as many students do when they have met others with whom they want to share.

The number of students living at home has been rising for several years. A report published by the Sutton Trust in 2008 found that those choosing this option tended to be state school or college students, and usually not those with the highest grades. There was also a strong representation of Asian students in the sample. But it is reasonable to assume that, in future, more applicants of all backgrounds will be considering student life at home.

The potential financial benefits of this are obvious, and there may also be advantages in terms of academic work if the alternative involves shopping, cooking and cleaning, as well as the other distractions of a student flat. The obvious downside is that you may miss out on a lot of the student experience, especially the social scene and the opportunity to make new friends.

There is no evidence that students living at home do any worse academically. The quality of your home environment should influence your decision when weighing up whether or not to take this option. If it is stressful or not conducive to studying then you are probably better off moving out, even if it means having to take a job to make ends meet. On the other hand, there is a lot to be said for making use of supportive and flexible home conditions where these exist. If you are studying at a "new" university, you are more likely to have fellow students who also live at home.

What universities offer

You might think that opting to live in university accommodation is the most straight-forward choice, especially since first-year students are invariably given priority in the allocation of places in halls of residence. Certainly if you go for university residences you benefit from being able to make arrangements in advance and at a distance, rather than having to be in the right place at the right time, as is often the way when searching for private housing. However, you may still need to select from a range of options because some universities will have a variety of accommodation on offer. You will need to consider which best suits your pocket and your preferred lifestyle.

New university accommodation

At the top end of the market, partnerships between universities and private firms have recently begun to lead the way. Private organisations such as UNITE plc (**www.unite-students.com**) and LibertyLiving (**www.libertyliving.co.uk**) have been paid by universities to

Money paid weekly for accommodation

	Overall	Catered halls	Self-catered halls/flats houses	Rented flats/ houses off campus	Own flats/ houses off campus	Home/ parents off campus
£0	14%	5%	2%	1%	33%	75%
£1–£40	3%	0%	0%	2%	6%	10%
£41–£60	16%	2%	10%	27%	13%	5%
£61–£80	32%	16%	35%	46%	9%	5%
£81–£100	18%	34%	38%	11%	10%	3%
£101–£150	10%	38%	12%	6%	14%	1%
over £150	7%	7%	3%	7%	14%	1%

Adapted from *Sodexo University Lifestyle Survey 2008*

build and manage some of the most luxurious student accommodation the UK sector has ever seen. Rooms in these complexes are typically en suite and include facilities such as your own phone line, satellite TV, and internet access. Shared kitchens are also top quality and fitted out with all the latest equipment. This kind of accommodation naturally comes at a higher price, but offers the advantages of flexibility both in living arrangements and through a range of payment options. Private companies have invested more than £5 billion into new student flats in recent years, continuing to do so even while the recession brought the rest of the construction business to a halt

Halls of residence

Many new or recently refurbished university-owned halls offer a standard of accommodation that is not far short of the privately built residences. One of the reasons for this is that rooms in these halls can be offered to conference delegates during vacations. Even though these halls are also at the pricier end of the spectrum, you will probably find that they are in great demand, and you may have to get your name down for one quickly to secure one of the fancier rooms. That said, you can often get a guarantee of some kind of university accommodation if you give a firm acceptance of an offered place by a certain date in the summer. This may not be the case, however, if you have gained your place through Clearing – although rooms in private halls might still be on offer at this stage.

While a few halls are single-sex, most are mixed, and often house over 500 students. They are therefore great places for making friends and becoming part of the social scene. One possible downside is that they can also be noisy places where it can be difficult at times to get down to some work. The more successful students learn, before too many essay deadlines and exams start to loom, to get the balance right between all-night partying and escaping to the library for some undisturbed study time. Many libraries, especially new ones, are also now open 24 hours a day. If you feel in need of either personal or study support, this is often at hand either through a counselling service or from fellow students.

Most popular place for private study
It is important that wherever you live, it will be easy for you to work, as much of your private study will be done there.

Own accommodation	63%
Library	26%
Resource Centre	4%
Social space (refectory, coffee shop, etc.)	3%
Other	4%

Sodexo University Lifestyle Survey 2008

University self-catering accommodation

An alternative to halls, offered particularly by some older universities, are smaller, self-catering properties fitted out with a shared kitchen and other living areas. Students looking for a more independent and flexible lifestyle may prefer this option. Remember that if you choose this kind of university housing, you will be responsible for feeding yourself, and you may also have heating and lighting bills to pay. University properties are often on campus or nearby, and so travel costs should not pose a problem.

Catering in university accommodation

Many universities have responded to a general increase in demand from students for a more independent lifestyle, by providing more flexible catering facilities. A range of eateries, from fast food outlets to more traditional refectories, can usually be found on campus. Students in university accommodation may now be offered pay-as-you-eat deals as an alternative to full-board packages.

What after the first year?

After your first year of living in university residences you may well wish, and will probably be expected, to move out to other accommodation. The only exceptions are in collegiate universities – particularly Oxford and Cambridge – which may allow you to stay on in college halls for another year or two, and particularly for your final year. Students from outside the EU are also sometimes guaranteed accommodation. There are also some universities, such as Loughborough, where it is not uncommon for students to move back in to halls for their final year.

Practical details

If you have decided to start out in university accommodation, then you will probably be expected to sign an agreement to cover rent. These contracts can be for around 40 weeks, which includes the Christmas and Easter holiday periods or for just the length of the three university terms. These term-time contracts are common when a university uses its rooms for conferences during vacations. You will be required to leave your room empty during vacations. It is therefore advisable to check whether the university has storage space for you to leave your belongings – otherwise you will have to make arrangements to take all your belongings home between terms. Depending on where you are in the country, it may be possible to pay to store you belongings somewhere privately, such as Big Yellow Self Storage, but this will not necessarily be cheap. International students may be offered special arrangements, in which they can stay in halls during the short vacation periods. Organisations like **www.hostuk.org** can also arrange for overseas students to stay in a UK family home at holiday times such as the Christmas break.

Being a lodger or staying in a hostel

A small number of students live as a lodger in a family home, an option most frequently taken up by international students. The usual arrangement is for a study bedroom and some meals to be provided, while other facilities such as a washing machine are shared. Students with particular religious affiliations or those from certain countries may wish to consider living in one of a number of hostels run by charities catering for certain groups. Most of these can be found in London.

Type of accommodation by year of study

1st year		2nd year onwards	
Self-catered halls	27%	Privately let flats/houses	52%
University self-catered flats/houses	19%	At home with parents/family	12%
At home with parents/family	15%	Commercially let flats/houses	10%
Privately let flats/houses	14%	Own flat/house	9%
Catered halls	13%	University self-catered flats/houses	8%
Own flat/house	10%	Self-catered halls	7%
Commercially let flats/houses	3%	Catered halls	3%

Sodexo University Lifestyle Survey 2008

Renting from the private sector

Every university city or town is awash with privately owned accommodation available via agencies or direct from individual landlords. Indeed, there has been so much of it that so-called "student ghettoes", where local residents feel outnumbered, have become hot political issues. Into this traditional market in rented flats and houses have come the new private-sector complexes and residences, often created in partnership with universities, adding considerably to the private-sector options. Examples can be seen online through sites such as www.accommodationforstudents.com, which are listed at the end of this chapter.

While there are always exceptions, a much more professional attitude and approach to managing rented accommodation has emerged among smaller providers, thanks to a combination of greater regulation and increasing competition. Nevertheless, it is wise to take certain precautions when seeking out private residences.

How to start looking for rented property

Contact your university's accommodation service and ask for their list of approved rented properties. Some have a Student Accommodation Accreditation Scheme, run in collaboration with the local council. To get onto an approved list under such schemes, landlords must show they are adhering to basic standards of safety and security, such as having an up-to-date gas and electric safety certificate. University accommodation officers should also be able to advise you on any hidden charges. For instance, you may be asked to pay a booking or reservation fee to secure a place in a particular property, and fees for references or drawing up a tenancy agreement are also sometimes charged. The practice of charging a "joining fee", however, has been outlawed. It would also be wise to speak to older students with first-hand experience of renting in the area. Certain companies in the area will often be notorious among second and third years and therefore you can seek to avoid them.

Making a choice

Once you have made an initial choice on the area you would like to live in and the size of property you are looking for, the next stage is to look at possible places. If you plan to share, it is important that you all have a look at the property. If you will be living by yourself, take a friend with you when you go to view a property, since he or she can help you assess what you see objectively, and avoid any irrational or rushed on-the-spot decisions. Don't let yourself be pushed into signing on the dotted line there and then. Take time to visit and consider a number of options. It is often helpful to spend some time in the area in which you may be living, to check out the local facilities, transport, and the general environment at various times of the day and different days of the week. If you can stay in the area for a few days, this will help you get a more accurate idea of what living in the district will be like.

If you are living in private rented accommodation, it is likely that at least some of your neighbours will not be students. Local people often welcome students, but resentment sometimes builds up, particularly in areas of towns and cities that are dominated by student housing. It is important to respect your neighbours' rights, and not to behave in an anti-social manner.

Preparing for sharing

The people you are planning to share a house with may not be as unsavoury as the characters in the TV comedy "The Young Ones", but you can be sure they will have some habits that you find at least mildly irritating. How well you cope with some of the downsides of co-habiting will be partly down to the kind of person you are – where you are on the spectrum between laid back and highly strung – but it will help a lot if you are sharing with people whose outlook on day-to-day living is not too far out of line with your own. Some students sign for their second year houses as early as November and while it is good to be ahead of the rush, in such a short time at the university you may not have met your best friends yet. If you have not already selected your own group of friends, universities and landlords can help by taking personal preferences and lifestyle into account when grouping tenants together. You can make this task easier if you give full details about yourself when filling in accommodation applications forms.

Potential issues to consider when deciding whether to move into a shared house include whether any of the housemates smoke, own a loud musical instrument that they may decide to play at any time of the day or night, or have a habit of spending hours on the telephone. With most students owning a mobile phone, the latter should not be a problem unless someone decides to save on their mobile bills by using a landline phone in your shared house instead. If this is the case, then you should arrange for individual billing, provided by a number of phone companies such as The Phone Co-op (**www.thephone.coop**). It will also be important to sort out broadband arrangements that will work for everyone in the house, and that you will be able to arrange access to the university system. It may seem like a drag, but it is usually a good idea to agree from the outset a rota for everyone to share in the household cleaning chores. Otherwise it is almost certain that you will live in a state of permanent unhygienic squalor or that one or two individuals will be left to clear up everyone else's mess.

The practical details about renting

It is a good idea to ask whether your house is covered by an accreditation scheme or code of standards. Such codes provide a clear outline of what constitutes good practice and the responsibilities of both landlords and tenants. Adhering to schemes like the National Code of Standards for Larger Student Developments compiled by Accreditation Network UK (**www.anuk.org.uk**) may well become a requirement for larger properties, including those managed by universities, now that the Housing Act is in force.

At the very least, make sure that if you are renting from a private landlord, you have his or her telephone number and home address. Some can be remarkably difficult to contact when repairs are needed or deposits returned.

HMOs

If you are renting a private house it may be is subject to the rules and regulations of the 2004 Housing Act in England and Wales (similar legislation applies in Scotland and Northern Ireland). Licenses are compulsory for all private Houses in Multiple Occupation (HMOs) with three or more stories that house five or more unrelated residents. The provisions of the Act also allow local authorities to designate whole areas in which HMOs of all sizes must be licensed. The good news is that these regulations are likely to be applied in sections of university towns and cities where most students live. This means that a house must be licensed, well-managed and must meet various health and safety standards, and its owner subject to various financial regulations. The bad news is that this could lead to a reduction in the number and range of privately rented properties on the market, or an increase in rental prices.

Tenancy agreements

Whatever kind of accommodation you go for, you must be sure to have all the paperwork in order and be clear about what you are signing up to before you move in. If you are taking up residence in a shared house, flat or bedsit, the first document you will have to grapple with is a tenancy agreement or lease offering you an "assured shorthold tenancy". Since this is a binding legal document you should be prepared to go through every clause with a fine-tooth comb. Remember that it is much more difficult to make changes or overcome problems arising from unfair agreements once you are a tenant than before you become one.

You would be well advised to seek help, in the likely event of your not fully understanding some of the clauses. Your university accommodation office or students' union are a good place to start, since they should know all the ins and outs, and have model tenancy agreements to refer to. A Citizens Advice Bureau or Law Advice Centre should also be able to offer you free advice. Watch out in particular for clauses that may make you jointly responsible for the actions of others with whom you are sharing the property. If you name your parent as a guarantor to cover any costs not covered by you, then they may also be liable for charges levied on all tenants for any damage that might not be your fault. A rent review clause could allow your landlord to increase the rent at will, whereas without such a clause, they are restricted to one rent rise a year. Make sure you keep a copy of all documents, and get a receipt (and keep it somewhere safe) for anything you have to pay for.

Contracts tend to be longer than for university accommodation – they will frequently commit you to paying rent for 52 weeks of the year. There are probably more advantages than disadvantages to this kind of arrangement. It means you don't have to move out in vacation periods, which you might have to in university halls to make way for conference delegates. You can store your belongings in your room when you go away (but don't leave anything really valuable behind if you can help it). You may be able to negotiate a rent discount for those periods when you are not staying in the property. The other advantage, particularly important for cash-strapped students, is that you have a base from which to find work and hold down a job during the vacations. Term dates are also not as dictatorial as they might be in halls; if you rent your own house then you can come back when you wish.

Deposits

On top of the agreed rent, you will need to provide a deposit or bond to cover any possible breakages or damage. This will probably set you back the equivalent of another month's rent. The deposit should be returned, less any deductions, at the end of the contract. However, be warned that disputes over the return of deposits are quite common, with the question of what constitutes reasonable wear and tear often the subject of disagreements between landlords and tenants. To protect students from unscrupulous landlords who withhold deposits without good reason, the 2004 Housing Act has introduced a National Tenancy Deposit Scheme under which deposits are held by an independent body rather than by the landlord. This is designed to ensure that deposits are fairly returned, and that any disputes are resolved swiftly and cheaply.

Inventories and other paperwork

You should get an inventory and schedule of condition of everything in the property. This is another document that you should check very carefully – and make sure that everything listed is as described. Write on the document anything that is different. The National Union of Students even suggests taking photographs of rooms and equipment when you first move in (putting the date on the pictures if you are using a digital camera), to provide you with additional proof should any dispute arise when your contract ends and you want to get your deposit back. If you are not offered an inventory, then make one of your own. You should have someone else witness and sign this, send it to your landlord, and keep your own copy. Keeping in contact with your landlord throughout the year and developing a good relationship with him her will also do you no harm, and may be to your advantage in the long run.

You should ask your landlord for a recent gas safety certificate issued by a qualified CORGI engineer, a fire safety certificate covering the furnishings, and a record of current gas and electricity meter readings. Take your own readings of meters when you move in to make sure these match up with what you have been given, or make your own records if the landlord doesn't supply this information. This also applies to water meters if you are expected to pay water rates (although this isn't usually the case).

If you are sharing a house only with other full-time students, then you will not have to pay Council Tax. However, you may be liable to pay a proportion of the Council Tax bill if you are sharing with anyone who is not a full-time student. You may need to get a Council Tax exemption certificate from your university as evidence that you do not need to pay Council Tax or should pay only a proportion, depending on the circumstances.

Security in rented accommodation

As students living in private housing are twice as likely to be burgled as those in university halls, it is worth running through this security checklist provided by the NUS:

» Check that the front and back doors are fitted with five-lever mortise locks in addition to standard catch locks.
» Make sure the door to your room has a lock, and always lock up when you leave it, especially for long periods such as during vacations.
» Check the locks and catches on accessible windows, especially those at ground-floor level.
» Before you move in, try to talk to neighbours about how safe the area is and whether there have been many instances of burglary or car crime.
» Ask your landlord to ensure that all previous tenants and holders of keys no longer have copies.
» If you find a property that you are keen to rent, but you are unsure about some of the security aspects, speak to the letting agency or landlord to discuss your concerns. They may be able to make the necessary changes to make the property more secure before you move in.

Safety and security

Once you have arrived and settled in, remember to take care of your own safety and the security of your possessions. You are particularly vulnerable as a fresher, when you are still getting used to your new-found independence. This may help explain why a fifth of students are burgled or robbed in the first six weeks of the academic year. Take care with valuable portable items such as mobile phones, iPods and laptops, all of which are tempting for criminals. Ensure you don't use them or have them obviously on display when you are out and about. If your mobile phone is stolen, call your network or 08701 123 123 to immobilise it.

Students' unions, universities and the police will provide plenty of practical guidance when you arrive. Following their advice will reduce the chance of you becoming a victim of crime, and so able to enjoy living in the new surroundings of your chosen university town.

Insurance

It is a false economy not to have adequate insurance to cover you for the loss or theft of valuable items. Your students' union will probably be able to advise you on where to go for the best deals and there may even be a shop on campus that can help you. It may be that your parents' insurance will cover you when you are a student, and you should certainly check this. You should also keep a record somewhere safe of the serial and model numbers of expensive electrical equipment. If you have to claim on your insurance for these items you will need these details. Remember that whether you say it out loud or subconsciously think it, courting the notion that "it won't happen to me" is one of the best ways to ensure that it probably will.

Useful websites
The following websites will help you find out more about the topics discussed in this chapter. In the university profiles later in this book, we give an indication of costs for university-provided accommodation and details of university accommodation websites.

For advice on a range of housing issues, visit:
www.nus.org.uk/en/Student-Life/Housing-Advice
The 2009/10 *Accommodation Costs Survey* carried out by the NUS and Unipol can be read online at the NUS website (**www.nus.org.uk**) or the Unipol website (**www.unipol.org.uk**) The Shelter website has separate sections covering different housing regulations in England, Wales, Scotland and Northern Ireland: **www.shelter.org.uk**

Private accommodation
As examples of a provider of private hall accommodation, visit:
www.unite-students.com
www.libertyliving.co.uk

There are a number of sites that will help you find accommodation, among which are:
www.accommodationforstudents.com
www.homesforstudents.co.uk
www.studentaccommodation.org
www.studentpad.co.uk

For guidance on private accommodation:
Accreditation Network UK runs an accreditation scheme for larger schemes (with Unipol):
www.anuk.org.uk
www.unipol.org.uk/national

To find your nearest Citizen's Advice Bureau, visit: **www.citizensadvice.org.uk**
To find your nearest Law Centre, visit: **www.lawcentres.org.uk/lawcentres**

For security advice on renting, visit the NUS security checklist:
www.nus.org.uk/en/Student-Life/Housing-Advice/House-hunting-checklist

For telephone sharing, visit the Phone Co-op: **www.thephone.coop**

For general advice on safety, this Home Office site gives practical advice:
www.homeoffice.gov.uk/crime-victims/how-you-can-prevent-crime/student-safety

9 Sporting Opportunities

If some of the sportsmen and women to be found on university campuses next year look a cut above the average, it may be because they are internationals training for the 2012 Olympic Games. It is a measure of their investment in sports facilities that half of all universities were chosen as training bases for Great Britain squads and several expect to host national teams in the run-up to the Games themselves.

Higher education's involvement in London 2012 has been carefully planned – the subject of a report to the Prime Minister, with separate organisations formed to coordinate activity and £10 million set aside for collaborative projects. The scale of universities' success speaks volumes about the quality and range of facilities available to ordinary students, not just elite performers. Some of the biggest multi-sports developments in recent years have been on university campuses, where facilities nationally are said to be worth an astonishing £20 billion.

Where universities have been able to attract Lottery funding or have made sport a priority in their portfolio of subjects, the standard of facilities can be breathtaking. Naturally, not all can aspire to those heights, but most now offer facilities to compare with the best available commercially – and usually at a fraction of the price. So many facilities are also available to local communities that a recent survey of usage found that more than 20 per cent of bookings were by non-students.

Sporting opportunities
Being a full-time student offers unrivalled opportunities to discover and play a vast range of sports. Many universities still encourage departments not to schedule lectures and seminars on Wednesday afternoons, to give students free time for sport. Even those who spend long hours in the laboratory have more time for leisure activities now than they will be able to spare later in life.

There are student-run clubs for all the major sports and – particularly at the larger universities – a host of minor ones, or you can content yourself with high-quality gyms, with staff on hand to devise personalised training regimes. The cost varies widely between universities, and membership fees can represent a large amount to lay out at the start of the year, but most provide good value if you are going to be a regular.

The course is rightly still top of most students' priorities when choosing a university, but sporting options play a growing role in the process. Gone are the days when only those aiming for university teams took them into account. More and more students want to keep fit, even if they don't play competitive sport, and universities have joined a race of their own to provide the best facilities. Sport may still be a secondary consideration for most applicants, but particularly good (or particularly poor) facilities can sometimes tip the balance.

Sport for all

For most universities, it is in the area of "sport for all" that most attention has been focused. Beginners are welcomed and coaching provided in a range of sports, from ultimate Frisbee to tai-chi, that would be difficult to match outside the higher education system. Check on university websites to see whether your usual sport is available, but don't be surprised if you come across a new favourite when you have the opportunity to try out some new sports as a student. Many universities have programmes designed to encourage students to take up a new sport, with expert coaching provided.

All universities are conscious of the need to provide for a spread of ability. Sports scholarships for elite performers are now commonplace, but there will be plenty of opportunities, too, for beginners. University teams demand a hefty commitment in terms of training and practice sessions – often several a week – and in many sports standards are high. University teams often compete in local and national leagues.

For those who don't aspire to such heights, or whose interests are primarily social, there are thriving internal, or intramural, leagues. These provide opportunities for teams from halls of residence or faculties, or even a group of friends, to form a team and participate on a regular basis. Nor is university sport a male preserve – student teams were among the pioneers in mixed sport and are still strong in areas such as women's cricket, football and rugby.

First year student-run sport

Halls of residence and university-owned flats will generally offer an array of sports teams. These are normally organised by the Sports Captain, elected the year previously as part of the Junior Common Room, whose responsibility it is to organise trials and pick the teams, as well as to arrange fixtures for the year. Hall sport is a great way of meeting like-minded people from your accommodation and over the course of the years, friendly rivalries often develop with other halls or flats. These competitions will take place over all three terms and will culminate with a winning team in each sport so, while it may start as a great way of playing sport and making friends, it will end very competitively. In the summer term, there is also often a Sports Day that is either restricted to your particular hall of residence, or one that is organised against another hall.

Generally there will be teams for football (both five- and 11-a-side), hockey, netball, cricket, tennis, squash, badminton and even golf. If your lodgings are smaller then don't worry, they are often twinned with similar flats to enable as many first-year students as possible to get involved in freshers' sport. The number and variety of teams will often depend on what has gone on in years gone by, as well as on the enthusiasm and dedication of the Sports Captain, so it is also up to you to make sure that he or she is doing a good job.

Intramural sport

As university numbers have increased, so has the standard of student sports teams and, while there are many keen sportsmen and women in higher education, most won't quite have the ability to play for a university team. This is where intramural (Latin for "inside the wall") competitions come in. Intramural sport allows students to compete against their fellow students in an organised league, something that has proved massively popular. From hall, subject and society teams, to corridor, house and simply 'mates' teams', intramural sport can be taken as seriously as you wish, but offers everybody the opportunity to get out there and play.

Unsurprisingly, the main winner in this set-up has been football. Most teams will offer both a five-a-side and 11-a-side option, with the former proving particularly successful. In large universities, the big departments have been known to field as many as 15 five-a-side teams. The competitions tend to span all three terms, giving you a lot of playing time over the year. If you want to get involved, there should be little to stop you and the cost is generally very reasonable.

For women, hockey and netball have led the way and there are also many unisex hockey and football leagues. Whilst each university will vary, badminton, basketball, cricket, tennis and squash are also all common in most campuses' intramural set ups.

Other opportunities

You may even end up wanting to coach, umpire or referee – and this is another area in which higher education has much to offer. Many university clubs and sports unions provide subsidised courses for students to gain qualifications that may be of use to the individual in later life, as well as benefiting university teams in the short term. Or you might want to try your hand at some sports administration, with an eye to your career. In most universities there is a sports (or athletic) union, with autonomy from the main students' union, which organises matches and looks after the wider interests of those who play. There are plenty of opportunities for those seeking an apprenticeship in the art of running a club, or larger organisation.

Universities that excel

A few universities are known particularly for sport – the University of London women's volleyball team has won the English Volleyball Championships, for example, and Bath University's "Team Bath" have tasted success in the FA Cup – and are benefiting from its increasing popularity as a degree subject, as well as an extra-curricular activity. Several of this elite group had a head start as former physical education colleges. Loughborough is probably the best-known of them, but Leeds Metropolitan and Brunel are others with a similar pedigree. Other universities with different traditions, such as Bath and the University of East Anglia, also have a variety of outstanding facilities, while the likes of Stirling and UWIC have the same in a narrower range of sports.

As in so much else, Oxford and Cambridge are in a category of their own. The Boat Race and the Varsity Match (in rugby union) are the only UK university sporting events with a regular popular following, and there is a high standard of competition in other sports, although there is an ambivalent attitude to them in many colleges. While star rowers and rugby players do turn up on postgraduate diploma courses, the days of special consideration for sporty undergraduates appear to be over, and there are few of the sports scholarships offered at other universities.

British Universities and College Sport

British university sport has not become big business, as it is in the United States of America, but competitive standards have been rising. British Universities and Colleges Sport (BUCS) runs competitions in almost 50 sports, and ranks participating institutions. There is also international competition in a number of sports, and numerous examples of students being selected for Olympic and professional teams. The World Student Games have become one of the biggest occasions in the international sporting calendar.

Formed in 2008, BUCS has brought together the administration of university sport and the job of lobbying for the best possible facilities. The new organisation has a student membership, but will also play a role in the wider sporting community, as well as negotiating with the Government and other national and international bodies to promote, develop and enable participation in sport and active recreation.

University sports facilities

Even the smallest university should provide reasonable indoor and outdoor sports facilities – a sports hall, modern gym equipment and outdoor pitches (usually including an all-weather surface and floodlights). Most will also have a swimming pool and extras such as climbing walls, but the smaller universities tend to make arrangements for students to use local sports centres and clubs when it is not feasible to provide for minority sports. The same goes for the really expensive ones, like golf, which is usually the subject of an arrangement with one or more local clubs that give students a discount. Specialist facilities, like boat houses and climbing huts, obviously depend on location, but the most landlocked university is likely to have a sailing club that organises regular activities away from campus, and a skiing club that runs at least annual trips to the mountains.

Many of the larger universities have spent millions of pounds improving their sports facilities, sometimes in partnership with local authorities, national sporting bodies or the Lottery. University campuses are ideal locations for national coaching centres, and many have been established in recent years. While some of the facilities are naturally reserved for elite performers, opportunities always exist for ordinary students to make use of them at reasonable rates, as well as occasionally rubbing shoulders with star players.

It is estimated that about £400 million has been spent on new or upgraded sports facilities at UK universities over the past seven years. Universities now boast a significant proportion of the UK's 50-metre pools, for example, and more are planned. Other innovative schemes include Leeds Metropolitan's development of the Headingley cricket and rugby league grounds, providing teaching space for students during the week and improved facilities for players and spectators on match days.

Both the scale of investment and the emphasis on sport has increased as the 2012 Olympics have come closer. The legacy for students – not just in London - should be considerable, as it was at the Commonwealth Games in Manchester and the World Student Games in Sheffield.

Beyond scrutinising the prospectus for the extent of university facilities, there are two important questions to ask: how much do they cost and where are they? Neither is easy to track down on the average university website.

How much?

Students who are used to free (if inferior) facilities at school often get a nasty surprise when they find that they are expected to pay to join the Athletic Union and then pay again to use the gym or play football. Because most university sport is subsidised, the charges are reasonable compared to commercial facilities, but the best deal may require a considerable outlay at the start. Some campus gyms and swimming pools now charge more than £300 a year, for example, which is still considerably cheaper than paying per visit if you intend to use the facilities regularly (and provides an incentive to carry on doing so). Most universities offer a variety of peak and off-peak membership packages – some for the entire length of your course.

Outdoor sports are usually charged by the hour, although clubs will also charge a membership fee. You may be required to pay up to £25 for membership of the Athletic Union (although not all universities require this). Fees for intramural sport are seldom substantial; teams will usually pay a fee for the season, while courts for racket sports tend to be marginally cheaper per session than in other clubs.

How far away?

University prospectuses tend to major on the quality of the five-a-side pitches without being as forthcoming about the prices. The other common complaint by students is that the playing fields are too far from the campus – understandable in the case of city centre universities, but still aggravating if you have to arrange your own transport. This is where campus universities have a clear advantage.

For the rest, there has to be some trade-off between the quality of outdoor facilities and the distance you have to travel to use them. But universities are beginning to realise that long journeys depress usage of important (and expensive) facilities, and some have tried to find suitable land closer to lectures and halls of residence. Indoor sports centres should all be within easy reach.

Sport as a degree subject

Sports science and other courses associated with sport have seen big increases in recent years – so much so that the subject was eleventh in terms of popularity, with close to 50,000 applications at the start of 2010. A separate ranking for the subject is published on page 178.

As those who have taken sports science at A level will know, an interest in sport is invaluable but far from sufficient. The same goes for sporting excellence. If you are hoping to be rewarded with an academic qualification for three years on the sports field, you will be disappointed because there is serious science involved.

However, sport is a growing employment field and one that demands qualifications like any other. Entrance requirements vary widely, with some of the top courses asking for 360 points on the UCAS tariff, while others ask half this number or less.

Other degrees in the sports area are more closely focused on management, with careers in the leisure industry in mind – golf course management, for example, has proved popular with students despite being a target of those who see anything beyond the traditional academic portfolio as "dumbing down". Such courses are usually no less rigorous than general management degrees. The question is not whether the courses are up to standard, but whether a less specialised one will offer more career flexibility if a decline in popularity for the particular sport limits future opportunities. The chance to combine work and play for three years holds obvious attractions, but there will be opportunities to pursue your chosen sport at university in any case.

Sports scholarships

The number and range of sports scholarships have expanded just as rapidly as courses in the subject, but the two are usually not connected. Sports scholarships are for elite performers, regardless of what they are studying – indeed, they exist at universities with barely any degrees in the field. Imported from the USA, scholarships now exist in an array of sports. At Birmingham University, for example, there are specialist golf awards (as there are at ten other universities) and a scholarship for triathletes, as well as others open to any sport.

The value of scholarships varies considerably – sometimes according to individual prowess. The Royal and Ancient scholarships for golfers, for example, range from £500 for promising handicap golfers to £10,000 for full internationals. All of them demand that you meet the normal entrance requirements for your course and maintain the necessary academic standards, as well as progressing in your sport. In practice, most departments will be flexible about attendance and deadlines, as long as you make your requests well in advance.

Many sports scholarships offer benefits in kind, in the form of coaching, equipment or access to facilities. The Government-funded Talented Athlete Scholarship Scheme (TASS), which is restricted to students at English universities who have achieved national recognition at under-18 level and are eligible to represent England, is one such example. The scholarships are worth £3,000 a year and can be put towards costs such as competition and training costs, equipment or mentoring. A more selective TASS 2012 scholarship is also available, valued at £10,000. Further details are available at **www.tass.gov.uk.**

Part-time work
University sports centres are an excellent source of term-time (and out-of-term) employment. They beat other campus jobs, such as bar work, in terms of enjoyment and healthiness. Depending on your qualifications, you could earn up to £17 an hour for coaching, or more like £7 an hour as a receptionist or for other forms of assistance. You may also be trained in first aid, fire safety, customer care and risk assessment – all useful skills for future employment. The experience will help you secure employment in commercial or local authority facilities – and even for jobs such as stewarding at football grounds and music venues.

Administrative work within the Athletic Union of university sports organisation, is more likely to be unpaid, but may still provide useful experience that will add to your CV. So, indeed, does a position of responsibility in a club, or even captaining a team. Many employers value sport as an indication of self-confidence and team-working qualities. Most universities also have a sabbatical post in the Athletic Union or similar body, a paid position with responsibility for organising university sport and representing the sporting community within the university.

Useful websites
The following websites will help you find out more about the topics discussed in this chapter.

BUCS (British Universities and Colleges Sports)
www.bucs.org.uk
UK Sport
www.uksport.gov.uk
London 2012
www.london2012.com
Talented Athlete Scholarship Scheme
www.tass.gov.uk

Table of university sporting facilities

The following six pages outline the sporting facilities at each of the universities covered in this book that were available in 2007. The information was compiled from a survey undertaken by University and College Sport (now absorbed into BUCS). The information only covers the facilities that universities provide centrally for all their students, and ignores any facilities there may be in halls of residence or colleges. At Oxford and Cambridge, for example, many colleges have facilities that are not reflected in the table. The table also contains the most recent BUCS League Ranking and websites correct as of April 2010.

The table provides the following information:
» British Universities and Colleges Sports (BUCS) League Rankings 2008–09, based on all sports. Teams get points each year for their success in inter-university competitions and BUCS uses them to compile an annual league table. The universities with the highest rankings (eg, Loughborough, Bath and Birmingham) are therefore overall the most successful competitively. A number of institutions with teams in BUCS are not universities and so do not appear in the following table. The BUCS rankings are based on all teams in the leagues.
» An indication of whether the university has (Y for "yes") or does not have (N for "no") the following facilities:
  Sports hall
  Swimming pool
  Squash courts
  Climbing wall
  Indoor tennis courts
  Fitness facilities
  Winter grass pitches (eg, for football, rugby, etc.)
  Cricket pitches
  Artificial turf pitches
» The number of different sports with student clubs.
» The number of indoor sports with intramural competitions.
» The number of outdoor sports with intramural competitions.
» Whether instruction classes are available to encourage new participants (Y = yes; N = no).
» Whether sports scholarships or bursaries are available. Full details will need to be checked on university websites.
» Details of university websites devoted to sports. Students' unions websites usually have sports information as well. Where the main university website is given, visit that site and search for sports. The full web address is too long to give in this table.

Grey boxes show where information is not available.

University sporting facilities

Universities	BUCS ranking 2008–09	Sports hall?	Swimming pool?	Squash courts?	Climbing wall?	Indoor tennis court(s)?	Fitness facilities?	Winter grass pitch(es)?
Aberdeen	24	Y	Y	Y	N	N	Y	Y
Abertay	103	N	N	N	N	N	Y	N
Aberystwyth	55	Y	Y	Y	Y	Y	Y	Y
Anglia Ruskin	87	Y	Y	Y	Y	Y	Y	Y
Aston	90	Y	Y	Y	Y	N	Y	Y
Bangor	74	Y	N	Y	Y	N	Y	Y
Bath	2	Y	Y	Y	Y	Y	Y	Y
Bath Spa	136	No further information reported						
Bedfordshire	68	Y	Y	N	Y	Y	Y	Y
Birmingham	4	Y	Y	Y	Y	N	Y	Y
Birmingham City	124	N	N	N	N	N	N	Y
Bolton	117	Y	Y	Y	Y	N	Y	N
Bournemouth	36	Y	Y	Y	Y	N	Y	Y
Bradford	94	Y	Y	Y	Y	Y	Y	Y
Brighton	32	Y	N	N	Y	N	Y	Y
Bristol	13	Y	Y	Y	N	Y	Y	Y
Brunel	18	Y	N	Y	Y	N	Y	Y
Buckinghamshire New	85	No further information reported						
Cambridge	9	N	Y	Y	N	N	Y	Y
Canterbury Christ Church	86	Y	N	N	N	N	Y	Y
Cardiff	16	Y	N	N	N	N	Y	Y
Cardiff Institute	14	Y	Y	Y	N	Y	Y	Y
Central Lancashire	43	Y	N	N	N	Y	Y	Y
Chester	76	Y	Y	Y	N	N	Y	Y
Chichester	57	Y	N	N	Y	Y	Y	Y
City	115	Y	N	N	N	N	Y	N
Coventry	63	Y	N	N	N	N	Y	Y
Cumbria	98	Y	N	N	N	N	Y	N
De Montfort	92	Y	N	Y	N	N	Y	N
Derby	104	No further information reported						
Dundee	35	Y	Y	Y	N	Y	Y	Y
Durham	6	Y	N	Y	Y	N	Y	Y
East Anglia	67	Y	Y	Y	Y	N	Y	Y
East London	127	No further information reported						
Edge Hill	95	Y	Y	Y	N	N	Y	Y
Edinburgh	5	Y	Y	Y	Y	N	Y	Y
Edinburgh Napier	78	No further information reported						
Essex	50	Y	N	Y	Y	N	Y	Y
Exeter	12	Y	Y	Y	Y	Y	Y	Y
Glamorgan	54	Y	N	Y	Y	N	Y	Y

Cricket pitch(es)?	Artificial turf pitch(es)?	Number of different sports with student clubs	Number of indoor sports with intra-mural competitions	Number of outdoor sports with intra-mural competitions	Instruction classes available?	Sports scholarships or bursaries available?	Sport website
Y	Y	53	0	2	Y	Y	www.abdn.ac.uk/sportandexercise
N	N	16	3	3	Y	Y	http://sport.abertay.ac.uk
Y	Y	50	0	1	Y	N	www.aber.ac.uk/en/sportscentre
N	N	60	5	5	Y	Y	www.anglia.ac.uk
Y	Y	37	0	0	Y	Y	www.aston.ac.uk/sport
N	Y	39	3	3	Y	Y	www.maesglas.co.uk
Y	Y	47	8	6	Y	Y	www.teambath.com
							www.bathspa.ac.uk
Y	N	11	4	2	Y	Y	www.beds.ac.uk/studentlife/town
Y	Y	43	3	4	Y	Y	www.sport.bham.ac.uk
N	Y	20	1	1	Y	N	www.birminghamcitysu.com/sports
N	N	9	3	0	Y	N	www.bolton.ac.uk/sport
Y	N	15	7	3	Y	Y	www.bournemouth.ac.uk/sports
Y	Y	34	13	14	Y	N	www.brad.ac.uk/sports
Y	N	24	0	4	Y	Y	www.brighton.ac.uk/sport
Y	Y	56	7	4	Y	Y	www.bris.ac.uk/sport
N	Y	39	3	2	Y	Y	www.brunel.ac.uk/sport
							www.bucks.ac.uk
Y	Y	53	12	7	Y	Y	www.sport.cam.ac.uk
N	N	15	0	4	Y	Y	www.canterbury.ac.uk/sport
Y	Y	59	0	3	Y	Y	www.cardiff.ac.uk/sport
Y	Y	19	0	0	Y	Y	www3.uwic.ac.uk/English/sport
Y	Y	35	0	1	Y	Y	www.uclan.ac.uk/uclansport
N	Y	33	3	3	Y	Y	www.chester.ac.uk
N	Y	17	0	1	Y	Y	www.chi.ac.uk/SportAtChichester.cfm
N	N	16	5	0	Y	N	www.city.ac.uk/studentcentre
Y	Y	34	4	2	Y	Y	www.coventry.ac.uk/cu/sport
N	N	12	8	2	Y	Y	www.cumbria.ac.uk
N	N	26	0	0	Y	N	www.dmu.ac.uk
							www.derby.ac.uk/sports
Y	N	44	5	3	Y	Y	www.dundee.ac.uk/ise
Y	Y	51	8	9	Y	Y	www.teamdurham.com
Y	Y	46	18	8	Y	Y	www.sportspark.co.uk
							www.uel.ac.uk/sports
N	Y	12	0	0	Y	Y	www.edgehill.ac.uk/sportingedge
Y	Y	59	3	5	Y	Y	www.eusu.ed.ac.uk
							www.napier.ac.uk
Y	Y	45	15	7	Y	Y	www.essex.ac.uk/sport
Y	Y	47	6	6	Y	Y	www.sport.ex.ac.uk
N	Y	25	6	1	Y	Y	http://sport.glam.ac.uk

University sporting facilities cont.

Universities	BUCS ranking 2008–09	Sports hall?	Swimming pool?	Squash courts?	Climbing wall?	Indoor tennis court(s)?	Fitness facilities?	Winter grass pitch(es)?
Glasgow	33	Y	Y	Y	N	N	Y	Y
Glasgow Caledonian	81	Y	N	N	N	N	Y	N
Gloucestershire	38	No further information reported						
Glyndŵr	140	No further information reported						
Goldsmiths College	126	Y	N	N	N	N	Y	Y
Greenwich	111	Y	N	N	N	Y	Y	Y
Heriot-Watt	47	Y	N	Y	Y	N	Y	Y
Hertfordshire	40	Y	Y	Y	Y	N	Y	Y
Huddersfield	110	Y	N	Y	N	N	Y	N
Hull	71	Y	N	Y	Y	N	Y	Y
Imperial College	22	Y	Y	Y	Y	N	Y	Y
Keele	72	Y	Y	Y	Y	N	Y	Y
Kent	34	Y	N	Y	Y	Y	Y	Y
King's College	52	N	N	Y	N	N	Y	Y
Kingston	83	N	N	N	N	N	Y	Y
Lampeter (Trinity Saint David)	142	No further information reported						
Lancaster	45	Y	Y	Y	Y	N	Y	Y
Leeds	15	Y	N	Y	Y	N	Y	Y
Leeds Metropolitan	3	Y	Y	Y	Y	Y	Y	Y
Leicester	76	Y	N	Y	N	Y	Y	Y
Lincoln	59	Y	N	Y	N	N	Y	Y
Liverpool	26	Y	Y	Y	Y	N	Y	Y
Liverpool Hope	100	No further information reported						
Liverpool John Moores	61	Y	Y	N	Y	N	Y	Y
London Metropolitan	21	No further information reported						
London School of Economics	49	No further information reported						
London South Bank	91	Y	N	N	N	N	Y	Y
Loughborough	1	Y	Y	Y	Y	Y	Y	Y
Manchester	11	Y	Y	Y	N	N	Y	Y
Manchester Metropolitan	64	Y	N	Y	N	N	Y	N
Middlesex	79	Y	N	N	N	N	Y	Y
Newcastle	10	Y	N	Y	N	N	Y	Y
Northampton	96	Y	N	N	N	N	Y	Y
Northumbria	19	Y	N	Y	N	N	Y	Y
Nottingham	7	Y	Y	Y	Y	Y	Y	Y
Nottingham Trent	27	Y	N	Y	Y	N	Y	Y
Oxford	8	Y	Y	Y	Y	N	Y	Y
Oxford Brookes	46	Y	N	Y	Y	N	Y	Y
Plymouth	51	N	N	Y	N	N	Y	N
Portsmouth	25	Y	N	Y	N	N	Y	Y

Cricket pitch(es)?	Artificial turf pitch(es)?	Number of different sports with student clubs	Number of indoor sports with intra-mural competitions	Number of outdoor sports with intra-mural competitions	Instruction classes available?	Sports scholarships or bursaries available?	Sport website
Y	Y	46	2	2	Y	Y	www.gla.ac.uk/services/sport
N	N	24	0	0	Y	Y	www.gcal.ac.uk/arc
							www.yourstudentsunion.com
							www.glyndwr.ac.uk
Y	N	17	1	1	Y	N	www.gold.ac.uk/sports
N	N	7	0	0	N	Y	www.gre.ac.uk/about/sports
N	Y	32	3	2	Y	Y	www.hw.ac.uk/sports
N	Y	24	1	2	Y	Y	http://student.hertssportsvillage.co.uk
N	N	28	0	0	Y	N	www2.hud.ac.uk/estates/sports
Y	Y	38	1	1	Y	N	www.hullstudent.com/au
Y	Y	73	5	4	Y	Y	www3.imperial.ac.uk/sports
Y	Y	32	2	1	Y	N	www.kususport.net
Y	Y	40	5	4	Y	Y	www.kent.ac.uk/sports
Y	N	51	0	0	Y	N	www.kclsu.org
Y	N	27	0	1	Y	Y	www.kingston.ac.uk/sport
							www.lampetersu.co.uk
Y	Y	30	7	7	Y	N	www.sportscentrelancaster.co.uk
Y	Y	63	9	6	Y	Y	www.leeds.ac.uk/sport
N	Y	40	1	2	Y	Y	www.leedsmet.ac.uk/sport
Y	Y	32	8	4	Y	Y	www.le.ac.uk/sports
N	Y	40	2	1	Y	Y	www.lincoln.ac.uk
Y	Y	43	3	3	Y	Y	www.liv.ac.uk/sports
							www.hope.ac.uk/hopeparksports
N	Y	30	0	3	Y	Y	www.ljmu.ac.uk/sport
							www.londonmet.ac.uk/sports
							www.lsesu.com
Y	N	13	1	0	Y	Y	www.lsbu.ac.uk/sports
Y	Y	53	28	14	Y	Y	http://sdc.lboro.ac.uk
Y	Y	44	5	7	Y	Y	www.manchester.ac.uk/sport
N	N	35	2	2	Y	N	www.mmu.ac.uk/sport
Y	N	12	2	2	Y	Y	www.mdx.ac.uk/sport
Y	Y	65	2	4	Y	Y	www.ncl.ac.uk/cprs
N	N	15	0	1	Y	Y	www.northamptonunion.com/clubs
Y	Y	27	4	2	Y	Y	www.teamnorthumbria.com
Y	Y	73	4	6	Y	Y	www.nottingham.ac.uk/sport
Y	Y	38	3	1	Y	Y	www.ntu.ac.uk/sport
Y	Y	81	28	18	Y	Y	www.sport.ox.ac.uk
Y	Y	30	1	1	Y	Y	www.brookes.ac.uk/sport
N	N	57	2	3	Y	Y	www.plymouth.ac.uk/recreation
N	Y	49	6	3	Y	Y	www.port.ac.uk/sport

University sporting facilities cont.

Universities	BUCS ranking 2008–09	Sports hall?	Swimming pool?	Squash courts?	Climbing wall?	Indoor tennis court(s)?	Fitness facilities?	Winter grass pitch(es)?
Queen Margaret, Edinburgh	122	Y	N	N	N	N	Y	N
Queen Mary, London	82	Y	N	Y	N	N	Y	N
Queen's, Belfast	107	Y	Y	Y	Y	N	Y	Y
Reading	44	Y	N	Y	N	N	Y	Y
Robert Gordon	66	Y	Y	Y	Y	Y	Y	N
Roehampton	101	Y	N	N	N	N	Y	Y
Royal Holloway	62	Y	Y	Y	N	N	Y	Y
St Andrews	29	Y	N	Y	Y	N	Y	Y
Salford	105	No further information reported						
Sheffield	23	Y	Y	Y	Y	N	Y	Y
Sheffield Hallam	30	Y	N	N	N	N	Y	Y
SOAS	123	No further information reported						
Southampton	20	Y	Y	Y	Y	N	Y	Y
Southampton Solent	70	Y	N	N	N	N	Y	Y
Staffordshire	97	Y	N	N	Y	Y	Y	Y
Stirling	28	Y	Y	Y	N	Y	Y	Y
Strathclyde	53	Y	Y	Y	N	N	Y	Y
Sunderland	80	Y	Y	N	N	N	Y	N
Surrey	60	Y	N	Y	Y	N	Y	Y
Sussex	58	Y	N	Y	N	N	Y	Y
Swansea	31	Y	Y	Y	Y	N	Y	Y
Swansea Metropolitan	135	No further information reported						
Teesside	73	Y	N	Y	Y	N	Y	Y
Thames Valley	120	No further information reported						
Ulster	112	Y	N	Y	N	Y	Y	Y
University of the Arts London	129	N	N	N	N	N	N	N
University College London	37	Y	N	Y	N	N	Y	Y
UWE, Bristol	39	Y	N	N	N	N	N	Y
Wales, Newport	109	Y	N	N	N	N	N	N
Warwick	17	Y	Y	Y	Y	Y	Y	Y
Westminster	131	No further information reported						
West of Scotland	128	No further information reported						
Winchester	108	Y	N	Y	N	N	Y	Y
Wolverhampton	88	Y	N	Y	N	N	Y	N
Worcester	48	Y	Y	N	N	N	Y	Y
York	41	Y	N	Y	N	N	Y	Y
York St John	84	Y	N	N	Y	N	Y	Y

Cricket pitch(es)?	Artificial turf pitch(es)?	Number of different sports with student clubs	Number of indoor sports with intra-mural competitions	Number of outdoor sports with intra-mural competitions	Instruction classes available?	Sports scholarships or bursaries available?	Sport website
N	Y	12	0	0	Y	N	www.qmu.ac.uk/sports
N	N	30	4	7	Y	N	www.qmsu.org
Y	Y	53	6	5	Y	Y	www.qub.ac.uk/sport
Y	Y	50	5	2	Y	Y	www.sport.reading.ac.uk
N	N	30	0	0	Y	Y	www.rgu.ac.uk/rgusport
N	N	20	0	3	Y	N	www.roehampton.ac.uk
Y	N	36	0	0	Y	Y	www.rhul.ac.uk/sports
Y	Y	46	7	7	Y	Y	www.st-andrews.ac.uk/sport
							www.salfordstudents.com
Y	Y	48	4	4	Y	Y	www.usport.co.uk
Y	Y	38	3	2	Y	Y	www.shu.ac.uk/sporthallam
							http://soasunion.org
Y	Y	70	7	9	Y	Y	www.sportrec.soton.ac.uk
Y	N	27	16	5	Y	Y	www.solent.ac.uk/sport
N	Y	35	0	0	Y	N	www.staffs.ac.uk
Y	Y	38	0	7	Y	Y	www.stir.ac.uk/sport
Y	Y	36	3	0	Y	Y	www.strath.ac.uk/sport
N	N	33	3	0	Y	N	www.unisportsunderland.com
Y	Y	35	7	1	Y	Y	www.unisport.co.uk
Y	Y	20	5	1	Y	Y	www.sussex.ac.uk/sport
Y	Y	50	6	1	Y	Y	www.swan.ac.uk/sport
							www.metsu.org
N	Y	40	0	1	Y	Y	www.tees.ac.uk/sections/sport
							www.tvu.ac.uk/students
Y	Y	42	2	0	Y	Y	www.uusport.com
N	N	17	0	0	N	N	www.suarts.org
Y	N	33	3	0	Y	Y	www.uclunion.org/sport-fitness
Y	N	40	2	0	Y	Y	www.uwe.ac.uk/sport
N	N	0	2	1	Y	N	www.newport.ac.uk
Y	Y	75	2	5	Y	Y	warwicksport.warwick.ac.uk
							www.westminster.ac.uk
							www.sauws.org.uk
Y	N	27	3	2	Y	N	www.winchesterstudents.co.uk
N	N	28	7	0	Y	Y	www.wlv.ac.uk/sport
Y	Y	42	0	0	Y	Y	www.worc.ac.uk/student/sports
Y	Y	58	5	9	Y	N	www.york.ac.uk/univ/sports
N	Y	23	1	0	Y	Y	www.yorksj.ac.uk

10 What Parents Should Do

This chapter looks at where to draw the line between constructive involvement and unwelcome interference. Nearly all students are adults, and university offers an environment where they can begin to make their own decisions and develop as individuals. A good starting point is to offer advice only when it is sought, and to leave direct contact with university administrators and academics to the student. It should go without saying that, throughout the *Guide*, all references to parents apply equally to guardians and step-parents.

Student finance and parental involvement
No matter how independent students are meant to be, most parents still feel obliged to do what they can to help their children through university. In these straitened times, however, many families will find that is rather less than they would have hoped. The system is designed to enable undergraduates to pay their own way through a degree course – albeit building up considerable debts along the way – and it will simply have to work that way for more students than was the case in the prosperous years.

One interesting side-effect of this change might be to reduce the involvement of parents in other aspects of their children's higher education – something that has been growing noticeably in recent years. Many parents took responsibility for the original £1,000 fees introduced when Labour came to power because they had to be paid up-front. But the more costly "top-up" fees are now met through loans that are only repayable after graduation, when the graduate's salary reaches £15,000. Parents will not even know when repayments begin, let alone be required to make a contribution.

"Helicopter parents"
However, universities have found that, in the controversy over the scale of top-up fees, the fact that mum and dad are no longer involved has passed many parents by. Anxious mothers and fathers are more inclined than ever to question what their children are getting for their £3,290 a year. There have been stories of parents challenging not just the amount and quality of tuition, but even the marking of essays and exams. The phenomenon, first reported in the USA, has given rise to the phrase "helicopter parents" – so called because they hover over their children's education when they should be letting go. No one wants to think of themselves in that category, but it is not surprising – or reprehensible – that parents are taking more of an

interest. Many more of today's parents have been to university themselves, so have the knowledge and confidence to offer advice, both in choosing where and what to study, and in the decisions facing students at university. One of the reasons that some then overstep the mark is that they are shocked that the amount of teaching and size of seminar groups are not what they recall from their own "free" higher education.

An associated reason is that family relationships have changed. Many teenage applicants are happy to accept a lift to an open day to get a second opinion on a university and their prospective course.

The family budget
Undoubtedly the main spur for heightened parental interest, however, is that, regardless of who pays the fees, higher education has been taking a bigger share of family budgets. Hundreds of thousands of students – particularly mature students – pay their own way through university. But every survey shows that families play an important (and, until now, growing) role where students move straight from school to higher education. Even at today's rates, fees remain a much less significant burden than living costs.

Laying the ground
The first thing any parent can do to smooth the path to university is to be encouraging about the value of higher education. Ideally, this should have started long before the application process, but it is especially important at this point. Particularly now that student debt has become a frequent media topic and the economic downturn has hit graduate employment prospects, it is only natural for sixth-formers and others thinking of higher education to have second thoughts.

The lure of a regular wage packet will be tempting, and there are plenty of young people who are not suited to full-time higher education. Even after the years of rapid university expansion, most people still do not go to university, but those who are capable of going generally do not regret the decision. Many people look back on their student days as the best period of their life, as well as the one that shaped their personality and their career.

Time as a student should still pay off for the individual in terms of lifetime earnings, as well as personal development. A little reassurance at this stage may make all the difference.

Making the choice
Any parent wants to help a son or daughter through the difficult business of choosing where and what to study. How big a role you play will depend on a number of factors, not the least of which is the extent to which your advice is wanted. In the end, it is the student's decision, and you can do no more than offer relevant information.

One important factor is the quality of advice available at school or college. If this is good, parental involvement should be marginal. But often that is not the case, and you may have to call on other resources, including your own research.

A second factor is your own level of expertise: you may have opinions about particular universities or subjects, but are they up-to-date and based on evidence? Try not to give advice that is coloured by memories of your own student days. That was probably a quarter of a century ago, and higher education has changed out of all recognition in the intervening years.

Avoid second-hand opinions gleaned through the media or dinner party gossip. You may think that some subjects are a sure-fire route to lucrative employment, while others are shunned by employers, but are you right? And do you really know the strengths and weaknesses of more than 100 universities? The tables in chapters 2 and 4 offer a reality check, but even they cannot take account of the differences within institutions. The subject tables in chapter 5 show that the best graduate employment rates are often not at the obvious universities.

Above all, do not try to rewind your own career decisions through your children. The fact that you enjoyed – or hated – a subject or a university does not mean that they will. You may have always regretted missing out on the chance to go to Oxbridge, or to become a brain surgeon, but they have their own lives to lead. Students who switch courses or drop out of university frequently complain that they were pressured into their original choice by their parents.

Check that choices are being made for sensible reasons, not on the basis of questionable gossip or trivial criteria. But beyond that, you should stay in the background unless there is a very good reason to play a more substantive role. Make a point of looking for important aspects of university life that the applicant might miss. Security, for example, usually does not feature near the top of a teenager's list of priorities, and likewise other practical issues, such as the proximity of student accommodation to lectures, the library and the students' union.

Many universities now publish guides specifically for parents and put on programmes for them at Open Days. The latter may be a way of separating prospective applicants from their more demanding "minders", but the programmes themselves can be interesting and informative. Do not worry that you will be an embarrassment by attending Open Days – thousands of parents do so, and you may add a critical edge to the proceedings. Like prospectuses, Open Days are part of the sales process, and it is easy for a sixth former to be carried away by the excitement surrounding a lively university. You are much more likely to spot the defects – even if they are ignored in the final decision.

Finding a place

Once the choices have been made, get to know the UCAS system and quietly ensure that deadlines are being met. The school should be doing this, but there is no harm in providing a little back-up, especially on parts of the process that take time and thought, such as writing the personal statement. There is little a parent can do as the offers and/or rejections come rolling in, other than to be supportive. If the worst happens and there are five rejections, you may have to start the advice process all over again for a new round of applications through UCAS Extra. If so, a cool head is even more necessary, but the same principles apply.

Results day

Then, before you know it, results day is upon you. Make sure you are at home, rather than in some isolated holiday retreat. Your son or daughter needs to have access to instant advice at school or college, and to be able to contact universities straight away if Clearing or Adjustment is required. And your moral support will be much more effective face to face, rather than down a telephone line. Whatever happens, try not to transmit the anxiety that you will inevitably be feeling to your son or daughter, especially if the results are not what was wanted. It is easy to make rash decisions about re-sitting exams or rejecting an insurance offer in the heat of the moment. Try to slow the process down and encourage clear and realistic thinking. As at other stages in the application, make sure you know in advance what might be required, such as where to access Clearing lists. After that, if it is Clearing or Adjustment, you will need to be on hand to offer advice and again provide a taxi service for visits to possible universities. Clearing or Adjustment is all but over in a week, so the agony should be short-lived.

Before they go

Little more than a month after the tension of results day, everything should be ready for the start of term. Unless your son or daughter is one of the growing band choosing to stay at home to study, there will be forms to fill in to secure university accommodation, as well as student loans to sort out and registration to complete. You can perform useful services, like supplying recipe books if the first year is to be spent in self-catering accommodation, but now is the time for independence to become reality. Make sure that important details like insurance are not forgotten, but otherwise stand clear.

The one thing parents must do before the fledgling student flies the nest, however, is to agree a budget – and make clear that it is a real one. How large that budget is will depend on family circumstances and your attitude to independent living. Some parents want to ensure that their children leave university debt-free; others could never afford to do that, while yet others believe that paying your own way is part of the learning experience. The important thing is that student and parents know where they stand.

After they've left

Any new student is going to be nervous if they are leaving home for the first time and having to settle into a strange environment. But in most cases it isn't going to last long because everyone is in the same boat and freshers' weeks hardly leave time for homesickness. In any case, they won't want to let their apprehension show. The people who are likely to be emotional are the parents – especially if they are left with an empty nest for the first time. It can take a while to get used to an orderly, quiet house after all those years of mayhem.

Resist any temptation to decorate their bedroom and turn it into an office – it is more common than you might think, and psychologists say it can do lasting damage to family relationships. Keep in touch by phone, text or email, but try not to pry. You're not going to be told everything anyway – which is probably just as well. They will be back soon enough: many more students go home at weekends than used to be the case and, just as you were getting used to having the place to yourself, the Christmas vacation will remind you of how things used to be. If things are not going smoothly at university, this may be the time for more reassurance – more students drop out at Christmas of their first year than at any other time.

Lastly, do not become a helicopter parent. Your son or daughter may well seek your advice if they are dissatisfied with the course, their accommodation or some other aspect of university life. By all means, give advice, but leave them to sort the problem out. Universities will cite the Data Protection Act, for example, to say they can only deal with students, not parents. What they really mean is that students are adults and should look after themselves.

Useful websites

Many universities now have special sections on their websites for parents of prospective students.
UCAS has a Parents section on its website: **www.ucas.com/parents**
To find out more about open days, visit: **www.opendays.com**
There is a useful selection of information and links to further advice within the direct.gov.uk website: **www.direct.gov.uk/parentsguidetohe**

The Department of Business, Innovation and Skills publishes *Help your Child into Higher Education*, which is also available as a download from **www.bis.gov.uk**

11 Coming to the UK to Study

UK universities have been growing in popularity among international students for many years – and the trend has accelerated as the value of the pound has made courses more affordable. Higher visa charges and changes in immigration regulations have not dimmed global enthusiasm for UK higher education. The country's international student population rose by 8 per cent in 2008–09 and overseas applications for undergraduate places were up again by nearly 29 per cent at the start of 2010.

Both EU students (who pay the same fees as their British counterparts) and those from the rest of the world (who pay considerably more) have shared in the boom. Indeed, the latest applications figures to show the largest numbers continuing to come from outside the EU, although there is a growing flow from Baltic countries such as Lithuania and Latvia.

Nearly all UK universities are cosmopolitan places that welcome international students in large numbers. Britain is the world's second most popular study destination, and recent surveys suggest that, in the eyes of international students, it is almost as attractive as the market leader, the USA. More than 340,000 international students were taking higher education courses in the UK in 2008–09. They now make up over 18 per cent of all students at UK universities and colleges. More full-time postgraduates – the fastest-growing group – come from outside the UK than within it.

Large numbers of students continue to come from China, Malaysia, Hong Kong, India, Nigeria, the USA, Pakistan and Singapore. Within the EU, the largest numbers are from France, Germany, Ireland and Poland. There has also recently been a significant influx of students from many of the new member states. In many UK universities you can expect to have fellow students from over 100 countries from around the world.

The results of studies by the British Council and the International Graduate Insight Group (i-graduate) suggest that international students are attracted to the UK chiefly because of the worldwide reputation of its universities and qualifications, high standards of teaching and research, and a perception that it is a safe place to live. Even after the decline in the value of the pound, the cost of studying and living in the UK remains relatively high, although courses are often shorter than in other parts of the world.

Within the UK, the cost of living varies by geographical area. Although London is the most expensive, accommodation costs in particular can also be high in many other major cities. You will want to factor into your decision:

» The availability, type and cost of accommodation.
» What financial and personal support is available.
» How easy it will be to find work if you need to supplement your income or broaden your experience.
» The location of your university, both within the UK and in relation to local facilities.

This chapter alone cannot provide all the answers, but it is a good place to start, pointing you in the direction of other useful sources of information. You should certainly find out as much as you can about what living in Britain will be like. Further advice and information is available through the British Council at its offices worldwide, at more than 60 university exhibitions that it holds around the world every year, or at its Education UK website (**www.educationuk.org**). Another useful website for international students is provided by the

The top countries for sending international students to the UK*

EU countries		%	Non-EU countries (Top 25)		%
France	6,593	11.2	China	19,457	21.7
Germany	6,367	10.9	Malaysia	8,378	9.4
Ireland	6,251	10.7	Hong Kong	6,993	7.8
Poland	5,327	9.1	India	4,626	5.2
Greece	4,549	7.8	Nigeria	3,985	4.5
Cyprus (Other*)	4,186	7.1	United States	3,357	3.8
Cyprus (EU)	2,636	4.5	Pakistan	2,849	3.2
Spain	2,327	4.0	Singapore	2,166	2.4
Sweden	2,032	3.5	Norway	1,841	2.1
Italy	1,970	3.4	South Korea	1,812	2.0
Lithuania	1,921	3.3	Sri Lanka	1,805	2.0
Belgium	1,585	2.7	Canada	1,805	2.0
Bulgaria	1,469	2.5	Saudi Arabia	1,553	1.7
Romania	1,280	2.2	Japan	1,448	1.6
Portugal	1,237	2.1	Bangladesh	1,362	1.5
Netherlands	1,190	2.0	Kenya	1,336	1.5
Finland	1,086	1.9	Russia	1,280	1.4
Latvia	1,047	1.8	United Arab Emirates	1,218	1.4
Slovakia	871	1.5	Brunei	1,171	1.3
Austria	688	1.2	Mauritius	1,031	1.2
Czech Republic	686	1.2	Switzerland	997	1.1
Hungary	661	1.1	Vietnam	965	1.1
Luxembourg	643	1.1	Iran	880	1.0
Estonia	622	1.1	Kazakhstan	849	0.9
Denmark	585	1.0	Thailand	787	0.9
Malta	226	0.4	**All non-EU students**	**89,507**	
Slovenia	106	0.2			
All EU Students	**58,653**				

*Note: First degree non-UK students

UK Council for International Student Affairs (UKCISA) at **www.ukcisa.org.uk**. We recommend some further websites at the end of the chapter.

Where to study in the UK

The UK is made up of three countries: England, Scotland and Wales – which collectively may be referred to as Great Britain – plus the province of Northern Ireland. The vast majority of the UK's universities and other higher education institutions are in England. Of the 119 universities covered in *The Times Good University Guide*, 93 are in England, 14 in Scotland, ten in Wales and two in Northern Ireland. It is now over a decade since Scotland gained its own parliament and Wales formed a National Assembly Government. Each has devolved powers and sets fee limits for higher education, which in some cases has brought benefits for EU students. All undergraduates from other EU countries are charged the same fees as those from the part of the UK where their chosen university is located, so the rate was £3,290 in England, Wales and Northern Ireland in 2010. EU students pay no tuition fees in Scotland.

The origins of UK universities can be traced back to the ancient seats of learning at Oxford (1096) and Cambridge (1209) – known collectively as "Oxbridge" – and St Andrews (1411) in

The universities most favoured by EU and non-EU students

Institution (Top 25)	EU students	Institution (Top 25)	Non-EU students
Edinburgh Napier	1,475	Manchester	3,343
University of the Arts London	1,190	Nottingham	2,579
Manchester	1,164	University of the Arts London	2,512
Westminster	1,094	University College London	2,168
Edinburgh	1,085	Imperial College	2,160
Coventry	1,080	Northumbria	2,153
Aberdeen	1,072	Warwick	1,804
University College London	1,018	Central Lancashire	1,557
Bedfordshire	1,011	Greenwich	1,540
Ulster	970	Edinburgh	1,490
Middlesex	956	Hertfordshire	1,482
Kingston	943	East London	1,464
Brighton	925	London School of Economics	1,451
Anglia Ruskin	905	Sheffield	1,317
Kent	897	Middlesex	1,285
Nottingham	885	Leeds	1,214
Glasgow	832	Birmingham	1,211
Surrey	830	Bath	1,185
King's College London	824	St Andrews	1,183
Imperial College	814	King's College London	1,173
Portsmouth	803	Kingston	1,168
Robert Gordon	801	Cardiff	1,166
Warwick	800	Coventry	1,137
Bath	771	Southampton	1,133
Manchester Metropolitan	768	Cambridge	1,126

Scotland. Although many people from outside Britain associate British universities with the Oxbridge image, in reality most higher education institutions in the UK are nothing like this. Some universities do still maintain a traditional culture, but most are modern institutions that place at least as much emphasis on teaching as research and offer many vocational programmes, often with close links with business, industry and the professions. The table opposite shows the universities that are most popular with international students.

UK universities have a worldwide reputation for high quality teaching and research. They maintain this position by investing heavily in the best academic staff, buildings and equipment, and by taking part in rigorous quality assurance monitoring. The main regulatory bodies include the Quality Assurance Agency for higher education (QAA), higher education funding councils for each country of the UK, and the Office for Standards in Education. Professional bodies also play an important role, and there is an Independent Adjudicator for Higher Education that handles student complaints that have not been resolved by universities' own internal complaints procedures.

What subjects to study?

You will find that strongly vocational courses are favoured by international students. Many of these in professional areas such as architecture, dentistry or medicine take one or two years longer to complete than most other degree courses. Traditional first degrees are mostly

The most popular subjects for international students

Subject Group	EU students	Non-EU students	Total	%
Business and administrative studies	13,607	26,083	39,690	27%
Engineering and technology	6,033	14,893	20,925	14%
Social studies	5,778	7,855	13,633	9%
Creative arts and design	4,881	5,173	10,053	7%
Law	3,119	5,983	9,102	6%
Subjects allied to medicine*	3,931	4,592	8,523	6%
Biological sciences	4,495	3,557	8,052	5%
Computer science	2,804	4,683	7,487	5%
Languages	3,859	2,182	6,041	4%
Medicine and dentistry	989	3,131	4,120	3%
Architecture, building and planning	1,968	2,116	4,084	3%
Physical sciences	1,781	2,038	3,818	3%
Mathematical sciences	993	2,761	3,754	3%
Mass communications and documentation	1,793	1,634	3,428	2%
Historical and philosophical studies	1,521	1,412	2,933	2%
Education	492	428	920	1%
Agriculture and related subjects	325	327	652	0%
Veterinary science	100	460	560	0%
Combined	185	200	385	0%
Total	**58,653**	**89,507**	**148,160**	**100%**

Note: First degree non-UK students
*Subjects allied to medicine include Pharmacy and Nursing.

awarded at Bachelor level (BA, BEng, BSc, etc.) and last three to four years. There are also some "enhanced" first degrees (MEng, MChem, etc.) that take four years to complete. The relatively new Foundation degree programmes are mostly vocational and take two years to complete as a full-time course, with an option to study for a further year to gain a full degree.

The tables at the end of this chapter select the 20 most popular subjects and show which universities for each subject have the greatest numbers of students. Remember, though, that you need also to consider the details of any course that you wish to study and to look at the overall ranking of that university as given in our main league table in chapter 4 and in the subject tables in chapter 5.

English language proficiency

The universities maintain high standards by generally setting high entry requirements, including proficiency in English. For international students, this usually includes a score of 6 or 7 in the International English Language Testing System (IELTS), which assesses English language ability through listening, speaking, reading and writing tests. New visa regulations introduced in 2010 will require English language proficiency at Level 3 of the UK qualifications system – equivalent to GCSE.

There are many private and publicly funded colleges throughout the UK that run courses designed to bring the English language skills of prospective higher education students up to the required standard. However, not all of these are Government approved. The web address for the list of Tier–4 Government approved education and training centres in the UK is given at the end of this chapter. Some private organisations such as INTO (**www.into.uk.com**) have joined with universities to create centres running programmes preparing international students for degree-level study. The British Council also runs English language courses at its centres around the world.

How to apply

You should read the information below in conjunction with that provided in chapter 6, which deals with the application process in some detail.

Some international students apply directly to a UK university for a place on a course, and others make their applications via an agent in their home country. But most applying for a full-time first degree course do so through the Universities and Colleges Admissions Service (UCAS). If you take this route, you will need to fill in an online UCAS application form at home, at school or perhaps at your nearest British Council office. There is lots of advice on the UCAS website about the process of finding a course and the details of the application system (**www.ucas.com/students/wheretostart/nonukstudents**).

Whichever way you apply, the deadlines for getting your application in are the same. For those applying from within an EU country, application forms must be received at UCAS by 15 January for most courses. Note that applications for Oxford and Cambridge and for all courses in medicine, dentistry and veterinary science have to be received at UCAS by 15 October. Some art and design courses also have a later deadline of 24 March (see chapter 6 for more details).

If you are applying from a non-EU country, you can submit your application to UCAS at any time between 1 September and 30 June preceding the academic year in which you plan to begin your studies. Most people apply well before the 30 June deadline to make sure that places are still available and to allow plenty of time for immigration regulations, and to make arrangements for travel and accommodation.

Entry and employment regulations

Since various high profile terrorist attacks in the UK and USA, visa regulations have been tightened. However, the main countries that welcome international students – including the UK, the USA, Australia and Canada – have made serious efforts to streamline visa processes and entry requirements to make them appear more welcoming. Students in some countries can also study for a degree qualification provided by a British university by enrolling at a university in their home country.

A global drive to promote the UK's universities was introduced in June 1999 and was later expanded, setting the target of recruiting an additional 100,000 international students to the UK's universities by 2011. Streamlining visa and entry procedures have been a key part of the initiative. However, since then, many new rules and regulations have been introduced, and it remains to be seen what effect they will have on recruitment. The British Government has been criticised for increasing visa fees, doubling fees for visa extensions, and ending the right to appeal against refusal of a visa. The most recent development is the introduction of a points system for entry – known as Tier 4, which came into effect in March 2009. Under this scheme, prospective students will be able to check whether they are eligible for entry against published criteria, and so assess their points score. Universities are also required to provide a Certificate of Acceptance for Study to their international student entrants and they have to be on the Register of Sponsors (details of where to find this list are given at the end of the chapter). Prospective students have to demonstrate that, as well as the necessary qualifications, they have English language proficiency and enough money for the first year of their specified course.

Since September 2007, all students wishing to enter the UK to study have been required to obtain entry clearance before arrival. The only exceptions are British nationals living overseas, British overseas territories citizens, British Protected persons, British subjects, and non-visa national short-term students who may enter under a new Student Visitor route. The details of the regulations are frequently reviewed by the UK Border Agency and you must always check changes. You can find more about all the latest rules and regulations for entry and visa requirements at **www.ukba.homeoffice.gov.uk/studyingintheuk**.

Changes are also being made to make it easier for international student to work in the UK during and after their studies. The rules and regulations governing permission to work vary according to your country of origin. If you are from a European Economic Area (EEA) country (the EU plus Iceland, Liechtenstein and Norway), you don't need permission to work in the UK, although you will need to be ready to show an employer your passport or identity card to prove you are a national of an EEA country. Students from outside the EEA who are here as Tier 4 students are allowed to work part-time for up to 20 hours a week during term time and to work full-time during vacations. These arrangements apply to students of degree courses; stricter limits were introduced in 2010 for lower level courses. If you wish to stay on after you have graduated, you can apply for permission under Tier 1 (Post-Study Work) under the new points-based immigration system. This scheme replaces the International Graduate Scheme in England, Wales and Northern Ireland and the Fresh Talent initiative in Scotland. Full details can be found at **www.ukba.homeoffice.gov.uk/workingintheuk/tier1/poststudy**. Post-study workers can look for employment without the need for a sponsor, but once in work will be expected to transfer to another tier within the points-based system. In Scotland, since the post-study scheme stated in 2008, over 4,000 graduates have taken advantage of it.

Bringing your family

In the UK, most universities can help to arrange facilities and accommodation for families as well as for single students. The family members you are allowed to bring with you are your husband or wife, civil partner (a same-sex relationship that has been formally registered in the UK or your home country) and dependent children.

If you are a national of any country from outside the EEA, your family will be subject to immigration policy. You will need to show that you can support them financially, that you can arrange appropriate accommodation, and that they will leave the UK when you have finished your studies. Your family members will usually be able to study (children under 16 are required to attend full-time education), and any over the age of 16 should be able to work as long as you have permission to stay for over 12 months and are following a degree or Foundation degree course. You can find out more about getting entry clearance for your family at
www.ukcisa.org.uk/student/info_sheets/your_family.php.

Support from British universities

Support for international students is more comprehensive than in many countries, and begins long before you arrive in the UK. Many universities have advisers – and sometimes offices or even whole campuses – in other countries. Some will arrange to put you in touch with current students or graduates who can give you a first-hand account of what life is like at a particular university. Pre-departure receptions for students and their families, as well as meet-and-greet arrangements for newly arrived students, are common. You can also expect an orientation and induction programme in your first week, and many universities now have "buddying" systems where current students are assigned to new arrivals to help them find their way around, adjust to their new surroundings, and make new friends. Each university also has a students' union that organises social, cultural and sporting events and clubs, including many specifically for international students. Both the university and the students' union are likely to have full-time staff whose job it is to look after the welfare of students from overseas.

International students also benefit from free medical and subsidised dental and optical care and treatment under the UK National Health Service, plus access to a professional counselling service and a university careers service.

At university, you will naturally encounter people from a wide range of cultures and walks of life. Getting involved in student societies, sport, voluntary work, and any of the wide range of social activities on offer will help you gain first-hand experience of British culture, and, if you need it, will help improve your command of the English language.

The 20 most popular subjects and universities for international students

Business Studies

	EU	Non-EU
Aston	204	609
Northumbria	233	570
Westminster	403	338
Middlesex	225	504
Bedfordshire	296	386
Anglia Ruskin	464	214
Sunderland	83	589
Manchester	173	454
Royal Holloway	197	407
Coventry	245	304
All overseas students	**10,074**	**16,193**

Computer Science

	EU	Non-EU
East London	31	392
Greenwich	33	317
Middlesex	48	198
Portsmouth	64	142
Coventry	101	100
Imperial College	101	90
Manchester	73	113
Teesside	71	113
Northumbria	26	157
Bedfordshire	95	77
All overseas students	**2,804**	**4,683**

Accounting and Finance

	EU	Non-EU
Manchester	83	426
City	109	358
Essex	64	341
London School of Economics	33	326
Lancaster	82	258
Warwick	57	251
Durham	18	246
Kent	21	211
Manchester Metropolitan	51	170
Bangor	1	218
All overseas students	**1,658**	**7,786**

Economics

	EU	Non-EU
University College London	78	438
London School of Economics	91	366
Warwick	76	297
Manchester	66	278
Royal Holloway	84	192
Essex	97	166
York	59	168
Bath	43	152
Nottingham	88	105
Leicester	13	168
All overseas students	**2,012**	**4,747**

Law

	EU	Non-EU
Northumbria	19	807
King's College London	195	199
Leicester	176	167
Kent	125	200
Warwick	67	211
Manchester	54	222
London School of Economics	37	211
Essex	160	67
Buckingham	18	207
Sheffield	89	132
All overseas students	**3,119**	**5,983**

Art and Design

	EU	Non-EU
University of the Arts London	667	1,792
University for Creative Arts	165	101
Nottingham Trent	41	149
Birmingham City	71	115
Middlesex	113	69
Kingston	44	120
Northumbria	31	120
Goldsmiths College	54	83
Coventry	42	76
West of England	64	47
All overseas students	**2,521**	**3,556**

The 20 most popular subjects and universities for international students cont.

Electrical and Electronic Engineering

	EU	Non-EU
Imperial College	85	308
Birmingham City	28	238
Manchester	43	191
Sheffield	16	186
Northumbria	14	181
Birmingham	16	175
Central Lancashire	6	166
Strathclyde	21	144
Nottingham	14	132
Southampton	34	110
All overseas students	**1,050**	**4,693**

Politics

	EU	Non-EU
St Andrews	77	218
Kent	223	52
London School of Economics	78	183
Warwick	61	87
Aberdeen	117	26
Edinburgh	34	103
Sussex	79	38
Aberystwyth	82	32
Birmingham	79	31
Nottingham	77	29
All overseas students	**2,203**	**1,718**

Mechanical Engineering

	EU	Non-EU
Imperial College	80	202
Nottingham	24	189
Central Lancashire	8	156
Coventry	41	122
Bradford	53	106
Bath	43	91
King's College London	34	98
Birmingham	5	124
Sheffield	11	116
Hertfordshire	19	104
All overseas students	**1,144**	**3,407**

Medicine

	EU	Non-EU
King's College London	84	188
Manchester	52	210
Nottingham	38	152
University College London	58	119
Imperial College	49	123
Glasgow	38	126
Leicester	31	131
Edinburgh	30	131
Southampton	29	132
Birmingham	19	140
All overseas students	**917**	**2,872**

Biological Sciences

	EU	Non-EU
Edinburgh	196	96
Imperial College	80	195
University College London	69	96
Manchester	49	90
Aberdeen	97	36
Cambridge	56	69
Nottingham	37	80
Glasgow	70	33
Oxford	43	51
St Andrews	41	48
All overseas students	**2,028**	**2,170**

Mathematics

	EU	Non-EU
Imperial College	77	271
University College London	56	262
Warwick	52	193
Manchester	72	169
Oxford	38	184
Cambridge	65	111
Bath	56	88
Southampton	20	102
Loughborough	11	104
London School of Economics	11	102
All overseas students	**993**	**2,761**

The 20 most popular subjects and universities for international students cont.

Civil Engineering

	EU	Non-EU
Edinburgh Napier	272	8
Bradford	147	64
Imperial College	46	126
Nottingham	43	119
East London	36	121
Cardiff	34	91
Coventry	56	58
Salford	60	49
Surrey	83	25
Leeds	27	79
All overseas students	**1,819**	**1,932**

Other Subjects Allied to Medicine

	EU	Non-EU
Bournemouth	152	165
Queen Margaret Edinburgh	113	87
Imperial College	48	123
Greenwich	60	81
Cambridge	57	71
Cardiff	20	104
Salford	68	29
Manchester Metropolitan	54	37
Robert Gordon	85	1
East London	42	33
All overseas students	**1,730**	**1,416**

Hospitality, Leisure, Recreation and Tourism

	EU	Non-EU
Thames Valley	162	319
University College Birmingham	126	202
University of the Arts London	33	171
Surrey	66	103
Queen Margaret Edinburgh	22	137
Brighton	124	33
Edinburgh Napier	57	93
Bedfordshire	115	27
Oxford Brookes	82	58
Bournemouth	61	76
All overseas students	**1,791**	**1,933**

Communication and Media Studies

	EU	Non-EU
University of the Arts London	77	114
Liverpool John Moores	17	167
Westminster	111	69
Goldsmiths College	69	99
Middlesex	75	49
Thames Valley	65	32
Coventry	30	62
Bedfordshire	67	16
Southampton Solent	59	23
Oxford Brookes	33	46
All overseas students	**1,651**	**1,411**

Psychology

	EU	Non-EU
East London	70	86
University College London	35	98
Aberdeen	95	21
Glasgow	89	18
Middlesex	48	50
Nottingham	30	68
York	11	87
Royal Holloway	60	34
St Andrews	47	46
Westminster	60	14
All overseas students	**2,004**	**1,300**

Pharmacology and Pharmacy

	EU	Non-EU
Sunderland	131	173
Brighton	187	54
Nottingham	16	211
Robert Gordon	212	15
Liverpool John Moores	41	137
Manchester	24	124
Strathclyde	6	142
Bath	16	118
Kingston	61	65
School of Pharmacy	13	102
All overseas students	**998**	**1,742**

The 20 most popular subjects and universities for international students cont.

Architecture	EU	Non-EU
Nottingham	48	157
Manchester Metropolitan	41	105
Robert Gordon	72	71
Greenwich	83	34
East London	74	42
Plymouth	89	11
University College London	11	85
Oxford Brookes	45	48
Portsmouth	57	36
Brighton	67	23
All overseas students	1,391	1,245

English	EU	Non-EU
Portsmouth	90	215
Central Lancashire	73	231
St Andrews	16	85
Edinburgh	22	69
Salford	44	36
Anglia Ruskin	50	22
Bedfordshire	58	10
Canterbury Christ Church	50	7
Cardiff	1	56
Glasgow	49	6
All overseas students	1,173	1,237

Useful websites

For information about studying in Britain, visit:
The British Council, with its dedicated Education UK site designed for those wishing to find out more about studying in the UK:
www.educationuk.org

The UK Council for International Student Affairs (UKCISA) produces a wide range of factsheets on all aspects of studying in the UK:
www.ukcisa.org.uk

UCAS, for full details of courses available and an explanation of the application process:
www.ucas.com/students/wheretostart/nonukstudents

For the latest information on entry and visa requirements, visit:
www.ukba.homeoffice.gov.uk/studyingintheuk

Register of Sponsors for Tier-4 educational establishments:
www.bia.homeoffice.gov.uk/sitecontent/documents/employersandsponsors/pointsbasedsystem/registerofsponsorseducation

UK Student Life, a guide designed to explain British daily life and culture to international students:
www.ukstudentlife.com

For a general guide to Britain, available in many languages:
www.visitbritain.com

12 Applying to Oxbridge

Oxbridge (as Oxford and Cambridge are called collectively) not only dominates UK higher education; the two universities are recognised as among the best in the world, regularly featuring among the top five in global rankings. But that is not why they merit a separate chapter in this *Guide*.

The two ancient universities have different admissions arrangements to the rest of the higher education system. Although part of the UCAS network, they have different deadlines from other universities, you can only apply to one or the other, and selection is in the hands of the colleges rather than the university centrally. Most candidates apply to a specific college, although you can make an open application if you are happy to go anywhere.

There have been reforms to the admissions system at both universities in recent years, in order to make the process more user-friendly to those who do not have school or family experience to draw upon. In particular, the business of choosing a college has been intimidating for many prospective applicants. Candidates are now distributed around colleges more efficiently, regardless of the choices they make initially.

There is little to choose between the two universities in terms of entrance requirements, and a formidable number of successful applicants have the maximum possible grades. However, that does not mean that the talented student should be shy about applying: both have fewer applicants per place than many less prestigious universities, and admissions tutors are always looking to extend the range of schools and colleges from which they recruit. For those with a realistic chance of success, there is little to lose except the possibility of one wasted space out of five on the UCAS application.

Overall, there are about four applicants to every place at Oxford and Cambridge, but there are big differences between subjects and colleges. As the tables in this chapter show, competition is particularly fierce in subjects such as medicine and English, but those qualified to read geology or classics have a much better chance of success. The pattern is similar to that in other universities, although the high degree of selection (and self-selection) that precedes an Oxbridge application means that even in the less popular subjects the field of candidates is certain to be strong.

The two universities' power to intimidate prospective applicants is based partly on myth. Both have done their best to live down the "Brideshead Revisited" image, but many sixth-formers still fear that they would be out of their depth there, academically and socially. In fact, the state sector produces nearly 55 per cent of entrants to Oxford and over 59 per cent to Cambridge, and the dropout rate is lower than at almost any other university. The "champagne set" is still present and its activities are well publicised, but most students are hard-working high achievers with the same concerns as their counterparts on other campuses. A joint poll by the two universities' student newspapers showed that undergraduates were spending much of their time in the library or worrying about their employment prospects, and relatively little time on the river or even in the college bar.

State school applicants

Both universities and their student organisations have put a great deal of effort into trying to encourage applications from state schools, and many colleges have launched their own campaigns. Such has been the determination to convince state school pupils that they will get a fair crack of the whip that a new concern has grown up of possible bias against independent school pupils. In reality, however, the dispersed nature of Oxbridge admissions rules out any conspiracy. Some colleges set relatively low standard offers to encourage applicants from the state sector, who may reveal their potential at interview. Some admissions tutors may give the edge to well-qualified candidates from comprehensive schools over those from highly academic independent schools because they consider theirs the greater achievement in the circumstances. Others stick with tried and trusted sources of good students. The independent sector still enjoys a degree of success out of proportion to its share of the school population.

Choosing the right college

Simply in terms of winning a place at Oxford or Cambridge, choosing the right college is not quite as important as it used to be. Both universities have got better at assessing candidates' strengths and finding a suitable college for those who either make an open application or are not taken by their first-choice college.

Cambridge: The Tompkins Table 2009

College	2009	2008	College	2009	2008
Trinity	1	3	Peterhouse	16	18
Emmanuel	2	2	King's	17	19
Selwyn	3	1	Clare	18	13
Gonville and Caius	4	4	Robinson	19	17
St Catharine's	5	11	Girton	20	22
Pembroke	6	10	Fitzwilliam	21	21
Churchill	7	6	Sidney Sussex	22	29
Magdalene	8	5	Murray Edwards (New)	23	23
Trinity Hall	9	15	Newnham	24	24
Corpus Christi	10	9	Homerton	25	25
Jesus	11	7	Hughes Hall	26	26
Queens'	12	16	Wolfson	27	27
Christ's	13	8	St Edmund's	28	29
St John's	14	20	Lucy Cavendish	29	28
Downing	15	12			

At Oxford, subject tutors from around the university put candidates into bands at the start of the selection process, using the results of admissions tests as well as exam results and references. Applicants are spread around the colleges for interview and may not be seen by their preferred college if the tutors think their chances of a place are better elsewhere. Almost a quarter of last year's successful candidates were offered places by a college other than the one they applied to.

Cambridge relies on the "pool", which gives the most promising candidates a second chance if they were not offered a place at the college to which they applied. Those placed in the pool are invited back for a second round of interviews early in the new year. The system lowers the stakes for those who apply to the most selective colleges – out of 4,016 offers made in 2008, a total of 743 came via the pool. Cambridge still interviews about 90 per cent of applicants, whereas the new system at Oxford has resulted in more immediate rejections in some subjects. In medicine, fewer than half of Oxford's applicants were interviewed in 2007, while in biochemistry almost all were.

However, most Oxbridge applicants still apply direct to a particular college, not only to maximise their chances of getting in, but because that is where they will be living and socialising, as well as learning. Most colleges may look the same to the uninitiated, but there are important differences. Famously sporty colleges, for example, can be trying for those in search of peace and quiet.

Thorough research is needed to find the right place. Even within colleges, different admissions tutors may have different approaches, so personal contact is essential. The tables in this chapter give an idea of the relative academic strengths of the colleges, as well as the varying levels of competition for a place in different subjects. But only individual research will suggest where you will feel most at home. For example, women may favour one of the few remaining single-sex colleges (Murray Edwards, Newnham and Lucy Cavendish at Cambridge). Men have no such option.

Oxford: The Norrington Table 2009

College	2009	2008	College	2009	2008
St John's	1	2	St Catherine's	16	26
Merton	2	1	Jesus	17	8
Magdalen	3	4	Exeter	18	19
Corpus Christi	4	11	Somerville	19	28
New College	5	6	St Anne's	20	12
Hertford	6	17	Lady Margaret Hall	21	30
University	7	18	St Hugh's	22	9
Lincoln	8	10	Pembroke	23	25
Wadham	9	16	Oriel	24	14
Queen's	10	7	St Peter's	25	20
Trinity	11	15	Brasenose	26	21
Christ Church	12	5	St Edmund Hall	27	22
Keble	13	13	Mansfield	28	23
Balliol	14	3	St Hilda's	29	29
Worcester	15	27	Harris Manchester	30	24

Oxford applications and acceptances by course

Arts	Applications 2009	Applications 2008	Acceptances 2009	Acceptances 2008	Acceptances to Applications % 2009	Acceptances to Applications % 2008
Ancient and Modern History	69	79	13	20	18.8	25.3
Archaeology and Anthropology	73	78	24	21	32.9	26.9
Classical Archaeology and Ancient History	95	78	18	22	18.9	28.2
Classics	267	259	110	122	41.2	47.1
Classics and English	23	33	5	6	21.7	18.2
Classics and Modern Languages	25	36	12	10	48.0	27.8
Economics and Management	1,171	939	92	73	7.9	7.8
English	1,122	1,090	242	227	21.6	20.8
English and Modern Languages	153	145	25	26	16.3	17.9
European and Middle Eastern Languages	51	47	13	7	25.5	14.9
Fine Art	155	175	20	19	12.9	10.9
Geography	310	272	82	78	26.5	28.7
Modern History	890	780	242	233	27.2	29.9
Modern History and Economics	75	57	13	8	17.3	14.0
Modern History and English	79	80	6	9	7.6	11.3
Modern History and Modern Languages	92	78	14	17	15.2	21.8
Modern History and Politics	282	240	46	48	16.3	20.0
History of Art	77	69	14	12	18.2	17.4
Law	1,078	935	191	179	17.7	19.1
Law with Law Studies in Europe	321	254	30	27	9.3	10.6
Mathematics and Philosophy	86	87	24	21	27.9	24.1
Modern Languages	554	553	175	178	31.6	32.2
Modern Languages and Linguistics	75	71	16	23	21.3	32.4
Music	158	165	68	70	43.0	42.4
Oriental Studies	163	150	42	42	25.8	28.0
Philosophy and Modern Languages	73	78	17	20	23.3	25.6
Philosophy and Theology	105	103	21	29	20.0	28.2
Physics and Philosophy	86	100	14	18	16.3	18.0
PPE	1,503	1,192	248	232	16.5	19.5
Theology	114	115	42	39	36.8	33.9
Total Arts	**9,325**	**8,338**	**1,879**	**1,836**	**20.2**	**22.0**

The findings in the Tompkins Table (see page 260) are not officially endorsed by Cambridge University itself. However, since 2007 we have been able to publish the "official" Norrington Table from Oxford. Sanctioned or not, both tables give an indication of where the academic powerhouses lie – information which can be as useful to those trying to avoid them as to those seeking the ultimate challenge. Although there can be a great deal of movement year by year, both tables tend to be dominated by the rich, old foundations. Both tables are compiled from the degree results of final-year undergraduates. A first is worth five points; a 2:1, four; a 2:2, three; a third, one point. The total is divided by the number of

Oxford applications and acceptances by course cont.

Sciences	Applications 2009	Applications 2008	Acceptances 2009	Acceptances 2008	Acceptances to Applications % 2009	Acceptances to Applications % 2008
Biochemistry	315	200	105	86	33.3	43.0
Biological Sciences	344	315	108	111	31.4	35.2
Chemistry	474	478	192	193	40.5	40.4
Computer Science	126	109	16	22	12.7	20.2
Earth Sciences (Geology)	69	74	31	34	44.9	45.9
Engineering Science	606	534	134	166	22.1	31.1
Engineering, Economics and Management	140	91	16	9	11.4	9.9
Experimental Psychology	215	190	57	48	26.5	25.3
Human Sciences	111	78	31	29	27.9	37.2
Materials Science; Materials, Economics and Management	78	66	31	30	39.7	45.5
Mathematics	917	836	174	169	19.0	20.2
Mathematics and Computer Science	78	68	18	28	23.1	41.2
Mathematics and Statistics	166	145	23	26	13.9	17.9
Medicine	1293	975	156	151	12.1	15.5
Physics	765	662	175	173	22.9	26.1
Physiological Sciences	79	61	23	23	29.1	37.7
PPP	176	168	33	36	18.8	21.4
Total Sciences	**5,952**	**5,050**	**1,323**	**1,334**	**22.2**	**26.4**
Total Arts and Sciences	**15,277**	**13,388**	**3,202**	**3,170**	**21.0**	**23.7**

Note: the dates refer to the year in which the acceptances were made.

candidates to produce each college's average.

In both universities, teaching for most students is based in the colleges. In practice, however, this arrangement holds good in the sciences only for the first year. One-to-one tutorials, which are Oxbridge's traditional strength for undergraduates, are by no means universal. However, teaching groups remain much smaller than in most universities, and the tutor remains an inspiration for many students. Both Oxford and Cambridge give applicants the option of leaving the choice of college to the university. For those with no ready source of advice on the colleges, this would seem an attractive solution to an intractable problem, but it is also a risky one: a slightly lower proportion succeeds in this way than by applying to a particular college and, inevitably, you may end up somewhere that you hate.

The applications procedure

Both universities have set a UCAS deadline of 15 October 2010 for entry in 2011. You may also need to take a written test and submit examples of your work – the exact requirements vary depending on the course you select, so check this carefully. See page 20 for details of application tests. In addition, once Cambridge receives your UCAS form, you will be asked to complete an online Supplementary Application Questionnaire. The deadline for this will be October 22 in most cases.

Cambridge Applications and Acceptances by Course

Arts	Applications		Acceptances		Acceptances to Applications %	
	2009	2008	2009	2008	2009	2008
Anglo-Saxon, Norse and Celtic	52	51	25	19	48.1	37.3
Archaeology and Anthropology	163	164	69	81	42.3	49.4
Architecture	499	392	43	40	8.6	10.2
Asian and Middle Eastern Studies	188	185	61	59	32.4	31.9
Classics	173	158	88	81	50.9	51.3
Classics (4 years)	34	37	11	13	32.4	35.1
English	1,035	880	221	204	21.4	23.2
Geography	332	356	99	120	29.8	33.7
History	772	758	210	220	27.2	29.0
History of Art	126	110	34	30	27.0	27.3
Modern and Medieval Languages	605	564	191	188	31.6	33.3
Music	182	165	71	66	39.0	40.0
Philosophy	312	240	52	47	16.7	19.6
Theology and Religious Studies	124	155	58	55	46.8	35.5
Total Arts	*4,597*	*4,215*	*1,233*	*1,223*	*26.8*	*29.0*
Social Science						
Economics	1,396	1,264	178	185	12.8	14.6
Land Economy	261	262	56	60	21.5	22.9
Law	1,062	1,075	219	220	20.6	20.5
Social and Political Sciences	689	638	110	112	16.0	17.6
Total Social Sciences	*3,408*	*3,239*	*563*	*577*	*16.5*	*17.8*
Science and Technology						
Computer Science	329	231	69	73	21.0	31.6
Engineering	1,546	1,364	307	332	19.9	24.3
Mathematics	1,177	1,174	244	257	20.7	21.9
Medical Sciences	1,857	1,680	299	310	16.1	18.5
Natural Sciences	2,278	2,111	647	640	28.4	30.3
Veterinary Medicine	414	3,75	75	76	18.1	20.3
Total Science and Technology	*7,601*	*6,935*	*1,641*	*1,688*	*21.6*	*24.3*
Education	98	109	42	43	42.9	39.4
Total	**15,704**	**14,498**	**3,479**	**3,531**	**22.2**	**24.4**

Note: the dates refer to the year in which the acceptances were made.

Mathematics includes mathematics and mathematics with physics. Medical sciences includes medicine and the graduate course in medicine.

The Tripos courses in chemical engineering, management studies and manufacturing engineering can be taken only after Part 1 in another subject. Applications and acceptances for these courses are recorded under the first year subjects taken by the applicants involved.

Linguistics could only be taken after Part 1 of another Tripos for 2009 entry. From 2010 entry onwards, however, this subject became available as a full three-year degree programme.

You may apply to either Oxford or Cambridge (but not both) in the same admissions year, unless you are seeking an Organ award at both universities. Interviews take place in September for those who have left school or applied early, but in December for the majority. By the end of October, the first group can expect an offer, a rejection or deferral of a decision until January. The main group of applicants to Oxford will receive either a conditional offer or a rejection by Christmas, while in Cambridge the news arrives early in the new year.

For more information about the application process and preparation for interviews, visit **www.cam.ac.uk/admissions** and **www.ox.ac.uk/admissions**.

Oxford College Profiles

Balliol
Balliol College, Oxford OX1 3BJ
01865 277777 undergrad.admissions@balliol.ox.ac.uk www.balliol.ox.ac.uk
Undergraduates: 383 Postgraduates: 316

Famous as the alma mater of many prominent post-war politicians, Balliol has maintained a strong presence in university life and is usually well represented in the Union and most other societies. Academic standards are formidably high, as might be expected in the college of Wycliffe and Adam Smith, notably in the classics and social sciences. PPE is notoriously oversubscribed. Library facilities are good and include the Tylor law library. Balliol began admitting overseas students in the 19th century and has cultivated an attractively cosmopolitan atmosphere. It is one of only two colleges to have an entirely student-run bar, the focal point for evening socialising. Most undergraduates are offered accommodation in college for three years, with second year accommodation off-site. Graduate students are usually lodged in the Graduate Centre at Holywell Manor. Centrally located, with a JCR pantry that is open all day, Balliol is convenient as well as prestigious.

Brasenose
Brasenose College, Oxford OX1 4AJ
01865 277510 (admissions) admissions@bnc.ox.ac.uk www.bnc.ox.ac.uk
Undergraduates: 365 Postgraduates: 209

Brasenose may not be the most famous Oxford college, but it makes up for its discreet image with an advantageous city-centre position. The *alma mater* of David Cameron, Brasenose was one of the first colleges to admit women in the 1970s, and now usually has a near-even split within each year. But BNC, as the college is often known, still has the image of a rugby haven, and has the lowest proportions of students from state schools in the university. Named after the door knocker on the 13th-century Brasenose Hall, the college has a pleasant, intimate ambience which most find conducive to study. Law, PPE, medicine and modern history are traditional strengths, and competition for places in these subjects is intense. Its library is open 24 hours a day and there is a separate law library. All undergraduate rooms have internet connections. Sporting standards are as high as at many much larger colleges and the college's rowing club is one of the oldest in the university. Two annexes, the St Cross Building and Frewin Court, mean nearly all undergraduates can live in.

Christ Church

Christ Church, Oxford OX1 1DP
01865 276181 (admissions) admissions@chch.ox.ac.uk www.chch.ox.ac.uk
Undergraduates: 438 Postgraduates: 223

The college founded by Cardinal Wolsey in 1525 and affectionately known as The House has come a long way since Evelyn Waugh mythologised its aristocratic excesses in *Brideshead Revisited*, although it is still heavily dominated by students from private schools. Academic pressure is reasonably relaxed, although natural high-achievers prosper and the college's history and law teaching is highly regarded. The college is now twelfth in the Norrington Table. The magnificent 18th-century library is one of the best in Oxford. It is supplemented by a separate law library. Christ Church has its own art gallery, which holds over 2,000 works of mainly Italian Renaissance art. Sport, especially rugby, is an important part of college life. The river is close by for the aspiring oarsman, and the college has good squash courts. Accommodation for all three years is rated by Christ Church undergraduates as excellent and includes flats off Iffley Road as well as a number of beautifully panelled shared sets (double rooms) in college. The modern bar adds to the lustre of a college justly famous for its imposing architecture. Its chapel is also the cathedral of the Diocese of Oxford – England's smallest medieval cathedral.

Corpus Christi

Corpus Christi College, Oxford OX1 4JF
01865 276693 (admissions) admissions.office@ccc.ox.ac.uk www.ccc.ox.ac.uk
Undergraduates: 248 Postgraduates: 105

Corpus, one of Oxford's smallest colleges, is naturally overshadowed by its Goliath-like neighbour, Christ Church, but makes the most of its intimate, friendly atmosphere and exquisite beauty. Like The House, it has an exceptional view across the Meadows. Although the college has only around 350 students including postgraduates, it has an admirable library open 24 hours a day. Academic expectations are high and English, Classics, PPE and medicine are especially well-established. Perhaps unsurprising, then, that Corpus has stormed to victory in *University Challenge* twice in recent years, although after their 2008 win the team were subsequently disqualified and stripped of their title. Corpus is able to offer accommodation to all its undergraduates, one of its many attractions to those seeking a smaller community in Oxford. The college is also one of the most generous with bursaries, giving travel, book and vacation grants at an almost unparalleled level across the university. Scholars are particularly well rewarded.

Exeter

Exeter College, Oxford OX1 3DP
01865 279648 (academic secretary) admissions@exeter.ox.ac.uk www.exeter.ox.ac.uk
Undergraduates: 343 Postgraduates: 201

Exeter is the fourth oldest college in the university and was founded in 1314 by Walter de Stapeldon, Bishop of Exeter. Nestling between the High Street and Broad Street, site of most of the city's bookshops, it could hardly be more central. The college boasts handsome buildings, the exceptional Fellows' garden and attractive accommodation for most undergraduates for all three years of their university careers, although many second year students currently live out. The college is in the process of refurbishing its graduate accommodation in the east of the city, which will be ready for the start of the 2010–11 academic year. Exeter does have academic pedigree, but has slipped down the Norrington Table in recent times. It is, however, often accused of being rather dull. Given its glittering roll-call of alumni, which includes Martin Amis, J.R.R. Tolkien, Alan Bennett, Richard Burton, Imogen Stubbs and Tariq Ali, this seems an accusation that, on the face of it at least, is hard to sustain. The arrival of Frances Cairncross, the former managing editor of *The Economist*, in 2004 has created a new dynamic at the college, with regular, high-profile, speaker events and the incorporation of a college careers service. The college recently took over the buildings of Ruskin College in Walton Street, which will provide further accommodation, although complete occupation is not expected until 2014.

Harris Manchester

Harris Manchester College, Oxford OX1 3TD
01865 271009 (admissions tutor)   enquiries@hmc.ox.ac.uk   www.hmc.ox.ac.uk
Undergraduates: 85   Postgraduates: 108

Founded in Manchester in 1786 to provide education for non-Anglican students, Harris Manchester finally settled in Oxford in 1889 after spells in both York and London. A full university college since 1996, its central location with fine buildings and grounds in Holywell Street is very convenient for the Bodleian, although the college itself does have an excellent library. Harris Manchester admits only mature students of mostly 25 years and above to read for both undergraduate and graduate degrees, predominantly in the arts. All students must be 21 or older. There are also groups of visiting students from American universities and some men and women training for the ministry. Most of its members live in and all meals are provided, indeed the college encourages its members to dine regularly in hall. The college has few sporting facilities (a croquet lawn and a college punt), but members can use two central Oxford gyms without charge and can play football, cricket, swimming and chess as well as playing on other college or university teams. Other outlets include the college Drama Society and also the chapel, a focal point to many there.

Hertford

Hertford College, Oxford OX1 3BW
01865 279404 (admissions)   admissions@hertford.ox.ac.uk   www.hertford.ox.ac.uk
Undergraduates: 396   Postgraduates: 172

Though tracing its roots to the 12th century, Hertford is determinedly modern. It was one of the first colleges to admit women (in 1976). Hertford also helped set the trend towards offers of places conditional on A-levels, which paved the way for the abolition of the entrance examination. It is still popular with state school applicants, and is one of the least stuffy colleges, with a reputation for attracting students from a broad range of backgrounds. The college lacks the grandeur of Magdalen, of which it was once an annex, but has its own architectural trademark in the Bridge of Sighs. It is also close to the History Faculty library (Hertford's neighbour), the Bodleian and the King's Arms, perhaps Oxford's most popular pub. Academic pressure at Hertford is relaxed, but the quality of teaching, especially in English, is generally thought admirable. Accommodation has improved, thanks in part to the Abingdon House and Warnock House complex close to the Thames near Folly Bridge, and the college can now lodge all of its undergraduates at any one time, albeit in disparate parts of the city. The bar, offering some notorious cocktails, serves as a central social hub, and is popular with students across the university. Like most congenial colleges, Hertford is often accused of being claustrophobic and inward-looking – a charge most Hertfordians would ascribe simply to jealousy.

Jesus

Jesus College, Oxford OX1 3DW
01865 279721 (admissions)   admissions.officer@jesus.ox.ac.uk   www.jesus.ox.ac.uk
Undergraduates: 347   Postgraduates: 168

Jesus, the only Oxford college to be founded in the reign of Elizabeth I, suffers from something of an unfair reputation for insularity. Its students, whose predecessors include T.E. Lawrence and Harold Wilson, describe it as "friendly but gossipy" and shrug off the legend that all its undergraduates are Welsh. Close to most of Oxford's main facilities, Jesus has three compact quads, the second of which is especially enticing in the summer. The college's JCR is well-equipped, with a pool table, large projector screen television, and a hatch serving tea and toast throughout the day. Academic standards are high and most subjects are taught in college. Physics, chemistry and engineering are especially strong. Rugby and rowing also tend to be taken seriously. Accommodation is almost universally regarded as excellent and relatively inexpensive. Self-catering flats in north and east Oxford have enabled every graduate to live in throughout his or her Oxford career. The range of accommodation available to undergraduates is similarly good and is available for the full length of any course. The college's Cowley Road development, also the site of the college's sports ground, has been described by the students' union as "some of the plushest student housing in Oxford".

Keble

Keble College, Oxford OX1 3PG
01865 272711 (admissions)   college.office@keble.ox.ac.uk   www.keble.ox.ac.uk
Undergraduates: 423   Postgraduates: 200

Keble, named after John Keble, the leader of the Oxford Movement, was founded in 1870 with the intention of making Oxford education more accessible, and the college remains proud of "the legacy of a social conscience". With around 400 undergraduates, Keble is one of the biggest colleges in Oxford, while its uncompromising Victorian Gothic architecture also makes it one of the most distinctive. Once famous for the special privileges it extended to rowers, the college's academic performance varies from year to year. It is strong in the sciences, where it benefits from easy access to the Science Area, the Radcliffe Science Library and the Mathematical Institute. The college's sporting record remains exemplary, with the rugby team regularly dominating university competitions, although some students find the overflow of the sporting ethos into the college's social life overbearing. Undergraduates are guaranteed accommodation in their first two years and the college can also accommodate most undergraduates in their final year. Its library is open 24 hours a day and all rooms have internet connections. The college hall, where students wishing to dine must wear gowns six nights a week, has recently been intensively cleaned to restore it to its former glory and is one of the most impressive in the university. The refurbished "spaceship" and Café Keble are particular attractions. The college also has a well-equipped gym and a modern theatre, the acoustics of which are rated the best in the university.

Lady Margaret Hall

Lady Margaret Hall, Oxford OX2 6QA
01865 274310 (admissions)   admissions@lmh.ox.ac.uk   www.lmh.ox.ac.uk
Undergraduates: 400   Postgraduates: 185

Lady Margaret Hall, Oxford's first college for women, has been co-educational since 1978 and now enjoys an equal gender balance. For many students, LMH's comparative isolation – the college is three quarters of a mile north of the city centre – is a real advantage, ensuring a clear distinction between college life and university activities, and a refuge from tourists. For others it means a long journey to central library facilities. Although the neo-Georgian architecture is not to everyone's taste, the college's beautiful gardens back onto the Cherwell river, allowing LMH to have its own punt house and 12 acres of land. The students' union describes life at the college as "relaxed". It generally hovers around the lower reaches of the Norrington Table, although English is strong, producing a high proportion of firsts each year. Accommodation is guaranteed for first and third years, and for the great majority of second years. The new Pipe Partridge Building has considerably enlarged undergraduate accommodation and houses a new JCR, dining hall and lecture theatre. Ongoing building works aim to provide further graduates rooms as well as a new gym. LMH shares most of its sports facilities with Trinity College, though it has squash and tennis courts on site and has become a leading rowing college. The library is open 24 hours and is well-stocked for English and Classics, with a separate law library. It has long been one of Oxford's dramatic centres, and has recently attained a strong presence in student journalism and the Oxford Union.

Lincoln

Lincoln College, Oxford OX1 3DR
01865 279836 (admissions)   admissions@lincoln.ox.ac.uk   www.lincoln.ox.ac.uk
Undergraduates: 318   Postgraduates: 291

Small, central Lincoln cultivates a lower profile than many other colleges with comparable assets. The college's 15th-century buildings and beautiful library – a converted Queen Anne church – combine to produce a delightful environment in which to spend three years. Academic standards are high, particularly in arts subjects, although the college's relaxed atmosphere is justly celebrated. Accommodation is provided by the college for all undergraduates throughout their careers and includes rooms above the Mitre, a medieval inn. Students parade around Oxford in sub fusc (formal wear) on Ascension Day while choristers from the University Church beat the parish bounds. The college has a healthy rivalry with neighbouring Brasenose. Historically, Lincoln students must invite their Brasenose counterparts into the bar for free drinks every Ascension Day, in recognition of a time when a Lincoln man was saved from a town mob by the college's neighbours. Graduate students have their own centre a few minutes' walk away in Bear Lane and at the EPA Science Centre close to the university science area. Finalists live in a recently refurbished complex on Museum Road, by Keble and the University Parks. Lincoln's small size and self-sufficiency have led to the college being accused of insularity. Lincoln's food is outstanding, among the best in the university. Sporting achievement is impressive for a college of this size, in part a reflection of its good facilities.

Magdalen

Magdalen College, Oxford OX1 4AU
01865 276063 (admissions) admissions@magd.ox.ac.uk www.magd.ox.ac.uk
Undergraduates: 415 Postgraduates: 189

Perhaps the most beautiful college in Oxford or Cambridge, Magdalen is known around the world for its tower, its deer park and its May morning celebrations – when students threw themselves off Magdalen Bridge into the river Cherwell. This practice has now been banned after shallow water resulted in a large number of injuries. The college has shaken off its public school image to become a truly cosmopolitan place, with a large intake from overseas and an increasing proportion of state school pupils. Magdalen's record in English, history and law is second to none, while its science park at Sandford is bound to bolster its reputation in these subjects. The college is academically very strong and is now third in the Norrington Table. Library facilities are excellent, especially in history and law. First-year students are accommodated in the Waynflete Building and are allocated rooms in subsequent years by ballot. Undergraduates can be housed in college for the full length of their course. Rents are not cheap compared to other colleges, but there is always financial help on offer. Sets in cloisters and in the palatial New Buildings are particularly sought after. Magdalen is also conveniently placed between the city centre and east Oxford, where there is a plethora of pubs and restaurants and a lively music scene. The college bar is one of the best in Oxford and the college is a pluralistic place, proud of its drama society and choir. In recent years the college has become particularly strong at rowing. Elsewhere, enthusiasm on the sports field makes up for a traditional lack of athletic prowess.

Mansfield

Mansfield College, Oxford OX1 3TF
01865 270920 (admissions) admissions@mansfield.ox.ac.uk www.mansfield.ox.ac.uk
Undergraduates: 226 Postgraduates: 81

Mansfield's graduation to full Oxford college status in 1995 marked the culmination of a long history of development since 1886. Its spacious, attractive site is fairly central, close to the libraries, the shops, the University Parks and the river Cherwell. With just over 200 undergraduates, the community is close-knit, although this can verge on the claustrophobic. Recent moves to increase intake numbers may change that. The less intimidating atmosphere of Mansfield is, perhaps, helped by its strong representation of state-school students. First and third years live in college accommodation. The library is open 24 hours. Mansfield students share Merton's excellent sports ground and have numerous college teams. In recent years the college has produced many student journalists. The twice-termly champagne and chocolate parties held in the chapel are hugely popular and very cheap. Despite its former theological background, students are not admitted on the basis of religion and can read a wide variety of subjects. Mansfield is home to the Oxford Centre for the Environment, Ethics and Society (OCEES) and the American Studies Institute backs onto its gardens, evidence of the strong links between Mansfield and the USA, which is reflected by some 35 visiting students annually. It also spearheads the Oxford FE Initiative, which encourages applications to the university from further education colleges.

Merton

Merton College, Oxford OX1 4JD
01865 276299 (admissions)   admissions@admin.merton.ox.ac.uk   www.merton.ox.ac.uk
Undergraduates: 314   Postgraduates: 289

Founded in 1264 by Walter de Merton, Bishop of Rochester and Chancellor of England, Merton is one of Oxford's oldest colleges and one of its most prestigious. Quiet and beautiful, with the oldest quad in the university, Merton has high academic expectations of its undergraduates, consistently reflected in a position at or near the top of the Norrington Table. It is currently in second place. History, English, physics, PPE and chemistry all enjoy a formidable track record. The medieval library is the envy of many other colleges. Accommodation is some of the cheapest in the university, of a good standard and offered to students for all three years. Merton's food is well-priced and among the best in the university; formal Hall is served six times a week. Kitchens are provided for the first and third years who live in college. Merton's many diversions include the Merton Floats, its dramatic society, the Neave (Politics) Society, an excellent Christmas Ball and the peculiar Time Ceremony, which celebrates the return of GMT. Sports facilities are excellent, although participation tends to be more important than the final score.

New College

New College, Oxford OX1 3BN
01865 279512 (admissions)   admissions@new.ox.ac.uk   www.new.ox.ac.uk
Undergraduates: 418   Postgraduates: 217

New College is old (founded in 1379 by William of Wykeham), large and much more relaxed than most expect when first confronting its daunting facade. It is a bustling place, as proud of its excellent music and its bar as of its strength in law, history and PPE. The college came fifth in the Norrington Table last year. Traditionally in the bottom third of colleges for attracting state-school students, the college has been making particular efforts to increase this proportion, inviting applications from schools that have never sent candidates to Oxford. The Target Schools Scheme, designed to increase applications from state schools, is well established. Almost all undergraduates will be able to have college accommodation for three years. The college's library facilities are impressive, especially in law, classics and PPE. The sports ground is nearby and includes good tennis courts. Women's sport is particularly strong, especially on the river. A sports complex, named after Brian Johnston, opened in 1997, at St Cross Road. The sheer beauty of New College remains one of its principal assets and the college gardens are a memorable sight in the summer. In spite of these traditional charms, the college has strong claims to be considered admirably innovative. Music is a feature of college life, and the college has some of the best practice facilities in the university. The Commemoration Ball, held every three years, is a highlight of Oxford's social calendar.

Oriel

Oriel College, Oxford OX1 4EW
01865 276522 (admissions)   admissions@oriel.ox.ac.uk   www.oriel.ox.ac.uk
Undergraduates: 302   Postgraduates: 158

In spite of its reputation as a bastion of muscular privilege, Oriel is a friendly college with a strong sense of identity. In recent years the college has succeeded in ridding itself of its image of being home to the archetypal "Tory boy" characters. The college is sometimes described as having "a strong crew spirit" reflecting its traditions on the river. Academic pressure is relaxed by Oxford standards and it tends to inhabit the bottom third of the Norrington Table. The well-stocked library is open 24 hours a day. Oriel's sporting reputation is certainly deserved and its rowing eight is rarely far from the head of the river. Other sports are well catered for, even if their facilities are considerably farther away than the boathouse, which is only a short jog away. Accommodation is of variable quality, but Oriel can provide rooms for all three years for those students who require them. Extensive new accommodation has been completed one mile away off the Cowley Road and at the Island Site on Oriel Street. Oriel also offers a lively drama society, a Shakespearian production taking place each summer in the front quad. College meals are cheap, with students charged little more than £6 for three meals a day in hall.

Pembroke

Pembroke College, Oxford OX1 1DW
01865 276412 (admissions)   admissions@pmb.ox.ac.uk   www.pmb.ox.ac.uk
Undergraduates: 367   Postgraduates: 141

Although its alumni include such extrovert characters as Dr Johnson and Michael Heseltine, Pembroke is one of Oxford's least dynamic colleges. The college is historically poor financially, but academic results are solid. The college has Fellows and lecturers in almost all the major university subjects. Pembroke expects to accommodate all first years and most final-year undergraduates. Planning permission has been given for an extension that will allow all undergraduates up to three years of college accommodation from 2012. The Sir Geoffrey Arthur building on the river, ten minutes' walk from the college, offers excellent facilities; in addition to 100 student rooms there is a concert room, computer room and a multigym. College food is reasonable, though some find formal Hall every evening rather too rich a diet. Rugby and rowing are strong, with Pembroke usually behind only Oriel and Magdalen on the river, and squash and tennis courts are available at the nearby sports ground. Over the past few years Pembroke's intake has had among the lowest proportion of state-school students in the university.

Queen's

Queen's College, Oxford OX1 4AW
01865 279161   admissions@queens.ox.ac.uk   www.queens.ox.ac.uk
Undergraduates: 343   Postgraduates: 124

One of the most striking sights of the High Street, Queen's has now shed its exclusive "northern" image to become one of Oxford's liveliest and most attractive colleges. The college's academic record is average, although results have improved recently and it is now placed tenth in the Norrington Table. Modern languages, chemistry and mathematics are reckoned among the strongest subjects. Queen's does not normally admit undergraduates for the single honour schools of English language and literature, theology, computer science or geography, and is seen as strong in history and politics. The library is as beautiful as it is well stocked. All students are offered accommodation, first years being housed in modernist annexes in east Oxford, and the college is in the process of converting all rooms into en-suite facilities. Queen's can be insular and is largely apolitical, but has a strong college enthusiasm for sport, particularly rugby and netball. The college's beer cellar is one of the most popular in the university and the JCR facilities are also better than average. An annual dinner commemorates a student who is said to have fended off a bear by thrusting a volume of Aristotle into its mouth. Postgraduates are accommodated in St Aldate's House, a modern building close to the centre of town.

St Anne's

St Anne's College, Oxford OX2 6HS
01865 274840 (admissions)   enquiries@st-annes.ox.ac.uk   www.st-annes.ox.ac.uk
Undergraduates: 444   Postgraduates: 233

Architecturally uninspiring (a Victorian row with concrete "stack-a-studies" dropped into their back gardens), St Anne's makes up in community spirit what it lacks in awesome grandeur. One of the largest colleges, it has a relatively high proportion of state-school students. A women's college until 1979, its academic standing has fluctuated, having been in last place in the Norrington Table in the middle of the last decade, but now scoring around mid-table. PPE is particularly strong. The library, which is now open 24 hours, is very well-stocked and is rich in law, Chinese and medieval history texts. The college has a strong presence in the university journalism scene and its football teams usually do very well. Accommodation is guaranteed to all undergraduates, and the college also operates an equalisation scheme which gives up to £800 to students wishing to live out. It is situated to the north of the city centre, although not as far out as St Hugh's. Three new accommodation blocks contain 150 student rooms, including four for disabled students, while the older rooms have been refurbished. Half of all rooms are en suite.

St Catherine's

St Catherine's College, Oxford OX1 3UJ
01865 271703 (admissions)   admissions@stcatz.ox.ac.uk   www.stcatz.ox.ac.uk
Undergraduates: 499   Postgraduates: 216

Arne Jacobsen's modernist design for "Catz", one of Oxford's youngest and largest undergraduate colleges, has attracted much attention as the most striking contrast in the university to the lofty spires of Magdalen and New College. Close to the Law, English and Social Science faculties, the university science area and the pleasantly rural Holywell Great Meadow, St Catherine's is nevertheless only a few minutes' walk from the city centre. Academic standards are especially high in mathematics and physics. The well-liked Wolfson library is open till midnight on most days. Rooms are small but tend to be warmer than in other, more venerable colleges, and are now available on site for first, second and third years. There is an excellent theatre, as well as an on-site punt house, gym and squash courts. The college is host to the Cameron Mackintosh Chair of Contemporary Theatre, currently held by Michael Frayn. Previous incumbents include Kevin Spacey, Arthur Miller and Sir Ian McKellen. St Catherine's has one of the best JCR facilities in Oxford.

St Edmund Hall

St Edmund Hall, Oxford OX1 4AR
01865 279011 (admissions)   admissions@seh.ox.ac.uk   www.seh.ox.ac.uk
Undergraduates: 404   Postgraduates: 166

St Edmund Hall – "Teddy Hall" – has one of Oxford's smallest college sites but also one of its most populous. The college offers students the chance to live in its medieval quads right in the heart of the city. With the male/female ratio nearly equal, the college is shedding its image as a home for "hearties", and the authorities have gone out of their way to tone down younger members' rowdier excesses. Nonetheless, the sporting culture is still vigorous and the college usually does well in rugby, football and hockey. The college is also known across the university for its "bops" – the name given to student discos. Academically, Teddy Hall tends to yo-yo between the middle and the bottom of the Norrington Table. It is currently four from the bottom. But the college has some impressive names among its fellowship as well as a marvellous library, originally a Norman church. It hosts three annual prizes for journalism, including a £500 award for a student from St Edmund Hall. College accommodation is reasonable and can be offered for three years, either on the main site or in North or East Oxford. The college has three annexes, one near the University Parks, and two on Iffley Road, where many of the rooms have private bathrooms. Hall food is better than average.

St Hilda's

St Hilda's College, Oxford OX4 1DY
01865 286620 (admissions)   college.office@st-hildas.ox.ac.uk   www.st-hildas.ox.ac.uk
Undergraduates: 398   Postgraduates: 139

October 2008 marked a milestone for St Hilda's and the university as a whole, as the college welcomed its first mixed sex intake. Although the college, founded in 1893, lasted more than 100 years as an all-female institution, the governing body voted in 2006 to admit men. Male students now make up nearly half of the first year. The college has long languished at the bottom end of the Norrington Table, but is a distinctive part of the Oxford landscape and is usually well represented in university life. The 65,000-volume library is growing fast and accommodation for readers was extended in 2005. St Hilda's also boasts one of the largest ratios of state-school to independent undergraduates in Oxford. Accommodation is guaranteed to first years and finalists. The JCR has its own punts, which are available free for college members and their guests. Many of the rooms offer some of the best river views in

Oxford. Social facilities are limited, but this is expected to change with the influx of men. The standard of food is high.

St Hugh's

St Hugh's College, Oxford OX2 6LE
01865 274910 (admissions)   admissions@st-hughs.ox.ac.uk   www.st-hughs.ox.ac.uk
Undergraduates: 397   Postgraduates: 219

One of the lesser-known colleges, St Hugh's was criticised by students in 1987 when it began admitting men. There is now an equal male/female ratio, a better balance than at most Oxford colleges. Like Lady Margaret Hall, St Hugh's picturesque setting is a bicycle ride from the city centre. It is an ideal college for those seeking a place to live and study away from the madding crowd, and is well liked for its pleasantly bohemian atmosphere and beautiful gardens. Academic pressure remains comparatively low. After a brief jump up the Norrington table last year the college is now back in the lower regions. History is particularly strong. St Hugh's guarantees accommodation to undergraduates for all three years, although the standard of rooms is variable. Sport, particularly football, is taken quite seriously. As the college enjoys extensive grounds compared to most colleges, there is space for a croquet lawn and tennis courts.

St John's

St John's College, Oxford OX1 3JP
01865 277317 (admissions)   admissions@sjc.ox.ac.uk   www.sjc.ox.ac.uk
Undergraduates: 399   Postgraduates: 213

St John's is one of Oxford's powerhouses, excelling in almost every field and boasting arguably the most beautiful gardens in the university. Founded in 1555 by a London merchant, it is richly endowed and makes the most of its resources to provide undergraduates with an agreeable and challenging three years. The work ethic is very much part of the St John's ethos, and academic standards are high, with English, chemistry and history among the traditional strengths, though all students benefit from the impressive library. The college is Merton's main rival for the top of the Norrington Table and this year it was St John's that claimed the coveted number one spot. It also has one of the highest proportions of state-school students in Oxford. As might be expected of a wealthy college, the accommodation is excellent and guaranteed for three or four years. The college's riches allow it to subsidise accommodation costs to a large degree, as well as providing generous book grants and prizes. St John's has a strong sporting tradition and offers good facilities, but the social scene is limited. As befits such an all-round strong college, entry is fiercely competitive. The college is very close to two of Oxford's landmark pubs: the Eagle and Child and the Lamb and Flag.

St Peter's

St Peter's College, Oxford OX1 2DL
01865 278863 (admissions)   admissions@spc.ox.ac.uk   www.spc.ox.ac.uk
Undergraduates: 348   Postgraduates: 92

Opened as St Peter's Hall in 1929, St Peter's has been an Oxford college since 1961. Its medieval, Georgian and 19th-century buildings are in the city centre and close to most of

Oxford's main facilities. Though still young, St Peter's is well represented in university life and has pockets of academic excellence, rising to tenth in the Norrington Table in 2004, although it has since fallen far back into the bottom half. History tutoring is particularly good. There are no Fellows in classics at the college. Accommodation is offered to students for first and third years and about 60 per cent of second years. Although previously prohibited from cooking on the main site, students now have a kitchenette with limited facilities. Student rooms vary from traditional rooms in college to new purpose-built rooms a few minutes' walk away. The college's facilities are impressive, including one of the university's best JCRs. The college has a proud sporting heritage, being particularly strong at rugby and rowing. St Peter's is known as one of Oxford's most vibrant colleges socially. It is strong in acting and journalism, and has a recently refurbished bar, although the college has recently suffered from a severe shortage in funding.

Somerville

Somerville College, Oxford OX2 6HD
01865 270619 (admissions) secretariat@some.ox.ac.uk www.some.ox.ac.uk
Undergraduates: 401 Postgraduates: 80

The announcement, early in 1992, that Somerville was to go co-educational sparked an unusually acrimonious and persistent dispute within this most tranquil of colleges. Protests were doomed to failure, however; the first male undergraduates arrived in 1994 and now account for half the students. Lady Thatcher was one of those who flocked to their old college's defence, illustrating the fierce loyalty Somerville inspires. The college's atmosphere appears to have survived the momentous change, although the culture of protest reappeared when a number of students refused to pay the Government's tuition fees in 1998. The college has relatively strong state-school representation. Accommodation, including 30 small flats for students, is of a reasonable standard, and is guaranteed for first years and students sitting university examinations, as well as roughly a third of all other students. The JCR operates a rent equalisation scheme for those who live out in their second year. There are kitchens in all college buildings, but hall food is towards the cheaper end of the university. Sport is strong at Somerville and the women's rowing eight usually finishes near the head of the river. The college's hockey pitches and tennis courts are nearby. The 100,000-volume library is open 24 hours a day and is one of the most beautiful in Oxford. The college also has an active music society.

Trinity

Trinity College, Oxford OX1 3BH
01865 279860 (admissions) admissions@trinity.ox.ac.uk www.trinity.ox.ac.uk
Undergraduates: 300 Postgraduates: 98

Architecturally impressive and boasting beautiful lawns (which you can walk on), Trinity is one of Oxford's least populous colleges, admitting some eighty undergraduates each year. It is ideally located, beside the Bodleian, Blackwell's bookshop and the White Horse pub. Cardinal Newman, an alumnus of Trinity, is said to have regarded Trinity's motto as "Drink, drink, drink". Academic pressure varies, but the college has recently made impressive steps up the ranks of the Norrington Table of academic performance and the college produces its fair share of firsts, especially in arts subjects. Trinity has shaken off its reputation for apathy, and whilst members are active in all walks of university life, the college has its own debating and drama societies, as well as sharing a fierce rivalry with neighbouring Balliol. Usually, all undergraduates are given a room on the main site in their first and second years, with the majority of third and forth years living in a purpose-built block a mile and a half north of the main site. Students rate the food highly.

University

University College, Oxford OX1 4BH
01865 276959 (admissions)   admissions@univ.ox.ac.uk   www.univ.ox.ac.uk
Undergraduates: 364   Postgraduates: 205

University is the first Oxford college to be able to boast a former student in the Oval Office. Indeed, the college seems certain to benefit from its unique links with former President Clinton, a Rhodes Scholar at University in the late 1960s. The college is probably Oxford's oldest, though highly unlikely to have been founded by King Alfred, as legend claims. Academic expectations are high and the college prospers in most subjects, and it is currently seventh in the Norrington Table. Physics, PPE and maths are particularly strong. That said, University has fewer claims to be thought a powerhouse in the manner of St John's, arguably its greatest rival. Students who are accepted to read courses with a mathematical element are invited to a free week-long maths course just before the beginning of their first term, providing a head-start in their studies. Accommodation is guaranteed to undergraduates for all three years, with third years lodged in an annexe in north Oxford about a mile and a half from the college site on the High Street, although the vast majority of third years choose to live out in rented accommodation. Sport is strong and University has been well represented and successful on the rugby field in the last few years, but the college has a reputation for being quiet socially. Students from the state sector are poorly represented, despite a generous bursary scheme.

Wadham

Wadham College, Oxford OX1 3PN
01865 277545 (admissions)   admissions@wadh.ox.ac.uk   www.wadh.ox.ac.uk
Undergraduates: 458   Postgraduates: 125

Founded by Dorothy Wadham in 1609, Wadham is known in about equal measure for its academic track record – the college generally ranks in the top third in examination performance – and its leftist politics. The JCR – or student union as it has rebranded itself – is famously dynamic and politically active, although the breadth of political opinion is greater than its left-wing stereotype suggests. Wadham students are notoriously trendy, although some in the university find the atmosphere at the college slightly forced. That said, the college is very strong on admitting students from state schools. And for somewhere supposedly unconcerned with such fripperies, its gardens are surprisingly beautiful. The somewhat rough-hewn chapel is similarly memorable. The college has a good 24-hour library. Accommodation is guaranteed for at least two years and there are many large, shared rooms on offer. Journalism, music and drama play an important part. Highlights in the social calendar are Queer Festival, a riotous celebration of all things gay, and Wadstock, the college's open-air summer music festival. Tickets to both are always sold out.

Worcester

Worcester College, Oxford OX1 2HB
01865 278391 (admissions)   admissions@worc.ox.ac.uk   www.worc.ox.ac.uk
Undergraduates: 416   Postgraduates: 186

Worcester is to the west of Oxford what Magdalen is to the east: an open, rural contrast to the urban rush of the city centre. The college's rather mediocre exterior conceals a delightful environment, including some characteristically muscular Baroque Hawskmoor architecture, a garden and a lake. The college has been rising up the Norrington Table and this year sits firmly in the middle. The 24-hour library is strongest in the arts. Accommodation, guaranteed for two years and provided for the majority of third years, varies in quality from ordinary to conference standard in the Canal Building. More en-suite accommodation, next to the new gym, is now available. Sport plays an important part in college life, as befits the only college with playing fields on site. Worcester has had recent successes in football, hockey and cricket. Formal halls are available six nights a week and a bargain at less than £3. Like Magdalen and New, it is home to the Commemoration Ball once every three years, a highlight of the Oxford social calendar. More than half of the 2008 intake was from the state system, but the average over the last three years (which the university considers more representative) is still just over 50 per cent.

Cambridge College Profiles

Christ's

Christ's College, Cambridge CB2 3BU
01223 334983 (admissions)   admissions@christs.cam.ac.uk   www.christs.cam.ac.uk
Undergraduates: 412   Postgraduates: 100

Christ's prides itself on its academic strength, but offers one third of places on "easy offers", anything as low as two E grades at A-levels. The college is confident of its ability to identify potential high-flyers at interview and, in effect, prepared to circumvent A-levels as the principal criteria for entry to ease the pressure on good applicants and allow them to read around their subject. However, to receive an "easy offer", applicants need "an outstanding record of GCSE grades and strong support from your school". Some 57 per cent of students accepted come from the state sector, and the college has been active in outreach and access work this year. Women make up about 40 per cent of the students. Christ's has a reputation for being dominated by hard-working medics, natural scientists and mathematicians, although it is also strong in history and English. Students love the location, right in the middle of the city, and describe the atmosphere at the college as intimate and cosy, but some complain of short bar opening hours, particularly in the exam term. College–owned accommodation is guaranteed to all undergraduates in college for the duration of the course. Rooms on offer vary from the gothic splendour of some of the old buildings on site to the more modern New Court "Typewriter", which has been recently refurbished, offering students en-suite accommodation and private balconies. The college has a visual arts centre where the college's artist in residence works, and a newly refurbished gallery and performance space, the Yusuf Hamied Centre. Christ's Films – widely considered to be one of the best film societies in the university – and the Christ's Amateur Dramatics Society are active student groups. College sport has flourished in recent years with teams competing to a good standard, particularly in rowing and football. The playing fields, shared with St Catharine's, are situated on Barton Road, about two miles away. Notable alumni include Charles Darwin and the poet John Milton.

Churchill

Churchill College, Cambridge CB3 0DS
01223 336202 (admissions)   admissions@chu.cam.ac.uk   www.chu.cam.ac.uk
Undergraduates: 480   Postgraduates: 238

Students at Churchill claim they are the most unpretentious of Cambridge colleges – and are proud of the fact the college allows its students to walk on the grass. This informality stems from the youth of the college, as well as its relatively high state-school intake. In 2008, the latest data available, some 70 per cent of students accepted came from the state sector. Founded in 1958 to help meet "the national need for scientists and engineers and to forge links with industry", Churchill has seen a recent rise up the Tompkins Table, finishing seventh last year. The college has a noticeably high proportion of scientists and men: only one in three students are female. Compared to the breathtaking architecture of other Cambridge colleges,

Churchill's modern and functional architecture strikes many as ugly, with some students saying the "1960s brutalism is something you get used to". Another perceived flaw is its distance from the city centre – the college is a 15-minute walk from the centre of the City. Others argue that the distance offers much-needed breathing space, and rate the college's spacious and leafy grounds. One undeniable advantage is Churchill's ability to provide every undergraduate with a room in college for all three years. Also, the college's weekly "pav" dances have become popular amongst Cambridge students in recent years. There are extensive on-site playing fields, and the college does well in rugby, hockey and rowing. The university's only student radio station (broadcasting to Churchill and New Hall) is based here, and they have recently developed new state of the art music facilities. The College Archive Centre houses the papers of both the college's namesake, Winston Churchill, and former prime minister Margaret Thatcher.

Clare

Clare College, Cambridge CB2 1TL
01223 333246 (admissions)   admissions@clare.cam.ac.uk   www.clare.cam.ac.uk
Undergraduates: 493   Postgraduates: 258

One of the most beautiful Cambridge colleges, Clare occupies a quiet yet central position behind Caius and looking onto the "backs". It is also one of the oldest of the colleges, founded in 1326. Despite these accomplishments, Clare is known among students as one of the friendliest and most welcoming places to study, with an active bar and frequent live music. Accommodation is guaranteed for all three years, either in college – where life centres around the 17th-century Old Court – or nearby hostels. The college has recently finished the Gillespie Centre, which houses undergraduates and provides conference facilities. Clare has a 50:50 ratio of male to female students, better than many colleges, and the college has made systematic attempts to raise the proportion of state-educated students. Almost 50 per cent of undergraduates accepted in 2008 came from the state sector. Clare's extracurricular life is a big attraction. Music thrives, and the choir records and tours regularly. Clare Cellars (comprising the bar and JCR) has fast become one of the best run student venues in the university – providing everything from jazz to hip hop to comedy. The student acting group, the Clare Actors, are well-known in college, whilst Clare Comedy provides a night of stand-up every month. One of the few gripes amongst students is that its playing fields, which are shared with Peterhouse and Clare Hall, are well away from its location in the centre of the city. Clare isn't known for its sporting prowess: instead, emphasis is placed on participation and "the social elements of sport".

Corpus Christi

Corpus Christi College, Cambridge CB2 1RH
01223 338057 (admissions)   admissions@corpus.cam.ac.uk   www.corpus.cam.ac.uk
Undergraduates: 261   Postgraduates: 178

One of the oldest Cambridge colleges, Corpus Christi's small size inevitably makes it one of the more intimate colleges. Some argue that allows for a cohesive community, others feel it can become a goldfish bowl. Although small, it is traditionally broad-based academically. Mixed with the old architecture, however, is a state-of-the-art undergraduate library – which has improved study facilities in the college – and a new student centre, both of which opened recently. The college's formal halls have a good reputation – and were recently voted sixth best by one student magazine. Students are offered a range of accommodation, from the old-fashioned to the modern: all undergraduates are allocated a room in college or neighbouring hostels for at least three years. Some students dislike the college's policy to allocate rooms partly on academic results. One student wrote in the Union's unofficial prospectus that, "as one of the highest colleges on academic results, the college does not react well to poor grades during your degree." There is a fairly even social balance at Corpus: the latest data showed 63 per cent of undergraduates at the college came from the state sector. The sporting facilities, at Leckhampton (just over a mile away), are among the best in the university and include a popular outdoor swimming pool. The size of the college means that its sporting reputation owes more to enthusiasm than success, however. Drama is also well catered for, with The Fletcher Players performing a number of plays each term, and the college owns The Playroom, the university's best small theatre. Music is strong at Corpus – although some students complain about the practice rooms, the college has one of the best student-run choirs and a beautiful chapel in which to practise.

Downing

Downing College, Cambridge CB2 1DQ
01223 334826 (admissions)   admissions@dow.cam.ac.uk   www.dow.cam.ac.uk
Undergraduates: 442   Postgraduates: 241

Hidden away behind the bustle of Regent Street, close to the city centre yet off the tourist trail, lies Downing College. As a result, its neo-Classical quadrangle and beautiful architecture is easily missed by anyone not looking for it. Founded in 1800 for the study of law, medicine and natural sciences, these are still thought to be the college's strong subjects. Indeed Downing is often called "the law college", and also has something of a reputation for hard-playing, hard-drinking rugby players and oarsmen. The college has many successful sports teams – with its own on-site tennis, netball and squash courts, a gym and plenty of open space (The Paddock), whilst the College is one of the best on the river. Downing currently guarantees a place in college accommodation for three years; the completion of a new accommodation block in 2000 allowed students to be housed throughout a first degree. The library, opened in 1993, has won an award for its architecture. There is a good mix between students with state and independent school backgrounds among new undergraduates (59:41). The student-run bar/party room has improved college social life, and the college "slops", or meals, are said to be improving. For those of a less sporting persuasion, meetings of the student debating society and the Blake Society, named after alumnus Quentin Blake, are important events in the student calendar. Music at the College is strong, and a new student theatre, providing a venue for drama, music and exhibitions, opened last year.

Emmanuel

Emmanuel College, Cambridge CB2 3AP
01223 334290 (admissions)   admissions@emma.cam.ac.uk   www.emma.cam.ac.uk
Undergraduates: 530   Postgraduates: 154

Despite being one of the most academically successful colleges, Emmanuel, more commonly known as "Emma", is keen to present itself as the "friendly" Cambridge college. The college is proud of students' achievements in sport and music, as well as their academic success. Emmanuel has topped the unofficial Tompkins Table of Cambridge colleges for academic achievement for a number of years, but for the last two years has been pushed into second place, last year by Trinity College. Despite its academic success, and being one of the wealthiest of the colleges, Emma has an unpretentious atmosphere: students and fellows share an open-air pool in the Fellows garden, the college bar is stylish and strikingly modern. For the last few years Emma has consistently kept the state to independent student ratio at about 60:40, and around half of all undergraduates are women. All students are guaranteed accommodation for the duration of their course. Second years can choose to stay on site or in nearby in college-owned houses. With self-catering facilities limited, most students eat in Hall. Although Formal Hall is good, most popular is the Sunday brunch: a late-morning affair with fry-ups or pastries and the Sunday papers. The college offers expedition grants to undergraduates every year, and has a large hardship fund. In the summer, the college gardens, with tennis courts and a duck pond, offer a welcome haven from exam pressures. The sports grounds are excellent, if some distance away, and the women's rowing team have excelled in recent years.

Fitzwilliam

Fitzwilliam College, Cambridge CB3 0DG
01223 332030 (admissions)   admissions@fitz.cam.ac.uk   www.fitz.cam.ac.uk
Undergraduates: 494   Postgraduates: 216

Based in the city centre until 1963, Fitzwilliam now occupies a large, modern site on the Huntingdon Road, a ten-minute cycle ride from the centre. What it may lack in architectural splendour (one student said that the main building resembles a multistorey carpark), "Fitz" makes up in friendly informality. The college was established in 1869, with the aim of widening access to the university. They are proud of this tradition, and have consistently attracted a larger than average proportion of talented applicants from the state sector. The college is notably "unstuffy", with a good college bar, popular ENTS events and a strong sporting reputation. The football and rugby teams have enjoyed great success, and there are extensive and well-kept sports facilities close by, including gym, football, rugby, cricket, hockey and tennis grounds – as well as squash courts on site. Music also thrives at the college: Fitz is the only college in Cambridge to have access to a professional string quartet. The college has a 250-seater auditorium for performances, and will this year open a state-of-the-art new library and IT centre, designed by the award-winning architect Edward Cullinan. Undergraduates are guaranteed college accommodation for three or four years, either on site or in nearby housing, where the modern facilities are particularly good. What the food lacks in reputation (cheap, was the best one student could say,) is made up in the Ents department – Andy C and Annie Mac have played in College recently.

Girton

Girton College, Cambridge CB3 0JG
01223 338972 (admissions)   admissions@girton.cam.ac.uk   www.girton.cam.ac.uk
Undergraduates: 541   Postgraduates: 179

Students at Girton readily admit: "You've probably never heard of Girton, half of Cambridge students haven't." Its anonymity is due to its distance from the city centre. Admittedly, the centre is only a 15-minute bike ride away, but in Cambridge terms that is as long a commute as you can get. However, its comparative isolation inevitably encourages a strong community spirit, and students get to enjoy its beautiful grounds away from the tourists and the relative bustle of the city. Girton stands on a 50-acre site – complete with woods and orchards – so there is no question of overcrowding: rooms are available for the entire course. The majority of second-year students live in Wolfson Court (near the University Library, closer to town). Some find that the long corridors remind them of boarding school, but accommodation at the College, which includes a number of self-contained houses on site, is noticeably cheaper than some other colleges. Since becoming coeducational in 1977, the college has maintained a balanced admissions policy. Around 60 per cent of the undergraduates admitted are from state schools, and just under half are women. Girton also has one of the highest proportion of women Fellows in any mixed college. Sporting facilities on site, which include sports pitches, a gym, squash court, tennis courts an indoor swimming pool, are excellent. The college is active in most sports and particularly strong in football, and many students go on to represent the University. Given its comparative isolation, many people eat and socialise in college. The food is reported to be excellent.

Gonville and Caius

Gonville and Caius College, Cambridge CB2 1TA
01223 332440 (admissions)   admissions@cai.cam.ac.uk   www.cai.cam.ac.uk
Undergraduates: 545   Postgraduates: 233

Gonville and Caius College – to confuse the outsider, the college is usually known as Caius (pronounced "keys") – is among the most beautiful of Cambridge's colleges, as well as one of the most central. It has an excellent academic reputation, especially in medicine and history, although maths and law are also highly rated. Caius also has one of the largest and most architecturally impressive student libraries in Cambridge, housed in the Cockerell Building next door to the college. Accommodation, though guaranteed for three years, varies in quality depending on how lucky you are. Most first years are housed in Harvey Court, a five-minute walk away across the river. Adjacent to Harvey Court is the £13-million Stephen Hawking Building, named after the college's most famous fellow, which opened in October 2006. Providing en-suite accommodation for 75 students and eight fellows, the building boasts some of the highest-standard student accommodation in Cambridge. Third years live in the idyllic surroundings of the old courts. Those unlucky in the room ballot though, especially second years, live in college hostels over a mile away. An ongoing gripe is that undergraduates are obliged to eat in Hall most nights of the week. Although the food itself is apparently nothing to write home about, and "on the pricey side", some argue that enforced Halls ensure that students meet regularly, and they tend to be louder and more informal than at other colleges. The college is working to diminish its public school reputation –more than half of new students now come from state schools. Academically, the college is a consistently strong performer, and has been in the top third of the Tompkins Table since 2001. Caius has one of the best and most competitive boat clubs in the university, and has won the "bumps" numerous times over the last few years. A lively social scene is helped by the fortnightly "bops".

Homerton

Homerton College, Cambridge CB2 8PH
01223 747252 (admissions)   admissions@homerton.cam.ac.uk   www.homerton.cam.ac.uk
Undergraduates: 604   Postgraduates: 448 PGCE and other graduate courses

Homerton's origins were in 18th-century London, and it moved to Cambridge in 1894. Although the college has been part of the university for over 30 years, where it is known primarily as a teaching college, in 2010 it was awarded full college status. Homerton now accepts students onto a wide range of courses offered by the University, although it continues to specialise in education, including teacher training – through the BA degree and the postgraduate certificate in education (PGCE) courses. Homerton was recently voted the "friendliest college in Cambridge", and its position, a mile from the city centre in its own large grounds, means that the onus is on Homerton students to take the initiative and get involved in university activities. Many do. That said, there are some great facilities on site and some popular societies. The Music Society – comprising of an orchestra, swing band, choir and even a steel-pan group – hold regular concerts, whilst the Amateur Dramatic Society performs several times throughout the year. All first years have rooms in college in new accommodation blocks. In the second year, accommodation may be in college or in private rented houses, but final-year students can live in if they wish. Homerton remains one of the few mixed colleges with more women than men.

Hughes Hall

Hughes Hall, Wollaston Road, Cambridge CB1 2EW
01223 334897 (admissions)   admissions@hughes.cam.ac.uk   www.hughes.cam.ac.uk
Undergraduates: 119   Postgraduates: 391

Hughes Hall admits mature undergraduates over the age of 21 and affiliated students (who already have a good honours degree from another university). The college is the oldest graduate college in the university, founded in 1885 for the training of graduate women teachers. Since then it has become a lively and cosmopolitan community of 500 mature undergraduate and graduate students studying for nearly all the degrees Cambridge offers. It has a large international community, and supports the applications of overseas students. Accommodation within the college is available for all single undergraduates and affiliated students throughout their course. The college is centrally located, with a new accommodation block, new library and attractive gardens. Students must be happy – they say the worst thing about the college is that no one knows where it is. "Whilst we are not the biggest, richest or most famous college in Cambridge," one student said, "we are very social and diverse, with students from a range of personal and academic backgrounds."

Jesus

Jesus College, Cambridge CB5 8BL
01223 339455 (admissions)   undergraduate-admissions@jesus.cam.ac.uk
www.jesus.cam.ac.uk
Undergraduates: 525   Postgraduates: 277

For those of a sporting inclination Jesus is perhaps the ideal college. Within its spacious grounds there are football, rugby and cricket pitches, as well as three squash courts and no less than ten tennis courts, while the Cam, and the university boat houses, are just a few hundred yards away. With these facilities, it is hardly surprising that sports, in particular rowing, rugby and hockey, rate high on many students' agendas. That said, sporting prowess is far from the whole story. The music society thrives, and has extensive practice facilities. Although Jesus lacks a theatre of its own, the college is active in university drama. On the academic front, the Fellows-to-undergraduates ratio is generous. There is an excellent and stylish new library which, unlike many college libraries, is open 24 hours. Accommodation is another plus, and the college recently spent £10 million renovating some quarters. Rooms in college are guaranteed for all first and half of third-year students, whilst all other students live in attractive college houses, or "external staircases", directly opposite the college. Regardless of where you are placed though, you are likely to have good lodgings, though first years have complained that their cooking facilities are poor. Just over half of new undergraduates are state educated and the college is keen to encourage more applications from the state sector. The college grounds – particularly The Chimney walkway to the porter's lodge – are attractive and the college boasts some of the oldest buildings anywhere in the university, with parts dating to the 12th century.

King's

King's College, Cambridge CB2 1ST
01223 331255 (admissions)   undergraduate.admissions@kings.cam.ac.uk
www.kings.cam.ac.uk
Undergraduates: 424   Postgraduates: 232

It is rather ironic that King's, for many outsiders the quintessential Cambridge college, is in fact, one of the university's most radical. King's has an unrivalled reputation for shaking the foundations of tradition: despite its grand surroundings, it has done away with many Cambridge traditions. Gone are gowns, a Fellows' "High Table" at dinner and superior rooms to reward good results. Formal Halls are banned, and May Balls replaced by the more casual June Events. The college was one of the first of the all-male colleges to admit women, and is actively involved in an initiative to increase the number of candidates from socially and educationally disadvantaged backgrounds. The college has a reputation for accepting a high proportion of state-school applications, usually over 70 per cent. The students' union is active politically, campaigning on issues such as top-up fees and the arms trade. The famous King's Bar is painted a socialist red, with some students insisting on painting on a yellow hammer and sickle for the full effect. The college has fewer undergraduates than the grandeur of its buildings might suggest, one result being that accommodation is guaranteed, either in college or in hostels. With the highest ratio of Fellows to undergraduates in Cambridge, it is not surprising that King's has a strong academic reputation. The world-famous chapel and choir form the heart of an outstanding music scene – stroll past the 15th-century chapel some evenings to hear them practicing.

Lucy Cavendish

Lucy Cavendish College, Cambridge CB3 0BU
01223 330280 (admissions)   lcc-admissions@lists.cam.ac.uk   www.lucy-cav.ac.uk
Undergraduates: 116 (women only)   Postgraduates: 109

Lucy Cavendish pitches itself as the college for "smart, inspirational women". Since its creation in 1965, Lucy Cavendish has given hundreds of women over the age of 21 the opportunity to read for Tripos subjects. A number of its students had already started careers and/or families when they decided to enter higher education. The college has a number of bursaries available, including some that give preference to single parents and applicants from the north-west of England. The college has particularly strong provision for the teaching of medicine and veterinary medicine. Accommodation is provided for all who request it, either in the college's three Victorian houses or in its three modern residential blocks. The college's small size enables all students to get to know one another within an intimate and informal atmosphere, although some find it a little too quiet: the college bar only really comes to life on Thursday's after formal Hall. However others appreciate a more relaxed, egalitarian atmosphere, with the lack high table in the dining hall a prime example. The College typically admits a large number of students from the state sector. In 2008, the number was 81 per cent, the year before, it was 100 per cent. All the Fellows are women, and there is a well-established network of university teachers for subjects not taught in college.

Magdalene

Magdalene College, Cambridge CB3 0AG
01223 332135 (admissions)   admissions@magd.cam.ac.uk   www.magd.cam.ac.uk
Undergraduates: 372   Postgraduates: 165

As the last college to admit women (1988), Magdalene has still to throw off a lingering image as the home to hordes of public school hearties. However, times are changing: now the number of female undergraduates just exceeds the number of male undergraduates, and more than half of new undergraduates come from the state sector. That said, the sporty emphasis, on rugby and rowing in particular, is undeniable. The nearby playing fields are shared with St John's and the college has its own Eton fives court. Magdalene's academic standing has improved of late – previously the college languished towards the bottom of the Tompkins Table, but it has steadily improved and finished eighth last year. Students are heavily involved in university-wide activities from drama to journalism, as well as sport. Accommodation is provided for all undergraduates, either in college or in one of 21 houses and hostels, "mostly on our doorstep". Magdalene is proud of its river frontage, the longest in the university, which is especially memorable in the summer when students take to the "beach" to relax.
Magdalene is unique in that formal hall takes place by candlelight every night. One attractive prospect for undergraduates is that they may also be eligible for travel grants from the college, ranging from £50 to £2,000.

Murray Edwards

Murray Edwards College, New Hall, Cambridge CB3 0DF
01223 762229 (admissions)   admissions@murrayedwards.cam.ac.uk
www.murrayedwards.cam.ac.uk
Undergraduates: 380 (women only)   Postgraduates: 78

Murray Edwards College was until last year known as New Hall. The college was established in 1954 to allow more young women to study in Cambridge, and unsurprisingly became known as "New Hall", remaining officially unnamed for more than 50 years. In 2008 however, Ros

Smith, a New Hall graduate, and her husband, Steve Edwards, gave the college a £30-million endowment, and, at last, a new name. One of three remaining all-women colleges, Murray Edwards enjoys a largely erroneous reputation for feminism and academic underachievement. The college is particularly proud of its collection of contemporary women's art, the second largest in the world, and students are politically active, recently hosting an exhibition celebrating the works of female Iranian film directors and photographers. Although modern – the college's signature building is the "dome", the central building where students take their meals – the grounds are lovely. There are also practice rooms for musicians and an art room with dark room facilities for the artistically inclined. The college is known for its unusual split-level bar, but many students choose to socialise elsewhere. Accommodation has improved in recent years, with new rooms, many en suite, now on offer. Sport is a good mixture of high-fliers and enthusiasts, with grounds, shared with Fitzwilliam, half a mile away.

Newnham

Newnham College, Cambridge CB3 9DF
01223 357898 (admissions)   admissions@newn.cam.ac.uk   www.newn.cam.ac.uk
Undergraduates: 393 (women only)   Postgraduates: 162

Newnham has long had to battle with a blue-stocking image. Its entry in the university prospectus used to insist that it was "not a nunnery" and that the atmosphere in this all-women college was no stricter than elsewhere. It even has a "Newnham Nuns" drinking club to make the point. Newnham was founded in 1871 to help women to reach their full academic and personal potential in what was then an all-male university. The college still has all-women Fellows, and Newnham is in the perfect location for humanities students, with the lecture halls and libraries of the Sidgwick Site just across the road. Sylvia Plath is perhaps the college's most famous alumna. Nearly all students live in for all three years. This is not to say that ventures into the social, sporting and artistic life of the university are the exception rather than the rule. Newnham students are anything but insular. As well as being blessed with the largest and most beautiful lawns in Cambridge, Newnham has its playing fields and tennis courts on site. The boat club has been notably successful, while the college competes to a high standard in tennis, cricket and a number of minority sports.

Pembroke

Pembroke College, Cambridge CB2 1RF
01223 338154 (admissions)   adm@pem.cam.ac.uk   www.pem.cam.ac.uk
Undergraduates: 446   Postgraduates: 197

Another college with a reputation for public school dominance, Pembroke's image is changing: today, 57 per cent of its intake come from state schools. Rowing and rugby still feature prominently, but with women undergraduates recently outnumbering men for the first time, its traditional reputation is giving way to a more relaxed atmosphere. Around two thirds of all undergraduates live in college, including all first years. The rest are housed in fairly central college hostels, though the standards of these are variable. That said, the college has recently completed a new student accommodation block that contains a gym, music rooms, and a new art room. Academically, Pembroke is towards the top of the Tompkins Table, steadily featuring in the top ten over the last decade, with traditional strengths in engineering and natural sciences. The bar is inevitably the social focal point, but a restriction on advertising means that Pembroke "bops" attract few students from other colleges. The Pembroke Players generally stage one play a term in the Old Reader, which also doubles as the college cinema, and many Pembroke students are involved in university dramatics. The Old Library is a popular venue for classical concerts. Indeed music is a Pembroke strength. Nestled in one of the quads is the college chapel, designed by Sir Christopher Wren. In a city of memorable college gardens, Pembroke's are among the best.

Peterhouse

Peterhouse, Cambridge CB2 1RD
01223 338223 (admissions)   admissions@pet.cam.ac.uk   www.pet.cam.ac.uk
Undergraduates: 264   Postgraduates: 132

The oldest and smallest of the undergraduate colleges, Peterhouse has for many years had to contend with an image problem. With an unwelcome reputation for being public school and male dominated, the college has been trying to restore the balance. Nowadays, the male–female ratio is about 60:40, but at last count the ratio of state–independent backgrounds in new undergraduates was 42:58, one of the lowest number of state-school acceptances among the colleges. The college's diminutive size inevitably makes for an intimate atmosphere, but this does not mean that its undergraduates never venture beyond the college bar. Peterhouse is known above all as "the history college", and while history is indeed seen as a traditional strength, there are thought to be no more historians than physicists or engineers. Academically, the college is generally a mid-table performer, coming 16th in the Tompkins Table last year. The 13th-century candle-lit dining hall provides what is by common consent one of the most impressive formal halls in the university. The college's rents are famously affordable – and most first years are housed in a row of houses just beside College or in the more modern William Stone Building. During the remaining years students live on site or in college hostels, most within ten minutes' walk. The sports grounds are shared with Clare and are about a mile away, although the college teams have a less than glittering reputation, not surprisingly, given its size. "Bops" are held around twice a term, and the student bar, has been recently refurbished.

Queens'

Queens' College, Cambridge CB3 9ET
01223 335540 (admissions)   admissions@queens.cam.ac.uk   www.queens.cam.ac.uk
Undergraduates: 530   Postgraduates: 339

There is a strong case for claiming that Queens' is the most tightly knit college in the university. With all undergraduates housed in college for the full three years, a large and popular bar (open all day) and outstanding facilities, including Cambridge's first college nursery, it is easy to see why. More than half of new undergraduates come from the state sector, and about 45 per cent of undergraduates are women. Though not to all tastes, the mix of architectural styles, ranging from the medieval Old Court to the 1980s Cripps Complex, is as great as any in the university. The college spans the River Cam, the two sides connected by its world famous

Mathematical Bridge. In addition to three excellent squash courts, the Cripps Complex is also home to Fitzpatrick Hall, a multipurpose venue containing Cambridge's best-equipped college theatre and the hub of Queens' renowned social scene. Friday and Saturday night "bops" are extremely popular – as is the Friday night sushi option at the canteen. The college has an excellent academic record. Apart from squash, Queens' is not especially sporty, although there is a gym and a dance studio on site. The playing fields (one mile away) are shared with Robinson, but the college does keeps its own punts, popular in the summer for trips up the river.

Robinson

Robinson College, Cambridge CB3 9AN
01223 339143 (admissions)   apply@robinson.cam.ac.uk   www.robinson.cam.ac.uk
Undergraduates: 419   Postgraduates: 99

Robinson is one of the youngest colleges in Cambridge and admitted its first students in 1979. Its unspectacular architecture has earned it the unfortunate nickname "the car park". On the other hand, having been built with one eye on the conference trade, what Robinson lacks in grand architecture, it makes up for with excellent facilities. Rooms are more comfortable than most, and the majority have their own bathrooms and balcony. Almost all students live in college or in nearby houses, and the college is one of the few with rooms adapted for disabled students. Academically, Robinson tends to be found in the middle of the Tompkins Table. One in four Fellows are women, one of the highest proportions in any mixed college. Its youth and admissions policy (the College typically accepts around 60 per cent from state schools) ensure that Robinson has one of the more unpretentious atmospheres – students are allowed to walk on the lawns, unusual for Cambridge. The auditorium is the largest of any college and is a popular venue for films, plays and concerts. The college fields (shared with Queens') are home to excellent rugby and hockey sides, and the boat club is also successful. The college has optional twice-weekly formal halls where students describe the atmosphere as "very down to earth". The college has two newly built graduate buildings providing state-of-the-art facilities as well as 48 new graduate rooms.

St Catharine's

St Catharine's College, Cambridge CB2 1RL
01223 338319 (admissions)   undergraduate.admissions@caths.cam.ac.uk
www.caths.cam.ac.uk
Undergraduates: 466   Postgraduates: 166

Known to everyone as "Catz", this medium-sized, 17th-century college stands opposite Corpus Christi on King's Parade. The principal college site, with its distinctive three-sided main court, though small, provides accommodation for all its first and third years. The majority of second years live in flats at St Chad's Court, a ten-minute walk away. Once not considered one of the leading colleges academically, its status is much changed. Having been top of the Tompkins Table in 2005, the college has hovered around top ten ever since. It has a reputation as a friendly place. About half of the students are women, and the split between independent and state-school undergraduates accepted to the college is 40:60. A new library and JCR have improved the facilities considerably, and there is a strong musical tradition. College social life centres on the large bar, which has been likened, among other things, to a ski chalet or sauna. St Catharine's recently proudly announced that it was the first college to be awarded Fair Trade status. With a reputation for being sporting rather than sporty, Catz is one of the few colleges that regularly puts out three rugby XVs, has a history of success at hockey and is the only Cambridge college with its own world-class astroturf pitch. The playing fields are a ten-minute walk from the college.

St Edmund's College

St Edmund's College, Mount Pleasant, Cambridge CB3 0BN
01223 336086 (admissions)   admissions@st-edmunds.cam.ac.uk
www.st-edmunds.cam.ac.uk
Undergraduates: 147   Postgraduates: 275

St Edmund's is primarily a graduate college, with over half its students coming from overseas. Students say this diversity gives the college a unique atmosphere. The college is set in quiet grounds and is conveniently placed to the northwest of the city centre. The college buildings currently house more than 200 single students, and some of the accommodation has been constructed specifically for students with physical disabilities. In addition there are a small number of maisonettes suitable for students with children or married couples. A new building with an additional 70 student rooms opened in 2006, and the college has recently invested in a new library, teaching rooms, a gym and music practice rooms. In recent times, St Edmund's students have become regulars in the university sports team, earning an impressive number of "blues" (awarded for competing in a varsity match against Oxford), whilst a number of the college's international students also represent their own countries as well. The college's lively student executive organise regular social events in the Teddies bar and pool room.

St John's

St John's College, Cambridge CB2 1TP
01223 338703 (admissions)   admissions@joh.cam.ac.uk   www.joh.cam.ac.uk
Undergraduates: 606   Postgraduates: 325

Second only to Trinity in size and wealth, St John's has an enviable reputation in most fields and is sometimes resented for it. The wealth translates into excellent accommodation in college, as well as book grants and a new 24-hour library. St John's riches ensure the best possible facilities, both academic and social. Its May Ball, a biennial end-of-year party was recently voted the "seventh-best party in the world". St John's has a formidable academic record, and English and natural sciences have been recent strengths. However, a reputation for heartiness persists and the female intake is below average at just below 40 per cent. St John's receives relatively few applications from state-school students, and the latest figures saw the intake of state students fall to 45 per cent, among the lowest among the colleges, and some students say they find the atmosphere "posh" and the college's events "terribly formal". The boat club has a powerful reputation, but rugby, hockey and cricket are all traditionally strong. In such a large community, however, all should be able to find their own level. Extensive playing fields shared with Magdalene are a few hundred yards away, and the boathouse is extremely good. The college film society organises popular screenings in the Fisher Building, which also contains an art studio and drawing office for architecture and engineering students. Music is dominated by the world-famous choir. Excellent as the facilities are, some students find that the sheer size of St John's can be daunting, making it hard to settle into. Others argue that such a large college provides a diverse atmosphere where "everybody can find their niche".

Selwyn

Selwyn College, Cambridge CB3 9DQ
01223 335896 (admissions)   admissions@sel.cam.ac.uk   www.sel.cam.ac.uk
Undergraduates: 386   Postgraduates: 156

Despite its reputation as one of the more relaxed and down-to-earth colleges, Selwyn made an appearance in 2008 at the top of the Tompkins Table. Nearly a third of all its undergraduates received a first class degree that year, cementing its reputation as a heavyweight academic college. Before then, the college had made a slow creep up the table, finishing fourth in 2007 from midway down the table the year before. Nonetheless, one undergraduate described the college as "the least overtly intellectual college". Selwyn has a relatively unpressured atmosphere behind "the Backs", and near the Sidgwick site where most humanities are taught, making it an ideal position for arts and humanities students, though engineering is also a perceived strength. One of the first colleges to admit women (1976), now almost half of Selwyn's undergraduates are female. Its state–independent ratio among new undergraduates stands at 68:32. A major new development means the college can now provide undergraduate accommodation to all students on site for the whole time they are at Selwyn. Students also claim that the food at hall has improved dramatically following a joint effort with the head chef. The college was a leader in IT provision, being one of the first to provide all college rooms with online connections, and there are two well-stocked computer rooms. As well as the usual college groups, the music society is especially well supported. The bar is popular if a little "hotel-like". Selwyn bucks the trend for a summer ball or June event, and hosts the popular snow ball each December. In sport, the novice boat crews have done well in recent years, as have the hockey and badminton sides, but the emphasis is as much on enjoyment as achievement. The grounds are shared with King's and are three quarters of a mile away.

Sidney Sussex

Sidney Sussex College, Cambridge CB2 3HU
01223 338846 (admissions)   admissions@sid.cam.ac.uk   www.sid.cam.ac.uk
Undergraduates: 385   Postgraduate: 158

Students at this small, central college are forever the butt of jokes about Sidney being mistaken for the branch of Sainsbury's over the road. Despite its location in the heart of the city, the college's large private gardens award the college an unexpectedly tranquil environment behind the redbrick walls. All students are housed either in college or one of 11 nearby hostels. The college's unpretentious atmosphere is cultivated by the students, where 73 per cent of new undergraduates are now from state schools, and half of whom are women. Despite its size, Sidney has an active social life, boasting one of the few student-run bars in the university and maintaining fortnightly "bop" dances like many of the larger colleges. The college choir has produced critically acclaimed recordings, and tours regularly in the UK and overseas. Sports are taken less seriously, with enthusiasm and enjoyment the focus of the students' sporting endeavours. Exam results at the college improved steadily for a number of years, although the last two years have seen a decline: the college fell from 9th, its best score in the Tompkins Table in 2006, to 29th in 2008, but rose to 22nd the following year. Sports grounds are shared with Christ's and are a 10-minute cycle ride away. Sidney's size means that the college is a tight-knit community, although some students find such insularity suffocating rather than supportive.

Trinity

Trinity College, Cambridge CB2 1TQ
01223 338422 (admissions) admissions@trin.cam.ac.uk www.trin.cam.ac.uk
Undergraduates: 721 Postgraduates: 331

The legend that you can walk from Oxford to Cambridge without ever leaving Trinity land typifies Cambridge undergraduates' views about the college, even if it is not true. Indeed, the college is almost synonymous with size and wealth – it is the largest and wealthiest of all Cambridge colleges. Founded by Henry VIII, its endowment is almost as big as the other colleges' put together. There was a view that every Trinity student was an arrogant public schoolboy. Though less true than it was, the number of students from the state sector has been historically low – the figure rose from 38 per cent in 2007 to 53 per cent at last count, and only 36 per cent of undergraduates are women. Being rich, Trinity offers book grants to every student as well as generous travel grants. The rooms are amongst the cheapest at the university as they are subsidised by the college, and are also known for being spacious. The huge number of rooms at Trinity means students can stay in residence for the duration of their undergraduate. Consistently strong academically, last year the college reclaimed the top position in the Tompkins Table. Trinity has a well-established reputation as a centre of excellence for sciences and maths, but is also strong in a number of arts subjects. Keen to dispel a reputation for being overly serious and academic, students have set up a new society: the Cocktail Society. Christopher Wren designed the college's iconic library, which backs onto the river. Trinity rarely fails to do well in most sports, with cricket in the forefront. The playing fields are half a mile away.

Trinity Hall

Trinity Hall, Cambridge CB2 1TJ
01223 332535 (admissions) admissions@trinhall.cam.ac.uk www.trinhall.cam.ac.uk
Undergraduates: 390 Postgraduates: 221

Trinity Hall or "Tit Hall" is one of the oldest and smallest colleges in Cambridge, resulting in a remarkably close community of students. The outstanding performance of its oarsmen has ensured the prevailing view of Trinity Hall as a "boaty" college, but it is also known for its drama, music and bar. The Preston Society is one of the better college drama groups, and stages regular productions. Weekly recitals keep the music society busy. The small bar is invariably packed. Not surprisingly, many undergraduates rarely feel the need to go elsewhere for their entertainment. The college is strong academically, and at ninth in the Tompkins Table in 2009, it reversed an unusually low position in the recent past. It has equal numbers of students studying arts and sciences. Just over half of the undergraduates are women, and in recent years the college has increased the number of state-school students at the college. Fifty-five per cent of new undergraduates come from the state sector. All first years and approximately half the third years live in college, which is situated on the Backs behind Caius. The remainder take rooms either in two large hostels close to the sports ground, or in college accommodation about five minutes' walk away. The college offers a number of travel bursaries and hardship funds for current students.

Wolfson

Wolfson College, Barton Road, Cambridge CB3 9BB
01223 335918   ugadministrator@wolfson.cam.ac.uk   www.wolfson.cam.ac.uk
Undergraduates: 110   Postgraduates: 486

Wolfson, although primarily a graduate college, has around 100 mature or affiliated undergraduates. Wolfson is one of three colleges that admit students for the graduate course in medicine. Life is enriched by the high proportion (about 50 per cent) of overseas students, reflected in popular societies and events, such as the salsa night. The relationship between senior and junior members is informal; common rooms, facilities and social activities are equally open to both. The college has a relaxed atmosphere. The average age is 27, and last year the number of students accepted from the state sector surged from 50 to 79 per cent. The college regularly hosts senior academic visitors, journalists and specialists, many of whom give open talks at the college. Wolfson is situated in west Cambridge, close to the University Library and the arts faculties – or as the students say, nearer to the M11 than the Cam. The location, however, means the green fields and popular pathway to nearby Grantchester are a short hop away. The main buildings of Wolfson College were built in the 1970s around attractive garden courts. The college has accommodation for most students who want to live in college. There is also some accommodation for couples.

13 University Profiles

The following profiles contain valuable information about each university. Each profile includes some standard information, including the postal address, the telephone number for admission enquiries, the e-mail or web address for admissions and prospectus enquiries, the address of the main university website and the address of the students' union website. In addition, each profile provides:

The Times rankings These figures are taken from the main league table. See chapter 4, The Top Universities, for this table and the sources of the data. The headings follow those in the main league table.

Undergraduates The first figure is for full-time undergraduates. The second figure (in brackets) gives the number of part-time undergraduates. The figures are for 2008–09, and are the most recent provided by HESA.

Postgraduates The first figure is for full-time postgraduates. The second figure (in brackets) gives the number of part-time postgraduates. The figures are for 2008–09, and are the most recent provided by HESA.

Mature students The percentage of first degree entrants who were 21 or over at the start of their studies. The figures are from 2008–09, and are from HESA.

Overseas students The number of undergraduate overseas students (both EU and non-EU) as a percentage of full-time undergraduates. The figures relate to 2008–09, and are based on HESA data.

Applications per place The number of applicants per place for 2009 as calculated by UCAS.

From state-school sector The number of young full-time undergraduate entrants from state schools or colleges in 2008–09 as a percentage of total young entrants. The figures are published by HESA.

From working-class homes The number of young full-time first degree entrants in 2008–09 whose parental occupations are small employers, self-employed, lower supervisory, technical, semiskilled and unskilled (NS-SEC classes 4–7) as a percentage of total young entrants. The figures are published by HESA.

Accommodation The information was obtained through a survey made of all university accommodation services, and their help in compiling this information is gratefully acknowledged.

Undergraduate fees and bursaries A summary of the fees and bursaries being offered in 2010 unless otherwise indicated. This is not comprehensive, so check the details with the individual universities and see chapter 7, *The Cost of Studying*. The information was obtained with the assistance of the individual universities and their help is gratefully acknowledged. Bursary schemes can change every year and must be checked with universities. Universities also have many scholarship schemes, for example, to encourage applicants for particular subjects or from particular areas. Again, it is essential to check university websites for further information. Wherever possible, a specific website address for financial information is given.

Comments on campus facilities apply to the universities' own sites only. Newer universities, in particular, operate "franchised" courses at further education colleges, which are likely to have lower levels of provision. Prospective applicants should check out the library and social facilities before accepting a place away from the parent institution.

Some famous names are missing from our university listings: the Open University, the separate business and medical schools, Birkbeck College and Cranfield University among them. Their omission is no reflection on their quality, simply a function of their particular roles. The *Guide* is based on provision for full-time undergraduates and the factors judged to influence this. The Open University (**www.open.ac.uk**), though Britain's biggest university, with 75,000 students, is not included because most of the measures used in our listing do not apply to it. As a non-residential, largely part-time institution, Birkbeck College, London (**www.bbk.ac.uk**), could also not be compared in many key areas. Cranfield (**www.cranfield.ac.uk**) now only offers postgraduate degrees. Manchester Business School (**www.mbs.ac.uk**) and London Business School (**www.lbs.ac.uk**) were excluded for the same reason. Specialist institutions such as the Royal College of Art (**www.rca.ac.uk**) and St George's Hospital Medical School (**sgul.ac.uk**) could not fairly be compared with generalist universities. A number of colleges with degree-awarding powers also do not appear because they have yet to be granted university status. However, at the end of the book, we list higher education colleges with their addresses and websites.

The University of Wales, founded in 1893, remained a federal university until 2007. It is now the degree-awarding authority to accredited higher education institutions in Wales. In addition it plays an active role in promoting Welsh language and culture. See **www.wales.ac.uk**.

University of Aberdeen

Aberdeen marked the early years of its sixth century with the recruitment of high-quality academics and a series of big capital projects. Now the university has turned its attention to the curriculum with a new range of "Sixth Century Courses", cross-disciplinary degrees such as risk in society, sustainability, and the digital society. They will include the option of "sustained study programmes" in a language, computing or a business-related subject. The aim is to give graduates broader knowledge and more intellectual flexibility.

Aided by one the most successful fundraising schemes at any UK university, Aberdeen has spent £28 million on a sports centre that opened in 2009 and made a start on a futuristic new library that will cost £57 million and is scheduled to open in 2011. Student services had already been transformed and some high-quality academics attracted from the United States and other countries.

The university registered some good results in the 2008 Research Assessment Exercise, when more than half of the work submitted was judged to be "world-leading" or internationally excellent. Health services research and theology, divinity and religious studies produced the best results in the UK, while computer science and informatics, anthropology, English and history also did particularly well. Research income grew by more than a third over five years, cementing Aberdeen's ambitions to be recognised among the top 100 universities in the world.

The 7.5 per cent growth in applications in 2009 was among the biggest in Scotland and Aberdeen shared in the applications boom at the start of 2010, with an increase of almost a third. Female students now outnumber the men, but Aberdeen still considers itself a "balanced" university because roughly half of its students study medicine, science or engineering, half the arts or social sciences. Even on traditional degree programmes, students can try out three or four subjects before committing themselves at the end of their first or even second year. The modular system, covering almost 600 first-degree programmes, is so flexible that the majority of students change their intended degree before graduation.

Medicine, law and divinity head Aberdeen's traditional strengths – the university established the English-speaking world's first chair in medicine and has produced its share of advances since. The Institute of Medical Sciences, which has brought together all Aberdeen's work in this area, boasts state-of-the-art laboratory facilities. Another £20 million has been invested in the Suttie Centre, which opened in 2009 as a new teaching and learning centre for medical education and clinical skills.

Education is now also considered among

King's College
Aberdeen AB24 3FX

01224 272090/91 (admissions)
sras@abdn.ac.uk
www.abdn.ac.uk
www.ausa.org.uk

The Times Rankings
Overall Ranking: **33**

Student satisfaction:	=9	(82%)
Research quality:	=33	(2.1)
Entry standards:	36	(357)
Student–staff ratio:	=28	(14.9)
Services & facilities/student:	55	(£1,344)
Expected completion rate:	78	(80.0%)
Good honours:	40	(67.6%)
Graduate prospects:	15	(76.8%)

Aberdeen's strengths, while the university is also the main centre for agriculture in Scotland. Biological sciences have developed considerably in recent years, becoming second only to the social sciences in terms of size. Biomedicine is particularly strong, and the university's links with the oil industry show in geology's high reputation.

Today's university is a fusion of two ancient institutions which came together in 1860. With King's College dating back to 1495 and Marischal College following almost a century later, Aberdeen likes to boast that for 250 years it had as many universities as the whole of England. The original King's College buildings are the focal point of an appealing campus, complete with cobbled main street and some sturdily handsome Georgian buildings, about a mile from the city centre.

Medicine is at Foresterhill, a 20-minute walk away, adjoining the Aberdeen Royal Infirmary. Buses link the two sites with the Hillhead residential complex. Almost a third of all students come from the north of Scotland, but taking one in six from outside Britain ensures a cosmopolitan atmosphere. Students from England and the 120 nationalities from further afield are generally prepared for Aberdeen's remote location and, although the winters are long, the climate is warmer than the uninitiated might expect. As the energy capital of Europe, transport links are good. Students find the city lively and welcoming but expensive: the JobLink service does provide a good selection of part-time jobs.

Student facilities are good and the new students' centre – The Hub – brings together dining and retail outlets with support services, including the Students' Association and the careers service. There is also a city centre bar and first-class sports facilities, which have improved still further with the opening of the Aberdeen Sports Village, part-funded by the City Council and Sports Scotland. The university ICT network has over 1,500 computers for student use. The university's residential stock has been growing and all new undergraduates are guaranteed a place. A £20-million phased investment in accommodation added over 500 new single study en-suite bedrooms at Hillhead in 2008.

Undergraduate Fees and Bursaries

» Scottish-domiciled and EU students: no fees payable.
» Non-Scottish UK-domiciled student fees: £1,820
£2,895 (medicine)
» International student fees: £9,500–£11,800
£23,625 (medicine)
» Scholarships based on circumstances or by competition.
» For full details see the university's website:
www.abdn.ac.uk/undergraduate/scholarships.php

Students		
Undergraduates:	**9,590**	(1,170)
Postgraduates:	**2,715**	(1,380)
Mature students:	**17.5%**	
Overseas students:	**16.0%**	
Applications per place:	**4.2**	
From state-sector schools:	**79.5%**	
From working-class homes:	**25.6%**	

For detailed information about fees, grants and bursaries and how they work, see chapter 7.

Accommodation

Number of places and costs refer to 2009–10
University-provided places: about 2,780
Percentage catered: 35%
Catered costs: £124.40–£145.40 a week (38 weeks).
Self-catered costs: £72–£116 a week (38–40 weeks).
First-year students are guaranteed accommodation.
International students: as above.
Contact: studentaccomm@abdn.ac.uk

University of Abertay Dundee

Abertay doubled in size during the 1990s and has grown further since up-front tuition fees were abolished for Scottish students. There are now more than 4,000 students, mainly in Dundee, but with several hundred in locations as far afield as Malaysia, India and Singapore. Applications were up by more than a quarter at the start of 2010. There have been dramatic improvements to dropout rate that once stood at more than one in three of all those starting degrees: the latest rate was less than one in ten. Almost a quarter of the undergraduates come from socially deprived areas and practically all attended state schools. More than a third come from working-class homes.

The former Dundee Institute of Technology had already established its academic credentials when university status arrived in 1994, with teaching in economics rated more highly than in some of Scotland's elite universities. Subsequent assessments were solid, without living up to that early promise, but economics, engineering and environmental sciences were given the highest possible rating in later inspections. More recently, two of the first four degree accreditations awarded by Skillset, the Government-sponsored training council for the creative industries, went to Abertay courses. The university has since been accredited as the first Interactive Media Academy in the UK. Staff and students in the Institute for Art, Media and Computer Games work with industrial partners from across the broadcast, interactive and wider digital media sectors. The university even has a partnership with Beijing University (one of China's top two) on computer games.

Research is not being ignored. Abertay is proud of its record in establishing a series of specialist centres, in areas as diverse as wood technology, urban water systems, bioinformatics, earth systems and environmental sciences. The university opened Europe's first research centre dedicated to computer games and digital entertainment, and a major environmental science centre. Earth systems and environmental sciences and general engineering, mineral and mining engineering produced the best scores in the latest research assessments. Environmental sciences also had the best rating in Scotland in the 2001 RAE.

Abertay plays to its strengths with a limited range of courses, and is not shy about its achievements. Among them is a high-tech approach that permeates all four of the university's schools, while spending on libraries and computers is among the highest per student in Britain, providing one computer for every four students.

Based mainly in the centre of Dundee, all

Bell Street
Dundee DD1 1HG
01382 308080

sro@abertay.ac.uk
www.abertay.ac.uk
www.abertaystudents.com

The Times Rankings
Overall Ranking: **102**

Student satisfaction:		n/a
Research quality:	=77	(0.4)
Entry standards:	89	(256)
Student-staff ratio:	99	(20.8)
Services & facilities/student:	=52	(£1,361)
Expected completion rate:	109	(70.1%)
Good honours:	83	(54.0%)
Graduate prospects:	99	(56.6%)

the university's buildings are within 15 minutes' walk of each other. The imposing Dudhope Castle is a conference and events venue, but the other buildings are more modern and functional. New facilities have been added gradually, from the £6-million student centre, which opened in 2005, to the innovative White Space facility, the university's flagship creative learning and working environment, where students study alongside industry professionals who are working on real commercial or broadcast projects. A 500-bed student village is next on the list, due to open at the start of the academic year in 2010.

Entrance requirements have been rising, although for most courses other than high-demand areas such as computer games, they are still modest. Well-qualified A-level students are eligible for direct entry into second year. Degrees are predominantly vocational, with more subjects being added every year. Forensic science, mental nursing, visual communications and media design, computer arts, and sports coaching and development have been followed recently by the likes of food and consumer sciences, creative sound production, and ethical hacking and countermeasures. All courses can be taken on a part-time basis, and the aim is for new programmes to offer students the chance to spend at least 30 per cent of their time in industry.

The university's revamped modular degree scheme means that undergraduates take a maximum of eight modules a year. First-year students are assessed by coursework alone in the first semester, with examinations at the end of the year. Students can complete a Certificate of Higher Education after one year, a diploma after two, an ordinary degree after three, or honours in four years. Abertay is piloting a new problem-based learning approach among first-year students focusing on real-world issues and learning by doing rather than sitting in lectures.

Dundee has a large student population and is improving as a youth centre where the cost of living is modest. More than 30 per cent of the undergraduates are over 21 on entry, many living locally. This lifts the pressure on university-owned beds sufficiently to allow all first years to be guaranteed accommodation.

Undergraduate Fees and Bursaries
» Scottish-domiciled and EU students: no fees payable.
» Non-Scottish UK-domiciled student fees: £1,820
» International student fees: £9,250
» Scholarships based on circumstances or by competition.
» For full details see the university's website: www.abertay.ac.uk/studying/studentlife/money

Students
Undergraduates:	**3,280**	(280)
Postgraduates:	**315**	(175)
Mature students:	**31.5%**	
Overseas students:	**17.0%**	
Applications per place:	**3.3**	
From state-sector schools:	**97.9%**	
From working-class homes:	**36.7%**	

For detailed information about fees, grants and bursaries and how they work, see chapter 7.

Accommodation
Number of places and costs refer to 2010–11
University-provided places: 568
Percentage catered: 0%
Self-catered costs: £45.00–£99.50 a week (38, 42 or 51 weeks).
New first years are given priority provided conditions are met. Some residential restrictions.
International students: prioritised by distance from Dundee.
Contact: accommo@abertay.ac.uk
www.abertay.ac.uk/studying/accommodation

Aberystwyth University

Aberystwyth has by far the most satisfied students of any university in Wales and is among the top five in the UK, according to the National Student Survey. Agriculture, cinematics, physical geography, sport and exercise science all registered outstanding results in the 2009 survey, when nine out of ten final-year undergraduates throughout the university declared themselves satisfied. The oldest of the Welsh universities, Aberystwyth has changed its title from the University of Wales, Aberystwyth, to emphasise its independence and is now awarding its own degrees. It has long prided itself on a modern outlook: it was among the pioneers of the modular degree system and allowed students flexibility between subjects even before that. Uniquely in the UK, every student is offered the opportunity of a year's work experience in commerce, industry or the public sector, either at home or abroad. Those who have taken advantage of the scheme have achieved better than average degrees and enhanced their employment prospects.

Aber is always heavily oversubscribed even though the number of places has increased. Over a third of the students are from Wales. An agreement to collaborate with Bangor University in a range of subjects, from business to science, emphasises teaching in Welsh. An attractive seaside location does the university no harm when the applications season comes around. The demand for places has grown substantially in each of the last three years, with a 16 per cent increase in 2009 followed by an even larger increase in the latest round of applications.

The university has grown significantly in recent years, with a £1.5m Student Welcome Centre opening in 2009, bringing together services such as the fees office and student support services that were previously distributed around the campus or in town. A purpose-built sports and exercise science centre has been added on the Penglais campus, which overlooks the town, and a new student health centre and crèche will open soon. A new building for the highly rated international politics department opened in 2006 and a £10-million Visualisation Centre followed in 2007, providing virtual reality facilities for academic and industrial partnerships. A new psychology department is the latest addition.

More than 90 per cent of the undergraduates come from state schools or colleges – a far higher proportion than the mix of subjects would imply – but in previous years around 30 per cent of the intake has come from working-class homes and only about half that number hail from areas that send few students to higher education. However, the dropout rate of less than 9 per cent is one of the lowest in Wales.

In 2008 Aberystwyth established the new

Old College
King Street,
Aberystwyth, Ceredigion
SY23 2AX

01970 622021 (admissions)
ug-admissions@aber.ac.uk
www.aber.ac.uk
www.aberguild.co.uk

The Times Rankings
Overall Ranking: **40**

Student satisfaction:	=7	83
Research quality:	=33	(2.1)
Entry standards:	55	(292)
Student–staff ratio:	46	(16.0)
Services & facilities/student:	57	(£1,320)
Expected completion rate:	=42	(85.8%)
Good honours:	62	(60.1%)
Graduate prospects:	70	(61.5%)

Institute of Biological, Environmental and Rural Sciences (IBERS) following a merger with the Institute of Grassland and Environmental Research. With over 300 staff and an annual budget in excess of £25 million, IBERS is one of the largest groups of scientists and support staff working in this field in Europe, and caters for more than 1,000 undergraduate and research students. Its remit is to look for creative solutions to some of the major challenges facing the world in sustainable land use, climate change, renewable energy and the security of food and water supplies. The institute, which won a Queen's Anniversary Prize for its work in 2010, gives Aber the widest range of land-related courses in the UK.

Over the next four years, £55 million will be invested in new teaching and research facilities and academic appointments. International politics produced the best results in the 2008 research assessments, with 40 per cent of work rated world-leading. Computer science, geography and earth sciences, Welsh, and theatre, film and television also did well.

Entrance scholarships and bursaries are available in a range of subjects, even though Welsh students have been spared the full impact of top-up fees. Aber boasts one of higher education's most informative websites and also publishes a 12-page guide for parents. There is 24-hour access to the computer network, and the four university libraries are complemented by the National Library of Wales.

The town of Aberystwyth is compact and travel to other parts of the UK slow, so applicants should be sure that they will be happy to spend three years or more in a tight-knit community. The students' guild is the largest entertainment venue in the region and the arts centre has been extended at a cost of £3.5 million. The seaside town of 25,000 people was placed among the top ten university locations in the UK in one 2009 survey and in the top three by another. There is plenty of out-of-season accommodation to supplement the university's 3,700 places, all of which are now online. Sports facilities are good for the size of institution, with 50 acres of pitches, a newly refurbished swimming pool, a climbing wall and specialist outdoor facilities for water sports.

Undergraduate Fees and Bursaries

- » Fees for UK/EU students: £3,290
- » International student fees: £8,870–£11,250
- » Bursary £1,000 (household income up to £18,370), then sliding scale to £200.
- » Scholarships based on circumstances or by competition.
- » For full details see the university's website: www.aber.ac.uk/en/scholarships/

Students

Undergraduates:	**6,250**	(2,135)
Postgraduates:	**1,025**	(800)
Mature students:	**10.9%**	
Overseas students:	**11.0%**	
Applications per place:	**3.3**	
From state-sector schools:	**94.4%**	
From working-class homes:	**33.3%**	

For detailed information about fees, grants and bursaries and how they work, see chapter 7.

Accommodation

Number of places and costs refer to 2010–11
University-provided places: 3,560
Percentage catered: 15%
Catered costs: £90.45–£103.80 a week (31 weeks or 37 weeks).
Self-catered costs: £70.00–£97.75 a week (37 weeks).
First years are guaranteed accommodation if conditions are met.
International students: accommodation guaranteed.
Contact: www.aber.ac.uk/residential
accommodation@aber.ac.uk

Anglia Ruskin University

The last university to retain the polytechnic title discarded it in 2005 to avoid confusion among employers and overseas applicants. The former APU took the name of John Ruskin, who founded the Cambridge School of Art, which evolved into the university. Under both names, the university has sometimes struggled to fill its places, reflecting the region's traditionally low participation rate in higher education. But that appears to have changed: applications were up by more than 16 per cent in 2009 and there was an unprecedented increase of more than 50 per cent at the start of 2010.

Campus developments have continued apace since the change of name. A new student centre on the larger of the university's two main sites, in Chelmsford, houses support services as well as union facilities, while the arts, law and social sciences faculty building in Cambridge has new and enhanced teaching and practice facilities.

The university has also acquired the former Homerton College School of Health Studies in Cambridge, after a long period of partnership. A new health and social care building was added in Chelmsford in 2007, with bespoke counselling rooms, simulated hospital wards, operating theatres, and a complementary medicine suite. A £15-million faculty building, which includes a mock courtroom for law students, followed in September 2008. The 22-acre Rivermead campus also boasts an impressive business school and a sports hall.

The region's first polytechnic was an amalgamation of two well-established higher education colleges, but the twin bases in Chelmsford and Cambridge remain distinct. The two very different locations are far enough apart to limit contact, although electronic networking and a central administration mean that key academic facilities are available throughout the university.

The university has more than 28,000 full and part-time students who are taught primarily on the two main campuses, but also through a growing network of regional partners. Anglia Ruskin has signed up to deliver higher-education courses in Peterborough, Harlow and King's Lynn in partnership with local further education colleges.

Nearly all the students attended state schools or colleges and more than a third are from working-class homes. The dropout rate has fluctuated over recent years, and the latest projection, that nearly 16 per cent of the 2007 entrants will fail to complete degrees in the expected time, is a marked improvement on nearly 25 per cent the previous year.

There have been good reports, under the

Rivermead Campus: Bishop Hall Lane, Chelmsford, Essex CM1 1SQ
Cambridge Campus: East Road, Cambridge CB1 1PT

0845 271 3333 (enquiries)
answers@anglia.ac.uk
www.anglia.ac.uk
www.angliastudent.com

The Times Rankings
Overall Ranking: **107**

Student satisfaction:	109	67
Research quality:	=95	(0.2)
Entry standards:	=91	(254)
Student–staff ratio:	=82	(19.6)
Services & facilities/student:	95	(£1,049)
Expected completion rate:	=99	(75.8%)
Good honours:	80	(55.4%)
Graduate prospects:	=87	(58.5%)

new healthcare assessments, for nursing and midwifery and allied health professions. But only three universities had lower satisfaction levels in the National Student Survey published in 2009, despite some improvement on the previous year. Physical science and forensic and archaeological science produced the best results but, for the second year in a row, the score for teacher training was one of the lowest in any subject at any university.

Only 71 academics were entered for the Research Assessment Exercise in 2008, but almost a third of their work was considered world-leading or internationally excellent. All but one of the nine subject areas had some top-rated research, with history, English and psychology producing the best grades. Psychology produced the best results among the new universities.

Each undergraduate has an adviser to help compile a degree package which looks at the chosen subject from different points of view to maximise future job prospects. There is also an employer mentoring scheme for second-year undergraduates planning for the transition from study to work. Each student is carefully matched with a mentor from their chosen career field who volunteers time to provide skills-building, support and encouragement.

Employers play a part in planning courses which are integrated into a modular system which extends from degree level to professional programmes, including a modest selection of vocational two-year Foundation degrees. The Business School, for example, has developed a work-based course with Barclays Bank, where the students are sponsored and salaried for all three years of their course. The programme is now being offered to other businesses in order to aid retention and staff development.

The social scene varies between the two campuses. There is limited collaboration with Cambridge University, for example on the new Cambridge Centre for Cricketing Excellence, and a base for Anglia Ruskin's Rowing Club. Some students find Chelmsford dull, but the social scene is said to be improving. Neither base is far from London by train.

Undergraduate Fees and Bursaries

» Fees for UK/EU students: £3,290
» International student fees: £9,500–£10,500
» Bursary on full grant: household income up to £25K: £329
» The university does not award bursaries for students on partial maintenance grants.
» Scholarships based on circumstances or by competition.
» For full details see the university's website: www.anglia.ac.uk/ruskin/en/home/student_essentials/student_finance.html

Students

Undergraduates:	**10,100**	**(7,515)**
Postgraduates:	**800**	**(1,415)**
Mature students:	**35.7%**	
Overseas students:	**11.5%**	
Applications per place:	**3.9**	
From state-sector schools:	**97.0%**	
From working-class homes:	**39.1%**	

For detailed information about fees, grants and bursaries and how they work, see chapter 7.

Accommodation

Number of places and costs refer to 2010–11
University-provided places: Cambridge, 826 plus 294 referral rooms; Chelmsford, 511
Percentage catered: 0%
Self-catered costs: Cambridge: £66.00 – £122.50 a week; Chelmsford: £86 – £93 a week
Most first years are accommodated (35-mile eligibility radius restriction at Cambridge campus only).
International students: conditions and deadline apply
Contact: cambaccom@anglia.ac.uk; essexaccom@anglia.ac.uk

Aston University

Aston has always gloried in its role as a tight-knit, vocational, urban university, which has swum against the tide of British higher education over the past decade. Small and lively, set in the heart of Birmingham, it has remained resolutely specialist in science and technology, business and languages, concentrating on the sandwich degrees which have served its graduates so well in the employment market. But its strategy up to 2012 is for "sustainable growth in key areas" to provide financial security and the size necessary to boost research performance and become a top ten university.

Aston did break into the top 20 in *The Times* table, although it has slipped back in the past three years, mainly due to less favourable staffing levels and lower spending on student facilities. Despite some modest growth recently, the university still has little more than 7,000 undergraduates. But, with healthy funding from industry and commerce, Aston has been investing in its future, boosting staffing in business, engineering and languages, and developing the campus with a £215 million programme of improvements.

Applications have been steady in recent years, the start of 2010 seeing a 14 per cent increase that was substantial but still below the national average. The general trend has been upwards for most of the decade, despite consistent increases in entry grades. New undergraduates take 12 study skills modules before the formal start of their course, covering areas such as essay-writing.

Business and management led the way in the 2008 Research Assessment Exercise, with health subjects also producing good grades from a smaller submission. The university submitted far more staff for assessment than in 2001 but, while 45 per cent of the work in the four subject areas was judged to be world-leading or internationally excellent, the results placed Aston near the bottom of the tables of pre-1992 universities.

As befits a one-time college of advanced technology, Aston is strong in the sciences, although the highly rated business school accounts for almost half of the students. A £20-million extension to the business school has seen an increase in staff from 80 to over 120.

There is a wide range of combined honours programmes for those who prefer not to specialise. More than 80 per cent of Aston graduates – far more than the national average – go straight into jobs, often returning to the scene of work placements, which have become the norm for seven out of ten undergraduates. At the forefront of employer-led degrees, Aston was awarded £1.6 million to set up a Foundation Degree Centre to establish new courses and explore other ways of delivering qualifications. The

Aston Triangle
Birmingham B4 7ET

0121 204 3000 (course enquiries)
ugenquiries@aston.ac.uk
www.aston.ac.uk
www.astonguild.org.uk

The Times Rankings
Overall Ranking: **29**

Student satisfaction:	=15	(80%)
Research quality:	50	(1.4)
Entry standards:	35	(364)
Student–staff ratio:	=59	(17.8)
Services & facilities/student:	24	(£1,718)
Expected completion rate:	28	(91.6%)
Good honours:	30	(70.1%)
Graduate prospects:	21	(75.2%)

foundation degree in electrical power engineering has attracted several large companies, while others include hearing aid technology and pharmaceutical technology.

The university's dropout rate has been improving and, at 6.8 per cent in the latest statistics, is almost half the national average for Aston's subjects. Socially, the intake is diverse, with more than a third of the undergraduates coming from working-class homes. Nearly one student in five comes from Birmingham and about four in ten are from the West Midlands more broadly. More than half of the undergraduates are from ethnic minorities.

The 40-acre campus, a ten-minute walk from the centre of Birmingham, is barely recognisable from the university's early days. Recent building programmes have brought all Aston's residential and academic accommodation onto one carefully landscaped site. Almost half of the undergraduates live on campus, with places guaranteed for first years. A new phase of construction for residential accommodation began in 2008 and will have added 2,400 en-suite rooms by 2014. The first block should be open in 2010. Recent developments in sporting facilities have included the addition of a new gymnasium, while an £8-million Academy of Life Sciences merges research with private practice in eye care and brain imaging. Another £4 million has been spent upgrading the IT and computing network.

Aston was among the pioneers of "smart cards", giving students access to university facilities and enabling them to make purchases on campus, once they have money in their accounts. There is plenty of opportunity to use them in a buzzing social scene, which most students find to their taste. The guild of students has always been very active, both socially and politically.

Undergraduate Fees and Bursaries
- Fees for UK/EU students: £3,290
- International student fees: £10,700–£12,250
- Bursary on full grant: household income up to £28K: sliding scale £800–£480.
- Bursary on partial grant: household income up to £39,333: sliding scale £320–£160.
- Scholarships based on circumstances or by competition.
- For full details see the university's website: www1.aston.ac.uk/study/undergraduate/student-finance

---

Students

Undergraduates:	**7,235**	(525)
Postgraduates:	**1,855**	(875)
Mature students:	**9.0%**	
Overseas students:	**20.1%**	
Applications per place:	**6.2**	
From state-sector schools:	**91.3%**	
From working-class homes:	**37.1%**	

For detailed information about fees, grants and bursaries and how they work, see chapter 7.

Accommodation

Number of places and costs refer to 2010–11
University-provided places: 2,300
Percentage catered: 0%
Self-catered accommodation: range £68 (standard) – £119 (en-suite deluxe) a week.
First years are guaranteed accommodation if they fulfil requirements and apply by the deadline.
International fee-paying students: as above.
Contact: accom@aston.ac.uk; www.aston.ac.uk/accommodation

Bangor University

Bangor has the "fairest" workload of any UK university, according to a poll of students published in 2009, although it was only just in the top 40 for overall satisfaction levels in the National Student Survey of that year. The university has generally performed well in the annual satisfaction survey, with those in business, education, history, languages and sports science giving particularly high marks in the most recent edition. The "small and friendly" nature of the university and the city no doubt helped.

Bangor's community focus dates back to a 19th-century campaign which saw local quarrymen putting part of their weekly wages towards the establishment of a college. The College of Education and Lifelong Learning continues the tradition with courses across North Wales, but the university has also built a worldwide reputation in areas such as environmental studies and ocean sciences. Like Aberystwyth and Swansea, it is another part of the University of Wales to have asserted its independence, taking the title of Bangor University while continuing to award degrees through the University of Wales.

The 2008 research assessments identified world-leading work in all Bangor's 19 subject areas. The university claimed the grades for accounting and finance to be the best in the UK, with electronic engineering second and both sports science and Welsh in the top ten in their respective subjects. Teaching assessments were impressive, with half of the subjects rated as excellent. There is a high proportion of small-group teaching and tutorials, as well as one of Britain's largest peer guiding schemes, which sees senior students mentoring new arrivals.

Bangor merged with a nearby teacher training college, Coleg Normal, in 1996, and that site is now part of the university. The 26 academic schools are grouped into six colleges: arts and humanities; business, social sciences and law; education and lifelong learning; natural sciences; health and behavioural sciences; and physical and applied sciences. All schools are within walking distance of each other, apart from ocean sciences, which is two miles away in Menai Bridge.

The university estate has been re-developed, with the addition of a £5-million environmental sciences building, while a £3.5-million Cancer Research Institute is attracting specialists of international repute. A combination of private funds and a £5-million European grant was used to establish a new Business Management Development Centre on a waterfront site. The next – and biggest – project will be the construction of a £35-million Arts and Innovation Centre that will form a bridge between the university's upper campus and

Bangor
Gwynedd LL57 2DG

01248 382017 (admissions)
admissions@bangor.ac.uk
www.bangor.ac.uk
www.undeb.bangor.ac.uk

The Times Rankings
Overall Ranking: **54**

Student satisfaction:	=32	(78%)
Research quality:	=44	(1.7)
Entry standards:	57	(284)
Student–staff ratio:	54	(17.1)
Services & facilities/student:	91	(£1,082)
Expected completion rate:	40	(86.4%)
Good honours:	=71	(56.9%)
Graduate prospects:	90	(57.8%)

the nearby science site. Part-funded by the Welsh Assembly, it will include a new students' union and an innovation hub, as well as teaching and performance spaces.

Based little more than a stone's throw from Snowdonia with its attractions for sports enthusiasts, Bangor is an expanding centre for Welsh-medium teaching. Although a majority of students come from outside Wales – there is a strong link with Ireland, for example – more than 10 per cent of the students speak the language and one of the halls of residence is Welsh-speaking. The university also has a flourishing international exchange programme. Spain and Germany are favourite destinations for linguistics students; biologists tend to head for the USA or France.

Bangor does better than most traditional universities when judged against access benchmarks. More than nine out of ten students come from state schools or colleges, and one in three come from working-class homes. The university is spending £2.8 million a year on bursaries and scholarships, offering students from low-income families up to £1,000 a year on some courses, as well as merit scholarships of £3,000 for high-fliers and excellence scholarships worth up to £5,000 each in seven subject areas. The university's Talent Opportunities Programme, which operates in 11 schools across North Wales, targets potential applicants from lower socio-economic families, who have little or no history of going on to university. Applications have increased steadily in recent years. The demand for degree places was up by almost 7 per cent at the start of 2010 – healthy growth, but modest in comparison with most universities at that time.

There is a strong focus on student support – the pioneering dyslexia unit, for example, offers individual and group support throughout students' courses. Six new halls of residence opened in 2008 and another five followed 12 months later. The work was part of a £35-million upgrade at the main university accommodation site. Bangor is also one of the most cost-effective places in which to study – one survey made it the second-cheapest university in the UK.

Undergraduate Fees and Bursaries
» Fees for UK/EU students: £3,290
» International student fees: £8,800–£9,900*
» Bursary of £1,000 (household income up to £18,370).
» Bursaries on partial grant: household income up to £39.7K: either £500 or £1,000.
» Scholarships based on circumstances or by competition.
» For full details see the university's website: www.bangor.ac.uk/studentfinance

*Figures for 2009–10

Students
Undergraduates:	6,945	(1,855)
Postgraduates:	1,395	(1,000)
Mature students:	25.7%	
Overseas students:	7.5%	
Applications per place:	3.5	
From state-sector schools:	95.1%	
From working-class homes:	33.5%	

For detailed information about fees, grants and bursaries and how they work, see chapter 7.

Accommodation
Number of places and costs refer to 2009–10
University-provided places: approx 2,400
Percentage catered: 8%
Catered costs: £98.50 (31-week contract) a week.
Self-catered costs: £66.50 – £103.50 (40-week contract) a week.
All first-year students are guaranteed places.
International students: as above.
Contact: accommodation@bangor.ac.uk
www.bangor.ac.uk/accommodation

University of Bath

Bath is in the throes of a £70-million "campus enhancement plan" which will add further facilities for teaching and research, as well as extra student accommodation and social space. A new student centre is under construction and should be open in October 2010. Bath is a relatively small university with 9,000 undergraduates and nearly 4,000 postgraduates. The additional facilities will cater to some degree for the burgeoning demand at an institution that enjoys both an attractive location and a high academic reputation. Although applications have slipped in the past two years and were up by less than 2 per cent at the start of 2010, this followed a succession of increases during a period of rising entrance requirements. Bath's healthy showing in league tables may be one reason for its popularity – it has never been out of the top 20 in *The Times* League Table.

Students like the community feel of campus life, and one of the lowest dropout rates in Britain suggests that they are well supported. The library is open 24 hours a day, seven days a week. Few can fail to be impressed by the magnificence of the city's architecture. The modern campus on the edge of Bath, with some undistinguished buildings dating from its origins as a technological university in the 1960s, is hardly in the same league. But the 200-acre site has pleasant grounds and is functional, with academic, recreational and residential facilities in close proximity. More lecture theatres and computer laboratories have eased the pressure on teaching space and 468 new study bedrooms have also been added recently. The university has launched a rolling programme to refurbish and update all its teaching facilities. Its central Parade now features a lively and contemporary café, while a new building opened in April 2010 provides additional research and teaching space, as well as a new postgraduate centre.

Research is Bath's greatest strength: 60 per cent of the work submitted for the 2008 Research Assessment Exercise was judged to be world-leading or internationally excellent. Social work and social policy, business and management, physics, pharmacy and maths did particularly well, but there were good results in a number of areas. Bath was also in the top 30 universities in the 2009 National Student Survey. Sports science produced the best results, but pharmacology, toxicology and pharmacy, Iberian studies, and civil and mechanical engineering all showed high levels of satisfaction.

Most courses have a practical element, and assessors have praised the university for the work placements it offers. The majority of students take sandwich courses or include a period of study abroad, which helps to produce consistently outstanding graduate

**Claverton Down
Bath BA2 7AY**

01225 383019 (admissions)
admissions@bath.ac.uk
www.bath.ac.uk
www.bathstudent.com

The Times Rankings
Overall Ranking: **13**

Student satisfaction:	=15	(80%)
Research quality:	=24	(2.3)
Entry standards:	9	(451)
Student–staff ratio:	42	(15.7)
Services & facilities/student:	31	(£1,610)
Expected completion rate:	=11	(94.8%)
Good honours:	=16	(74.2%)
Graduate prospects:	6	(80.9%)

employment figures. Student entrepreneurship is actively encouraged through a number of initiatives and projects. A recent success story involved two students who set up their own frozen yoghurt range, Arctic Farm, which is now on the shelves of Harrods.

The university's other great claim to fame lies in its sports facilities, which were already among the best in Britain before the addition of a £30-million training village, funded with Lottery money. The campus acquired a 50-metre swimming pool by this route, to which it has added an indoor running track, a new multipurpose sports hall, eight indoor tennis courts, an indoor jumps and throws hall, air pistol and fencing sale, a judo dojo and even a simulated bobsleigh and skeleton start area, as used by Amy Williams, 2010 Olympic gold medallist for the skeleton. There is a strong tradition in competitive sports: the university pioneered sports scholarships more than 20 years ago. There are also courses to do the facilities justice, as recognised in a near-perfect score for teaching quality in sport and leisure. Bath claims that its students have access to more free sports facilities than any other university in Britain, from the swimming pools to badminton, squash and tennis courts to grass and astroturf pitches. The campus will also host the British paralympic team in the run up to London 2012.

Students – nearly a quarter of whom were educated at independent schools – may find the campus quiet at weekends and struggle to afford some of Bath's attractions, but they value its location. When they tire of the beauty of Bath, the nightlife of Bristol is only a few minutes away. The two cities have a combined student population of more than 50,000. The students' union is active and the university has been upgrading its student support services, for example through the introduction of a new virtual learning environment and establishment of a centrally based one-stop centre for student services. More than nine out of ten students surveyed say they would recommend the university to family and friends.

Undergraduate Fees and Bursaries

- » Fees for UK/EU students: £3,290
- » International student fees: £11,000–£14,000
- » Bursary on full grant: household income up to £25K: £1,200*
- » Bursary on partial grant: household income up to £50K: sliding scale £900–£300.*
- » Scholarships based on circumstances or by competition.
- » For full details see the university's website: www.bath.ac.uk/study/ug/finance

*Figures for 2009–10

Students

Undergraduates:	**8,890**	(415)
Postgraduates:	**1,545**	(2,525)
Mature students:	**8.1%**	
Overseas students:	**21.6%**	
Applications per place:	**6.8**	
From state-sector schools:	**76.8%**	
From working-class homes:	**19.0%**	

For detailed information about fees, grants and bursaries and how they work, see chapter 7.

Accommodation

Number of places and costs refer to 2010–11
University-provided places: 3,354
Percentage catered: 0%
Self-catered cost: £85–£135 a week.
First years guaranteed accommodation if conditions are met, and applications received by 13 August.
International students: as above. Exchange students are housed on a reciprocal basis.
Contact: www.bath.ac.uk/accommodation/enquiry

Bath Spa University

Bath Spa is one of a number of "teaching-led" universities created since the millennium under Government reforms. But it is far from new in other respects and not without research strengths. The history of the predecessor colleges goes back 150 years, and it boasts some famous alumni, including Body Shop founder Anita Roddick and Turner Prize winner Sir Howard Hodgkin. Its Newton Park headquarters, four miles outside the World Heritage city of Bath, is in grounds landscaped by Capability Brown in the eighteenth century, with a handsome Georgian manor house owned by the Prince of Wales as its centrepiece.

In recent years, the new university has undertaken its biggest-ever building programme to cater for growing student numbers. However, applications were down in 2008 and a 3 per cent increase at the start of 2009 was well below that national average. With around 7,000 students, it is still comparatively small, but the range of courses has been growing steadily. At Newton Park, the base for all students except those taking art and design subjects, the students' union has practically doubled in size, a library extension has added about 120 workstations and £4.8 million has been spent on an impressive university theatre with a 200-seat auditorium. A new creative writing centre is housed in the 14th-century gatehouse, bringing it into student use for the first time. Further development is planned at Newton Park over the next five years, encompassing both teaching and residential facilities.

A second campus at Sion Hill, in Bath itself, which houses the Bath School of Art and Design, has recently undergone a £6-million redevelopment and boasts facilities that are among the most modern in the country. Meanwhile, the university has established a postgraduate centre at Corsham Court, a 16th-century manor house near Chippenham that previously housed the Bath Academy of Art, and there is a teacher training centre in the grounds of Culverhay School, in Bath. About a third of the students are postgraduates, including a large cohort training to be teachers.

Bath Spa has been awarding its own degrees since 1992 – much longer than some of the other new arrivals on the university scene – and now also has the power to award research degrees. Results in all the National Student Surveys have been good, especially for teaching quality. Business and management, sociology and social studies, and philosophy, theology and religious studies produced the best results in 2009. The university has been designated a national centre for excellence in teaching and learning in the creative industries, bringing significant investment in the Schools of Music and Performing Arts, English and Creative

Newton Park
Newton St Loe
Bath BA2 9BN

01225 875609 (admissions)
admissions@bathspa.ac.uk
www.bathspa.ac.uk
www.bathspasu.co.uk

The Times Rankings
Overall Ranking: **80**

Student satisfaction:	=32	(78%)
Research quality:	=77	(0.4)
Entry standards:	58	(283)
Student–staff ratio:	111	(24.2)
Services & facilities/student:	113	(£653)
Expected completion rate:	=30	(90.3%)
Good honours:	45	(65.9%)
Graduate prospects:	104	(55.1%)

Studies, and Art and Design. Half of the subjects in which the university entered the 2008 Research Assessment Exercise (art and design, communication, cultural and media studies, English, history and music) were judged to have some world-leading work.

Despite a setting that would seem to be a magnet for applicants from independent schools, 95 per cent of the home intake is state-educated and over 34 per cent are from working-class homes. Two thirds of the students are female, reflecting the arts and social science bias in the curriculum, and 25 per cent are over 25. The latest projected dropout rate, of 8.3 per cent, is significantly better than the national average for the university's courses and entry grades. There are about 500 overseas students from a variety of countries.

The university has a number of partner further education colleges in the region, where a range of two-year Foundation degrees are delivered, the latest of which include musical theatre, professional musicianship, contemporary circus and physical performance, and further education management. Many students then progress to the university campuses to complete an honours degree. About 85 per cent of first years attending Bath Spa itself are offered hall places and more places are available off-campus through a partnership with Unite, a private company specialising in student accommodation. Students like the "small and friendly" atmosphere, which the university is anxious to retain in spite of the temptation to go for more substantial growth. Sports facilities are not extensive, but a new gym in the students' union has improved them, and a number of the university's sports teams fare well in local competitions. The countryside – on and off campus – is a major draw.

Undergraduate Fees and Bursaries

» Fees for UK/EU students: £3,290
» International student fees: £9,000–£9,580*
» Bursary on full grant: household income up to £25K: sliding scale £1,200–£350.
» Bursary on partial grant: household income up to £39K: sliding scale £200–£100
» Scholarships based on circumstances or by competition.
» For full details see the university's website: www.bathspa.ac.uk/services/student-services/prospective-students/your-money

*Figures for 2009-10

Students

Undergraduates:	4,775	595
Postgraduates:	710	(2,080)
Mature students:	21.7%	
Overseas students:	3.1%	
Applications per place:	5.4	
From state-sector schools:	95.3%	
From working-class homes:	34.6%	

For detailed information about fees, grants and bursaries and how they work, see chapter 7.

Accommodation

Number of places and costs refer to 2010–11
University provided places: 979 in halls; 100 in Accredited Independent Housing
Percentage catered: 0%
Self catered: £72 – £118 a week (40 or 45 weeks)
First years are housed provided requirements are met. Residential restrictions apply. Students with a disability, impairment or medical condition have priority.
International students: as above; Homestay option available
Contact: accommodation@bathspa.ac.uk

University of Bedfordshire

Bedfordshire has suffered a big fall in this year's *Times* league table, reversing the strong upward progress it made last year. But in other respects the former Luton University has never looked back since taking over De Montfort University's Bedford campus and establishing its new identity in 2006. The move made the new university the main provider of higher education in a relatively prosperous county and allowed it to shed a name that – however unfairly – had become a liability. The university's decline in our table stems from a drop in staffing levels and lower spending on facilities after the first phase of a big campus development programme. But applications for courses beginning in 2009 were 29 per cent up and the increase at the start of 2010 was one of the largest at any university, at 54 per cent.

With two quite different sites to its name, the new university is expanding and developing. It has already spent £60 million on the two main campuses, adding a well-equipped media arts centre and an impressive learning resources centre in Luton. The Bedford redevelopment is now complete, with a new campus centre comprising a 280-seat auditorium and a students' union, as well as an accommodation block for 500 students. Two new gyms and a series of sports science laboratories opened in 2006.

Work is now underway to plough a further £74 million into the Luton campus, building a new campus centre, which is due to open in September 2010, and new student accommodation which should be ready a year later.

The Bedford campus, once a teacher training college, is a 20-minute walk from the town centre in a "self-contained leafy setting". It houses the Faculty of Education and Sport, with 3,000 students and plans for more. Although there are partner colleges in Bedford, Dunstable and Milton Keynes, the bulk of the students remain in Luton. The centrepiece of the campus, in the midst of the shopping area, is the striking atrium which leads into the learning resources centre.

There is also an attractive management centre and conference venue at Putteridge Bury, a neo-Elizabethan mansion three miles outside Luton. Nursing and midwifery students in the growing Faculty of Health and Social Sciences are based at the Butterfield Park campus, near Luton, which opened in 2008, or at the even newer Oxford House development, in Aylesbury, Buckinghamshire. There are additional teaching facilities at Stoke Mandeville and Wycombe General hospitals. A postgraduate medical school is run in partnership with Hertfordshire and Cranfield universities, as part of the Government's £1-billion

Park Square
Luton
Bedfordshire
LU1 3JU

0844 848 2234
enquiries via website
www.beds.ac.uk
www.ubsu.co.uk

The Times Rankings
Overall Ranking: **101**

Student satisfaction:	=69	(75%)
Research quality:	=95	(0.2)
Entry standards:	110	(200)
Student–staff ratio:	78	(19.3)
Services & facilities/student:	112	(£728)
Expected completion rate:	63	(82.7%)
Good honours:	111	(44.5%)
Graduate prospects:	=76	(60.2%)

investment in healthcare across Bedfordshire and Hertfordshire.

Courses in the new university maintain the vocational character that Luton pursued after dropping a number of traditional academic subjects. The portfolio of two-year Foundation degrees, for example, is among the largest in the country, stretching from football studies and specialist make-up design to sustainable construction and animation for industry. The university pioneered electronic assessment, with more than 10,000 students in disciplines from accountancy to biology tested by computer. Bedfordshire also hosts a national centre of excellence in personal development planning and employability, which aims to link student learning with life after university.

Almost all of Bedfordshire's entrants are from state schools and nearly 47 per cent come from working-class backgrounds. Around a half are mature students, many taking access courses to bring them up to degree or diploma standard, and about a third take part-time courses. The numbers entering through clearing have dropped from nearly one in three to only one in ten. Surprisingly high numbers – nearly one in five – are from outside the EU, many of them taking postgraduate courses.

The university celebrated much-improved results in the 2008 Research Assessment Exercise, registering at least some world-leading work in earth systems and environmental science, social work, social policy and administration, sport, tourism and leisure, English language and literature, and communications, cultural and media studies. Scores in the National Student Survey have also been improving. Bedfordshire was ranked second in the country for marketing and equal second for journalism, fourth for human resource management and seventh in the results published in 2009.

Neither Luton nor Bedford is particularly famous for its social scene, but both have their share of pubs, clubs and restaurants. London is only half an hour away by train for those seeking something livelier. The number of residential places has been increasing but has not kept pace with enrolments, so the university is no longer able to guarantee accommodation for all first years. The sports facilities are improving, albeit from a low base in Luton.

Undergraduate Fees and Bursaries

» Fees for UK/EU students: £3,290
» International student fees: £8,590
» Bursary on full grant: household income up to £25K: £329
» Bursary on partial grant: £329
» Scholarships based on circumstances or by competition.
» For full details see the university's website: www.beds.ac.uk/howtoapply/money/fees/ug

Students

Undergraduates:	**8,735**	**(4,505)**
Postgraduates:	**2,770**	**(1,270)**
Mature students:	**44.9%**	
Overseas students:	**18.9%**	
Applications per place:	**3.4**	
From state-sector schools:	**98.9%**	
From working-class homes:	**46.7%**	

For detailed information about fees, grants and bursaries and how they work, see chapter 7.

Accommodation

Number of places and costs refer to 2010–11
University-provided places: about 1,617
Percentage catered: 0%
Self-catered costs: £77.00–£92.50 a week.
First years cannot be guaranteed a place but help is available to find alternative housing in the private sector.
International students: as above.
Contact: www.beds.ac.uk/studentlife/accommodation
studentservices.bedford@beds.ac.uk
accommodation@beds.ac.uk

University of Birmingham

Birmingham is the original "redbrick" university and remains a source of great civic pride in the second city. To those outside the West Midlands, however, it has been a quiet achiever, lacking the glamour of some of its Russell Group counterparts. The university recruited Professor David Eastwood, chief executive of the Higher Education Funding Council for England, to maximise its undoubted potential. He has said he wants Birmingham to be "the best of the rest" after Oxbridge and the top London colleges.

There are plans for more postgraduates, greater investment in research and major changes to the university's estate. The university will be the national hub for a new STEM programme, a national initiative to promote interest in science, technology, engineering and maths among young people and enhance higher level skills in the workplace. It will also be the first link in a chain of Cancer Research UK Centres, while a £60-million fundraising campaign will support projects ranging from research into brain injury, ageing and clean energy to scholarships, a new concert hall and a centre for heritage and cultural learning.

Students come to Birmingham from more than 150 countries. Entry standards are high, averaging the equivalent of more than ABB at A level. With over six applicants for each place, they are likely to remain so, but aspiring students still flock to the largest open days in Britain each June. There is also an additional open day for upper sixth-formers in September. Applications have been increasing and were up 10 per cent at the start of 2010.

The university's enduring reputation is based on its research, with 16 per cent of the work submitted for the 2008 Research Assessment Exercise regarded as world-leading. Birmingham took satisfaction from the broad range of subjects in which it produced good results, with music, physics, computer science, mechanical engineering, European studies and law all doing well. The university finished in the top 30 in the 2009 National Student Survey, faring better than most of the big city universities. Classics produced a rare 100 per cent satisfaction rating, while physics and astronomy, dentistry, French and other European languages were the other top performers. Birmingham encourages interdisciplinary study, for example allowing undergraduates to combine technology with subjects ranging from Latin or modern Greek to the management of floods and other natural disasters.

In recent years, the university has added a student facilities building at the Medical School, a new home for Sport and Exercise Sciences and a well-equipped learning centre, as well as spending £47.5 million on

Edgbaston
Birmingham B15 2TT

0121 415 8900 (admissions)
admissions@bham.ac.uk
www.bham.ac.uk
www.guildofstudents.com

The Times Rankings
Overall Ranking: **22**

Student satisfaction:	=22	(79%)
Research quality:	=20	(2.4)
Entry standards:	19	(404)
Student–staff ratio:	32	(15.1)
Services & facilities/student:	15	(£1,893)
Expected completion rate:	18	(93.3%)
Good honours:	21	(72.2%)
Graduate prospects:	43	(69.9%)

refurbishing student accommodation. The full investment programme in staff, buildings and equipment is costing a total of £225 million. In the latest phase, the Muirhead Tower has been refurbished at a cost of £40 million to house the College of Social Sciences, providing facilities for staff, postgraduate research students, teaching rooms and a 200-seat lecture theatre.

The 230-acre campus in leafy Edgbaston is dominated by a 300-foot clocktower, which is one of the city's best-known landmarks, and boasts its own station. Dentistry is located in the city, while part of the School of Education is in Selly Oak, a mile from the Edgbaston campus. Drama is also located there, along with the BBC Drama Village, which is part of a strategic alliance between the university and the corporation.

Most of the halls and university flats are conveniently located in an attractive parkland setting near the main campus. There are more than 4,000 university-owned beds, following a ten-year programme of expansion, and accommodation in the private sector is also plentiful.

The campus is less than three miles from the centre of Birmingham, but the area has plenty of shops, pubs and restaurants of its own. With its own nightclub among the facilities on campus, some students do not even stray that far, but the city is acquiring a growing reputation among the young, which is helping to make the university even more popular. Some 40 per cent of Birmingham graduates choose to make the city their home.

Student facilities on campus are on a par with the best in the country, and include a medical practice. An outdoor pursuits centre is on Coniston Water, in the Lake District. Birmingham has traditionally been concerned with the body as well as the mind, and the voluntary Active Lifestyles Programme attracts 4,000 students to 150 different courses. Tutors with national qualifications run classes from beginner to advanced level. In addition, Birmingham has ranked in the top four in British Universities competitions for the past 15 years.

Undergraduate Fees and Bursaries
» Fees for UK/EU students: £3,290
» International student fees: £10,800–£13,950
   £25,685 (clinical)
» Bursary on full grant: household income up to £25K: £877
» Bursary on partial grant: household income up to £36,170: £877
» Scholarships based on circumstances or by competition.
» For full details see the university's website: www.as.bham.ac.uk/study/support/finance

Students
Undergraduates:	**16,740**	(1,755)
Postgraduates:	**5,685**	(5,005)
Mature students:	**7.7%**	
Overseas students:	**9.8%**	
Applications per place:	**7.1**	
From state-sector schools:	**81.0%**	
From working-class homes:	**23.3%**	

For detailed information about fees, grants and bursaries and how they work, see chapter 7.

Accommodation
Number of places and costs refer to 2010–11
University-provided places: 4,267
Percentage catered: 42%
Catered costs: £108.64–£162.19 a week
Self-catered costs: £77.60–£128.05 a week
All first years are guaranteed housing (subject to conditions).
International students: as above
Contact: ugradaccomm@bham.ac.uk
www.has.bham.ac.uk/studentaccom

Birmingham City University

Birmingham City University has never looked back since adopting its new name in 2007. Applications were up by a third at the start of 2010, following an even bigger increase – the largest in the UK – 12 months earlier. Improved grades have doubled the university's research income, leading to the establishment of 11 new research centres. The transformation of the university's facilities has continued, although the Government's plans for a high-speed rail terminal in Birmingham appear to have scuppered its most ambitious project by taking the intended site of a new city centre campus.

The switch from the previous identity as UCE Birmingham (in turn originally the University of Central England) was designed to emphasise the university's location, reinforce its close links with the city and give the university a stronger identity. The Vice-Chancellor's strategy has been to build on the university's tradition-ally close links with business and the professions. An emphasis on employability is underlined by a £300,000 project to create "future-proof" graduates with training and education resources to help develop skills and knowledge for the workplace.

The annual satisfaction survey goes to half of the student body, and the results are taken seriously: a recent exercise led to the introduction of internet tutorials in engineering and new help with research for undergraduates in law and social science. The long-standing initiative is just one of the activities of the influential Centre for Research into Quality, headed by one of the university's most senior academics.

The university has a proud record of extending access to higher education: over 44 per cent of its students come from working-class homes and 97 per cent attended state schools or colleges. The drop-out rate has risen to nearly 18 per cent in the latest figures, slightly worse than the national average for the university's courses and entry grades. About half of the full-time students come from the West Midlands, many from ethnic minorities. The university also has one of the largest programmes of part-time courses in Britain, making it the biggest provider of higher education in the region. Entrance is through the network of associated further education colleges, which run foundation and access programmes.

Eight campuses straggle across the city, but about half of students are concentrated on the modern City North Campus at Perry Barr. The planned city-centre campus in the Eastside district, near Millennium Point, already had planning permission and was intended to form the centrepiece of a sustained programme of capital investment. If the rail project goes ahead, an alternative site will be sought for the creative and

---

Perry Barr
Birmingham B42 2SU

0121 331 5595 (enquiries)
choices@bcu.ac.uk
www.bcu.ac.uk
www.birminghamcitysu.com

The Times Rankings
Overall Ranking: **=81**

Student satisfaction:	=89	(73%)
Research quality:	=88	(0.3)
Entry standards:	=91	(254)
Student–staff ratio:	=62	(18.0)
Services & facilities/student:	36	(£1,554)
Expected completion rate:	94	(77.4%)
Good honours:	=74	(56.2%)
Graduate prospects:	=45	(69.1%)

performing arts, media, technology and design. The relocation of engineering and computing to Millennium Point in 2001 provided a new focus for the university. Facilities in the £114-million Lottery-funded centre are open to the public. The Birmingham School of Acting also moved into £4-million purpose-built facilities at Millennium Point in 2007.

The Edgbaston campus has been refurbished for the Faculty of Health, with a prize-winning library, IT suites, teaching facilities and recreational space. The Birmingham Institute of Art and Design spreads over four campuses from Gosta Green and the impressive listed Venetian gothic fine art campus at Margaret Street, both in the city centre, to Bournville. This facility was refurbished at a cost of £20 million and occupies part of the Cadbury village. The largest institute of its kind outside London, it also includes the world famous and newly refurbished School of Jewellery in the city's famous Jewellery Quarter.

One of the university's best-known features is its Conservatoire, housed in part of Birmingham's smart convention centre. Courses from opera to world music have given it a reputation for innovation. Teacher education courses consistently produce among the best scores in Ofsted inspections. The university was awarded a national centre for excellence in teaching and learning for health and social care.

The university has been increasing its portfolio of high-tech degree courses like electronic commerce, communications and network engineering, and electronic systems. The 2008 Research Assessment Exercise recorded some world-leading work in all seven areas covered by the university's submission. In art and design, 30 per cent were given the top grade, placing Birmingham City in the top ten for the subject.

University-owned accommodation is guaranteed for first years, and there is a relatively cheap and plentiful private housing sector. The Pavilion, adjacent to the City North Campus, has added £4.5 million of conference and sports facilities, comprising 43 acres. The city's youth scene is highly rated.

Undergraduate Fees and Bursaries
» Fees for UK/EU students: £3,290
» International student fees: £9,250–£13,770
» Bursary on full grant: household income up to £25K: £525
» Bursary on partial grant: sliding scale £525–£300
» Scholarships based on circumstances or by competition.
» For full details see the university's website:
www.bcu.ac.uk/student-info/finance-and-money-matters

Students
Undergraduates:	**14,220**	(6,410)
Postgraduates:	**1,380**	(2,345)
Mature students:	**32.4%**	
Overseas students:	**5.7%**	
Applications per place:	**4.4**	
From state-sector schools:	**97.3%**	
From working-class homes:	**44.7%**	

For detailed information about fees, grants and bursaries and how they work, see chapter 7.

Accommodation
Number of places and costs refer to 2010–11
University-provided places: 2,400
Percentage catered: 0%
Self-catered costs: £64–£103.50 a week (40 weeks).
Accommodation guaranteed for first years if conditions are met.
International students are guaranteed accommodation.
Contact: www.bcu.ac.uk/accommodation
accommodation@uce.ac.uk

University of Bolton

Applications to Bolton were up by almost a third at the start of 2010 – a welcome return to the boom years that followed the granting of university status in 2005. The university now has a single campus in the centre of the town, as well as a branch campus in the United Arab Emirates that is part of a longer-term internationalisation strategy. The rationalisation of sites in Bolton has provided additional and enhanced teaching space, facilities to interact with industry and a new students' union.

The university traces its roots back as far as 1824 to one of the country's first three mechanics institutes. There are now more than 13,000 students but there are no plans for further dramatic growth. The university sees itself as a regional institution, with three quarters of the students coming from the North West, many through partner colleges. But the international dimension includes long-established links in Malaysia, China, Zambia, Malawi and Vietnam, as well as a regular contingent of overseas students from 60 different countries. The Ras as Khaimah campus opened in 2008, offering a range of undergraduate and postgraduate courses identical to those taught at Bolton. The £1-million development near Dubai has 270 students and is intended to take 700 within five years. Students at Bolton will also have the opportunity to study in the UAE for part of their degree course.

Student satisfaction scores have slipped a little since the early days of the National Student Survey, when Bolton almost made the top ten. It has now dropped into the bottom half of the table on this measure, although there was a good score in 2009 for maths and statistics. At the other end of the scale, design students were among the least satisfied in the whole survey. The university has done better in the International Student Barometer, which tracks the views of overseas students at UK institutions.

The university is not research-driven, but engineering, architecture and the built environment, social work and social policy all contained some world-leading research in the 2008 assessments. A centre for research and innovation in materials which opened in 2003 is to be the first of a series of "knowledge exchange zones". Bolton is not one of the new breed of "teaching-only" universities; it has been accredited for research degrees for more than ten years and acquired its new status under the old rules. About 2,200 of the students are postgraduates, taking qualifications up to and including PhDs.

The £11.3-million building programme at the Deane campus has included a design studio and three floors of teaching and learning space where students work on actual briefs for companies seeking design solutions,

---

Deane Road
Bolton BL3 5AB

01204 903903 (course enquiries)
contact via website
www.bolton.ac.uk
www.ubsu.org.uk

The Times Rankings
Overall Ranking: **108**

Student satisfaction:	=89	(73%)
Research quality:	=88	(0.3)
Entry standards:	107	(209)
Student–staff ratio:	=62	(18.0)
Services & facilities/student:	111	(£734)
Expected completion rate:	113	(62.6%)
Good honours:	105	(48.5%)
Graduate prospects:	=100	(56.5%)

an Innovation Factory housing, among others, special effects laboratories and a product design studio. Also included within this development is a new social learning zone which includes a students' union bar and social facilities, a computer access room and new students' union offices and advice centre. Now completed, this combined student services covers floor space equivalent to the size of a football pitch. A multifaith chaplaincy opened in 2010, with a resources area, a quiet room and a prayer room. A swimming pool and sports complex built in partnership with the local authority is due to be completed in 2012 and will offer students access to the pool, gym, sports courts, teaching facilities and equipment, physiotherapy and rehabilitation facilities, an NHS surgery and emergency walk-in centre. The 702 reasonably priced residential places go a long way in an institution with a high proportion of home-based students. Nearly 47 per cent of the students are over 21 at entry.

The university exceeds all the access measures designed to widen participation in higher education: nearly all the students are state-educated, over half are from working-class homes and the proportion from areas without a tradition of higher education is almost twice the national average for Bolton's subjects and entry qualifications. The downside – and an important one – is that the dropout rate remains the highest in England. The university has an action plan to bring the rate down to the national average for its courses and qualifications by 2012, but almost 30 per cent of undergraduates who entered in 2007 are projected to leave without a qualification.

Undergraduate Fees and Bursaries
» Fees for UK/EU students: £3,290
» International student fees: £7,900*
» Bursary on full grant: household income up to £39,333: £350
» Bursary on partial grant: household income up to £60, 032: £120.
» Scholarships based on circumstances or by competition.
» For full details see the university's website: www.bolton.ac.uk/ProspectiveStudents/Undergraduate/Finance/Home.aspx

*Figures for 2009–10

Students
Undergraduates:	**3,705**	(3,080)
Postgraduates:	**520**	(865)
Mature students:	**46.9%**	
Overseas students:	**7.1%**	
Applications per place:	**4.7**	
From state-sector schools:	**99.7%**	
From working-class homes:	**52.3%**	

For detailed information about fees, grants and bursaries and how they work, see chapter 7.

Accommodation
Number of places and costs refer to 2009–10
University-provided places: 702
Percentage catered: 0%
Self-catered costs: £2,665 annually (40 weeks); £65 a week. There is a £200 discount if the full rent is paid in one lump sum.
All first years are generally accommodated.
International students: accommodation is secured for these students.
Contact: accomm@bolton.ac.uk

Bournemouth University

Once a university that gloried in the absence of traditional academic disciplines, Bournemouth has been subtly changing its image. Its latest corporate plan speaks of a university "geared to the professions with passionate commitment to academic excellence". Research moved up the agenda with a £1-million investment in 80 PhD studentships, and the aim is to increase undergraduates' entry qualifications. The university had risen 27 places up *The Times* league table in the four years up to last year; this year it fell back just one place.

Bournemouth's forte has always been in identifying gaps in the higher education market and then filling them with innovative programmes. Degrees in public relations, retail management, scriptwriting and tax law are among the examples. The university also boasts the National Centre of Computer Animation. The mix has been popular with students: applications were up by more than a third at the start of 2010, the latest in a series of increases. Attendance at open days has tripled in four years.

The university claims a number of firsts in its growing portfolio of courses, notably in the area of tourism, media-related programmes and conservation. It was no surprise to find Bournemouth among the pioneers of two-year Foundation degrees.

Now much expanded, the courses are being delivered in further education colleges from Somerset to Wiltshire, supporting the needs of business in the creative arts, media and tourism. One even serves soldiers based in Afghanistan, who are studying business and management via the internet to boost their employment prospects when they leave the military.

A majority of undergraduates take sandwich courses, and 70 per cent do work placements. The result is that nearly four out of five graduates went straight into jobs at the time of the latest survey. The retail management degree notched up eight successive years of full employment and is still running at over 90 per cent. Virtually all students take up the offer of personal development planning, both online and with trained staff, while 1,400 first years also take advantage of peer-assisted learning, receiving advice and mentoring from more experienced undergraduates.

Archaeology, fine art, complementary medicine, management and psychology all achieved high scores in the National Student Survey published in 2009, although the university remained in the bottom half of the table overall. Media courses are a particular strength, with entry requirements well above the average for Bournemouth – itself now among the highest in the post-1992 universities. State-of-the-art equipment includes a motion capture facility for real-

Fern Barrow
Talbot Campus
Poole
Dorset BH12 5BB

01202 961961 (enquiries)
askBUenquiries@
  bournemouth.ac.uk
www.bournemouth.ac.uk
www.subu.org.uk

The Times Rankings
Overall Ranking: **=59**

Student satisfaction:	=69	(75%)
Research quality:	=69	(0.5)
Entry standards:	54	(297)
Student–staff ratio:	110	(23.8)
Services & facilities/student:	62	(£1,282)
Expected completion rate:	=49	(85.3%)
Good honours:	57	(61.5%)
Graduate prospects:	38	(70.8%)

time animation, which is used in teaching and available for use by outside companies. The university has been designated as England's only centre for excellence in media practice.

Computer animation was the star performer in the 2001 research assessments, which saw much-needed improvement on the previous exercise. In 2008, eight of the ten subject areas contained at least some world-leading research, with art and design and communication, cultural and media studies producing the best grades. The results have tripled Bournemouth's research grant, which is being invested in new posts.

New teaching and residential accommodation has been added in recent years, with more to come. Recent developments include a new Executive Business Centre, which is a focus for services to local companies. An additional large, modern lecture theatre will be completed in 2010 and new residential accommodation has been added. Students based in halls of residence in Poole enjoy a millionaire's view of Poole Harbour. There are now two campuses – the original Talbot site in Poole and a dedicated campus in Bournemouth – with partner colleges in Bridgwater, Yeovil, Bournemouth and Poole, Dorchester, Salisbury and Weymouth.

The southern seaside location and the subject mix attract more middle-class students than most new universities, although over 95 per cent attended state schools and colleges. Students are discouraged from bringing cars, but many still do. The campuses are served by a subsidized bus service. The area has plenty to offer students during the summer season. Although it naturally becomes less lively in the winter months, Bournemouth no longer shuts up when the tourists go home. The students' union's Old Fire Station bar is the favourite among many nightlife options. The new surf reef, recently completed off Boscombe seafront, is helping to transform Bournemouth into the UK's latest surfing hotspot and other watersports are catered for in Poole Harbour. There is a wide range of accommodation, from around 2,300 places in university halls to bed-and-breakfast lets and shared houses.

Undergraduate Fees and Bursaries

» Fees for UK/EU students: £3,290
» International student fees: £9,000–£14,000
» Bursary on full grant: household income up to £25K: £329
» The university does not award bursaries for students on partial maintenance grants.
» Scholarships based on circumstances or by competition.
» For full details see the university's website: www.bournemouth.ac.uk/futurestudents/undergraduate/funding/index.html

Students

Undergraduates:	11,565	(4,070)
Postgraduates:	1,305	(1,025)
Mature students:	20.9%	
Overseas students:	6.0%	
Applications per place:	4.9	
From state-sector schools:	95.2%	
From working-class homes:	31.0%	

For detailed information about fees, grants and bursaries and how they work, see chapter 7.

Accommodation

Number of places and costs refer to 2010–11
University-provided places: about 2,910 (2,310 in halls; 600 head tenancy)
Percentage catered: 0%
Self-catered costs: £78–£95 a week.
The university expects to offer all first years a place to live.
Residential restrictions apply.
International students: guaranteed if conditions are met.
Contact: accommodation@bournemouth.ac.uk

University of Bradford

Bradford has been a leading light in the green movement in higher education, with its "ecoversity" programme addressing issues of sustainable development in all the university's practices, including the curriculum. The most visible sign will be the opening of a sustainable student village in 2010, which will cater mainly for first-year and international students. The development is part of a £70-million modernisation plan that includes a £7-million investment in new and upgraded teaching facilities. Another project produced the distinctive four-storey Atrium, which has brought together all student support services in a single, open-plan social space.

Still a relatively small university of 12,000 students, Bradford has carved out a niche for itself with mature students, who now make up over a quarter of all undergraduates. They relish the vocational slant and the accent on work experience and placement courses, which regularly place Bradford towards the top of the graduate employment tables. More than half of the undergraduates are from working-class homes – by far the biggest proportion of any pre-1992 university. Demand for places has recovered after a difficult period: applications were up by 23 per cent at the start of 2010 and admission requirements have been rising.

Nearly 20 per cent of the university's students are from overseas, many of them taught in partner institutions in locations as diverse as Poland, India, Iceland and Hong Kong. Nearer home, there are alliances with a number of further education colleges to help boost participation in a region where it is well below the national average. The colleges offer eight Foundation degrees in areas such as public sector administration, community justice, engineering technology and enterprise in IT. Perhaps the best known is in health and social care, where the university was already expanding opportunities locally, bringing about a fourfold increase in enrolments by young women from South Asian families.

The relatively small, lively campus is close to the city centre. Health students have their own building a few minutes' walk away, while a shuttle bus service runs to the highly rated management school two miles away in a 14-acre parkland setting. The eventual aim is to develop a health and science quarter, with the School of Health Studies housed in its own building on campus. Improvements in recent years have included upgraded laboratories for chemical and forensic science, and new sports facilities including a gym and climbing wall and an improved sports hall.

The university improved its scores considerably in the 2009 National Student Survey, climbing into the top 50 with good

Richmond Road
Bradford
West Yorkshire BD7 1DP

0800 073 1225 (freephone)
course-enquiries@bradford.ac.uk
www.bradford.ac.uk
www.ubuonline.co.uk

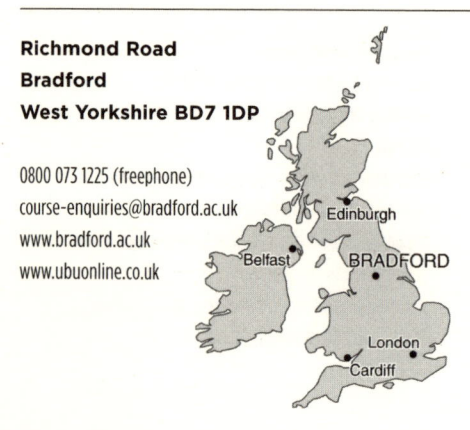

The Times Rankings
Overall Ranking: **=57**

Student satisfaction:	=59	(76%)
Research quality:	=54	(1.1)
Entry standards:	63	(275)
Student–staff ratio:	43	(15.8)
Services & facilities/student:	74	(£1,170)
Expected completion rate:	=80	(79.8%)
Good honours:	55	(62.2%)
Graduate prospects:	=35	(71.1%)

results in medical technology, ophthalmics and nursing. Bradford is harnessing the power of technology: it operates an online social network for prospective students before they even apply to the university. A so-called "e-induction" acts as a preparation for university life, while those who do win a place are offered a "self-audit" that gauges new students' levels of confidence in different academic areas and allows them to develop an action plan with their personal tutor.

Some 80 per cent of the work submitted for the 2008 Research Assessment Exercise was placed in the top two categories, although more than a third of the academics were not entered. Social work and social policy, politics, civil engineering and pharmacy produced the best results. Politics includes the university's best-known offering of peace studies, which has acquired an international reputation, while the human studies programme, which combines psychology, literature and sociology with philosophy, is another imaginative construct.

The university has launched suites of ICT and media studies courses to add to those in e-commerce and internet computing, computer animation and special effects, interactive systems and video games design. Computer-assisted learning is increasing in many subjects, making use of unusually extensive IT provision and a new wireless network. Some courses feature online assessment and the use of laptops in lectures.

More southerners are being attracted to Bradford's status as Britain's cheapest student city. The 1,000 places in halls are reasonably priced and all have internet connections. There is particularly good provision for disabled students, who account for 6 per cent of the university population. Bradford's senior management group includes a Director of Student Engagement to ensure that the student voice is heard in future developments.

Undergraduate Fees and Bursaries
» Fees for UK/EU students: £3,290
» International student fees: £9,000–£11,400
» Bursary of £900–£500 for those on a full grant, depending on year in course.
» Bursaries for those on partial grant based on household income up to £40K, depending on year in course £900–£500; up to £60K, £600–£400.
» Scholarships based on circumstances or by competition.
» For full details see the university's website: www.bradford.ac.uk/external/tuitionfees

Students
Undergraduates:	**8,130**	**(1,350)**
Postgraduates:	**1,440**	**(1,815)**
Mature students:	**26.6%**	
Overseas students:	**19.3%**	
Applications per place:	**3.8**	
From state-sector schools:	**94.4%**	
From working-class homes:	**52.4%**	

For detailed information about fees, grants and bursaries and how they work, see chapter 7.

Accommodation
Number of places and costs refer to 2010–11
University-provided places: 1,000
Percentage catered: 0%
Self-catered costs: £53.50 – £94.00 (deluxe en-suite) a week (42-week contracts)
All first-year undergraduate students are guaranteed accommodation (terms and conditions apply).
Contact: halls-of-residence@bradford.ac.uk
www.brad.ac.uk/accommodation

University of Brighton

A series of new developments will be ready by the time students arrive at Brighton in 2011. Languages and literature students, as well as those in the School of Education, have already moved into the smart new Checkland Building, on the Falmer campus, which will also boast a £7.6-million sports centre. Meanwhile, at the Moulsecoomb site, the £23m Huxley Building, with its living roof, will provide a new home for pharmacy and biosciences. £10 million has been spent on sports facilities in the last three years.

Brighton came of age as one of the first new universities to be awarded a medical school, but is equally well known for imaginative initiatives in its region. It has set up a centre in Hastings and runs a number of schemes, both to draw people from the region into higher education and to help them with practical problems. The £28.5-million medical school, run jointly with neighbouring Sussex University, is training 128 doctors a year and has proved popular with applicants. Brighton was already heavily engaged in other health subjects, such as nursing and midwifery. The medical school's headquarters, on Brighton's Falmer campus, has also provided a new base for applied social sciences, such as criminology and applied psychology, which are among the university's most sought-after degrees.

The two universities have been collaborating since Brighton was a polytechnic. There is a joint research building for science policy and management studies, and a joint accord guarantees the offer of a place to all suitably qualified applicants from the Channel Island of Jersey. Brighton does the same for applicants from Sussex and leads a Learning Network for the county. Almost a third of undergraduates now come through these accords.

Brighton was again one of the top new universities in the 2008 Research Assessment Exercise. Art and design produced the best results, with two thirds of the work submitted considered world-leading or internationally excellent. Business management, sports studies and mechanical and aeronautical engineering also did well. Geography and environmental science, medicine and sports science achieved the best scores in the latest National Student Survey. The plaudits have not gone unnoticed: a rise in applications of almost a third at the start of 2010 was just the latest in a series of impressive figures.

Brighton's strengths in art and design – recognised in the award of national teaching centres in design and creativity – have been at the forefront of the university's rise. But the university also has a growing reputation in areas such as sport and hospitality, as well as scoring well in teacher education rankings. It was the first university to achieve an "outstanding" rating from the Office for Standards in Education for management and

Mithras House
Lewes Road
Brighton BN2 4AT

01273 600900
enquiries@brighton.ac.uk
www.brighton.ac.uk
www.bsms.ac.uk
www.ubsu.net

The Times Rankings
Overall Ranking: **71**

Student satisfaction:	=69	(75%)
Research quality:	=56	(1.0)
Entry standards:	59	(281)
Student–staff ratio:	=85	(19.7)
Services & facilities/student:	106	(£931)
Expected completion rate:	=57	(83.5%)
Good honours:	64	(58.9%)
Graduate prospects:	69	(61.6%)

quality assurance across the full range of primary, secondary and post-compulsory teacher education courses.

The Design Council's national archive is lodged on campus, and the four-year fashion textiles degree offers work placements in the USA, France and Italy, as well as Britain. Teaching facilities include a flight simulator, a fully functional newsroom for the university's sports journalists, modern clinical skills laboratories for pharmacy, and a custom-designed culinary arts studio. At Eastbourne there is a new library and extensive sports and leisure facilities, including a sports centre with three gymnasia and a dance studio, a refurbished swimming pool and fitness facilities. Sport-science laboratories and 354 en-suite residential places have been added, and improvements made to the learning resources centre, lecture theatres and refectory.

Four sites house the five faculties. Art and Design has the prime location opposite the Royal Pavilion, with sports science, service management and the health professions at Eastbourne and the other subjects on the outskirts of Brighton, at Falmer and Moulsecoomb, the university's headquarters. The university has a cosmopolitan air, with more overseas students and a more middle-class UK intake than most of the former polytechnics. Over a quarter of the full-time undergraduates are over 21 on entry, often attracted by strongly vocational courses and the prospect of three years at "London by the sea". Most students have a personal tutor to advise on combinations within the modular degree scheme.

Students have taken to the "managed learning environment", known as Studentcentral, an interactive service providing online access to teaching materials and other information. Most also like Brighton, although the cost of living is high for those not in hall. There is a lively social scene. Eastbourne is also surprisingly popular, and both towns offer plentiful accommodation to supplement the university's stock, which is being expanded considerably.

Undergraduate Fees and Bursaries
» Fees for UK/EU students: £3,290
» International student fees: £9,600–£11,160
£23,678 (medicine)
» Bursary on full grant: household income up to £25K: £1,080
» Bursary on partial grant: household income up to £40.3K: sliding scale £860–£540.
» Scholarships based on circumstances or by competition.
» For full details see the university's website: www.brighton.ac.uk/studentlife/money

Students
Undergraduates:	**13,110**	(3,735)
Postgraduates:	**1,510**	(2,615)
Mature students:	**27.3%**	
Overseas students:	**10.2%**	
Applications per place:	**5.6**	
From state-sector schools:	**93.1%**	
From working-class homes:	**34.7%**	

For detailed information about fees, grants and bursaries and how they work, see chapter 7.

Accommodation
Number of places and costs refer to 2009–10
University-provided places: 2,000; 270 in private sector university-managed houses or flats.
Percentage catered: 43%
Catered costs: £115–£133 a week.
Self-catered costs: £70–£106 a week.
First years have priority for housing if conditions are met.
International students: guaranteed accommodation if conditions are met.
Contact: accommodation@brighton.ac.uk

University of Bristol

Bristol is the most popular multi-faculty university in Britain, judged in terms of applications per place – over 11 hopefuls vie for every degree slot. It has long been a natural alternative to Oxbridge, favoured particularly by independent schools, whose pupils take more than a third of the places. In order to broaden the intake, departments are encouraged to make slightly lower offers to the most promising applicants from schools and colleges with poor records at A level. Applications were down at the start of 2010, when most universities registered big increases, but competition remained intense.

The university's academic credentials are not in doubt – it broke into the top 35 in the *Times Higher Education/QS* world rankings for 2009. But it has found it difficult to attract working-class teenagers, who fear that they would be out of place socially, if not academically. In 2008–09 only about one in seven came from a working-class home – almost the lowest proportion outside Oxbridge. Tiny numbers are recruited from the schools in the bottom half of the A-level league tables and few come from Scotland or the north of England, but £1 million a year is being spent on efforts to recruit more widely.

Overall entry standards remain among the highest at any university. A modular course system is now well established, although the majority of students still take single or dual honours degrees. Bristol has no intention of aping the growth plans of some of its rivals, but there has been modest expansion to nearly 13,000 full-time undergraduates and the university has continued to live up to expectations in assessments of teaching and research. Almost two thirds of the work submitted for the 2008 Research Assessment Exercise was rated in the top two categories, with epidemiology and public health, health services research, chemistry, mathematics, drama, mechanical engineering and economics producing the best results. Four research projects involving the university were included in *Time* magazine's top ten medical breakthroughs and scientific discoveries of 2008. There are 31 Fellows of the Royal Society and similar numbers in other learned societies.

Bristol was given the best rating among the small group of universities seeking to demonstrate their creditworthiness to the money markets. The university celebrated its centenary in 2009 and launched a new fundraising campaign with a target of £100 million by 2014. The previous campaign helped the university to create new chairs and embark on a number of building projects. The highly rated chemistry department, for example, moved into a well-appointed new centre in 2000, allowing new medical science laboratories to be constructed in the department's former premises. Both

Senate House
Tyndall Avenue
Bristol BS8 1TH

0117 928 9000 (admissions)
ug-admissions@bristol.ac.uk
www.bristol.ac.uk
www.ubu.org.uk

The Times Rankings
Overall Ranking: **14**

Student satisfaction:	=79	(74%)
Research quality:	=7	(3.0)
Entry standards:	10	(448)
Student–staff ratio:	17	(13.6)
Services & facilities/student:	11	(£2,015)
Expected completion rate:	=7	(95.1%)
Good honours:	10	(78.6%)
Graduate prospects:	11	(78.3%)

chemistry and medical sciences now have national teaching and learning centres, and the university has also been chosen to host four centres to train doctoral scientists and engineers.

An impressive sports complex at the heart of the university precinct opened in 2004 and new buildings for neuroscience and dynamics engineering opened in the same year. The £11-million Centre for Nanoscience and Quantum Information, which opened in 2008, contains some of the "quietest" labs in the world, with extremely low levels of vibrational and acoustic noise, and tight controls on temperature and air movement. The first stage of a programme of refurbishment for the university's library facilities was completed in 2009 and there are plans for a new boathouse and a health and fitness centre. Facilities at the underused students' union building are set for radical improvement and planning approval has been obtained for a major new centre for biological sciences as part of an ambitious, ongoing investment plan.

The city is one of the most attractive in Britain, as well as possessing a vibrant youth culture. An academic think tank named it European City of the Year in 2009. It is also relatively prosperous, offering job opportunities to students and graduates alike. The university merges into the centre, its famous gothic tower dominating the skyline from the junction of two of the main shopping streets. Despite its hills, Bristol is England's first Cycling City and was the only UK city to be shortlisted for the European Green Capital Award 2010.

The current students' union is less of a social centre than in some universities, partly because of the intense competition from nightclubs. Most students enjoy life in Bristol, although the high cost of living can be a serious drawback. The dropout rate is among the lowest in Britain. Parts of the city suffer from the same security concerns as any big conurbation, but the university won a police-approved Secured Environments award in 2009 for its crime protection work.

Undergraduate Fees and Bursaries

» Fees for UK/EU students: £3,790
» International student fees: £11,900–£14,950
£27,600 (medicine)
» Bursary on full grant: £1,230 + £1,100 (local students)
» Bursary on partial grant: household income up to £40K: £790; up to £50K: £320, all plus £1,100 (local students)
» Scholarships based on circumstances or by competition.
» For full details see the university's website: www.bristol.ac.uk/studentfunding

Students

Undergraduates:	**12,465**	**(2,740)**
Postgraduates:	**4,050**	**(1,735)**
Mature students:	**5.2%**	
Overseas students:	**10.3%**	
Applications per place:	**11.7**	
From state-sector schools:	**60.0%**	
From working-class homes:	**14.2%**	

For detailed information about fees, grants and bursaries and how they work, see chapter 7.

Accommodation

Number of places and costs refer to 2009–10
University-provided places: about 3,827
Percentage catered: 47%
Catered costs: £104–£162 a week.
Self-catered costs: £58–£130 a week.
First years are guaranteed one offer of accommodation provided conditions are met.
International students: accommodation is guaranteed provided conditions are met.
Contact: www.bristol.ac.uk/accommodation

Brunel University

Brunel's investment in teaching, research and sporting facilities over the last five years is now approaching £300 million. The building programme has included a £6.5-million outdoor sports complex and a £7-million indoor athletics and netball centre, making a fitting home for the former Borough Road College and its illustrious sporting traditions. There is also a hugely extended university library, increased residential accommodation, more catering and social amenities and enhanced teaching and research facilities. A new accommodation complex comprising 1,188 en-suite rooms, 40 specially adapted rooms for students with disabilities and 112 studio flats opened in 2008.

For the first time since its early years, the whole university is located on the main Uxbridge campus. But there is still plenty of scope for development. Still less than 50 years old, Brunel has 13,000 students who share a spacious, but hitherto uninspiring, main campus that had an isolated feel despite affording easy access to central London. Among the recent additions have been a new engineering and design annex, including an impressive exhibition space, and a student facilities complex, also featuring an atrium entrance that opens onto a dining area, bars, the students' union and retail outlets.

In recent years, Brunel has introduced more variety into a portfolio of degrees that was once given over almost entirely to sandwich courses. About a third of all undergraduates still take four-year degrees that incorporate work placements, but new developments have tended to be conventional three-year arts, humanities, social science or sports programmes. There has also been significant growth in courses specialising in new technologies, such as multimedia design and broadcast media, as well as and health and social care. Other innovations include creative writing, journalism, sonic arts, aviation engineering and pilot studies, motorsport engineering and games design.

Work placements and the inclusion in degree courses of skills modules (such as oral and written communication, business and computer literacy) in degree courses have helped maintain a consistently good record in the graduate employment market. Many courses are validated by professional institutions. A recent survey placed Brunel graduates 13th in the UK for average starting salaries. At more than £22,000, the figure was almost £3,000 above the national average.

Substantial investment in research centres and academic recruitment produced significant improvements in the latest Research Assessment Exercise, when Brunel registered one of the biggest increases in the numbers of staff entered. Almost nine out of ten academics were assessed, compared with

Uxbridge
Middlesex UB8 3PH

01895 265265 (admissions)
admissions@brunel.ac.uk
www.brunel.ac.uk
www.brunelstudents.com

The Times Rankings
Overall Ranking: **50**

Student satisfaction:	=89	(73%)
Research quality:	=41	(1.9)
Entry standards:	45	(315)
Student–staff ratio:	=85	(19.7)
Services & facilities/student:	=37	(£1,531)
Expected completion rate:	41	(86.2%)
Good honours:	=41	(66.8%)
Graduate prospects:	57	(66.1%)

barely more than six out of ten in 2001. With 43 percent of the work submitted judged to be world-leading or internationally excellent, the outcome was a 54 per cent increase in Brunel's research allocation from the Higher Education Funding Council for England.

A recent review of all aspects of learning in NHS-funded health programmes produced a "commendable" rating and Brunel also scored well in its last institutional audit. Sporting excellence is also being maintained, with four graduates winning Olympic medals in 2008 and several students competing in the games – notably Montell Douglas, who broke the British 100 metres record on the day before she graduated. Brunel has also been selected as a pre-training site for the 2012 Olympics and is likely to be a training base for international teams in the run-up to the London Games.

Nearly four out of ten undergraduates are from working-class homes – significantly more than the national average for the subjects on offer – and more than half come from ethnic minorities. The level of applications has been rising, despite increased entry scores, which now average 320 points, but there was a surprise drop at the start of 2010, when most universities were recording big increases. The projected total of nearly 11 per cent leaving without a qualification is much better than the UK average for Brunel's subjects and entry grades.

Student union facilities are good and students like Brunel's intimacy, although the university has not done well in National Student Surveys. It was among the bottom 30 universities in the 2009 survey, although design and biomedical students were among the most satisfied in the country. The university's residential stock has been greatly increased in recent years and all new undergraduates are guaranteed accommodation on campus. Brunel won an award for its provision for disabled students.

Undergraduate Fees and Bursaries

» Fees for UK/EU students: £3,290
» International student fees: £9,750–£11,765
» Bursary on full grant: household income up to £25K £1,000
» Bursary on partial grant: household income up to £33K: £500
» Scholarships based on circumstances or by competition.
» For full details see the university's website: www.brunel.ac.uk/ugstudy/finance

Students

Undergraduates:	**10,185**	(645)
Postgraduates:	**2,645**	(1,610)
Mature students:	**15.5%**	
Overseas students:	**11.6%**	
Applications per place:	**6.2**	
From state-sector schools:	**95.7%**	
From working-class homes:	**37.8%**	

For detailed information about fees, grants and bursaries and how they work, see chapter 7.

Accommodation

Number of places and costs refer to 2009–10
University-provided places: 4,549
Percentage catered: 0%
Self-catered costs: £84.49–£105.00 a week (36 weeks).
All new full-time first-year students are eligible for on-campus accommodation.
International students: as above.
Contact: www.brunel.ac.uk/life/accommodation
accom-uxb@brunel.ac.uk

University of Buckingham

Britain's only private university describes itself as the country's smallest and friendliest – a claim borne out by the National Student Surveys published in 2008 and 2009, in which Buckingham students emerged as the most satisfied in England. Accounting, economics, social studies and psychology all produced unusually high levels of satisfaction in 2009.

Even before the advent of top-up fees elsewhere, Buckingham claimed to be no more expensive than other universities because its intensive two-year degrees cut maintenance costs and accelerate entry into employment. Total fees for UK undergraduates taking the two-year degree are now £17,280, and there are further discounts for payment in advance. Foreign students pay £27,900 and there is a range of scholarships for both home and overseas candidates.

The university, which celebrated its 30th anniversary in 2006, has no ambitions to follow its peers into the mass higher education market: it values the personal approach that comes with having fewer than 10 students to each member of staff, when the UK average is 17. One-to-one tutorials, which have all but disappeared outside Oxbridge and are by no means universal there, are common at Buckingham. The average teaching group contains about six students.

A Conservative-backed experiment of the 1970s, Buckingham had to wait almost ten years for its royal charter, but is now an accepted part of the university system. Although in 1992 it installed Baroness Thatcher as Chancellor, the university has no party political ties. Dr Terence Kealey, a biochemist from Cambridge University, became the latest Vice-Chancellor in April 2001, declaring an ambition for Buckingham to "one day" challenge the cream of American higher education. He has recruited a number of high-profile libertarians, including Chris Woodhead, the commentator and former Chief Inspector of Schools.

Buckingham's private status excludes it from the funding council's assessment of teaching and research, making it impossible to place in our league table. However, the university commissioned its own audit of teaching standards from the Quality Assurance Agency, which gave it a clean bill of health in 2004. The university's degrees carry full currency in the academic world and teaching standards are high. Education courses now have accreditation from the Training and Development Agency for Schools. Student numbers have increased by 25 per cent over the past three years, despite falling applications in 2008 and 2009. The latter trend had been reversed at the start of 2010, when applications were up by more than a quarter.

The university runs on calendar years, rather than the traditional academic variety, although some courses give the option of

Hunter Street
Buckingham MK18 1EG

01280 814080
info@buckingham.ac.uk
www.buckingham.ac.uk
www.buckingham.ac.uk/life/social/su

The Times Rankings
Not applicable

entering in July or September. Most degree courses run for two 40-week years, minimising disruptive career breaks for the many mature students. Over 60 per cent of the students are from overseas, but the proportion from Britain has been growing. Students have the option of a three-year degree in the humanities and other schools will be offering this option in 2010.

Even before the QAA audit, the two-year degree had been fully assessed by Professor John Clarke, a founder member of the university staff. Although hardly neutral, he concluded that the individual tuition given to Buckingham students, made possible by unusually generous staffing levels, allowed the system to succeed. He acknowledged that "undercapitalisation" had prevented the university achieving as much as it hoped, although only four universities spend as much per student on information technology.

Recent additions to the subjects on offer include a BSc in business enterprise and an MSc in international financial services. Masters programmes in biography, military history and decorative arts are now taught in London. The most striking development, however, is the postgraduate medical school launched in 2008 with a two-year MD in clinical medicine. The course is expected to attract overseas medical graduates who find it difficult to secure junior doctor posts as a result of recent Government restrictions.

Campus facilities have improved considerably in recent years, although they cannot compare with those available at traditional universities. Buckingham operates on two sites, within easy walking distance of each other. An academic centre containing computer suites, lecture theatres and student facilities provides a focal point that was missing previously.

The social scene is predictably quiet, given the size of the university and the workload, especially at weekends. There is a university cinema and the town is pretty with a good selection of pubs and restaurants. Milton Keynes or Oxford are near, although Buckingham has no rail station. A good bus service operates throughout the week with extra buses at weekends.

Undergraduate Fees and Bursaries

» Fees for UK/EU students:	£8,640*
» International student fees:	£19,677*
» Bursary on full grant:	n/a
» Bursary on partial grant:	n/a
» Scholarships based on circumstances or by competition.	
» For full details see the university's website: www.buckingham.ac.uk/study/fees	

*Duration of the degree course is 8 terms over two years.

Students

Undergraduates:	695	(45)
Postgraduates:	285	(30)
Mature students:	45.2%	
Overseas students:	61.5%	
Applications per place:	5.8	
From state-sector schools:	86.8%	
From working-class homes:	n/a	

For detailed information about fees, grants and bursaries and how they work, see chapter 7.

Accommodation

Number of places and costs refer to 2009–10
University-provided places: 465
Percentage catered: 0%
Self-catered accommodation: £929–£1,584 a term (4 terms)
Most first years are accommodated.
International students: same as above.
Contact: accommodation@buckingham.ac.uk

Buckinghamshire New University

Having waited a couple of years longer for university status than the group of higher education colleges promoted in 2005, Buckinghamshire New University has been making up for lost time. The first phase of a £200-million campus redevelopment was completed in 2009 and students have been responding enthusiastically to a portfolio of innovative courses and an attractive package of financial support and extra-curricular benefits for students. The 33 per cent rise in applications in 2009 was one of the biggest ever recorded by a UK university and even this was bettered by the 54 per cent increase at the start of 2010.

The redevelopment allows most students to be based at the main campus in High Wycombe – the exception being those taking nursing, who have moved into a new building in nearby Uxbridge. The new Gateway Building at High Wycombe has transformed the town-centre campus with improved teaching, social and administrative space. The complex includes a new sports hall, gym, treatment rooms and sports laboratory, which are available to the public as well as to students. At the same time, collaboration with two of the world's biggest IT companies is developing one of the most advanced student networks in UK higher education.

Sport is an important part of life at the new university, which partners the London Wasps rugby union team in a relationship which trades coaching for Bucks students for courses for Wasps players. But the university's main aim is to contribute to the social and economic life of the region, embracing workplace learning and close ties with local businesses. Employees of the bed company, Dreams, which is based in High Wycombe, take a new Foundation degree in retail management while at work, for example. Bucks has also won awards for its training of commercial pilots and its courses for music industry management. Other Foundation degrees include one for the motorsport industry and another in "protective security management".

There are more than 9,000 full and part-time students, 77 per cent of whom are taking first degrees and 45 per cent of whom are over 25. Nearly 60 per cent of the students are female. Academic departments are divided into two faculties: Design, Media and Management, and Society and Health. The extensive nursing provision has growing links with the Imperial College London Healthcare Trust, including a joint appointment designed to promote innovation. Only 26 staff were entered for the 2008 Research Assessment Exercise – half of them in art and design, which registered the only world-leading research. However, an institutional

Queen Alexandra Road
High Wycombe
Buckinghamshire
HP11 2JZ

0800 0565 660 (enquiries)
advice@bucks.ac.uk
www.bucks.ac.uk
www.bucksstudent.com

The Times Rankings
Overall Ranking: **112**

Student satisfaction:	=105	(69%)
Research quality:	=107	(0.1)
Entry standards:	108	(207)
Student–staff ratio:	96	(20.5)
Services & facilities/student:	61	(£1,283)
Expected completion rate:	91	(77.9%)
Good honours:	112	(43.8%)
Graduate prospects:	112	(45.7%)

audit expressed "broad confidence" in academic standards.

The projected dropout rate for undergraduates entering in 2007 rose to 14.5 per cent, considerably lower than at most comparable institutions and around 1.5 percentage points better than the national average for its subjects and entry qualifications. Nor was this achieved by neglecting the Government's widening participation agenda: almost all the entrants are from state schools or colleges, and nearly 40 per cent are from working-class homes.

The university has a particular focus on student support, devoting more than a third of its fee income to bursaries – one of the biggest proportions in England. In 2009–10, all full-time UK undergraduates (apart from nursing students, who are eligible for Government bursaries) received an annual, non means-tested £500 cash award. In addition, the Big Deal scheme offers free entry to all entertainment events, free participation in competitive sport and a programme of extra-curricular activities such as lessons in cookery and motor mechanics, as well as course-related materials. The university also pays student representatives.

One disappointment has been consistently low scores in the National Student Survey, which has left Bucks in the bottom ten for the last three years. The extensive building work on the main campus may have been a factor. Its own annual survey, carried out by independent academics, has been more complimentary. Beyond the campus, High Wycombe might not be an iconic student destination, but it has the usual range of pubs and clubs for a medium-sized town and central London is only 40 minutes away by train. The university has opened an art gallery in the main shopping centre to showcase students' work, as part of its efforts to maintain a strong relationship with the town.

Undergraduate Fees and Bursaries
» Fees for UK/EU students: £3,290
» International student fees: £8,100–£8,850
» Bursary on full grant: household income up to £25K: £500
» Bursary on partial grant: £500
» Scholarships based on circumstances or by competition.
» For full details see the university's website: www.bucks.ac.uk/courses/undergraduate/fees_bursaries.aspx

Students
Undergraduates:	**4,600**	**(4,165)**
Postgraduates:	**220**	**(480)**
Mature students:	**32.7%**	
Overseas students:	**12.5%**	
Applications per place:	**3.1**	
From state-sector schools:	**96.9%**	
From working-class homes:	**39.7%**	

For detailed information about fees, grants and bursaries and how they work, see chapter 7.

Accommodation
Number of places and costs refer to 2009–10
University-provided places: 780
Percentage catered: 0%
Self-catered costs: a week: £80–£105 a week (42 or 44 weeks)
First-year students cannot be guaranteed accommodation.
Residential restrictions apply.
International students: priority allocation for first years.
Contact: accom@bucks.ac.uk

University of Cambridge

Cambridge already has the highest entry standards of any UK university and, having become the first institution announce its intention to use the new A* grade for admissions, the standard offer for entry in 2011 will be AAA* at A level. The only good news for applicants is that, for most degrees, the top grade can come in any subject. The bad news is that there will still be additional tests, such as Cambridge's own STEP papers, in a number of subjects.

Until 2001, Cambridge had also enjoyed an unbroken run at the top of *The Times* league table, and even now it is practically inseparable from first-placed Oxford. The university produced the best results in the 2008 Research Assessment Exercise and the university still tops far more of our subject tables than any of its rivals. Nearly a third of its research was considered world-leading and over 70 per cent was rated in the top two categories.

Traditionally supreme in the sciences, where it is heads the field in the QS World University Rankings, Cambridge has also strengthened the arts and social sciences. Cambridge has been in the top three overall every year that the rankings have been published and was second in 2009.

At first, Cambridge students did not respond in sufficient numbers for the university to be included in the National Student Survey. But the 2009 results put Cambridge second in the UK, with undergraduates in anthropology, politics, archaeology, psychology and sociology particularly satisfied. The tripos system was a forerunner of the currently fashionable modular degree, allowing students to change subjects (within limits) midway through their courses. Students receive a classification for each of the two parts of their degree.

More students now come from state schools than the independent sector – a trend the university is keen to continue – but the proportion of working-class undergraduates remains low, at only 12.6 per cent. Summer schools, student visits and, in some colleges, sympathetic selection procedures, are helping to attract more applications from comprehensive schools and further education colleges.

The application system has been simplified slightly, with candidates no longer required to complete an initial Cambridge form, as well as their UCAS form. However, they are still sent the Supplementary Application Questionnaire, after they have submitted their UCAS form, covering the applicant's academic experience in more detail.

A lively alternative prospectus, available from the students' union, used to say there was no such thing as Cambridge University, just a collection of colleges. Where

The Old Schools
Trinity Lane
Cambridge CB2 1TN

01223 333308 (admissions)
admissions@cam.ac.uk
www.cam.ac.uk
www.cusu.cam.ac.uk

The Times Rankings
Overall Ranking: **2**

Student satisfaction:	=1	(85%)
Research quality:	1	(4.3)
Entry standards:	1	(547)
Student–staff ratio:	6	(11.6)
Services & facilities/student:	3	(£2,635)
Expected completion rate:	1	(98.6%)
Good honours:	2	(87.3%)
Graduate prospects:	4	(82.3%)

applications are concerned, this is still true, as it is to some extent socially. Making the right choice of college is crucial, both to maximise the chances of winning a place and to ensure an enjoyable three years if you are successful. Applicants can take pot luck with an open application if they prefer not to opt for a particular college. But, though the statistics show that this route is equally successful, only a minority takes it. Most teaching is now university-based, especially in the sciences, and a shift of emphasis towards the centre has been taking place more generally. The trend may accelerate if a £1-billion funding appeal to mark the university's 800th anniversary, in 2009, is successful. It had reached £940 million early in 2010.

Cambridge boasts numerous successful partnerships with the private sector, several of which benefit undergraduates as well as researchers. The university was also chosen for a Government-sponsored partnership with the Massachusetts Institute of Technology to promote entrepreneurship and, more recently, was selected to host one of five Academic Health Science Centres to lead biomedical innovation.

Such is the scale of development that almost £500-million worth of building is either planned or under construction. The university is looking to the outskirts of the city to expand. The West Cambridge site will take a mixture of teaching and research buildings, and there are plans for more on green-belt land further north. In the long term, up to three new colleges could be built, but there will be few extra places for undergraduates in the foreseeable future.

With around four applicants for each place – fewer still if you choose your subject carefully – the competition for places appears less intense than at the popular civic universities, but the real difference is that nine out of ten entrants have at least three A grades at A level. The pressure does not end there: the amount of high-quality work to be crammed into eight-week terms can prove a strain, although the projected dropout rate of 1.4 per cent is the lowest at any university offering conventional degrees.

Undergraduate Fees and Bursaries
- Fees for UK/EU students: £3,290
- International student fees: £10,752–£14,073 £26,028 (medicine)
- Bursary on full grant: household income up to £25K: £3,400
- Bursary on partial grant: household income up to £50K: sliding scale £3,150–£50.
- Scholarships based on circumstances or by competition.
- For full details see the university's website: www.cam.ac.uk/admissions/undergraduate/finance

Students
Undergraduates:	11,910	(3,815)
Postgraduates:	5,615	(1,480)
Mature students:	4.8%	
Overseas students:	13.2%	
Applications per place:	4.6	
From state-sector schools:	59.3%	
From working-class homes:	12.6%	

Accommodation
See chapter 12 for information about individual colleges.

For detailed information about fees, grants and bursaries and how they work, see chapter 7.

Canterbury Christ Church University

This former Church of England college started branching out well before university status arrived in 2005. There is a network of campuses right across Kent, the most populous county in England but, until recently, one of the most sparsely provided with higher education. At the purpose-built campus at Broadstairs, for example, the university offers subjects as diverse as commercial music, digital media, photography, and child and youth studies. There is also an imposing country house outside Tunbridge Wells, mainly for postgraduates, as well as a newly expanded Medway site at Chatham that is shared with Greenwich and Kent universities, and a University Centre at Folkestone, offering performing and visual arts, also developed in partnership with Greenwich. The Medway campus offers education and health programmes at a variety of levels, from foundation degree to postgraduate.

The majority of the 17,000 students, however, are at the university's Canterbury headquarters. The main campus, which dates from 1962, is a few minutes' walk from the city centre, but the university has several buildings in other parts of Canterbury. A £35-million library and student services centre, with specialist teaching and IT facilities, opened in 2009. It includes a café, two garden terraces, an atrium and multipurpose floor space for public events, conferences, exams, teaching and exhibitions. A new sport centre, a short walk from the main campus, also opened in the same year, while planning permission has been given for a purpose-built music venue to open in 2012.

The Church of England link was underlined with the installation of the Archbishop of Canterbury as the university's Chancellor in 2005. Religious studies is available as a single-honours degree or as part of the modular scheme, which covers the arts and humanities, business and management, social and applied sciences, education, and health and social care. The large health and teacher training programmes make the university the largest provider of higher education to the public services in Kent. Canterbury is one of the few Grade 1 providers of teacher training offering the full range of courses from early years to primary, secondary, further and higher education. Sport and exercise science and history are other degrees that recruit strongly.

The results from successive National Student Surveys have been good. Geography registered a rare 100 per cent satisfaction rate in 2009, when architecture, history and sports science also produced particularly good scores. Canterbury Christ Church was one of the new "teaching-led" universities, but still

North Holmes Road
Canterbury CT1 1QU

01227 782900 (prospectus)
admissions@canterbury.ac.uk
www.canterbury.ac.uk
www.ccsu.co.uk

The Times Rankings
Overall Ranking: **97**

Student satisfaction:	=79	(74%)
Research quality:	=95	(0.2)
Entry standards:	=94	(247)
Student–staff ratio:	=94	(20.3)
Services & facilities/student:	108	(£919)
Expected completion rate:	77	(80.5%)
Good honours:	=102	(49.2%)
Graduate prospects:	60	(64.7%)

entered staff in seven areas in the 2008 Research Assessment Exercise. The best grades came in education and music, both of which had 10 per cent of their work assessed as world-leading.

The subject mix, with an emphasis on health subjects and education, means that seven out of ten students are female. Nearly 97 per cent of the undergraduates are state-educated and over 39 per cent come from working-class homes. The dropout rate of 16 per cent is above average for the university's courses and entry qualifications. The university's applications were up by more than 30 per cent at the start of 2010, the fourth successive increase. Graduates' job prospects are relatively good, with three-quarters going straight into employment and only 4 per cent unemployed six months after completing a degree.

All campuses are interconnected by a high speed regional data network, providing access to online teaching and learning materials, the student web portal and email. A new student and staff support service – i-zone – was introduced in 2009, which can be accessed online or via staff at the i-zone desks. The new Drill Hall Library at Medway provides 90,000 items, 400 computers and 250 study spaces.

Social and sports facilities naturally vary between the campuses, although the students' union is present on all of them. The new sports centre in Canterbury includes a fitness suite and a hall big enough for eight badminton courts. There is also a tennis court and netball court on campus and the university also has facilities at Polo Farm Sports Club close to the city. Residential accommodation is not plentiful, but first years are given priority. The pressure is eased to some extent because nearly 60 per cent of the students come from Kent, many of them among the 7,600 taking part-time courses.

Undergraduate Fees and Bursaries
» Fees for UK/EU students: £3,290
» International student fees: £8,880–£9,130
» Bursary on full grant: household income up to £25K: £880
» Bursary on partial grant: household income up to £50K: partial award on a sliding scale.
» Scholarships based on circumstances or by competition.
» For full details see the university's website: www.canterbury.ac.uk/support/student-support-services/students/finance/index.asp

Students
Undergraduates:	7,665	(4,955)
Postgraduates:	1,465	(2,670)
Mature students:	25.7%	
Overseas students:	8.1%	
Applications per place:	4.3	
From state-sector schools:	96.5%	
From working-class homes:	39.2%	

For detailed information about fees, grants and bursaries and how they work, see chapter 7.

Accommodation
Number of places and costs refer to 2010–11
University-provided places: 1,450
Percentage catered: 0%
Self-catered costs: £80–£105 a week.
Accommodation guaranteed for first years if conditions are met.
International students: as above.
Contact: accommodation@canterbury.ac.uk
www.canterbury.ac.uk/support/accommodation

Cardiff University

Cardiff is long established as the front-runner in Welsh higher education and a leading player in the UK and beyond. It is a member of the Russell Group of 20 research-led universities and has two Nobel Laureates on its staff. No longer a member of the University of Wales, Cardiff now has more than 27,000 students and nearly 6,000 staff, making it a match for most of its peers in teaching and research. A third of the students come from Wales, but the 3,000 from overseas testify to Cardiff's international reputation.

The 2008 Research Assessment Exercise rated almost 60 per cent of the work submitted in the top two categories, with 33 of the 34 subject areas containing some world-leading research. Journalism, media and cultural studies, English, city and regional planning, and business produced the best results.

Teaching quality is also highly rated, with courses accredited by 42 different professional bodies. An audit by the Quality Assurance Agency complimented the university on its "powerful academic vision and well-developed and effectively articulated mission to achieve excellence in teaching and research". Student support services, including counselling facilities and the help offered to dyslexics, were among the features singled out for praise.

Cardiff has done well in every edition of the National Student Survey, finishing just outside the top 30 in 2009. Genetics produced a rare 100 per cent satisfaction rate and there were high scores, too, in geography and environmental science, communication, linguistics and ophthalmics. Cardiff is the first Welsh university to be awarded the Frank Buttle Trust Quality Mark which recognises support for looked after children in higher education.

Many full-time degrees share a common first year, and the modular system of courses makes undergraduate study flexible thereafter. Recent additions at degree level include electronic and communication engineering, medical pharmacology, marine geoscience, and politics and international relations, as well as an MMath degree.

The university occupies a significant part of the civic complex around Cathays Park in the Welsh capital. The five healthcare schools at the Heath Park campus share a 53-acre site with the University Hospital of Wales. In recent years, there has been major investment in new buildings and equipment, and extensive refurbishment. Almost £30 million was invested in brain and body imaging facilities at the medical school. Library services are being transformed in order to improve access to resources, increase the range of electronic resources, extend self-service provision and improve the environment for the study of rare collections. The

Cardiff
Wales CF10 3XQ

029 2087 4455 (enquiries)
enquiry@cardiff.ac.uk
www.cardiff.ac.uk
www.cardiffstudents.com

The Times Rankings
Overall Ranking: **34**

Student satisfaction:	=46	(77%)
Research quality:	=33	(2.1)
Entry standards:	25	(392)
Student–staff ratio:	=28	(14.9)
Services & facilities/student:	54	(£1,348)
Expected completion rate:	17	(93.4%)
Good honours:	33	(69.0%)
Graduate prospects:	27	(72.8%)

School of Optometry and Vision Sciences moved into a £21-million building in 2007 and a new Medical School building opened in 2008. There are also plans for a new Medical Education Centre on the Heath Park campus.

A new IT working environment gives students online access to information about their studies and social life, from reading lists and timetables to social events and networking groups. Other recent developments include the establishment of the International Academy of Voice, providing individual training for opera stars of the future, while the School of Earth, Ocean and Planetary Sciences has invested in its own research vessel for a programme of research and teaching voyages. In 2009, Cardiff Business School launched a state-of-the-art trading room which allows students to gain the practical skills needed for life at the Stock Exchange.

With nearly 5,200 study bedrooms, the university can accommodate all first years. Rents are among the lowest in the UK, according to a National Union of Students survey.

Entry requirements have been rising, despite recent expansion, and the graduate employment record is good. The demand for places was static at the start of 2010, but Cardiff remained among the top 20 for total applications. The university has been bucking the national trend with increases in applications in science, technology, engineering and maths. One undergraduate in seven comes from an independent school, but still more than one in five have a working-class background. The projected dropout rate has fluctuated over recent years, and in the latest survey dropped back down to 6 per cent from 9 per cent.

The city of Cardiff is popular with students. The main residential site at Talybont boasts a "sports village", and there is also a city-centre fitness suite and a sports ground available to students. The university is continuing to update its sports facilities across the three sites, one being an upgrade of the floodlit grass training pitch to a new 3G rubber crumb synthetic pitch.

Undergraduate Fees and Bursaries

- » Fees for UK/EU students: £3,290
- » International student fees: £10,100–£12,950 £23,500 (medicine)
- » Bursary on full grant: household income up to £25K: £1,000
- » Bursary on partial grant: household income up to £50K: sliding scale £500–£350.
- » Scholarships based on circumstances or by competition.
- » For full details see the university's website: www.cardiff.ac.uk/for/prospective/ug/scholarships/index.html

Students			Accommodation
Undergraduates:	**16,245**	**(4,085)**	Number of places and costs refer to 2009–10
Postgraduates:	**3,805**	**(3,805)**	University-provided places: 5,172
Mature students:	**11.0%**		Percentage catered: 5.4%
Overseas students:	**8.2%**		Catered costs: £73–£88 a week.
Applications per place:	**6.3**		Self-catered costs: £64–£88 a week.
From state-sector schools:	**85.2%**		All first years (except Clearing students) are guaranteed
From working-class homes:	**22.9%**		accommodation if conditions are met.
			Policy for international students: as above
			Contact: residences@cardiff.ac.uk

For detailed information about fees, grants and bursaries and how they work, see chapter 7.

University of Wales Institute, Cardiff (UWIC)

The University of Wales Institute in Cardiff has an international reputation for sport, but other areas are also benefiting from a £50-million programme of improvements. The £20-million Cardiff School of Management will open on the Llandaff campus for the start of the 2010–11 academic year, offering improved facilities for business, hospitality and tourism. A Food Industry Centre opened in 2009 and the Cyncoed campus has a new student centre with a nightclub and all the normal catering and leisure facilities.

UWIC's scores slipped slightly in the 2009 National Student Survey, but it was the most improved university in Wales and had one of the biggest rises in the UK in the previous year. Accounting, food studies and social work produced good scores, but sociology students were among the least satisfied in any subject in the UK. There was a 12 per cent increase in applications at the start of 2010, but even that was well below the UK average.

Two thirds of UWIC's 11,000 students are Welsh, half of them from Cardiff or the Vale of Glamorgan. Some 95 per cent attended state schools and nearly 40 per cent come from working-class homes. The dropout rate had been improving and is still better than at the other new universities in Wales, but the latest figure of more than 16 per cent is higher than the UK average for UWIC's subjects and entry grades.

UWIC is one of Britain's leading centres for university sport, with team performances to match some excellent facilities. In recent years, the Institute has had British university champions in gymnastics, trampolining, athletics, rugby union, rugby league, boxing, squash, archery, weightlifting and judo. More than 300 past or present students are internationals in 30 sports, world and Olympic champions among them. The £7-million National Indoor Athletics Centre is UWIC's pride and joy, but other facilities are also of high quality.

Academically, the large Cardiff School of Art and Design is the star performer, with 70 per cent of the work submitted to the 2008 Research Assessment Exercise rated either world-leading or internationally excellent. Sport also registered some world-leading research and all six teacher training courses are rated as excellent by Estyn, the school inspectorate. UWIC also did well in the Higher Education Academy's satisfaction survey of postgraduate research students.

Entrance requirements are generally modest, but the menu of largely vocational courses means that many students come with qualifications other than A levels. About a quarter are mature students and more than 1,000 are international students from 125 different countries. Many are among the

---

Cardiff Institute
Western Avenue
Cardiff CF5 2YB

029 2041 6044 (enquiries)
uwicinfo@uwic.ac.uk
www.uwic.ac.uk
www.uwicsu.co.uk

The Times Rankings
Overall Ranking: **=67**

Student satisfaction:	=59	(76%)
Research quality:	=77	(0.4)
Entry standards:	=85	(260)
Student–staff ratio:	=91	(20.0)
Services & facilities/student:	44	(£1,432)
Expected completion rate:	=66	(82.5%)
Good honours:	82	(54.5%)
Graduate prospects:	=71	(61.1%)

23 per cent postgraduates – the largest proportion in Wales. UWIC courses are also taught at partner colleges in Kuala Lumpur, Singapore and Dhaka.

The four Cardiff sites are all within three miles of the city centre. The Cyncoed campus, which houses education and sport, is the centre of activity, particularly for first-year students. As well as the new student centre, the athletics centre is there, together with a multitude of outdoor facilities and also the Welsh Sports Centre for the Disabled. Student facilities, including the Institute's largest bar, have been upgraded recently. A £2-million learning centre opened in 2005; the IT suite has 250 computers available 24 hours a day.

Howard Gardens is the home of fine art, while the Llandaff campus hosts design, engineering, food science and health courses. A £3-million student centre at Llandaff, which opened in 2003, includes a dyslexia support unit among a number of advice and representation services, and a learning centre with more than 300 computers.

Students tend to like Cardiff as a city, and UWIC's enterprising union does its best to make their time there as lively as possible. It owns a nightclub and bar in the city centre to add to the campus choices. During term-time, the UWIC Rider bus service links all the campuses with other parts of Cardiff at a cost to students of £5.26 a week in 2009-10. The 929 UWIC hall places, plus rooms in privately run residences, accommodate most first years, but recent expansion means that some have to rely on the private sector. UWIC is the only university to have been awarded the Government's Charter Mark four times, the judges commenting particularly on the level of satisfaction among students.

Undergraduate Fees and Bursaries

» Fees for UK/EU students: £3,290
» International student fees: £8,000–£9,200
£11,200 (podiatry)
» Bursary on full grant: household income up to £25K: household income up to £18.3K: £500.*
» Bursary on partial grant: household income up to £39.3K: £300.*
» Scholarships based on circumstances or by competition.
» For full details see the university's website: www3.uwic.ac.uk/english/studyatuwic/finance

*Figures for 2009-10

Students

Undergraduates:	7,215	(825)
Postgraduates:	1,220	(1,785)
Mature students:	25.9%	
Overseas students:	10.1%	
Applications per place:	3.8	
From state-sector schools:	94.4%	
From working-class homes:	38.4%	

For detailed information about fees, grants and bursaries and how they work, see chapter 7.

Accommodation

Number of places and costs refer to 2010–11
University-provided places: 929
Percentage catered: 34%
Catered cost: £111–£121 a week.
Self-catered costs: £76.50–£95.00 a week.
First-year students have no guarantee, terms and conditions apply.
International students: accommodation is reserved, subject to availability and if conditions are met.
Contact: accomm@uwic.ac.uk

University of Central Lancashire (UCLan)

A big university at the heart of England's newest city, only six English institutions have a bigger teaching budget than UCLan. A total of £120 million has been spent on the modern, town-centre campus, as the university has doubled in size – and still the building continues. The new £5-million dental school was one of the first to open in over a century, while the £15-million Media Factory, with facilities for music, theatre, dance, film, photography and media studies, has prompted a surge in applications for arts and fashion courses. The campus boasts the largest 3D lecture theatre in Europe and the library has been upgraded. A new £12.5 million facility for forensic science courses is due for completion in 2011.

An extended and refurbished students' union boasts one of the largest student venues in the country, and well-equipped new buildings have opened recently for science, health and business subjects. A new Futures Centre brings together advice on careers and work placements, employability and enterprise course electives, business start-up and self-employment services. All students are encouraged to develop their CVs, and to draw on the experience of local employers and alumni. The university produces the most graduate business start-ups in the North West and is in the top five nationally. In a new development, UCLan students are being offered the opportunity to study a range of world languages, including Arabic, Chinese, Japanese and Russian.

Amid the expansion, the university has revamped its pioneering credit accumulation and transfer system, allowing undergraduates to mix and match from a menu of more than 3,000 courses. Electives are used to broaden the curriculum, so that up to 11 per cent of students' time is spent on subjects outside their normal range. The university has also launched two unusual scholarships: the Gilbertson Award, offering free postgraduate study to every UCLan undergraduate achieving a First; and the Internationalisation Bursary, giving students the opportunity to study or work abroad.

The former polytechnic has acquired a high reputation in some apparently unlikely fields. Astrophysics benefits from two observatories in Britain and a share in the Southern African Large Telescope. Following dentistry, the UK's first new architecture degree for ten years was launched in 2009. Linguistics and journalism produced the best results in the 2008 Research Assessment Exercise, when 17 areas contained work considered world-leading or internationally excellent. The university has since invested £10 million in ten research centres in areas as diverse as philosophy and nuclear science.

Preston
Lancashire PR1 2HE

01772 892400 (enquiries)
cenquiries@uclan.ac.uk
www.uclan.ac.uk
www.yourunion.co.uk

The Times Rankings
Overall Ranking: =69

Student satisfaction:	=46	(77%)
Research quality:	=77	(0.4)
Entry standards:	=82	(263)
Student–staff ratio:	=52	(17.0)
Services & facilities/student:	32	(£1,606)
Expected completion rate:	106	(73.9%)
Good honours:	101	(49.7%)
Graduate prospects:	73	(61.0%)

The Confucius Institute promotes and supports the development of Chinese language and culture throughout the North West region.

UCLan opened a £10-million campus in Burnley in 2009, in partnership with Burnley College, which already offers a number of the university's degree and Foundation degree courses. A new Centre for Outdoor Education has been developed at Llangollen, in north Wales, enabling the university to launch a degree in the subject. UCLan is one of only two universities to be awarded the Carbon Trust Standard and now runs modules in sustainability, as well as claiming to have the most solar panels of any UK university.

Scores in the National Student Survey have been steady, with engineering, journalism, maths, philosophy, physical geography, social policy and sports science all in the top ten for their subject in 2009. Over four out of ten Central Lancashire students come from working-class homes. A high proportion are local people in their twenties or thirties, many of whom come through the well-established lifelong learning networks run in colleges throughout the North West. No fewer than 14 per cent of the university's students are taught in colleges but, unlike some institutions involved in "franchising", Central Lancashire has won official praise for the quality of its external programmes. Applications were up by 37 per cent at the start of 2009, following an impressive increase in the previous year.

The social scene in Preston may not compare with Manchester or Liverpool, but neither do the security risks, and the cost of living is low. Both cities are within easy reach, and the student union's "Feel" club nights have won national recognition. UCLan commands great loyalty among its students.

Rents for the nearly 2,000 places in university accommodation are among the lowest in Britain and the 60-acre Preston Sports Arena has some of the best outdoor facilities in higher education. Work has started on a new £16 million indoor sports centre on campus, which is due for completion early 2011.

Undergraduate Fees and Bursaries
» Fees for UK/EU students: £3,290
» International student fees: £8,950–£9,500
» Bursary on full grant: household income up to £25K: £500 (£329 from Year 2).
» Bursary on partial grant: household income up to £60K: £500 (£329 from Year 2).
» Scholarships based on circumstances or by competition.
» For full details see the university's website: www.uclan.ac.uk/study/fees_and_finance/index.php

Students
Undergraduates:	**16,265**	(8,330)
Postgraduates:	**1,270**	(2,265)
Mature students:	**28.8%**	
Overseas students:	**10.2%**	
Applications per place:	**3.7**	
From state-sector schools:	**97.9%**	
From working-class homes:	**43.7%**	

For detailed information about fees, grants and bursaries and how they work, see chapter 7.

Accommodation
Number of places and costs refer to 2009–10
University-provided places: around 2,000
Percentage catered: 0%
Self-catered costs: £75.50 – £89.00 a week.
The Student Accommodation Service will assist all first years find suitable accommodation either in University owned/leased halls of residence, private sector registered halls, or shared houses.
International students: as above.
Contact: saccommodation@uclan.ac.uk

University of Chester

The picturesque Roman city of Chester is one of those places that outsiders probably always expected to have its own university. Indeed, William Gladstone was among the founders of the first Church of England teacher training college there in 1839. Although it took until 2005 for that college to achieve university status, it had been building up a solid reputation in a number of subjects beyond education. Applications were up by more than 30 per cent at the start of 2010, following a string of increases that has taken the demand for places far above that in pre-university days.

The main campus is only a short walk from the centre of Chester, a 32-acre site boasting manicured gardens and a number of new developments. A new students' union is just one of a stream of improvements, the latest of which is the purchase of historic County Hall in Chester, which from September 2010 will house the faculties of Health and Social Care and Education and Children's Services.

The Warrington campus, which has eight halls of residence, focuses on the creative industries and public services. It has seen the addition of state-of-the-art production facilities in collaboration with Granada Television and a new students' union. The university has also signed a partnership agreement with the BBC, which is intended to open up new employment opportunities in the media industry and develop new talent ahead of the transfer of parts of the corporation to Salford in 2011. The library has been extended to three times its original size and a business centre opened for students and local firms. The campus is expected to be the focus of future development to accommodate modest increases in student numbers.

Chester was among the top ten universities in the first National Student Survey but has since slipped out of the top 50. Archaeology, psychology, law and English all achieved good results in the 2009 survey. Chester was the first of the universities created in 2005 to be granted the power to award research degrees. Four of the ten subject areas entered for the 2008 Research Assessment Exercise contained at least some world-leading work. History was the most successful, with nearly half of its submission placed in the top two categories.

With 15,600 students, including part-timers, Chester is among the biggest of the new universities established in 2005. Over a quarter of undergraduates are mature students and two thirds are female. Nearly all are state-educated, and more than a third have working-class roots. The projected dropout rate of over 17 per cent is above the national average for the university's courses and entry standards in the latest statistics.

Parkgate Road
Chester CH1 4BJ

01244 512175 (admissions)
enquiries@chester.ac.uk
www.chester.ac.uk
www.chestersu.com

The Times Rankings
Overall Ranking: **83**

Student satisfaction:	=69	(75%)
Research quality:	=95	(0.2)
Entry standards:	=76	(268)
Student–staff ratio:	56	(17.5)
Services & facilities/student:	110	(£854)
Expected completion rate:	=88	(79.0%)
Good honours:	73	(56.7%)
Graduate prospects:	59	(65.6%)

About a third of the undergraduates take combined honours degrees and many courses of all types include a period of extended work experience. There is also a limited range of foundation degrees, mainly in health subjects but now including courses in business or leadership and management for RAF personnel. The Foundation degree in Muslim youth work is the first of its kind, as is one in mortuary science. Even the more traditional degrees have been designed to support the practical and vocational demands of the professions.

A student contract of the type that is likely to become commonplace elsewhere in the higher education sector sets out clear conditions on the offer of a place, as well as detailing the university's responsibilities. Students promise to "study diligently, and to attend promptly and participate appropriately at lectures, courses, classes, seminars, tutorials, work placements and other activities which form part of the programme." The university undertakes to deliver the student's programme, but leaves itself considerable leeway beyond that.

However, Chester offers considerable support and facilities for its students. It was the first UK university to receive the maximum five-star rating from the British Quality Foundation for its student support and guidance and its careers and employability departments. There are libraries on both sites and extensive sports facilities, especially on the main campus, catering partly for the large physical education programme. Most first years are offered one of the growing number of hall places, although there is not yet enough university accommodation to make this a guarantee. Student union facilities form the basis of the social scene on both campuses, but Chester has more to offer for those looking further afield.

Undergraduate Fees and Bursaries
» Fees for UK/EU students: £3,290
» International student fees: £7,614–£8,892
» Bursary on full grant: household income up to £25K: £1,000
» The university does not award bursaries for students on partial maintenance grants.
» Scholarships based on circumstances or by competition.
» For full details see the university's website: www.chester.ac.uk/campus-life/finance

Students
Undergraduates:	7,245	(3,025)
Postgraduates:	655	(2,560)
Mature students:	19.8%	
Overseas students:	1.8%	
Applications per place:	5.8	
From state-sector schools:	97.6%	
From working-class homes:	39.2%	

For detailed information about fees, grants and bursaries and how they work, see chapter 7.

Accommodation
Number of places and costs refer to 2010–11
University-provided places: approx 1,000
Percentage catered: 46%
Catered costs: £66.85–£132.30 a week.
Self-catered costs: £66.15–£89.95 a week.
First years cannot be guaranteed accommodation.
International students: guaranteed accommodation if they apply by the advertised date.
Contact: www.chester.ac.uk/campus-life/accommodation

University of Chichester

Chichester is the smallest of the nine universities created in 2005, but it features consistently among the leading modern universities in league tables. It headed the post-1992 foundations in the National Student Survey published in 2009, finishing in the top 20 overall, with drama, education, English and history all showing very high levels of satisfaction. *The Times Higher Education* student experience survey also rated Chichester the top modern university. Similarly good results in 2008 helped produce a big rise in applications, but even this was been outdone by a 27 per cent increase at the start of 2010.

The university traces its history back to 1839, when the college that subsequently bore his name was founded in memory of William Otter, the education-minded Bishop of Chichester. It became a teacher training college for women, who still account for two thirds of the places. Two further stages preceded university status – twenty years as the West Sussex Institute of Higher Education, following an amalgamation with the nearby Bognor Regis College of Education, and then seven as University College Chichester. The Chichester campus – now the larger of two – continues to carry the Bishop Otter name, signifying a continuing link with the Church of England.

The two faculties operate on both sites, one covering business, arts and the humanities; the other sport, social sciences and education. The portfolio of some 300 courses ranges from adventure education to humanistic counselling, fine art and the psychology of sport and exercise. The PE teacher training course is the largest in the country – the university now trains one in five PE teachers in England – and is highly rated by Ofsted. Sport was the only area in which the university registered any world-leading work in the 2008 Research Assessment Exercise, but history and drama, dance and performing arts also produced good results.

The Alexandra Theatre, in Bognor, is used as a base for the musical theatre programme and there are links, too, with the Chichester Festival Theatre. The Mathematics Centre, at Bognor, has an international reputation, working with over 30 countries as well as teaching the university's own students. It has become a focal point for curriculum development in Britain and elsewhere. Chichester runs short courses for education ministries in countries as diverse as Bhutan, Russia and the Seychelles.

Graduate employment rates have been good for a number of years, with only 4 per cent thought to be jobless in the last survey published, but a relatively high proportion staring off in non-graduate work pushes Chichester down our table on this measure. About 22 per cent of the 5,000 students are

Bishop Otter Campus
College Lane
Chichester
W. Sussex PO19 6PE

01243 816002 (admissions)
admissions@chi.ac.uk
www.chi.ac.uk
www.chisu.org

The Times Rankings
Overall Ranking: **53**

Student satisfaction:	=9	(82%)
Research quality:	=95	(0.2)
Entry standards:	=73	(270)
Student–staff ratio:	=36	(15.3)
Services & facilities/student:	=88	(£1,105)
Expected completion rate:	37	(87.0%)
Good honours:	99	(50.2%)
Graduate prospects:	80	(59.9%)

over 21 on entry. Almost all are state educated and, despite the comfortable south coast location, the proportions from working-class homes and areas of low participation in higher education are both close to the national average for the university's courses and entry grades. The projected dropout rate has fallen to under 8 per cent in the latest survey, approaching half the benchmark figure. The university runs summer taster sessions and has a series of partnerships with schools in the Channel Islands and Sussex to encourage a broader intake. Courses are also run in collaboration with Isle of Wight College, where fees were pegged at £1,200 in 2009–10.

Both of the university's campuses are within ten minutes' walk of the sea and the 647 residential places are roughly equally divided between them. There is a university bus service linking the two and student union bars at each. Sports facilities are good and competitive teams surprisingly successful for such a small university. The university has been chosen to provide training facilities for competitors in athletics, boxing, road cycling and table tennis before the 2012 Olympic Games. The bid was based on Chichester's expertise in sports science, as well as its facilities.

The small cathedral city of Chichester is best known as a yachting venue and, while Bognor's days as a leading holiday resort are well in the past, it is said to have the longest stretch of coastline in the south where all types of watersports are available. Both locations offer a good supply of private housing and some student-oriented bars. Much of the surrounding countryside has been designated an area of outstanding natural beauty.

Undergraduate Fees and Bursaries

» Fees for UK/EU students: £3,290
» International student fees: £8,500–£9,700
» Bursary on full grant: household income up to £25K: £1,077*
» Bursary on partial grant: household income up to £50K: sliding scale £1,026–£256.*
» Scholarships based on circumstances or by competition.
» For full details see the university's website: www.chi.ac.uk/studentfinance

*Figures for 2009–10

Students

Undergraduates:	**3,185**	(705)
Postgraduates:	**310**	(805)
Mature students:	**21.8%**	
Overseas students:	**3.1%**	
Applications per place:	**5.2**	
From state-sector schools:	**96.7%**	
From working-class homes:	**34.5%**	

For detailed information about fees, grants and bursaries and how they work, see chapter 7.

Accommodation

Number of places and costs refer to 2009–10
University-provided places: 647
Percentage catered: 66.5%
Catered costs: £107 (twin) – £142 (single, en suite) a week (37 or 40 weeks).
Self-catered costs: £83.75 (shared) – £129.50 (en suite) a week (37 or 40 weeks).
First years are accommodated on a first come, first served basis.
International students: as above.
Contact: www.chi.ac.uk/accomm/index.cfm

City University London

Having marketed itself as the "international university in the heart of London", City added the name of the capital to its title to make the most of its greatest asset. Students come from more than 150 different countries to study on the borders of the financial district. Once a college of advanced technology, City now has roughly a quarter its students taking business courses, another quarter health and community subjects and the remaining half law, computing, mathematics, engineering, journalism, and the arts.

The university has maintained its links with business, industry and the professions, reaping the benefits with consistently good graduate employment figures. The university's graduates play their part, with nearly 2,000 of them offering practical help to current students through an online careers network. Courses have a practical edge, and many of the staff hold professional, as well as academic, qualifications.

Student numbers doubled during the 1990s, partly due to the incorporation of colleges of radiography and nursing and midwifery. There are now more than 21,000 students, including large contingents of postgraduates and part-timers. City is among the most popular universities in London, with nearly eight applications for each undergraduate place. There was an 18 per cent rise in applications at the start of 2010, the latest in a series of increases.

A number of interdisciplinary centres have been launched more recently, designed to increase collaborative teaching and research, as well as to build stronger links between industry and academia. These include the Centre for Creativity in Professional Practice, the Centre for Information Leadership, the Centre for Performance at Work and the City Collaborative Transport Hub.

Development is continuing at the university's Islington headquarters. Some £20 million went into an impressive new building for the School of Social Sciences, the students' union has been refurbished and £12 million invested in a new School of Arts with well-equipped recording and television studios. The School of Engineering and Mathematical Sciences added four new interactive classrooms and a modern electronics laboratory in 2009, and the library has been renovated at a cost of £2.3 million, giving students more space, upgraded technology and better support.

The most ambitious project, however, was the £42-million Cass Business School, which opened in 2002 and is one of City's great strengths. It has 3,000 students and is ranked among the top 50 business schools in the world. Based in the heart of the financial district, it has built up an impressive cadre of

Northampton Square
London EC1V 0HB

020 7040 5060
ugadmissions@city.ac.uk
www.city.ac.uk
www.culsu.co.uk

The Times Rankings
Overall Ranking: **47**

Student satisfaction:	=97	(72%)
Research quality:	=48	(1.5)
Entry standards:	40	(340)
Student–staff ratio:	74	(18.6)
Services & facilities/student:	50	(£1,381)
Expected completion rate:	62	(82.8%)
Good honours:	38	(68.2%)
Graduate prospects:	10	(79.4%)

visiting practitioner lecturers who find it easy and convenient to visit. City has links with 50 European universities and many more further afield, and many students spend a year of their course abroad.

The university boosted its legal provision by incorporating the Inns of Court School of Law in 2001. The City Law School, which includes the university's original department, was the first in London to offer a "one-stop shop" for legal training, from undergraduate to professional courses.

City is also working with Queen Mary, University of London, in a range of subjects, starting with medicine and other health subjects, journalism and engineering. The two universities jointly host a national centre for teaching and learning in nursing and midwifery. Journalism is highly regarded and the university has launched the UK's first graduate school of journalism in new £12-million facilities. There is also a flourishing sub-degree programme for adults, which ranges from sitcom writing to e-business.

City also has a particularly high reputation in music, where it is associated with the Guildhall School of Music and Drama. Together with nursing and midwifery, music achieved the university's best results in the 2008 Research Assessment Exercise. Social work and social policy also produced good results. Like other universities in London, City has struggled to make an impression in the National Student Survey, finishing low down the table in 2009. Aerospace engineering and music received high marks for teaching, while finance and mathematics produced high overall satisfaction levels.

Official performance indicators show the dropout rate falling, although the projection of just over 15 per cent is still high for a traditional university. City has a good record among its peers for widening participation in higher education, with four out of ten undergraduates coming from working-class homes. The students' union is popular, but sports facilities are poor by current standards; the indoor sports centre is conveniently located.

Undergraduate Fees and Bursaries
» Fees for UK/EU students: £3,290
» International student fees: £8,900–£11,500
» Bursary on full grant: household income up to £25K: £770
» Bursary on partial grant: household income up to £30K: £360
» Scholarships based on circumstances or by competition.
» For full details see the university's website: www.city.ac.uk/study/money/undergraduate

Students
Undergraduates:	8,050	(6,625)
Postgraduates:	4,265	(2,785)
Mature students:	24.4%	
Overseas students:	15.6%	
Applications per place:	7.9	
From state-sector schools:	92.5%	
From working-class homes:	39.6%	

For detailed information about fees, grants and bursaries and how they work, see chapter 7.

Accommodation
Number of places and costs refer to 2010–11
University-provided places: 1,360
Percentage catered: 0%
Self-catered costs: £106–£198 a week.
Accommodation is guaranteed for first years if conditions are met.
Residential restrictions apply.
International students: preference is given to new overseas students.
Contact: accomm@city.ac.uk
www.city.ac.uk/studentcentre/housing

Coventry University

Coventry is still in the process of rejuvenating its campus with an investment of £160 million over ten years in its 33-acre campus close to the city centre, much of it going on student facilities. The showpiece turreted library cost £20 million and is almost entirely naturally ventilated and lit. The £5-million student centre, opened in 2006, contains everything from the accommodation and careers services to the finance and academic registry, as well as lounge space. Next on the list are a student enterprise centre, containing a new students' union and featuring a roof garden among its many facilities, and a new home for the faculty of engineering and computing.

The campus is now fully WiFi enabled and there are 2,400 PCs for student use. The university has already added other facilities, including more residential accommodation, a £7-million arts centre and a sports centre, during a decade in which student numbers doubled to more than 20,000.

Coventry traces its origins back to 1843 with the foundation of the College of Design and its links with the motor industry of the Midlands were reflected in its earlier title of Lanchester Polytechnic, named after a leading engineering figure. It has adopted an innovative approach to computer-assisted learning, supported by an expanded computer network. The university was chosen to house national centres of excellence in teaching for e-learning in health and social care, as well as in maths, and transport and product design.

The university has a focus on employment, which is reflected in a predominantly vocational curriculum. The Start-Up Café encourages business networking and local employers are engaging with the programme of work-based learning. The Add+vantage scheme is designed to help full time undergraduate students improve their employability whilst studying. Its modules cover a wide range of skills and help students gain work-related knowledge and prepare for a career.

The majority of students exercise their right to take "free-choice modules" that cover the full range of university provision, with IT skills and languages particularly popular. Coventry has been building up its portfolio of courses, introducing eye-catching degrees in subjects such as ethical hacking and network security, disaster management, forensic chemistry, criminology and boat design.

The 2009 National Student Survey showed 100 per cent satisfaction in human and social geography, with good scores in physical geography and environmental science, nutrition and physiology. But the overall score still left the university towards the bottom of the table. Research grades

Priory Street
Coventry CV1 5FB

024 7615 2222 (admissions)
studentenquiries@coventry.ac.uk
www.coventry.ac.uk
www.cusu.org

The Times Rankings
Overall Ranking: **84**

Student satisfaction:	=79	(74%)
Research quality:	=88	(0.3)
Entry standards:	=64	(274)
Student–staff ratio:	61	(17.9)
Services & facilities/student:	78	(£1,155)
Expected completion rate:	97	(76.4%)
Good honours:	48	(64.9%)
Graduate prospects:	61	(64.2%)

improved in the 2008 assessment exercise, when small amounts of world-leading work were recognised in seven of the sixteen areas in which the university made submissions. Art and design and electrical and electronic engineering produced the best results. Design benefits from a revolutionary £1.6-million digital modelling workshop, sponsored by the Bugatti Trust, which provides full-scale vehicle modelling facilities for undergraduates as well as researchers.

Among the initiatives to improve the student experience has been the introduction of tangible rewards for excellent teaching and further development of electronic learning. The Centre for Academic Writing offers advice on essays and theses, with group sessions and one-to-one appointments, while the Maths Support Centre includes a statistics advisory service and specialist support service for students with dyslexia.

Over 40 per cent of the undergraduates have working-class backgrounds, many from areas of low participation in higher education. Applications have been healthy and were up by 30 per cent – more than the national average – at the start of 2010, following a good year in 2009. The projected dropout rate fell back a little in the latest survey, and now stands at 19 per cent.

More than most universities, Coventry is a creature of its city, and the civic-minded approach of the university has created many town–gown links. The 20-acre Coventry University Technology Park has benefitted both the university and the city. It houses the TechnoCentre and the £3-million Enterprise Centre as well as the Coventry and Warwickshire New Technology Institute. The university's main buildings open out from the ruins of the bombed cathedral, as university and public facilities mingle in the city. Student residences are within easy walking distance of the campus and city centre. Students welcome the relatively low cost of living in Coventry, and, as at most modern universities, the student body encompasses a wide range of ages.

Undergraduate Fees and Bursaries

» Fees for UK/EU students: £3,290
» International student fees: £8,560–£9,100
» Bursary on full grant: household income up to £25K: £329
» Bursary on partial grant: household income up to £50K: £329
» Scholarships based on circumstances or by competition.
» For full details see the university's website: wwwm.coventry.ac.uk/studentlife/Pages/StudentFunding.aspx

Students

Undergraduates:	**12,055**	(3,990)
Postgraduates:	**2,160**	(1,910)
Mature students:	**24.6%**	
Overseas students:	**12.9%**	
Applications per place:	**3.9**	
From state-sector schools:	**97.2%**	
From working-class homes:	**40.8%**	

For detailed information about fees, grants and bursaries and how they work, see chapter 7.

Accommodation

Number of places and costs refer to 2010–11
University-provided places: 2,386
Percentage catered: 24.4%
Catered costs: £105 a week (10 meals).
Self-catered costs: £87–£136
First-year students are guaranteed housing provided conditions are met.
International students: as above.
Contact: accomm.ss@coventry.ac.uk;
www.coventry.ac.uk/cu/accommodation

University of Cumbria

One of the largest counties without a university of its own put that right through the amalgamation of a former teacher training college and an arts institute, with the addition of the two Cumbrian campuses of the University of Central Lancashire. The new University of Cumbria was divided between Carlisle, Penrith, Ambleside and Lancaster, as well as running a specialist teacher education centre in east London. There are also partnerships with the four further education colleges in the county to provide higher education locally.

The new university, which has more than 12,000 students, was finally established in 2007, after a series of false starts. It is the largest provider of higher education in Cumbria by a considerable margin and growing in popularity. Applications were up by 17 per cent at the start of 2010, following an increase of similar proportions in the previous year. However, these successes were tempered by financial problems, which led to plans to "mothball" the Ambleside campus and cut a number of courses.

The biggest of the component parts was the former St Martin's College, which was founded in Lancaster by the Church of England in 1964 to train teachers and expanded during the 1990s with the addition of a nursing college. It forms the new university's main base, a ten-minute walk from Lancaster town centre, with a modern library and excellent sports facilities, including a £2.5-million sports complex, gymnastics centre and fitness centre. The Ambleside campus, which has an outdoor studies centre and a new learning resources centre, was also part of St Martin's.

There are two main sites in Carlisle, the larger of which is in a parkland setting close to the River Eden. The second campus, closer to the city centre, boasts a new Learning Gateway, an innovative multi-media learning resource centre, and a sports centre with a four-court sports hall and well-equipped fitness room. The former Cumbria Institute of the Arts can trace its history in Carlisle back to 1822, eventually becoming the only specialist institute of the arts in North West England and one of only a small number of such institutions in the country. The creative arts are one of the main areas for development in the university's initial planning.

A review was under way as the *Guide* went to press into the future of the other main campus, at Newton Rigg, a mile outside Penrith. Acquired from the University of Central Lancashire, it is set in landscaped gardens overlooking the fells, and caters mainly for agriculture and forestry. A former agricultural college, it has broadened into related areas such as environmental management and other subjects not directly related to land-based industries. Courses

Fusehill Street
Carlisle
Cumbria CA1 2HH

01228 616234
contact via website
www.cumbria.ac.uk
www.thestudentsunion.org.uk

The Times Rankings
Overall Ranking: **78**

Student satisfaction:	=89	(73%)
Research quality:	=107	(0.1)
Entry standards:	=64	(274)
Student–staff ratio:	=33	(15.2)
Services & facilities/student:	81	(£1,148)
Expected completion rate:	=64	(82.6%)
Good honours:	97	(50.6%)
Graduate prospects:	=52	(67.2%)

include outdoor education and leadership, sport, forensic science and conservation biology. Library and learning resource facilities have been improved and residential accommodation expanded. There are also two farms, one adjacent to the campus and a working hill farm 15 miles away within the national park.

Cumbria had been planning a £160-million development of its estate, including a new campus in Carlisle, but these await the verdict of the review. The university will be anxious to maintain a "Cumbria-wide presence" and is not planning to close Newton Rigg. There are four faculties: arts, design and media; business, social sciences and sport; health, medical science and social care; and science and natural resources.

Cumbria made its debut in the lower reaches of *The Times* league table and made some progress, now being out of the bottom 30. However, the university was bottom of the initial rankings from the 2008 Research Assessment Exercise, recording only a small amount of world-leading research in theology, divinity and religious studies. There has been some improvement in National Student Survey, but the university remained close to the bottom 20 in 2009. Nursing, medical technology and other subjects allied to medicine produced the most satisfied students.

The early focus of the university has been on attracting more students from a region of low participation in higher education, as well as on serving the social and economic needs of the county. Almost all the undergraduates are from state schools and colleges and over 43 per cent are from working-class homes. The proportion from areas without a tradition of higher education is also well above the national average for the university's subjects and entry grades.

Undergraduate Fees and Bursaries
» Fees for UK/EU students: £3,290
» International student fees: £8,325
» Bursary on full grant: household income up to £25K: £1,100
» Bursary on partial grant: household income up to £50K: £500.
» Scholarships based on circumstances or by competition.
» For full details see the university's website: www.cumbria.ac.uk/FutureStudents/FeesFinance

Students
Undergraduates:	**5,205**	(5,210)
Postgraduates:	**1,075**	(1,615)
Mature students:	**30.3%**	
Overseas students:	**1.9%**	
Applications per place:	**3.3**	
From state-sector schools:	**98.0%**	
From working-class homes:	**43.7%**	

For detailed information about fees, grants and bursaries and how they work, see chapter 7.

Accommodation
Number of places and costs refer to 2009–10
University-provided places: 821
Percentage catered: 65%
Catered costs: £90.95–£103.95 (41 weeks).
Self-catered costs: £50–£82 a week.
First years are guaranteed housing if Cumbria is first choice.
International students: guaranteed halls accommodation if conditions are met.
Contact: www.cumbria.ac.uk/FutureStudents/Accommodation

De Montfort University

De Montfort was among a handful of universities to enjoy growth in applications of more than 50 per cent at the start of 2010, following a 14 per cent increase in 2009. Although the university benefited from the boom in applications for nursing and a change in deadlines for arts and design, there were increases across the board.

An emphasis on research paid off spectacularly for De Montfort in the 2008 official assessments, when the university achieved the best results of any post-1992 university. Some 43 per cent of the work submitted was rated world-leading or internationally excellent. Almost all the subject areas contained some world-leading research and in the case of English language and literature the proportion reached an outstanding 40 per cent. Communication and media studies and drama, dance and performing arts also produced excellent results.

Accolades in the previous Research Assessment Exercise helped to bring in annual research income of about £10 million a year in external research grants and contracts. The university has 1,500 staff engaged in research and 450 research degree students. Much of the successful work took place in the Institute of Creative Technologies, which acts as a catalyst for research that defies the traditional boundaries of computer science, the digital arts and humanities, and is already exciting the interest of the business world.

Another £3.7 million was spent on creative technology studios, which feature video, audio and radio production suites, recording studios and laboratories with the latest broadcast and audio analysis technology. A Performance Arts Centre for Excellence (PACE) had already opened, allowing the university to deliver innovative teaching for students of dance, drama and music technology.

Once a network of campuses, De Montfort is concentrating its efforts on its original base in Leicester. The university is putting more than £100 million into consolidating a more manageable estate, some of it provided by the city council and local businesses. There are now only two campuses, both in Leicester itself, following the relocation of health and life sciences to the university's headquarters. Another 11 colleges are associates, linked into the university's network and offering its courses. A formal agreement commits the colleges, which stretch from north Oxfordshire to Liverpool, to work with each other as well as with De Montfort.

Campus developments include the diversion of part of the ring road to allow the university to open up the 15th-century Magazine Gateway building, which will become the focal point of a university quarter with public open spaces and new links to the city centre. A £35-million building for

The Gateway
Leicester LE1 9BH

08459 454647 (enquiries)
enquiry@dmu.ac.uk
www.dmu.ac.uk
www.demontfortstudents.com

The Times Rankings
Overall Ranking: **=57**

Student satisfaction:	=22	(79%)
Research quality:	=60	(0.6)
Entry standards:	=94	(247)
Student–staff ratio:	=47	(16.3)
Services & facilities/student:	92	(£1,078)
Expected completion rate:	70	(82.0%)
Good honours:	94	(51.5%)
Graduate prospects:	44	(69.4%)

business and law, which opened in 2009, is at its heart. The 24-hour library has been remodelled with wireless networks and rooms equipped with audio visual and IT facilities.

The professional accounting courses were awarded "premier" status in a worldwide accreditation scheme, and the university houses a national teaching centre for drama, dance and theatre studies. Recent results in the National Student Survey have seen a big improvement on the first two rounds, with English, history, music, politics and business producing the highest levels of satisfaction.

The university launched the Leicester Centre for Journalism in 2009. Among the recent additions to the portfolio of courses is a BSc in green energy technology and another in public and community health, tackling issues such as increases in sexually transmitted infections and obesity.

The dropout rate has improved considerably: at under 15 per cent, it is now around the national average for the university's courses and entry grades. De Montfort has abandoned semesters and gone back to a three-term year, partly because it believed the prospect of imminent assessment encouraged some students to give up at Christmas in their first year. The university has a proud record for widening access to higher education with 41 per cent of students coming from working-class homes. It was one of the first to set up an employment agency to help students find part-time work as well as find careers upon graduation. Strong links with local business and industry manifest themselves in courses such as the BSc in media production, run in conjunction with the BBC, and in the provision of facilities such as the telematics laboratory sponsored by Orange, the mobile telephone company.

Accommodation difficulties have been addressed, with the addition of new halls within walking distance of lectures, although all first years cannot be guaranteed a place in halls. Rents in the private sector are among the lowest in England.

Undergraduate Fees and Bursaries
» Fees for UK/EU students: £3,290
» International student fees: £8,750–£9,250
» Bursary on full grant: household income up to £25K: £600
» Bursary on partial grant: household income up to £40K: £600; household income up to £50K: £300.
» Scholarships based on circumstances or by competition.
» For full details see the university's website: www.dmu.ac.uk/study/applicants/ug/fees/

Students
Undergraduates:	13,835	(3,255)
Postgraduates:	1,055	(2,765)
Mature students:	21.6%	
Overseas students:	4.5%	
Applications per place:	3.4	
From state-sector schools:	97.7%	
From working-class homes:	41.2%	

For detailed information about fees, grants and bursaries and how they work, see chapter 7.

Accommodation
Number of places and costs refer to 2010–11
University-provided places: around 3,500
Percentage catered: 0%
Self-catered costs: £65–£155 a week.
First years cannot be guaranteed accommodation. Residential restrictions apply.
International students: guaranteed accommodation.
Contact: housing@dmu.ac.uk

University of Derby

Derby sees itself as a prototype for the modern university, providing courses at all levels from the age of 16 into retirement. Although not as extensive as the original plans for spanning further and higher education in the same institution, a merger with High Peak College and the subsequent creation of the University of Derby Buxton have stayed true to the model. While accepting that Derby will never scale the heights in league tables such as ours, the university set itself the target of becoming the pre-eminent university of its type by 2020. Its yardsticks are student satisfaction, employability and cost-effectiveness. Applications were up by 38 per cent at the start of 2010.

The university takes pride in its record for widening access, although higher entry grades have coincided with the recruitment of more students from affluent families. Derby still has a high proportion of state-educated undergraduates, approaching four in ten are from working-class homes and two in ten are from areas of low participation in higher education – well above the national average for the courses and entry qualifications. But the latest projected dropout rate was more than 24 per cent, a fall on the previous year but still above the benchmark figure for the university.

Campus developments are continuing: a £21-million art, design and technology building opened in 2007 and £5 million has been spent on refurbishing the nearby Britannia Mill where social science courses and some health-related courses are based. This is all part of a £75-million estates strategy that has created a University Quarter for the city of Derby. The second campus in Buxton is based in what used to be the Devonshire Royal Hospital and provides an ideal centre for courses in spa, outdoor recreation and hospitality management, as well as further education programmes. The landmark building, which has a bigger dome than St Paul's Cathedral, houses a training restaurant, a beauty salon and a health spa, as well as more conventional teaching facilities.

There are three main sites in Derby. Kedleston Road, two miles north of the city centre, is the largest, catering for most of the main subjects including all business, computing and law courses. The students' union, multi-faith centre and main sports facilities are here. The £1.5-million clinical skills suite was built to NHS "Red Book" standards, featuring hospital wards, counselling rooms and diagnostic radiography facilities. The site's three tower blocks are being refurbished and made greener in a £13.5-million project to be completed by 2010, which will make them more energy efficient with the installation of photovoltaic panels to generate some of their own

**Kedleston Road
Derby DE22 1GB**

01332 59116 (admissions)
askadmissions@derby.ac.uk
www.derby.ac.uk
www.udsu.co.uk

The Times Rankings
Overall Ranking: **=104**

Student satisfaction:	=79	(74%)
Research quality:	=107	(0.1)
Entry standards:	102	(237)
Student–staff ratio:	=82	(19.6)
Services & facilities/student:	51	(£1,367)
Expected completion rate:	105	(74.2%)
Good honours:	109	(46.2%)
Graduate prospects:	97	(56.8%)

electricity. A new all-weather sports pitch was added in 2009.

The Mickleover campus, which specialises in education and health, is also in a suburban location. All three sites in Derby are within 10 minutes walk of each other as well as being linked by free shuttle buses and the UniBus service, which also connects the halls of residence. Derby also has a £400,000 centre in Chesterfield to teach nursing.

A foundation programme allows students to begin work at a partner college before transferring to the university. Derby has also awarded more work-based qualifications than any other UK university. Business and management is by far the university's biggest academic area, but work placements are encouraged in all subjects. The accent on employability continues through the "Skillbuilder" career development programme, which covers a range of transferable skills to give graduates an edge in the employment market.

Derby has been in the forefront of the adoption of new teaching methods, pioneering the use of interactive video for a national scheme. Distance learning is a growth area, either online or through Derby's nine regional centres. Prospective students can even sample a virtual open evening. A variety of courses, from foundation degrees to postgraduate qualifications, are available online. The School of Flexible and Partnership Learning, which spans the entire university, won an award for the imaginative use of distance learning.

The university has spent £30 million in five years to maintain its guarantee of accommodation for all first years. Students seem to appreciate the university's efforts because Derby comes out well in its own satisfaction surveys, although this has not been reflected in the national equivalent. Scores improved in the 2009 National Student Survey, but the university remained well down the table. History, teacher training, law and biology recorded the best results, with law again producing some of the most satisfied students in the country.

Undergraduate Fees and Bursaries

» Fees for UK/EU students: £3,290
» International student fees: £8,500–£8,800
» Bursary on full grant: £850 + £300 (local address) or £850 + £400 (partner school).
» Bursary on partial grant: household income £25K–£35K: £530; £35K–£51K: £215; All + £300 or £400 local bursary.
» Scholarships based on circumstances or by competition.
» For full details see the university's website: www.derby.ac.uk/fees

---

Students

Undergraduates:	**10,015**	**(4,115)**
Postgraduates:	**640**	**(2,265)**
Mature students:	**33.7%**	
Overseas students:	**8.7%**	
Applications per place:	**4.4**	
From state-sector schools:	**97.0%**	
From working-class homes:	**37.9%**	

For detailed information about fees, grants and bursaries and how they work, see chapter 7.

Accommodation

Number of places and costs refer to 2010–11
University-provided places: 2,500
Percentage catered: 0%
Self-catered costs: £70.00–£97.02.
First-year students are guaranteed accommodation if they apply before 31 July.
Policy for international students: as above.
Contact: www.derby.ac.uk/accommodation
Student Living – tel: 01332 594111 (126 Nuns St, Derby, DE1 3LQ)

University of Dundee

Dundee has enjoyed a surge in popularity in recent years. Applications shot up by 88 per cent in five years, ending with by far the biggest rise in Scotland in 2008. And at the start of 2010, there was another bumper increase – this time of nearly 42 per cent, again one of the largest north of the border. Dundee describes itself as "Scotland's most enterprising university" and, while there would be other claimants to that title, it has certainly been among the liveliest in recent years. A long series of good quality ratings and the acquisition of education, nursing and art colleges, which doubled its size and greatly increased its scope, have been complemented by high-profile research successes, especially in medicine and the life sciences.

The university now has about 16,000 students, of whom two thirds are undergraduates, including a healthy number from overseas. It has been looking outwards to achieve the "critical mass" which experts regard as essential to break into the higher education elite, appointing professors at the rate of one a month for four years.

A £200-million campus redevelopment designed by the leading architect, Sir Terry Farrell, is now complete. Almost £40 million of this was spent on wireless-networked student residences. The IT facilities include a "superfast" broadband network and are among the best in the UK, allowing the latest technologies to be used to enhance teaching. Education and social work moved into a new teaching block on the main campus in 2008, and there have been extensions to the library and the sports centre. Best-known for the life sciences, where research into cancer and diabetes is recognised as world-class, the university had already opened new buildings for interdisciplinary research, applied computing and clinical research.

Set in 20 acres of parkland, the medical school is the one of the few components of the university outside the compact city-centre campus – some of the nursing and midwifery students are 35 miles away in Kirkcaldy. Biochemistry is the flagship department, housed in the £13-million Wellcome Trust Building. Its academics were the first in Britain to be invited to take part in Japan's Human Frontier science programme and are now the most-quoted researchers in their field.

More than half the work submitted for the 2008 Research Assessment Exercise was rated world-leading or internationally excellent. Dundee recorded the best results in Scotland for art and design, civil engineering, biological and laboratory-based clinical sciences. Undergraduates in pharmacy and zoology produced rare 100 per cent satisfaction ratings in the National Student Survey published in 2009.

Nethergate
Dundee DD1 4HN

01382 383838 (enquiries)
contactus@dundee.ac.uk
www.dundee.ac.uk
www.dusa.co.uk

The Times Rankings
Overall Ranking: **44**

Student satisfaction:	=15	(80%)
Research quality:	47	(1.6)
Entry standards:	39	(344)
Student–staff ratio:	=23	(14.0)
Services & facilities/student:	56	(£1,333)
Expected completion rate:	84	(79.5%)
Good honours:	36	(68.4%)
Graduate prospects:	=47	(68.6%)

Finance and accounting, biology, planning and teacher training also recorded extremely high scores.

Vocational degrees predominate, helping to produce the university's consistently good graduate employment record. The university sends more graduates into the professions than any other institution in Scotland and only Oxbridge graduates came out ahead of Dundee's in a national survey of starting salaries. All degrees include a career planning module and an internship option, and students are now provided with their own personal development website. Among the new courses introduced recently are forensic anthropology, sports biomedicine and innovative product design. The highly rated design courses are taught at the former Duncan of Jordanstone College of Art.

There has been an emphasis on opportunities for women ever since Dundee's separation from St Andrews University, in 1967, and the addition of teacher training has increased the female majority. Two thirds of Dundee's students are from Scotland and nearly one in ten from Northern Ireland. One in five come from areas with little tradition of higher education and more than a quarter are from working-class homes. They enjoy a welcoming atmosphere and a cost of living which is lower than in most university cities. Private accommodation is plentiful for those who are not housed by the university. New students even have their own website.

The city is profiting from recent regeneration programmes and becoming more fashionable. The university has been at the heart of a successful campaign to bring the Victoria and Albert Museum to Dundee by 2014. Spectacular mountain and coastal scenery are close at hand, but social life tends to be concentrated on the students' union, which is one of the largest and most active in Scotland.

Undergraduate Fees and Bursaries

» Scottish-domiciled and EU students: no fees payable.
» Non-Scottish UK-domiciled student fees: £1,820
  £2,895 (medicine)
» International student fees: £8,925–£11,025
  £16,000–£23,000 (medicine)
» Scholarships based on circumstances or by competition.
» For full details see the university's website:
  www.dundee.ac.uk/undergraduate/fees_funding

Students

Undergraduates:	8,735	(1,815)
Postgraduates:	1,570	(3,400)
Mature students:	30.1%	
Overseas students:	7.9%	
Applications per place:	5.7	
From state-sector schools:	90.5%	
From working-class homes:	25.4%	

For detailed information about fees, grants and bursaries and how they work, see chapter 7.

Accommodation

Number of places and costs refer to 2010–11
University-provided places: 1,809
Percentage catered: 0%
Self-catered costs: £72.94 – £111.58 a week.
Entrant students guaranteed accommodation if conditions are met.
No residential restrictions.
International students are guaranteed accommodation if conditions are met.
Contact: residences@dundee.ac.uk
www.dundee.ac.uk/studentservices/residences

Durham University

Long established as a leading alternative to Oxford and Cambridge, Durham has a collegiate structure and picturesque setting that attracts a largely middle-class student body. However, although more than a third of undergraduates come from independent schools, the university has been attracting more applicants from non-traditional backgrounds. All those who receive an offer are invited to a special open day to see if Durham is the university for them. Since around 80 per cent come from outside the northeast of England, most are seeing the small cathedral city for the first time.

Undergraduates apply to one of 14 colleges, all of which have been mixed since 2004. The newest, Josephine Butler College – a self-catering college with around 400 bedrooms – accepted its first intake of students in 2006. Colleges range in size from 300 to 1,100 students and are the focal point of social life, although all teaching is done in central departments. There are significant differences in atmosphere and student profile, ranging from the historic University College, in Durham Castle, to modern buildings on the city's outskirts and on the Queen's Campus, 23 miles away at Stockton-on-Tees.

Durham has been among the top 20 universities for student satisfaction for the last three years. History recorded a 100 per cent overall satisfaction rate in 2009, while archaeology, education, linguistics, molecular biology and teacher training all scored highly. Winning a place is far from easy – entrance requirements are among the highest in Britain – but the dropout rate of less than 2 per cent is also among the lowest in any university. Durham has seldom been out of the top ten in *The Times* league table and has been moving up the world rankings, finishing just outside the top 100 in the QS World University Rankings of 2009.

More than 60 per cent of the work submitted for the 2008 Research Assessment Exercise was rated world-leading or internationally excellent. Applied maths, archaeology and theology and religion achieved among the best results in the UK. Music, English and geography and environmental science also did well. A £3-million grant to establish a centre for fundamental physics should place Durham at the forefront of world research on the structure of the universe. The Calman Learning Centre, on the Science Site, incorporates lecture theatres, seminar and conference facilities and a "techno café". The site will also see the opening of a landmark "Gateway" development, containing a new law school and student services centre, in 2012.

Durham is generally quite traditional. Wherever possible, teaching takes place in

University Office
Old Elvet
Durham DH1 3HP

0191 334 6123 (admissions office)
admissions@dur.ac.uk
www.dur.ac.uk
www.dsu.org.uk

The Times Rankings
Overall Ranking: **6**

Student satisfaction:	=11	(81%)
Research quality:	=7	(3.0)
Entry standards:	5	(468)
Student–staff ratio:	39	(15.4)
Services & facilities/student:	8	(£2,084)
Expected completion rate:	3	(97.8%)
Good honours:	9	(79.0%)
Graduate prospects:	13	(77.8%)

small groups and most assessment is by written examination. However, the establishment of the Queen's Campus in Stockton-on-Tees broke the mould. Initially a joint venture with Teesside University, Stockton is now home to a wide range of courses including applied psychology, biomedical sciences, business and business finance, anthropology and primary education. The campus has also seen the fulfilment of Durham's long-held ambition to restore the medical education it lost when Newcastle University went its own way 45 years ago. An innovative joint project allows students to do the first two years of their training at Stockton, concentrating on community medicine, before transferring to Newcastle to complete their degree.

Significant investment has been made to improve social facilities for the 2,000 students on the Queen's Campus, and £5.5million has been earmarked for improved sporting facilities, relocating some of the university's elite sports activities as part of a strategy to increase integration between Durham and Stockton. The campus is at the heart of a planned £300-million redevelopment of the surrounding North Shore area, in which the university will play a key role, extending its academic facilities and social spaces.

The university dominates the city of Durham to an extent which sometimes causes resentment, but adds considerably to the local economy. The latest National Student Housing Survey rated Durham top for private sector accommodation and second for halls of residence. For those looking for nightlife, or just a change of scene, Newcastle is a short train journey away. Sports facilities are excellent, and Durham is among the premier universities in national competitions: it came sixth in national student championships in 2009. Among the alumni are the current and former England cricket captains, Andrew Strauss and Nasser Hussain, and rugby World Cup winner, Will Greenwood. The university runs centres of excellence in cricket and fencing, and has plans to build on its existing strengths in rowing, rugby and hockey.

Undergraduate Fees and Bursaries

» Fees for UK/EU students: £3,290
» International student fees: £12,400–£14,865
» Bursary on full grant: household income up to £25K: £1,000
» The university does not award bursaries for students on partial maintenance grants.
» Scholarships based on circumstances or by competition.
» For full details see the university's website: www.dur.ac.uk/undergraduate/finance/dgs

Students

Undergraduates:	**11,145**	**(225)**
Postgraduates:	**3,800**	**(1,675)**
Mature students:	**6.2%**	
Overseas students:	**8.6%**	
Applications per place:	**6.5**	
From state-sector schools:	**59.2%**	
From working-class homes:	**16.8%**	

For detailed information about fees, grants and bursaries and how they work, see chapter 7.

Accommodation

Number of places and costs refer to 2010–11
University-provided places: 5,758
Percentage catered: 67%
Catered costs: £4,854 (3 terms, Durham)
Self-catered costs: £4,278 (3 terms, Durham)
£4,227 (38-week contract, Stockton campus)
All full-time students become members of one of the university's colleges or societies.
International students: first years are guaranteed housing.
Contact: admissions@dur.ac.uk

University of East Anglia

UEA has been one of the big winners in the National Student Survey, finishing in the top ten every year that results have been published. The 90 per cent satisfaction rating among final-year undergraduates placed it among the top five non-specialist universities in 2009. Pharmacy registered 100 per cent satisfaction for the second year in a row and was joined by the innovative programme in society, culture and media, with maths and statistics, geology and archaeology also scoring well. Students appear to like the scale of this relatively small campus university, as well as the quality of its courses. The news appears to be getting through to many sixth-formers: applications were up by 35 per cent – the biggest rise at any pre-1992 university in England – at the start of 2010.

The university has been engaged in an ambitious building and refurbishment programme on the 320-acre site on the outskirts of Norwich. It has included the provision of 700 more en-suite student bedrooms, a new health centre and the extension and refurbishment of the central library, catering facilities and students' union. The Square, the university's social centre, has been regenerated and new buildings added for the schools of Nursing and Midwifery and Medicine, as well as for an INTO English language centre for overseas students. In the latest developments, a £3.9-million extension to the Sportspark has opened, together with a new lecture theatre and seminar building. In keeping with the university's strong "green" credentials, a biomass generator facility has been provided that should reduce the university's carbon emissions dramatically.

Some of the broad subject combinations that the university pioneered from its origins in the 1960s – such as development studies and environmental sciences – are highly regarded in the academic world. With successive 5* ratings for research followed by a good result in the 2008 Research Assessment Exercise, environmental sciences is the flagship school. The Climatic Research Unit and the Government-funded Tyndall Centre for Climate Change Research are among the leaders in the investigation of climate change. Although the university has been at the centre of international controversy over allegations that climate data were manipulated, UEA contributed more than any other university in the world to the 2007 Nobel Prize-winning Intergovernmental Panel on Climate Change.

History of art and culture and media did even better in the latest RAE, with half of their research considered world-leading. Art history has the benefit of the Sainsbury Centre for the Visual Arts, perhaps the greatest resource of its type on any British campus. The centre, which has been refurbished and extended, houses a priceless collection of modern and tribal art, in a building designed by Lord (Norman) Foster.

Norwich NR4 7TJ

01603 591515 (admissions office)
admissions@uea.ac.uk
www.uea.ac.uk
www.ueastudent.com

The Times Rankings
Overall Ranking: **=23**

Student satisfaction:	=7	(83%)
Research quality:	=33	(2.1)
Entry standards:	=33	(366)
Student–staff ratio:	=36	(15.3)
Services & facilities/student:	30	(£1,617)
Expected completion rate:	=30	(90.3%)
Good honours:	25	(71.2%)
Graduate prospects:	=45	(69.1%)

Creative writing is another star-studded area, with authors Andrew Cowan, Giles Foden and Lavinia Greenlaw taking up where Andrew Motion, the former Poet Laureate, and the late Malcolm Bradbury left off.

Health studies have been among UEA's fastest-developing areas. The university was awarded one of the first new medical schools for 20 years, graduating its first doctors in 2007, and has since added pharmacy and speech and language therapy degree courses.

Almost nine out of ten undergraduates come from state schools or colleges, and over a quarter have a working-class background. Since 1999, most have had the opportunity of work experience as part of their course. An academic adviser guides all students on their options under the modular course system and monitors their progress right through to graduation.

Dropout rates have fluctuated, but the latest projected figure of less than 9 per cent was below the national average for the university's subjects and entry standards. Most students come from outside the region, although there is an unusually large contingent of mature students for a traditional university, who tend to be more local. UEA opened University Campus Suffolk in 2007, in partnership with Essex University, with a main site in Ipswich and smaller bases in Bury St Edmunds, Great Yarmouth, Lowestoft and Otley.

The university is situated in parkland, with easy access to the medieval city of Norwich, which can boast a pub for every day of the year and has been voted one of the best small cities in the world. Rail links to London now take less than two hours, while Norwich airport offers flights through Amsterdam and Paris worldwide. The Sportspark boasts an Olympic-sized swimming pool, fitness and aerobics centres, athletics track, climbing wall, courts and pitches. The university was chosen as the base for the English Institute of Sport in the East, developing a sports science network for the region.

Undergraduate Fees and Bursaries

» Fees for UK/EU students: £3,290
» International student fees: £10,400–£13,000
  £20,225 (clinical medicine)
» Bursary on full grant: household income up to £25K: £600
» Bursary on partial grant: household income up to £50K: £300
» Scholarships based on circumstances or by competition.
» For full details see the university's website: www.uea.ac.uk/sixthform/finance

Students

Undergraduates:	**10,035**	(2,175)
Postgraduates:	**2,200**	(880)
Mature students:	**20.6%**	
Overseas students:	**11.0%**	
Applications per place:	**5.0**	
From state-sector schools:	**89.2%**	
From working-class homes:	**27.6%**	

For detailed information about fees, grants and bursaries and how they work, see chapter 7.

Accommodation

Number of places and costs refer to 2010–11
University-provided places: 3,457
Percentage catered: 0%
Self-catered costs: £1,981.70–£3,775.92 (38 weeks)
First years guaranteed accommodation if conditions are met.
Distance restrictions.
International students (non EU) are guaranteed accommodation if conditions are met.
Contact: accom@uea.ac.uk
www.uea.ac.uk/accommodation

University of East London

The University of East London (UEL) has spent more than £190 million on its Docklands campus, and is now unrecognisable from its early days as a pioneering polytechnic. Student residences and recreational facilities sit side by side with academic buildings in a prize-winning waterside development for more than 7,000 students. The final pieces in the jigsaw were the business school and Knowledge Dock, a support centre for local companies, which opened in 2006, and a £40-million student village on the Royal Albert Dock, which added 800 more beds in 2007. The campus has helped to attract substantial growth in applications to UEL – there was a 49 per cent increase at the start of 2010. Student numbers have almost doubled since 2001, with students coming from 120 countries.

The capital's first new campus for 50 years gave the university a new focal point, with its modern version of traditional university features like cloisters and squares. Students of fashion, fine art, graphic design, product design, media and cultural studies were first into new premises, followed by UEL's highly rated School of Architecture and the Visual Arts and electrical and manufacturing engineering in 2005. Business, computing and technology have now completed the academic set.

The United States Olympic team is to be based at UEL for the 2012 Olympic Games. More than 1,000 competitors, coaches and medical staff will use a new £18-million sports and academic centre at the Docklands campus, provisionally named the Sports Dock, which is due to open in late 2011. UEL's new Vice-Chancellor, Professor Patrick McGhee, has said that that the university's Olympic and Paralympic involvement, together with its location and the diversity of its students, give it a unique role in the regeneration of the area.

The university's original Stratford campus is also being redeveloped, with a new library and learning centre, student residences and facilities for part-time and evening courses. The Centre for Clinical Education in Podiatry, Physiotherapy and Sports Sciences, incorporating the new London Foot Hospital, opened there in 2006. The Great Hall in University House boasts a high-tech, 230-seat fully retractable lecture theatre, while the health and bioscience laboratories have been refurbished and refitted. New buildings for education and law are next on the development plan.

All but one of the nine subject areas in which UEL entered the 2008 Research Assessment Exercise contained at least some world-leading research. In communication, culture and media studies, the proportion was 20 per cent, with another 60 per cent of work rated internationally excellent. Art and design

Stratford Campus
Water Lane
London E15 4LZ

020 8223 3333 (admissions)
study@uel.ac.uk
www.uel.ac.uk
www.uelunion.org

The Times Rankings
Overall Ranking: **111**

Student satisfaction:	=105	(69%)
Research quality:	=69	(0.5)
Entry standards:	112	(187)
Student–staff ratio:	105	(22.3)
Services & facilities/student:	87	(£1,117)
Expected completion rate:	85	(79.4%)
Good honours:	108	(46.4%)
Graduate prospects:	109	(52.9%)

and sociology also produced good results.

Teacher training courses have been given good marks by the Office for Standards in Education. Accounting and languages achieved the best results in an otherwise poor set of scores in the 2009 National Student Survey, which left UEL among the bottom ten universities.

UEL's focus is more concerned with extending access to higher education than competing with the elite universities. Barely more than half of new first years now arrive with A levels and a majority are over 21 on entry – many choosing to start courses in February. Many degrees are vocational and employers are closely involved in course planning. The university has pioneered a work-based learning initiative, offering accredited placements with local employers.

Almost half of UEL's students come from working-class homes and over 98 per cent are state-school educated, many from the area's large ethnic minority populations. A successful mentoring scheme for black and Asian students has become a model for other institutions. A guidance unit advises local people considering returning to education. UEL is also strong on provision for disabled students and houses the new Rix Centre for Innovation and Learning Disability. The projected dropout rate has been improving – the latest figure of 15.5 per cent is better than the national average for UEL's courses and entry qualifications. Graduate employment rates have also been improving, with the university operating mentoring and placement programmes that involve almost 1,000 businesses, including many in the City or Canary Wharf.

University-owned accommodation is still not plentiful, although there are now more than 1,100 flats and studios on the Docklands campus and the rents are good value for London. All first years who request accommodation are housed. The social mix means that UEL has not been the place to look for the archetypal partying student lifestyle, although the Docklands campus is beginning to change this. Sports facilities and new students' union premises have been added at both Stratford and Docklands.

Undergraduate Fees and Bursaries
» Fees for UK/EU students: £3,290
» International student fees: £9,990–£13,800
» Bursary on full grant: household income up to £25K: £319*
» The university does not award bursaries for students on partial maintenance grants.*
» Scholarships based on circumstances or by competition.
» For full details see the university's website: www.uel.ac.uk/studentservices/moneymatters/index.htm

*Figures for 2009–10

Students
Undergraduates:	**13,055**	**(6,460)**
Postgraduates:	**3,485**	**(3,310)**
Mature students:	**54.5%**	
Overseas students:	**11.5%**	
Applications per place:	**3.1**	
From state-sector schools:	**98.3%**	
From working-class homes:	**47.2%**	

For detailed information about fees, grants and bursaries and how they work, see chapter 7.

Accommodation
Number of places and costs refer to 2009–10
University-provided places: 1,100
Percentage catered: 0%
Self-catered costs: £101–£125 a week (39 weeks)
New students, those living furthest away and disabled students have priority.
International students: same as above.
Docklands Campus 020 8223 5093/4
dlres@uel.ac.uk

Edge Hill University

Based at Ormskirk, near Liverpool, Edge Hill is one of the fastest growing universities in the UK, as well as one of the newest. It has almost doubled its complement of students since the millennium to reach 23,000 mark, although only 8,000 of them are on full-time courses. Rapid growth often does universities no favours in rankings, but Edge Hill moved up ten places in last year's *Times* league table. Applications increased three-fold in that time, culminating in a 45 per cent rise at the start of 2010. It has moved up a further 12 places this year.

There are plans for significant expansion with the purchase of land adjoining the existing site, but the next generation of students will have to make do with improvements to the current campus. Over £100 million has been spent on it already and more is on the way. A £14-million home to house the Faculty of Health, the SOLSTICE e-learning centre and a 900-seat theatre were completed in 2007. A new £8-million Business School opened in 2009, when additional student residences also came on stream.

Although university status arrived only in 2005, Edge Hill has been training teachers since the 19th century. Having moved to its 75-acre landscaped campus in the 1930s, it has long since expanded into other subjects, but it remains the largest provider of secondary teacher training and courses for classroom assistants. It has also won the lion's share of funding to deliver further training for qualified secondary school teachers.

A £5-million expansion of resources for the performing arts opened in 2005 and there are industry-standard facilities for animation, TV and other media areas. SOLSTICE (which stands for Supported Online Learning for Students using Technology for Information and Communication in their Education) is recognised officially as a national centre of excellence in teaching and learning. It has a particular focus on learning in the workplace, but is involved with curriculum development and delivery in all three of the university's faculties.

Other big recruiters are health, business, sport and media courses. Nursing, midwifery and other health care programmes were commended by inspectors in 2005 and the university's primary and secondary teacher training courses have been rated as outstanding by Ofsted. Courses are determinedly job-related – three quarters of graduates leave with professional accreditation. Among the latest additions is Chinese studies, which is available as a joint honours programme with English or business.

All students have a personal tutor, as well as access to counsellors and financial advice. Satisfaction levels have been above average in the National Student Survey, with good

St Helens Road
Ormskirk
Lancashire L39 4QP

01695 575171
enquiries@edgehill.ac.uk
www.edgehill.ac.uk
www.edgehillsu.com

The Times Rankings
Overall Ranking: **76**

Student satisfaction:	=32	(78%)
Research quality:	=107	(0.1)
Entry standards:	87	(259)
Student–staff ratio:	=62	(18.0)
Services & facilities/student:	45	(£1,425)
Expected completion rate:	=88	(79.0%)
Good honours:	106	(47.6%)
Graduate prospects:	62	(63.9%)

scores for students' personal development, as well as for assessment and feedback – the main bone of contention for undergraduates at most universities. Subjects allied to medicine and physical geography and environmental science produced the best results in 2009.

Beyond Ormskirk, there are seven satellite campuses in Liverpool, Manchester and other parts of the North West to facilitate local learning. The largest is based in the grounds of University Hospital Aintree, where students in the Faculty of Health can see at first-hand how a busy hospital runs. In addition, a range of further education colleges in the North West teach the university's Foundation degrees.

Edge Hill has one of the highest proportion of state-educated students in England – nearly 99 per cent. Over four in ten undergraduates have a working-class background and almost a quarter come from areas without a tradition of higher education. Almost two thirds of the university's fee income goes on bursaries and outreach activities. Edge Hill won an award for a student finance support package that rewards achievement, as well as encouraging students to complete their studies, rather than simply offering incentives for enrolling. The dropout rate has been falling: the latest projection of 12.5 per cent is well below the national average for the university's courses and entry qualifications.

The university has been rated among the cheapest in the UK for accommodation and overall cost of living. There are now almost 850 hall places on the Ormskirk campus and 25 acres of sporting facilities. The £3.9-million Sporting Edge complex, which was part funded by a Lottery grant, is open to staff, students and the local community. The university has been chosen as a pre-Olympic training centre for athletics, road cycling and archery.

Undergraduate Fees and Bursaries
» Fees for UK/EU students: £3,290
» International student fees: £8,600
» Bursary on full grant: household income up to £25K: £500 + £200 learning support bursary.
» Bursary on partial grant: £200 learning support bursary.
» Scholarships based on circumstances or by competition.
» For full details see the university's website: http://www.edgehill.ac.uk/study/fees

---

Students
Undergraduates:	6,905	(6,700)
Postgraduates:	640	(10,100)
Mature students:	24.3%	
Overseas students:	0.9%	
Applications per place:	3.2	
From state-sector schools:	98.9%	
From working-class homes:	44.0%	

For detailed information about fees, grants and bursaries and how they work, see chapter 7.

Accommodation
Number of places and costs refer to 2010–11
University provided places: 1,046
Percentage catered: 41%
Catered costs: £87 a week (38–40 weeks)
Self-catered costs: £54–£93 a week (40 weeks)
First years cannot be guaranteed housing. Residential restrictions apply.
International students: guaranteed accommodation if conditions are met.
Contact: www.edgehill.ac.uk/study/accommodation

University of Edinburgh

Edinburgh retains a special status in Scotland, where the university is regarded as the nearest thing to Oxbridge north of the border. Despite having to play second fiddle to St Andrews in our league table recently, it is seldom far from the top ten in the UK and was in the top 20 universities in the world in the last QS global rankings. The presence of more than 6,000 international students testifies to its worldwide reputation.

Edinburgh is now the largest university in Scotland, with nearly 27,000 students. The university's buildings are scattered around the city, but most border the historic Old Town. These include the university's main library, which has been redeveloped at a cost of £60 million. The science and engineering campus is two miles to the south.

Like Oxbridge, Edinburgh has been trying to widen its intake, especially since the arrival of Sir Tim O'Shea as Principal – the first non-Scot to hold the post in modern times. More than £10 million has been raised for access bursaries of £1,000 a year, with the university steadily increasing number of awards, which now stand at 180. Other measures include an eight-week summer school for teenagers from local schools and support for students in the transition to higher education and later in their courses. The university has always attracted a high proportion of middle-class candidates – many from England – and is a favourite in independent schools, whose students take about three places in ten. Selection guidelines aim to look more broadly at candidates' potential. The university reduced its minimum entry requirements to consider a wider pool of candidates and place more weight on references and personal statements. It also gives extra credit in some oversubscribed programmes to applicants from Scotland and the north of England, from Teesside to Cumbria.

The measures appeared to have an instant impact, with a succession of big increases in applications at a time when most Scottish universities were experiencing declines. The demand for places has held up in generally problematic areas such as engineering and modern languages although, like a number of universities at the top of the league tables, Edinburgh did not share in the 2010 applications boom. There was an increase of less than 1 per cent at the start of the year, although at nine candidates to every place, standards remain extremely high.

The university, which is a member of the Russell Group of 20 UK research universities, has stepped up its fund-raising activities. They have already contributed to a new informatics building, as well as to the development of a "BioQuarter", a groundbreaking collaboration between the university and a number of public bodies that is intended to consolidate Scotland's

Old College
South Bridge
Edinburgh EH8 9YL

0131 651 1905 (admissions)
sra.enquiries@ed.ac.uk
www.ed.ac.uk
www.eusa.ed.ac.uk

The Times Rankings
Overall Ranking: **11**

Student satisfaction:	=79	(74%)
Research quality:	=4	(3.2)
Entry standards:	11	(439)
Student–staff ratio:	12	(13.3)
Services & facilities/student:	4	(£2,572)
Expected completion rate:	26	(92.0%)
Good honours:	5	(80.2%)
Graduate prospects:	17	(76.2%)

reputation as a world leader in biomedical science. A 100-acre site for biomedical research is located alongside the medical school and the new Royal Infirmary. A new building for the Scottish Centre for Regenerative Medicine, housing researchers from a range of disciplines including those from the university's renowned Institute for Stem Cell Research, will open in 2010. Elsewhere a £100 million redevelopment of the university's Easter Bush site is underway, which will include a vet school building, a research building for the recently incorporated Roslin Institute and a cancer centre.

Almost two thirds of the work submitted for the 2008 Research Assessment Exercise was rated as world-leading or internationally excellent, the highest proportion in Scotland. The university's entry was among the largest in the UK and produced strong results across the board. The College of Medicine and Veterinary Medicine was the star performer, with all of the work in hospital-based clinical subjects rated at the international level and 40 per cent at the highest grade. Informatics, linguistics and English literature also produced outstanding results.

Departments organise visiting days in October for those thinking of applying and in the spring for those holding offers. There is also an annual open day in June. New undergraduates generally take three subjects in both their first and second years. Every student has a Director of Studies to help them narrow down the selection of a final degree and give personal advice when necessary.

Considerable sums have been spent making the university more accessible to the 1,600 disabled students, who can also call on the services of a disability office. All students are issued with a smart card for access to university facilities. The students' union operates on several sites and sports facilities are excellent.

The city is a treasure-trove of cultural and recreational opportunities. Most students thrive on Edinburgh life, even though the cost of living can make it difficult to do it justice. Some scientists complain of isolation, although there is a regular bus link with the main university area around George Square. The plentiful stock of residential accommodation has been increased recently.

Undergraduate Fees and Bursaries

» Scottish-domiciled and EU students: no fees payable.
» Non-Scottish UK-domiciled student fees: £1,820
  £2,895 (medicine)
» International student fees: £11,600–£15,250
  £15,250–£31,900 (medicine)
» Scholarships based on circumstances or by competition.
» For full details see the university's website:
  www.scholarships.ed.ac.uk/undergraduate/index.htm

Students

Undergraduates:	**16,590**	**(695)**
Postgraduates:	**5,200**	**(2,035)**
Mature students:	**9.4%**	
Overseas students:	**15.0%**	
Applications per place:	**8.6**	
From state-sector schools:	**70.8%**	
From working-class homes:	**18.6%**	

For detailed information about fees, grants and bursaries and how they work, see chapter 7.

Accommodation

Number of places and costs refer to 2009–10
University-provided places: about 6,300
Percentage catered: about 30%
Catered costs: £148–£184 a week
Self-catered costs: £81–£106 a week.
First years are guaranteed an offer of accommodation providing they fulfil requirements. Residential restrictions apply.
International students: accommodation guaranteed if conditions are met.
Contact: www.accom.ed.ac.uk

Edinburgh Napier University

Edinburgh Napier had the biggest increase in applications of any non-specialist UK university at the start of 2010. Indeed, the 78 per cent rise was probably the largest in any year. Although partly fuelled by UK-wide changes in art and design deadlines and nursing qualifications, the unprecedented demand for places was a reflection of the university's growing popularity over several years. A 14 per cent rise in 2009 was the latest in a series of healthy increases, buoyed by strong international recruitment.

Once Scotland's first and largest polytechnic, Napier has added the name of its home city to underline a location in the capital that helps to attract 4,000 international students from more than 100 countries. With nearly 15,000 students in all, it is now one of Scotland's biggest universities. Professor Dame Joan Stringer, who was the first woman to lead a university north of the border, has set Edinburgh Napier the target of becoming "one of the leading modern universities in the United Kingdom". It is now in the midst of a £100-million redevelopment programme to help achieve that ambition.

Edinburgh Napier is a multi-campus university, with its headquarters in Merchiston, the city's main student district. The campus has a purpose-built music centre and the £5-million, 500-seat Jack Kilby Computing Centre is open 24 hours a day. The Craiglockhart campus houses Scotland's biggest business school and features a glass atrium housing a cyber café and two spherical lecture theatres with a total of 600 seats, as well as a new fitness suite.

The latest phase of the development programme will see the reopening in January 2011 of the Sighthill Campus, bringing the Faculty of Health, Life and Social Sciences together on one site for the first time. The £30-million development includes a learning resource centre, clinical skills laboratories, IT-enabled lecture theatres and seminar rooms, as well as integrated sports facilities. A new clinical skills suite will be equipped with advanced technology to give the university a lead in Scotland on cross-sector clinical skills education.

The university is named after John Napier, the inventor of logarithms. The tower where he was born still sits among the concrete blocks of the Merchiston campus. There are several smaller sites, mainly in the leafy south of Edinburgh, ranging from a converted church to a former school and two hospitals, as well as outposts in Melrose and Livingston.

An International College, launched in 2007, offers overseas students a dedicated service, with pastoral and recruitment

Craiglockhart Campus
Edinburgh EH14 1DJ

08452 606040 (switchboard)
admissions@napier.ac.uk
also contact via website
www.napier.ac.uk
www.napierstudents.com

The Times Rankings
Overall Ranking: **66**

Student satisfaction:	=59	(76%)
Research quality:	=77	(0.4)
Entry standards:	=80	(264)
Student–staff ratio:	77	(19.2)
Services & facilities/student:	75	(£1,162)
Expected completion rate:	102	(75.6%)
Good honours:	=50	(63.9%)
Graduate prospects:	32	(72.0%)

activities, as well as support for Napier's programmes in China, Hong Kong and India. Closer to home, there are links with more than 100 colleges in Scotland, England and Ireland (both north and south) to encourage progression from further to higher education. Widening participation is high on the university's list of priorities: more than a third of the undergraduates come from working-class homes.

Most of Edinburgh Napier's avowedly vocational courses include a work placement, and the close relationship with industry and commerce helps to produce consistently good graduate employment figures. The modular course system allows movement between courses at all levels and has allowed students the option of starting courses in February, rather than September.

Edinburgh Napier has been held up as a model to other universities trying to reduce non-completion rates. The university uses its own students to mentor newcomers, runs bridging programmes and offers pre-term introductions to staff and information on facilities, as well as running summer top-up courses in a variety of subjects. The Confident Futures programme helps students make the transition to higher education and teaches employability skills and personal development. However, the latest projected dropout rate of 16 per cent is above the UK average for the subjects on offer.

Library and information management achieved by far the best results in the 2008 Research Assessment Exercise, when just over a fifth of the university's submission was considered world-leading or internationally excellent. The Edinburgh Skillset Screen and Media Academy, run in partnership with Edinburgh College of Art, reflects the university's strong reputation in film education.

The dispersed nature of the university does nothing for the social scene, although Edinburgh is hardly dull. Some students find life too quiet in the evenings and at weekends, although the students' association, in partnership with local clubs, organises regular party nights in the city centre.

Undergraduate Fees and Bursaries
» Scottish-domiciled and EU students: no fees payable.
» Non-Scottish UK-domiciled student fees: £1,820
» International student fees: £9,120–£10,600
» Scholarships based on circumstances or by competition.
» For full details see the university's website: www.napier.ac.uk/napierlife/money/Pages/default.aspx

Students
Undergraduates:	**9,215**	**(2,240)**
Postgraduates:	**1,090**	**(1,105)**
Mature students:	**47.2%**	
Overseas students:	**20.0%**	
Applications per place:	**3.4**	
From state-sector schools:	**94.4%**	
From working-class homes:	**34.9%**	

For detailed information about fees, grants and bursaries and how they work, see chapter 7.

Accommodation
Number of places and costs refer to 2010–11
University-provided places: 900
Percentage catered: 0%
Self-catered costs: £89–£94 average cost a week.
First years are guaranteed a place provided requirements are met.
Residential restrictions apply.
International students are guaranteed a place as long as requirements are met.
Contact: accommodation@napier.ac.uk

University of Essex

Essex has sometimes struggled to attract enough applicants to do justice to the high quality of its teaching and research. But a 33 per cent increase in applications at the start of 2010 – one of the biggest rises among pre-1992 universities and building on substantial growth in the previous year – suggests this may be a thing of the past. The university has acquired a reputation for high-quality research, especially in the social sciences, which led to a strong set of results in the 2008 Research Assessment Exercise (RAE). Essex has also been doing well in the National Student Survey.

There are still only 9,700 full-time students, about a fifth of whom are postgraduates. The student population is unusually diverse for a traditional university, with high proportions of mature and overseas students. More than a third of the undergraduates are from working-class homes and 96 per cent went to state schools or colleges – a significantly higher proportion than the subject mix would suggest.

Economics and politics led the way in the latest RAE where almost two thirds of the work submitted by the university was found to be world-leading or internationally excellent. Both politics and sociology produced the best results in the country, while the newly formed Essex Business School ranked second in the UK for accounting and finance. Philosophy, electronic engineering and technology boasted the most satisfied students in the 2009 National Student Survey, which showed that 85 per cent of Essex's final-year undergraduates were generally satisfied with their course.

The university has been building up its science departments – the biological sciences department is one of its largest. Computer science is also strong and a BSc in computer games and internet technology shows Essex keeping pace with changing demands in graduate employment. But improvements in the university's academic performance could not disguise the fact that the glass and concrete campus, set in 200 acres of parkland on the outskirts of Colchester, was showing distinct signs of wear and tear. The university has been carrying out a programme of refurbishment at the same time as expanding student facilities. Teaching and administration blocks cluster around a network of squares, and are gradually being transformed with extra catering and residential facilities.

The University has announced a major capital development programme in the lead up to its 50th anniversary. Recent developments on the Colchester campus include a new Centre for Brain Science and a health and human sciences building. The library has been extended and is open for over 84 hours a week, with the Large Reading Room open

Wivenhoe Park
Colchester
Essex CO4 3SQ

01206 873778 (admissions)
admit@essex.ac.uk
www.essex.ac.uk
www.essexstudent.com

The Times Rankings
Overall Ranking: **41**

Student satisfaction:	=46	(77%)
Research quality:	=29	(2.2)
Entry standards:	48	(311)
Student–staff ratio:	=21	(13.8)
Services & facilities/student:	=25	(£1,672)
Expected completion rate:	39	(86.5%)
Good honours:	65	(58.3%)
Graduate prospects:	=76	(60.2%)

24 hours a day, Monday to Thursday, and seven days a week in the summer term. Sustainable energy and technology are being used whenever possible, with recent projects featuring ground source heat pumps and a wind turbine.

Essex champions academic breadth, and in each of the four faculties, students follow a common first year before specialising. They may take four or five different subjects before committing themselves to a particular degree. Social and sporting facilities are good, the more so following an extension of the Sports Centre and the refurbishment of the students' union bars. There are now four bars, an enlarged and refurbished nightclub and numerous cafés on campus. Some 40 acres of land are devoted to sports facilities, used extensively by individual students and over 40 university sports clubs.

First years new to Colchester and all overseas students are guaranteed university accommodation, which in 2009 won the "best halls of residence" category in the National Student Housing survey. All university accommodation is now net-worked to the IT system and equipped with telephones giving free access to the internal phone system. Some ground-floor flats have been adapted for disabled students.

The incorporation of the East 15 acting school, in Loughton, enhanced the university's provision in theatre studies, and was the university's first venture beyond Colchester. A third campus opened in Southend in 2007, offering courses in business, health education and the arts. It also includes health and dental facilities, the latter staffed by senior dental students from Barts and the London School of Medicine and Dentistry. Colourful new student accommodation containing 561 rooms is due for completion in September 2010.

Another regional project sees Essex collaborating with the University of East Anglia on University Campus Suffolk, which offers courses in Ipswich and at smaller centres across the county. Essex degrees are also taught at Writtle College, near Chelmsford, the Colchester Institute and South East Essex College, in Southend.

Undergraduate Fees and Bursaries
» Fees for UK/EU students: £3,290
» International student fees: £9,250–£11,990*
» Bursary on full grant: household income up to £25K: £384
» Bursary on partial grant: household income from £25.5K: £484; increasing to max. £2,184 at £34K; decreasing to £52 at £50K.
» Scholarships based on circumstances or by competition.
» For full details see the university's website: www.essex.ac.uk/studentfinance/ug

* Figures for 2009–10

Students
Undergraduates:	**7,945**	(1,610)
Postgraduates:	**1,805**	(940)
Mature students:	**20.3%**	
Overseas students:	**20.1%**	
Applications per place:	**4.3**	
From state-sector schools:	**96.1%**	
From working-class homes:	**38.9%**	

For detailed information about fees, grants and bursaries and how they work, see chapter 7.

Accommodation
Number of places and costs refer to 2010–11
University-provided places: 4,166
Percentage catered: 0%
Self-catered costs: £64.75–£125.02 a week.
New first years living outside the borough of Colchester are guaranteed accommodation if conditions are met.
International students: new students are guaranteed accommodation if conditions are met; priority given to students in final year.
Contact: admit@essex.ac.uk

University of Exeter

Already one of Britain's most popular universities in terms of first-choice applications, last year Exeter broke into the top ten in *The Times* league table for the first time, but slipped back to 12th this year. Good results in the National Student Survey (NSS) and the Research Assessment Exercise (RAE) were largely responsible, but the university has also seen its applications rising consistently. English literature, drama, law, history and psychology are among the most heavily subscribed courses in their fields and the university has been investing heavily in the sciences.

Exeter has been among the top five universities in the NSS for the past two years and has never been out of the top ten since the survey began. There was a 100 per cent satisfaction rate among final-year finance and accounting undergraduates in 2009, when business and management, physics and theology all produced extremely high scores.

The latest RAE saw Exeter move up the pecking order of research universities, with most of its work judged to be world-leading or internationally excellent despite a much larger submission (involving 95 per cent of academics) than most of its peers. English, classics, archaeology, and accounting and finance did particularly well. The successes produced a 26 per cent increase in research funding, one of the biggest at any university in England.

Exeter boasts one of the most attractive settings of any university, and is currently investing more than £270 million on its main campus. This includes £130 million for student residences, substantial investment in the business school and new facilities for biosciences. The jewel in the crown of the new developments is the Forum, a new £48-million student services centre which will include an extended library and more learning, social and retail facilities.

More than a quarter of the undergraduates come from independent schools – a much higher proportion than the national average for Exeter's subjects, although this figure has been dropping. Professor Steve Smith, the Vice-Chancellor, has put broadening the social mix at the top of his agenda, particularly targeting schools and colleges in the rural South West. Location is partly responsible for the relatively rarefied social mix. There is no large centre of population and despite sophisticated shopping and a lively entertainment scene, South West cathedral cities are not what every teenager is looking for. Nevertheless, the city has been attracting new businesses like the Met Office and benefiting from major investment such as the £235-million Princesshay shopping centre.

A £100-million campus near Falmouth, in Cornwall, has helped boost applications.

Northcote House
The Queen's Drive
Exeter, Devon EX4 4QJ

01392 263855 (admissions)
ug-ad@exeter.ac.uk
www.exeter.ac.uk
www.pcmd.ac.uk
www.exeterguild.org
www.fxu.org.uk

The Times Rankings
Overall Ranking: **12**

Student satisfaction:	=5	(84%)
Research quality:	=10	(2.8)
Entry standards:	17	(408)
Student–staff ratio:	72	(18.4)
Services & facilities/student:	22	(£1,732)
Expected completion rate:	4	(95.8%)
Good honours:	8	(79.6%)
Graduate prospects:	55	(66.8%)

Shared with University College Falmouth, the campus offers Exeter degrees in bioscience, geography, English, law, history and politics plus a range of degrees, such as mining engineering not available in Exeter.

The other big development of recent years was the opening of Peninsula College of Medicine and Dentistry, in association with Plymouth University. Recruitment has been strong and Peninsula was the only successful bidder for a new dental school in 2006. The four-year Bachelor of Dental Surgery has an annual intake of 64 science graduates or health service professionals. Applications more than doubled in its second year when the increase was 10 per cent nationally.

Arabic and Islamic studies have benefited from support from the Middle East. A longstanding focus is exemplified by the growing range of four-year programmes "with international study" and its 180 partner universities worldwide. All students are offered tuition in foreign languages and even some three-year degrees include the option of a year abroad.

Career management skills are built into degree programmes and students can gain work experience through the university's employability and business project programmes. The Careers and Employment Service has been expanded to increase the work experience and placement opportunities available to students. The university's Exeter Awards provide official recognition of all the extra-curricular activities that students undertake to enhance their employability.

The main Streatham Campus is close to the centre of Exeter and has a lively social scene. The highly rated schools of education, sport and health sciences are a mile away in the former St Luke's College. Some £11 million has been invested in sports facilities, which are among the best in the country. Exeter is one of only nine UK universities to have indoor tennis facilities to national competition standards and a new £2-million cricket centre opened in 2009. Exeter is one of the UK's top sporting universities and was placed twelfth in the 2008–09 national rankings.

Undergraduate Fees and Bursaries

» Fees for UK/EU students: £3,290
» International student fees: £11,100–£13,200
   £13,200–£21,500 (medicine)
» Bursary on full grant: household income up to £25K: £1,500
» Bursary on partial grant: household income up to £35K: £750
» Scholarships based on circumstances or by competition.
» For full details see the university's website: http://admin.exeter.ac.uk/academic/scholarships

Students

Undergraduates:	**11,065**	**(420)**
Postgraduates:	**3,275**	**(1,435)**
Mature students:	**7.6%**	
Overseas students:	**12.2%**	
Applications per place:	**6.8**	
From state-sector schools:	**71.0%**	
From working-class homes:	**20.8%**	

For detailed information about fees, grants and bursaries and how they work, see chapter 7.

Accommodation

Number of places and costs refer to 2010–11
University-provided places: 4,309
Percentage catered: 37%
Catered costs: £112.91–£179.20 a week (31 weeks)
Self-catered costs: £73.01–£123.00 a week (40, 44 or 51 weeks).
Unaccompanied first years are guaranteed accommodation provided conditions are met.
International students: as above.
Contact: accommodation@exeter.ac.uk

University of Glamorgan

Glamorgan has been growing in popularity, with a series of increases in applications. The opening of a striking new £35-million campus in the centre of Cardiff in 2007 has made all the difference, increasing the demand for courses based in the capital by more than 60 per cent. The university's Cardiff School of Creative and Cultural Industries offers an "eclectic mix of teaching and research in the theory and practice of media, design and the arts". Students work in an ultra-modern new building, known as the ATRiuM, and have access to 1,350 rooms in privately run halls of residence.

The new development followed a merger with the Royal Welsh College of Music and Drama, with its conservatoire courses. However, most of Glamorgan's 21,000 students will remain on the Treforest campus, 20 minutes by train from Cardiff, overlooking the market town of Pontypridd. Others take Glamorgan courses in five overseas centres or in a growing number of further education colleges across Wales. Four have become accredited colleges, guaranteeing places on degree courses if students meet set conditions, while Merthyr Tydfil College has become the university's Faculty of Further Education.

The university produced good results in the 2008 Research Assessment Exercise, albeit from a low entry in most subjects. Almost a third of the work submitted was judged to be world-leading or internationally excellent, with English and nursing and midwifery doing especially well.

Originally based in a large country house, Glamorgan now has a large, modern campus. The Law School moved to new premises on the main campus in 2008 with upgraded facilities including a moot courtroom, while accommodation for mathematics and computing has had a £5-million refurbishment. The Faculty of Health Sport and Science are on the Glyntaff site, a short walk from the main campus. They are housed in new buildings and restored tramsheds, a reminder of the industrial past of the area. The popular Institute of Chiropractic is one of only two university-based centre for training chiropractors in the UK.

The business school is the largest in Wales, and the university was among the first providers of the Foundation degree. The range of two-year courses has since expanded rapidly, covering subjects as diverse as football and rugby coaching, surveying and costume construction. The vocational approach pays dividends for graduate employment, which is consistently good, although the projected dropout rate is the highest in Wales and among the worst in the UK, at over 26 per cent. The intake is more socially diverse than elsewhere in the Principality. Almost 40 per cent of

Pontypridd
Mid Glamorgan CF37 1DL

0800 716925 (enquiries)
enquiries@glam.ac.uk
www.glam.ac.uk
www.glamsu.com

The Times Rankings
Overall Ranking: **94**

Student satisfaction:	=79	(74%)
Research quality:	=69	(0.5)
Entry standards:	72	(271)
Student–staff ratio:	=67	(18.1)
Services & facilities/student:	66	(£1,244)
Expected completion rate:	110	(69.8%)
Good honours:	=78	(56.0%)
Graduate prospects:	103	(56.1%)

undergraduates come from working-class homes and 14 per cent are from areas with no tradition of higher education.

Glamorgan did well in the early rounds of the National Student Survey, but the university has since slipped into the bottom half of the table. There were some good scores in 2009, however. There was 100 per cent satisfaction among final-year undergraduates in creative writing and high levels in accountancy, English, history and languages. The picture was spoiled for the second year in a row by unusually low scores on some technology courses. However, the Faculty of Advanced Technology has been designated a centre of excellence for Wales, while three National Partnership awards testify to high standards in course design and delivery. Degrees in computer forensics, computer games development, lighting and design technology and aerospace courses are all designed with employers' needs in mind.

Many of the 9,000 full-time undergraduates live around Pontypridd, while others choose Cardiff, which is both livelier and a better source of accommodation. However, the Pontypridd campus has been developing. A new students' union building will open on the Treforest campus in September 2010, providing all the normal facilities, including a nightclub. There is also a modern a recreation centre on campus.

The sports facilities are good enough for Glamorgan to have been awarded the 2001 British University Games and to become one of six centres of excellence in cricket. The university's playing fields have been used for training purposes by leading football and rugby teams. Glamorgan is successful in student competitions, especially in rugby, and offers a number of sports bursaries for students with international potential. There is also a wide range of health and fitness classes for those with lower aspirations.

Undergraduate Fees and Bursaries

» Fees for UK/EU students: £3,290
» International student fees: £9,500
» Bursary on full grant: household income up to £25K: £329
» The university does not award bursaries for students on partial maintenance grants.
» Scholarships based on circumstances or by competition.
» For full details see the university's website: http://money.glam.ac.uk

---

Students

Undergraduates:	**11,205**	**(6,435)**
Postgraduates:	**1,340**	**(1,925)**
Mature students:	**35.8%**	
Overseas students:	**15.8%**	
Applications per place:	**3.5**	
From state-sector schools:	**98.2%**	
From working-class homes:	**39.1%**	

For detailed information about fees, grants and bursaries and how they work, see chapter 7.

Accommodation

Number of places and costs refer to 2009–10
University-provided places: 1,108
Percentage catered: 0%
Self-catered accommodation: £59 (standard) and from £82 (en suite) a week (39 weeks).
First-year students are offered accommodation. Local restrictions apply.
International students are guaranteed housing.
Contact: accom@glam.ac.uk

University of Glasgow

More distinctively Scottish than its rivals in Edinburgh or St Andrews, almost half of Glasgow's students come from within 30 miles of the city and two thirds are from north of the border. There was always a high proportion of home-based students, but the university also attracts students from 116 countries. They seem to enjoy the experience, voting Glasgow fourth in the UK in i-graduate's independent International Student Barometer. British students are also pretty satisfied – Glasgow was in the top five in the National Student Survey published in 2009, after a big improvement on the previous year. The four 100 per cent satisfaction ratings – in classics, genetics, molecular biology and physics – were the most at any university.

Glasgow enjoys the rare distinction of having been established by Papal Bull, and began its existence in the Chapter House of Glasgow Cathedral in 1451. Since 1871 it has been based next to Kelvingrove Park in the city's fashionable west end on the Gilmorehill campus, with its 104 listed buildings – more than any other British university. A major addition, opened in 2002, houses the prestigious medical school, while a £15-million cancer research centre followed in late 2006. A new student centre opened in 2008, with student services and catering facilities.

Education occupies a separate campus nearby, while the Vet School and outdoor sports facilities are located at Garscube, four miles away. A £15-million small animal hospital for the Vet School opened in 2009, with state-of-the-art facilities including a radioactive iodine unit for cats, and an underwater treadmill. The centre will have 11,000 visits annually from all over the UK, and has already won two architecture awards. The environmental research building has also won awards as one of the "greenest" in Scotland.

Glasgow has adopted an increasingly outward-looking style in recent years, marked by the launch of the Common-wealth Scholarship scheme in 2008, which celebrates the city's success as host of the 2014 Commonwealth Games by offering 53 students from developing countries the chance to study at the university. The Centre for International Development, which is the first of its kind in Scotland and the largest in the UK, has helped to secure more than £20-million of research income, including a £4.7-million grant from the Wellcome Trust to enable African scientists to complete research fellowships. The university also has a campus at Dumfries, which is taking liberal arts and teacher education degrees to southwest Scotland.

Not that Glasgow is a stranger to innovation: it was the first university in Britain to have a school of engineering,

University Avenue
Glasgow G12 8QQ

0141 330 2000 (switchboard)
prospectus via website
www.gla.ac.uk
www.theguu.com
www.qmu.org.uk

The Times Rankings
Overall Ranking: **=23**

Student satisfaction:	=11	(81%)
Research quality:	=20	(2.4)
Entry standards:	=21	(399)
Student–staff ratio:	=23	(14.0)
Services & facilities/student:	16	(£1,888)
Expected completion rate:	53	(84.3%)
Good honours:	=28	(70.3%)
Graduate prospects:	31	(72.1%)

for example, and the first in Scotland to have a computer. Today it is a member of the Russell Group of 20 leading research universities. More than half of the work submitted for the 2008 Research Assessment Exercise was considered world-leading or internationally excellent. Art history was the most highly rated in the UK and the Vet School joint top in its field, while the university finished in the top ten in 18 subject areas.

Almost half of the university's applications are for arts or sciences degrees, reflecting the popularity of a flexible system of study where students can delay choosing a subject in which to specialise until the end of their second year. Total applications were up by more than 15 per cent at the start of 2010, following the biggest increase in Scotland in the previous year. But the projected dropout rate of over 15 per cent is above the average for the subjects on offer and entry qualifications.

Overseas recruitment has remained strong, as Glasgow has moved into the top 80 in the QS world university rankings. But the home market has not been overlooked. The Club 21 programme, which provides students with paid work experience placements, involves more than 100 employers from Santander to T-Mobile, some of whom sponsor undergraduates at £1,000 a year, as part of an arrangement to forge closer links with local business.

Nearly a quarter of the students are from working-class homes. The university operates a number of access initiatives, including the Top Up programme, which has been working with schools in the West of Scotland since 1999, and the Talent Awards, 50 annual awards of £1,000 a year for academically able entrants who could face financial difficulties in taking up a place at Glasgow.

Most students like the combination of campus and city life, with the added bonus that Glasgow has been rated among the most cost-effective cities in which to study. Undergraduates have the choice of two students' unions, plus a sports union supporting 46 clubs and activities.

Undergraduate Fees and Bursaries

» Scottish-domiciled and EU students: no fees payable.
» Non-Scottish UK-domiciled student fees: £1,820
   £2,895 (medicine)
» International student fees: £10,750–£14,000
   £20,000 (veterinary medicine)
   £24,750 (medicine)
   £25,750 (dentistry)
» Scholarships based on circumstances or by competition.
» For full details see the university's website: www.gla.ac.uk/scholarships

Students

Undergraduates:	**14,865**	(4,145)
Postgraduates:	**3,375**	(1,855)
Mature students:	**13.9%**	
Overseas students:	**7.9%**	
Applications per place:	**5.5**	
From state-sector schools:	**86.9%**	
From working-class homes:	**24.5%**	

For detailed information about fees, grants and bursaries and how they work, see chapter 7.

Accommodation

Number of places and costs refer to 2010–11
University-provided places: 3,521
Percentage catered: 6.7%
Catered costs: £118.51–£131.39 a week.
Self-catered costs: £70.00 – £105.77 a week.
First years are guaranteed accommodation if conditions are met. Deadline applies.
International students: first years are guaranteed accommodation if conditions are met; 20% of returners are also housed.
Contact: accom@gla.ac.uk

Glasgow Caledonian University

Glasgow Caledonian has spent more than £70 million transforming previously mediocre facilities into a single campus that does justice to a modern university of more than 16,000 students. Over 80 per cent of the buildings are new or have been upgraded, and improvements are still being made. The health building brings together teaching and research facilities and includes a virtual hospital, where students can hone their clinical and interpersonal skills. The Saltire Centre, which has brought all library and student services together for the first time, opened in 2006 with study spaces for 1,800 students.

With the accent firmly on widening participation in higher education, the university will always struggle in league tables such as ours, but it is well-regarded by employers, and applications have been healthy. There was a 48 per cent increase at the start of 2010, buoyed by changes in the applications process for nursing. Caledonian is among the top UK universities for attracting students from areas without a tradition of higher education, and more than a third of its undergraduates come from working-class homes. The university has argued forcefully that extending access should be rewarded more generously if such students are to receive the support they need to make a success of higher education.

The projected dropout rate came down to 19 per cent in the most recent survey, but still above the UK average for Caledonian's courses and entry qualifications. Caledonian has introduced a series of measures designed to improve retention. Telltale signs are monitored, such as non-attendance at lectures, and better academic, social and financial support offered to those at risk of dropping out.

The compact, modern city-centre campus is a big advantage for the university. Sports and social facilities have been among the priorities in the building programme and a learning café combines enhanced-learning technology with an informal cyber-café atmosphere.

Half of the 14 subject areas in which the university entered the 2008 Research Assessment Exercise contained at least some world-leading work, with 30 per cent of all researchers judged to have produced world-leading or internationally excellent work. Health subjects registered the best results and entered the largest numbers for assessment. The university has among the most extensive health programmes in Britain and produced particularly good results in rehabilitative health sciences, which covers long-term health conditions such as arthritis and strokes.

Cowcaddens Road
Glasgow G4 0BA

0141 331 8681 (enquiries)
helpline@gcal.ac.uk
www.gcu.ac.uk
www.caledonianstudent.com

The Times Rankings
Overall Ranking: **65**

Student satisfaction:	=46	(77%)
Research quality:	=77	(0.4)
Entry standards:	42	(328)
Student–staff ratio:	108	(23.1)
Services & facilities/student:	77	(£1,158)
Expected completion rate:	82	(79.7%)
Good honours:	=43	(66.0%)
Graduate prospects:	=66	(62.6%)

Business is the other big area, the Caledonian Business School boasting more undergraduates than any other institution in Scotland, with almost 1,000 in each year group. The university pioneered subjects such as entrepreneurial studies and risk management – the only university in the country to do so – and offers highly specialist degrees, such as tourism management, fashion marketing, leisure management and consumer protection.

Caledonian has extended its offering this year with the establishment of a London campus providing a range of specialist postgraduate courses and professional development programmes in business, finance and risk, retailing and tourism from the heart of the City. The new venture makes Caledonian the first Scottish university to have a campus in London. It also has a long-established engineering college in Oman, part of an international network that includes partners in China, India, Pakistan and South America. The most significant of these involves joint degrees with the University of Jinan, in China's Shandong province.

Degrees in all areas are strongly vocational, and are complemented by a wide portfolio of professional courses. A high proportion of students choose sandwich courses, which help to boost graduates' prospects in the employment market.

The legacy of Queen's College, which catered mainly for women, has continued with Caledonian registering one of the highest proportions of female students at any university in Britain. Sports and social facilities have been among the priorities in the building programme. Some students find that the high proportion of their peers living at home detracts from the social scene, but Glasgow is a very lively city with a large student population. The university is consistently rated top in Scotland for international student experience, according to independent education researchers i-graduate.

Undergraduate Fees and Bursaries
» Scottish-domiciled and EU students: no fees payable.
» Non-Scottish UK-domiciled student fees: £1,820
» International student fees: £9,500–£10,500
» Scholarships based on circumstances or by competition.
» For full details see the university's website: www.gcu.ac.uk/student/money/index.html

Students
Undergraduates:	**11,305**	(3,830)
Postgraduates:	**1,700**	(1,575)
Mature students:	**37.2%**	
Overseas students:	**4.2%**	
Applications per place:	**4.7**	
From state-sector schools:	**97.0%**	
From working-class homes:	**36.8%**	

For detailed information about fees, grants and bursaries and how they work, see chapter 7.

Accommodation
Number of places and costs refer to 2010–11
University-provided places: 660
Percentage catered: 0%
Self-catered costs: £83.46–£96.21 a week.
Students under 19 living outside the Glasgow area have priority for accommodation.
International students: non-EU students given priority if conditions are met.
Contact: www.gcu.ac.uk/study/undergraduate/accommodation

University of Gloucestershire

Gloucestershire is closing two campuses and dividing its courses between the university's three remaining sites in time for the 2011 intake. The reorganisation, in response to financial problems that have seen the departure of the Vice-Chancellor, will reduce the four faculties to three, but maintain the full range of subjects. One casualty is a London campus for teacher training, which only opened in 2003. The other is the Pittville campus, in Cheltenham, whose art and design students will transfer to the nearby Francis Close Hall, which they will share with a new Institute of Education and Public Services, covering education, health and social care.

The main Park Campus, on the site of a former botanical garden, will be the main base for the Faculty of Professional Studies for students in accounting, law and business management. Sport and exercise sciences, playwork, leisure, tourism, hospitality and event management will continue to be based at the Oxstalls campus in Gloucester, which will also house the Countryside and Community Research Institute and the International Research Institute in Sustainability.

Gloucestershire has had a focus on green issues, topping the Green League of Universities in 2008 for its all-round environmental performance and finishing in the top five in 2009. There are allotments for students and a bike loan scheme, as well as diplomas in environmentalism and an International Research Institute in Sustainability. Students are discouraged from bringing cars to university and, although a free bus service has been scrapped, fares between campuses are subsidised. This approach may be a factor in the growing popularity of the university: although applications only rose by 3 per cent at the start of 2010, the 20 per cent increase in 2009 was one of the biggest in the UK.

One of the more recent additions to the list of universities, Gloucestershire is also the first for more than a century to have formal links with the Church of England. Although its religious origins have been played down in recent years and students of all faiths are welcomed, the university includes church appointees on its governing body. Lord Carey, the former Archbishop of Canterbury, is its first Chancellor. This did not prevent the university dropping theology at degree level as part of a curriculum review, although the subject returned to the prospectus for 2010–11.

Before university status in 2001, Cheltenham and Gloucester College of Higher Education had been the product of a merger between a church college and the higher education wing of a college of arts and

The Park Campus
The Park
Cheltenham GL50 2RH

0844 8011100 (prospectus)
admissions@glos.ac.uk
www.glos.ac.uk
www.yourstudentsunion.com

The Times Rankings
Overall Ranking: **64**

Student satisfaction:	=69	(75%)
Research quality:	=88	(0.3)
Entry standards:	90	(255)
Student–staff ratio:	=67	(18.1)
Services & facilities/student:	49	(£1,397)
Expected completion rate:	71	(81.8%)
Good honours:	59	(60.9%)
Graduate prospects:	75	(60.3%)

technology. After considerable expansion during the 1990s, there are now about 9,200 students, including 2,800 part-timers, and over 1,300 academic and support staff. The university prides itself on a good range of work placements, which include Microsoft and Disneyworld.

The main campus is on the attractive site of the former College of St Paul and St Mary, a mile outside Cheltenham. There has also been considerable development of the Gloucester campus, on the site of a former domestic science college which became part of the university in 2002. Although middle-class Cheltenham is a world away from more working-class Gloucester socially, the two centres are only seven miles apart and students are not as isolated as they are in some split-site institutions.

Gloucestershire did not quite repeat the success it enjoyed in the previous research assessments when the exercise was repeated in 2008. Some world-leading research was found in five of the 12 areas in which the university submitted work, with the small education entry producing the best results. But less than 20 per cent of all work reached the top two categories. Results in the National Student Survey improved in 2009, with English, teacher training, languages, marketing, theology and tourism recording the highest satisfaction levels.

The university's intake is diverse, with over 95 per cent of undergraduates from state schools and over a third from working-class homes. The projected dropout rate has improved dramatically, with the latest projection of 8 per cent well below the national average for the university's subjects and entry qualifications. The well-equipped Gloucester campus, where participation in higher education has always been low, focuses particularly on access initiatives.

The sports facilities include a sports hall, gym and tennis courts. First years are given preference for the 1,350 hall places, and the university assures its students that it has access to enough private sector places to meet their needs. At both sites facilities overall are improving.

Undergraduate Fees and Bursaries
» Fees for UK/EU students: £3,290
» International student fees: £8,615
» Bursary on full grant: household income up to £25K: £385
» The university does not award bursaries for students on partial maintenance grants.
» Scholarships based on circumstances or by competition.
» For full details see the university's website: www.glos.ac.uk/money

Students
Undergraduates:	**5,820**	(1,205)
Postgraduates:	**635**	(1,595)
Mature students:	**17.3%**	
Overseas students:	**5.5%**	
Applications per place:	**4.2**	
From state-sector schools:	**95.4%**	
From working-class homes:	**36.1%**	

Accommodation
Number of places and costs refer to 2009–10
University-provided places: about 1,350
Percentage catered: 0%
Self-catered costs: £71–£104 a week.
First-year undergraduates have priority for halls.
International students: first-year undergraduates are guaranteed accommodation if conditions are met.
Contact: accommodation@glos.ac.uk

Glyndŵr University

The former North East Wales Institute of Higher Education took the name of the medieval Welsh prince Owain Glyndŵr, who championed the establishment of universities throughout Wales in the early 15th century, when it was awarded university status in 2008. The new university is based on two campuses in Wrexham and one at Northop, in Flintshire, on the site of the former Welsh College of Horticulture. The Flintshire campus is the first university presence in the county, and £1.7 million has been invested to make it a centre of excellence for land and animal-based studies.

Glyndŵr has fewer than 3,000 full-time students and another 4,900 part-timers, whose qualifications will continue to be awarded by the University of Wales. Nearly two thirds of the undergraduates are over 21 on entry and nearly a third of all students are from overseas, many from other EU countries, India or China. As NEWI, there were only two applications per place – a lower ratio than at any UK university. But in 2009 Glyndŵr enjoyed the customary boost that accompanies a change of status, and applications had risen by another 38 per cent at the start of 2010.

Sports science produced one of the few 100 per cent satisfaction ratings in the National Student Survey published in 2009. There were good scores, too, for education, English, biology and business studies. Many of the results were an improvement on the previous year, but not enough overall to escape the lower reaches of the table.

Fewer than half of the undergraduates are school-leavers and nearly all of them are state-educated. More than half are from working-class homes – easily the biggest proportion in Wales and far in excess of the UK average for the university's subjects and entry grades. Glyndŵr also has the largest proportion of disabled students in Wales and was nominated for an award for its provision for them. There is a dedicated centre for students with disabilities that assesses students' needs before they embark on a course.

Among a raft of new courses for 2009–10 were a Foundation degree in floristry and floral design and degrees in mobile computing and therapeutic childcare. The university has even launched a degree in equestrian psychology, examining the way in which horses learn and investigating their bond with humans. Only Cardiff has a better graduate employment rate among universities in Wales.

Glyndŵr entered only 27 academics for the 2008 Research Assessment Exercise, but almost a quarter of their work was judged to be world-leading or internationally excellent. Computer science and materials both reached the top grade for a small proportion

Mold Road
Wrexham
N. Wales LL11 2AW

01978 293469 (student enquiries)
sid@glyndwr.ac.uk
www.glyndwr.ac.uk
www.glyndwr.ac.uk/
 Studentsupportservices/
 en/StudentsGuild

The Times Rankings
Overall Ranking: **93**

Student satisfaction:	=69	(75%)
Research quality:	=95	(0.2)
Entry standards:	=106	(232)
Student–staff ratio:	101	(21.0)
Services & facilities/student:	34	(£1,561)
Expected completion rate:	=95	(77.2%)
Good honours:	88	(52.8%)
Graduate prospects:	=66	(62.6%)

of their work, and the university's research funding more than doubled as a result. A new Creative Industries Centre is due to open on the Wrexham campus in 2011, bringing together art, design, media, engineering and computing to train a new generation of multi-skilled graduates. A Centre for the Child will open in the same year, promising a new outlook on child development and education studies.

The two campuses in Wrexham are within five minutes' walk of each other. Most courses are taught at the larger Plas Coch site, next to the Wrexham FC ground. The university's art school is based at the Regent Street campus, nearer the town centre.

The modern sports centre, in Wrexham, is one of the features of the university. There are two floodlit artificial pitches with different surfaces, including an international standard hockey pitch, a human performance laboratory and indoor facilities that include a sports hall with a 1,000 square-metre sprung floor. The centre has hosted a number of big sporting events, as well as conferences.

Bursaries of up to £1,000 a year are available for all UK students, dependant on family income, and entrants to full-time courses with more than 300 UCAS points are eligible for one-off scholarships of another £1,000. Two thirds of the students are from the local area, many living at home, which inevitably affects the social scene. But Wrexham is not without nightlife, and both Manchester and Liverpool are within reach for those in search of more sophisticated shopping or clubbing.

Undergraduate Fees and Bursaries
» Fees for UK/EU students: £3,290
» International student fees: £6,950*
» Bursary of £500 (household income up to £18,370)
» Bursary of £450 (household income up to £22,000)
» Bursary of £350 (household income up to £95,000)
» Scholarships based on circumstances or by competition.
» For full details see the university's website: www.glyndwr.ac.uk/en/Feesandstudentfinance

*Figures for 2009-10

Students
Undergraduates:	**2,540**	**(4,275)**
Postgraduates:	**450**	**(465)**
Mature students:	**61.9%**	
Overseas students:	**33.7%**	
Applications per place:	**2.1**	
From state-sector schools:	**99.1%**	
From working-class homes:	**54.5%**	

Accommodation
Number of places and costs refer to 2010-11
University-provided places: 459
Percentage catered: 0%
Self-catered costs: £58.50-£82.95 a week (37 weeks)
First-year undergraduates are guaranteed accommodation.
International students: guaranteed housing.
Contact: www.glyndwr.ac.uk/Studentsupportservices/en/Accommodation
accommodation@glyndwr.ac.uk

Goldsmiths, University of London

Dubbed the "campus of cool", Goldsmiths is best known for excellence in the arts, but it stresses that it brings the same creative approach to a wider range of subjects, spanning humanities, social sciences and teacher training. Although it did not take part in the Brand Council's most recent exercise, Goldsmiths' nickname came from its inclusion alongside MTV, Apple and the Tate among 50 previous "cool brand leaders". Alumni include Mary Quant and Damien Hirst among many other famous names, such as Antony Gormley, Julian Clary, Malcolm McLaren and Linton Kwesi Johnson. Graduates of the college have won the Turner Prize no fewer than six times.

There is another side to Goldsmiths, however, in its tradition of community-based courses, which predates membership of the University of London. Evening and other part-time classes are still as popular as conventional degree courses and many subjects can be studied from basic to postgraduate levels. A history of providing educational opportunities for women is reflected in one of the largest proportions of female students in the British university system – nearly two thirds at the last count.

Determinedly integrated into its southeast London locality, the campus has a cosmopolitan atmosphere. Nearly a third of all undergraduates are over 21 on entry (a large proportion of these over 30), many coming from the area's ethnic minorities, and there is a growing proportion of overseas students. The age profile helped Goldsmiths to a rise in applications of more than 26 per cent at the start of 2010.

The older premises have been likened to a grammar school, with their long corridors of classrooms. But the Rutherford Building, containing library and IT services, won an award from the Royal Institute of British Architects, and a Grade II listed former baths building has been converted to provide more space for research and art studios. The Ben Pimlott Building, which features a dramatic metal "scribble" by the acclaimed architect Will Alsop, contains state-of-the-art studio facilities and two multi-disciplinary centres for interaction between the arts and social sciences.

Although dominated by the arts, Goldsmiths' portfolio of subjects stretches through the humanities and social sciences as far as computing and psychology. More than half of the work submitted for the 2008 Research Assessment Exercise was considered world-leading or internationally excellent. Indeed, it was among the top ten universities for the proportion of work (22 per cent) placed in the highest category. Communication, cultural and media studies

Lewisham Way
New Cross
London SE14 6NW

020 7078 5300
admissions@gold.ac.uk
www.gold.ac.uk
http://goldsmithsstudents.org

The Times Rankings
Overall Ranking: **52**

Student satisfaction:	=89	(73%)
Research quality:	=18	(2.5)
Entry standards:	44	(318)
Student–staff ratio:	=50	(16.8)
Services & facilities/student:	109	(£911)
Expected completion rate:	=66	(82.5%)
Good honours:	=43	(66.0%)
Graduate prospects:	98	(56.7%)

led the way, but there were good results, too, in music, sociology and art and design.

There are only 6,200 full-time students and around 1,400 part-timers. Undergraduates have shown themselves generally been satisfied in the National Student Survey although, in common with other London universities, really high scores have been hard to come by. Only education, sociology, social policy and anthropology reached satisfaction levels of 90 per cent in 2009.

Employment prospects are good, especially for an institution with such a high proportion of students taking performing arts subjects, where a period of unemployment after graduation is commonplace. Indeed, on postgraduate courses, recent success rates have been among the best in Britain.

Student politics has survived at Goldsmiths to an extent not seen at many universities – the union building was given the name Tiananmen – while a college in which Alex James and Graham Coxon, from Blur, are just two of a number of successful rock alumni cannot fail to have a thriving music scene. The union has a strong tradition in volunteering and an award-winning newspaper, and in recent years have been winners of several Sound Impact Awards, recognising work on ethical and environmental issues.

The surrounding area enjoyed a mini-boom before the recession as a prime location for loft apartments. Although sky-high prices put them way beyond the reach of the student housing market, there are plenty of more reasonably priced options in the vicinity. Most first years are allocated one of the 971 residential places within walking distance of the campus and overseas students can be housed throughout their course. Sports enthusiasts have been less well provided for, although there is a well-equipped and affordable gym on campus. There is also a swimming pool and indoor complex in Deptford, but the main pitches are eight miles away.

Undergraduate Fees and Bursaries
» Fees for UK/EU students: £3,290
» International student fees: £10,170–£13,680
» Bursary on full grant: household income up to £25K: household income up to £19K: £1,000 then £500.
» Bursary on partial grant: household income up to £40K: £329.
» Scholarships based on circumstances or by competition.
» For full details see the university's website: www.gold.ac.uk/ug/costs

Students
Undergraduates:	**4,905**	(595)
Postgraduates:	**1,330**	(825)
Mature students:	**30.1%**	
Overseas students:	**12.8%**	
Applications per place:	**5.9**	
From state-sector schools:	**89.9%**	
From working-class homes:	**31.6%**	

Accommodation
Number of places and costs refer to 2009–10
University-provided places: 971 (college halls); 83 studio flats through McMillan Student Village (private hall provider)
Percentage catered: 0%
Self-catered costs: £88.90–£119.20 a week (studio flats in McMillan Student Village are £156–£200 a week)
Priority is given to new full-time students.
International students will be given priority for accommodation throughout their degree programme.
Contact: www.goldsmiths.ac.uk/accommodation

University of Greenwich

Greenwich was one of three universities charging British and EU undergraduates less than £3,000 when top-up fees were introduced, but it finally raised them to the maximum for new undergraduates in 2010–11. Those taking Foundation degrees and HNDs will continue to receive a hefty discount, paying £2,300 a year for full-time courses. The change hardly seemed to deter prospective students – applications were up by almost 40 per cent at the start of 2010.

The university's move, completed in 2002, into the former Royal Naval College buildings designed by Sir Christopher Wren provided a campus worthy of one of the most desirable titles in the higher education world. Its name has always conjured up images of history and science in equal measure, and the main campus is now part of a World Heritage site. Wren's baroque masterpiece is being used, with the former Dreadnought Hospital, to teach over half the university's students in humanities, business, law, maths, computing and maritime studies. Four halls provide around 2,300 places.

Under the leadership of Baroness Blackstone, the former Higher Education Minister, Greenwich has dropped the soubriquet of "regional university" but still draws primarily from southeast London and Kent, a populous county that until recently had only a single university. The prize-winning Medway campus, centred on the former naval base at Chatham, has been developed in partnership with Kent and Canterbury Christ Church universities. New student accommodation for an additional 140 students opened there in 2008, together with an improved café for Greenwich students in the main Pembroke building. Greenwich put £20 million into the campus, which houses one of the first new schools of pharmacy for 20 years, as well as the schools of science and engineering, the Natural Resources Institute, nursing and some business courses. A joint learning resources centre serves Chatham Maritime and the University of Kent's neighbouring premises. Another shared facility has improved teaching facilities and expanded student services, the campus having already exceeded the original target of 6,000 students.

Other schools are situated at Avery Hill, a Victorian mansion on the outskirts of southeast London, where a £14-million sports and teaching centre opened in 2006, with a new gym and refurbished café following in 2008. As well as a sports hall and 220-seat lecture theatre, there are laboratories for health courses that replicate NHS wards. A neighbouring building is now the main base for the School of Health and Social Care. The campus also contains a student village of 1,300 rooms, as well as teaching accommodation for the social sciences, architecture, landscape and construction, and the large education faculty, which is one of the few to offer both primary

Old Royal Naval College
Park Row,
Greenwich
London SE10 9LS

0800 005 006 (course enquiries)
courseinfo@greenwich.ac.uk
www.gre.ac.uk
www.suug.co.uk

The Times Rankings
Overall Ranking: **103**

Student satisfaction:	=32	(78%)
Research quality:	=77	(0.4)
Entry standards:	=98	(241)
Student–staff ratio:	113	(25.1)
Services & facilities/student:	99	(£1,023)
Expected completion rate:	101	(75.7%)
Good honours:	107	(47.4%)
Graduate prospects:	82	(59.7%)

and secondary teacher training courses. The Avery Hill TV studio has also been refurbished to meet current industrial standards.

The university has also bought a large site in Greenwich town centre, where it plans to invest £60 million in a new library and a new home for the School of Architecture and Construction. The development will increase student numbers in the town by about 20 per cent.

Student satisfaction rates have improved dramatically since the early years of the National Student Survey, with Greenwich now outscoring most universities in the capital. The Medway pharmacy students were the most satisfied in the country in 2009, while philosophy, nursing, law, economics and maths all produced good results.

The university achieved mixed results from a large entry to the 2008 Research Assessment Exercise, which showed a quarter of the work reaching world-leading or internationally excellent levels. The small mechanical engineering group produced by far the best results, but architecture and history also did well. A fifth of the university's income is from research and consultancy – the largest proportion at any former polytechnic.

Eleven associated colleges in Kent and London teach the university's courses, while strong links with institutions in Europe and further afield provide a steady flow of overseas students, as well as exchange opportunities for those at Greenwich. The university is the UK's top recruiter of students from India, and also takes large numbers from Mauritius and Nigeria.

A commitment to extending access has led to low entrance requirements in many subjects and a relatively high proportion of mature students. At present 98 per cent of undergraduates are state-educated, and over 55 per cent come from working-class homes. Both figures are significantly higher than the national average for Greenwich's courses and entrance qualifications. The downside has been the dropout rate. However, the latest projection of 15 per cent, while not low, is better than the university's benchmark.

Undergraduate Fees and Bursaries

» Fees for UK/EU students: £3,290
» International student fees: £8,950
» Bursary on full grant: household income up to £25K: £400; £550 for mature students.
» Bursary on partial grant: household income up to £34K: sliding scale £375–£350; for mature students, sliding scale £535–£500.
» Scholarships based on circumstances or by competition.
» For full details see the university's website: www.gre.ac.uk/students/finance

Students

Undergraduates:	**13,700**	(6,850)
Postgraduates:	**2,795**	(2,775)
Mature students:	**45.1%**	
Overseas students:	**12.7%**	
Applications per place:	**5.7**	
From state-sector schools:	**98.0%**	
From working-class homes:	**55.5%**	

Accommodation

Number of places and costs refer to 2009–10
University-provided places: 2,300
Percentage catered: 0%
Self-catered costs: £87.08–£156.52 a week.
First years are guaranteed a place. Conditions apply.
International students: new students get priority.
Contact: www.gre.ac.uk/about/accommodation;
accommodation-AH@gre.ac.uk (Avery Hill)
accommodation-GM@gre.ac.uk (Greenwich)
accommodation-ME@gre.ac.uk (Medway)

Heriot-Watt University

Heriot-Watt is investing £10 million to increase its academic staff by 50 per cent, boosting teaching and research in business and technology in order to become a world-leading university within ten years. The university is already Scotland's most international institution, with a campus in Dubai and a total of almost 12,000 students in approved learning centres overseas or taking distance learning courses in 150 different countries.

Heriot-Watt also produces more graduates than any of its rivals north of the border in the physical sciences, mathematics, engineering and in the built environment. Concentration on these areas is fitting for a university which commemorates James Watt, the pioneer of steam power, and George Heriot, financier to King James VI. The university has fostered inter-disciplinary teaching and research, with a battery of employment-related degrees.

Heriot-Watt is also one of the most commercially diversified universities in Britain, with the share of private research funding consistently among the highest in the UK per member of academic staff. About half of the university's income, around £70 million, comes from research, training and commercial services.

More than half of the work in a larger-than-average submission for the 2008 Research Assessment Exercise was rated world-leading or internationally excellent. Mathematics produced by far the best results, but there were good grades, too, in petroleum engineering, physics, general engineering, the built environment, and art and design. The results helped propel the university seven places up last year's *Times* league table and into the top 40, although it has slipped back a little to 43 this year.

The last institutional review of the university's quality, in 2006, produced the top grade of "broad confidence". Heriot-Watt has also done well in the National Student Survey, although its scores slipped in the 2009 publication. Civil and chemical engineering, accounting and chemistry produced the best results.

The main campus, at Riccarton, close to Edinburgh Airport and 20 minutes drive from the city centre, still has a modern feel more than 40 years after it opened. The university remains small in terms of full-time students – there are about 6,900 on the Edinburgh campus, with another 1,300 in Dubai taking business, engineering, science, technology or textiles and design courses. Overseas students also fill a quarter of the places at Riccarton. Heriot-Watt won the Scottish Council of Development and Industry's 2007 award for Outstanding International Achievement in Scotland's Universities, partly for its support for

Riccarton
Edinburgh EH14 4AS

0131 449 5111
enquiries@hw.ac.uk
www.hw.ac.uk
www.hwusa.org

The Times Rankings
Overall Ranking: **43**

Student satisfaction:	=79	(74%)
Research quality:	=41	(1.9)
Entry standards:	41	(338)
Student–staff ratio:	=50	(16.8)
Services & facilities/student:	23	(£1,726)
Expected completion rate:	=64	(82.6%)
Good honours:	34	(68.6%)
Graduate prospects:	=22	(74.7%)

international students.

Science, engineering, management and languages are located on the Edinburgh campus. There is a postgraduate campus at Stromness in Orkney, specialising in renewable energy, and a Scottish Borders Campus in Galashiels, 35 miles south of Edinburgh, which specialises in textiles, fashion, textiles design and management. Heriot-Watt and Borders College have signed a partnership agreement for a long-term collaboration to deliver higher and further education in the historically under-provided region, both institutions now sharing £34 million of new campus facilities.

The subject mix serves graduates well: Heriot-Watt is seldom far from the top of the graduate employment league tables. The latest projected dropout rate of less than 10 per cent is well below the UK average for the university's subjects and entrance qualifications. More than half of the undergraduates are from Scotland, and 17 per cent from other parts of Britain, over 90 per cent of them from state schools and colleges.

The Edinburgh campus has an attractive parkland setting, with the students' union at its heart and halls of residence conveniently placed. Students have complained that the six-mile journey to the city centre leaves them isolated, but there are now frequent bus services. Sports enthusiasts are well provided for, and representative teams do well. Hearts, one of Edinburgh's two Scottish Premier League football clubs, have their sports academy on campus, which is used by students and local people as well as the young professionals. Music also thrives: there is a professional musician-in-residence and a number of music scholarships, as well as a varied programme of events.

Undergraduate Fees and Bursaries

» Scottish-domiciled and EU students: no fees payable.
» Non-Scottish UK-domiciled student fees: £1,820
» International student fees: £9,730–£12,270
» Scholarships based on circumstances or by competition.
» For full details see the university's website: www.hw.ac.uk/student-life/scholarships-fees.htm

Students

Undergraduates:	**5,360**	(425)
Postgraduates:	**1,575**	(3,070)
Mature students:	**16.9%**	
Overseas students:	**25.2%**	
Applications per place:	**3.6**	
From state-sector schools:	**90.4%**	
From working-class homes:	**29.7%**	

Accommodation

Number of places and costs refer to 2010–11
University places provided: 1,624
Percentage catered: 19%
Catered costs: £120 a week.
Self-catered costs: £69–£98 a week.
All new first years are guaranteed accommodation provided conditions are met and applications in place by 22 August.
International students: as above.
Contact: halls@hw.ac.uk

University of Hertfordshire

Hertfordshire has become a model for the "business-facing" university, serving the needs of local employers and improving the job prospects of its students in the process. The university even runs the local bus service and plays an important role in steering the local economy. A purpose-built £120-million campus, close to the existing Hatfield headquarters, opened in 2003, bringing the university together for the first time and providing outstanding facilities. The de Havilland campus, named after the aircraft manufacturer which once occupied the site, houses business, education and the humanities. It has a 24-hour learning resources centre, £15-million sports complex and 1,600 networked, en-suite residential places. The two sites are linked by cycleways, footpaths and university-owned shuttle buses.

As Hatfield Polytechnic, the university's reputation was built on engineering and computer science, but health subjects now account for by far the largest share of places. An innovative degree in paramedic science was Britain's first, its students using the UK's largest medical simulation centre to train how to treat patients in emergency situations. The university is still hoping for a medical school, although its last bid was not successful. A new School of Pharmacy and a postgraduate medical school have strengthened its position. Increased research activity resulted in the establishment of the Health and Human Sciences Institute.

Art and design is also growing, particularly the multimedia courses. In 2005, the university launched a School of Film, Music and New Media and in 2007 built a £10-million media centre, with the latest technology for the teaching of music, animation, film, television and multimedia, based on the College Lane campus. This includes one of the largest art gallery in the eastern region, which mounts regular public exhibitions, while a 460-seat auditorium enhances the cultural programme. An Automotive Centre has upgraded the teaching facilities for that branch of engineering, as well as boosting interaction with industry.

Professor Tim Wilson, the Vice-Chancellor, has been trying to widen the university's base through collaboration with local further education colleges. The intake is more diverse than might be expected, given the location and subject mix: 40 per cent of undergraduates come from working-class homes and 97 per cent are state-educated. The projected dropout rate declined a little in the latest survey to nearly 16 per cent, a little above the national average of 15.5 percent for the subject mix and entry grades.

Applications were up by 36 per cent at the start of 2010, following a healthy increase in

College Lane
Hatfield
Herts AL10 9AB

01707 284800 (admissions)
admissions@herts.ac.uk
www.herts.ac.uk
www.uhsu.co.uk

The Times Rankings
Overall Ranking: **63**

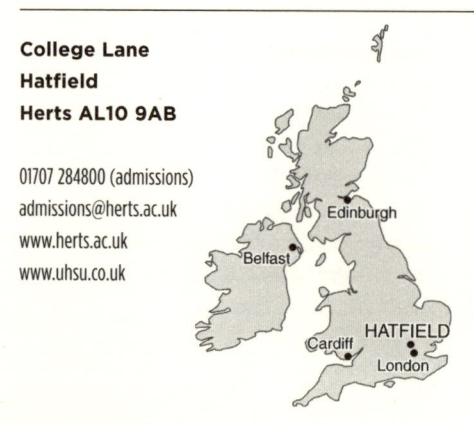

Student satisfaction:	=69	(75%)
Research quality:	=77	(0.4)
Entry standards:	=98	(241)
Student–staff ratio:	=40	(15.6)
Services & facilities/student:	27	(£1,644)
Expected completion rate:	=73	(81.3%)
Good honours:	63	(59.5%)
Graduate prospects:	64	(62.9%)

the previous year which led to the recruitment of 500 students more than the university's official target. Many Hertfordshire students include work placements in their degrees, the close links with employers sometimes bringing in valuable research and consultancy contracts, and contributing to a consistently good graduate employment record. Last year the university launched Graduate Futures, a new programme offering graduates lifelong support on employment and career development issues.

Hertfordshire's record in the National Student Survey has been disappointing, although there was some improvement in 2009. The most satisfied students were in creative writing, communications, pharmacy, physiology and human resource management.

Hertfordshire produced some of the best results of any post-1992 university in the 2008 Research Assessment Exercise, when approaching half of its submission was judged to be world-leading or internationally excellent. History, nursing and midwifery, engineering and computing collected the highest grades. The results helped the university to a rise of 13 places in last year's *Times* league table and a further three places this year.

The award-winning library and resource centre on the main campus is Britain's biggest, offering 24-hour access to hundreds of computer workstations. A second centre on the de Havilland campus provides another 1,100 workstations. The StudyNet information system has been a leader in its field, giving all staff and students their own storage space. Students can use it for study, revision or communication, as well as to access university information.

In September 2009, the university opened the Forum, a new student venue on the College Lane campus. It includes an auditorium for live gigs and club nights, a nursery, a convenience store and a multi-storey car park, as well as quiet areas. A £15-million sports complex, the Hertfordshire Sports Village, boasts some of the best university-based facilities in Britain. Although principally for student use, it is also open to local residents.

Undergraduate Fees and Bursaries

» Fees for UK/EU students: £3,290
» International student fees: £8,000
» Bursary on full grant: household income up to £25K: £1,000
» The university does not award bursaries for students on partial maintenance grants.
» Scholarships based on circumstances or by competition.
» For full details see the university's website: www.herts.ac.uk/courses/fees-and-funding

Students

Undergraduates:	**15,800**	**(4,040)**
Postgraduates:	**2,580**	**(2,700)**
Mature students:	**26.0%**	
Overseas students:	**12.1%**	
Applications per place:	**3.6**	
From state-sector schools:	**97.7%**	
From working-class homes:	**40.4%**	

Accommodation

Number of places and costs refer to 2010–11
University-provided places: 3,300
Percentage catered: 0%
Self-catered costs: £68–£112 a week.
First years are guaranteed accommodation if conditions are met.
International students: as above.
Contact: Accommodation@herts.ac.uk

University of Huddersfield

Official performance indicators for higher education have shown Huddersfield living up to its mission to help produce a more diverse student population. More than four out of ten full-time students are from working-class homes – far in excess than the national average for the university's courses and entry qualifications – and the numbers coming from areas without a tradition of higher education are among the highest in the country. The university has opened satellite centres in Barnsley and Oldham to widen participation further.

Imaginative conversions and new buildings have finally allowed the university to come together on one town-centre campus. The university capitalised on Huddersfield's industrial past to ease the strain on facilities that were struggling to cope with expansion which reached 13 per cent a year at its peak. There are now more than 21,000 students. Canalside, a refurbished mill complex, provided extra space for mathematics and computing, and education occupies another mill site – this time a £4-million re-creation of the original. The university is even creating "pocket parks" and a landscaped area along the reopened Narrow Canal to provide additional green space. Human and health sciences have also acquired new premises,
and an additional £4 million has been spent on a new students' union, allowing drama courses to take over the existing union complex. The new union includes alcohol-free social areas to encourage participation by those overseas students and ethnic minorities who would otherwise avoid the facilities.

The most recent addition is a striking Creative Arts Building, which cost some £16 million. A similar sum is being spent on a new Business School, due to open in 2010. The 19th-century Ramsden Building – the historical heart of the university, in use for 125 years – has now been refurbished and there are up-to-the-minute facilities behind its carefully preserved exterior.

A tradition of vocational education dates back to 1841, and the university has a long-established reputation in areas such as textile design and engineering. But there are less obvious gems such as music and social work, as well as teacher training, for which Huddersfield was awarded a national centre of excellence. Scores in the National Student Survey improved in 2009, although the university remained in the bottom half of the table. History produced by far the best score, close to 100 per cent satisfaction, while physiology, finance, teacher training and subjects allied to medicine also did well. The university's own satisfaction surveys suggest that students value the friendliness and helpfulness of staff. The dropout rate had

**Queensgate
Huddersfield
West Yorkshire HD1 3DH**

0870 901 5555 (prospectus)
prospectus@hud.ac.uk
www.hud.ac.uk
www.huddersfield
   student.com

The Times Rankings
Overall Ranking: **73**

Student satisfaction:	=69	(75%)
Research quality:	=95	(0.2)
Entry standards:	71	(272)
Student–staff ratio:	=44	(15.9)
Services & facilities/student:	48	(£1,409)
Expected completion rate:	93	(77.7%)
Good honours:	69	(57.3%)
Graduate prospects:	=71	(61.1%)

been improving, but the latest projection of 20 per cent is higher than the national average for Huddersfield's courses and entry qualifications.

Most of the areas in which Huddersfield entered the 2008 Research Assessment Exercise contained at least some world-leading work. A third of the university's submission was placed in the top two categories, with music producing by far the best results and social work also doing well. The results brought a 45 per cent increase in research funding. A flourishing relationship with industry produces more private income than is achieved in many larger institutions, as well as influencing courses. The university has sealed partnerships recently with the National Physical Laboratory, the Food and Environment Research Agency and the Royal Armouries in developments that it expects to benefit undergraduates as well as researchers.

The most popular courses are in human and health sciences. Many arts and social science courses have a vocational slant. Politics, for example, includes a six-week work placement, which often takes students to the House of Commons. The university's Chancellor, the actor Sir Patrick Stewart, coaches drama students in his capacity as professor of performing arts, as well as performing his ceremonial duties.

A third of the students in all subjects take sandwich courses, one of the highest proportions in Britain, and more than 4,000 have some element of work experience. The approach has been paying off in terms of graduate employment figures and applications, which were up by almost 25 per cent at the start of 2010.

Most residential accommodation is now concentrated in the Storthes Hall Park student village, but additional housing is available at Ashenhurst, just over a mile from the campus. Recent developments mean the 1,711 residential places are enough to guarantee accommodation to first years, and private housing is cheap and plentiful in Huddersfield. Town–gown relations are good and most students like the town's friendly atmosphere, although they tend to base their social life on the students' union.

Undergraduate Fees and Bursaries
» Fees for UK/EU students: £3,290
» International student fees: £10,500–£11,500
» Bursary on full grant: household income up to £25K: £500
» The university does not award bursaries for students on partial maintenance grants.
» Scholarships based on circumstances or by competition.
» For full details see the university's website: www2.hud.ac.uk/student_finance

---

Students
Undergraduates:	**11,790**	(5,945)
Postgraduates:	**1,110**	(2,745)
Mature students:	**28.8%**	
Overseas students:	**4.6%**	
Applications per place:	**4.2**	
From state-sector schools:	**98.4%**	
From working-class homes:	**43.4%**	

Accommodation
Number of places and costs refer to 2009–10
University-provided places: 1,711 in privately-owned halls
Percentage catered: 0%
Self-catered costs: £65.95–£82.95 a week.
First years are guaranteed accommodation provided conditions are met.
International students: as above.
Contact: info@campusdigs.com; www.campusdigs.com

University of Hull

Hull recorded one of the biggest ever rises in applications at a traditional university in 2009, so it did well to attract another big increase of 20 per cent at the start of 2010. A string of excellent performances in the National Student Survey will have done the university no harm. Hull has been near the top for overall student satisfaction in every round of the survey, and made the top 20 again in 2009. Music, physical science and astronomy returned good scores, while French studies and chemistry produced satisfaction ratings of 100 per cent.

The university and the city have always commanded loyalty among students, who appreciate the modest cost of living and ready availability of accommodation, as well as the quality of courses. Research plaudits have been more elusive, however. No subject was rated internationally outstanding in the 2001 assessments and Hull had the lowest proportion of world-leading research among England's older universities the 2008 exercise. Health subjects, geography and environmental science, and drama, dance and performance achieved the best grades. An Institute for Learning encourages academics to put research findings into practice, developing training courses and developing the university's interest in lifelong learning.

A longstanding focus on Europe shows in the wide range of languages available at degree level, with the purpose-built Language Institute heavily used by students of all subjects. Strength in politics – confirmed by one of three grade 5 is reflected in a steady flow of graduates into the House of Commons. The Westminster Hull Internship Programme (WHIP) offers a year-long placement and month-long internships for British politics and legislative studies students. However, the university was criticised for deciding to close mathematics following poor recruitment to the honours degree.

After years of relative stability, Hull expanded rapidly, both on its spacious home campus and through mergers. First it added nursing to its portfolio of courses with the acquisition of the former Humberside College of Health, then it took in University College Scarborough and finally the university bought the adjacent campus of the former Humberside (now Lincoln) University. There are now over 19,000 undergraduates, including part-timers. The main academic development has been the establishment of a medical school in conjunction with York University, which takes 150 students a year and handles its own admissions. Hull's patient development, in collaboration with the local health authority, of a postgraduate medical school was rewarded with the award of a traditional school housed in a landmark building on the

Cottingham Road
Hull HU6 7RX

01482 466100 (admissions)
admissions@hull.ac.uk
www.hull.ac.uk
www.hyms.ac.uk
www.hullstudent.com

The Times Rankings
Overall Ranking: **48**

Student satisfaction:	=11	(81%)
Research quality:	=52	(1.2)
Entry standards:	56	(290)
Student–staff ratio:	=79	(19.5)
Services & facilities/student:	70	(£1,216)
Expected completion rate:	68	(82.4%)
Good honours:	66	(58.0%)
Graduate prospects:	42	(70.0%)

former Humberside (West) campus. The West Campus also contains a Business Quarter, incorporating the Business School and a new Enterprise Centre to support local business.

The original 94-acre main campus has also seen considerable development, with improvements to social facilities, new buildings for languages and chemistry, a Graduate Research Institute and a state-of-the-art sport, health and exercise science laboratory. The campus, with its art gallery and highly automated library, is less than three miles from the centre of Hull. In early 2010 the university opened a history centre in partnership with the city council, telling the story of the city over the centuries. It attracted 10,000 visitors in its first six weeks.

The Scarborough campus has also seen investment, with new laboratories for music technology and digital arts, and a renovated café bar. A new enterprise lab opened on the campus in 2010, helping new start-up firms and existing businesses to harness their innovations. Hull has always maintained a roughly equal balance between science and technology and the arts and social sciences, but the Scarborough campus has tipped the scales towards the arts.

Almost 95 per cent of the undergraduates are state-educated – one of the highest proportions at any pre-1992 university – while over a third are from working-class homes. The projected dropout rate of 14 per cent, was above the 13 per cent benchmark for the university's courses and entry qualifications.

Student leisure facilities, which were always good but becoming crowded, have been upgraded as part of the campus building programme. The students' union, which was rated the second best in Britain in a new awards scheme in 2008, has been refurbished and features the popular Asylum nightclub. New football pitches have been added recently on campus and the Sports and Fitness Centre has been attracting praise.

Undergraduate Fees and Bursaries
» Fees for UK/EU students: £3,290
» International student fees: £9,800–£11,900
  £22,700 (medicine)
» Bursary on full grant: household income up to £25K: £1,000
» Bursary on partial grant: household income up to £40K: £500
» Scholarships based on circumstances or by competition.
» For full details see the university's website: www2.hull.ac.uk/student/money.aspx

Students
Undergraduates:	**11,585**	**(7,460)**
Postgraduates:	**2,025**	**(1,300)**
Mature students:	**19.8%**	
Overseas students:	**8.9%**	
Applications per place:	**3.5**	
From state-sector schools:	**94.8%**	
From working-class homes:	**34.9%**	

Accommodation
Number of places and costs refer to 2010–11
University-provided places: 2,601 (owned stock); 150 (leased/associated stock)
Percentage catered: 49%
Catered costs: £78.96–£126.63 (31 weeks).
Self-catered costs: £52.36–£88.83 a week (34–50 weeks).
Unaccompanied first years are guaranteed accommodation if conditions are met.
International students: as above.
Contact: www2.hull.ac.uk/student/accommodation.aspx

Imperial College of Science, Technology and Medicine

Regularly in the top three in *The Times* league table, London's specialist university of science, engineering and medicine is also in the top five in the QS world rankings. Over 6,000 academic staff include 67 Fellows of the Royal Society, 69 Fellows of the Royal Academy of Engineering and 78 Fellows of the Academy of Medical Sciences. Imperial's submission for the 2008 Research Assessment Exercise contained a higher proportion of world-leading or internationally excellent work (73 per cent) than any other university's submission. The college achieved the best results in the UK for pure mathematics, chemical engineering, civil engineering, mechanical, aeronautical and manufacturing engineering, and history of science.

Imperial is not recommended for academic slouches, but tough entrance requirements ensure that they are a rare breed in any case. The projected dropout rate of less than 5 per cent is among the lowest in the country. Competition for places is high. There were more than 14,500 applications for 2,400 places in 2009 and demand was up by 8 per cent at the start of 2010. Even in subjects that struggle for candidates elsewhere, entrants average better than two As and a B at A level. The average points score on the UCAS tariff of entrants in 2009 was 357. More than a third of the undergraduates are from independent schools – one of the highest proportions at any university and considerably more than the national average for Imperial's courses. Approaching 4,000 of the 9,000 full-time students are from outside the EU.

Medicine has been the main area of development recently: mergers with the St Mary's, Charing Cross and Westminster, and Royal Postgraduate teaching hospitals produced one of the biggest faculties of medicine in the UK. In 2007, Imperial formed the UK's first Academic Health Science Centre in partnership with Imperial College Healthcare NHS Trust in order to translate research advances into patient care. The partnership was named as one of the UK's five Academic Health Science Centres (AHSC) in 2009, denoting international excellence in biomedical research, education and patient care. The medical school has teaching bases attached to a number of hospitals in central and west London, and facilities at Hammersmith are currently being redeveloped to accommodate the AHSC.

Engineering degrees last four years and lead to an MEng. The college has been expanding its range of European exchanges, with a variety of prestigious technological institutions available for courses such as the MSci in physics.

Exhibition Road
South Kensington
London SW7 2AZ

020 7594 8014
contact via website
www.imperial.ac.uk
www.imperialcollege
union.org

The Times Rankings
Overall Ranking: **3**

Student satisfaction:	=59	(76%)
Research quality:	6	(3.1)
Entry standards:	3	(504)
Student–staff ratio:	2	(10.4)
Services & facilities/student:	1	(£4,090)
Expected completion rate:	=7	(95.1%)
Good honours:	20	(72.7%)
Graduate prospects:	1	(88.9%)

Imperial celebrated its centenary in 2007 and has left the University of London to trade on its global reputation. It has been redeveloping and expanding facilities on its main campus, in the heart of South Kensington's museum district, most recently with the construction of a new sports centre and a second complex of halls of residence. The growing business school is Imperial's main concession to the academic world beyond science, technology and medicine. There is also an environmental research campus at Silwood Park, 25 miles west of London.

The Undergraduate Research Opportunities Programme provides opportunities for "hands-on" experience of the research activities of college staff and postgraduates. A voluntary scheme open to all undergraduates, it is especially popular in the summer vacation, when students can be paid bursaries and international undergraduates can participate without needing a work permit. There is also a vacation placement scheme during the summer for undergraduates to acquire work experience.

Imperial's specialisms have the effect of making it one of the most male-dominated university institutions in Britain, although the number of female students doubled during the 1990s and now stands at more than a third. The social scene has improved and Imperial claims to have the largest selection of clubs and societies in the country to add to the many attractions that London has to offer. Outdoor sports facilities are remote, but there is a well-equipped sports centre at the South Kensington campus offering students free gym and swimming facilities. Wednesday afternoons are left free to encourage participation in sporting activities.

Student satisfaction levels are well above the national average and good for London, where many universities have struggled in the National Student Survey. Aerospace engineering, biology, computer science and medicine produced the best results in the survey published in 2009. There were high levels of satisfaction on the quality of the library and IT resources, but more concern about academics' feedback on students' work.

Undergraduate Fees and Bursaries
» Fees for UK/EU students: £3,290
» International student fees: £19,800–£21,850
  £26,250–£39,150 (medicine)
» Bursary on full grant: household income up to £25K: £3,500
» Bursary on partial grant: household income up to £50K: sliding scale £2,500–£500.
» Scholarships based on circumstances or by competition.
» For full details see the university's website: www3.imperial.ac.uk/ugprospectus/money

Students
Undergraduates:	**8,580**	**(0)**
Postgraduates:	**4,345**	**(1,225)**
Mature students:	**5.2%**	
Overseas students:	**34.7%**	
Applications per place:	**5.9**	
From state-sector schools:	**62.1%**	
From working-class homes:	**18.7%**	

Accommodation
Number of places and costs refer to 2010–11
University-provided places: 2,497
Percentage catered: 0%
Self-catered costs: £55.30 – £227.36 a week.
First-year undergraduates are guaranteed accommodation provided all conditions are met.
International students: as above.
Contact: accommodation@imperial.ac.uk

Keele University

Keele has set itself the goal of becoming the "ultimate 21st-century campus university" and is committing more than £70 million of public and private investment to provide the necessary facilities. The broad Foundation course and four-year degree that made the university's name is a fading memory, but it remains committed to breadth of study in order also to be the leading interdisciplinary institution in Britain.

The majority of the degree courses are two-subject dual honours degrees, with single honours degrees in professional subjects like health and law. Popular combinations include criminology and psychology, geology and physical geography, history and politics, and biology and forensic science. More unusual pairings include geology and music, and mathematics and sociology. Students have a choice of over 500 degree combinations, most giving the opportunity of a semester abroad.

An emphasis on research since an improved set of results in the 2001 assessments brought limited success in the 2008 exercise. A total of 45 per cent of the work submitted was judged to be world-leading or internationally excellent, but Keele was still towards the bottom of the traditional universities on this measure. The most successful subjects were history and music.

Green issues have been rising up the university's agenda as it achieved the Carbon Trust Standard. Within five years, the university aims to have at least halved its reliance on external energy supplies, and a number of initiatives are being developed to ensure that Keele gains international recognition for expertise in sustainability. A degree in environment and sustainability was introduced in 2009 and all undergraduates can take a module in sustainability or environmental studies.

However, health subjects have been the main focus of development in recent years. First degrees in physiotherapy and nursing and midwifery were added to the well-established postgraduate medical school. Keele also offers a five-year undergraduate medical course. Some 130 students each year are taught in new facilities on the Keele campus, at the University Hospital of North Staffordshire NHS Trust, three miles away, and at the Associate Teaching Hospital at the Shrewsbury and Telford Hospitals NHS Trust in Shropshire. Students take the new Keele undergraduate degree programme (MBChB), which is in the process of validation by the GMC. A part-time BSc in osteopathy has been introduced in collaboration with the College of Osteopaths and the School of Pharmacy, which opened in 2006, has already moved to larger premises with additional seminar rooms and upgraded lecture theatres in a £2.2-million development.

Keele
Staffordshire ST5 5BG

01782 734005 (admissions)
undergraduate@keele.ac.uk
www.keele.ac.uk
www.kusu.net

The Times Rankings
Overall Ranking: **42**

Student satisfaction:	=22	(79%)
Research quality:	51	(1.3)
Entry standards:	50	(302)
Student–staff ratio:	=10	(13.0)
Services & facilities/student:	82	(£1,141)
Expected completion rate:	34	(88.5%)
Good honours:	46	(65.6%)
Graduate prospects:	49	(68.3%)

All Keele's courses are modular, with the academic year divided into two 15-week semesters, with breaks at Christmas and Easter. The university remains small by modern standards – under 7,000 full-time students – despite 75 per cent growth during the 1990s. The proportion of postgraduates has also been growing, with a quarter of the students now taking higher degrees, many on a part-time basis. Applications for undergraduate places were up by 33 per cent at the start of 2010 – one of the biggest rises among pre-1992 universities – building on a big increase in 2009.

Keele has a good record in the National Student Survey, with 88 per cent of final-year undergraduates satisfied in 2009, placing it in the top 20 on this measure. There was total satisfaction in American studies, and close to that level in anatomy, physiology and pathology, biology, chemistry, pharmacy and forensic science. The projected dropout rate has increased a little in the latest survey to 9 per cent – still below the national average for the university's subjects and entry qualifications. Nine out of ten undergraduates are state-educated, and around a third come from working-class homes. Keele has been proactive in trying to broaden its intake, targeting 12 and 13-year-olds with a special website, as well as running masterclasses in local schools and hosting a summer school at the university.

Nearly 70 per cent of all undergraduates live on the attractive 617-acre campus, which inevitably dominates the social scene as well as providing part-time employment for hundreds of students. The students' union offers entertainment on campus every night of the week and houses five bars and two purpose-built entertainment venues. The university's sports facilities have benefited from investment in a new all-weather pitch, and the leisure centre has recently refurbished its fitness suite. Keele has an active athletic union. The cost of living in the Potteries and the surrounding area is also relatively low.

Undergraduate Fees and Bursaries
» Fees for UK/EU students: £3,290
» International student fees: £9,500–£11,800
£19,000–£22,250 (medicine)
» Bursary on full grant: household income up to £25K: £800
» The university does not award bursaries for students on partial maintenance grants.
» Scholarships based on circumstances or by competition.
» For full details see the university's website: www.keele.ac.uk/studentfunding

Students
Undergraduates:	**6,160**	(2,270)
Postgraduates:	**590**	(1,345)
Mature students:	**13.1%**	
Overseas students:	**6.6%**	
Applications per place:	**4.6**	
From state-sector schools:	**91.9%**	
From working-class homes:	**33.1%**	

Accommodation
Number of places and costs refer to 2010–11
University-provided places: 3,200
Percentage catered: 0% (optional meal plan available)
Self-catered costs: £66–£109 a week.
First years are guaranteed accommodation on campus if Keele is first choice university.
International students: guaranteed accommodation for the duration of their course.
Contact: accomenq@keele.ac.uk

University of Kent

Kent has capitalised sensibly on its position near the Channel ports, specialising in international programmes, as well as in the flexible degree structures that have been the hallmark of most 1960s universities. Styling itself "the UK's European university", Kent now has postgraduate sites in Brussels and Paris, as well as giving many undergraduates the option of a year spent elsewhere in Europe or the USA. There are partnerships with over 100 European universities and Kent is one of the UK's most enthusiastic participants in the EU's Erasmus exchange programme, providing its undergraduates with study or work opportunities in countries from Spain to the Czech Republic.

The university has been broadening its horizons at home as well, however, assuming a regional role. Access courses throughout the county allow students to upgrade their qualifications to university standard, but the main focus is on the Medway towns, where Kent is involved in ambitious projects with Greenwich and Canterbury Christ Church universities and Mid-Kent College. The Medway campus, based in the old Chatham naval base, has already exceeded its target of 6,000, a third of whom are Kent students. A new School of Pharmacy is the main feature of a £50-million development. The school now has more than 550 undergraduates and 100 postgraduates students and boasted the highest satisfaction rating of any pharmacy department in the 2009 National Student Survey.

The original low-rise campus, set in 300 acres of parkland overlooking Canterbury, is tidy rather than architecturally distinguished. The student centre has a nightclub big enough to attract big-name bands, as well as a theatre, cinema and bars. The university has another base in Tonbridge serving part-time students, of whom there are 3,000 across Kent, mainly taught in associate colleges. Entry grades for full-time degrees are variable, with offers pitched according to the UCAS points tariff, although those taking A levels are expected to pass at least three subjects (one of which may be general studies).

Applications have been increasing, partly thanks to the Medway development. The demand for places was up by 26 per cent at the start of 2010 – the third successive big increase. Kent is strongest in the social sciences, although biosciences, philosophy, and drama, dance and theatre studies took pride of place in the old system of teaching assessments, each registering a maximum score. The university takes teaching standards seriously, encouraging all academics to take a Postgraduate Certificate in Higher Education. Kent academics have been awarded National Teaching Fellowships in each of the last three years.

Canterbury
Kent CT2 7NZ

01227 827272 (admissions)
information@kent.ac.uk
www.kent.ac.uk
www.kentunion.co.uk

The Times Rankings
Overall Ranking: **39**

Student satisfaction:	=15	(80%)
Research quality:	=44	(1.7)
Entry standards:	43	(319)
Student–staff ratio:	=26	(14.8)
Services & facilities/student:	65	(£1,245)
Expected completion rate:	38	(86.8%)
Good honours:	=50	(63.9%)
Graduate prospects:	=47	(68.6%)

The university was also much more successful in the 2008 research assessments than in previous exercises, with more than half of its submission placed in the top two categories. Thirty per cent of research in social policy was considered world-leading.

Kent has been building up its science departments, among which computing is particularly well regarded, but still a majority of the students take arts or social sciences. Graduates of all disciplines fare well in the employment market – the university regularly features among the top 20 for graduate starting salaries. It is also in the top ten for student satisfaction, with particularly high levels in health subjects, anthropology and finance.

The university has a more mixed intake than many in the south of England: over nine out of ten undergraduates are from state schools and a over quarter come from working-class homes. Significant numbers of American and European students give the university a cosmopolitan feel and campus security is good, but some complain that Canterbury itself is expensive and limited socially.

Students on the main campus are attached to one of four colleges, although they do not select it themselves. There is a separate college for postgraduates. The colleges act as the focus of social life, and include academic as well as residential facilities. They provide accommodation for all first years. Among £100 million of completed or planned capital developments has been an expansion of sports facilities and residential accommodation at the Parkwood student village, bringing the total number of residential places to 4,300. Developments in 2008 included more study bedrooms, a 480-seat lecture theatre and more seminar rooms on the main campus, and further development of the Medway campus, which now has 600 residential places. Subsequent developments on the main campus have included a new School of Arts building, the Canterbury Innovation Centre and a new sports pavilion.

Undergraduate Fees and Bursaries
» Fees for UK/EU students: £3,290
» International student fees: £10,350–£12,590*
» Bursary on full grant: household income up to £25K: £1,000
» Bursary on partial grant: household income up to £40K sliding scale: £750–£250.
» Scholarships based on circumstances or by competition.
» For full details see the university's website: www.kent.ac.uk/studying/funding

*Figures for 2009–10

Students
Undergraduates:	**11,920**	(3,715)
Postgraduates:	**1,395**	(1,260)
Mature students:	**14.1%**	
Overseas students:	**13.5%**	
Applications per place:	**4.8**	
From state-sector schools:	**93.2%**	
From working-class homes:	**28.3%**	

Accommodation
Number of places and costs refer to 2009–10
University-provided places: 4,300
Percentage catered: 18%
Catered costs: £107–£120 a week.
Self-catered costs: £89–£128 a week.
First years are guaranteed accommodation provided applications received before 31 July.
International students: as above
Contact: hospitality-enquiry@kent.ac.uk

King's College London

One of the oldest and largest of London University's colleges, King's has been cementing its reputation among the elite of British higher education. Ranked among the top 25 universities in the world, it is Europe's largest centre for the education of doctors, dentists and other healthcare professionals and home to six Medical Research Council centres. Sixty per cent of the work submitted to the 2008 Research Assessment Exercise was judged to be world-leading or internationally excellent, with cardiovascular medicine, dentistry, nutritional sciences, philosophy, languages and the Centre for Computing in the Humanities among the leaders in their fields.

Applications were up by almost 18 per cent at the start of 2010, with strong demand from international students. About one student in five is from outside the European Union, many of them among the 8,000 postgraduates. King's has done well in the National Student Survey, generally finishing among the leading institutions in London. Biomedical Sciences, music, French, linguistics, classics and nutrition were among 11 subject areas recording satisfaction levels in excess of 90 per cent in 2009. An institutional audit by the Quality Assurance Agency gave King's the highest mark, stressing the excellence of the student support services.

King's is now concentrated on four main campuses close to the Thames, within walking distance of each other. The original Strand site and the Waterloo campus, which includes the largest university building in London, house most of the non-medical departments. Nursing and midwifery and some biomedical subjects are also based at Waterloo, while medicine and dentistry are mainly at Guy's Hospital, near London Bridge, and in the St Thomas' Hospital campus, across the river from the Houses of Parliament. A fifth site, at Denmark Hill, in south London, houses the Institute of Psychiatry and more medicine and dentistry. Information services centres on each campus provide students with integrated library and computing facilities. There are over 1,600 PC workstations and computer rooms are open 24 hours a day, seven days a week. An extensive wireless internet also covers much of the college.

A £500-million transformation of the college estate is still in progress, particularly at the St Thomas' site. The conversion of the former Public Record Office in Chancery Lane created the largest new university library in Britain since World War II. A donation of £4 million by a graduate allowed the spectacular Maughan Library to be equipped with 1,400 networked reader places. And a £40-million redevelopment of the Grade I listed King's Building has provided new teaching facilities, wireless internet access, social and catering facilities.

Strand
London WC2R 2LS

020 7848 7070 (enquiries)
thecompass@kcl.ac.uk
www.kcl.ac.uk
www.kclsu.org

The Times Rankings
Overall Ranking: **=16**

Student satisfaction:	=59	(76%)
Research quality:	=24	(2.3)
Entry standards:	13	(421)
Student–staff ratio:	4	(11.1)
Services & facilities/student:	9	(£2,060)
Expected completion rate:	=14	(94.1%)
Good honours:	12	(75.6%)
Graduate prospects:	8	(80.5%)

Once known primarily for science, King's now excels in a wide range of subjects in nine schools of study, including such unusual features as Britain's only department devoted entirely to Portuguese – one of four language departments rated internationally outstanding in the latest research assessments. War studies is another unusual and well-regarded department. Medical subjects have been the main growth point in recent years. Clinical psychology, nursing, midwifery, health visiting and physiotherapy did well in a major review in 2005.

The full extent of the college's ambitions is clear from its mission statement, which includes having all its departments rated as excellent for both teaching and research. Graduates enjoy one of the best employment rates in the UK and typically, also earn among the highest starting salaries. King's was ranked eighth for graduate prospects in this year's *Times* league table.

More than a quarter of the undergraduates come from independent schools, despite the college's efforts to widen its intake. Among the medical courses, for example, are successful programmes catering for mature students and school-leavers who have attended London comprehensives with generally poor A level results. Much of the teaching is in small groups and every student is allocated a personal tutor,

Student facilities on the Strand and Guy's campuses have been upgraded recently and the active students' union puts on an extensive programme of events. King's has 2,654 residential places of its own, as well as access to 677 places in the intercollegiate halls of London University and another 175 in Liberty Living residences. Some of the outdoor sports facilities are a long way from the college, but are accessible by train. The three sports grounds have facilities for all the main sports, while there are also rifle ranges, two gyms and a swimming pool.

Undergraduate Fees and Bursaries

» Fees for UK/EU students: £3,290
» International student fees: £12,500–£15,850
  £29,400 (medicine)
» Bursary on full grant: household income up to £25K: £1,350
» Bursary on partial grant: household income up to £50K: sliding scale: £1,050–£100.
» Scholarships based on circumstances or by competition.
» For full details see the university's website: www.kcl.ac.uk/ug/funding

Students

Undergraduates:	**12,085**	**(2,070)**
Postgraduates:	**4,690**	**(3,430)**
Mature students:	**16.2%**	
Overseas students:	**15.1%**	
Applications per place:	**8.4**	
From state-sector schools:	**72.9%**	
From working-class homes:	**24.2%**	

Accommodation

Number of places and costs refer to 2009–10
University-provided places: 2,654; 677 intercollegiate.
Percentage catered: 17.7% King's Residences; 100% intercollegiate
Catered costs: £114.24 King's Residence; £109.90–£198.45 intercollegiate a week
Self-catered costs: £70.49–£249.50 (40 weeks).
New full-time undergraduate students are guaranteed the offer of one year in accommodation if specific conditions are met.
International students: priority for new students to the UK.
Contact: 020 7848 2759; www.kcl.ac.uk/accomm

Kingston University

Kingston's new strategic plan stresses its mission to be an inclusive university, open to all who can benefit from higher education. It has one of the most ethnically mixed student populations of any UK university and many undergraduates are the first in their family to experience higher education. Applications have been buoyant, enabling the university to reduce the numbers recruited through Clearing. Kingston has been one of the UK's fastest-growing universities over recent years and saw a 36 per cent increase in the demand for places at the start of 2010.

The university has revitalised its four campuses, opening three impressive new buildings as part of a £123-million programme which will run to 2018. The new facilities, which include multiple projection systems, video conferencing, interactive displays and built-in voting systems, have won plaudits from staff and students alike. The centrepiece is the £20-million John Galsworthy Building at the heart of the Penrhyn Road campus, which incorporates lecture theatres, flexible teaching space and information technology suites as well as a "Knowledge Centre" giving students a spacious setting, including at a laptop bar, in which to do course work.

There have been extensive upgrades of the library facilities on each campus. Learning resource centres bring together library, computing and multimedia facilities to encourage interactive and group learning. There are bookable study rooms with multimedia facilities and specially equipped spaces dedicated to meeting the needs of disabled users. The main LRCs are open 24 hours a day during term weekdays and a high-tech self issue system makes borrowing books, DVDs and other resources much quicker and easier.

The university markets itself as in "lively, leafy London", making a virtue of its suburban location southwest of central London as well as its proximity to the bright lights. Two of its four campuses are close to Kingston town centre; another, two miles away, is at Kingston Hill; and the fourth is in Roehampton Vale, where a site once used as an aerospace factory now contains a new technology block. A flight simulator and the university's own Learjet continue the tradition, and a Foundation degree in aeronautical engineering is ministers' favourite example of the two-year course. Kingston boasts the third largest engineering faculty in London, behind Imperial College and Brunel.

Elsewhere, new buildings under way include a new home for the Business School and extensive refurbishment at the Knights Park site, home to the Faculty of Art, Design and Architecture. Other developments include a three-storey teaching extension at

---

River House
53–57 High Street
Kingston upon Thames
Surrey KT1 1LQ

0844 855 2177 (application enquiries)
aps@kingston.ac.uk
www.kingston.ac.uk
www.kusu.co.uk

The Times Rankings
Overall Ranking: **92**

Student satisfaction:	=79	(74%)
Research quality:	=77	(0.4)
Entry standards:	104	(235)
Student–staff ratio:	=91	(20.0)
Services & facilities/student:	83	(£1,134)
Expected completion rate:	72	(81.5%)
Good honours:	60	(60.7%)
Graduate prospects:	=91	(57.7%)

the Faculty of Engineering's Roehampton Vale site. The university also contributed to the £11-million cost of the Rose Theatre in Kingston, where students and staff use performance and exhibition space.

Approaching a third of the university's submission to the 2008 Research Assessment Exercise was rated world-leading or internationally excellent. The star performance was in history of art, architecture and design, where half of the submission was at least internationally excellent. In nursing, 15 per cent of the work reached the top level, and in business and management studies, the proportion was 10 per cent, making Kingston the highest-rated new university in the field.

Nursing is part of the Faculty of Health and Social Care Sciences, a collaboration with St George's Hospital Medical School, which recently added pharmacy to its course portfolio. A new £420,000 purpose-built pharmacy practice laboratory, opened in 2009. Radiotherapy students are among the first in the country to hone their clinical skills in a simulated cancer treatment room. The Centre for Paramedic Science serves as a hub for course delivery and a raft of revolutionary research projects positions the two institutions at the forefront of paramedic education.

A quarter of Kingston's places go to mature students and around 40 per cent to those from working-class families – both groups with low completion rates nationally. Students get extra support in their first year. The latest projected dropout rate is just over 15 per cent and lower than the national average for the subjects on offer. Results in the National Student Survey have been variable, although medical technology produced a 100 per cent satisfaction rating in 2009, when drama, mathematics, molecular biology and other subjects allied to medicine all scored well.

A "one-stop shop" deals with student issues ranging from careers and accommodation to complaints and financial advice. Kingston's responsiveness and the accessibility of staff were singled out for praise in a quality audit. Over £20 million has been spent on halls of residence. Students like the location, although complain about the high cost of living.

Undergraduate Fees and Bursaries

» Fees for UK/EU students: £3,290
» International student fees: £9,600–£10,650
» Bursary on full grant: household income up to £25K: household income up to £1K: £1,000, then £600.
» Bursary on partial grant: household income up to £39.7K: £384.
» Scholarships based on circumstances or by competition.
» For full details see the university's website: www.kingston.ac.uk/undergraduate/money-matters

Students

Undergraduates:	**17,475**	**(2,060)**
Postgraduates:	**2,760**	**(3,495)**
Mature students:	**25.1%**	
Overseas students:	**11.7%**	
Applications per place:	**4.6**	
From state-sector schools:	**96.5%**	
From working-class homes:	**40.5%**	

Accommodation

Number of places and costs refer to 2010–11
University-provided places: 2,360; private hall: 214
Percentage catered: 0%
Self-catered costs: £90.50–£113.50 a week (university provided); £148.50–£175 (private hall).
Offers accommodation to many first-years who make Kingston their firm choice through UCAS. All other applicants will be offered accommodation subject to availability.
International students: offered places if conditions met.
Contact: www.kingston.ac.uk/accommodation

Lancaster University

Lancaster has enjoyed one of the biggest rises of any university in this year's *Times* league table, breaking into the top 10 for the first time. It has improved on almost every measure, but owes its 13-place leap above all to higher spending on facilities and better graduate destinations, even in the teeth of a recession. Having celebrated its 45th birthday and almost completed a £300-million makeover for its campus, Lancaster has been expanding its overseas activities in line with its ambition to be truly international. The campus hosts students from more than 100 countries, but there will soon be more graduating with the university's degrees in India, Malaysia and Pakistan than in Lancaster itself. In the latest development, the university has opened a campus near Delhi in partnership with an Indian group, becoming the first UK university on the sub-continent.

At home, recent campus developments will increase its capacity by up to 50 per cent. Still a relatively small institution, Lancaster has established itself in among the leading research universities, with Vice-Chancellor Professor Paul Wellings chairing the 1994 Group. It is a member of the N8 Group of northern research universities and is invariably the highest-placed institution in the northwest in league tables.

Lancaster has done well in all five National Student Surveys, finishing in the top ten in the rankings published in 2009. The best results came in drama, history and molecular biology. The university has also won nine National Teaching Fellowships since the scheme was launched in 2000.

Lancaster did not quite repeat the scale of success achieved in the 2001 Research Assessment Exercise in 2008, but more than 60 per cent of its work was rated as world-leading or internationally excellent. Physics was the star performer, with the best results in the country, but there were good results in health studies, computer science, art and design, management and sociology. Specialising in environmental research, Lancaster has won both a Queen's Anniversary Prize and the *Times Higher* research project of the year award for the development of water-saving techniques which help farmers in some of the world's driest regions.

A new 24-hour student learning space at the centre of the campus will provide students with flexible learning environments and social space with up-to-date technology. Infolab 21, the £15-million centre of excellence in information communication technology, acts as a technology transfer and incubation facility and houses a training facility for high-tech businesses. Other recent developments include a leadership centre for the highly rated Management School, while

Bailrigg
Lancaster LA1 4YW

01524 592028 (admissions)
ugadmissions@lancaster.ac.uk
www.lancaster.ac.uk
www.lusu.co.uk

The Times Rankings
Overall Ranking: **10**

Student satisfaction:	=15	(80%)
Research quality:	=10	(2.8)
Entry standards:	24	(393)
Student–staff ratio:	=14	(13.4)
Services & facilities/student:	20	(£1,746)
Expected completion rate:	=14	(94.1%)
Good honours:	37	(68.3%)
Graduate prospects:	14	(77.6%)

work has begun on a £10-million building for the Lancaster Institute for the Contemporary Arts, which has brought together art, music and theatre studies with the university's public art gallery, concerts and theatre.

Lancaster is another of the campus universities which has always championed a flexible degree structure. Most undergraduates can broaden their first-year studies by taking a second or third subject. The final choice of degree comes only at the end of that year. Combined degree programmes, with 200 courses to choose from, are especially popular. The degree portfolio now includes medicine, with students taking a five-year course following the Liverpool University curriculum. The first students will graduate in 2011 and new developments include a research centre specialising in bipolar disorder and a new Centre for Organisational Health and Wellbeing.

The projected dropout rate of 6 per cent is lower than the average for the subjects on offer. Lancaster also exceeds expectations for the recruitment of state-school students and the proportion from working-class homes is only marginally below the benchmark for the university's courses and entry grades.

Students join one of nine residential colleges, which become the centre of most students' social life. Most house between 800 and 900 students in self-catering accommodation. The pioneering 800-room Eco Residence, which opened in 2008, has won an environmental award. Students can live in town houses with shared facilities and monitor their bills. As part of the developments, Cartmel and Lonsdale colleges have transferred to the New Alexandra Park area of the campus with enhanced social facilities.

The campus has been praised by students, especially for its refurbished lecture theatres and academic areas. Lancaster itself is a ten-minute bus ride away. Both the campus and city have been rated among the safest in the UK. Sports facilities are good and conveniently placed. Work on a £20-million sports centre with climbing wall (built to Chancellor Chris Bonington's specifications) started in 2009. For the outdoor life, the Lake District is within easy reach. Road and rail communications are good, but Lancaster is inevitably more limited than larger university centres in terms of off-campus life.

Undergraduate Fees and Bursaries
- Fees for UK/EU students: £3,290
- International student fees: £10,500–£13,060
- Bursary on full grant: household income up to £25K: £1,000
- Bursary on partial grant: household incomes up to £34K: £1,000.
- Scholarships based on circumstances or by competition.
- For full details see the university's website: www.lancaster.ac.uk/ugfinance

Students
Undergraduates:	**8,040**	**(1,390)**
Postgraduates:	**1,865**	**(1,400)**
Mature students:	**5.1%**	
Overseas students:	**14.7%**	
Applications per place:	**5.0**	
From state-sector schools:	**92.0%**	
From working-class homes:	**25.5%**	

Accommodation
Number of places and costs refer to 2009–10
University-provided places: 6,700 (plus 600 places in university-managed houses)
Percentage catered: 0%
Self-catered costs: £70.00–£95.90 a week; £113.40 for a student apartment.
All first years are normally accommodated; no formal guarantee for Insurance, Clearing and late applicants.
International students are guaranteed accommodation.
Contact: CRO@lancaster.ac.uk

University of Leeds

The rise of Leeds as a shopping and clubbing centre has added to the attractions of a university which has long been one of the giants of the higher education system. It is second only to Manchester University in terms of applications received, although the 5 per cent increase at the start of 2010 was lower than that at other civic universities. Leeds has scaled back its campus development plan and cut a number of academic posts to cope with a looming deficit, but is still spending £195 million on new facilities that are designed to propel it into the top 50 universities in the world. It broke into the top 100 in the QS world rankings in 2009.

An unusually wide range of degrees gives applicants more than 650 undergraduate programmes to choose from, with over 2,000 academic staff teaching 30,000 students, including more than 8,000 postgraduates.

The university occupies a 98-acre site within walking distance of the city centre. The buildings are a mixture of Victorian and modern, the latest of which are Leeds' newest theatre and a £16-million building to house student services. Other improvements include a new swimming pool and fitness centre, which is under construction, and new buildings for the schools of earth and environment and law.

Nine other colleges in various parts of Yorkshire offer Leeds courses, but handle their own admissions. Further afield, Leeds is also part of the Worldwide Universities Network, which brings together 16 research-led universities to collaborate on research, postgraduate degree programmes and continuing professional development. There is a thriving study abroad programme and the university has links with over 250 universities around the world. A free-standing language unit caters for casual learners as well as specialists.

Leeds operates a modular course system, enabling its students to take elective modules or combine complementary subjects. Almost a quarter now take dual honours or interdisciplinary combinations such as nanotechnology, women's studies or international studies. The university was chosen to house a national centre of excellence in interdisciplinary teaching and another in assessment and learning in medical practice settings.

The 2008 Research Assessment Exercise scores showed improvement since 2001, with over 60 per cent of the university's submission rated as world-leading or internationally excellent. Electrical and electronic engineering produced the best results in the country, with social work and social policy, English, Italian, geography and nursing also highly rated. Leeds also has 15 National Teaching Fellows - more than any other university in England.

Leeds
West Yorkshire LS2 9JT

0113 343 2336
study@leeds.ac.uk (enquiries)
www.leeds.ac.uk
www.leedsuniversityunion.org.uk

The Times Rankings
Overall Ranking: **26**

Student satisfaction:	=32	(78%)
Research quality:	=24	(2.3)
Entry standards:	23	(397)
Student–staff ratio:	24	(14.1)
Services & facilities/student:	42	(£1,484)
Expected completion rate:	=21	(92.6%)
Good honours:	=16	(74.2%)
Graduate prospects:	=40	(70.5%)

The Quality Assurance Agency gave Leeds the best possible verdict on its academic processes in 2008. Scores in the National Student Survey published in 2009 slipped back after two years of improved satisfaction levels, but were still in the top half of the table. Pharmacists were 100 per cent satisfied and microbiologists not far behind. The verdict on learning resources was especially positive, thanks to one of the largest libraries at any UK universities and an extensive IT network.

Sports and social facilities are also first rate. Leeds teams regularly excel in competition and the university hosts one of five centres of cricketing excellence. Sustainability is a key strategic aim of the university, and Leeds has won more environmental awards than any other UK university, including the 2007 Green Gown Award for continuous improvement.

National statistics show more than a quarter of the undergraduates coming from independent schools, although the university says its own more recent survey puts the figure at one in five – the same proportion as come from working-class homes. The projected dropout rate has improved and, at less than 8 per cent, is below the national average for the university's courses and entry grades. The already large students' union, famous for its long bar and big-name rock concerts, has been extended to cope with the latest phase in the university's expansion. It was named the NUS Students' Union of the Year 2009–10 and is the UK's only gold accredited students' union under a national evaluation scheme. A £4.5-million upgrade has provided a new venue, more shops and catering facilities.

Town–gown relations are generally good, although residents in Headingley, the main student area for both of the city's universities, have complained about the impact on their neighbourhood. The wider local community benefits from 2,000 student volunteers, almost five times the national average.

Undergraduate Fees and Bursaries
» Fees for UK/EU students: £3,290
» International student fees: £10,900–£14,200 £25,970 (medicine)
» Bursary on full grant: household income up to £25K: £1,540
» Bursary on partial grant: household income up to £36.6K: sliding scale £1,540–£335.
» Scholarships based on circumstances or by competition.
» For full details see the university's website: www.leeds.ac.uk/yourfinances

Students
Undergraduates:	**22,015**	(1,680)
Postgraduates:	**6,140**	(2,535)
Mature students:	**7.0%**	
Overseas students:	**7.2%**	
Applications per place:	**7.2**	
From state-sector schools:	**74.6%**	
From working-class homes:	**21.6%**	

Accommodation
Number of places and costs refer to 2010–11
University-provided places: 7,700
Percentage catered: 23%
Catered costs: £96–£158 a week.
Self-catered costs: £70–£134 a week.
Single first years are guaranteed a place provided conditions are met.
International students: guaranteed to full fee-paying undergraduates if conditions are met.
Contact: www.leeds.ac.uk/accommodation

Leeds Metropolitan University

Leeds Met took the bold step of becoming the first university to set fees below the £3,000-a-year maximum allowed in 2006, and for four years was by far the cheapest in England at which to take a full-time degree. But the university has now joined the rest of the system in charging the maximum. Both applications and enrolments hit record levels initially and further increases followed, but the university's finances felt the strain. Other promotional ventures, such as the sponsorship of professional rugby league, and penalties for the misreporting of student numbers have left the university with considerable financial problems.

Nevertheless, applications were up by 24 per cent at the start of 2010. Leeds Met has a longstanding reputation for widening participation in higher education: it is one of the largest providers of Foundation degrees and has more than 27,000 students (17,000 of whom are full-time undergraduates). Four out of ten students come from the Yorkshire and Humberside region, and around a quarter are over 21 on entry. More than nine out of ten are state-educated and almost a third come from working-class homes. Partnerships with 24 colleges from Belfast to Nottinghamshire are designed to produce the equivalent of an American state university system, enabling students to take Leeds Met courses locally.

Some 2,500 students come from 90 countries outside the UK. Only just over half are taking conventional full-time degrees, such is the popularity of sandwich and part-time courses. The projected dropout rate of 17 per cent is above the official benchmark based on the university's courses and entry qualifications. As part of its efforts to widen access, Leeds Met runs a course for sixth-formers from the region, awarding UCAS points for those who complete successfully. There is also a wide range of summer schools, including one for Asian women and one for Afro-Caribbean boys.

There are two bases in Leeds: the Civic Quarter Campus, close to the city centre, and the Headingley Campus, three miles away in the 100 acres of park and woodland of Beckett Park. The latter boasts outstanding sports facilities, including the £2-million Carnegie Regional Tennis Centre, as well as teaching accommodation for education, informatics, law and business. Over 7,000 students take part in some form of sporting activity, and there is a range of £2,000 sports scholarships. The university has been named a UK centre for coaching excellence.

The Civic Quarter campus is the subject of a £100-million development programme, which began with the opening in 2005 of a new film school. A futuristic lecture theatre

Civic Quarter
Leeds
West Yorkshire LS1 3HE

0113 812 3113 (enquiries)
www.experience.leedsmet.ac.uk
www.lmu.ac.uk
www.leedsmetsu.co.uk

The Times Rankings
Overall Ranking: **99**

Student satisfaction:	108	(68%)
Research quality:	=95	(0.2)
Entry standards:	=82	(263)
Student–staff ratio:	102	(21.2)
Services & facilities/student:	102	(£941)
Expected completion rate:	=73	(81.3%)
Good honours:	87	(53.4%)
Graduate prospects:	=52	(67.2%)

complex next to Leeds Civic Hall now houses the business school. The former BBC building has reopened as Old Broadcasting House, while next door Broadcasting Place has become the new home of the Faculty of Arts and Society. In the first development of its kind, a new stand has been built at the Headingley rugby ground, with classrooms, coaching facilities and social space for use by the university and the two professional clubs. A new pavilion is planned for the nearby Test and County Cricket ground with similar multi-use facilities.

Relatively few academics were entered for the 2008 Research Assessment Exercise, but nearly a third of their work was judged to be world-leading or internationally excellent. Communication, cultural and media studies, sport and library and information management produced the best results. Students are included on the committees that design and manage courses, although the impact has not been obvious in the National Student Survey. Leeds Met was again among the bottom three universities in the 2009 results, although physiotherapists were 100 per cent satisfied with their course.

A growing emphasis on educational technology is enhanced by a £20-million learning resources centre. More than 400 computers, audiovisual presentation studios and study areas are available all hours. Contacts with small and medium-sized businesses have been carefully fostered as part of the university's successful attempts to maintain a good record in graduate employment. Like its older neighbour, Leeds Met is benefiting from the city's growing reputation for nightlife, but it is making its own contribution with a famously lively entertainments scene. With 4,500 bed spaces, those who accept places before Clearing are guaranteed university accommodation. Carnegie Village, a self-contained residential facility on the Headingley campus, has added to the places available. The Athletic Union, founded in 2005, hosts 32 clubs and came third in the BUCS competitions in 2008–09. A season pass for both the Headingley Campus and Civic Quarter facilities cost £100 in 2009–10.

Undergraduate Fees and Bursaries

» Fees for UK/EU students: £3,290
» International student fees: £8,250–£9,500
» Bursary on full grant: household income up to £25K: Year 1: £500; Year 2: £800; Year 3 or above: £1,000.
» The university does not award bursaries for students on partial maintenance grants.
» Scholarships based on circumstances or by competition.
» For full details see the university's website: www.leedsmet.ac.uk/study/bursaries.htm

Students

Undergraduates:	17,775	(5,885)
Postgraduates:	1,515	(2,620)
Mature students:	20.1%	
Overseas students:	4.3%	
Applications per place:	5.5	
From state-sector schools:	93.0%	
From working-class homes:	36.9%	

Accommodation

Number of places and costs refer to 2010–11
University-provided places: 4,500
Percentage catered: 0%
Self-catered costs: £78.98–£140.00 a week (41–51 weeks).
First years with Conditional Firm or Unconditional Firm offers guaranteed accommodation.
International students: guaranteed accommodation if conditions are met.
Contact: www.leedsmet.ac.uk/accommodation

University of Leicester

Leicester has been enjoying a period of unprecedented success, after many years living in the shadow of the big city universities. Consistently in the top five in the National Student Survey (NSS) and named as the *Times Higher Education* University of the Year in 2008, it has shown the scale of its ambitions with a £1-billion development plan. The Queen opened the university's new £32-million library in 2008 and another £15 million is being spent on a new students' union. The university's qualities are being recognised by applicants: a 14 per cent rise at the start of 2010 continued a run of increases. Leicester's scores in the 2009 NSS were bettered only by Cambridge, of the mainstream universities. There was 100 per cent satisfaction in pharmacy and physiology and 91 per cent of final-year undergraduates across the university declared themselves satisfied overall with their course. The university is trialling the use of social media to improve feedback in an attempt to increase satisfaction levels even more. A new web technologies facility opened in 2010 to keep staff up to date with the latest developments in e-learning and web technologies more generally.

Although Leicester will celebrate its 90th anniversary in 2011, it only approaches the size of other big city universities by dint of rapid growth in postgraduate and distance learning programmes. The 8,700 full-time undergraduates based on the main campus represent much less than half of the student population. Professor Robert Burgess, the Vice-Chancellor, has focused on strengthening research, and Leicester entered a much larger proportion of its academics than many of its peers in the 2008 Research Assessment Exercise. As a result of the large entry, less than half of the university's submission was considered world-leading or internationally excellent, but there was a big increase in research funding. The star performer was the small department of museum studies, which produced the highest proportion of world-leading research in any subject at any UK university, with almost two thirds of its work placed in that top category.

The university has scaled down its programme of two-year Foundation degrees. But efforts continue to broaden Leicester's intake, for example through a summer school for local teenagers. Nine out of ten undergraduates come from state schools and more than a quarter come from working-class homes. The 7.4 per cent projected dropout rate falls below the national average for the university's courses and entry grades.

Leicester hosts national centres of excellence for teaching and learning in geography, genetics and physics. The university also has a long-established reputation in space science, with Europe's

University Road
Leicester LE1 7RH

0116 252 5281 (admissions)
admissions@le.ac.uk
www.le.ac.uk
http://leicesterunion.com

The Times Rankings
Overall Ranking: **15**

Student satisfaction:	=1	(85%)
Research quality:	=29	(2.2)
Entry standards:	=28	(372)
Student–staff ratio:	25	(14.4)
Services & facilities/student:	29	(£1,618)
Expected completion rate:	=21	(92.6%)
Good honours:	24	(71.6%)
Graduate prospects:	25	(74.2%)

largest university-based space research facility, including the £52-million National Space Centre.

The medical school, which allows graduates in the health and life sciences to qualify in four years, has among the most modern facilities in Britain. The siting of a medically based interdisciplinary research centre at the university was another indication of strength. The genetics department, where DNA genetic fingerprinting was discovered, has helped make Leicester's academics among the most cited in Britain, according to Thomson Scientific, which monitors research.

Other than clinical medicine which is taught at the city's three hospitals, all teaching and much residential accommodation is concentrated in a leafy suburb a mile from the city centre. Its location, adjacent to one of Leicester's main parks, is popular with students. The new library has doubled the available space and brought the total number of workspaces to 1,500.

The students' union already runs one of the most popular university nightclubs. Its new building will feature a spectacular new atrium with communal social space for students and improved catering and retail facilities, a 1,750-capacity nightclub, bars, extra space for student societies, and increased provision for welfare and support services.

Extensive residential accommodation includes a £21-million 600-bed en-suite development. First years are guaranteed a residential place and many second and third-year students also live in hall, although the majority choose to live in the reasonably priced private accommodation available nearby. The main sports facilities are conveniently located; in 2009–10, students paid £60 a year to use them.

Undergraduate Fees and Bursaries
» Fees for UK/EU students: £3,290
» International student fees: £9,825–£13,150
£23,820 (medicine)
» Bursary on full grant: household income up to £20K: £1,384; household income up to £25K: £1,084.
» Bursary on partial grant: household income up to £40K: sliding scale £400–£100.
» Scholarships based on circumstances or by competition.
» For full details see the university's website: www.le.ac.uk/fees

Students
Undergraduates:	**8,705**	**(1,405)**
Postgraduates:	**2,590**	**(3,805)**
Mature students:	**9.8%**	
Overseas students:	**12.4%**	
Applications per place:	**6.7**	
From state-sector schools:	**89.4%**	
From working-class homes:	**26.4%**	

Accommodation
Number of places and costs refer to 2010–11
University-provided places: 4,345
Percentage catered: 33%
Catered costs: £105.00–£160.30 a week (30 weeks).
Self-catered costs: £76.30–£154.00 (42 weeks).
First-year students are guaranteed accommodation if conditions are met.
International students: as above, with priority to those returning.
Contact: www.le.ac.uk/accommodation

University of Lincoln

Lincoln has achieved the biggest rise of any university in this year's *Times* league table, leaping 24 places as a result of better staffing levels, more satisfied students and higher spending on facilities. The opening of an impressive purpose-built campus alongside a marina in the centre of Lincoln in 1996 brought about the most dramatic transformation of any university in recent times. Humberside University, as it had been, even gave its new location pride of place in its title. Five years later it went a step further, selling the previous head-quarters campus in Hull and becoming the University of Lincoln. While not moving out of Hull entirely, the university is concentrating its activities there on a much smaller city-centre site.

The switch has paid undoubted dividends, helping to attract high-quality academics. The number of professors grew from eight to 87 in four years. Student applications have increased practically throughout the decade, despite rising admission requirement, and the start of 2010 produced another record with the demand for places up by almost a third.

New science laboratories, sports facilities, an architecture school, a library in a converted warehouse and a students' union and entertainment venue in a former railway engine shed have taken the cost of the development in Lincoln to over £100 million, and another £30 million has been committed to complete the main campus. A £6-million performing arts centre contains a 450-seat theatre and three large studio spaces, while the Human Performance Centre is a regional facility for excellence in sport, coaching and exercise science. The latest developments are the new School of Engineering, the relocation of the Lincoln Business School to its own dedicated building and the opening of the Enterprise building – a one-stop-shop for students to get careers advice, enhance their CVs or find work, as well as for graduates who are supported in setting up their own businesses.

The various projects have won two regeneration awards. The campus now has around 1,000 beds, while purpose-built private developments in close proximity to the university now provide well over 2,000 further residential places. Only the School of Health and Social Care remains in Hull, following the transfer of art and design degree provision in the city to Hull College.

Lincoln initially concentrated on social sciences, but the university now has a wider range of courses. Following the acquisition of former art and design and agriculture colleges from De Montfort University in 2001, the university now has more than 8,000 students in and around Lincoln. The School of Architecture has over 400 students. Art and design is based in the city centre, while animal, biological and equine studies are at

Brayford Pool
Lincoln LN6 7TS

01522 882000 (enquiries)
contact via website
www.lincoln.ac.uk
www.lincolnsu.com

The Times Rankings
Overall Ranking: **62**

Student satisfaction:	=32	(78%)
Research quality:	=60	(0.6)
Entry standards:	=68	(273)
Student–staff ratio:	=94	(20.3)
Services & facilities/student:	93	(£1,073)
Expected completion rate:	=57	(83.5%)
Good honours:	=74	(56.2%)
Graduate prospects:	74	(60.6%)

Riseholme Park, a 1,000-acre site ten minutes outside Lincoln. Riseholme has been chosen as one of the training centres for equine events ahead of the 2012 Olympic Games.

The university was determined to achieve a high-profile return in the Research Assessment Exercise in 2008 to match a sharp rise in its research income over recent years. Lincoln entered more of its academics for assessment than many institutions in its peer group and improved on previous results, with 28 per cent of its submission judged to be world-leading or internationally excellent. The result was a £2-million boost in research grants. Communication, cultural and media studies and computer science and informatics produced the highest grades. The university has also had successes in applied research and knowledge transfer, notably with the National Centre for Food Manufacturing, based in Holbeach, which specialises in the production of chilled foods.

All students take the Effective Learning Programme, which uses computer packages backed up by weekly seminars to develop necessary study skills, and produce a detailed portfolio of all their work. Some degrees can be taken as work-based programmes, with credit awarded for relevant aspects of the jobs. Lincoln was the first university to win a Charter Mark for exceptional service. Results in the National Student Survey have improved and are now close to the average for all universities. English, forensic science, human resource management and law produced the best results in 2009.

Around 40 per cent of the undergraduates come from working-class homes and the projected dropout rate of 13.9 per cent is just below the average for the subjects on offer, given the entry standards. Only three universities devote as much of their tuition fee income to bursaries and scholarships as Lincoln. The city is adapting to its new student population with new bars and clubs, although the social scene there is not the prime draw for students.

Undergraduate Fees and Bursaries
» Fees for UK/EU students: £3,290
» International student fees: £10,292–£10,914
» Bursary on full grant: household income up to £25K: £600*
» Bursary on partial grant: household income up to £50K: sliding scale £370–£20.*
» Scholarships based on circumstances or by competition.
» For full details see the university's website: www.lincoln.ac.uk/home/fees

*Figures for 2009–10

Students
Undergraduates:	8,025	(1,975)
Postgraduates:	490	(970)
Mature students:	18.4%	
Overseas students:	6.1%	
Applications per place:	3.3	
From state-sector schools:	97.7%	
From working-class homes:	40.4%	

Accommodation
Number of places and costs refer to 2009–10
University-provided places: Lincoln, 1,037; Riseholme Park, 180
Percentage catered: 13% (Riseholme Park only)
Catered costs: £91–£129 a week (half-board)
Self-catered costs: £85–£99 a week.
Student accommodation prioritised by distance.
International students are given detailed information and assistance.
Contact: www.lincoln.ac.uk/accommodation

University of Liverpool

Liverpool has invested more than £200 million to improve its 100-acre precinct for a growing student population, and there is more work in progress. The dozen projects included the expansion and refurbishment of the library, restructuring of the Faculty of Engineering, and the transformation of the redbrick Victoria Building into a public gallery and museum during Liverpool's year as the Capital of Culture in 2008. There have been new facilities for chemistry and a one-stop shop for student services, while sports facilities have been renovated and extended. A £9-million refurbishment of the guild of students should be complete in 2011, when new teaching laboratories for science subjects are also due to open. The 15 laboratories, several of which will accommodate more than 200 students, will be focused on undergraduate teaching and will facilitate the introduction of innovative new teaching modules that promote inter-disciplinary science.

In addition, more than £100 million is being invested in new facilities for research and teaching in the Faculty of Medicine. A Centre for Personalised Medicines will open in 2010 in the old Liverpool Royal Infirmary, developing treatments tailored to a patient's individual genetic make-up. The first phase of a centralised clinical research facility will open in 2011 and will accommodate more than 600 scientists when it is complete in 2013.

The university is among the top 15 recipients of research funds, with outside income increasing dramatically in recent years. There has also been substantial investment in new educational technology, helping to cope with the demands of extra undergraduates. The university has been awarded a national centre of excellence to develop professionalism in medical students. Full-time numbers throughout the university are almost exactly balanced between the sexes. Publicity studies produced 100 per cent satisfaction in the 2009 National Student Survey, when the other top scores were in chemistry and pharmacy.

A £50-million fundraising drive aims to establish world-class centres of excellence in management, law, medicine, engineering, veterinary science and architecture. More than half of the work submitted for the 2008 Research Assessment Exercise was judged to be world-leading or internationally excellent. Computer science, materials, architecture, English and history produced particularly good results. But the RAE results have also resulted in closure proposals for five departments, including politics and philosophy, where relatively low grades left future financial question marks.

Liverpool prides itself on strength across the board and opened a new university in

Liverpool L69 3BX
0151 794 5927 (enquiries)
ugrecruitment@liv.ac.uk
www.liv.ac.uk
www.lgos.org.uk

The Times Rankings
Overall Ranking: **28**

Student satisfaction:	=46	(77%)
Research quality:	=33	(2.1)
Entry standards:	20	(403)
Student–staff ratio:	7	(12.5)
Services & facilities/student:	12	(£1,994)
Expected completion rate:	=32	(89.6%)
Good honours:	26	(71.1%)
Graduate prospects:	39	(70.6%)

Suzhou, China, in partnership with Xi'an Jiaotong University, in 2006. Chinese students can complete the latter part of their studies in Liverpool, while Liverpool-based students are offered work experience at Suzhou Industrial Park, which is home to 53 "Fortune 500" companies. The university is planning further collaborations with universities in Chile, Mexico and Spain that will allow Liverpool students to complete part of their degree at one or more of these institutions via a range of options such as projects or placements. Students will have access to a full range of support services while abroad. Liverpool is popular with international students, 88 per cent of whom were satisfied with their experience in 2008.

Applications from home and overseas were up by almost 12 per cent at the start of 2010. Physics with nuclear science, e-finance and a BSc in dental hygiene and dental therapy were among the new degrees for 2010–11. One of Europe's largest facilities for training dentists opened in 2007, marking the start of another big investment programme following the award of an additional 125 dental places from 2009.

Liverpool was among the first traditional universities to run access courses for adults without traditional qualifications. The projected dropout rate fell back from 10 per cent to 8.6 per cent in the latest survey, below the national average for the courses and entry grades. Even before the introduction of top-up fees, the university was awarding record numbers of scholarships and bursaries to widen opportunities further. They include 30 in memory of John Lennon, mainly for Merseyside residents. The proportion of state-educated students is higher than at the other civic universities and over a quarter of the undergraduates are from working-class homes.

A total of £45 million will be invested in the new Eco Residences, which are due to open in September 2011 with 700 en-suite study bedrooms, shops and a 250-seat restaurant. There will be more than 4,000 places – enough to guarantee accommodation to all first years. The suburban setting of the main halls complex means the focus of social life is on the guild of students, but there is no shortage of nightlife.

Undergraduate Fees and Bursaries

» Fees for UK/EU students: £3,290
» International student fees: £9,870–£12,000
  £19,530 (medicine)
» Bursary on full grant: household income up to £25K: £1,400
» The university does not award bursaries for students on partial maintenance grants.
» Scholarships based on circumstances or by competition.
» For full details see the university's website: www.liv.ac.uk/study/undergraduate/money

Students

Undergraduates:	**13,480**	**(2,920)**
Postgraduates:	**2,150**	**(1,395)**
Mature students:	**12.9%**	
Overseas students:	**9.1%**	
Applications per place:	**7.2**	
From state-sector schools:	**84.7%**	
From working-class homes:	**25.2%**	

Accommodation

Number of places and costs refer to 2010–11
University-provided places: 3,357
Percentage catered: 59%
Catered costs: £111.30–£126.35 a week.
Self-catered costs: £81.20–£91.70 a week.
First-year students are guaranteed accommodation if requirements are met.
International students: as above.
Contact: accommodation@liverpool.ac.uk
www.liv.ac.uk/accommodation

Liverpool Hope University

Liverpool Hope continues to opt out of league tables after finishing at the bottom of our table on its only appearance in *The Times Good University Guide*. It has improved some scores since then, but the university believes that the criteria used in league tables are biased in favour of wealthier institutions with a longer history. It insists that its objections "can't be summed up in one sentence." Hope even hides its application rates from public view, although it admits that they fell in 2008 and 2009.

Hope is a unique ecumenical institution formed from the merger of two Catholic and one Church of England teacher training colleges in 1980. The two churches' leading figures on Merseyside described the union as a "sign of hope", unintentionally providing the title for one of the nine new universities created in 2005. It describes itself as "teaching led, research informed and mission focused" and includes "taking faith seriously" among its five key values. The university is opening its own joint Church of England and Roman Catholic academy in September 2011, replacing two comprehensive schools.

Student satisfaction rates had improved since the early years of the National Student Survey, but slipped back in 2009, leaving the university in the lower reaches of the table. Music and physical geography and environmental science produced good scores, but no other subjects reached 90 per cent overall satisfaction. Only just over a third of final-year undergraduates were satisfied with the IT provision – something on which most universities score highly – and little more than half were satisfied with the library and other learning resources.

More than a quarter of the academics were entered for the 2008 Research Assessment Exercise – a higher proportion than at most comparable institutions. Theology was again the top scorer, although a small amount of world-leading work was found in applied social sciences. Overall, only 12 per cent of the university's submission reached the top two grades – placing it among the bottom five on this measure.

Most students opt for combined subject degrees, choosing after the first year whether to give them equal weight or to go for a major/minor arrangement. Environ-mental management and dance is one of the more unusual combinations suggested. Subjects are grouped into four "deaneries": arts and humanities; education; business and computing; sciences and social sciences.

Nearly 30 per cent of the undergraduates are over 21 on entry and female students outnumber their male counterparts by more than two to one. Hope comfortably exceeds all of the official benchmarks for widening participation in higher education. Almost all

Hope Park
Liverpool L16 9JD

0151 291 3295 (admissions)
admission@hope.ac.uk
www.hope.ac.uk
www.hopesu.com

The Times Rankings
Liverpool Hope blocked the release of data from the Higher Education Statistics Agency and so we cannot give any ranking information.

the undergraduates attended state schools or colleges, over four out of ten are from working-class families and almost one in five is from an area with little tradition of higher education – one of the highest proportions in England. This is partly the result of the Network of Hope, which brings university courses to sixth-form colleges across the northwest of England, in areas where there is limited higher education. Single honours and Foundation degrees are taught in Bury and Blackburn. The projected dropout rate has improved dramatically and, at just over 8 per cent, is nearly half the national average for the courses and entry qualifications.

The university's own premises are now concentrated on two sites in Liverpool, with a residential outdoor education centre set in 20 acres of woodland in the heart of Snowdonia, North Wales. The main campus – Hope Park – is three miles from the city centre in the suburb of Childwall, while the creative and performing arts are based at the more central Cornerstone campus, at which a new performance centre opened in January 2010. The £5-million main library, on the Hope campus, has 250,000 items and 700 study spaces, with electronic access from other sites.

Sports facilities have been improving and there are student union facilities on both campuses. The university has a range of residential accommodation, some of it provided by a private firm, and is able to guarantee places for first years and all overseas students.

Undergraduate Fees and Bursaries
- Fees for UK/EU students: £3,290
- International student fees: £6,980
- Bursary on full grant: household income up to £25K: £500
- Bursary on partial grant: household income up to £39.3K: £500.
- Scholarships based on circumstances or by competition.
- For full details see the university's website: www.hope.ac.uk/studentfinance

Students
From state-sector schools:	**98.3%**
From working-class homes:	**45.8%**

Accommodation
Number of places and costs refer to 2010–11
University-provided places: 1,000
Percentage catered: 0%
Self-catered costs: £74–£98 a week.
First years are guaranteed accommodation if Liverpool Hope is their first choice and they apply before Clearing.
International students: housing is subject to availability, but demand is usually met.
Contact: accommodation@hope.ac.uk

Liverpool John Moores University (LJMU)

Naming itself after a football pools millionaire was just the start for one of the most innovative of the new universities. Always keen to portray itself as "forward-thinking", LJMU is focusing on giving its graduates the skills to succeed in an increasingly competitive employment market. Work-related learning is included in every degree and all undergraduates are encouraged to become expert in up to eight transferable skills, applicable to a wide range of professions and careers. They can have their abilities verified through an employer-validated skills statement. The initiative to give degrees the WoW (world of work) factor won a coveted business award.

Earlier innovation included Britain's first student charter, which became a template for others. LJMU also launched the first distance learning degree in astronomy and the first degree in criminal justice. It has been investing £180 million to transform its three campuses by 2013. An Art and Design Academy opened in 2009 and a £25-million life sciences building opened in 2010.

The two learning resource centres serving different academic areas and a state-of-the-art media centre are open all hours. The university's Virtual Learning Environment enables students to access most teaching materials and a range of other support features online. Student numbers increased substantially in the early years of the decade and applications were up again by 17 per cent at the start of 2010.

Mainly concentrated in an area between Liverpool's two cathedrals, the university is now one of Britain's biggest with 26,000 students in the city and another 4,500 taking LJMU courses overseas. Arts and science courses occupy separate sites within easy reach of the city centre, with the IM Marsh campus three miles away for education and community studies. Nearly half of the students are drawn from the Merseyside area. A "learning federation" embracing four further education colleges in St Helens, Southport and Liverpool itself adds to the regional flavour.

A growing research reputation is a source of particular pride: LJMU was one of only two new universities to have a subject (sports science) rated internationally outstanding in the 2001 Research Assessment Exercise. There is now a national centre of excellence in teaching and learning in PE, dance, sport and exercise sciences. The new life sciences building houses the School of Sports and Exercise Sciences and the School of Natural Sciences and Psychology, offering some of the best facilities in the world. These include appetite laboratories, psychology testing labs, neuroscience labs, an indoor 70-metre

---

Roscoe Court
4 Rodney Street
Liverpool L1 2TZ

0151 231 5090 (course enquiries)
courses@livjm.ac.uk (enquiries)
www.livjm.ac.uk
www.l-s-u.com

The Times Rankings
Overall Ranking: **98**

Student satisfaction:	=79	(74%)
Research quality:	=77	(0.4)
Entry standards:	96	(246)
Student–staff ratio:	=85	(19.7)
Services & facilities/student:	80	(£1,150)
Expected completion rate:	=95	(77.2%)
Good honours:	=84	(53.6%)
Graduate prospects:	107	(54.2%)

running track, physiology suites, a scanner for measuring body fat, muscles and bone density, a driving simulator and a chronobiology lab.

A third of the research assessed in 2008 was rated as world-leading or internationally excellent, with 12 of the 17 subject areas having some work in the top category. The built environment, electrical and electronic engineering, general engineering and sport-related studies produced the best results. The university did well in areas such as astrophysics and biological anthropology, where post-1992 rarely conduct research.

The International Centre for Digital Content has been developing a range of new courses, including masters programmes in computer games design and e-commerce. A £1.6-million maritime centre features the UK's most advanced 360-degree ship-handling simulator.

The university's efforts to extend access to higher education are successful: there are significantly more state-educated undergraduates than average for the subjects offered and four in ten are from working-class homes. Two thirds of undergraduates qualify for bursaries and there is a range of scholarships, including six worth £10,000 a year. LJMU has also been addressing concerns about its dropout rate, which is now the official benchmark for the university.

Student facilities have been improving. The university has partnerships with a range of private accommodation providers so that all new students are guaranteed accommodation if they require it, even if they enter through Clearing.

Undergraduate Fees and Bursaries

» Fees for UK/EU students: £3,290
» International student fees: £9,950–£10,600
» Bursary on full grant: household income up to £25K: £1,075
» Bursary on partial grant: household income £25–£50K: £430
» Scholarships based on circumstances or by competition.
» For full details see the university's website: www.ljmu.ac.uk/StudyLJMU/Fees

Students

Undergraduates:	**15,990**	**(5,080)**
Postgraduates:	**2,040**	**(2,885)**
Mature students:	**18.4%**	
Overseas students:	**8.6%**	
Applications per place:	**5.1**	
From state-sector schools:	**95.4%**	
From working-class homes:	**41.0%**	

Accommodation

Number of places and costs refer to 2009–10
University-provided places: 3,300 plus 15,000 through Liverpool Student Homes.
Percentage catered: 0%
Self-catered costs: £64–£104 a week.
All new students are guaranteed a place in university accommodation.
International students: as above
Contact: www.ljmu.ac.uk/accommodation
accommodation@ljmu.ac.uk; (0151) 231 4166

University of London

The federal university is Britain's biggest by far, despite the loss of Imperial College in 2007. Some other prestigious members have considered going their own way and applied for their own degree-awarding powers to hold in reserve, but they are bound together by the London degree, which enjoys a high reputation worldwide. Reforms to the university's governance have given the colleges more autonomy and look to have staved off further departures for now.

London students do have access to some joint residential accommodation, sporting facilities and the University of London Union. But most identify with their college.

The following colleges – some of which have dropped the word "college" from their title to underline their university status – have separate entries, and each also appears within the main university league table.

Goldsmiths, University of London
King's College London
London School of Economics and Political Science
Queen Mary
Royal Holloway
School of Oriental and African Studies
University College London

Many of London's teaching hospitals have now merged with colleges of the university:

King's College now incorporates Guys and St Thomas's (the United Medical and Dental Schools of Guys and St Thomas's).

Queen Mary now incorporates St Bartholomew's and the Royal London School of Medicine and Dentistry.

University College now incorporates the Royal Free Hospital Medical School and the Eastman Dental Hospital.

In addition, the School of Slavonic and Eastern European Studies is now part of University College.

Eleven colleges do not have separate entries in the *Guide*. These are listed below and opposite, with useful postal, telephone and electronic contacts.

Birkbeck College
Malet Street, Bloomsbury
London WC1E 7HX
0845 601 0174 (course enquiries)
info@bbk.ac.uk
www.bbk.ac.uk
14,645 undergraduates, mainly part-time.
Apply direct, not through UCAS.

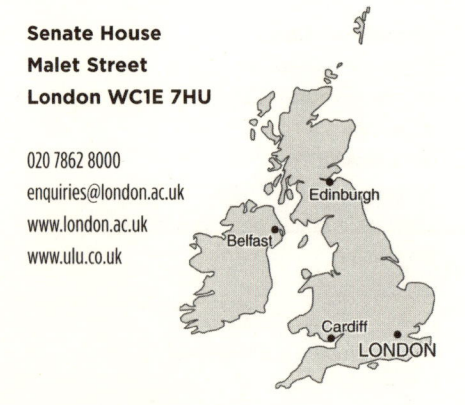

Senate House
Malet Street
London WC1E 7HU

020 7862 8000
enquiries@london.ac.uk
www.london.ac.uk
www.ulu.co.uk

Enquiries: to individual colleges, institutes or schools.

Central School of Speech and Drama
Eton Avenue
London NW3 3HY
020 7559 3912 (admissions)
admissions@cssd.ac.uk
www.cssd.ac.uk
540 undergraduates. Acting and theatre practice.

Courtauld Institute of Art
Somerset House, Strand
London WC2R 0RN
020 7848 2645 (degree programmes)
ugadmissions@courtauld.ac.uk
www.courtauld.ac.uk
165 undergraduates. History of art degree.

Heythrop College
Kensington Square
London W8 5HN
020 7795 4202 (admissions enquiries)
enquiries@heythrop.ac.uk
www.heythrop.ac.uk
430 undergraduates. Degrees in theology and philosophy.

Institute of Education
20 Bedford Way
London WC1H 0AL
020 7612 6000 (switchboard)
info@ioe.ac.uk
www.ioe.ac.uk
750 undergraduates; mainly postgraduate education courses.

London Business School
Regent's Park
London NW1 4SA
020 7000 7000 (switchboard)
webenquiries@london.edu
www.london.edu
Postgraduate MBA and other courses.

London School of Hygiene and Tropical Medicine
Keppel Street
London WC1E 7HT
020 7299 4646 (admission enquiries)
registry@lshtm.ac.uk
www.lshtm.ac.uk
Postgraduate medical courses.

Royal Academy of Music
Marylebone Road
London NW1 5HT
020 7873 7393 (registry)
registry@ram.ac.uk
www.ram.ac.uk
320 undergraduates. Degrees in music.

Royal Veterinary College
Royal College Street
London NW1 0TU
020 7468 5147 (undergraduate admissions)
enquiries@rvc.ac.uk
www.rvc.ac.uk
1,495 undergraduates. Degrees in veterinary medicine.

St George's, University of London
Cranmer Terrace
London SW17 0RE
020 8725 2333 (admissions enquiries)
enquiries@sgul.ac.uk
www.sgul.ac.uk
3,960 undergraduates. Degrees in medicine.

School of Pharmacy
29–39 Brunswick Square
London WC1N 1AX
020 7753 5831 (enquiries)
registry@pharmacy.ac.uk
www.pharmacy.ac.uk
740 undergraduates. Degrees in pharmacy.

London Metropolitan University

London Met has boycotted league tables since making its debut in our *Guide* five years ago, perilously close to the bottom of *The Times* ranking. It has announced a change of heart since the arrival of a new Vice-Chancellor, Professor Malcolm Gillies, and will make a welcome reappearance next year. But for this edition the university continued to block the release of data from the Higher Education Statistics Agency. Those figures that are available paint a mixed picture. Student satisfaction levels had been increasing, for example, but dipped again in the National Student Survey published in 2009, when London Met was in the bottom four.

The immediate difficulty facing the university is a cut of at least £15 million in its grant over the misreporting of student numbers. Hundreds of staff posts will be lost and the previous Vice-Chancellor, Professor Brian Roper, has resigned. The last projected dropout rate was 24 per cent – significantly above the national average for the university's courses and entry qualifications.

London Met specialises in extending higher education boundaries to bring in groups who are under-represented at traditional universities. Since its establishment from the merger of London Guildhall and North London universities, it has developed hundreds of new degree courses, described as both intellectual and vocational, and which allow students to study citizenship, ethics or enterprise alongside their main subject. Many prepare students for professional qualifications and gain credit for work experience or volunteering.

Recent developments have seen four "business-related" departments join together to form the London Metropolitan Business School which, with 10,000 students and more than 100 courses, will be one of Europe's largest. An "international medical degree" was launched in September 2008, through the University of Health Studies, in Antigua. The five-year programme will be based in London and graduates will complete the United States Medical Licensing Examination, enabling them to practise in America.

With over 28,000 students, 7,000 of whom are from other countries, it has become the biggest single institution in the capital. However, applications have been uneven: although the demand for places had risen by nearly 5 per cent at the start of 2009, this followed a 17.5 per cent decline in the previous year. Fortunately, overseas recruitment has remained healthy. London Met has more undergraduates from other EU countries than any university.

The university's sites are centred on the

---

31 Jewry Street
London EC3N 2EY

020 7133 4200 (enquiries)
admissions@londonmet.ac.uk
www.londonmet.ac.uk
www.londonmetsu.org.uk

The Times Rankings
London Metropolitan's decision to release data from the Higher Education Statistics Agency came too late this year for any rankings to be produced.

City of London and north London's Holloway Road. A new graduate school, designed by Daniel Libeskind, opened soon after the merger, and an impressive £30-million science centre followed in 2006. This features a "superlab" of 280 workstations that is Europe's largest, as well as a multipurpose gym and sports therapy facilities.

Among a variety of craft subjects, the silversmithing and jewellery courses are the largest in Britain, with facilities to match, while those in furniture restoration and conservation were the first of their kind in Europe.

Courses are also directed at the local community. More than a third of the students are Afro-Caribbean and the proportion of mature students is among the highest in England. One of London Met's first objectives was to improve student retention: student support services, from admission to careers advice, have been remodelled and there is a particular emphasis on academic and pastoral counselling on entry and at other key points of courses.

London Met entered more academics than most former polytechnics in the 2008 Research Assessment Exercise, when almost a quarter of the work submitted was placed in the top two categories. About half of the 21 subject areas contained some world-leading research, with architecture, media studies, education and social studies producing the best results. Education, maths and statistics and sociology had the most satisfied undergraduates.

Residential accommodation is limited, but many of London Met's students live at home. Sports facilities are still not extensive, although competitive teams are successful. However, the social scene is lively, particularly in north London.

Undergraduate Fees and Bursaries

» Fees for UK/EU students: £3,290
» International student fees: £9,600
» Bursary on full grant: household income up to £25K: Sliding scale: £1,000–£325.*
» The university does not award bursaries for students on partial maintenance grants.*
» Scholarships based on circumstances or by competition.
» For full details see the university's website: http://intranet.londonmet.ac.uk/studentservices/aifs

* Figures for 2009–10

Students

Undergraduates:	**13,310**	(6,195)
Postgraduates:	**3,175**	(3,700)
Mature students:	**47.7%**	
Overseas students:	**n/a**	
Applications per place:	**7.3**	
From state-sector schools:	**97.0%**	
From working-class homes:	**57.2%**	

Accommodation

Number of places and costs refer to 2009-10
University-provided places: Students have access to accommodation in a wide range of halls of residences provided by specialist student accommodation providers.
Percentage catered: 0%
Self-catered costs: approximately £102–£260 a week.
The university cannot guarantee a place in halls.
All students have access to halls spaces
International students: first years given priority.
Contact: accommodation@londonmet.ac.uk

London School of Economics and Political Science

Always one of the big names of British higher education, the LSE is in the top five social science institutions in the world, according to the QS global rankings. Like most of the universities at the top of the league tables, LSE did not share in the 2010 applications boom. But with around 14 applications for every place, competition for admission remains tougher than at any UK university. Only Oxford, Cambridge and Imperial College London have higher average entry grades. The school has added 1,000 places in recent years, having seized the chance to tackle a longstanding shortage of teaching space by acquiring former Government buildings near the school's Aldwych headquarters. However, most of the extra capacity has gone on postgraduate courses.

Sir Howard Davies, the Director, has built on the progress made by his predecessor, Professor Anthony Giddens, the academic face of Tony Blair's Third Way, who brought in a number of big names from other top universities. The LSE does not hide its light under a bushel: it describes itself as "the world's leading social science institution for teaching and research". A pan-European survey also showed the school's students to be more active in student associations, more entrepreneurial and more open to opportunities to work abroad than those at other leading universities. The students' union claims to be the only one in Britain to hold weekly general meetings at which every student may attend and vote.

The school has a cosmopolitan feel that derives from the highest proportion of overseas students at any publicly funded university. Due to national funding restrictions, only a relatively small proportion of the extra places have been for UK undergraduates. More than 30 past or present heads of state have either been students at, or taught at the university, as have 15 Nobel prizewinners in economics, literature and peace – including George Bernard Shaw, Bertrand Russell, Friedrich von Hayek and Amartya Sen. Before the 2010 General Election, 31 MPs had the same association with LSE, as did 42 members of the House of Lords. The nationals of more than 140 countries take up half of the 9000 places. At the undergraduate level, only the much larger Manchester University has more applications from overseas. Its international character not only gives the LSE global prestige but also an unusual degree of financial independence. Less than a fifth of its income is from the Higher Education Funding Council for England, although the LSE will still be affected by cuts of more than 6 per cent from that source in 2010–11.

More than a third of British students are

Houghton Street
London WC2A 2AE

020 7955 7125
stu.rec@lse.ac.uk (pre-application)
ug-admissions@lse.ac.uk
(post-application)
www.lse.ac.uk
www.lsesu.com

The Times Rankings
Overall Ranking: **5**

Student satisfaction:	=97	(72%)
Research quality:	3	(3.7)
Entry standards:	4	(494)
Student–staff ratio:	11	(13.2)
Services & facilities/student:	5	(£2,232)
Expected completion rate:	6	(95.2%)
Good honours:	11	(76.5%)
Graduate prospects:	5	(81.9%)

from independent schools – one of the highest ratios in the country and higher than the funding council's benchmark figure. Efforts are being made to attract a broader intake with Saturday classes and summer schools. The projected dropout rate of less than 5 per cent is among the lowest at any university. However, average scores in the National Student Survey published in 2009 were again the lowest of any pre-1992 university. There was still no subject in which more than 85 per cent of students were satisfied with their course. However, the percentage of leavers securing graduate-level employment is impressive, with management studies and history outstanding at 100 per cent and 95 per cent respectively.

Areas of study range more broadly than the name suggests: law, management and history are all on the curriculum and there is even a small contingent of scientists. Only Cambridge recorded higher average scores than the LSE in the 2008 Research Assessment Exercise, which saw almost 70 per cent of the work submitted rated world-leading or internationally excellent. Ninety-five per cent of the economics submission, 80 per cent in social policy and 75 per cent in law reached the top two categories.

Improvements were being made to the campus long before the opportunity arose to expand. A £30-million Norman Foster-designed redevelopment of the Lionel Robbins Building houses a much-improved library. The move was a welcome one since the number of books borrowed by LSE students is more than four times the national average, according to a recent survey. Routes between most of the buildings have been pedestrianised and a new student services centre has opened. In 2008 the Queen opened LSE's £71-million eco-friendly academic building, which helped the LSE to second place in the "Green League" of universities in the following year.

Partying is not the prime attraction of the LSE for most applicants, who tend to be serious about their subject, but London's top nightspots are on the doorstep for those who can afford them. The 3,650 residential places for 8,500 full-time students offer a good chance of avoiding central London's notoriously high private sector rents.

Undergraduate Fees and Bursaries

» Fees for UK/EU students: £3,290
» International student fees: £13,680
» Bursary on full grant: household income up to £25K: sliding scale £2,500–£1,000.
» Bursary on partial grant: household income up to £50K: sliding scale £1,000–£100.
» Scholarships based on circumstances or by competition.
» For full details see the university's website: www2.lse.ac.uk/intranet/students/studentFinance.aspx

Students

Undergraduates:	4,200	50
Postgraduates:	4,815	(505)
Mature students:	2.4%	
Overseas students:	47.5%	
Applications per place:	13.8	
From state-sector schools:	70.7%	
From working-class homes:	18.7%	

Accommodation

Number of places and costs refer to 2009–10
University-provided places: 3,650
Percentage catered: about 36%
Catered costs: from £67–£160 a week.
Self-catered costs: £73–£199 a week.
First years are guaranteed an offer of accommodation.
Policy for international students: same as above.
Contact: accommodation@lse.ac.uk
to apply online: www.lse.ac.uk/accommodation

London South Bank University

Once marketed as "the university without ivory towers", London South Bank University's mission statement underlines the point with an emphasis on wealth creation and the labour market. The university was in the top ten in the last survey of graduate starting salaries. A PricewaterhouseCoopers study in 2007 found that a LSBU degree increased lifetime earnings by more than £185,000, which was nearly £26,000 more than the national average. LBSU is the number one university in the UK for "knowledge transfer partnerships" with firms and other outside organisations, its projects spanning construction, manufacturing, energy and environment, food, information technology, health and the creative industries.

Over 70 per cent of students are from the capital, most of them from south London and especially from the area's wide range of ethnic minorities. Of nearly 17,000 undergraduates, over a third are part-time and half are on sandwich courses. Fewer than half enter with traditional academic qualifications. Applications were buoyant throughout the period following the introduction of top-up fees and the start of 2010 saw another big increase, of 38 per cent.

The proportion of mature entrants is among the highest in Britain, encouraged by initiatives such as the summer school for local people to upgrade their qualifications. Six out of ten students are over 25. The Fast Track to Higher Education programme has been expanded to include English, IT and science, as well as the original mathematics. The courses, some of which are tailored to the needs of mature students and some for younger students, start at the end of June and are limited to 15 hours a week so as not to affect students' benefit entitlement.

LBSU gives a high priority to widening participation in higher education, something for which it won a London education award for its work with non-traditional learners who have no family history or aspirations to apply to university. Diploma and degree courses run in parallel so that students can move up or down if they are better suited to another level of study. The university offers a wide range of Foundation and pre-degree courses in business and accounting, law, tourism and hospitality, design and engineering, and science and technology for international students

Specialist facilities, such as the Centre for Explosion and Fire Research, show that the vocational theme carries through into research. Although the university entered only 87 academics for the 2008 Research Assessment Exercise, their average grades were among the best of the new universities. More than 40 per cent of the submission was rated as world-leading or internationally excellent, with social policy, engineering and communication,

---

103 Borough Road
London SE1 0AA

020 7815 7815
course.enquiry@lsbu.ac.uk
www.lsbu.ac.uk
www.lsbsu.org

The Times Rankings
Overall Ranking: **113**

Student satisfaction:	=97	(72%)
Research quality:	=88	(0.3)
Entry standards:	111	(192)
Student–staff ratio:	109	(23.4)
Services & facilities/student:	102	(£976)
Expected completion rate:	112	(66.4%)
Good honours:	110	(45.8%)
Graduate prospects:	=87	(58.5%)

culture and media studies leading the way.

LSBU is in the midst of a 15-year programme to develop its campus in Southwark, near the Elephant and Castle, and not far from the South Bank arts complex. The nine-storey Keyworth Centre upgraded much of the teaching accommodation and provided a new focal point for the university. The flagship building "K2" opened in 2009, housing the Faculty of Health and Social Care, and the Department of Education. By summer 2010, K2 will also accommodate the Centre for Efficient and Renewable Energy in Buildings, a teaching, research and demonstration resource for the built environment

Some health students are based on the other side of London, in hospitals in Romford and Leytonstone, where there are smaller satellite campuses to supplement those in Southwark. The university now trains 40 per cent of London's nurses. It topped the list of London universities for midwifery and was rated third for nursing in NHS London's new Higher Education Quality Assurance assessment.

The capital's attractions are on the doorstep of the main campus but, with nearly half of the students coming from working-class homes, many cannot afford them. The official projected dropout rate is nearly 30 per cent, a proportion exceeded by only one university in England. But LSBU insists that the true rate is less than half that figure because most students do complete their courses eventually; they just take longer than the standard course length.

A new hall of residence means that the university now has residential places within ten minutes' walk of the main campus. There are not enough rooms to guarantee places for all first years, but the 2,000 overseas students are all given places if they want them. Sports facilities improved considerably with the extension of the campus sports centre and the launch of the Academy of Sport. Representative teams have been quite successful in recent years – especially in basketball – and sports bursaries of £3,000 are available for elite performers.

Undergraduate Fees and Bursaries

» Fees for UK/EU students: £3,290
» International student fees: £8,300–£8,600*
» Bursary on full or partial grant: Year 1 £500; Year 2 £750; Year 3 £750 (+ £250 graduation bonus for Hons graduates).*
» Scholarships based on circumstances or by competition.
» For full details see the university's website: www1.lsbu.ac.uk/fees

* Figures for 2009–10

Students

Undergraduates:	**9,965**	(8,200)
Postgraduates:	**1,625**	(4,215)
Mature students:	**57.4%**	
Overseas students:	**8.8%**	
Applications per place:	**5.1**	
From state-sector schools:	**98.8%**	
From working-class homes:	**49.1%**	

Accommodation

Number of places and costs refer to 2010–11
University-provided places: 1,400
Percentage catered: 0%
Self-catered costs: £95–£97 (standard) – £116 (en suite) a week.
First-year UK students are not guaranteed accommodation, but high priority is given to those who live outside Greater London area.
International students: first years are guaranteed accommodation if conditions met.
Contact: accommodation@lsbu.ac.uk

Loughborough University

Loughborough celebrated its centenary in the top 20 in every UK league table, partly thanks to its own students. It has been in the top ten universities for student satisfaction every year since the National Student Survey was launched. Scores dipped slightly in 2009, but the university was still among the top five in England. There was 100 per cent satisfaction on the courses listed under anatomy, pathology and nearly nine out of ten undergraduates throughout the university declared themselves satisfied overall. Loughborough has also won the first four *Times Higher Education* awards for best student experience, after separate national polls of undergraduates.

Still best known for its successes on the sports field, Loughborough has enhanced its academic reputation recently, consistently finishing well up *The Times* rankings and improving its performance in the 2008 Research Assessment Exercise. Although the results were patchy, more than half of the research in art and design was considered world-leading, and there were particularly good results in architecture and sport. The Office for Standards in Education also rates Loughborough in its top category for teacher training in physical education, design and science.

The university remains a major centre of engineering with more than 2,800 students in a £20-million integrated engineering complex. Loughborough headquarters the £1 billion national Energy Technologies Institute, as part of a consortium with Birmingham and Nottingham universities concentrating on low-carbon energy. Civil, aeronautical and automotive engineering are particularly strong, although art and design, business and sports science now all have more students than any single branch of the discipline. Like most universities in the top 20, Loughborough did not share in the applications boom, but still registered a 5 per cent rise at the start of 2010.

The original 216-acre campus has benefited from a sustained construction programme which included a large student union extension and a new business school, as well as the gradual refurbishment of residential accommodation. The first phase of a £68-million on-campus accommodation development opened in 2008 and more than 5,000 rooms now all have telephone and internet connections. The development will eventually provide another 1,300 new bedrooms in four new halls.

The purchase of the adjacent Holywell Park site increased the size of the campus by 75 per cent. This will become the focus for research and collaboration with industry, including a £59-million BAE-sponsored Systems Engineering Innovation Centre. The university prides itself on a close relationship

---

Ashby Road
Loughborough
Leicestershire LE11 3TU

01509 223522 (admissions)
admissions@lboro.ac.uk
admissions
www.lboro.ac.uk
www.lufbra.net

The Times Rankings
Overall Ranking: **=16**

Student satisfaction:	=1	(85%)
Research quality:	=18	(2.5)
Entry standards:	31	(370)
Student–staff ratio:	=62	(18.0)
Services & facilities/student:	60	(£1,288)
Expected completion rate:	16	(93.8%)
Good honours:	31	(69.9%)
Graduate prospects:	34	(71.3%)

with industry, which accounts for its record haul of six Queen's Anniversary Prizes. Arts facilities are improving with the upgrading of the Cope Auditorium to serve the campus and local community. The business school is being extended, and an £8-million building for Health, Exercise and Biosciences opened in 2010.

Most subjects are available either as three-year full-time or four-to-five-year sandwich courses, which includes a year in industry. This has helped to give graduates an outstanding employment record, as well a dropout rate of less than 4 per cent, which is particularly low for the subjects Loughborough offers. The university is a leader in the use of computer-assisted assessment, offering students the chance to gauge their own progress online.

Loughborough remains pre-eminent in British university sport, both in terms of facilities and performance. More than 50 past and present students took part in the 2008 Beijing Olympic and Paralympic Games, reaching 19 finals and winning three Olympic medals. Representative teams have a record second to none – the women won the national title for the 31st successive year and the men for the 29th in 2009 – and the programme of sports scholarships is the largest in the university system.

The campus boasts a 50-metre swimming pool, national academies for cricket and tennis, a gymnastics centre and a high-performance training centre for athletics. The university also opened the UK's only centre for disability sport in 2005 and was shortlisted as a possible training camp for the British team ahead of the 2012 Olympics in London. Joining the Olympic effort will be the new £15-million Sports Technology Institute, as well as enhanced research, innovation and enterprise in sport and leisure in the longer term.

Social activity is concentrated on the students' union. The relatively small town of Loughborough, a mile away, is never going to be a clubber's paradise, but both Leicester and Nottingham are within easy reach.

Undergraduate Fees and Bursaries

» Fees for UK/EU students: £3,290
» International student fees: £10,990–£14,400
» Bursary on full grant: household income up to £25K: household income up to £24.6K: sliding scale £1,420–£800 (doubled for mature students).
» Bursary on partial grant: household income up to £36.3K: sliding scale £660–£220 (doubled for mature students).
» Scholarships based on circumstances or by competition.
» For full details see the university's website: www.lboro.ac.uk/admin/ar/funding

---

Students

Undergraduates:	**11,810**	**(305)**
Postgraduates:	**2,325**	**(1,690)**
Mature students:	**3.5%**	
Overseas students:	**9.8%**	
Applications per place:	**6.9**	
From state-sector schools:	**82.8%**	
From working-class homes:	**22.7%**	

Accommodation

Number of places and costs refer to 2010–11
University-provided places: 5,592
Percentage catered: 42%
Catered costs: £4039.20 – £5593.20
Self-catered costs: £2,659.80 – £5,608.20
First-year first-choice students are guaranteed accommodation.
International students: guaranteed housing in same residence for two years.
Contact: SAC@lboro.ac.uk
http://accommodation.lboro.ac.uk

University of Manchester

Always among the giants of British higher education, with 23 Nobel prizewinners to its credit, Manchester became larger and more powerful in 2004 through a merger with neighbouring UMIST. The largest conventional university in Britain kept its familiar name, but is now headed by a Vice-Chancellor from the other side of the world. Professor Alan Gilbert arrived from the University of Melbourne shortly before the new institution was formed.

Some departments were already administered jointly with UMIST and the two institutions only separated fully in 1993, so the new institution has been able to avoid some of the problems associated with other university mergers. A £400-million building and refurbishment programme, the largest ever in UK higher education has been completed and another £250 million of investment is planned by 2015. At the same time, a raft of new professors has been appointed. The aim is not only to break into higher education's "golden triangle" of Oxford, Cambridge and London, but to make Manchester one of the top 25 universities in the world by 2015. By then, the aim is to have at least five Nobel laureates on the staff. Nobel laureates now on the staff include the economist Joseph Stiglitz and the scientist Sir John Sulston, who specialises in science and ethics. There have been other high-profile appointments, such as the novelist Martin Amis as Professor of Creative Writing.

Manchester was among the top ten universities in the 2008 Research Assessment Exercise, with almost two thirds of its submission considered world-leading or internationally excellent. The university's claim to have "smashed the golden triangle" may have been wishful thinking, but there were particularly strong performances in cancer studies, nursing, biology, dentistry, engineering, sociology, development studies, Spanish, and music and drama. Google are helping to fund new research that could help blind people to find their way around the worldwide web.

The university has produced consistently good scores in the National Student Survey, with 99 per cent satisfaction in anatomy, physiology and pathology as well as physics and astronomy in 2009, and high scores in classics and biology.

Manchester has reclaimed its place as the university with the largest number of applicants since the merger. The demand for places had been growing, and applications were up 5.5 per cent at the start of 2010, as most universities saw substantial increases. One of the priorities in the new institution's founding strategy is to broaden the undergraduate intake, with a particular focus on increasing recruitment from the city and its surrounding area. However, in addition to

Oxford Road
Manchester M13 9PL

0161 275 2077 (admissions)
ug-admissions@manchester.ac.uk
www.manchester.ac.uk
www.umsu.manchester.ac.uk

The Times Rankings
Overall Ranking: **30**

Student satisfaction:	=89	(73%)
Research quality:	=10	(2.8)
Entry standards:	14	(416)
Student–staff ratio:	16	(13.5)
Services & facilities/student:	19	(£1,777)
Expected completion rate:	24	(92.3%)
Good honours:	=28	(70.3%)
Graduate prospects:	=35	(71.1%)

the normal bursary package for British students, Manchester is aiming eventually to have 750 awards for students from educationally deprived backgrounds in developing countries.

UMIST's legacy was a strong reputation among academics and employers alike in its specialist areas of engineering, science and management. Surveys of employers frequently placed UMIST among their favourite recruiting grounds, helping to produce an unrivalled network of industrial sponsorship. Employers have rated Manchester's careers service the best at any university. The merger also produced the largest engineering school in the UK, with a £20-million budget and 1,200 students.

A £14-million extension to the School of Chemistry, the second-largest in Britain, opened in 2007. A new £39 million research centre dedicated to Biomedical Science was opened in May 2009, making it one of the largest complexes of its kind in Europe, housing 300 scientists and 50 research groups. There already was a federal business school, which is among the strengths of the merged institution, as is the medical school, which was rewarded for impressive teaching ratings with extra places. A new teaching block helps to cater for 2,000 undergraduates following a problem-based curriculum.

The city's famed youth culture and the university's position at the heart of a huge student precinct already help to ensure keen competition for places – and hence high entry standards in most subjects. Sports facilities, which were already first rate, have improved still further since the city hosted the Commonwealth Games. Students get discount rates at the aquatics centre opened for the games on campus, for example. The university sports teams are also high achievers, ranking 11th overall in the BUCS league. The city's reputation for violent crime has subsided, but the students' union (which has the largest premises in the country) runs late-night minibuses, self-defence classes, and regular safety campaigns. Students tend to be

Undergraduate Fees and Bursaries
» Fees for UK/EU students: £3,290
» International student fees: £11,300–£14,200
£25,900 (medicine)
» Bursary on full grant: household income up to £25K: £1,250
» The university does not award bursaries for students on partial maintenance grants.
» Scholarships based on circumstances or by competition.
» For full details see the university's website: www.manchester.ac.uk/undergraduate/funding

Students
Undergraduates:	26,070	(1,575)
Postgraduates:	6,900	(3,645)
Mature students:	9.1%	
Overseas students:	16.5%	
Applications per place:	6.2	
From state-sector schools:	78.9%	
From working-class homes:	24.4%	

Accommodation
Number of places and costs refer to 2010–11
University-owned/managed places: 9,200
Percentage catered: (approx) 30%
Catered costs: £4,269–£5,790 (40 weeks).
Self-catered costs: £3,204–£5,313 (40 weeks).
All first years are guaranteed accommodation provided conditions are met.
International students paying overseas fees are guaranteed accommodation if conditions met.
Contact: www.manchester.ac.uk/accommodation

Manchester Metropolitan University

With over 34,000 students, including more than 7,000 part-timers, Manchester Metropolitan is neck and neck with its neighbour, Manchester, for the title of the largest conventional higher education institution in Britain. But the giant institution boasts quality as well as quantity: more than a third of the work entered for the 2008 Research Assessment Exercise was rated as world-leading or internationally excellent. Education, English and art and design produced the best results.

Although the former polytechnic has not been able to sustain the lead it held briefly over Manchester University in applications, still only a handful of institutions are more popular. The demand for places has grown throughout most of the decade and there had been an increase in applications of almost 30 per cent at the start of 2010. Longstanding commitments to extending access are being continued: even among the full-time undergraduates, a fifth are over 25 and more than a third come from working-class homes.

Almost 1,000 courses cover more than 70 subjects, with the menu of programmes including a growing range of two-year Foundation degrees. The university takes teaching seriously: small groups are used whenever possible and staff are encouraged to take a three-year MA in teaching. Many courses also involve work placements. MMU has more professionally accredited courses than any other university. Scores improved a little in the 2009 National Student Survey, but the university still found itself towards the bottom of the table. Maths and statistics, biology, chemistry and philosophy were the only subjects to achieve satisfaction levels of more than 90 per cent.

Education courses have also fared well in the Teacher Training Agency's performance indicators, especially for primary training. The university trains more teachers than any other and has launched a Centre for Urban Education to develop its expertise further. Some 800 trainees and other students taking contemporary arts and sports science are at the former Crewe and Alsager College campuses, 40 miles south of Manchester and now rebranded as MMU Cheshire. The remaining education students are based at Didsbury, five miles out of the centre of Manchester, with those taking community studies. A single Institute of Education covers both centres.

The two Cheshire campuses are being merged into one at Crewe in the area of the town now known as the University Quadrant. A £30-million student village has already opened and arts facilities have switched to Crewe with the opening of a £6-million drama, music and dance centre. Exercise and

---

All Saints Building
All Saints
Manchester M15 6BH

0161 247 6969 (enquiries)
enquiries@mmu.ac.uk
www.mmu.ac.uk
www.mmunion.co.uk

The Times Rankings
Overall Ranking: **95**

Student satisfaction:	=97	(72%)
Research quality:	=69	(0.5)
Entry standards:	=76	(268)
Student–staff ratio:	89	(19.8)
Services & facilities/student:	85	(£1,127)
Expected completion rate:	90	(78.8%)
Good honours:	70	(57.2%)
Graduate prospects:	94	(57.5%)

sport science students will be the final group to make the six-mile move and will be based at Crewe before autumn 2011, after which only sports fields will remain at Alsager.

The five sites in Manchester will eventually be reduced to two linked campuses. The university will move from leafy Didsbury in the southern suburbs and create a £120-million "campus for the professions" in the city centre that will be one of the most environmentally sustainable in the UK, uniting provision for teachers, nurses, health and youth workers. The new site is close to the existing All Saints campus, on the university's border with Hulme and Moss Side.

New science and engineering buildings at All Saints cost £42 million – part of a £300-million building programme for the university as a whole. The large business school will benefit from a new £65-million building next to the Mancunian Way. Overseas links have expanded rapidly in recent years, offering exchange opportunities in Europe and farther afield, as well as establishing teaching bases abroad.

However, more than half of the students come from the Manchester area, easing the pressure on accommodation in a city of nearly 70,000 students. Some 85 per cent of hall places are reserved for first years, with priority going to the disabled and those who live furthest from the university. The city's attractions do no harm to recruitment levels, but much depends on where the course is based; students at Crewe can feel isolated. Some potential applicants are daunted by the sheer size of the university, but individual courses and sites usually provide a social circle.

Undergraduate Fees and Bursaries

» Fees for UK/EU students: £3,290
» International student fees: £8,555–£14,200
» Bursary on full grant: household income up to £21K: £1,025; household income up to £25K: £475.
» Bursary on partial grant: household income up to £40K: £475.
» Scholarships based on circumstances or by competition.
» For full details see the university's website: www.mmu.ac.uk/studentfinance

---

Students

Undergraduates:	**24,245**	(3,475)
Postgraduates:	**2,810**	(3,800)
Mature students:	**21.1%**	
Overseas students:	**7.1%**	
Applications per place:	**5.2**	
From state-sector schools:	**96.0%**	
From working-class homes:	**38.7%**	

For detailed information about fees, grants and bursaries and how they work, see chapter 7.

Accommodation

Number of places and costs refer to 2010–11
University provided places: 4,324
Percentage catered: 3%
Catered Costs: Manchester £95.46 a week
Self-catered costs: Manchester £77.04–£103.03 a week; Cheshire £77.04– £86.99 a week
All new full-time students will be housed if requirements are met. Local restrictions apply.
International students: as above.
Contact: www.mmu.ac.uk/accommodation

Middlesex University

Middlesex had the biggest increase in applications of any university in London at the start of 2010 – more than 50 per cent. Although helped by changes in nursing and art and design, the unprecedented rise marked the culmination of a programme of reorganisation that has seen a new pattern of courses and more international recruitment. The university has rationalised its schools to focus on its strengths in business, computing and the arts. Now almost 25,000 strong, including part-timers, it would like to carry on growing, partly through partner colleges at home and abroad that participate in exchanges and/or offer Middlesex qualifications.

Overseas recruitment was Middlesex's salvation when it found UK students more difficult to attract: foreign undergraduates now make up 15 per cent of its intake. A longstanding commitment to Europe sees more than 1,000 students arriving from the Continent, and even more come from further afield. There is a network of 11 regional offices, producing a student population drawn from 130 countries, which won the university a Queen's Award for Enterprise. Middlesex has its own campus in Dubai and has just become the first UK university to open a campus in Mauritius.

The highly flexible course system allows students to start some courses in January if they prefer not to wait until autumn, and offers the option of an extra five-week session in the summer to try out new subjects or add to their credits. The introduction of year-long modules have the benefit of instilling a deeper level of learning, allowing students to get to grips with a subject before assessment.

Nine out of ten students take vocational courses, many at postgraduate or sub-degree level. Media students, for example, benefit from a new Skillset Academy. The business school is the biggest subject area, but almost half of the undergraduates are on multidisciplinary programmes. About 42 per cent are over 21 on entry and half of the full-timers come from London. Almost all of the British students are from state schools, 48 per cent of them from working-class homes.

The projected dropout rate has dropped back to around 21 percent, but is still worse than the national average for the university's subjects and entry qualifications. Even before the introduction of top-up fees, Middlesex was attempting to attract better-qualified students by offering £1,000-a-year scholarships for UK entrants with 300 UCAS points (the equivalent of three Bs). There are now awards for community engagement and sporting achievement, as well as bursaries for students from non-traditional backgrounds.

For some time, the university has been reducing the number of campuses dotted

North London Business Park
The Burroughs
London NW4 4BT

020 8411 5555 (enquiries)
enquiries@mdx.ac.uk
www.mdx.ac.uk
www.musu.mdx.ac.uk

The Times Rankings
Overall Ranking: **=104**

Student satisfaction:	104	(70%)
Research quality:	=60	(0.6)
Entry standards:	113	(184)
Student–staff ratio:	107	(22.8)
Services & facilities/student:	6	(£2,128)
Expected completion rate:	=99	(75.8%)
Good honours:	98	(50.3%)
Graduate prospects:	=100	(56.5%)

around London's North Circular Road. A building programme that has already cost £100 million will eventually concentrate the university on three sites in north London. The latest to close will be the Cat Hill site, whose students will move into a new Art and Design Centre on the Hendon campus in September 2011. Some £50 million has already been invested at Hendon on a library, learning resources centre and roofing in the main quadrangle to provide social space. New student facilities, including an entertainment venue, expanded nursery and refectory have been added to meet the demand from the extra students and staff. The campus, which boasts one of the country's few Real Tennis courts, already housed the business school, also has a new teaching and learning centre that includes biomedical, psychology, sports and computing science laboratories.

The other locations include a picturesque country estate at Trent Park, which includes a gym and multi-purpose sports hall, outdoor swimming pool, outdoor fitness trail and access to the on-site hockey training ground of Southgate hockey club. Nurses and other health students are based in four London teaching hospitals and on a campus at Archway which is shared with the University College and Royal Free Hospital medical schools. There is also a joint degree in veterinary nursing run with the Royal Veterinary College.

Middlesex did well in the first of the new institutional audits in 2003, but results from National Student Surveys have been disappointing. It was in the bottom ten in 2009. Architecture registered the best results, while philosophy and fine art were the only other subjects to achieve 90 per cent overall satisfaction among final-year undergraduates.

The number of residential places is planned to double in the next few years from the current 1,350 beds. Priority is given to first-years who live outside London and international students. Sports facilities have been improving and now includes a "fitness pod" at Hendon with a gym and multipurpose outdoor courts.

Undergraduate Fees and Bursaries

» Fees for UK/EU students: £3,290
» International student fees: £9,900
» Bursary on full grant: household income up to £25K: £329
» The university does not award bursaries for students on partial maintenance grants.
» Scholarships based on circumstances or by competition.
» For full details see the university's website: www.mdx.ac.uk/courses/undergraduate/fees

Students

Undergraduates:	13,120	(3,335)
Postgraduates:	2440	(2,455)
Mature students:	36.4%	
Overseas students:	15.3%	
Applications per place:	5.8	
From state-sector schools:	98.9	
From working-class homes:	48.4	

For detailed information about fees, grants and bursaries and how they work, see chapter 7.

Accommodation

Number of places and costs refer to 2010–11
University-provided places: 1,350
Percentage catered: 0%
Self-catered costs: £89–£107 a week.
Full-year international students have priority; residential restrictions apply.
International students are guaranteed a room provided they apply by the deadline.
Contact: accomm@mdx.ac.uk; www.mdx.ac.uk/accommodation

Newcastle University

Twice recently, Newcastle has been named as the best university city in the UK, but the message was slow to get through to sixth-formers. The university had seen below-average increases for several years until an 11.5 per cent rise at the start of 2010 that was better than several comparable institutions.

The university has practically completed the first phase of a £200-million programme of investment in its campus and facilities. The five-storey, glass-fronted King's Gate building cost £35 million and is intended to create a "welcoming front door" to the university, as well as housing all the main student services and a visitor centre. New buildings have opened for music and medical sciences, and a new accommodation block has added nearly 100 study bedrooms on campus. In addition, the business school has taken 100,000 square feet of space in a new city-centre development and a partner-ship with a private languages firm is putting £49 million into accommodation and teaching facilities for international students.

Science and engineering laboratories have already been upgraded, disabled access improved and thousands of students provided with internet connections in university-owned flats and halls of residence. And the university's museum has been redeveloped into the £24-million Great North Museum: Hancock, taking in collections from two other museums and a gallery from the city.

Another significant development will be the opening of an international branch campus in Johor, Malaysia, in 2011. Newcastle University Medicine Malaysia (NUMed) will offer degrees in medicine and biomedical science, adding to the courses in naval architecture that are already provided in Singapore. For those who prefer to come to the UK, the university has been placed seventh in the world in i-graduate's International Student Barometer for the quality of the student experience.

Originally Durham University's medical school until going its own way in 1937, Newcastle's excellence in that area was confirmed by its selection as a national centre to disseminate best teaching practice in medicine. The school has gone back into partnership with Durham, with about a third of trainees spending their first two years at Durham's Stockton campus.

Newcastle was also chosen to house a national centre of teaching excellence in music. Other academic developments include the creation of nine new research institutes, housed in new buildings costing over £30 million. Research grades improved in the 2008 assessments, although Newcastle entered fewer academics than most members of Russell Group universities. Almost 60 per cent of the work reached the top two

Kensington Terrace
Newcastle upon Tyne
NE1 7RU

0191 208 3333 (enquiries)
www.ncl.ac.uk/enquiries
www.ncl.ac.uk
www.unionsociety.co.uk

The Times Rankings
Overall Ranking: **25**

Student satisfaction:	=22	(79%)
Research quality:	=29	(2.2)
Entry standards:	=21	(399)
Student–staff ratio:	31	(15.0)
Services & facilities/student:	28	(£1,624)
Expected completion rate:	20	(92.9%)
Good honours:	22	(72.0%)
Graduate prospects:	29	(72.4%)

categories, with 90 per cent of research in cancer research rated world-leading or internationally excellent. Art and design, music and English also produced outstanding results.

Recent additions to the portfolio of courses have included Britain's first degree in folk and traditional music, and an MEng in drug development. Newcastle already had a number of unusual features for a traditional university, such as a fine art degree which attracts up to 15 applicants for each place. It also has a longstanding reputation for agriculture, which benefits from two farms in Northumberland.

The campus is spacious and varied, occupying 45 acres close to the main shopping area, civic centre and Newcastle United's ground. The university also boasts an art gallery, the Hatton Gallery, and an expanded and refurbished theatre. Tyneside has plenty more culture to offer in the riverside Sage Gateshead music centre and the BALTIC Centre for Contemporary Art.

The university is popular with independent schools, whose applicants take three in ten places, but the university has stepped up its contacts with local state schools in order to broaden its intake. Alumni and other friends of the university raised £6 million in two years to add to the bursaries available for students from less affluent backgrounds. Official performance indicators reveal a healthy 93 per cent completion rate – better than anticipated, given the subject mix.

Few students regret choosing Newcastle for a degree, even if southerners can find the winter temperatures a shock. The city's nightlife is legendary and the cost of living is reasonable. Town–gown relations are better than in many cities.

Sport is a particular strength, Newcastle claiming to be one of the top ten universities both in terms of performance and facilities. A new £5.5-million sports centre supplements two older centres, which have refurbished fitness suites, massage clinics and all the normal indoor services. The main outdoor pitches are two miles from the university. Over £30,000 is awarded annually in sports bursaries for elite athletes.

Undergraduate Fees and Bursaries
» Fees for UK/EU students: £3,290
» International student fees: £10,525–£13,765
£25,480 (medicine)
» Bursary on full grant: household income up to £25K: £1,500
» Bursary on partial grant: household income £25K–£32.2K: £750.
» Scholarships based on circumstances or by competition.
» For full details see the university's website: www.ncl.ac.uk/undergraduate/finance

Students
Undergraduates:	**14,325**	(90)
Postgraduates:	**3,695**	(1,465)
Mature students:	**7.4%**	
Overseas students:	**12.5%**	
Applications per place:	**5.6**	
From state-sector schools:	**69.2%**	
From working-class homes:	**21.9%**	

For detailed information about fees, grants and bursaries and how they work, see chapter 7.

Accommodation
Number of places and costs refer to 2010–11
University-provided places: 4,375
Percentage catered: 26%
Catered costs: £98.84–£116.55 a week.
Self-catered costs: £69.79–£107.17 a week.
All single undergraduates are guaranteed a room in university-managed accommodation provided requirements are met. Local restrictions apply.
International students: as above.
Contact: accommodation-enquiries@ncl.ac.uk

University of Wales, Newport

A futuristic £35-million riverside campus that will be a focal point for Newport, as well as its university, will be open in time to welcome new entrants in 2011. The City Campus will house the Business School and part of the School of Art, Media and Design. The city council has contributed £10 million towards the development, which will be at the heart of a new Cultural Quarter designed to attract inward investment and strengthen the local economy.

Newport had already embarked on an ambitious expansion strategy before attaining full membership of the University of Wales. Full-time student numbers rose by more than 50 per cent in the five years ending in 2007–08. But the demand for places really took off after the change of status from college to university. Applications were up by 19 per cent at the start of 2010. Students have been attracted by a range of new courses in areas such as photography for fashion and advertising, creative therapies in education, and applied drama.

At the same time, Newport will pursue closer links with the University of Wales Institute Cardiff (UWIC) and Glamorgan University, which it already partners in a number of subjects. A joint submission with UWIC in art and design was particularly successful in the 2008 Research Assessment Exercise. Newport entered only 28 staff for the RAE, but their work was highly rated compared with most of their peers in similar institutions. More than half of it was considered world-leading or internationally excellent, with mechanical engineering and social work doing especially well.

Newport also did well in the first National Student Survey, finishing in the top ten, but it has slipped down the table subsequently and was close to the bottom in 2009. Only accounting, business studies, English, history and philosophy recorded satisfaction levels of more than 85 per cent. A poll of local employers was particularly positive about the university, however, and Estyn, the Welsh schools inspectorate, gave the best grades in Wales to the teacher-training courses. Newport achieved the highest possible rating in its last audit of academic processes by the Quality Assurance Agency.

The university, which was previously Gwent College of Higher Education, now has over 10,000 students. Virtually all the full-time undergraduates come from state schools and over four in ten come from working-class homes. The projected dropout rate of less than 20 per cent is much improved, but still higher than the benchmark set according to the subject mix. Newport operates a number of access schemes, and is a partner in the University of the Heads of the Valleys

Caerleon Campus
Lodge Road
Newport
South Wales NP18 3QT

01633 432030
admissions@newport.ac.uk
www.newport.ac.uk
www.newportunion.com

The Times Rankings
Overall Ranking: **96**

Student satisfaction:	=69	(75%)
Research quality:	=88	(0.3)
Entry standards:	93	(249)
Student–staff ratio:	106	(22.6)
Services & facilities/student:	101	(£987)
Expected completion rate:	=86	(79.3%)
Good honours:	90	(52.5%)
Graduate prospects:	85	(58.7%)

Institute, a community education initiative expected to launch in 2011.

The university is actively involved with a range of local businesses. It was rated the number one university in Wales for enterprise education by the Knowledge Exploitation Fund for three years in a row, helping more than 70 new start-up businesses. Among its innovations were the Corus to Campus project for redundant steelworkers (previously employed by Corus). Newport is also well-known for photography and film, hosting the International Film School Wales, whose graduates include double-BAFTA winner Asif Kapadia, and Justin Kerrigan, director of the cult movie *Human Traffic*.

There are currently two campuses. The smaller, Allt-Yr-Yn, campus, will close during 2010–11 when its business, art, media and design students move into the new City Campus. The larger Caerleon campus is further out, with impressive views, and from 2010–11 will cater for humanities, education, health and social sciences, photography and fine art. This is also where the student village of 661 self-catered study bedrooms is located and where the Wales International Study Centre opened in 2008. Free buses link the campuses, which are officially among the safest in Britain: Newport was the first educational establishment to pass an industry-standard security inspection.

A well-equipped sports centre at Caerleon has transformed facilities that previously compared unfavourably with those of other universities. The city of Newport is undergoing a £2-billion regeneration programme and has established a reputation for producing successful rock bands and has plenty of clubs and entertainment venues, but students in search of serious cultural or clubbing activity gravitate to nearby Cardiff.

Undergraduate Fees and Bursaries
- Fees for UK/EU students: £3,290
- International student fees: £7,950–£8,950
- Bursary on full grant: household income up to £25K: £329 plus £1,000 (limited)*
- Bursary on partial grant: household income up to £30K: £600 (limited); household income up to £40K: £300 (limited).*
- Scholarships based on circumstances or by competition.
- For full details see the university's website: www.newport.ac.uk and follow the link for 'Course funding'.

*Figures for 2009–10

Students
Undergraduates:	**3,285**	(4,075)
Postgraduates:	**615**	(1,090)
Mature students:	**32.2%**	
Overseas students:	**2.9%**	
Applications per place:	**3.7**	
From state-sector schools:	**99.5%**	
From working-class homes:	**43.4%**	

For detailed information about fees, grants and bursaries and how they work, see chapter 7.

Accommodation
Number of places and costs refer to 2010–11
University-provided places: 661
Percentage catered: 0%
Self-catered costs: £68–£82 a week.
First years guaranteed accommodation if requirements met.
International students: same as above.
Contact: accommodation@newport.ac.uk

University of Northampton

Northampton had a university in the thirteenth century, but it took until 2005 to get it back after Henry III dissolved the original version – allegedly because his bishops thought it posed a threat to Oxford. Nearly 90 places separate the two universities in *The Times* league table, but Northampton will hope to narrow that gap somewhat in years to come. Its aim is to "create a campus for creative technologies bringing together synergies between the arts and sciences". The university has already registered good results in the first four National Student Surveys, finishing in the top half of the table in 2009. Management produced the best score, but education, biology and geography all did well.

The modern university has its origins in teacher training, but had developed a wider range of degrees, including vocational courses for the leather industry, occupational therapy, nursing and midwifery, by the time university status arrived. All remain in a surprisingly broad portfolio of more than 100 degree and diploma courses. The university is taking part in a national pilot to develop fast-track degrees and extended work-based equivalents. The two-year route is available in law, management, marketing and sport development; the four-year option in a range of business, finance and marketing courses.

Specialisms such as leather technology, fashion, and waste management have helped to build up the recruitment of overseas students to some 700 a year from 100 different countries. Overall student numbers were steady for several years, but have now risen to about 12,000. Applications have been rising steadily and were up by more than 20 per cent at the start of 2010. Business is the most popular area, but teacher training and health subjects are not far behind – the university is the region's largest provider of teachers and healthcare professionals. The School of Education was awarded the Training and Development Agency's highest grade for quality, but the university was close to the bottom of the ranking for the 2008 Research Assessment Exercise. There was some world-leading research in four of the ten subject areas, with history producing by far the best results.

The university has two sites: an 80-acre campus on the edge of Northampton, where £73 million has been spent on improvements, and the smaller but more central Avenue campus, which specialises in art and design, media, technology and the performing arts. Both sites have new halls of residence, and the main Park Campus has also seen several new teaching developments, a management centre and a research centre. Another £80 million of investment was completed in 2010.

New arts facilities at Avenue will form the

Park Campus
Boughton Green Road
Northampton NN2 7AL

0800 358 2232 (courses freephone)
study@northampton.ac.uk
www.northampton.ac.uk
www.northampton
  union.com

The Times Rankings
Overall Ranking: **89**

Student satisfaction:	=46	(77%)
Research quality:	=95	(0.2)
Entry standards:	102	(240)
Student–staff ratio:	100	(20.9)
Services & facilities/student:	86	(£1,123)
Expected completion rate:	76	(80.6%)
Good honours:	67	(57.6%)
Graduate prospects:	105	(54.9%)

centrepiece of the town's "cultural mile", while an innovative student centre on the Park Campus will provide administrative and support services. Work has started on the conversion of a school next to the Avenue campus, which will house the School of Applied Sciences, as well as an £11-million Technology Realm project featuring the latest 3D visualisation technology and LCD presentation facilities.

Northampton takes its mission to widen participation in higher education seriously: almost all the undergraduates attended state schools or colleges, while over 40 per cent come from working-class homes. The projected dropout rate had been improving but, at 18 per cent, is now back above the national average for the university's courses and entry qualifications. Some of the degrees – such as podiatry and product design – recruit from all over Britain (and farther afield) but in other subjects most of the students are from the region. As a result, the 1,620 residential places are enough to guarantee accommodation for all first years who make Northampton their first choice.

Sports enthusiasts have a Premier League rugby club on their doorstep, as well as a more modest football club and first-class cricket. The university has added a £100,000 gym to its sports facilities, which include a sports hall and outdoor pitches. The town has a number of student-oriented bars, but the two campuses' union bars remain the hub of the social scene. Students receive a free discount card to use in Northampton's high street and independent shops, entertainment and health venues.

Undergraduate Fees and Bursaries

- » Fees for UK/EU students: £3,290
- » International student fees: £8,750
- » Bursary on full grant: household income up to £25K: £2,906
- » Bursary on partial grant: household income £30K–£50K: sliding scale £1,906–£50.
- » Scholarships based on circumstances or by competition.
- » For full details see the university's website: www.northampton.ac.uk/study/fees

Students

Undergraduates:	**7,100**	**(3,420)**
Postgraduates:	**800**	**(1,360)**
Mature students:	**35.7%**	
Overseas students:	**5.4%**	
Applications per place:	**5.0**	
From state-sector schools:	**97.8%**	
From working-class homes:	**41.7%**	

For detailed information about fees, grants and bursaries and how they work, see chapter 7.

Accommodation

Number of places and costs refer to 2010–11
University-provided places: 1,620
Percentage catered: 0%
Self-catered costs: £40.95 (small twin) – £93.00 (en-suite single) a week with network access included.
First years are guaranteed accommodation provided requirements are met.
International students: guaranteed housing.
Contact: www.northampton.ac.uk/study/accommodation

Northumbria University

Northumbria consistently ranks among the leading post-1992 universities and a £136-million investment in its city centre campus is producing facilities to match. The first phase was completed in 2007, when 9,000 design, law and business students moved into the new City Campus East development, which is linked to the existing main campus by an iconic new footbridge spanning Newcastle's central motorway. Extensive developments on the west side of the campus will be completed in 2010 and include a £6-million refurbishment of the library, which is open 24 hours a day, and a £30-million sports centre which will allow the university to become a pre-Olympics training centre.

With more than 32,000 students, 7,000 of whom are from overseas, Northumbria is the largest university in the region, both at undergraduate and postgraduate level. Three quarters of students are from the North East of England but numbers drawn from across the UK are rising year on year. A further 4,000 are studying Northumbria degrees in other countries. The demand for places has been growing for most of the decade and there had been another rise, of more than 23 per cent, at the start of 2010.

Entry grades for those with A levels are among the highest in the new universities, but many older students are admitted with other qualifications or on the strength of relevant work experience. Half of the mature students enter through the Higher Education Foundation Certificate, an access course system with modules in more than 30 subjects. Free one-day taster courses run throughout the year to give local people an idea of what studying at Northumbria would be like.

Over a third of the students come from working-class homes, 15 per cent from areas with little tradition of higher education. The projected dropout rate fell in the latest survey to 12.4 per cent, below the benchmark for Northumbria's courses and entry grades. Scores had improved in the National Student Survey, but the university was back in the bottom half of the table in 2009. Mathematics and statistics managed 100 per cent satisfaction, while French and Iberian studies, information services, nursing and law also did well.

Health subjects have now overtaken business studies in terms of student numbers. Many degrees are available as sandwich courses, with placements of up to a year in business or industry. The latest inspection by Ofsted rated the university's teacher training programmes as "outstanding". Northumbria also has a national centre of excellence in assessment, building on the university's attempts to give students more constructive feedback and teaching them how to assess themselves as future professionals. Five of

**Ellison Terrace
Newcastle upon Tyne
NE1 8ST**

0191 243 7420 (admissions)
er.admissions@northumbria..ac.uk
www.northumbria.ac.uk
http://mynsu.northumbria.
ac.uk

The Times Rankings
Overall Ranking: **=59**

Student satisfaction:	=32	(78%)
Research quality:	=88	(0.3)
Entry standards:	=51	(299)
Student–staff ratio:	102	(21.3)
Services & facilities/student:	76	(£1,160)
Expected completion rate:	=42	(85.8%)
Good honours:	=74	(56.2%)
Graduate prospects:	=40	(70.5%)

the university's academics have won National Teaching Fellowships.

The majority of subjects are based in the city centre, with health, education and community studies on the Coach Lane campus on the outskirts of the city, where £18 million has been spent upgrading facilities. Coach Lane now incorporates a learning resources centre with a fully integrated library, a clinical skills centre, where students can learn in simulated hospital environments, and new sports facilities, as well as teaching and seminar rooms.

Northumbria's best-known feature is its School of Design, which won the top national award for fashion design in 2006 and produced some of the university's best results in the 2008 Research Assessment Exercise. The university entered a comparatively low proportion of its academics, but more than a third of its submission was considered world-leading or internationally excellent. Architecture and the built environment, general engineering and nursing and midwifery were other high scorers. Northumbria intends to double its capacity in research and enterprise over the next five years.

Sport plays a growing role: Northumbria is consistently among the leaders in the British Universities and Colleges Sport rankings. The sports scholarship programme has supported over 250 athletes from over 40 sports in the past ten years, some going on to success at the highest level.

All new first years are offered places in university accommodation, although distance restrictions do apply, while others are assisted by the accommodation office. Two large residential developments with en-suite rooms opened in September 2005, bringing the total stock to over 3,500 places, and there is a plentiful supply of privately rented flats and houses.

Undergraduate Fees and Bursaries

» Fees for UK/EU students: £3,290
» International student fees: £9,000–£10,200
» The general bursary is £329; in addition, in the first year a further award is dependent on course of study: sliding scale £250–£1,000.
» The university does not award bursaries for students on partial maintenance grants.
» Scholarships based on circumstances or by competition.
» For full details see the university's website: www.northumbria.ac.uk/brochure/courses/ug/studfees

Students

Undergraduates:	**17,830**	(7,255)
Postgraduates:	**3,045**	(4,160)
Mature students:	**20.7%**	
Overseas students:	**11.6%**	
Applications per place:	**4.1**	
From state-sector schools:	**92.3%**	
From working-class homes:	**34.0%**	

For detailed information about fees, grants and bursaries and how they work, see chapter 7.

Accommodation

Number of places and costs refer to 2010–11
University-provided places: 3,580
Percentage catered: 8%
Catered costs: £102 or £113 a week.
Self-catered costs: £68–£107 a week.
First years who need accommodation can be offered rooms. Local restrictions apply.
International students: first years are guaranteed accommodation if requirements met.
Contact: rc.accommodation@northumbria.ac.uk

University of Nottingham

Nottingham is the nearest Britain has to a truly global university, with campuses in China and Malaysia modelled on a headquarters that is among the most attractive in Britain. For many years Nottingham has been among the institutions with the stiffest competition for each place, and a striking new campus and extra courses has made the university even more fashionable in recent years. Growth in applications of almost 13 per cent at the start of 2010 was higher than at most comparable universities.

The university enjoyed a spectacular rise up the pecking order of higher education. In less than 20 years, it went from being a solid civic university to a prime alternative to Oxbridge. Currently in the top 100 in the QS World University Rankings, it seldom stands still.

Nottingham describes itself as "research-led", with work carried out at the university winning two Nobel prizes in 2003. Professor Sir Peter Mansfield, who won the medicine prize for research leading to the development of the MRI scanner, has spent almost all his academic career there. The university's record-breaking research contracts brought in £140 million in 2008–09 and place it among the leading universities for private funding.

About £70 million was spent on a research recruitment initiative in advance of the 2008 Research Assessment Exercise, with 20 new research chairs and the equipment and support posts to accompany them. The investment paid off handsomely with sharply improved results in the RAE, which will bring long-term increases in funding. Almost 60 per cent of a big submission was judged to be world-leading or internationally excellent, with pharmacy and Spanish, Portuguese and Latin American studies producing the best results in the UK and chemistry and physics the second-best.

Physical expansion allowed the university to take almost 1,000 more students in recent years, but new undergraduates' average A-level grades have not dropped. Once in, they tend to stay the course – the dropout rate of 4 per cent is consistently among the best in the country. But the university is trying to broaden an intake which has more independent school students and fewer from working-class homes than the national average for the subjects offered. There is a well-established summer school for state-school teenagers and a bursary scheme, which pre-dated top-up fees, for Nottinghamshire students with no family history of higher education.

Consistently good National Student Survey results continued in 2009, when biology, theology and mechanical engineering produced the best scores, with pharmacy, German and chemistry close behind. The university has also stepped up its efforts to give students the best possible chance in the jobs market. The Nottingham Advantage Award offers a range of extra-curricular modules to

University Park
Nottingham NG7 2RD

0115 951 5559 (enquiries)
undergraduate-enquiries@
  nottingham.ac.uk
www.nottingham.ac.uk
www.su.nottingham.ac.uk

The Times Rankings
Overall Ranking: **20**

Student satisfaction:	=32	(78%)
Research quality:	=20	(2.4)
Entry standards:	15	(412)
Student–staff ratio:	18	(13.6)
Services & facilities/student:	33	(£1,574)
Expected completion rate:	13	(94.5%)
Good honours:	14	(75.0%)
Graduate prospects:	19	(75.7%)

enhance skills while students take their degree, as well as providing scores of internships for recent graduates.

The original University Park campus has won seven consecutive Green Flag awards for excellent parkland. A mile away is the 30-acre Jubilee campus, which cost £50 million and includes 750 residential places. Futuristic buildings clustered around an artificial lake house the schools of management and finance, computer science and education. An additional building for the fast-growing business school was added in 2004 and a new sports hall opened the following year. The campus is undergoing further £200-million expansion to accommodate an innovation park and has acquired a landmark sculpture towering 60 metres over its buildings.

The adjoining medical school is also close to University Park, although its recently established graduate-entry outpost is in Derby. The biosciences and the new veterinary school are at Sutton Bonington, ten miles south of the city. Recent developments include a £7-million biomedical sciences building on the main campus.

Nottingham has long-standing links with the Far East, which provides the majority of its 7,000 overseas students, and has a Chinese physicist, Professor Fujia Yang, as its Chancellor. The two branch campuses outside Kuala Lumpur, in Malaysia, and at Ningbo, in China, now host 7,500 students. The purpose-built campuses have echoes of Nottingham's distinctive clock tower. Students have the opportunity to move between the three countries.

Both main campuses are within three miles of the centre of Nottingham, with a good selection of student-friendly clubs. However, halls of residence and the students' union tend to be the centre of social life for students in both locations. New bars, café facilities and a nightclub were included in a £1-million makeover of student facilities in 2007. Sports facilities are excellent and expanding.

Undergraduate Fees and Bursaries

- » Fees for UK/EU students: £3,290
- » International student fees: £10,880–£14,260 £15,030–£19,450
- » Bursary on full grant: household income up to £25K: £1,100
- » Bursary on partial grant: household income £25K–$45.5K: sliding scale £1,100–£275.
- » Scholarships based on circumstances or by competition.
- » For full details see the university's website: www.nottingham.ac.uk/ugstudy/introduction/finance

Students

Undergraduates:	**21,710**	**(2,800)**
Postgraduates:	**6,235**	**(2,180)**
Mature students:	**7.1%**	
Overseas students:	**15.0%**	
Applications per place:	**6.1**	
From state-sector schools:	**71.6%**	
From working-class homes:	**19.1%**	

For detailed information about fees, grants and bursaries and how they work, see chapter 7.

Accommodation

Number of places and costs refer to 2009–10
University-provided places: 7,400
Percentage catered: 58%
Catered costs: £106.95–£172.99 a week (31 weeks).
Self-catered costs: £80.00–£101.50 a week (43–44 weeks).
First years are guaranteed accommodation if conditions are met.
International undergraduates: as above
Contact: www.nottingham.ac.uk/accommodation

Nottingham Trent University

Consistently among the leading new universities in *The Times* league table, as well as one of the biggest, Nottingham Trent has demonstrated high quality in an unusually wide range of disciplines. Best known for fashion and other creative arts, which have the largest number of students, it also boasts one of the UK's biggest law schools, offering legal practice courses for both solicitors and barristers as well as degrees. A four-year "exempting law degree", launched in 2009, combines both phases with an extended work placement, enabling students to qualify as solicitors without paying postgraduate fees.

Nottingham Trent has among the highest entry grades of any new university and one of the best employment records. It helps that the university has the third highest number of year-long placements in the UK through its working partnerships with more than 6,000 businesses and private sector organisations. More than a third of the undergraduates come from working-class homes and over nine out of ten attended state schools or colleges, while the projected dropout rate of less than 11 per cent is below the national average for the university's courses and entry grades.

An ambitious research programme attracted a £7.65 million donation – thought to be the largest to a post-1992 university – to advance the university's work in cancer diagnosis and therapy. A new conference centre, opened in 2010, will also help to boost income and investment. The university held its own in the 2008 Research Assessment Exercise, although it entered fewer academics than some of the other leading new universities. More than a third of its submission was rated world-leading or internationally excellent, with communication, culture and media studies, social policy, engineering and biomedical sciences producing the best results.

Scores have improved in the National Student Survey, leaving Nottingham Trent just below half way in the table. Economics, psychology and biology produced some the best results while history excelled with a 100 per cent satisfaction rating. The university has seen big rises in applications over the past three years and at the start of 2010 there was a 30 per cent increase on the previous year.

There are now nearly 25,000 students, including 5,000 part-timers. The extensive main city site boasts a mixture of Victorian and modern buildings. The schools of science and technology, education, and arts and humanities are five miles away on the Clifton campus. The university appointed its first Chancellor in 2008, the broadcaster and journalist, Sir Michael Parkinson.

The Brackenhurst campus, devoted to animal, rural and environmental studies, is 14 miles out of Nottingham and includes an equestrian centre with a purpose-built indoor riding area, a well-equipped veterinary nursing

Burton Street
Nottingham NG1 4BU

0115 848 2814 (admissions)
admissions@ntu.ac.uk
www.ntu.ac.uk
www.trentstudents.org

The Times Rankings
Overall Ranking: **55**

Student satisfaction:	=59	(76%)
Research quality:	=69	(0.5)
Entry standards:	=64	(274)
Student–staff ratio:	69	(18.2)
Services & facilities/student:	=52	(£1,361)
Expected completion rate:	47	(85.5%)
Good honours:	81	(55.1%)
Graduate prospects:	37	(71.0%)

building and an animal unit. Another 300 residential places were added there in 2006, following a £3-million renewal of the teaching facilities. A new £1.5-million unit houses state-of-the-art equipment and facilities and will be used to provide veterinary nursing courses

Art and design facilities on the city campus have been upgraded and both the Boots Library and the students' union refurbished. Computing and informatics have a new building on the Clifton campus and the university has launched a bus service linking Clifton and the city. A total of £130 million has been earmarked for building projects starting with a £90-million regeneration of the Newton and Arkwright buildings to produce a first-class working environment and student support facilities, completed in 2009.

The university was responsible for the largest programme of Foundation degrees when the two-year qualification was launched. Subjects ranging from forensic science to wildlife conservation saw another increase in applications early in 2009.

The university has a good sporting reputation and always fares well in the BUCS leagues, ranking 27th this year. The university opened a sport and lifestyles department in 2005 and offers a good number of government sports scholarships. It can also boast alumni such as marathon runner and Olympic silver-medalist Paula Radcliffe and Steve Trapmore, who has an Olympic gold medal in rowing. In the world of politics, former Cabinet Minister Hazel Blears is also an alumna.

The student body is diverse, with large numbers of mature and overseas students. The university's residential stock of 4,200 beds is sufficient to house all new first years and overseas students. Social life varies between campuses, but all have access to the city's lively cultural and clubbing scene. A late-night bus service links the main campuses and the city's new tram system serves the university.

Undergraduate Fees and Bursaries

- » Fees for UK/EU students: £3,290
- » International student fees: £9,600–£10,700
- » Bursary on full grant: household income up to £25K: £1,095
- » Bursary on partial grant: household income up to £35K: sliding scale £675–£525.
- » Scholarships based on circumstances or by competition.
- » For full details see the university's website: www.ntu.ac.uk/apps/applyingfees/prospective.cfm

Students

Undergraduates:	**17,840**	**(2,405)**
Postgraduates:	**1,975**	**(2,685)**
Mature students:	**12.5%**	
Overseas students:	**5.8%**	
Applications per place:	**4.5**	
From state-sector schools:	**93.2%**	
From working-class homes:	**35.5%**	

For detailed information about fees, grants and bursaries and how they work, see chapter 7.

Accommodation

Number of places and costs refer to 2010–11
University-provided places: 4,200
Percentage catered: 0%
Self-catered costs: £70–£135 (42–48 weeks).
First years and new students are guaranteed accommodation if conditions are met.
International students: guaranteed accommodation if conditions are met.
Contact: www.ntu.ac.uk/accommodation
accommodation@ntu.ac.uk

University of Oxford

Oxford has topped *The Times* league table since 2002, when it wrested first place from Cambridge. The oldest and probably the most famous university in the English-speaking world, Oxford remains almost inseparable from Cambridge in terms of overall quality. Both are among the top five universities in the world, according to the QS World University Rankings, and are head and shoulders above the other non-specialist universities in *The Times* table and in the view of most experts. Considerably higher spending on student facilities and more top degrees keep the university ahead of its ancient rival this year.

Applications were up by 12 per cent at the beginning of 2010, when Cambridge's increase was little more than 1 per cent. There were still fewer than five applicants to the place – a much more favourable ratio than at some of the top universities – but nearly all are predicted at least three As at A level, or their equivalent. Gradually, there may be more research students and marginally fewer UK undergraduates, making the competition for places still more intense.

The university is still struggling to broaden its intake and shake off allegations of social elitism. The long-term growth in demand for places (which is concentrated in the more job-oriented subjects) is due, at least partly, to more systematic attempts to get the message through to teenagers that Oxford is open to all who can meet the exacting entrance requirements. Student visits to comprehensive schools have been supplemented by summer schools, recruitment fairs and colleges' own initiatives, as well as tireless public statements of intent by the university.

For all the university's efforts to shed its "Brideshead Revisited" stereotype, however, official figures still show nearly 45 per cent of Oxford's students coming from independent schools – the largest proportion at any university. Just more than one student in ten comes from a working-class home, despite the introduction of bursaries worth £3,225 in 2009–10 for all undergraduates who are eligible for full fee remission. A projected dropout rate of 1.5 per cent is only eclipsed by Cambridge in the UK.

Applications must be made by mid-October – a month earlier if you wish to be interviewed overseas. There are written tests for some subjects and you may be asked to submit samples of work. Selection is in the hands of the 30 undergraduate colleges, which vary considerably in their approach to this issue and others. Sound advice on academic strengths and social factors is essential for applicants to give themselves the best chance of winning a place and finding a setting in which they can thrive. Only a

University Offices
Wellington Square
Oxford OX1 2JD

01865 288000 (admissions)
undergraduate.admissions
@admin.ox.ac.uk
www.ox.ac.uk
www.ousu.org

The Times Rankings
Overall Ranking: **1**

Student satisfaction:	=1	(85%)
Research quality:	2	(4.2)
Entry standards:	2	(532)
Student–staff ratio:	3	(10.8)
Services & facilities/student:	2	(£3,168)
Expected completion rate:	2	(98.5%)
Good honours:	1	(91.8%)
Graduate prospects:	3	(82.8%)

minority of candidates opt to go straight into the admissions pool without expressing a preference for a particular college. The choice is particularly important for arts and social science students, whose world-famous individual or small group tuition is based in college. Science and technology, which have benefited from Oxford's phenomenally successful fundraising efforts, are taught mainly in central facilities. All subjects operate on eight-week terms and assess students entirely on final examinations – a system some find too pressurised.

The development of a major new campus on the site of the Radcliffe Infirmary will be the first fruit of a £1.25-billion fundraising campaign. Oxford's biggest capital development for more than a century will provide more student accommodation for neighbouring Somerville College, a new Mathematical Institute building and a new building for the humanities. Recent developments include a £21-million social sciences library and animal research facilities that drew bitter (often illegal) protests from animal rights campaigners. There should be many more developments as a result of a commitment by Dr James Martin, the technology entrepreneur who was already the university's largest benefactor, to donate £50 million if others would match it. A year later and in the middle of an international financial crisis, the university raised the matching funds, and thus gained the full £100 million.

There was never much doubt about the strength of Oxford's research, but the 2008 Research Assessment Exercise found more than 70 per cent of it to be world-leading or internationally excellent. Oxford entered more academics for assessment than any other university – twice as many as some research-based universities of similar size. There were good results in all areas, but the university was pre-eminent in several medical specialisms, as well as statistics, development studies, education and French. Oxford also attracts the largest amount of research income.

Undergraduate Fees and Bursaries
» Fees for UK/EU students: £3,290*
» International student fees: £12,200–£14,000†
  £25,500 (medicine)†
» Bursary on full grant: household income up to £25K: £3,225
» Bursary on partial grant: household income up to £50K: sliding scale £3,290–£200.
» Scholarships based on circumstances or by competition.
» For full details see the university's website: www.ox.ac.uk/admissions/undergraduate_courses/student_funding

* UK & EU students eligible for tuition fee support not liable for College fees
† Plus College fees (£5,692)

Students
Undergraduates:	**11,500**	**(4,405)**
Postgraduates:	**6,635**	**(1,220)**
Mature students:	**8.2%**	
Overseas students:	**10.7%**	
Applications per place:	**4.9**	
From state-sector schools:	**54.7%**	
From working-class homes:	**11.5%**	

Accommodation
See chapter 12 for information about individual colleges.

For detailed information about fees, grants and bursaries and how they work, see chapter 7.

Oxford Brookes University

Now firmly established as England's leading post-1992 university in *The Times* league table, Oxford Brookes receives more than five applications to the place – a level of competition not unlike that at some Russell Group universities. The demand for places has been steady: although there was only a small increase in 2009 when most universities experienced substantial growth, applications were up by more than 18 per cent at the start of 2010.

Brookes is particularly popular with independent schools, which provide more than a quarter of the undergraduates – by far the highest proportion among the new universities and twice the national average for the university's subjects and entry grades. However, the proportion from working-class homes, at 44 per cent, is also considerably ahead of the official benchmark. The university has been trying to attract more students from state schools and has targeted areas in Oxfordshire and the wider region

The university's location has always been an advantage in student recruitment, but the quality of provision is the real draw. Its departments feature near the top of *The Times* rankings for several subjects. Ofsted rated primary teacher training outstanding and the university was in the top 40 in the 2009 National Student Survey. Business, English, marketing, media studies and accounting, all produced more than 95 per cent satisfaction levels.

The university houses national centres for hospitality, leisure and tourism, and the teaching of business and undergraduate research, as well as one for teacher training in partnership with Westminster University. The *Architect's Journal* rated the Department of Architecture the best outside London. Oxford Brookes, which has a consistently excellent record for graduate employment, is also partnering Warwick University in the Government's academy for gifted and talented schoolchildren.

Grades in the 2008 Research Assessment Exercise showed improvement, with more than a third of the work judged to be world-leading or internationally excellent. History, which made headlines in 2001 with a higher grade than its world-renowned neighbour, again produced the best results, but there were good performances, too, in history of art and computer science.

Brookes made a leap in size in 2000, taking in Westminster College, a merger which added 2,000 students, mainly in teacher training and the humanities, and forming a £2.5-million Institute of Education. As a polytechnic, Oxford pioneered the modular degree system that has swept British higher education. After more than 20 years' experience, the scheme has now trimmed the 2,000 modules it once offered, but

Headington Campus
Gypsy Lane
Oxford OX3 0BP

01865 484848 (enquiries)
query@brookes.ac.uk
www.brookes.ac.uk
www.thesu.com

The Times Rankings
Overall Ranking: **51**

Student satisfaction:	=32	(78%)
Research quality:	=60	(0.6)
Entry standards:	49	(309)
Student–staff ratio:	=57	(17.7)
Services & facilities/student:	71	(£1,206)
Expected completion rate:	=45	(85.6%)
Good honours:	=41	(66.8%)
Graduate prospects:	54	(67.0%)

undergraduates can pair subjects as diverse as history and biology, or catering management and environmental management. Each subject has compulsory modules in the first year and a list of others that are acceptable later in the course. Students are encouraged to take advantage of a range of placement and exchange opportunities as well as subjects outside their main area of study, such as additional language modules.

There are four main sites, two of which are only a mile from the city centre and linked to each other by a footbridge. Some £150 million has been earmarked for improvements to the Headington, Wheatley and Harcourt Hill campuses over the next few years. Older buildings on the original Gipsy Lane site, at Headington, dating from the 1950s and '60s will be replaced with flexible, functional buildings benefiting from the latest technology. This will provide social learning space that allows students to work together and engage with careers guidance, volunteering opportunities and student support services.

Maths and engineering have now joined computing and business five miles away at Wheatley. The new engineering building supports the university's status as a Government-designated regional centre for motorsport and high performance engineering. The Harcourt Hill campus at Botley, focuses on teacher education, human development and learning.

Oxford Brookes is the third greenest university in the UK and was one of the first universities in the world to be awarded Fairtrade status, in October 2003.

A 25-metre swimming pool and 9-hole golf course have been added to the already impressive sports facilities. The gym and climbing centre have recently undergone a £175,000 refurbishment. Representative teams have a good record, with the rowers particularly successful, winning medals at three consecutive Olympic games, and the cricketers now combining with Oxford University to take on county teams. The students' union runs the biggest entertainment venue in Oxford, a city that can be expensive, but which offers enough to satisfy most students. The university has 3,600 residential places, all with internet access – enough for all first-year undergraduates.

Undergraduate Fees and Bursaries

» Fees for UK/EU students: £3,290
» International student fees: £10,200–£11,740
» Bursary on full grant: household income up to £25K: sliding scale £1,800–£1,050.
» Bursary on partial grant: household income up to £36K: sliding scale £1,050–£150.
» Scholarships based on circumstances or by competition.
» For full details see the university's website: www.brookes.ac.uk/studying/finance

Students

Undergraduates:	**11,030**	**(2,955)**
Postgraduates:	**1,610**	**(2,575)**
Mature students:	**22.6%**	
Overseas students:	**14.6%**	
Applications per place:	**5.2**	
From state-sector schools:	**73.7%**	
From working-class homes:	**44.0%**	

For detailed information about fees, grants and bursaries and how they work, see chapter 7.

Accommodation

Number of places and costs refer to 2009–10
University-provided places: 3,600
Percentage catered: 15%
Catered cost: £4,600–£5,000
Self-catered cost £3,500–£5,000 (38 week contract)
All accommodation is allocated to first year who select Oxford Brookes as Firm choice through UCAS and meet all deadlines for application.
International students: as above.
Contact: accomm@brookes.ac

University of Plymouth

Now one of the UK's largest universities with nearly 30,000 students, Plymouth has restructured its activities to concentrate on its home city. The original aim was to break into the research elite while still serving the region through teaching, but the new Vice-Chancellor, Professor Wendy Purcell, who graduated from the university in the 1980s, has declared a new mission to make Plymouth the top "enterprise university". It was named as the most enterprising organisation in the southwest in 2008 and 2009. Some 12,000 students take advantage of work-based learning or placements and the university is the only one in the region to pilot fast-track, two-year degrees.

Plymouth entered by far the largest number of academics of any post-1992 university in the latest research assessments – twice the proportion entered by some of its peer group. More than a third of the submission was rated world-leading or internationally excellent. Computer science produced by far the best results, but civil engineering, geography and environmental science, and art and design also did well.

Following the closure of campuses in Exmouth, Exeter and near Newton Abbot, more than £100 million has been spent on the main North Hill campus in Plymouth. The library was extended and upgraded and the students' union refurbished. A £35-million arts complex opened in 2007, housing the Faculty of Arts and the Plymouth Arts Centre. Teaching facilities and residential accommodation for the education courses transferring from Exmouth cost another £40 million, while a £11-million building for the Faculty of Health and Social Work, overlooking the Drake Reservoir, includes sports facilities as well as teaching space.

Plymouth opened a £1-million Immersive Vision Theatre, thought to be the first of its kind at a UK university, in 2008. The IVT is used for a variety of subjects in the sciences, arts and medicine, with projection onto the dome giving the audience a strong feeling of being "in", rather than just observing, different types of image. The latest development saw the opening of the new School of Marine Science and Engineering, building on Plymouth's worldwide reputation in this field. With 1,400 students and 80 staff, the school will be the largest of its kind in Europe. It is also the base for the new Peninsula Research Institute for Marine Renewable Energy, a joint venture with the University of Exeter.

Plymouth and Exeter were already partners in the Peninsula College of Medicine and Dentistry, which has its headquarters and a second teaching building in the city. One of the new wave of medical schools, established in 2002, the Peninsula was the only successful bidder for a new

Drake Circus
Plymouth
Devon PL4 8AA

01752 588036 (admissions)
admissions@
 plymouth.ac.uk
www.plymouth.ac.uk
www.upsu.com

The Times Rankings
Overall Ranking: **61**

Student satisfaction:	=69	(75%)
Research quality:	59	(0.8)
Entry standards:	62	(279)
Student–staff ratio:	=36	(15.3)
Services & facilities/student:	69	(£1,222)
Expected completion rate:	=54	(83.8%)
Good honours:	56	(61.8%)
Graduate prospects:	=91	(57.7%)

dental school in the last national competition. The school, which will train 64 dentists a year, opened in 2007. With campuses in Plymouth, Exeter and Truro, along with teaching facilities in Bristol, the university's Faculty of Health and Social Work is the largest provider of nurse, midwifery and health professional education and training in the southwest.

The university is a partner in the Combined Universities in Cornwall, which is boosting further and higher education in one of the few counties without its own university. Plymouth has also established a unique relationship with its 18 partner colleges, which have become a faculty of the university, sharing £3.5 million in capital investment. They spread from Cornwall to Somerset, taking in Jersey, and have 10,000 students taking university courses.

The intake reflects Plymouth's position as the working-class hub of the southwest, with just over 95 per cent of students state-educated and a third from the poorest social classes. The projected dropout rate of 13 per cent is below the national average for the courses and entry grades.

Plymouth was chosen to house no fewer than four national teaching centres – in health and social care placements, experiential learning in environmental and natural sciences, institutional partnerships, and education for sustainable development – as well as a the national subject centre for geography, earth and environmental sciences and the Royal Statistical Society Centre for Statistical Education. No university has exceeded the 12 National Teaching Fellowships won by its academics.

A 1,300-bed student village costing £15 million, has greatly improved the university's residential stock. There is a lively social scene as well as a thriving nightlife. With excellent and recently upgraded facilities for water sports as well as an £850,000 fitness centre, the sports facilities have improved, while a range of sports scholarships and bursaries will help support high-fliers. The university has a partnership with Plymouth Albion Rugby Club to promote and support sport in the city.

Undergraduate Fees and Bursaries
» Fees for UK/EU students: £3,290
» International student fees: £8,925
£14,000–£21,500 (medicine)
» Bursary on full grant: household income up to £25K: £900
» Bursary on partial grant: household income up to £40K: £300
» Scholarships based on circumstances or by competition.
» For full details see the university's website: www.plymouth.ac.uk/fees

Students
Undergraduates:	**18,820**	**(8,020)**
Postgraduates:	**1,145**	**(2,945)**
Mature students:	**26.5%**	
Overseas students:	**5.3%**	
Applications per place:	**4.1**	
From state-sector schools:	**95.4%**	
From working-class homes:	**33.8%**	

For detailed information about fees, grants and bursaries and how they work, see chapter 7.

Accommodation
Number of places and costs refer to 2010–11
University-provided places: 2,500
Percentage catered: 0%
Self-catered costs: £85–£130 a week.
First years are not guaranteed university provided accommodation.
International students: overseas students have priority for allocation.
Contact: accommodation@plymouth.ac.uk

University of Portsmouth

Portsmouth registered what was then regarded as an extraordinary 25 per cent increase in applications in 2009 and practically repeated the feat in the boom year of 2010, attracting double the numbers received at the beginning of the decade. It has always been among the leaders of its generation of universities, but a wider portfolio of courses, a modernised campus and new facilities in the city are proving a powerful draw.

Strength in teaching has been recognised with the award of two national centres of excellence and 40 per cent of the work submitted for the 2008 Research Assessment Exercise was considered world-leading or internationally excellent. Applied mathematics and European studies achieved particularly good results, while biomedical and biomolecular sciences also did well. Portsmouth also has the best record of any of the post-1992 universities in the National Student Survey. Only one of its peer group produced better results in 2009, when there were satisfaction levels of more than 95 per cent in biology, accounting, geology, mathematics and statistics, law, and physical science, whilst finance excelled with 100 per cent.

Graduate employment has been harder recently, especially as the university has a high proportion of students who take arts subjects. Languages are Portsmouth's traditional strength – one student in five takes a language course at some level – and the facilities rival those of many traditional universities. About 1,000 Portsmouth students go abroad for part of their course, and at least as many come from the Continent.

However, it is in health subjects that the university's reputation has been growing most obviously. The School of Professionals Complementary to Dentistry is one of the first new dental education facilities in England for 50 years. There is also a centre for molecular design and the UK's first dedicated brain tumour research centre. The £9-million dental outreach centre, operated in partnership with King's College London, is scheduled to open in September 2010.

The main city-centre Guildhall campus has undergone extensive redevelopment. The £11-million library complex, integrated into its 1970s predecessor, was commended in the 2008 Civic Trust awards. Earlier developments included the aluminium-clad St Michael's Building and the eco-friendly Portland Building, with its solar panels. The business school has moved into a new £12-million building on the main campus. Other recent additions include a sports science building that houses laboratories, a swimming flume and two British Olympic Medical Centre accredited climatic

University House
Winston Churchill Avenue
Portsmouth
Hampshire PO1 2UP

023 9284 8484
info.centre@port.ac.uk
www.port.ac.uk
www.upsu.net

The Times Rankings
Overall Ranking: **=74**

Student satisfaction:	=15	(80%)
Research quality:	=60	(0.6)
Entry standards:	=68	(273)
Student–staff ratio:	93	(20.2)
Services & facilities/student:	67	(£1,242)
Expected completion rate:	=60	(82.9%)
Good honours:	95	(51.3%)
Graduate prospects:	106	(54.6%)

chambers. A new £9-million building for the internationally recognised Institute of Cosmology and Gravitation opened in 2009. And following the launch of the new School of Law, a state of the art courtroom will be ready by February 2011.

Teaching in all subjects is concentrated on the Guildhall campus, while much of the residential stock is a couple of miles away at Langstone. A £6.5-million student centre caters for the multicultural population of the university with alcohol-free areas, an international students' bar and a family area for students with children. There is also a new social learning space, modernised sport, exercise and fitness facilities which include resistance and cardiovascular training gyms, dance studios and a sports hall.

Just under a third of the undergraduates come from working-class homes, although this is still slightly below the national average for the subjects and entry qualifications. Efforts are being made to broaden the intake further through an award-winning membership club that introduces teenagers to higher education through workshops, holiday courses and access to university facilities. The projected dropout rate has improved considerably over the last decade and, at 14 per cent is now level with the university's benchmark.

Portsmouth has a larger working-class population and more deprivation than some applicants may realise. But the new 170-metre Spinnaker Tower is already a landmark and the city has a vibrant student pub and club scene to supplement a popular students' union. The cost of living is not as high as at many southern universities, and the sea is close at hand. Hall places are offered to 90 per cent of first years and the university runs "secure a home" days at the beginning of September to help the remaining new arrivals with house-hunting. The university is launching a new combined broadband, phone and TV service for students living in private accommodation, mirroring a similar offer for those in halls. Parents will be able to download software allowing them to call students at no cost, using a PC.

Undergraduate Fees and Bursaries

» Fees for UK/EU students: £3,290
» International student fees: £9,200–£10,500
» Bursary on full grant: household income up to £25K: £900
» Bursary on partial grant: household income up to £32K: £600
» Scholarships based on circumstances or by competition.
» For full details see the university's website: www.port.ac.uk/departments/studentsupport/studentfinancecentre

---

Students

Undergraduates:	**15,055**	**(2,210)**
Postgraduates:	**1,620**	**(2,490)**
Mature students:	**15.9%**	
Overseas students:	**9.8%**	
Applications per place:	**4.8**	
From state-sector schools:	**95.1%**	
From working-class homes:	**32.4%**	

For detailed information about fees, grants and bursaries and how they work, see chapter 7.

Accommodation

Number of places and costs refer to 2010–11
University-provided places: 2,987
Percentage catered: 25%
Catered costs: £86–£115 a week (37 weeks).
Self-catered costs: £74–£117 a week (37 weeks).
Majority of first years offered university accommodation.
International, Channel Island and Isle of Man students guaranteed university accommodation subject to terms and conditions.
Contact: Student.housing@port.ac.uk

Queen Margaret University

Scotland's first new university of the 21st century got a new campus to match, when Queen Margaret University moved into gleaming new premises in Musselburgh, to the southeast of Edinburgh, in September 2007. The "campus in the park", as it has been dubbed, was designed in consultation with students, and is only six minutes by train from the city centre.

In 2008, the university opened the first UK university campus in Singapore, a joint venture with the East Asia Institute of Management, which has taught Queen Margaret degrees for several years. Yet all has not been plain sailing. Queen Margaret has been struggling with debts of £7 million, although a merger with Edinburgh Napier has now been ruled out. Only one university had a lower average score in the 2008 Research Assessment Exercise. Applications dropped in 2009, mainly because of a reorganisation of "conservatoire" drama courses in Scotland, but they recovered with a 22 per cent increase at the start of 2010.

Named after Saint Margaret, the 11th-century Queen of Scotland, the institution dates back to 1875 and was originally a school of cookery for women. The college had been awarding its own degrees since 1992, but was too small to qualify for university status until 2007. Having achieved that ambition, the university made an auspicious debut in *The Times* league table and has been outscoring many of the former polytechnics.

Queen Margaret is the smallest university in Scotland and it says that it is likely to remain so. The strategic plan promises that the new university will be "smart, innovative and very clearly focused and above all relevant" to compensate for the limitations of size. Three quarters of the students are female, seven out of ten of them from north of the border. Over 3,000 students are in the health sciences faculty, with social sciences and media, followed in terms of size by business and enterprise, the other main areas. The four drama degrees have been consolidated into one interdisciplinary programme, under the title of drama and performance, which recruited successfully in its first year, building on the university's reputation in the creative industries.

Health is an area of particular strength: Queen Margaret offers courses in an unusually broad range of subjects, from dietetics, podiatry and audiology, to art therapy, music therapy and health psychology. There are also courses in the field of international health which attract students from all over the world as well as a specialism in international healthcare, with students in Angola, Guatemala, Uganda, Ethiopia, Gambia, India and Cuba. Other international programmes run in Egypt, Saudi Arabia, Greece and Switzerland, as well as on the

Queen Margaret University Drive
Musselburgh EH21 6UU

0131 474 0000
admissions@qmu.ac.uk
www.qmu.ac.uk
www.qmusu.org.uk

The Times Rankings
Overall Ranking: **=67**

Student satisfaction:		n/a
Research quality:	=69	(0.5)
Entry standards:	=51	(299)
Student–staff ratio:	=85	(19.7)
Services & facilities/student:	=88	(£1,105)
Expected completion rate:	83	(79.6%)
Good honours:	52	(63.4%)
Graduate prospects:	56	(66.3%)

new Singapore campus. QMU's international profile continues to grow, with partnerships established with universities in Egypt and Saudi Arabia.

The projected dropout rate of almost 16 per cent has improved slightly since the last survey, but is still higher than average for the university's courses and entry qualifications. Three undergraduates in ten come from working-class homes and a similar proportion are over the age of 21 on entry.

An impressive learning resource centre, parts of which are open 24 hours a day, offers a variety of study spaces Specialist laboratories and clinics are well equipped. The nursing simulation lab, for example, is set out exactly like a hospital ward, helping to instil students with the confidence to move on easily to a work placement or career in the NHS or private practice. There are also specially equipped rooms for podiatry, radiography, occupational therapy, physiotherapy and art therapy.

There are 800 residential places on the new campus, 500 of them reserved for undergraduates. Other features include a students' union building, indoor and outdoor sports facilities, a variety of catering outlets and landscaped gardens with a range of environmental features. Queen Margaret claims that the campus is the "greenest" in Scotland – a high priority among the students. The institution is particularly proud of Re:Use Project which they claim has diverted more than 18 tonnes of serviceable household waste from landfill. The campus has already won an award for sustainable design and has one of the lowest carbon footprints of any UK higher education establishment.

Undergraduate Fees and Bursaries
» Scottish-domiciled and EU students: no fees payable.
» Non-Scottish UK-domiciled student fees: £1,820
» International student fees: £9,250–£10,200*
» Scholarships based on circumstances or by competition.
» For full details see the university's website: www.qmu.ac.uk/prospective_students/funding.htm

*Figures for 2009–10

Students

Undergraduates:	**2,910**	**(960)**
Postgraduates:	**395**	**(780)**
Mature students:	**29.5%**	
Overseas students:	**12.9%**	
Applications per place:	**4.7**	
From state-sector schools:	**94.9%**	
From working-class homes:	**37.4%**	

For detailed information about fees, grants and bursaries and how they work, see chapter 7.

Accommodation
Number of places and costs refer to 2010–11
University-provided places: 800
Percentage catered: 0%
Self-catered costs: £3,900–£4,120 (40 weeks) to £4,875–£5,150 (50 weeks).
First years are guaranteed accommodation. Residential and age restrictions apply.
International students: guaranteed housing.
Contact: accommodation@qmu.ac.uk
www.qmu.ac.uk/services/student_accommodation.htm

Queen Mary, University of London

More than £150 million has been spent developing London University's East End base into a broadly based institution of 15,000 students and strengthening the academic staff. Some of the investment paid off in spectacularly improved grades in the 2008 Research Assessment Exercise, when almost two thirds of the work submitted was rated world-leading or internationally excellent. Linguistics, geography and drama produced the best results in their fields, with dentistry, English and several medical specialisms in the top five, propelling Queen Mary into the top 25 UK universities for research in our table.

Queen Mary is ranked among the top 200 universities in the world by QS, and has the capital's most extensive self-contained campus. It includes a state-of-the-art learning resource centre with 24-hour access and an award-winning student village with 2,000 en-suite rooms. An arts quarter, containing research facilities, a conference centre, drama studio and teaching space, was completed in 2006. A £15-million humanities building opened in early 2010 and a biosciences innovation centre is also under construction, next door to the £44-million Blizard Building – the striking home of Barts and the London School of Medicine and Dentistry, in Whitechapel.

The modern setting is a far cry from the People's Palace, which first used the site to bring education to the Victorian masses, but there is still a community programme as well as conventional teaching and research. The arts-based Westfield College and scientific Queen Mary came together in 1989, but it took time to mould the new institution and overcome financial difficulties. The sale of Westfield's Hampstead base released the necessary capital to begin to modernise the Mile End Road campus. Now the historic People's Palace building, which is still the college's most recognizable feature, is to be restored to host cultural events for the institution and the local community.

Already London University's fourth largest unit, Queen Mary is expected to carry on growing. It is one of London's designated points of expansion in the sciences, although its strength is more obvious on the arts side, which boasts a clutch of high-profile academics. The college is leading a national initiative to boost the number of maths graduates. It has also announced the launch of an innovative series of Olympics lectures which will take place during the run-up to London 2012.

Applications have risen at the rate of 7 per cent a year for most of the decade and had increased by 13 per cent at the start of 2010, when applications were up

---

Mile End Road
London E1 4NS

0800 376 1800 (prospectus)
admissions@qmul.ac.uk
www.qmul.ac.uk
www.qmsu.org

The Times Rankings
Overall Ranking: **=36**

Student satisfaction:	=46	(77%)
Research quality:	=24	(2.3)
Entry standards:	37	(354)
Student–staff ratio:	8	(12.9)
Services & facilities/student:	=37	(£1,531)
Expected completion rate:	=32	(89.6%)
Good honours:	49	(64.6%)
Graduate prospects:	18	(76.0%)

considerably all around the country. There has been further success in attracting overseas students, who make full use of a unit specialising in English as a foreign language and now fill about one place in six.

Results have been consistently good in the National Student Survey, with English, human and social geography, drama, languages, media studies and history producing the most satisfied students in 2009. The majority of undergraduates take at least one course in departments other than their own, under the modular course system. Most degrees are organised in units to allow maximum flexibility. Interdisciplinary study has always been encouraged: for example, medics can choose selected modules in English and drama. The medical school houses a national teaching centre for clinical and communications skills. There is a flourishing exchange programme, which includes universities in the USA and Japan, as well as Europe. Each student has an adviser to guide them through the possibilities. Language students can use the University of London Institute in Paris, while students at Beijing's University of Posts and Telecommunications can take double degrees (awarded by their own institution and Queen Mary) without leaving China.

Queen Mary attracts students from across the UK and over 120 countries around the world and has a socially diverse intake: more than a third of the undergraduates come from the two lowest socio-economic classes, many of them from local minority ethnic groups. Social life centres on the campus, which features a refurbished students' union with a subsidised health and fitness centre and a new bar, and the West End is easily accessible by tube. Students welcome the relatively low prices (for the capital) in east London, which has more to offer than many expect when they apply.

Undergraduate Fees and Bursaries
» Fees for UK/EU students: £3,290
» International student fees: £10,250–£12,500
£15,350–£24,480 (medicine)*
» Bursary on full grant: household income up to £25K: £1,100
» Bursary on partial grant: household income up to £34.6K: £878.
» Scholarships based on circumstances or by competition.
» For full details see the university's website: www.qmul.ac.uk/undergraduate/feesfinance

* Figures for 2009–10

Students
Undergraduates:	**10,905**	(50)
Postgraduates:	**2,010**	(1,060)
Mature students:	**16.5%**	
Overseas students:	**16.4%**	
Applications per place:	**6.9**	
From state-sector schools:	**85.8%**	
From working-class homes:	**36.6%**	

For detailed information about fees, grants and bursaries and how they work, see chapter 7.

Accommodation
Number of places and costs refer to 2009–10
University-provided places: 2,257
Percentage catered: 7.7%
Catered costs: £137 upwards a week.
Self-catered costs: £87–£118 a week.
First years giving Queen Mary as first choice get priority, if terms and conditions are met. Residential restrictions apply.
International students given priority if conditions are met and includes distance.
Contact: residences@qmul.ac.uk

Queen's University, Belfast

Generally regarded as Northern Ireland's premier university, Queen's became a member of the Russell Group of leading UK research institutions in 2006. The university has launched a major recruitment campaign to attract high-calibre academics from around the world and is investing heavily in new and improved facilities to improve the student experience and enhance its research performance. Now just outside the top 200 in the QS World University Rankings, the aim is to break into the top 100 in the world within five years. The 2008 Research Assessment Exercise showed some progress, with more than half of the university's submission rated as world-leading or internationally excellent and Queen's ranked in the UK's top 10 in 11 subject areas. Music, English and anthropology produced the highest grades and all branches of engineering were placed in the top 10 in their respective disciplines.

In recent years the Queen's campus has been transformed. The centrepiece is the new £50-million library, said to be one of the most ambitious building projects in Northern Ireland, which opened for business in the summer of 2009. The university's vision for the future also includes improvements in student facilities: a student village, costing £45 million, has replaced the existing tower block residences with three-storey self-catering "villas". A new student guidance centre is bringing services together at the heart of the campus and the students' union has had a £9-million refurbishment. It now includes Enterprise SU, an area for students to improve their enterprise and employability skills. Queen's has also introduced Degree Plus – a new award providing official recognition of extra-curricular activities and achievements and to help graduates in the job market.

Although it still finished comfortably in the top half of the table, the university dropped out of the top 30 in the 2009 National Student Survey. Physics and astronomy, aerospace engineering, chemistry, dentistry and academic studies in education all produced good results. Strictly non-denominational teaching is enshrined in a charter which has guaranteed student representation and equal rights for women since 1908. The charter even precluded the teaching of theology – this is done through a network of four associated colleges.

Queen's was one of four university colleges for the whole of Ireland in the 19th century, and still draws students from all over the island. Applications were up by 10 per cent at the start of 2010. The university has begun to attract more students from Great Britain, as well as boosting the numbers of international students. A variety of international agreements have been forged in the USA, Malaysia, China and

University Road
Belfast BT7 1NN

028 9097 2727 (admissions)
admissions@qub.ac.uk
www.qub.ac.uk
www.qubsu.org

The Times Rankings
Overall Ranking: **38**

Student satisfaction:	=46	(77%)
Research quality:	=39	(2.0)
Entry standards:	32	(368)
Student–staff ratio:	=33	(15.2)
Services & facilities/student:	21	(£1,745)
Expected completion rate:	=49	(85.3%)
Good honours:	35	(68.5%)
Graduate prospects:	=22	(74.7%)

India. However, the majority of students still come from Northern Ireland. Like the University of Ulster, Queen's suffers in comparisons of entry grades because most schools in the Province limit sixth-formers to three A levels.

The university district is amongst the most attractive in Belfast, and is one of the city's main cultural and recreational areas. Queen's runs a highly successful arts festival each autumn, as well as an art gallery and has the only full-time university cinema in the UK – one of the best in Ireland. Another £2 million has been invested in arts facilities recently, the lion's share of the cash going into a new drama and film centre. More teaching accommodation has been added, with better access for the disabled, and the university's great hall has had a £2.5-million refurbishment, courtesy of the university's own foundation.

Students are encouraged to take language programmes from a unique "virtual" language laboratory, which provides online tuition from any computer in the university. IT facilities are good: Queen's was the first institution to meet the national target of providing at least one computer workstation for every five undergraduate students. An unusually large proportion of graduates go on to further study, which does Queen's no harm in the employment league.

The city centre is not short of nightlife, but the social scene is still concentrated on the students' union and the surrounding area. Sports facilities, which include a university hut in the Mourne mountains, are of a high standard. A £7-million extension to the university's physical education centre has helped in Queen's selection as an official training camp for the 2012 Olympics. The university runs academies for rugby and Gaelic sports, which have strong external links. Numerous Queen's players are selected at club, provincial and national levels. First years have priority for university accommodation and there is plenty of reasonably priced private housing.

Undergraduate Fees and Bursaries
» Fees for UK/EU students: £3,290
» International student fees: £9,889–£12,115 £13,395–£25,270 (medicine)
» Bursary on full grant: household income up to £25K: household income up to £19,203: £1,100; household income up to £24.2K: £550.
» Bursary on partial grant: household income up to £40.2K: £320.
» Scholarships based on circumstances or by competition.
» For full details see the university's website: www.qub.ac.uk/home/TuitionFeesandStudentSupportArrangements201011

Students
Undergraduates:	**13,080**	**(4,430)**
Postgraduates:	**3,060**	**(2,240)**
Mature students:	**14.8%**	
Overseas students:	**6.0%**	
Applications per place:	**5.2**	
From state-sector schools:	**98.9%**	
From working-class homes:	**32.9%**	

Accommodation
Number of places and costs refer to 2010–11
University-provided places: around 2,000
Percentage catered: 0%
Self-catered costs: £65.80–£93.80 a week.
First-year students are guaranteed accommodation.
International students: as above.
Contact: accommodation@qub.ac.uk
www.stayatqueens.com

For detailed information about fees, grants and bursaries and how they work, see chapter 7.

University of Reading

Reading is another of the medium-sized campus universities that have demonstrated their appeal through the National Student Survey. Consistently in the top 20, it again satisfied almost 90 per cent of its final-year undergraduates in the results published in 2009. Archaeology, classics, finance, Italian studies, mathematical sciences, and management all scored well.

The university is ranked among the top 200 in the world and did well in the latest Research Assessment Exercise, despite entering a much higher proportion of its academics than many of its peers. More than half of their work was considered world-leading or internationally excellent, with archaeology and art and design doing particularly well. However, subsequent cuts in Government funding mean that the university is having to make savings worth more than £10 million by 2012. It has assured stakeholders that this had been anticipated and that the quality of teaching and research will be maintained.

There are three main sites within Reading, including the original 320-acre parkland site, and the university also owns 2,000 acres of farmland at nearby Sonning and Shinfield, where the renowned Centre for Dairy Research (CEDAR) is located. To these have been added the former Henley Management College, which became the university's business school in 2008. The Greenlands site, on the banks of the river at Henley-on-Thames, houses postgraduate and executive programmes, while undergraduates are taught at the university's Whiteknights campus. Plans to build a new Science and Innovation Park in Shinfield were given the go ahead in April 2010, creating more jobs for the local economy, bringing together academic expertise with local and international technology-based businesses.

Reading was the only university established between the two world wars, having been Oxford's extension college for the first part of the last century, but the attractive main campus now has a modern feel. A new School of Pharmacy opened in 2005 and sports facilities have been extended. A multimillion pound student services building, providing a one-stop shop for student support and welfare, followed in 2007.

The university's location, a bus ride away from Heathrow Airport, and an international reputation in key areas for developing countries have always ensured a healthy flow of overseas students. A series of increases in applications for full-time degree places came to an end at the start of 2010, when a tiny 1 per cent rise was far below national norms. However, little more than half of the students are full-time undergraduates.

About one undergraduate in five is from

Whiteknights
PO Box 217
Reading RG6 6AH

0118 378 8618/9
student.recruitment@
reading.ac.uk
www.reading.ac.uk
www.rusu.co.uk

The Times Rankings
Overall Ranking: **35**

Student satisfaction:	=22	(79%)
Research quality:	=20	(2.4)
Entry standards:	38	(350)
Student–staff ratio:	49	(16.7)
Services & facilities/student:	79	(£1,152)
Expected completion rate:	27	(91.8%)
Good honours:	32	(69.8%)
Graduate prospects:	58	(66.0%)

an independent school and just over a quarter come from working-class homes, rather less than average for the university's subjects and entry qualifications. However, the retention rate is better than the university's benchmark, with only 6 per cent of undergraduates expected to leave without a qualification.

The university is involved with a number of centres of excellence in teaching and learning, including one focusing on career management skills. All undergraduates take career management skills modules that contribute five credits towards their degree classification. The online system, which has 200 web pages of advice, exercises and information, has been bought by 30 other universities and colleges. Sessions are delivered jointly by academics and careers advisors, with input from alumni and leading employers.

The town – only a short walk from the campus – may not be the most fashionable, but it has plenty of nightlife and an award-winning shopping centre. It also offers temporary and part-time employment opportunities for students. London is easily accessible by train, but the cost of living is on a par with the capital. The more than 4,500 residential places include a landscaped student village, while first-rate sports provision includes accessible rowing and sailing boathouses, scholarships and an academy. Teams have a good record in inter-university competitions and the campus has been chosen as a pre-Olympics training camp for basketball and fencing.

Students praise the social scene, although the high proportion of students from the southeast of England means that many go home at the weekends. The large students' union had a £500,000 refit in 2007, improving and extending its popular main venue. The union has been voted among the best in Britain, and has won numerous awards including Best Bar None status for encouraging safe drinking. It has also been known to attract some big-name bands. Students who live in town can make use of the free night bus service to take them back into Reading.

Undergraduate Fees and Bursaries
» Fees for UK/EU students: £3,290
» International student fees: £10,200–£12,300
» Bursary on full grant: household income up to £25K: £1,385*
» Bursary on partial grant: household income up to £35K: £923; household income up to £45K: £462.*
» Scholarships based on circumstances or by competition.
» For full details see the university's website: www.reading.ac.uk/life/life-moneymatters.aspx

*Figures for 2009–10

Students
Undergraduates:	**9,030**	(1,835)	
Postgraduates:	**2,315**	(2,780)	
Mature students:	**12.1%**		
Overseas students:	**10.8%**		
Applications per place:	**6.5**		
From state-sector schools:	**81.9%**		
From working-class homes:	**26.4%**		

For detailed information about fees, grants and bursaries and how they work, see chapter 7.

Accommodation
Number of places and costs refer to 2009–10
University-provided places: about 4,500
Percentage catered: 25%
Catered costs: £105.23–£160.10 (30 weeks).
Self-catered costs: £68.18–£108.68 (38 weeks).
First-year undergraduate students are guaranteed a place if conditions are met.
International students: given priority if conditions are met.
Contact: www.reading.ac.uk/life/life-accommodation.aspx

Robert Gordon University

Robert Gordon is again the top post-1992 university in *The Times* league table and also features in the top half of the latest National Student Survey. It has improved substantially in research quality, one of its weaker areas in previous years, after a much better performance in the 2008 Research Assessment Exercise. Almost a third of its submission was considered world-leading or internationally excellent, with library and information management the star performer.

So close are links with the North Sea oil and gas industries that Robert Gordon used to dub itself the Energy University. But with nursing and the health sciences now equally important, it has gone for the broader soubriquet of the Professional University. The creative industries are a growth area and there is a full portfolio of courses in business, design and engineering.

Flexible programmes, with credit accumulation and transfer, make for easy movement in and out of the university for an often mobile local workforce. Work placements, lasting up to a year, are the norm, helping an employment record that has been Scotland's best for several years and consistently one of the UK's leaders.

Efforts to extend access beyond the normal higher education catchment have produced a diverse student population, with just over a third of the undergraduates coming from working-class homes and almost all attending state schools or colleges. The dropout rate has improved considerably over recent years and, at 11 per cent, is lower than the UK average for RGU's subjects and entry qualifications.

Robert Gordon has a pedigree in education that goes back 250 years. The School of Pharmacy is the oldest in the UK, Gray's School of Art is over 120 years old and the Scott Sutherland School of Architecture and the Built Environment has just celebrated its 50th anniversary. The university now offers about 140 degrees. Students from the city's two universities mix easily, and there is healthy academic rivalry in some areas, despite the obvious differences. There is also a partnership with Aberdeen College, which has become an associate college of the university to encourage progression from school to higher education.

Named after an 18th-century philanthropist, Robert Gordon has two sites around the city. The historic Schoolhill site adjoins Aberdeen Art Gallery in the city centre, while Garthdee, where 70 per cent of undergraduates are taught, is a mile away overlooking the River Dee. The university has spent £100 million on its buildings and facilities, with Norman Foster designing the business school, while other recent developments made room for art, architecture and

Schoolhill
Aberdeen AB10 1FR

01224 262728 (enquiries)
admissions@rgu.ac.uk
www.rgu.ac.uk
www.rgunion.co.uk

The Times Rankings
Overall Ranking: **46**

Student satisfaction:	=32	(78%)
Research quality:	=60	(0.6)
Entry standards:	=46	(314)
Student–staff ratio:	75	(18.7)
Services & facilities/student:	58	(£1,305)
Expected completion rate:	56	(83.6%)
Good honours:	=71	(56.9%)
Graduate prospects:	2	(83.4%)

the faculty of health and social care, which has recently launched the Centre of Obesity Research and Epidemiology (CORE). Another £110 million of improvements is planned for Garthdee over the next few years and their "estates masterplan" is hoping to give the university some of the best teaching and research facilities by 2015.

Like most new universities, especially in Scotland, RGU recruits most of its students locally, 60 per cent of them female. However, overseas student numbers have been growing sharply and the overall demand for places has been stronger than at most universities north of the border. The university offers four-week intensive access programmes in mathematics, engineering, chemistry and computing during August and September for applicants who narrowly miss the entry requirements to top up their qualifications. If they prefer, prospective students may take access units in these subjects by distance learning, using study packs and with the support of an assigned tutor. The scheme, which runs all year round, is recommended for aspiring students without traditional academic backgrounds.

The university is pinning many of its hopes on new technology. An award-winning virtual campus was launched with an online course in e-business for postgraduates. It also enables management undergraduates to receive course materials via an intranet, and other degree and short courses are available. The new Moodle system is used across Robert Gordon's courses for both on-campus and distance learning students.

Aberdeen is a long way to go for English students, but train and air links are excellent, and the city regularly features in the top 10 for quality of life. A £12-million sports and leisure centre opened in 2005, provides a centre of excellence for the region in hockey, as well as a 25-metre swimming pool, three gyms, a climbing wall and bouldering room, a café bar, three exercise studios and a large sports hall. Although accommodation can be expensive in the private sector, low prices in the students' union partially compensate, and there are enough residential places to guarantee housing to first years from outside the local area.

Undergraduate Fees and Bursaries
» Scottish-domiciled and EU students: no fees payable.
» Non-Scottish UK-domiciled student fees: £1,820
» International student fees: £8,950–£10,400
» Scholarships based on circumstances or by competition.
» For full details see the university's website: www.rgu.ac.uk/future-students/finance-and-scholarships

Students
Undergraduates:	**6,735**	(2,700)
Postgraduates:	**1,905**	(2,285)
Mature students:	**27.6%**	
Overseas students:	**10.7%**	
Applications per place:	**3.3**	
From state-sector schools:	**93.4%**	
From working-class homes:	**34.9%**	

For detailed information about fees, grants and bursaries and how they work, see chapter 7.

Accommodation
Number of places and costs refer to 2010–11
University-provided places: 1,481
Percentage catered: 0%
Self-catered costs: £84.50–£102.50 a week.
All first-year students are eligible to apply for student accommodation. Residential restrictions apply.
International students: given priority for accommodation.
Contact: accommodation@rgu.ac.uk
www.rgu.ac.uk/living/accommodation

Roehampton University

Fully independent since 2004, Roehampton is now making its mark as a university in its own right, after four years in a federation with Surrey University. There have been record intakes, with applications growing year on year despite rising entry requirements, although the 1.5 per cent increase in applications at the start of 2010 was well below the national average. Successes in the latest Research Assessment Exercise, when Roehampton entered a much higher proportion of its academics than most of its peer group, will add to the university's reputation. A third of the submission was judged to be world-leading or internationally excellent, with the university producing the best results in the country for dance and doing well in anthropology and drama, theatre and performance studies.

Roehampton is a collegiate university with four distinctive colleges, which still maintain some of the traditional ethos of their religious foundations: the Anglican Whitelands, the Roman Catholic Digby Stuart, the Methodist Southlands, and the Froebel, which follows the humanist teachings of Frederick Froebel. Students need not follow any of these denominations to enrol in the colleges. The university also has a Jewish resource centre and Muslim prayer rooms.

All four colleges are based in a 64-acre campus, with stunning parkland and lakes, on or adjacent to Roehampton Lane. Whitelands moved from Putney in 2004 to the 18th-century mansion, Parkstead House, overlooking Richmond Park, which also houses the School of Human and Life Sciences. The buildings have been refurbished with IT facilities, student accommodation, laboratories and teaching space. The colleges all have their own bars and other leisure facilities, although they are open to all members of the university.

A £6-million building, mainly for dance and PE, opened on the main campus in 2005. Recent projects include a £4-million facility for the School of Arts, which opened in 2006, and a new national centre of excellence for teaching on citizenship education, human rights and social justice. Over the summer of 2009 a fully functioning newsroom was opened for journalism and media students. A 15-year programme will bring further improvements, designed to enhance the student experience and provide an environment that can be enjoyed by the local community. The plans include a new library, halls of residence, a university congregation hall, more sports facilities, a new students' union hub, cloisters, piazzas and a performing arts centre.

The four schools of Arts, Education, Human and Life Sciences, and Business and Social Sciences encourage inter-disciplinary

Erasmus House
Roehampton Lane
London SW15 5PU

020 8392 3232 (enquiries)
enquiries@roehampton.ac.uk
www.roehampton.ac.uk
www.roehampton
student.com

The Times Rankings
Overall Ranking: **87**

Student satisfaction:	=97	(72%)
Research quality:	58	(0.9)
Entry standards:	97	(245)
Student–staff ratio:	=70	(18.3)
Services & facilities/student:	59	(£1,292)
Expected completion rate:	69	(82.1%)
Good honours:	92	(52.2%)
Graduate prospects:	=91	(57.7%)

work. Themes such as "creativity", "childhood", "wellbeing" and "social justice" are explored in two or more schools and permeate many of the university's activities. True to the university's origins, education remains the largest subject area, accounting for more than a quarter of the students.

The Quality Assurance Agency complimented Roehampton on the accessibility of academic staff to students and the positive ways in which they responded to student needs. One example has been the provision of enhanced sports facilities on campus, with a new gym, two football pitches, running track and a multi-use games area. Results in the National Student Survey are beginning to reflect these changes: business studies, theology and religious studies all did well in 2009, but classics stood out with 100 per cent satisfaction.

The sport performance and rehabilitation centre offers students, staff and local people physiotherapy, podiatry and sports massage, as well as access to physiological assessment, biomechanical analysis, sport psychology support and sports nutrition. The university offers four sports scholarships of £3,000 a year and is a high performance centre for British fencing.

More than nine out of ten undergraduates were educated in state schools and over 40 per cent come from working-class homes. The projected dropout rate had been coming down, but the latest figures suggest that 17 per cent of students will fail to graduate in the expected time – significantly more than average for the university's courses and entry grades.

About 80 per cent of first years who want a hall place are offered one, with priority going to those who make Roehampton their first preference. Rents are not cheap for those who miss out on a place or prefer the private sector, but students like the proximity of central London and the lively and attractive suburbs around Roehampton.

Undergraduate Fees and Bursaries
- » Fees for UK/EU students: £3,290
- » International student fees: £9,599
- » Bursary on full grant: household income up to £25K: £1,500
- » The university does not award bursaries for students on partial maintenance grants.
- » Scholarships based on circumstances or by competition.
- » For full details see the university's website: www.roehampton.ac.uk/admissions/finance

Students
Undergraduates:	6,050	(515)
Postgraduates:	1,320	(1,025)
Mature students:	23.4%	
Overseas students:	5.5%	
Applications per place:	4.7	
From state-sector schools:	97.4%	
From working-class homes:	41.6%	

For detailed information about fees, grants and bursaries and how they work, see chapter 7.

Accommodation
Number of places and costs refer to 2009–10
University-provided places: 1,600
Percentage catered: 12.5%
Catered costs: £126 a week
Self-catered costs: £91 (standard) – £112 (en suite) a week.
First years are given priority if conditions met. Local restrictions apply.
International students: guaranteed for first year
Contact: accommodation@roehampton.ac.uk

Royal Holloway, University of London

As the University of London's "campus in the country", Royal Holloway occupies 135 acres of woodland between Windsor Castle and Heathrow. The 600-bed Founder's Building, modelled on a French chateau and opened by Queen Victoria, is one of Britain's most remarkable university buildings. More than £100 million has been spent on the campus in the last five years, resulting in an impressive range of new and refurbished academic and social facilities. Recent projects have included a major auditorium, extensions to the School of Management and other academic buildings, an extension to the main library and new student residences, which have been praised for their comfort and eco-friendly features.

Other developments have included expansion of the academic staff, better student services and a portfolio of scholarships and bursaries that predated top-up fees. One offers free places or reduced fees to those who stay on for a postgraduate degree. The conversion of the huge Victorian boilerhouse into a performance space for drama and the establishment of formal links with institutions such as New York, Sydney and Yale universities, demonstrate that progress has not just been a matter of bricks and mortar. Closer to home, another link allows music students to take lessons at the Royal College of Music.

Both Bedford College and Royal Holloway, which amalgamated to form the existing college 25 years ago, were founded for women only, their legacy commemorated in the Bedford Centre for the History of Women. However, the gender balance in the student population is now roughly equal. Royal Holloway is not just about the arts: the college offers a science foundation year at further education colleges in the region, and the balance of disciplines is gradually shifting.

Of the work entered for the Research Assessment Exercise, 60 per cent was rated world-leading or internationally excellent, cementing Royal Holloway's place among the top 25 research universities. Music was ranked top in the UK, with 90 per cent of its research in the top two categories, while biology, drama, earth sciences, economics, geography, German, media arts and psychology were all in the top 10 in their fields.

The college has also had consistently good results in the National Student Survey, with 85 per cent of final-year undergraduates satisfied with their courses in 2009. History, human and social geography, historical and philosophical studies and psychology all produced high levels of satisfaction. All 18 departments encourage interdisciplinary work, which is facilitated by a modular course

University of London
Egham
Surrey TW20 0EX

01784 434455 (switchboard)
admissions@rhul.ac.uk
www.rhul.ac.uk
www.surhul.co.uk

The Times Rankings
Overall Ranking: **31**

Student satisfaction:	=59	(76%)
Research quality:	=10	(2.8)
Entry standards:	=33	(366)
Student-staff ratio:	=26	(14.8)
Services & facilities/student:	40	(£1,495)
Expected completion rate:	19	(93.1%)
Good honours:	27	(70.9%)
Graduate prospects:	65	(62.7%)

structure with examinations at the end of every year. An Advanced Skills Programme, covering information technology, communication skills and foreign languages, further encourages breadth of study.

Royal Holloway offers e-degrees in classics, history, business management and postgraduate courses in information security and management. It is also spearheading the development of the University of London Institute in Paris, allowing students to spend part of their course in France.

Applications dipped in 2009, following a large increase in the previous year, but a 19 per cent rise at the start of 2010 was the highest in the University of London and among the best returns at any pre-1992 university. The college still draws just over a fifth of its undergraduates from independent schools, although the proportion coming from working-class homes has been rising. The ethnic mix is above average and the projected dropout rate is back down to less than 7 per cent – well below the official benchmark.

Over 2,900 students are in halls of residence, many of them in the Founder's Building itself. The college's green belt location at Egham, Surrey, 35 minutes from the centre of London by rail, ensures that social life is concentrated on an extended students' union. However, the West End is close for those determined to seek the high life. Sports facilities are good and have been upgraded recently – Royal Holloway claims to be "the University of London's best sporting college", although three other colleges performed better in the BUCS league in 2008-09. It has had considerable success with its "student talented athlete award scheme" (STARS).

A high proportion of students come from London and the Home Counties, so many go home at the weekend, but the lively students' union puts on entertainment and activities seven days a week.

Undergraduate Fees and Bursaries

» Fees for UK/EU students: £3,290
» International student fees: £11,555–£13,120*
» Bursary on full grant: household income up to £25K: £750
» Bursary on partial grant: household income up to £39.3K: £750
» Scholarships based on circumstances or by competition.
» For full details see the university's website: www.rhul.ac.uk/Prospective-Students/finance

*Figures for 2009-10

Students

Undergraduates:	**6,590**	(370)
Postgraduates:	**1,335**	(470)
Mature students:	**10.6%**	
Overseas students:	**25.8%**	
Applications per place:	**5.1**	
From state-sector schools:	**78.3%**	
From working-class homes:	**25.4%**	

For detailed information about fees, grants and bursaries and how they work, see chapter 7.

Accommodation

Number of places and costs refer to 2010–11
University-provided places: 2,921
Percentage catered: 37%
Catered costs: £77.90–£130.05 a week (30–38 weeks).
Self-catered costs: £75.45–£132.43 a week (38–50 weeks).
First years are prioritised for accommodation provided conditions are met.
International students: non-EU students guaranteed accommodation.
Contact: Accommodation-Office@rhul.ac.uk

University of St Andrews

St Andrews has been the leading Scottish university in *The Times* league table for the last four years, reaping the benefits of outstanding scores in the National Student Survey (NSS). The university already had the highest entry standards, the best staffing levels and the lowest dropout rate north of the border. Now, the distinction of having the most satisfied students in the UK has taken St Andrews up to fourth in the table, eclipsed only by Oxbridge and Imperial College London.

Scotland's oldest university and the third oldest in the English-speaking world, St Andrews has long been both well known and fashionable among a mainly middle-class clientele. Applications were up by more than 6.5 per cent at the official deadline for courses beginning in 2010. While this year's rise does not stand out in comparison to the UK average, previous increases mean that selection is highly competitive in almost all subjects.

With nearly 30 per cent of the students coming from south of the border, St Andrews has earned the nickname of Scotland's English university. But another 26 per cent come from over 100 countries farther afield, giving the university a cosmopolitan feel. Fee concessions and exchange schemes have boosted applications, particularly from the USA, which provides nearly a fifth of first-year students on its own.

Peer assessments have shown that there is top quality behind the prestige. Nearly 60 per cent of the work submitted for the 2008 Research Assessment Exercise was rated as world-leading or internationally excellent. St Andrews was joint top in the UK for philosophy and top in Scotland for physics and astronomy, German, film studies, applied maths, French and psychology.

Just under 40 per cent of undergraduates come from independent schools, when the UK average for the university's courses and entry scores is just over 25 per cent. A dedicated schools liaison service has been trying to broaden the intake, and a fund-raising campaign is building up a bank of £3,000-a-year scholarships for students in need. Only four UK universities have a lower proportion of students from working-class backgrounds. Those who do come could hardly be more satisfied: the 2008 NSS showed 100 per cent satisfaction among theology and religious studies students whilst only seven of the 27 subjects with published ratings had satisfaction levels of less than 90 per cent.

The town of St Andrews is steeped in history, as well as being the centre of the golfing world. The university at its heart accounts for about a third of the 18,000 inhabitants. There are close cultural and social relations between town and gown. New

College Gate
St Andrews
Fife KY16 9AJ

01334 462150
admissions@st-andrews.ac.uk
www.st-andrews.ac.uk
www.yourunion.net

The Times Rankings
Overall Ranking: **4**

Student satisfaction:	=5	(84%)
Research quality:	=10	(2.8)
Entry standards:	8	(455)
Student–staff ratio:	=14	(13.4)
Services & facilities/student:	17	(£1,856)
Expected completion rate:	=9	(94.9%)
Good honours:	3	(85.6%)
Graduate prospects:	24	(74.4%)

students ("bejants" and "bejantines") acquire third and fourth-year "parents" to ease them into university life, and on Raisin Monday give their academic guardians a bottle of wine in return for a receipt in Latin, which can be written on anything. Another unusual feature is that all humanities students are awarded an MA rather than a BA.

Many of the main buildings date from the 15th and 16th centuries, but sciences are taught at the modern North Haugh site a few streets away. Everything is within walking distance, but bicycles are common. Although small, St Andrews offers a wide range of courses. The university's reputation has always rested on the humanities, which acquired a £1.3-million research centre recently. An £8-million headquarters for the School of International Relations opened in 2006, with Europe's first Centre for Syrian Studies, an Institute of Iranian Studies and a Centre for Peace and Conflict Studies. St Andrews has the largest mediaeval history department in Britain and has now added film studies and sustainable development. A full range of physical sciences is also on offer, with sophisticated lasers and the largest optical telescope in Britain.

A £45-million School of Medicine and the Sciences is due for completion in 2010. This will be one of the first UK medical schools whose research facilities are fully integrated with the other sciences and key university disciplines including physics, chemistry, biology and psychology, offering an important new dimension to medical training and research. A £5-million Bio-medical Sciences Research complex is also planned to lead the fight against superbugs and serious viral, bacterial and parasitic diseases.

Students do not come to St Andrews for the nightclubs, but there is no shortage of parties in a tight-knit community. The sports facilities are excellent and more than half of all students live in halls, the latest of which was opened by Gordon Brown in 2007, providing self-catering accommodation for 920 students during term and three-star accommodation for golfers and other tourists in vacations. Features such as the grass roof made it the first university residence to be awarded the Green Tourism Business Scheme's Gold Award. A further 250 residential places are also under construction and will be ready for use by September 2010.

Undergraduate Fees and Bursaries

» Scottish-domiciled and EU students: no fees payable.
» Non-Scottish UK-domiciled student fees: £1,820
£2,895 (medicine)
» International student fees: £12,600
£19,200 (medical science)
» Scholarships based on circumstances or by competition.
» For full details see the university's website: www.st-andrews.ac.uk/admissions/scholarships

Students

Undergraduates:	**7,080**	(345)
Postgraduates:	**1,565**	(285)
Mature students:	**3.3%**	
Overseas students:	**34.5%**	
Applications per place:	**8.0**	
From state-sector schools:	**60.7%**	
From working-class homes:	**13.1%***	

* 2007–08 figure

For detailed information about fees, grants and bursaries and how they work, see chapter 7.

Accommodation

Number of places and costs refer to 2010–11
University-provided places: 3,899
Percentage catered: 47%
Catered costs: £142.68–£190.87 a week (33 weeks).
Self-catered costs: £63.11–£137.75 a week (37 weeks).
First years guaranteed accommodation if conditions are met.
Policy for international students: as above.
Contact: studacc@st-andrews.ac.uk
www.st-andrews.ac.uk/admissions/ug/Accommodation

University of Salford

In the last five years, Salford has slipped below some of the new universities in *The Times* league table. But consistently good graduate employment rates, carefully targeted courses and an emphasis on the university's location close to the centre of Manchester appeal to students. Applications have been buoyant for several years and an increase of nearly 29 per cent at the start of 2010 was outstanding, even in a year when applications were up significantly nationwide.

The university has embarked on a £500-million investment programme that will take 15 years to complete. It will include a £47-million Arts and Media Centre on campus and a centre at the MediaCityUK development in Salford Quays – home to five BBC departments from 2011. Salford Law School opened in 2007 in a £10-million building featuring a Law Society-approved library. New acoustic laboratories opened in 2008, with a reverberation room capable of transforming the quality of sound and an anechoic chamber, which is said to be the quietest place in the world. Also new is the £22-million Mary Seacole building, which houses the Faculty of Health and Social Care.

Salford stresses its business links and modern portfolio of courses, including two-year Foundation degrees. The university does well on the Government's access measures: more than four in ten undergraduates come from working-class homes and there is a high proportion from areas sending few students to higher education. The projected dropout rate has fluctuated but, at 23 per cent, is well above the national average for the subjects and students' qualifications. A new Student Life Directorate has been charged with improving every aspect of the student experience, even planning events for students staying at Salford over the Christmas holiday closure.

Business and health subjects are now big recruiters. The university's growing involvement in health has seen the establishment of a national centre for prosthetics and orthotics, and Salford has a high reputation for the treatment of sports injuries. Another innovation was the launch of Europe's first nursing course for deaf students. There is also a BA in journalism and war studies – the only undergraduate degree in the UK to combine the two disciplines. In February 2010, the university became the first in the UK to launch a master's in psycho-oncology, which explores the psychological consequences of cancer and its treatment.

Engineering is the university's traditional strength, attracting many of the 3,000 overseas students. Two thirds of courses offer work placements, half of them abroad and almost all counting towards degree classifications. The tradition of sandwich

Salford
Greater Manchester M5 4WT

0161 295 4545
course-enquiries@salford.ac.uk
www.salford.ac.uk
www.salfordstudents.com

The Times Rankings
Overall Ranking: **88**

Student satisfaction:	=79	(74%)
Research quality:	=56	(1.0)
Entry standards:	79	(266)
Student–staff ratio:	73	(18.5)
Services & facilities/student:	84	(£1,133)
Expected completion rate:	104	(74.6%)
Good honours:	91	(52.3%)
Graduate prospects:	81	(59.8%)

courses always serves Salford well in terms of graduate employment. The Enterprise Academy scheme was commended by the EU after it helped 32 student businesses become established. Students are offered training in entrepreneurship and business skills, as well as a business mentor.

Online degrees have been introduced and the university has also made headlines with more unusual innovations, such as the appointment of Britain's first Professor of Pop Music. The university launched Salford Business School in 2006, formed from the merger of four existing schools and has several areas of expertise such as information management and operational research. A new Centre for Applied Archaeology has also been established.

Salford entered a relatively low proportion of its academics for the 2008 Research Assessment Exercise, but still had among the lowest grades of the pre-1992 universities. Architecture and business produced the best results. The university remains committed to research: it has established nine interdisciplinary research centres and a graduate school. It also led the way in formally recognising interaction with business and industry as of equal importance to teaching and research.

The modern landscaped campus, a haven of lawns and shrubberies along the River Irwell, is less than two miles from Manchester city centre and has a mainline railway station. The university also has its own TV and radio studios. The School of Media, Music and Performance plans to take full advantage of the move by the BBC of production facilities to nearby Salford Quays.

There has been some improvement in scores in the National Student Survey, although satisfaction levels are still below the national average. Only four subjects have an approval rating of 90 per cent or more, with accounting by far the highest-rated of these. Students like the friendly atmosphere and most of the residential places are either on campus or in a student village 15 minutes' walk away.

Undergraduate Fees and Bursaries
» Fees for UK/EU students: £3,290
» International student fees: £9,050–£11,250
» Bursary on full grant: household income up to £25K: £384
» Bursary on partial grant: (subject and academic bursaries available)
» Scholarships based on circumstances or by competition.
» For full details see the university's website: www.salford.ac.uk/study/undergraduate/money_matters

Students
Undergraduates:	12,010	(3,860)
Postgraduates:	2,010	(2,215)
Mature students:	34.1%	
Overseas students:	10.2%	
Applications per place:	3.9	
From state-sector schools:	98.1%	
From working-class homes:	43.1%	

For detailed information about fees, grants and bursaries and how they work, see chapter 7.

Accommodation
Number of places and costs refer to 2010–11
University-provided places: 1,309 plus 1,930 managed by specialist providers
Percentage catered: 0%
Self-catered costs: £58.52–£83.09 (standard); £82.04–£95.00 (en suite)
First years are guaranteed accommodation (terms and conditions apply).
International students: as above.
Contact: www.accommodation.salford.ac.uk

School of Oriental and African Studies, London

As the major national centre for the study of Africa, Asia and the Middle East, SOAS has a global reputation in subjects relating to two thirds of the world's population. Originally only a specialist Oriental college, the school now covers a much wider range of subjects. The library, which holds 1.2 million volumes, periodicals and audiovisual materials in 400 languages, attracts scholars from around the world is to get a makeover. The £12-million Library Transformation Project will provide a more modern environment as the School approaches its centenary in 2016. It is in the top 50 in the QS world rankings for the arts and humanities, and has been strengthening its academic staff in a variety of disciplines.

The 4,300 students on campus, plus over 2,000 studying distance learning programmes, come from over 130 countries. However, two thirds are from Britain and the rest of the EU – and the proportion is higher still among the undergraduates.

The school has a much wider portfolio of courses than its name would suggest, with more than 350 degree combinations on offer and 100 postgraduate programmes. Degrees are available in familiar subjects such as law, music, history and the social sciences, but with a different emphasis. There is also a more limited portfolio of Foundation programmes and language courses. Over 5,000 students (from inside and outside SOAS) take courses in one of the 50 languages on offer. The school was chosen to house a national teaching centre for languages.

Student recruitment remains healthy, especially among independent school candidates, who account for almost a quarter of the British entrants to undergraduate courses. Undergraduate applications grew strongly earlier in the decade, but showed only a modest increase of 2 per cent in the boom year of 2010, following a decline in the previous two years. The main growth area is in postgraduate courses, which have helped to tackle a financial deficit.

In addition, more than 2,000 students are now taking distance learning courses, mainly outside the UK. Numbers have risen with the transfer of University of London postgraduate programmes previously taught by Imperial College, making SOAS one of the world's largest providers of distance learning at this level.

Postgraduates are attracted by a research record which saw more than half of the work submitted for the 2008 Research Assessment Exercise rated world-leading or internationally excellent. SOAS was ranked top in the UK for Asian studies and did well in anthropology, politics, history and music.

There is an option of spending one, two or

Thornhaugh Street
Russell Square
London WC1H 0XG

020 7898 4301/4306
undergradadmissions@soas.ac.uk
www.soas.ac.uk
www.soasunion.org

The Times Rankings
Overall Ranking: **27**

Student satisfaction:	=89	(73%)
Research quality:	=29	(2.2)
Entry standards:	27	(387)
Student–staff ratio:	5	(11.2)
Services & facilities/student:	10	(£2,016)
Expected completion rate:	36	(87.9%)
Good honours:	18	(73.1%)
Graduate prospects:	26	(73.1%)

three terms of a degree course in one of the school's many partner universities in Africa or Asia. More than a fifth of the British undergraduates come from working-class homes. The dropout rate has fluctuated over recent years, but had dropped to 12 per cent in the latest statistics, just above the UK average for the subjects and entry qualifications at SOAS.

The school is located in Bloomsbury, but in 2001 a second campus opened at Vernon Square, Islington. Less than a mile from the main Russell Square site and adjacent to two of the three student residences, it provides student-orientated facilities such as a Learning Resource Centre and an internet café. The centrepiece of the main campus is an airy, modern building with gallery space as well as teaching accommodation, a gift from the Sultan of Brunei. There is no separate students' union building, although the students do have their own bar and catering facilities. The well-equipped and under-used University of London Union is close at hand, with swimming pool, gym and bars. The West End is also on the doorstep.

Nearly 1,000 residential places accommodate both undergraduates and postgraduates, and are within 15 minutes' walk of the school. Another 101 places are available in flats in Vernon Square. However, the school has few of its own sports facilities and the outdoor pitches are remote, with no time set aside from lectures. The ethnic and national mix has led to inevitable tensions at times, but SOAS is small enough for most students to know each other, at least by sight, and the atmosphere is normally friendly. Students tend to be highly committed – not surprising since many will return to positions of influence in developing countries – and the variety of cultures makes for lively debate.

Undergraduate Fees and Bursaries

» Fees for UK/EU students: £3,290
» International student fees: £12,600
» Bursary on full grant: household income up to £25K: £860
» Bursary on partial grant: household income to £39.3K: £420.
» Scholarships based on circumstances or by competition.
» For full details see the university's website: www.soas.ac.uk/registry/scholarships

Students

Undergraduates:	2,745	(100)
Postgraduates:	1,545	(500)
Mature students:	22.3%	
Overseas students:	36.2%	
Applications per place:	5.5	
From state-sector schools:	76.3%	
From working-class homes:	28.5%	

For detailed information about fees, grants and bursaries and how they work, see chapter 7.

Accommodation

Number of places and costs refer to 2010–11
University-provided places: 770 (Sanctuary Management Services); 186 (intercollegiate)
Percentage catered: 24%
Catered costs: £109.90–£266 a week
Self-catered costs: £123.69–£255.01 a week
Priority given to first years on first come basis. Residential restrictions apply.
International students: as above, although they are a high priority.
Contact: student@sanctuary-housing.co.uk

University of Sheffield

Sheffield has cemented its position in the top 20 of *The Times* league table and recorded high finishes in a number of subjects, following good results in the 2008 Research Assessment Exercise (RAE) and consistently high levels of satisfaction among the students. Student numbers reached 24,000 after 14 per cent growth in three years and the 22 per cent increase in applications for courses beginning in 2010 was the highest at any member of the Russell Group of leading research universities. A new student village and a high-tech library have added to the feeling of a university on the move. The £23-million Information Commons, opened in 2007, operates 24 hours a day, providing 1,300 study spaces and 500 computers linked to the campus network, as well as 110,000 books and periodicals.

More than 60 per cent of the work submitted for the RAE was judged to be world-leading or internationally excellent. Politics and information studies achieved the best results in the country, while town planning, philosophy, Russian, architecture, and mechanical and aeronautical engineering were near the top for their fields.

Sheffield was only just outside the top 10 in the National Student Survey in 2009, producing some of the best results among the big city universities. There was 100 per cent satisfaction in chemistry, computer science, theology, genetics, physical science, molecular biology, biophysics and biochemistry with several other subjects, such as dentistry, not far behind. The university houses national teaching centres for the arts and social sciences and for enterprise learning.

There has been sustained investment in facilities in recent years: £100 million for biological and physical sciences, medicine, engineering and social sciences, and £15 million on an advanced manufacturing research centre in which Boeing is the senior partner, and which forms the hub of a technology park. The university is the lead institution for systems engineering, smart materials and stem-cell technology in a research network of European, American and Chinese universities.

The conversion of the former Jessop hospital at the heart of the campus provides a new centre for the arts and humanities, which includes a visitor information centre and café. The new Soundhouse, clad in black rubber, provides ultra-modern music practice studios, rehearsal rooms and recording facilities. Another new site adjacent to the engineering departments will house high-tech multidisciplinary facilities.

The university has always enjoyed a high ratio of applications to places, despite recent expansion. There are more than 3,600 overseas students from 124 countries. Sheffield is in the top 80 universities in the

Western Bank
Sheffield S10 2TN

0114 222 8030 (admissions)
http://ask.sheffield.ac.uk/
www.shef.ac.uk
www.shef.ac.uk/union

The Times Rankings
Overall Ranking: **18**

Student satisfaction:	=15	(80%)
Research quality:	16	(2.7)
Entry standards:	16	(411)
Student–staff ratio:	=21	(13.8)
Services & facilities/student:	41	(£1,488)
Expected completion rate:	25	(92.1%)
Good honours:	19	(72.8%)
Graduate prospects:	30	(72.3%)

world, according to both the main global rankings.

Academic buildings are concentrated in an area about a mile from the city centre on the affluent west side of Sheffield, with most university flats and halls of residence a little further into the suburbs. Recent developments mean that the main university precinct now stretches into an almost unbroken mile-long "campus".

The intake is more diverse than at most leading universities: just over 87 per cent of undergraduates come from state schools or colleges and more than one undergraduate in five comes from a working-class home. A famously lively social scene is based on the students' union's extended facilities – twice voted the best in Britain – but also takes full advantage of the city's burgeoning club life. In addition to its own popular facilities, the union owns a pub in the western suburb where most students live and the students' union is renowned for attracting some big-name bands. Town–gown relations are much better and the crime rate lower than in most big cities. The university claims the highest proportion of graduates staying in the city after completing their studies.

Residential accommodation is plentiful, with most university-owned places within walking distance of lectures, and private housing reasonably priced as well as being available very close to lectures. First years from outside Sheffield are guaranteed accommodation. The new Endcliffe Village caters for about 3,500 students in a mix of refurbished Victorian houses and new flats. A second development will add another 1,000 places and take spending on accommodation to £200 million.

The university's excellent sports facilities have been the subject of a £6-million makeover, which includes a 170-station fitness centre and three astroturf pitches, one of which is specifically designed for soccer. A five-year student sports strategy was launched in 2007, aiming to boost participation at various levels of the sport and recreation. Intramural football has benefited the most from this scheme with large 5-a-side, 6-a-side and 11-a-side leagues spanning all three terms, as well as regular weekend tournaments.

Undergraduate Fees and Bursaries
» Fees for UK/EU students: £3,290
» International student fees: £10,940–£14,380 £25,990 (medicine)
» Bursary on full grant: household income up to £25K: household income up to £17.5K: £715; household income up to £25K: £440.
» Bursary on partial grant: household income up to £36.2K: £440 (subject and academic bursaries available).
» Scholarships based on circumstances or by competition.
» For full details see the university's website: www.shef.ac.uk/bursaries

Students
Undergraduates:	**15,665**	(1,930)
Postgraduates:	**5,475**	(1,640)
Mature students:	**8.5%**	
Overseas students:	**10.5%**	
Applications per place:	**6.5**	
From state-sector schools:	**87.1%**	
From working-class homes:	**22.6%**	

For detailed information about fees, grants and bursaries and how they work, see chapter 7.

Accommodation
Number of places and costs refer to 2010–11
University-provided places: 5,942
Percentage catered: 10%
Catered costs: £4,451.16 – £5,491.92 (42 weeks; 31 weeks of catering).
Self-catered costs: £3,116.40 – £4,551.12 (42 weeks).
First years are guaranteed accommodation if conditions are met.
International students: as above.
Contact: accommodationoffice@sheffield.ac.uk
www.shef.ac.uk/accommodation

Sheffield Hallam University

Sheffield Hallam has been undergoing a physical transformation designed to alter its image and cater for an even bigger student population. The university has two campuses, one in the heart of the city centre, near the railway station, and the other not far away in a leafy inner suburb. Developments have been continuing apace, with almost £100 million already spent on teaching and learning facilities and half as much again earmarked for the next five years.

An atrium provides social space for staff and students, and innovative library developments take pride of place on both campuses. Business and management courses, which account for easily the biggest share of places, have their own city-centre headquarters.

The Collegiate Crescent campus, a former teacher training college, houses education, health and community studies. The students' union has taken over the spectacular but ill-fated National Centre for Popular Music, with facilities described by the former higher education minister Kim Howells as the best he had seen. Environmentally, the university is ranked eighth in the "Green League 2009", as compiled by the campaigning website, People and Planet.

While most of the development has been on the main campus, the latest stage has seen the opening of a new social centre on the Collegiate Crescent site. A £14-million development that opened in 2005 has allowed the faculty of health and wellbeing to almost double in size, as extra provision is made for nursing, radiotherapy, physiotherapy and social work. The Centre for Sport and Exercise Science, with its £6-million research facility, won glowing praise from inspectors, and is one of the largest of its kind in Europe, with more than 2,000 students. The faculty is the biggest provider of health and social care training in the UK and offers the widest range of sports courses.

Another new development, combined with the refurbishment of existing city-centre buildings brought all the departments in the Faculty of Arts, Computing, Engineering and Sciences together on the main campus for the first time, placing them in the heart of Sheffield's thriving cultural industries quarter. The university also launched the Sheffield Business School in May 2009, bringing together academic and professional groups in business, finance, management and languages, with the university's specialisms of facilities management, food and nutrition, tourism, hospitality and events management.

Of the subjects available in 2010, chemistry and nursing produced the best results in the latest National Student Survey, boasting 100 per cent satisfaction among the undergraduates. Mathematical studies, technology, planning, architecture and

City Campus
Howard Street
Sheffield S1 1WB

0114 225 5555 (enquiries)
enquiries@shu.ac.uk
www.shu.ac.uk
www.hallamunion.org

The Times Rankings
Overall Ranking: **72**

Student satisfaction:	=89	(73%)
Research quality:	=77	(0.4)
Entry standards:	=64	(274)
Student–staff ratio:	=70	(18.3)
Services & facilities/student:	94	(£1,050)
Expected completion rate:	51	(85.2%)
Good honours:	53	(63.0%)
Graduate prospects:	63	(63.0%)

medical technology also produced high scores. Almost a third of the work submitted for the 2008 Research Assessment Exercise was rated as world-leading or internationally excellent, with planning and art and design achieving the highest grades.

Sheffield Hallam traces its origins in art and design back to the 1840s and celebrated the centenary of education and teacher training in 2005. It is now one of the largest of the new universities, with more than 30,000 students, including high proportions of part-time and mature students, and more than 1,000 taught on franchised courses in further education colleges. Business and industry are closely involved in the development hundreds of courses, with almost half of the students taking sandwich course placements with employers. More than 200 "specialist flexible courses" mix part-time study, distance learning and work-based learning. The university also has a growing international dimension: it celebrated its 5,000th Malaysian graduate in 2010 and has an office in India to facilitate research and faculty exchange through partnerships with universities on the sub-continent.

The university leads two national teaching centres, one for fostering employability and the other promoting autonomous learning. It is also a partner in a third, led by Coventry University, on e-learning in the professions. A "virtual campus" offers students e-mail accounts and cheap equipment to access the growing volume of online courses, assignments and discussion groups provided by the university, even when they are at home or on work placements.

Almost 97 per cent of the intake is from state schools, while over a third of the undergraduates come from working-class homes. Almost one in five students come from areas that send few students to higher education. The projected dropout rate of 12 per cent is lower than average for the subjects offered and the students' entry qualifications.

Such is Sheffield Hallam's size that it is not possible to guarantee all first years university-owned accommodation, although the large local intake means that many live at home. Transport in the city is excellent, with both a well-run bus and tram service. Sports facilities are supplemented by those provided by the city for the World Student Games. The impressive swimming complex, for example, is on the university's doorstep.

Undergraduate Fees and Bursaries
» Fees for UK/EU students: £3,290
» International student fees: £9,480–£11,280
» Bursary on full grant: household income up to £25K: £700
» The university does not award bursaries for students on partial maintenance grants.
» Scholarships based on circumstances or by competition.
» For full details see the university's website: www.shu.ac.uk/study/ug/money.html

Students
Undergraduates:	**19,895**	(5,665)
Postgraduates:	**3,110**	(5,160)
Mature students:	**20.8%**	
Overseas students:	**6.6%**	
Applications per place:	**4.7**	
From state-sector schools:	**96.8%**	
From working-class homes:	**35.0%**	

For detailed information about fees, grants and bursaries and how they work, see chapter 7.

Accommodation
Number of places and costs refer to 2009–10
University-provided places: 4,205
Percentage catered: 8%
Catered costs: £91.41 a week (39 weeks).
Self-catered costs: £49–£93 (42–44 weeks).
All first years offered university owned, managed, partnership or private housing.
International students: as above, providing conditions are met.
Contact: accommodation@shu.ac.uk
www.shu.ac.uk/accommodation

Southampton University

Southampton has seen applications increase steadily for the last few years, following substantial investment in campus facilities and good results in the National Student Survey (NSS). Growth in the demand for places was the biggest at any of the 20 Russell Group research-led universities in 2009 and there was another 11 per cent increase at the start of 2010. The university is more than half way through a £250-million programme to upgrade its six sites in Southampton and Winchester.

The university could not quite repeat its outstanding results in the 2001 Research Assessment Exercise, which took it into the top 10, when the 2008 RAE took place. However, more than 60 per cent of its work was considered world-leading or internationally excellent and it remained firmly entrenched among the research elite. The best grades came in music, sociology and social policy, computer science and nursing. The proportion of income derived from research at Southampton is among the highest in Britain.

Although the percentages of students from working-class homes and areas with little tradition of university education are lower than the national average for the subjects offered, the statistics agency concluded that this was largely a matter of location. The university does exceed the benchmark set for the number of state school pupils, as it does for the proportion of students who have a disability. Students act as ambassadors, associates and mentors in local schools and colleges, as part of the university's effort to broaden its intake. A range of Foundation degrees carefully tailored to industry needs offers students flexible ways of learning.

Chemistry and geology students gave their courses the highest rating in the country in the 2009 NSS, while the university also scored very highly in aerospace engineering, archaeology, geology, Iberian studies and sociology. The medical school, which features an innovative common core curriculum for the pre-registration programmes of over 3,000 medical, nursing and other health students from entry to internship, again scored well with students.

The main Highfield campus is in an attractive green location two miles from the city centre, adjoining Southampton Common. It has been the focus of recent development to cater for a considerable expansion in numbers during this decade. Education, engineering, health sciences, chemistry, electronics and computer science have all benefited. The library has been greatly extended and the campus now has an e-science centre, as well as a commercial services hub. A purpose-built student services centre provides learning support and other

University Road
Southampton SO17 1BJ

023 8059 5000
admissns@soton.ac.uk
www.soton.ac.uk
www.susu.org

The Times Rankings
Overall Ranking: **19**

Student satisfaction:	=22	(79%)
Research quality:	=24	(2.3)
Entry standards:	18	(407)
Student–staff ratio:	=14	(13.4)
Services & facilities/student:	18	(£1,854)
Expected completion rate:	=21	(92.6%)
Good honours:	15	(74.4%)
Graduate prospects:	16	(76.3%)

advisory facilities – most of which are backed up online for students in other areas of the university. The latest addition is the striking new £55-million Mountbatten Building for the School of Electronics and Computer Science and the Optoelectronics Research Centre and the £50-million Life Sciences Building. The latter is home to the Schools of Biological Sciences and Medicine.

The university has four other sites in Southampton. The Waterside Campus, in the city's revitalised dock area, houses the National Oceanography Centre, Southampton. A £50-million joint project with the Natural Environment Research Council, it is considered Europe's finest. The Avenue Campus, near the main site, is home to most of the arts departments. Clinical medicine is based at Southampton General Hospital, where a new research centre opened in 2007.

Winchester School of Art, which has been part of the university since 1996, has also enjoyed significant recent investment in new facilities. The arts are well represented in Southampton, too, with three nationally renowned arts centres: the Turner Sims Concert Hall, the Nuffield Theatre and the John Hansard Gallery all based at Highfield. The university has also been expanding its international activities, for example through the Centre for Contemporary China, which originated in law, the arts and social sciences, but which now links Southampton with a number of leading Chinese universities.

Social facilities for students have been expanded and refurbished, with the addition of a popular campus nightclub. Sports facilities are first-class, with an £8.4-million indoor sports complex and swimming pool next to the students' union and £4.5-million investment in outdoor facilities, with grass and synthetic pitches, a new pavilion, bar and meeting rooms. Student accommodation is plentiful and was improved in 2006 with the £20-million renovation and expansion of three halls of residence.

Undergraduate Fees and Bursaries

» Fees for UK/EU students: £3,290
» International student fees: £10,4000–£13,300
   £23,800 (medicine)
» Bursary on full grant: household income up to £25K: £1,200*
» Bursary on partial grant: household income up to £35K: £600*
» Scholarships based on circumstances or by competition.
» For full details see the university's website:
   www.soton.ac.uk/study/feesandfunding

* Figures for 2009–10

Students

Undergraduates:	**14,715**	**(2,085)**
Postgraduates:	**4,005**	**(1,875)**
Mature students:	**13.0%**	
Overseas students:	**11.5%**	
Applications per place:	**7.1**	
From state-sector schools:	**85.2%**	
From working-class homes:	**22.1%**	

For detailed information about fees, grants and bursaries and how they work, see chapter 7.

Accommodation

Number of places and costs refer to 2009–10
University-provided places: 5,200
Percentage catered: 15%
Catered costs: £103.95–£152.95 a week.
Self-catered costs: £71.40– £152.95 a week (self-contained flat)
All first years are guaranteed an offer of accommodation.
Conditions apply.
International students: All non-EU students are guaranteed accommodation (conditions apply).
Contact: www.southampton.ac.uk/accommodation

Southampton Solent University

The largest of the nine universities created in 2005, Southampton Solent also has the broadest range of programmes, stretching from Foundation courses for those without the qualifications to begin degrees, to PhDs. Around 11,000 students embrace civil and mechanical engineering, as well as media, arts and business, with a separate maritime centre capitalising on the coastal location. The subject mix explains why the former Southampton Institute is now one of the few universities with a majority of male students.

The rebranded Solent Curriculum plays to the university's strengths in vocational courses, with an eye to maintaining a good graduate employment record. There is a strong representation of "non-traditional" disciplines, such as yacht and powercraft design, computer and video games, and comedy writing and performance. A new range of courses in 2008 included degrees in fashion management, television and music production, and coaching and sport development. A Graduate Enterprise Centre provides advice and rent-free offices for those hoping to start their own businesses, while the Warsash Maritime Centre is an internationally renowned training and research facility for the shipping and offshore oil industries.

Solent entered fewer academics for the 2008 Research Assessment Exercise than any university in England – fewer than one in ten of those eligible. But two of the three areas in which it made a submission contained some world-leading research, with art and design achieving much the best results. It was also among the bottom 10 universities for student satisfaction in 2009, although the results were an improvement on the previous year. Sociology performed best with a 92 per cent satisfaction rating, but no other subject scored more than 85 per cent in 2009 and music managed less than 50 per cent.

Nevertheless, applications have been healthy and had risen by 19 per cent at the start of 2010, following another big rise in the previous year. Demand for places remains especially strong in marine-based courses. The university is higher education's premier yachting institution, with a world champion student team that has won the national championships four times in six years. Three new boats will support courses at the new, purpose-built Watersports Centre, where some of the activities are targeted on disadvantaged young people in the area. The centre now boasts seven powerboats, nine dinghies and three keelboats.

Almost a third of the students come from Hampshire and there has been a substantial increase in the proportion with working-class roots, almost reaching the national average

East Park Terrace
Southampton SO14 0YN

023 8031 9000 (main switchboard)
ask@solent.ac.uk
www.solent.ac.uk
www.solentsu.co.uk

The Times Rankings
Overall Ranking: **110**

Student satisfaction:	=102	(70%)
Research quality:	=107	(0.1)
Entry standards:	=100	(241)
Student–staff ratio:	104	(22.1)
Services & facilities/student:	90	(£1,085)
Expected completion rate:	103	(75.0%)
Good honours:	113	(42.3%)
Graduate prospects:	111	(49.2%)

for the university's subjects and entry qualifications. Solent's projected dropout rate had improved in the latest survey and, at just below 19 per cent, was fractionally better than the university's benchmark. Just over 13 per cent of undergraduates come from overseas, while a further 100 are enrolled on research degrees. There is a special link with Guernsey, which has no higher education of its own. Colleges on the island (and in various parts of the south of England) bring students for taster courses and provide evidence of academic potential that can lead to entry on criteria other than A level.

The main campus has few architectural pretensions, but is conveniently based in the city centre within walking distance of the station. Recent investment has included a new Centre for Professional Development in Broadcasting and Multimedia Production, which includes an online editing suite, digital television studio and gallery, for use by undergraduates as well as community groups and professionals. Media, arts and society courses now attract almost as many students as the consistently popular business school.

Other recent additions include the Centre for Health, Exercise and Sports Science, which enables sports science students to conduct the latest types of fitness testing, including ergonomic and biomechanical movement analysis. In September 2009, a new Centre for Football Research was opened in a development that university said would cement its position as a leading provider for football-related academic study. New music studios feature an industry-standard recording complex, while a performance space and dance studio, opened in 2008, includes a dance floor, tiered seating and a technical viewing gallery.

Students like the location, close to the city's growing complement of bars and nightclubs, as well as to the main shopping area. There are more than 2,300 hall places close to the campus, most of which are allocated to first years and almost half of which are en suite. A landlord accreditation scheme helps to guarantee standards of accommodation for those who rely on the private sector. Away from the water, there is the usual range of sports facilities, with a sports hall and fitness suite on campus and outdoor pitches, tennis and netball courts four miles away. Students living in hall and members of university sports clubs get free fitness classes and gym use.

Undergraduate Fees and Bursaries
» Fees for UK/EU students: £3,290
» International student fees: £8,600
» Bursary on full grant: household income up to £25K: £750
» The university does not award bursaries for students on partial maintenance grants.
» Scholarships based on circumstances or by competition.
» For full details see the university's website: www.solent.ac.uk/fees/info.aspx

Students
Undergraduates:	9,600	(1,410)
Postgraduates:	340	(400)
Mature students:	24.2%	
Overseas students:	13.5%	
Applications per place:	4.0	
From state-sector schools:	96.1%	
From working-class homes:	38.5%	

For detailed information about fees, grants and bursaries and how they work, see chapter 7.

Accommodation
Number of places and costs refer to 2009–10
University-provided places: 2,340 (majority are offered to first years).
Percentage catered: 0%
Self-catered costs: £87.85–£101.85 a week (40 weeks).
First years are guaranteed accommodation if conditions are met.
International students: some accommodation is set aside.
Contact: Accommodation@solent.ac.uk
www.solent.ac.uk/accommodation/accommodation_home.aspx

Staffordshire University

Staffordshire used to describe itself as a "university in the community" but it is increasingly reliant on overseas students, both at home and abroad. There are 6,000 students taking Staffordshire courses outside Britain, almost half of them located around the Pacific Rim, as well as a growing cohort of foreign students in the university's domestic campuses. There are more than 12,000 UK students, however, and the demand for places has grown substantially over the last two years, after a period of decline. Applications were up by more than 30 per cent at the start of 2010.

A quarter of the students taking qualifications either awarded or quality assured by the university are at partner institutions across Europe, in China, India or beyond. There are dedicated admissions offices in Oman, Sri Lanka, Singapore and Macedonia, and enrolment began in Slovenia and Kosovo last autumn.

The university is based on two main sites: in Stoke-on-Trent and 16 miles away in Stafford. Both have modern halls of residence, sports centres and lively students' union venues. There has been significant investment at the Stafford campus, which features the Octagon Centre, in which lecture theatres, offices and walkways surround one of the largest university computing facilities in Europe. The New Technologies Centre has some of the finest film production facilities at any university. Engineering and technology are based at Stafford, as well as the Faculty of Health, which has branches in Telford and Shrewsbury.

The large business school is based at Stoke, which also hosts the Law School, the Faculty of Arts, Media and Design and courses in sport and exercise. Developments are dominated by a £287-million plan to produce an attractive and thriving University Quarter – one of the largest collaborative projects of its kind in the UK. New science facilities are due for completion in 2011, focusing on the university's strengths in forensics, biology and psychology.

A third campus in Lichfield houses an integrated further and higher education centre, developed in partnership with Tamworth and Lichfield College, as well as 26 business start-up units. The Staffordshire University Regional Federation also involves partner colleges in delivering a range of higher education awards to around 3,000 students. A bespoke £520,000 higher education centre will open on the new Newcastle College campus in 2010.

The university is a pioneer of two-year fast-track degrees, which are now offered in accounting and finance, computing science, business, English, law, geography and motor sport technology. Staffordshire academics will also be evaluating the national

College Road
Stoke-on-Trent ST4 2DE

01782 294000 (enquiries)
admissions@staffs.ac.uk
www.staffs.ac.uk
www.staffsunion.com

The Times Rankings
Overall Ranking: **77**

Student satisfaction:	=59	(76%)
Research quality:	=107	(0.1)
Entry standards:	=100	(241)
Student–staff ratio:	76	(19.1)
Services & facilities/student:	63	(£1,274)
Expected completion rate:	=80	(79.8%)
Good honours:	96	(50.8%)
Graduate prospects:	51	(67.4%)

programme of accelerated degrees. There already was an extensive portfolio of two-year Foundation degrees. Many programmes are available with a January start, a popular arrangement with overseas students who often take English language courses before beginning a degree. However, after cuts of over £2 million from the Higher Education Funding Council for England (HEFCE), the university is facing the possibility of cutting some courses and moving more towards vocational subjects.

Staffordshire is in the top three universities for secondary teacher training courses. Fine art produced the best results in the 2008 National Student Survey and the only subject to register more than 90 per cent satisfaction. The university entered only a small proportion of its academics for the latest Research Assessment Exercise. Three of the ten subject areas had some world-leading research, with general engineering and education producing the best results. Accounting, finance and accounting, sports science and biology were the subjects that produced the best sets of results in the 2009 National Student Survey, all registering above 90 per cent satisfaction.

With 98 per cent of its undergraduates state-educated and more than four in ten coming from working-class homes, Staffordshire exceeds all the benchmarks set by the funding council for widening access to higher education. There is good provision for the 700 students with disabilities. The projected dropout rate has also improved, falling just below the average for the university's courses and entry qualifications.

Stoke is not the liveliest city of its size, but the University Quarter project should attract more social facilities to the area. The campus, which is close to the railway station, is within easy reach of the city centre and has a buzzing students' union. Stafford is much the more attractive setting and offers the best chance of a residential place, but the town is quiet and the campus is a mile and a half outside it. Sports facilities are good, especially in Stafford, where there is a new £1.4-million sports centre and all-weather pitches. Good coaching has helped attract some outstanding athletes, who have access to a sports performance centre to help with training schedules, psychological support and dietary assessments.

Undergraduate Fees and Bursaries

» Fees for UK/EU students: £3,290
» International student fees: £9,385*
» Bursary on full grant: household income up to £25K: household income up to £20.8K: £1,000; household income up to £25.5K: £850.*
» Bursary on partial grant: HI up to £30.8K: £500.*
» Scholarships based on circumstances or by competition.
» For full details see the university's website: www.staffs.ac.uk/study_here/fees_and_funding

* Figures for 2009-10

Students

Undergraduates:	**8,655**	**(4,730)**
Postgraduates:	**1,420**	**(2,185)**
Mature students:	**25.4%**	
Overseas students:	**5.4%**	
Applications per place:	**3.5**	
From state-sector schools:	**98.0%**	
From working-class homes:	**41.5%**	

For detailed information about fees, grants and bursaries and how they work, see chapter 7.

Accommodation

Number of places and costs refer to 2010-11
University-provided places: 1,090 (Stoke); 786 (Stafford)
Percentage catered: 0%
Self-catered accommodation: £51–£95 a week (36 weeks).
First years have priority, if conditions met.
International students: have priority, if conditions are met.
Contact: Accommodation_stoke@staffs.ac.uk
Accommodation_stafford@staffs.ac.uk
www.staffs.ac.uk/study_here/student_services/accommodation

University of Stirling

One of the most beautiful campuses in Britain is also one of the best provided for sports facilities. Stirling was designated Scotland's University for Sporting Excellence in 2008 and is home to national swimming and tennis centres, as well as a golf course and a football academy. The university, with its modern buildings in a loch-side setting beneath the Ochil Hills, has twice recently been voted the favourite UK destination of international students.

Stirling remains a relatively small institution with a strong community feel but has grown to 11,500 students. There are no faculties, but five "core areas" have been identified: health and well-being, culture and society, environment, enterprise and economy, and sport. Philosophy produced the best results in the 2008 Research Assessment Exercise, but nursing, film, media and journalism, economics, education and history all did well.

The university fared very well in the 2009 National Student Survey, finishing just outside the top 10 in the UK for the most satisfied students. History, sociology, law and accounting all scored highly. Investment is taking place in a number of academic areas, including teacher education, where there have been six new appointments to enhance a research-led approach to the subject.

Stirling was the British pioneer of the semester system, which has now become so popular throughout higher education. The academic year is divided into two 15-week terms, with short mid-semester breaks. Students have the option of starting courses in February, rather than September. Successful completion of six semesters will bring a General degree; eight semesters, Honours.

The emphasis on breadth is such that there are no barriers to movement between departments. Undergraduates can switch the whole direction of their studies, in consultation with their academic adviser, as their interests develop. The modular scheme allows students to speed up their progress on a Summer Academic Programme, which squeezes a full semester's teaching into July and August. Full-time students are not allowed to use the programme to reduce the length of their course, but part-timers can use it to make rapid progress.

Applications rose by a remarkable 41 cent at the start of 2010 – nearly twice the UK average. The intake is surprisingly diverse, with almost 93 per cent of undergraduates state-educated and nearly a third coming from working-class homes. Two thirds are from Scotland. International exchanges are common, with many students going to American, Asian and European universities each year.

Recent campus developments have

Stirling FK9 4LA

01786 467044 (admissions)
admissions@stir.ac.uk
www.stir.ac.uk
www.susaonline.org.uk

The Times Rankings
Overall Ranking: **45**

Student satisfaction:	=32	(78%)
Research quality:	=48	(1.5)
Entry standards:	=46	(314)
Student–staff ratio:	=52	(17.0)
Services & facilities/student:	72	(£1,205)
Expected completion rate:	=60	(82.9%)
Good honours:	47	(65.5%)
Graduate prospects:	50	(67.6%)

included the refurbishment of the School of Biological and Environmental Sciences. Journalism students have the use of a high-tech newsroom. In 2009, the university launched the UK's first degree in financial journalism. The library is also undergoing major refurbishment, in a £14-million programme that is due to be completed for the start of the 2010–11 academic year. The university has more than 700 computers for student use, many available 24 hours a day, and all rooms in halls are wired for internet use.

The sports facilities, which include a 50-metre pool and a golf centre with indoor facilities and a synthetic putting green, are used for teaching and research, as well as for training by elite athletes and recreation for the university community. Sports Studies are particularly popular, with 80 students in 2009 benefiting from a sports scholarships programme that is open to overseas, as well as UK students. It covers golf, swimming, disability swimming, tennis, triathlon and football.

Students appreciate the individual attention that a small campus university can offer, although some find the atmosphere claustrophobic. Stirling is not the top choice of nightclubbers, but the students' union won "Best Bar None" status for three years in a row and there is a lively social scene. The MacRobert Arts Centre offers a full programme of cultural activities, while the surrounding countryside offers its own attractions for walkers and climbers. The campus has been described by police as one of the safest in Britain, but a community policeman is based there and available to students for extra advice.

The Highland campus, for nurses and midwives, is based in the modern Centre for Health Science, in Inverness. There is also a Western Isles campus, located in Stornoway, where the teaching accommodation is an integral part of the Western Isles Hospital.

Undergraduate Fees and Bursaries

» Scottish-domiciled and EU students: no fees payable.
» Non-Scottish UK-domiciled student fees: £1,820
» International student fees: £9,900–£11,950
» Scholarships based on circumstances or by competition.
» For full details see the university's website: www.external.stir.ac.uk/undergrad/financial_info/index.php

Students

Undergraduates:	**6,540**	**(1,005)**
Postgraduates:	**1,470**	**(1,105)**
Mature students:	**26.4%**	
Overseas students:	**8.3%**	
Applications per place:	**5.7**	
From state-sector schools:	**92.5%**	
From working-class homes:	**30.5%**	

For detailed information about fees, grants and bursaries and how they work, see chapter 7.

Accommodation

Number of places and costs refer to 2010–11
University-provided places: 2,805
Percentage catered: 0%
Self-catered costs: £61.92–£97.41 a week.
All first years are guaranteed suitable housing arranged by the university.
International students: as above.
Contact: Accommodation@stir.ac.uk

University of Strathclyde

Even as Anderson's Institution in the 18th century, Strathclyde concentrated on "useful learning". Today's university has set itself the target of being recognised as one of the world's leading technological universities. The new Vice-Chancellor, Professor Jim McDonald, has called for improvements in research to achieve this goal, but has promised not to neglect the student experience.

Strathclyde aims to offer courses that are both innovative and relevant to 21st-century needs – hence product design and innovation, energy systems or international business with modern languages. Business and law were the main successes in the 2008 Research Assessment Exercise (RAE), when almost 60 per cent of the university's submission was rated as world-leading or internationally excellent. Pharmacy and some branches of engineering also achieved good results.

The business school, rated among the top 20 in Europe by *The Financial Times*, is normally considered Strathclyde's main strength. It is one of the largest in Europe and the only one in Scotland to be accredited by the European Quality Improvement System. Business studies students follow a Management Development programme, which is designed to place them in a realistic business environment from day one and involves work with a range of major companies.

The engineering faculty is also the largest in Scotland. The university is heavily involved in Scotland's "pooling" arrangement for research in potentially vulnerable science subjects. There were a number of joint submissions with neighbouring Glasgow University in the RAE.

European focus is evident throughout the university. Many students combine business or engineering with European studies or languages to give themselves an edge in the job market. Mature students account for nearly a fifth of the places and have a special organisation to look after their interests. With nearly 22,000 students, including part-timers, Strathclyde is the third-largest university in Scotland. but its numbers swell to more than 60,000 including short courses and distance learning programmes.

Strathclyde actively promotes wider access, comfortably exceeding national averages for state-educated students and the share of places going to applicants from working-class homes. The projected dropout rate had fallen to 13 per cent in the latest survey, but is still higher than the UK average for the university's subjects and entry qualifications.

The main John Anderson campus is in the centre of Glasgow, behind George Square and near Queen Street station. Apart from the Edwardian headquarters, the buildings

---

16 Richmond Street
Glasgow G1 1XQ

0141 552 4400 (main switchboard)
scls@strath.ac.uk
www.strath.ac.uk
www.strathstudents.com

The Times Rankings
Overall Ranking: **=36**

Student satisfaction:	=46	(77%)
Research quality:	43	(1.8)
Entry standards:	26	(388)
Student–staff ratio:	=57	(17.7)
Services & facilities/student:	35	(£1,558)
Expected completion rate:	52	(84.6%)
Good honours:	23	(71.7%)
Graduate prospects:	20	(75.5%)

are mostly modern. The site of a former maternity hospital in the centre of the campus will eventually provide extra teaching accommodation, but a £73-million refurbishment programme is taking priority.

The university, which has taken to adding Glasgow to its name recently, has unveiled ambitious plans to invest £350 million over the next ten years to transform the city centre campus. A range of new facilities will be added, including a Centre for Sport and Health. A new building for the Strathclyde Institute of Pharmacy and Biomedical Sciences – a centre for excellence in drug discovery and development research – will be open in 2011. In addition, a new Technology and Innovation Centre will enable companies to work side-by-side with university researchers and the graduates of tomorrow.

Strathclyde's Jordanhill campus on the west side of the city was acquired from a merger with Jordanhill College of Education in 1993. The 67-acre parkland site houses the Faculty of Education, which is breaking new ground with Scotland's first part-time teacher training degree and also offers courses in speech and language pathology, community arts, social work, sport and outdoor education. The Jordanhill site is scheduled to close, its education students moving to the main campus in September 2010. Strathclyde should have a unified, city-centre campus by 2012.

There is a student village on the main campus with 1,400 places, all with network access. Another 500 residential places are nearby in the trendy Merchant City. The ten-floor union building attracts students from all over Glasgow with its reputation for revelry. There are over 40 sporting clubs and teams and another 40 social, cultural and political clubs and societies, plus a student newspaper and radio station. Proximity to Glasgow's vibrant and celebrated music scene is a plus, and for those with more sophisticated tastes, there are numerous theatres and arts organisations, as well as standout museums such as the Kelvingrove Gallery, one of Scotland's top attractions.

Undergraduate Fees and Bursaries
- » Scottish-domiciled and EU students: no fees payable.
- » Non-Scottish UK-domiciled student fees: £1,820
- » International student fees: £11,000–£12,600
- » Scholarships based on circumstances or by competition.
- » For full details see the university's website: www.strath.ac.uk/studying/prospective/financingyoureducation

Students
Undergraduates:	**11,930**	**(2,680)**
Postgraduates:	**3,390**	**(3,300)**
Mature students:	**17.5%**	
Overseas students:	**6.7%**	
Applications per place:	**5.6**	
From state-sector schools:	**93.0%**	
From working-class homes:	**27.7%**	

For detailed information about fees, grants and bursaries and how they work, see chapter 7.

Accommodation
Number of places and costs refer to 2009–10
University-provided places: 1,979
Percentage catered: 0%
Self-catered costs: £74–£97 a week.
First years are offered accommodation if they live further than 25 miles from the university.
International students: as above.
Contact: student.accommodation@mis.strath.ac.uk
www.strath.ac.uk/accommodation

University of Sunderland

Sunderland already has one of the UK's newest campuses, having taken advantage of urban regeneration programmes to transform its facilities. Now the £75-million development of the original City Campus is well underway, after the £12-million CitySpace sports and social space opened in September 2009. Work has begun on a student village that will cost another £12 million, and a hotel and conference facility, landscaping, traffic calming measures and a restructuring of the sciences complex have also been announced. The main feature of the campus, right in the city centre, is the Gateway one-stop shop for student services, but there is a well-appointed science complex and design centre.

The university's other campus at St Peter's, an award-winning 24-acre site by the banks of the Wear, houses the business school and the faculties of applied sciences, law and arts, design and media. The Sir Tom Cowie campus is built around a 7th-century abbey described as one of Britain's first universities and incorporates a working heritage centre for the glass industry. A glass and ceramics design degree maintains a Sunderland tradition, while teaching and research in automotive design and manufacture serve the region's modern industrial base. The large pharmacy department is another strength and the well-equipped Faculty of Applied Sciences is one of the largest in the UK, with over 3,000 students.

Sunderland is making the most of the opportunity to link up with the multinational companies that have arrived on its doorstep. The Institute for Automotive and Manufacturing Advanced Practice has a team of 40 researchers and consultants working with local businesses, while nearby Nissan played an important role in designing a course in automotive product development. The media centre provides students with excellent television and video production facilities and is home to the student-run community radio station, Spark FM.

The university has a determinedly local focus, aiming to double the number of students coming from an area which has little tradition of sending students to higher education. Only one UK university recruits a higher proportion from "low participation neighbourhoods" – at 21 per cent, well above the national average for the subjects on offer. A pioneering access scheme offers places to mature students without A levels, as long as they reach the required levels of literacy, numeracy and other basic skills. The Learning North East initiative, based on Sunderland's successful pilot for the University for Industry, even offers free taster courses to take at home.

Almost half the undergraduates have a

**Chester Road
Sunderland SR1 3SD**

0191 515 3000 (course helpline)
student.helpline@sunderland.ac.uk
www.sunderland.ac.uk
www.sunderlandsu.co.uk

The Times Rankings
Overall Ranking: **79**

Student satisfaction:	=22	(79%)
Research quality:	=60	(0.6)
Entry standards:	=106	(232)
Student–staff ratio:	=40	(15.6)
Services & facilities/student:	105	(£932)
Expected completion rate:	98	(76.1%)
Good honours:	104	(48.6%)
Graduate prospects:	86	(58.6%)

working-class background, and the projected dropout rate has dropped from more than a quarter to around one in five in recent years but this is still well above the average for the subjects that they offer. Provision for disabled students is excellent, with award-winning information produced for those with disabilities, trained support staff in every academic school as well as in the libraries and special modules to help dyslexics. The campus also houses the North East Regional Access Centre, which assesses the learning support requirements of students with disabilities and specific learning difficulties. There is special provision among the 2,200 residential places.

The university is in the top half of the table for student satisfaction, with law undergraduates emerging as the most satisfied in the country in the 2009 National Student Survey. English, languages and psychology also produced high scores. Sunderland was less successful in the latest 2008 Research Assessment Exercise, although more than half of the 16 subject areas contained at least some world-leading work. Communication, cultural and media studies produced by the far best grades, but history and English also did well. The law department has now incorporated space law into their degree, the first module of its kind in the UK.

Sunderland itself is fiercely proud of its identity and has the advantage of a coastal location. The leisure facilities are better than one might imagine: the city has the north east's only Olympic-sized swimming pool and only dry ski slope, as well as Europe's biggest climbing wall and a theatre showing West End productions. Those in search of more cultural events or serious nightlife head for Newcastle, which is less than half an hour away by Metro.

Undergraduate Fees and Bursaries
» Fees for UK/EU students: £3,290
» International student fees: £8,550
» Bursary on full grant: household income up to £25K: £525
» Bursary on partial grant: household income up to £39.3K: £525.
» Scholarships based on circumstances or by competition.
» For full details see the university's website: www.sunderland.ac.uk/fees

Students
Undergraduates:	8,315	(8,845)
Postgraduates:	1,880	(990)
Mature students:	34.4%	
Overseas students:	15.1%	
Applications per place:	4.0	
From state-sector schools:	98.2%	
From working-class homes:	45.0%	

For detailed information about fees, grants and bursaries and how they work, see chapter 7.

Accommodation
Number of places and costs refer to 2010–11
University provided places: 1,640 beds in Halls, 105 (Managed Houses/Head Tenancy Scheme).
Percentage Catered: 0%
Self Catered Costs: £1852.62 (shared twin room; 40 weeks) – £3,948.35 (en suite; 50 weeks)
First-year undergraduates have priority, followed by all EU students (certain circumstances apply).
International students: as above
Contact: www.sunderland.ac.uk/residentialservices

University of Surrey

Surrey has been one of the recent success stories of the university world, remaining true to its technological history while building a strong research base and a degree of financial independence envied by its peers. Even some of the arts degrees carry a BSc and are highly vocational: four out of five undergraduates in all subjects undertake work experience. Placements of one (or two half) years, often taken abroad, mean that most degrees last four years. The format and the subject balance combine to keep Surrey near the top of the graduate employment league, as well as producing a healthy research income. Indeed, it has taken to describing itself as the "University for Jobs" to ram the point home. Recent expansion in healthcare, human sciences and performing arts has added to the traditional strengths in science and engineering.

The mix has been proving popular: applications were up 13 per cent at the start of 2010 in a unique year when that figure was actually below the national average. This followed growth of 60 per cent over the previous three years while average entry scores rose to 372 points on the UCAS tariff. The increased demand for places has come at an opportune time: the university is planning to boost its numbers further, partly through overseas ventures. An international institute in the Chinese city of Dalian, in partnership with Dongbei University, is the first of these. Nearer home, Surrey has taken in the Guildford School of Acting, launching its first degree in English literature in 2008.

All students are encouraged to enrol for a course at the European language centre, and a growing number of degrees, including a new range in engineering, have a language component. The cosmopolitan feel is enhanced by one of the largest proportions of overseas students at any university – a feat which won Surrey a Queen's Award for Export Achievement. The 2,700 foreign students come from 140 different countries.

More than half of the work submitted for the 2008 Research Assessment Exercise was considered world-leading or internationally excellent. Electrical and electronic engineering was ranked second in the country, while health and medical sciences, sociology and general engineering were in the top 10 in their fields. Another indication of the university's research strength lies in the growing proportion of income derived from sources other than Government grants: up from 10 per cent to about 70 per cent in little over a decade. The Surrey Research Park is one of only three science parks still owned, funded and managed by the university that opened it, helping Surrey to amass one of the highest proportions of private funding at any British university.

Scores in the National Student Survey

Guildford
Surrey GU2 7XH

0800 980 3200 (enquiries)
ug-enquiries@surrey.ac.uk
www.surrey.ac.uk
www.ussu.co.uk

The Times Rankings
Overall Ranking: **32**

Student satisfaction:	=32	(78%)
Research quality:	=33	(2.1)
Entry standards:	=28	(372)
Student–staff ratio:	=62	(18.0)
Services & facilities/student:	39	(£1,515)
Expected completion rate:	=57	(83.5%)
Good honours:	39	(68.1%)
Graduate prospects:	9	(79.6%)

have improved. Chemical, process and energy engineering received a 100 per cent rating, whilst civil engineering, aerospace engineering, economics, sociology, computer science and mechanically based engineering also produced very high levels of satisfaction in 2009. Both the proportions of undergraduates from working-class homes and from areas without a tradition of higher education are lower than average for the university's subjects and entry standards, but the statistics agency has acknowledged that the explanation lies largely in the university's location. The projected dropout rate, however, had risen to more than 14 per cent in the latest survey, slipping above the university's benchmark.

The compact campus is a ten-minute walk from the centre of Guildford. Most of the buildings date from the late 1960s, but the new business school and the gleaming European Institute of Health and Medical Sciences offer a striking contrast. Shaped like a giant ship's prow, the steel and glass building houses the large nursing and midwifery departments. The campus includes two lakes, playing fields and enough residential accommodation to enable all first years to live in. A second campus, adjacent to the Stag Hill headquarters, is now being developed.

The new postgraduate medical school is intended to be the first stage in the development of a health campus, which will also contain more residential places for students and staff, as well as other academic buildings, leisure and sporting facilities. The ambitious £35-million Surrey Sports Park development is well underway and is expected to be completed in 2010. The vast facilities will include three multipurpose halls and a 50-metre swimming pool as well as outdoor pitches, tennis and squash courts, two floodlit artificial pitches and a health and fitness suite.

Guildford has plenty of cultural and recreational facilities, but riotous nightclubs are not encouraged. The campus is the centre of social life, and has seen recent improvements to leisure facilities. The proximity of London (35 minutes by train) is an attraction to many students, but also helps account for the high cost of living, which is not mitigated by the allowances available in the capital.

Undergraduate Fees and Bursaries

» Fees for UK/EU students: £3,290
» International student fees: £10,000–£12,500
» Bursary on full grant: household income up to £25K: household income up to £10K: £2,100; household income up to £25K: sliding scale.
» Bursary on partial grant: household income up to £35K: sliding scale.
» Scholarships based on circumstances or by competition.
» For full details see the university's website: www2.surrey.ac.uk/undergraduate/fees

Students

Undergraduates:	**8,420**	**(1,855)**
Postgraduates:	**3,160**	**(2,315)**
Mature students:	**14.2%**	
Overseas students:	**15.4%**	
Applications per place:	**5.6**	
From state-sector schools:	**93.3%**	
From working-class homes:	**28.0%**	

For detailed information about fees, grants and bursaries and how they work, see chapter 7.

Accommodation

Number of places and costs refer to 2010–11
University-provided places: 4,851
Percentage catered: 0%
Self-catered costs: £61–£131 a week.
All first years are guaranteed a place.
International non-EU students are guaranteed accommodation for the whole of their course. Remaining places are allocated to final year students.
Contact: www.surrey.ac.uk/Accommodation

University of Sussex

Sussex is on the brink of the top 20 in this year's *Times* league table, after a prodigious rise of 14 places, the most by any university in the top half of the ranking. Its reputation was enhanced by good results in the 2008 Research Assessment Exercise, when almost 60 per cent of an unusually large submission was rated as world-leading or internationally excellent. But it has benefited this year from improved satisfaction levels and the impact of a major campus development project. The university, which also does well in world rankings, now generates more than a third of its income from private sources, largely in research contracts.

There has been dramatic improvement in Sussex's performance in the National Student Survey over the past three years, propelling the university towards the top 30 for satisfaction levels. The results in 2009 showed 100 per cent satisfaction in molecular biology, biophysics and biochemistry, while anatomy, physiology and pathology, history, chemistry and philosophy also scored well. Applications were up 32 per cent at the start of 2010, well above the national average, after reduced demand in the two previous years.

The university is aiming to improve the student experience further with the introduction of the Sussex Plus initiative, which will provide recognition for students' voluntary work and other extracurricular activities. As part of a focus on flexible learning, the library has introduced 24-hour opening during term-time and many lectures are available online for students to download. The interdisciplinary approach that has always been Sussex's trademark has been re-examined to adapt this 1960s concept for the 21st century. An academic restructuring exercise has produced 12 schools of study to improve students' access to support.

Arts and social science students take the biggest share of places, but the life sciences are not far behind. The newly created School of Business, Management and Economics, which opened in 2009, offers a portfolio of undergraduate and postgraduate business and management programmes. The new School of Global Studies was opened officially at the end of 2009 by CNN presenter and former student Becky Anderson, who anchored a live link-up to academic staff and students working in California and India.

Sussex is committed to taking candidates with no family tradition of higher education and has much larger numbers of mature students than most of its peer group of institutions. The proportion of working-class students is marginally lower than the national average for the university's subjects and entry grades, but this is attributed to the university's south coast location. The projected dropout rate has been improving

Sussex House
Falmer
Brighton BN1 9RH

01273 678416 (admissions)
ug.admissions@sussex.ac.uk
www.sussex.ac.uk
www.bsms.ac.uk
www.ussu.info

The Times Rankings
Overall Ranking: **21**

Student satisfaction:	=32	(78%)
Research quality:	17	(2.6)
Entry standards:	30	(371)
Student–staff ratio:	=33	(15.2)
Services & facilities/student:	45	(£1,428)
Expected completion rate:	29	(90.8%)
Good honours:	6	(80.0%)
Graduate prospects:	28	(72.6%)

and, despite rising to 9 per cent in the latest figures, remains below the university's benchmark.

The university is based within the South Downs, in a designated Area of Outstanding Natural Beauty, four miles from the centre of Brighton. The university is currently completing a £100-million campus development plan, which will refurbish Sir Basil Spence's original buildings and add new ones. A £10-million state-of-the-art teaching building is due for completion in 2010. Student accommodation has also been upgraded – there are more than 3,000 residential places on campus, including rooms in newly built halls offering en-suite rooms – and there are plans to increase campus accommodation still further. All first-year students are guaranteed a place in university-managed accommodation if they meet the deadline for applications.

Relations with neighbouring Brighton University are good. The two institutions succeeded in a joint bid for a medical school, which opened in 2003 and has since recorded big increases in applications. The Brighton and Sussex Medical School is split between the Royal Sussex County Hospital and the two universities' Falmer campuses.

Sussex has always attracted overseas students in large numbers (including former South African President, Thabo Mbeki) and has seen big increases recently. It was voted the best university experience in England for the third year running in the 2009 International Student Barometer. But a high proportion of the remaining students are from the London area, where many return at weekends. As a result, the well-appointed campus can be quiet then, although there is no shortage of social events, and Brighton has plenty to offer. Sports facilities are good, and the university has launched initiatives in basketball and hockey to entice top performers.

Undergraduate Fees and Bursaries

» Fees for UK/EU students: £3,290
» International student fees: £10,475–£14,050
   £23,678 (medicine)
» Bursary on full grant: household income up to £25K: £1,000
» Bursary on partial grant: subject and academic bursaries are available.
» Scholarships based on circumstances or by competition.
» For full details see the university's website: www.sussex.ac.uk/study/funding

Students

Undergraduates:	**8,045**	(1,590)
Postgraduates:	**1,795**	(930)
Mature students:	**16.7%**	
Overseas students:	**10.4%**	
Applications per place:	**4.7**	
From state-sector schools:	**88.2%**	
From working-class homes:	**23.8%**	

For detailed information about fees, grants and bursaries and how they work, see chapter 7.

Accommodation

Number of places and costs refer to 2010–11
University-provided places: 3,440
Percentage catered: 0%
Self-catered costs: £65–£110 a week.
First-year students are guaranteed accommodation if conditions are met.
International students: given priority providing conditions are met.
Contact: housing@sussex.ac.uk

Swansea University

Swansea's attractive coastal location and easy access from outside Wales have helped to make it a popular choice for students. Total applications were up by 24 per cent at the start of 2010, when those from overseas had risen by nearly half. Most of those who take up places seem to enjoy their time there: Swansea has won awards for the best student experience in the UK and has become established among the best performers in the National Student Survey. The university has been in and around the top 25 in every year of the survey, with archaeology, physical geography and environmental science, classics and zoology registering particularly high levels of satisfaction in 2009.

Swansea became independent of the University of Wales in 2007 and entrants in 2011 will receive a Swansea degree. Independence is intended to reflect confidence in the future, as well as helping with international recruitment and research partnerships. There are now about 500 degree courses in the modular scheme, and undergraduates are encouraged to stray outside their specialist area in their first year.

The university has links to more than 90 European institutions and offers many degrees that include opportunities to study abroad. It has won European funding for some of its projects, including Graduate Opportunities Wales, which steers students towards small firms through industrial placements and vacation jobs.

The most important academic development, however, has come with the opening of the School of Medicine and the subsequent development of a full four-year graduate entry medical degree, launched in 2009. Previous entrants have spent half of their course in Cardiff, but the new degree is linked to a new University NHS Trust and the £50-million Institute of Life Science. The institute's six-storey building is home to the IBM "Blue C" Supercomputer, one of the fastest computers in the world dedicated to life science research.

Another recent addition is the £4.3-million Digital Technium Building, housing the media and communication studies department. And the university's commitment to aerospace engineering recently included investment in a £250,000 single-seat flight simulator facility, housed in the School of Engineering. In April 2010 the university also submitted a planning application for a new science park. The university plans to develop a science and innovation campus within Swansea Bay and the Western Valleys region. If successful, work is expected to begin by 2013.

Despite its international links, Swansea has not forgotten its local responsibilities. The Department of Adult and Community Education teaches mature students in

Singleton Park
Swansea SA2 8PP

01792 295111
admissions@swansea.ac.uk
www.swansea.ac.uk
www.swansea-union.co.uk

The Times Rankings
Overall Ranking: **49**

Student satisfaction:	=22	(79%)
Research quality:	=44	(1.7)
Entry standards:	=51	(299)
Student–staff ratio:	=28	(14.9)
Services & facilities/student:	68	(£1,227)
Expected completion rate:	35	(88.1%)
Good honours:	=78	(56.0%)
Graduate prospects:	89	(58.4%)

locations throughout the Valleys and elsewhere in South Wales. Compacts with the region's schools encourage students in areas of economic disadvantage to aspire to higher education.

Swansea makes a particular effort to cater for disabled students, which are coordinated through a £250,000 assessment and training centre. Other access measures have been successful: almost 10 per cent of the students come from areas of low participation in higher education, while the 95 per cent share of places going to applicants from state schools and colleges is significantly higher than the UK average for the university's courses and entry grades. The projected dropout rate is below the benchmark set for the university, at less than 11 per cent.

The attractive parkland campus two miles from the centre of Swansea overlooks the sea and offers ready access to the Gower Peninsula, the UK's first Area of Outstanding Natural Beauty. Apart from Singleton Abbey, the neo-Gothic mansion which houses the administration, most of the buildings are modern. The 1,800 computers available for student use represent one of the best ratios at any university. The university has recently opened two new halls of residence, providing a further 350 study bedrooms that takes the total to over 3,000.

The university's £20-million Sports Village includes a 50-metre pool, a warm-up pool, athletics track, all-weather pitches, indoor athletics training centre and gym, which attract top performers. The swimming pool is the Wales National Pool and is one of only five facilities in the UK to be awarded Intensive Training Centre status. The campus is the focal point of most students' leisure activities, but the city has a good range of leisure facilities, including the new LC2 Leisure Centre, which includes Wales' largest indoor water-park and the world's first deep water standing wave machine – the Boardrider.

Undergraduate Fees and Bursaries

» Fees for UK/EU students: £3,290
» International student fees: £9,500–£12,200
» Bursary on full grant: household income up to £18,370: £329
» The university does not award bursaries for students on partial maintenance grants.
» Scholarships based on circumstances or by competition.
» For full details see the university's website: www.swansea.ac.uk/undergraduate/money

Students

Undergraduates:	**9,365**	(2,530)
Postgraduates:	**1,395**	(730)
Mature students:	**18.1%**	
Overseas students:	**8.1%**	
Applications per place:	**3.5**	
From state-sector schools:	**95.1%**	
From working-class homes:	**31.9%**	

For detailed information about fees, grants and bursaries and how they work, see chapter 7.

Accommodation

Number of places and costs refer to 2010–11
University-provided places: about 3,200
Percentage catered: 11%
Catered costs: £97.00 – £105.50 a week.
Self-catered costs: £71 (standard) – £105 (en suite) a week.
First-year students holding a firm offer are guaranteed accommodation if conditions are met.
International students: offered up to 3 years.
Contact: www.swansea.ac.uk/accommodation
accommodation@swansea.ac.uk

Swansea Metropolitan University

Although university status arrived only in 2008, Swansea Met can trace its history back more than 150 years. However, it does not appear in the main league table or in any of the subject tables because the new university has again instructed the Higher Education Statistics Agency not to release data on its performance. Those figures that are available suggest that it would have appeared in the lower reaches of the table, but not right at the bottom.

The 25 academics entered for the 2008 Research Assessment Exercise represented the smallest submission at any UK university, for example. But there was some world-leading research in three of the four subject areas in which the university was assessed. Engineering produced the best results. Every faculty has a research director, and a series of research centres is planned.

Similarly, results in the last four National Student Surveys have been disappointing, and Swansea Met ranked only just outside the bottom 10 universities in 2009. Business and administrative studies, along with tourism, transport and travel, were the only subjects to achieve a satisfaction rating of 85 per cent or higher in the survey.

Swansea Met is divided into three faculties: applied design and engineering, art and design, and humanities. Of around 5,500 students, just more than half are full-time undergraduates, almost half of whom are studying education or the humanities, and a third of whom are over 21 on entry. Surprisingly, given the mix of subjects, more of them are male than female. Two thirds of the undergraduates come from within 45 miles of Swansea, but there is also a long-established tradition of overseas recruitment, which accounts for almost 7 per cent of the places.

Based around the centre of Swansea, the new university is gradually developing an urban campus. There are four sites close to the city centre and another high above the city, overlooking Swansea Bay, for education and the humanities. The main Mount Pleasant campus is the largest in terms of student numbers, hosting design and engineering, business and leisure courses. Its automotive engineering degrees – especially those focused on motorsport – are probably now the best-known feature of the university.

The nearby Dynevor site has seen the most recent development, with £12.5 million spent on such ventures as an impressive new building for art, design and media, which was rated excellent in the now dated teaching quality assessments. All the faculty's students undertake an "external project" with a company or outside organisation, which has improved employment prospects in a

Mount Pleasant
Swansea SA1 6ED

01792 481010 (admissions)
enquiry@smu.ac.uk
www.smu.ac.uk
www.metsu.org

The Times Rankings

Swansea Metropolitan blocked the release of data from the Higher Education Statistics Agency and so we cannot give any ranking information.

notoriously difficult group of subjects. The two smaller sites are the former college of art, which focuses on the university's internationally rated work on architectural stained glass, and the former BBC building, where the music technology degree is located.

University status arrived at an opportune moment for, while other universities in Wales were experiencing a serious downturn in applications at the beginning of 2008, the decline was the smallest in the Principality. The demand for places dropped in 2009, when most universities saw healthy increases, but Swansea Met shared in the applications boom of 2010, with a 37 per cent increase at the start of the year.

Efforts to widen participation in higher education are high on the new university's agenda. More than four undergraduates in ten have a working-class background and a high proportion come from areas with little tradition of higher education. Almost all the students are state educated. However, the projected dropout rate is well above average for the university's courses and entry grades, with more than one in five, not expected to complete their course in the expected time.

There are fewer than 320 residential places – not enough for all first years – but private housing is plentiful and reasonably priced. The city has seen considerable development recently and has a good range of pubs and clubs. The university's sports facilities are not extensive, but the nearby Gower Peninsula, officially an Area of Outstanding Natural Beauty, is a prime location for surfers and walkers. A Swansea Met PGCE student from Mauritius will be part of the French sailing team's coaching staff for the 2012 Olympic Games.

Undergraduate Fees and Bursaries

- » Fees for UK/EU students: £3,290
- » International student fees: £7,500*
- » Bursary on full grant: household income up to £25K: £329 plus £500 if living more than 45 miles from university
- » Bursary on partial grant: £500 if living more than 45 miles from University (UK & EU students).
- » Scholarships based on circumstances or by competition.
- » For full details see the university's website: www.smu.ac.uk/index.php/potential-students/bursaries

*Figures for 2009–10

Students

From state-sector schools:	**98.7%**
From working-class homes:	**40.6%**

For detailed information about fees, grants and bursaries and how they work, see chapter 7.

Accommodation

Number of places and costs refer to 2009–10
University-provided places: 318
Percentage catered: 0%
Self-catered costs: £50.25 (twin) – £67.25 (en suite) a week (40 weeks).
First years cannot be guaranteed accommodation. Residential restrictions apply.
International students: guaranteed if conditions met and application received by 31 August.
Contact: accommodation@smu.ac.uk; 01792 482082

Teesside University

Teesside was *Times Higher Education*'s University of the Year for 2009, the first post-1992 institution to win the award, for its "outstanding regional economic strategy and strong financial performance." But if that sounds less than wholeheartedly student-focused, above average and improving results in the National Student Survey (NSS) suggest otherwise. The university's mission statement promises a "vibrant and effective learning community" with high academic standards that is committed to social inclusion, as well as benefiting the local economy.

The 2009 NSS showed 100 per cent satisfaction among the university's history students, with nursing, law and psychology all scoring around 95 per cent. Teesside is also the top-ranked UK university for learning, living and support in the International Student Barometer. Middlesbrough has never been considered a fashionable student destination, but the demand for places held up while some former polytechnics were having recruitment problems. Now the number of international students has soared and total applications were up by more than a third at the start of 2010.

Teesside has long been among the leading new universities for the proportion of leavers going into graduate-level jobs or further training. The university also improved its grades in the 2008 Research Assessment Exercise, albeit with only a small proportion of its academics submitting work. Thirty per cent of the research was considered world-leading or internationally excellent, with computer science and history achieving the best results. Five research-led institutes will focus on digital innovation, health, culture, social science and technology.

Official performance indicators also show the university well ahead of the access benchmarks calculated by the Higher Education Statistics Agency. It takes more undergraduates than any other UK university (over a quarter) from areas of low participation in higher education, while almost half come from working-class homes. The projected dropout rate has improved, partly because of a programme that supports non-traditional students, funded by the European Union, and is now well below the national average for the courses and entry qualifications.

Over 3,000 students are taking Teesside courses at local further education colleges, which are also involved in the growing range of full-time and part-time two-year Foundation degrees. The university has a higher education centre attached to one of the colleges in Darlington and is investing a new £13-million campus in Darlington. The Passport scheme offers help and guidance to students considering going to university. However, the university's best-known access

---

7 Borough Road
Middlesbrough TS1 3BA

01642 218121 (switchboard)
enquiries@tees.ac.uk
www.tees.ac.uk
www.utsu.org.uk

The Times Rankings
Overall Ranking: **=90**

Student satisfaction:	=22	(79%)
Research quality:	=95	(0.2)
Entry standards:	88	(258)
Student–staff ratio:	=79	(19.5)
Services & facilities/student:	96	(£1,043)
Expected completion rate:	108	(71.2%)
Good honours:	86	(53.5%)
Graduate prospects:	=78	(60.0%)

initiative targets a much younger age group. The prize-winning Meteor scheme gives primary school children a taste of higher education, with university students acting as mentors while earning some useful extra cash and gaining experience of working in schools.

There are more than 24,000 undergraduates, two thirds of them taking part-time courses, and around a third of full-time students are over 21 on entry. The 10,000 health students are by far the largest group in the university, but Teesside is also strong in niche markets such as computer games design and animation, sport and exercise, forensic science and health-related courses like physiotherapy and radiography. A new BA in economic crime management, to be launched in September 2010, will be the first of its kind in the UK.

More than £120 million has been spent in recent years on the town-centre campus. A new sport and health sciences building with dentistry training and hydrotherapy facilities is due to open in 2010. Recent developments include a £10-million centre for creative technologies, for computing, media and design students, and a £12-million Institute of Digital Innovation, which supports Teesside's bid to turn Middlesbrough into a Digital City. Over 180 new graduate businesses have been incubated on campus since 2001 and Teesside has been awarded £5 million to help it develop as a business-facing university.

Pioneering tailored-made courses with industry are proving popular. Computer provision is generous, with 2,500 workstations available for student use. Specialist facilities for those studying computer games design, animation and digital media include a new digital sound and TV studio which can create special effects.

Middlesbrough has more nightlife than sceptics might imagine, and the booming student population has attracted new pubs, cafés and student-orientated shops in and around the Southfield Road area. The cost of living is another attraction: university rents are reasonable and the lively students' union has twice won the title of Students' Union of the Year. Outdoor sports facilities, shared with Durham University, include a £1.5-million watersports centre on the River Tees and Elite Athlete bursaries are available. The new Middlesbrough Institute of Modern Art (mima) is also putting the town on the cultural map and there is a full programme of Culture on Campus events during the year.

Undergraduate Fees and Bursaries

» Fees for UK/EU students: £3,290
» International student fees: £8,950
» Bursary on full grant: household income up to £25K: £750
» Bursary on partial grant: household income up to £31K: £750
» Scholarships based on circumstances or by competition.
» For full details see the university's website: www.tees.ac.uk/funding

Students

Undergraduates:	**8,050**	**(15,345)**
Postgraduates:	**1,430**	**(2,145)**
Mature students:	**32.8%**	
Overseas students:	**6.7%**	
Applications per place:	**3.3**	
From state-sector schools:	**99.2%**	
From working-class homes:	**49.6%**	

For detailed information about fees, grants and bursaries and how they work, see chapter 7.

Accommodation

Number of places and costs refer to 2010–11
University-provided places: 1,124
Percentage catered: 0%
Self-catered costs: £49–£84 a week (residences, 37 weeks);
£54–£59 a week (managed housing, 38 weeks)
University managed residences are reserved exclusively for first years.
International students: as above.
Contact: 01642 342255; accommodation@tees.ac.uk; www.tees.ac.uk/sections/accommodation

Thames Valley University

Having tried the expansion route, Thames Valley has now decided to focus on its original home in Ealing, West London, while also building up its base in Reading. The Slough campus, where the university built an award-winning learning resources centre designed by Richard Rogers, will close in the summer of 2010. Its 1,000 full-time students, two thirds of whom are on pre-registration nursing courses, will move to Reading, leaving just part-time business courses and some post-registration nursing in Slough, at a different site. The restructuring will not alter TVU's aim to become the country's leading university for employer engagement, with an accent on the creative industries and entrepreneurship.

The Reading campus, a former college site that is still being redeveloped, has been mainly concerned with further education with some locally focused higher education. Now, however, it may host social work degrees transferred from Reading University, as well as the new nursing portfolio. The Ealing campus has a more traditional university feel and is being upgraded at a cost of almost £10 million. In addition, a landmark building in Brentford, not far from the Ealing campus, will remain the headquarters of one of the largest healthcare faculties in Britain. It contains 850 residential places, as well as teaching facilities.

The university has recovered from a traumatic period at the end of the 1990s, when barely 30 degrees were left, following official criticism of academic standards and a collapse in student demand. TVU is virtually unrecognisable from those dark days, but there was a hitch in its development when a failure to hit previous recruitment targets led to cuts of nearly 12 per cent in its budget for 2009–10. The university had to shed staff to balance the books, but it will have been delighted that applications were up at the start of 2010 by a staggering 75 per cent.

Courses are now concentrated in three faculties – arts, professional studies, and health and human sciences. Many further education programmes are being extended into degrees or professional qualifications. Amid the reconstruction, new honours degrees have been launched in areas such as video production, 3D design, entrepreneurship, computing and information systems. The portfolio of two-year Foundation degrees is growing, with employers such as Compaq, Ealing Studios and the Savoy Hotel Group helping to provide courses. Some are run in conjunction with Stratford-upon-Avon College – one of a number of partner institutions.

Nursing courses are popular and well regarded, while the School of Hospitality and Tourism is recognised by the Académie Culinaire de France for its culinary arts

St Mary's Road
Ealing
London W5 5RF

0800 036 8888 (admissions)
admissions@tvu.ac.uk
www.tvu.ac.uk
www.tvusu.co.uk

The Times Rankings
Overall Ranking: **106**

Student satisfaction:	=102	(72%)
Research quality:	=95	(0.2)
Entry standards:	109	(201)
Student–staff ratio:	97	(20.6)
Services & facilities/student:	47	(£1,421)
Expected completion rate:	111	(67.2%)
Good honours:	=102	(49.2%)
Graduate prospects:	83	(59.6%)

programmes. The London College of Music, which is part of TVU, has some of the longest-established music technology courses in the country. The university has improved its scores in the National Student Survey, but was still in the bottom 20 in 2009. Only tourism, transport and travel achieved a satisfaction rating of more than 90 per cent, although accounting and business studies managed better than 85 per cent. Fewer than half of the final-year undergraduates in film cinematics and photography, communications and information studies, and other creative arts were satisfied overall with their course.

A policy of open access puts the university at a disadvantage on other measures in our ranking. However, the projected dropout rate has fallen from almost 29 per cent to 22 per cent, almost in line the norm for a university with similar entry requirements and curriculum. Three quarters of the students are over 24, and about 60 per cent are female. Nearly half of the undergraduates come from working-class homes. The university is also very ethnically diverse with only one third of undergraduates of white, European origin.

TVU improved its ratings considerably in the 2008 Research Assessment Exercise, but entered only a small proportion of its academics. Only nursing and midwifery was judged to have world-leading research.

The town-centre sites in Ealing and Brentford are linked by a free bus service. The busy Ealing base is within easy reach of central London without the metropolitan hassle that students encounter at some institutions in the capital. Almost half of the students are from London or Berkshire, and there is an unexpectedly large contingent of international students.

Residential accommodation is growing and the Paragon building, in Brentford, won *Building* magazine's Major Housing Project of the Year award. However, students who rely on private housing find the cost of living high. There is a football ground and cricket pitch close to the Ealing campus, but otherwise sports facilities are limited.

Undergraduate Fees and Bursaries
- Fees for UK/EU students: £3,290
- International student fees: £7,830–£9,170*
- Bursary on full grant: household income up to £25K: £1,060*
- Bursary on partial grant: household income £25K–£40K: £530.*
- Scholarships based on circumstances or by competition.
- For full details see the university's website: www.tvu.ac.uk/students/undergraduate/Scholarships_and_bursaries.jsp

*Figures for 2009–10

Students
Undergraduates:	7,455	(7,580)
Postgraduates:	585	(1,490)
Mature students:	54.8%	
Overseas students:	15.2%	
Applications per place:	2.8	
From state-sector schools:	98.6%	
From working-class homes:	49.6%	

For detailed information about fees, grants and bursaries and how they work, see chapter 7.

Accommodation
Number of places and costs refer to 2009–10
University-provided places: 839
Percentage catered: 0%
Self-catered costs: £117–£161 a week.
First years will be prioritised for accommodation at Ealing if conditions are met; accommodation at Reading is also allocated on a distance from campus basis.
International students: same as above.
Contact: uas@tvu.ac.uk
reading.homes@tvu.ac.uk

Trinity Saint David, University of Wales

The new University of Wales Trinity Saint David will welcome its first students in September 2010. But approval by the Privy Council was still awaited as this *Guide* went to press and was already too late for a change to the UCAS process for entry in 2011. As a result, this year's applications will still go to Lampeter University of Wales or Trinity University College, the two partners in the merger that will form the new institution.

In the whole of England and Wales, only Oxford and Cambridge were awarding degrees before Lampeter, which claimed to be the smallest publicly funded university in Europe before the merger. It will continue to make a virtue of its size in the new collegiate set-up by stressing its friendly atmosphere and intimate teaching style. With the former Trinity University College 23 miles away in Carmarthen, Lampeter will remain a quiet, rural outpost.

The new institution will constitute a more substantial academic unit, with greater financial security, to serve West Wales. The Welsh Assembly Government and the Higher Education Funding Council for Wales have invested £18 million in the merger to produce a "distinctive and unique curriculum with a strong emphasis on Welsh cultural heritage and bilingualism". The aim is to serve the region, but also to attract students from all around the world through the Confucius Centre, the Islamic Studies Centre and the Welsh American Academy.

The new title echoes Lampeter's original name of St David's College. As the University of Wales, Lampeter, applications had been dropping, but that trend was reversed with a 38 per cent increase at the start of 2010. The number of entrants had already doubled in 2009, as more candidates accepted their offers. Those who go are enthusiastic about Lampeter: it has recorded high levels of satisfaction in every year of the National Student Survey, finishing in the top 20 in 2009, when history and media studies produced the best scores.

Based on an ancient castle and modelled on an Oxbridge college, St David's College was established to train young men for the Anglican ministry. The original quadrangle remains and the chapel is in daily use. There have been significant changes in recent few years – notably a big expansion in distance learning and the introduction of such subjects as Chinese studies, anthropology, IT, management, and film and media studies. A degree in Voluntary Sector Studies, which won a Queen's Anniversary Prize, is offered part-time and by distance learning so that students can combine study with volunteering and personal commitments.

Arts-dominated Lampeter is best known

College Street
Lampeter
Ceredigion SA48 7ED

01570 422351 (switchboard)
admissions@lamp.ac.uk
www.lamp.ac.uk
www.lampetersu.co.uk

The Times Rankings for Lampeter
Overall Ranking: **85**

Student satisfaction:	=46	(77%)
Research quality:	=54	(1.1)
Entry standards:	84	(262)
Student–staff ratio:	=59	(17.8)
Services & facilities/student:	98	(£1,029)
Expected completion rate:	107	(73.0%)
Good honours:	=84	(53.6%)
Graduate prospects:	95	(57.2%)

for theology, but archaeology produced the best results by far in the 2008 Research Assessment Exercise. The small campus includes a mosque for the growing number of Muslim students attracted by the well-endowed programme of Islamic studies. Media studies, which benefits from a well-equipped media centre for film and television students, is also growing in popularity. A new research centre opened in 2008, housing the Founders' Library collections and the historical archives.

Lampeter is deep in Welsh-speaking rural West Wales, like its new partner, the university has strong bilingual policies. The university also takes Welsh to a wider audience, with the only university course teaching the language over the internet. Although only four hours from London and two from Cardiff, Lampeter's geographical position could be a problem for the unprepared. The town has just 4,000 inhabitants, with among the lowest crime rates in Britain, and the nearest station is more than 20 miles away.

As a university college, Trinity did not qualify for inclusion in this *Guide*, although it was part of the University of Wales. With 2,200 students, including part-timer, it was hardly large, but still twice the size of Lampeter. Established in 1848, it is affiliated to the Church in Wales, but recruits students of all faiths and none. Trinity has a long history of teacher training, with arts and social studies the only other faculty. Results in the National Student Survey have not been as good as Lampeter's, but the overall satisfaction rate of 82 per cent was close to the average for Wales.

Carmarthen is a county town of 18,000 people with reasonably-priced accommodation for the few first-year students who fail to secure a place in one of the three halls of residence. Less remote as well as larger than Lampeter, it has a railway station and is not far from the end of the M4 for car drivers.

Undergraduate Fees and Bursaries
Lampeter and Trinity University College

- » Fees for UK/EU students: £3,290
- » International student fees: £9,348
- » Bursary on full grant; household income up to £25K: £329
- » Scholarships based on circumstances or competition.
- » For full details see:
  www.lamp.ac.uk/undergraduate/student_finance_ug.html
  www.trinity-cm.ac.uk/en/campuslife/studentfinance

Contact Details
Trinity Saint David
www.trinitysaintdavid.ac.uk

Trinity University College
Carmarthen SA48 7ED
01267 676767
registry@trinity-cm.ac.uk
www.trinity-cm.ac.uk
www.trinitysu.org

Students
Undergraduates:	**2,200***	**(4,730)***
Postgraduates:	**810***	**(765)***
Mature students:	**46.5%**	
Overseas students:	**15.1%**	
Applications per place:	**2.0**	
From state-sector schools:	**94.3%**	
From working-class homes:	**32.5%**	

*Combined student numbers. Other figures refer to Lampeter alone.

For detailed information about fees, grants and bursaries and how they work, see chapter 7.

Accommodation
Number of places and costs refer to 2010-11
L refers to Lampeter, CM to Carmarthen
University-provided places: 500 (L), 512 (CM)
Percentage catered: 0% (L), 44% (CM)
Catered costs: £98 a week; meals for 5 days (CM).
Self-catered costs: £2,171–£2,714 a year (L); £78 a week (CM).
First years can normally be placed in university accommodation.
International students: guaranteed housing for first year.
Contact: www.lamp.ac.uk/accommodation
www.trinity-cm.ac.uk/en/studentservices/accommodation

University of Ulster

Ulster is in the top 20 universities in terms of applications and registered another 14 per cent increase at the start of 2010. The university's reputation has been further enhanced by its strong performance in the 2008 Research Assessment Exercise. Nearly half of its submission was rated as world-leading or internationally excellent, with the University ranked in the top three for biomedical sciences, celtic studies and nursing and midwifery. Results improved in almost all areas, leaving Ulster within sight of neighbouring Queen's University in the research tables.

The university is the only one in Britain with a charter stipulating that there should be courses below degree level. Certificates, diplomas and integrated Foundation years lead on to Honours degrees. Plans to improve and expand all four main sites, at a cost of £200 million, are almost complete. With more Irish students now choosing to stay in the Province to study, there is plenty of scope for expansion, despite the fact that UU already has over 23,000 students, including almost 7,000 part-timers.

There are four campuses – at Coleraine, Jordanstown (seven miles outside Belfast), Magee in Londonderry, and in Belfast city centre. Each campus has a distinct character and while some courses are offered at more than one campus, there is a degree of specialisation across the campuses. Belfast concentrates on art and design, architecture and hospitality and tourism management. Jordanstown concentrates on business and management, the built environment, computing and engineering, health and sports sciences and social sciences. At Coleraine there is a focus on the environmental and life sciences, humanities and services management, whist at Magee there is a concentration on the creative and performing arts, nursing and social work, computing and engineering, business and management and social sciences.

All undergraduates complete their studies on a single campus which each have well-equipped learning resource centres. Accommodation is guaranteed for first-years students at all four campuses. The university did well in the 2009 National Student Survey, when tourism, transport and travel, sports science and marketing scoring the best individual results.

Early in 2009, the university announced ambitious £250-million capital development plans which will see most of the activity currently based at Jordanstown transferred to the university's Belfast campus, where it has acquired a substantial additional site in the city's Cathedral Quarter. Jordanstown will be retained and developed further as Ireland's sports campus. The university is already well positioned in this regard having

Cromore Road
Coleraine
Co. Londonderry
BT52 1SA

08700 400 700
enquiry via website
www.ulster.ac.uk
www.uusu.org

The Times Rankings
Overall Ranking: **56**

Student satisfaction:	=46	(77%)
Research quality:	=52	(1.2)
Entry standards:	75	(269)
Student–staff ratio:	=44	(15.9)
Services & facilities/student:	43	(£1,480)
Expected completion rate:	92	(77.8%)
Good honours:	58	(61.2%)
Graduate prospects:	84	(58.9%)

won 17 team or individual Irish Universities' Champion-ships across a range of sports during 2008–09. Over £20 million has already been invested here in a new high performance sports centre. Facilities include an indoor sports hall, outdoor and indoor sprint tracks, a strength and conditioning suite, water recovery area and sports science and sports medicine facilities.

A further expansion in student numbers is planned and will be concentrated at Magee where the university has recently signed an option agreement which will see UU almost double its physical footprint in the city. Plans for expansion at Magee include an Institute of Health and Wellbeing and an Institute of Sustainable Technologies. Magee also houses a Centre of Intelligent Systems and the historic Foyle Arts Centre. Further expansion is also planned in the schools of creative arts, computing and electronics as well as nursing.

Coleraine is home to the £11-million Centre for Molecular Biosciences. Building on its expertise, the university also introduced a new programme in pharmacy. A £7.6-million sports centre is also planned.

Ulster has a strong commitment to widening access and is consistently among the top ten universities in terms of admitting students from the less advantaged socio-economic groups. The projected dropout rate had improved in the latest survey but, at more than 21 per cent, was still considerably higher than the benchmark calculated according to the university's subjects and entry grades. A range of scholarships is available including sports scholarships and others for high achievers in economically relevant subjects such as engineering, computing, science and economics.

There has never been a big representation from mainland Britain, but the university's contingent of international students includes many from the Republic of Ireland as well as further afield. The Campus One programme provides an alternative mode of study, offering courses online to students all over the world. With more than half of Ulster's students home based, the university is not always the focus of social life. The exception is the Coleraine campus, although many gravitate towards the nearby seaside towns of Portrush and Portstewart.

Undergraduate Fees and Bursaries

» Fees for UK/EU students: £3,290
» International student fees: £9,020
» Bursary on full grant: household income up to £25K: household income up to £18.8: £1,095; household income up to £21.5K: £640.
» Bursary on partial grant: household income up to £40.2K: £320.
» Scholarships based on circumstances or by competition.
» For full details see the university's website: http://prospectus.ulster.ac.uk/geninfo/how-much-does-it-cost.html

Students

Undergraduates:	**14,925**	(3,490)
Postgraduates:	**1,645**	(3,100)
Mature students:	**20.1%**	
Overseas students:	**8.3%**	
Applications per place:	**5.0**	
From state-sector schools:	**100.0%**	
From working-class homes:	**46.8%**	

For detailed information about fees, grants and bursaries and how they work, see chapter 7.

Accommodation

Number of places and costs refer to 2010–11
University-provided places: 2,300
Percentage catered: 0%
Self-catered costs: average £75 a week (37 weeks).
First-year students are guaranteed accommodation if conditions are met.
International students: same as above.
Contact: accommodation@ulster.ac.uk

University of the Arts London

The collection of world-famous art, design, fashion and media colleges that constituted the London Institute became a university in 2005. With about 30,000 further and higher education students spread through 17 sites around central London, it is the largest arts university in Europe. Unlike the other new foundations of that year, it has a research remit and is already becoming a powerful "brand".

The five component colleges became six when Wimbledon College of Art joined in 2006, bringing an international reputation in theatre design and the UK's largest school of theatre. The founding members, which continue to use their own names and enjoy considerable autonomy, were Camberwell College of Arts, Central Saint Martins College of Art and Design, Chelsea College of Art and Design, London College of Fashion and London College of Communication (formerly the London College of Printing).

Big changes were already under way before the change of title was agreed: a £70-million development programme has produced prestigious new premises for Chelsea College next door to the Tate Gallery, on Millbank, with extensive workshop facilities, studios and an impressive new library. Another £32 million was spent on new headquarters for the College of Communication at the Elephant and Castle, south of the Thames, where a newly built Special Archives and Collections Centre will include the archives of the filmmaker Stanley Kubrick. The college now has Film Academy status.

London's largest open air art gallery was launched in July 2008 on the Parade Ground at the heart of the Chelsea College of Art and Design, funded by a £1.5-million gift from the Rootstein Hopkins Foundation. Summer 2008 also saw the launch of university's first virtual degree show, showcasing final-year students' work online. The Economic Challenge Investment Fund awarded the university £500,000 to support recent arts graduates and creative businesses during the economic downturn.

The next major project will bring Central Saint Martins together on one site for the first time, when it moves to the new King's Cross development in 2011. Published assessments have barely done justice to the eminence of the colleges. But the 2008 Research Assessment Exercise saw half of the university's submission rated as world-leading or internationally excellent – albeit one that involved a relatively low proportion of the academics.

Chelsea and London College of Fashion were jointly awarded a national teaching

---

65 Davies Street
London W1K 5DA

020 7514 6130 (enquiries)
info@arts.ac.uk
www.arts.ac.uk
www.suarts.org

The Times Rankings
Overall Ranking: **86**

Student satisfaction:	111	(63%)
Research quality:	=39	(2.0)
Entry standards:	=60	(280)
Student–staff ratio:	=82	(19.6)
Services & facilities/student:	100	(£1,008)
Expected completion rate:	44	(85.7%)
Good honours:	61	(60.5%)
Graduate prospects:	102	(56.2%)

centre for the arts, focusing on practice-based teaching and learning. All the colleges make good use of visiting lecturers, who keep students abreast of current developments in their field. Arts London had the second lowest score in the latest National Student Survey, but even this was an improvement after being rock bottom for the three previous years. Chemistry and media studies were the only subjects to have scored more than 70 per cent satisfaction in the 2009 survey.

The figures have not affected applications, which have risen every year since the university was established – none more so than at the start of 2010, when applications were up by more than 100 per cent, aided by a change in deadlines for art and design degrees. A number of two-year Foundation degrees have been introduced, including one in interactive games production and another in fashion styling and photography.

The university has been running weekend classes and summer schools in an attempt to broaden the intake, as well as organising a national event to help students with their portfolios, and the proportion of undergraduates from working-class homes is now over a quarter. The projected dropout rate of 13 per cent is slightly higher than average for the subjects on offer.

Students have access to the largest art and design specialist careers information centre in the country, while the pioneering Emerging Artists Programme continues to support graduates in the early years of their careers. A £2-million information technology system links all the sites. The colleges vary considerably in character and facilities, although a single students' union serves them all and a new Student Hub has brought all student services together at the university's central London headquarters. The university is not overprovided with residential accommodation, although there are 12 residences spread around the colleges, providing more than 2,900 beds. House-hunting workshops help those who have to rely on what is inevitably an expensive private housing market. Somewhat stereotypically, the university owns no sports facilities, although it has arranged student discounts with a number of providers.

Undergraduate Fees and Bursaries
» Fees for UK/EU students: £3,290
» International student fees: £12,250
» Bursary on full grant: household income up to £25K: £319*
» Bursary on partial grant: considered for £1,000 University Access Bursary.*
» Scholarships based on circumstances or by competition.
» For full details see the university's website: www.arts.ac.uk/student/money

*Figures for 2009–10

Students
Undergraduates:	12,350	(565)
Postgraduates:	2,045	(860)
Mature students:	23.5%	
Overseas students:	33.3%	
Applications per place:	5.5	
From state-sector schools:	90.6%	
From working-class homes:	29.4%	

For detailed information about fees, grants and bursaries and how they work, see chapter 7.

Accommodation
Number of places and costs refer to 2010–11
University-provided places: 2,774
Percentage catered: 0%
Self-catered costs: £83–£180 a week.

First-year students are offered accommodation if conditions are met. Priority for disabled students and those from outside London.
International students: guaranteed if conditions met.
Contact: www.arts.ac.uk/housing
accommodation@arts.ac.uk

University College London

Such is the breadth and quality of provision at University College London (UCL) that, although part of the University of London, it can fairly describe itself as one of the top multi-faculty institutions in England. Its position in *The Times* rankings has regularly confirmed this and it climbed to fourth place in the world in the QS World University rankings in 2009. UCL's excellence is built on a history of pioneering subjects that have become commonplace in higher education: modern languages, geography and fine arts among them.

The 2008 Research Assessment Exercise provided further confirmation of UCL's academic power, with two thirds of its submission judged to be world-leading or internationally excellent. The top scorers were economics, which saw 95 per cent of its work rated in the top two categories, and computer science and informatics, immunology and infection, environmental sciences and history of art, all of which had at least 80 per cent at this level. Architecture, chemical engineering, cancer studies, law, philosophy and psychology also produced outstanding results.

Already comfortably the largest of London University's colleges, UCL has grown rapidly in the past two decades and can now award its own degrees. It took in a number of specialist schools and institutes at the end of the 1990s. Most were medical or dental, and UCL's medical school is now a large and formidable unit. Its credentials have been strengthened still further with the announcement that UCL will be the sole university partner in the new national medical research centre to be constructed adjacent to St Pancras Station. The centre will undertake cutting-edge research to advance understanding of health and disease.

The various acquisitions mean that there are now outposts in several parts of central and north London, but the main activity remains centred on the original impressive Bloomsbury site. There have been discussions with Camden Council on the creation of a university quarter, linking UCL's buildings and the University College Hospital buildings, together with neighbouring parts of the University of London.

UCL has done better than most London universities in the National Student Survey, with 87 per cent of final-year undergraduates expressing satisfaction in the results published in 2009. Classics, forensic and archaeological science, molecular biology, biophysics and biochemsitry produced the best scores. A growing number of degrees take four years, and most are organised on a modular basis.

About 7,000 of UCL's students are from overseas, nearly half of them postgraduates and a third of them from other EU countries,

Gower Street
London WC1E 6BT

020 7679 2000 (main switchboard)
contact via website
www.ucl.ac.uk
www.uclu.org

The Times Rankings
Overall Ranking: **7**

Student satisfaction:	=32	(78%)
Research quality:	=4	(3.2)
Entry standards:	7	(458)
Student–staff ratio:	1	(8.9)
Services & facilities/student:	7	(£2,124)
Expected completion rate:	=11	(94.8%)
Good honours:	4	(81.0%)
Graduate prospects:	7	(80.8%)

reflecting the college's high international standing. The proportion is likely to rise further in the coming years. All first-year students are helped to make the academic and social adjustment to university life through UCL's Transition Programme, which includes a variety of activities such as peer mentoring and workshops. UCL stresses its commitment to teaching in small groups, especially in the second and subsequent years of degree courses. The approach seems to work: over four-fifths leave with a first or upper second. The projected dropout rate of 5.2 per cent is better than the national average for UCL's courses and entry grades. Applications were up by around 6 per cent at the start of 2010 but, like other universities at the top of the table, it could not match the increases seen elsewhere.

UCL is conscious of its traditions as a college founded to expand access to higher education, but the 35 per cent share of places going to independent school students is one of the highest in Britain. Around one undergraduate in five has a working-class background. Concerted attempts are being made to broaden the intake with summer schools for state-school students, outreach activities and campus-based programmes. UCL is sponsoring a new academy, which it sees as part of its contribution to the local community.

UCL is pioneering the idea of education for global citizenship, ensuring students are given opportunity and encouragement to explore academic ideas from different cultural perspectives and to work on problems of international importance, as well as contributing to their local community and the university's social and cultural life.

The academic pace can be frantic but, close to the West End and with its own theatre and recreational facilities, there is no shortage of leisure options. Students also have immediate access to London University's underused central students' union facilities. Residential accommodation is plentiful and of a good standard. Indoor sports and fitness facilities are close at hand, but the main outdoor pitches, though good enough to attract professional football clubs, are a (free) coach ride away in Hertfordshire. Hockey players have access to Astroturf pitches at the Old Cranleighans ground, in Thames Ditton.

Undergraduate Fees and Bursaries

- » Fees for UK/EU students: £3,290
- » International student fees: £12,770–£16,725 £24,940 (medicine)
- » Bursary on full grant: household income up to £25K: household income up to £14.1K: £2,220; household income up to £16.2K: £1,650 then at least 50% of maintenance grant.
- » Bursary on partial grant: at least 50% of maintenance grant.
- » Scholarships based on circumstances or by competition.
- » For full details see the university's website: www.ucl.ac.uk/prospective-students/undergraduate-study/fees-and-costs

Students

Undergraduates:	**11,820**	**(590)**
Postgraduates:	**6,080**	**(2,720)**
Mature students:	**11.3%**	
Overseas students:	**29.8%**	
Applications per place:	**9.4**	
From state-sector schools:	**64.1%**	
From working-class homes:	**21.1%**	

For detailed information about fees, grants and bursaries and how they work, see chapter 7.

Accommodation

Number of places and costs refer to 2009–10
University-provided places: 4,197 (including 500 intercollegiate places)
Percentage catered: 30%
Catered costs: £91.00–£166.60 a week (37 weeks).
Self-catered costs: £71.68–£153.44 a week (37 weeks).
First years are guaranteed accommodation if conditions are met.
International students: as above.
Contact: Residences@ucl.ac.uk
www.ucl.ac.uk/prospective-students/accommodation

University for the Creative Arts

England's newest university is the product of a merger between two well-established arts institutes straddling Kent and Surrey. Indeed, the first version of its title was the unwieldy University for the Creative Arts at Canterbury, Epsom, Farnham, Maidstone and Rochester, although the multiple locations have since been dropped. The constituent colleges all date back to Victorian times, but university status arrived only in 2008. The location of each college is given in the map below: Canterbury (1), Epsom (2), Farnham (3), Maidstone (4) and Rochester (5).

With about 6,000 students, UCA is already sizeable by the standards of specialist institutions. Applications for 2010 were up by nearly 94 per cent, aided by changes in deadlines for degrees in art and design, but still a staggering figure. With these figures, the university's plan to grow to 9,000 students by 2017 would not seem unrealistic if Government policy allowed. A new campus in Kent is expected by 2017, complementing the university's ambitious expansion aims.

By far the largest enrolment is at Farnham, in Surrey, where more than 2,000 students take courses in art, design, cinematics and communications. There is a purpose-built student village with 350 rooms in the centre of town and two galleries, as well as teaching space and a library and learning centre. The campus boasts Oscar and BAFTA winners in animation in its pre-university days. It is now home to research centres in animation, crafts and sustainable design. Courses range from pre-degree Foundation courses in art and design to degrees in film production, motoring journalism and three-dimensional design.

The other four sites are of similar size in terms of student numbers. The second base in Surrey, at Epsom, specialises in fashion, graphics and new media, although it offers general art and design courses at further education level. There is a modern library and learning resource centre for more than 1,200 students, a bar and café on campus and two halls of residence for 120 students. Degrees include music journalism and fashion promotion and imaging.

The largest of the three campuses in Kent is at Rochester, which offers a full range of art and design, including fashion, photography and specialist design courses. The purpose-built campus is set on a hillside overlooking the city centre and River Medway. Halls of residence with 214 places are close to the campus, which has studio space, library and learning resource centre and a gallery.

The Maidstone campus is in parkland, ten minutes from the centre of town, with

New Dover Road
Canterbury, Kent CT1 3AN

01252 892883 (enquiries)
contact via website
www.ucreative.ac.uk
www.uccasu.com

The Times Rankings
Overall Ranking: **109**

Student satisfaction:	110	(67%)
Research quality:	=60	(0.6)
Entry standards:	=80	(264)
Student–staff ratio:	112	(24.3)
Services & facilities/student:	=25	(£1,672)
Expected completion rate:	=54	(83.8%)
Good honours:	100	(50.0%)
Graduate prospects:	113	(45.3%)

another gallery and extensive library. The integrated teaching and research facilities include a multi-user video editing facility and video studio, printmaking area, animation resources and a specialist photography resource. Courses for more than 900 students encourage interdisciplinary study.

At Canterbury, the accent is on architecture, but there are also degrees in fine art, interior design and more general art and design. The modern site is close to the city centre and contains purpose-built studios, workshops and lecture theatres. The Canterbury School of Architecture is the only such school to remain within a specialist art and design institution, encouraging collaboration between student architects, designers and fine artists.

The university offers four-year degrees, incorporating a Foundation year, as well as the three-year format and two-year Foundation degrees, which can be topped up to produce Honours. However, results in the National Student Survey have been poor in all four years of polling. Although there was improvement in the results published in 2009, the university remained in the bottom three. Although architecture performed well with a 93 per cent satisfaction rating, other results were poor; no other course scored more than 70 per cent.

Many staff are practitioners as well as academics and the colleges have produced a string of famous graduates, such as Tracy Emin, Karen Millen and Zandra Rhodes. There is also a strong research culture, although UCA had only limited success in the 2008 Research Assessment Exercise. Thirty per cent of the university's submission was considered world-leading or internationally excellent, but this left it well down the ranking for art and design.

Undergraduate Fees and Bursaries
» Fees for UK/EU students: £3,290
» International student fees: £7,855–£10,500
» Bursary on full grant: household income up to £25K: £450
» Bursary on partial grant: subject and academic bursaries available.
» Scholarships based on circumstances or by competition.
» For full details see the university's website:
www.ucreative.ac.uk
and follow the "Undergraduate Fees and Finance" link.

Students
Undergraduates:	4,775	(295)
Postgraduates:	135	(80)
Mature students:	20.7%	
Overseas students:	10.9%	
Applications per place:	3.3	
From state-sector schools:	97.3%	
From working-class homes:	38.4%	

For detailed information about fees, grants and bursaries and how they work, see chapter 7.

Accommodation
Places and costs refer to 2009-10
University-provided places: 1,056
Percentage catered: 0%
Self catered costs: £50–£107 a week.
Priority is given to disabled students (new and returning) and new full-time students by distance.
International students: guaranteed housing if application received by mid June
Contact: accommodation@ucreative.ac.uk
www.ucreative.ac.uk

University of Warwick

The most successful of the first wave of new universities from the 1960s, Warwick was derided by many in its early years for its close links with business and industry. Few are critical today. Gordon Brown described it as "one of the great universities, absolutely central to the industrial, scientific and technological future of our country". Research was very highly rated in the 2008 assessments, but the university's mission statement still stresses the extension of access to higher and continuing education and community links.

There is a smaller proportion of independent school students than at most of the leading universities – less than a quarter – although this does not translate into large numbers of working-class undergraduates. The share of places going to students from the lowest social classes and the representation from areas sending few young people to higher education are both close to the national average for Warwick's subjects and entry qualifications. But the mix helps to produce one of the lowest dropout rates in Britain at less than 5 per cent. Warwick puts almost a third of its income from top-up fees into bursaries and financial support – one of the highest proportions among the old universities.

Almost two thirds of the work submitted for the 2008 Research Assessment Exercise was considered world-leading or internationally excellent, placing Warwick among the top 10 universities. Film and television studies, and horticultural research achieved two of the top scores for any subject at any university, while pure maths, French and Italian were in the top three. There were particularly high grades, too, for economics, applied maths, and theatre, performance and cultural studies.

The university was a late starter in the National Student Survey, due to opposition from the students' union, but is now in the top 20. Accounting, biology, chemistry, classics, drama, literary studies, finance, German, management studies and physics and astronomy produced good scores. Warwick was awarded a national teaching centre in theatrical performance, in partnership with the Royal Shakespeare Company, and is collaborating with Oxford Brookes University on another centre to "reinvent" undergraduate research. It has also been funded to help devise a blueprint for improving the undergraduate curriculum in research-led universities. The science park, one of the first in Britain, is among the most successful.

The university invested shrewdly in business, science and engineering and there is now a thriving graduate entry medical school, with more than 2,000 students and new professional courses in implant dentistry.

Coventry CV4 7AL

024 7652 3723 (admissions)
ugadmissions@warwick.ac.uk
www.warwick.ac.uk
www.warwicksu.com

The Times Rankings
Overall Ranking: **8**

Student satisfaction:	=22	(79%)
Research quality:	=10	(2.8)
Entry standards:	6	(464)
Student–staff ratio:	=10	(13.0)
Services & facilities/student:	13	(£1,927)
Expected completion rate:	5	(95.4%)
Good honours:	7	(79.9%)
Graduate prospects:	12	(77.9%)

Warwick is also one of the few leading universities to embrace two-year Foundation degrees, running courses in education and community enterprise, the latter taught by a local further education college.

With nearly nine applicants for every place on conventional degree courses, many departments stick rigidly to offers averaging more than an A and two Bs at A level. Applications have been buoyant but, like most of the universities at the top of *The Times* league table, Warwick did not see a big increase at the start of 2010, when the rise was only 1 per cent. Warwick has built up its numbers in science and engineering, however, as other universities have struggled to fill their places. The business school has grown rapidly, with a new £15-million extension, while chemistry and physics have acquired new, upgraded facilities.

Hundreds of millions of pounds have been spent on the campus, which has often resembled a building site. However, a second significant extension to students' union facilities will fully open in time for the start of the 2010–11 academic year. An £8-million extension to the university's already extensive Warwick Arts Centre, which attracts over 250,000 visitors a year, has just been completed. There is also a new £12.5-million building to house a "digital laboratory" for manufacturing and engineering research, a clinical trials unit and a new indoor tennis centre. The university will also benefit from one of the largest donations ever from a member of staff, after Professor Lord Bhattacharyya made a £1-million commitment and has asked that it be put towards research.

The 750-acre campus is three miles south of Coventry, where many students choose to live, and three times as far from Warwick. University accommodation is plentiful and the sports facilities are both extensive and conveniently placed on campus, where there is a sports centre with 25-metre swimming pool and a range of other facilities.

Undergraduate Fees and Bursaries

» Fees for UK/EU students: £3,290
» International student fees: £11,500–£15,000
» Bursary on full grant: household income up to £25K: £1,500
» Bursary on partial grant: household income up to £36K: £1,500.
» Scholarships based on circumstances or by competition.
» For full details see the university's website: www2.warwick.ac.uk/study/undergraduate/studentfunding

---

Students

Undergraduates:	**11,425**	(7,810)
Postgraduates:	**3,995**	(5,205)
Mature students:	**10.2%**	
Overseas students:	**17.3%**	
Applications per place:	**8.9**	
From state-sector schools:	**76.6%**	
From working-class homes:	**19.0%**	

For detailed information about fees, grants and bursaries and how they work, see chapter 7.

Accommodation

Number of places and costs refer to 2010–11
University-provided places: 5,779 (on campus); 1,750 (head leasing)
Percentage catered: 0%
Self-catered costs: £74–£125 a week (30, 39, 50 week contracts).
First-year undergraduates are prioritised for campus accommodation (terms and conditions apply).
International students as above
Contact: www2.warwick.ac.uk/services/accommodation

University of the West of England, Bristol (UWE)

The University of the West of England (UWE) is the largest provider of higher education in the southwest of England and one of the most popular post-1992 universities, both in terms of total applications and the proportion who subsequently choose to study there – one in four. Applications were up by 27 per cent in 2010, 6 per cent above the national average, following several years of increases earlier in the decade. The university is planning a £150-million extension and development of its main campus, eventually closing the three outlying sites, but many of the changes will not affect those admitted in 2011.

UWE has sometimes found itself in trouble for missing its benchmarks for widening access to higher education, but official reports now accept that this is largely due to its location. The proportion of independent school entrants has dropped to just over 11 per cent – still a figure exceeded by only one new university – while the share of places going to students from working-class homes is about one in three. UWE has one of England's largest bursary schemes, with annual bursaries of £1,000 going to about a third of its students. At 18 per cent, the projected dropout rate had been coming down, but is still well above the national average for the university's subjects and entry qualifications.

The university has improved its scores in the National Student Survey and is now in the top half of the table for the second year running. There were particularly high levels of satisfaction in history, forensic and archaeological science, anatomy, physiology and pathology, and initial teacher training in the results published in 2009. Unusually, the university trains and pays its 900 student representatives – the biggest such network in the country – while a development programme helps new students settle in and supports them throughout their studies. More than half of the students come from the West Country and there are close links with local business and industry. These provide guest lecturers, professors involved in practice, and thousands of part-time jobs and work placements for students, as well as helping to ensure that the curriculum is up-to-date and relevant.

A tradition of vocational education regularly helps the university to a healthy graduate employment record. The entrance system credits vocational qualifications and practical experience equally with traditional academic results. Law received a commendation from the Legal Practice Board and the degree in architecture and planning won a similar accolade from the Royal Town Planning Institute for bringing together the

Frenchay Campus
Coldharbour Lane
Bristol BS16 1QY

0117 328 3333 (admissions)
admissions@uwe.ac.uk
www.uwe.ac.uk
www.uwesu.org

The Times Rankings
Overall Ranking: **=69**

Student satisfaction:	=46	(77%)
Research quality:	=60	(0.6)
Entry standards:	=68	(273)
Student–staff ratio:	=79	(19.5)
Services & facilities/student:	73	(£1,184)
Expected completion rate:	74	(81.1%)
Good honours:	54	(62.9%)
Graduate prospects:	=78	(60.0%)

two disciplines in one joint-honours course giving dual professional qualifications. UWE is one of just four universities recognised by the Forensic Science Society for the quality of courses in the subject.

Only two new universities entered more academics than UWE in the 2008 Research Assessment Exercise. More than a third of the work was judged to be world-leading or internationally excellent. Physiotherapy and other health subjects, media studies and general engineering produced the best results.

For the moment, there are four sites in Bristol itself, mainly around the north of the city. Only Bower Ashton, which has new studio space and media suites for its art, media and design students, is in the south. The main campus at Frenchay, four miles out of the city centre, has already doubled in size and is to expand again after the purchase of adjoining land. It includes the largest exhibition and conference centre in the southwest, allowing it to stage major careers fairs for its students and enhance links with employers. The St Matthias campus is to close and its social sciences and humanities courses transferred to Frenchay over the next two years. Glenside (for midwifery, nursing, physiotherapy and radiography) will also close, but probably not before 2016.

A network of 15 colleges stretches into Somerset and Wiltshire, offering UWE programmes. Hartpury College, near Gloucester, has become an associate faculty of the university, specialising in agriculture, equine studies and other land-based courses, and there are university centres in hospitals in Bath and Swindon that concentrate nursing and allied health professions.

Bristol is a hugely popular student centre: an attractive and lively city, but not cheap. University accommodation has become more plentiful in recent years, with over 4,000 places available, including nearly 2,000 in a new £80-million student village on the Frenchay campus. Sports facilities were a bone of contention for students, but a new sports complex opened in 2006 as part of a £300-million investment programme, which is one of the largest in UK higher education. It has been chosen as a pre-Olympics training site for badminton, fencing, table tennis, indoor volleyball and wrestling.

Undergraduate Fees and Bursaries
» Fees for UK/EU students: £3,290
» International student fees: £9,250–£9,700
» Bursary on full grant: household income up to £25K: £1,000
» The university does not award bursaries for students on partial maintenance grants.
» Scholarships based on circumstances or by competition.
» For full details see the university's website: www.uwe.ac.uk/money

Students
Undergraduates:	**18,940**	**(6,415)**
Postgraduates:	**1,915**	**(4,370)**
Mature students:	**21.9%**	
Overseas students:	**6.6%**	
Applications per place:	**4.1**	
From state-sector schools:	**88.8%**	
From working-class homes:	**33.9%**	

For detailed information about fees, grants and bursaries and how they work, see chapter 7.

Accommodation
Number of places and costs refer to 2010–11
University-provided places: 4,079
Percentage catered: 0%
Self-catered costs: £91.00–£131.50 a week (41 weeks).
First-year students are guaranteed accommodation provided requirements are met.
International students are offered accommodation where possible.
Contact: accommodation@uwe.ac.uk

University of the West of Scotland

A merger between Paisley University and Bell College, in Hamilton, produced Scotland's largest new university, with more than 20,000 students and the largest School of Health, Nursing and Midwifery north of the border. The university is planning improvements of £250 million to its four campuses, with local provision within reach of nearly 40 per cent of Scots. However, it is not possible to monitor its progress in *The Times* league table since the university has blocked the release of data until all the statistics relate to the new, merged university.

Since the university's one appearance in the table, just outside the bottom ten, which was based on the Paisley campus alone, UWS has improved its research grades. A quarter of the work in a comparatively small submission was rated as world-leading or internationally excellent, with biomedical sciences and social policy and social work producing the best results. Paisley had enjoyed surges in popularity in the early years of the decade as students flocked to a new range of degree subjects such as computer animation, commercial music, computer games technology, sports studies and music technology. But the new university did not initially receive the boost in applications that new universities normally enjoy. The demand for places fell when there were rises elsewhere in Scotland. However, the start of 2010 saw a turnaround in fortunes, with applications up a staggering 65 per cent.

The two parent institutions had proud records in attracting under-represented groups onto courses. Almost two fifths of Paisley's entrants in the year before the merger were from working-class homes the proportion at Bell was close to half. Unfortunately, however, projected dropout rates on both campuses have been high at more than twice the 12.6 per cent benchmark set according to the subject mix and entry qualifications. Paisley introduced measures to address the problem, including a personal tutor system, strengthened counselling support and attendance monitoring. Access measures are continuing, with hundreds of youngsters aged 14 and 15 attending the "University Experience" and sampling a week of student life.

The new university's four bases are in Ayr, Dumfries, Hamilton and Paisley. Among the first developments were the £5.5-million library and student support services in Dumfries, a £2-million engineering centre at Hamilton and a £1-million employment centre for students across all campuses, which has its hub at the Paisley campus. The university's new £70-million Ayr Campus is currently under construction and is

Paisley Campus
Paisley
Renfrewshire PA1 2BE

0141 848 3000 (switchboard)
info@uws.ac.uk
contact via website
www.uws.ac.uk
www.sauws.org.uk

The Times Rankings
West of Scotland blocked the release of data from the Higher Education Statistics Agency and so we cannot give any ranking information.

scheduled for opening in September 2011. The new campus, which is being developed in partnership with the Scottish Agricultural College (SAC), will create an innovative learning environment, one of the most environmentally sustainable in the UK, for over 4,000 students. The new campus is adjacent to an 18th-century mansion that houses the West of Scotland Management Centre.

Paisley is Scotland's largest town, while Hamilton ranks fifth. Both draw a high proportion of the students from the local area, many on part-time courses. Paisley numbers at have grown rapidly in recent years, but staffing levels compare favourably with most new universities. There are around 1,100 international students, thanks to a growing number of Chinese and Indian nationals and long-established links with over 50 EU institutions.

Courses are strongly vocational, with business, multimedia and health subjects by far the most popular choices. There are close links with business and industry and all students are offered hands-on computer training. Paisley was the first UK university approved by Microsoft, Macromedia and Cisco, and has the status of Microsoft Academic Professional Development Centre. A games development laboratory, supported by Sony, is part of a £300,000 package of investment in multimedia and games facilities.

Paisley pioneered credit transfer in Scotland, including credit for non-academic achievement, and the modular course system covers day, evening and weekend classes. Most students either take sandwich degrees or have work placements built into their courses, earning an average of £10,000 in the process, but the impact on graduate employment has not been as great as elsewhere.

Over £9 million has been invested in student facilities in Paisley in recent years. The main campus, 20 acres in the town centre, has seen substantial development: a new library and learning resource centre, a £5-million students' union building, and recently upgraded indoor and outdoor sports facilities. The Dumfries campus, operated in partnership with Glasgow University, has over 400 students. The Hamilton campus contains teaching facilities, a students' union, an upgraded leisure centre and some accommodation. The Centre for Engineering Excellence is the newest addition.

Undergraduate Fees and Bursaries
» Scottish-domiciled and EU students: no fees payable.
» Non-Scottish UK-domiciled student fees: £1,820
» International student fees: £9,300–£10,050
» Scholarships based on circumstances or by competition.
» For full details see the university's website: www.uws.ac.uk/schoolsdepts/studentservices/fundingadvice

Students
From state-sector schools:	**98.5%**
From working-class homes:	**38.8%**

For detailed information about fees, grants and bursaries and how they work, see chapter 7.

Accommodation
Number of places and costs refer to 2009–10
University-provided places: 884 (628 at Paisley; 100 at Ayr; 156 at Hamilton)
Percentage catered: 0%
Self-catered costs: £60 a week.
First-year students have priority (conditions apply).
International students: single students guaranteed accommodation if conditions are met.
Contact: www.uws.ac.uk/about/facilities/accommodation.asp

University of Westminster

Westminster hit the headlines in the 2008 Research Assessment Exercise, when it was rated top in the UK for media studies with one of the highest proportions of world-leading research (60 per cent) in any subject. More than a third of all the work submitted by the university was rated in the top two categories, resulting a doubling of Westminster's research grants. Art and design, architecture and biomedical sciences all achieved good grades. The successes helped the university to a 27 per cent rise in applications at the start of 2010, well above the national average at that time.

The university is about to embark on an extensive redevelopment programme of its Harrow site, costing £40 million. This will include a new student centre with catering facilities and a student learning and social space. The internationally recognised School of Media, Arts and Design will remain at Harrow. The School of Electronics and Computer Science will be consolidated onto a single site in the West End, followed by a merging of the Harrow Business School with the Westminster Business School – also onto a single site in the West End. The School of Life Sciences, concentrated at the New Cavendish Street site near the BT Tower, has recently undergone a re-development of its facilities, costing £6 million.

The greenfield Harrow campus boasts a high-tech information resources centre with good facilities for the highly rated media studies courses. Computing and design are also based on a site designed for 7,500 students. The West End sites provide the perfect catchment area for part-time undergraduates, who account for about a third of the 17,000 undergraduate places. By no means all the students are Londoners, however: over 5,000 come from overseas – among the highest proportions among the post-1992 universities – and Westminster has the largest number of ethnic minority students in Britain. Westminster courses are also taught in nine overseas countries, from Sri Lanka to Uzbekistan, a characteristic which won the university a Queen's Award for Enterprise.

The university has launched a £5-million appeal to restore its main Regent Street building, which it claims as the birthplace of British cinema. The campaign was launched with a £1-million donation from the MBI Al Jaber Foundation. The historic headquarters building, near the BBC's Broadcasting House, houses social sciences and languages. Westminster claims to offer one of the widest ranges of language teaching of any British university, while science and health courses are concentrated on the Cavendish campus. The university's growing interest in health includes degrees from the British College of Naturopathy and Osteopathy and a range of

---

309 Regent Street
London W1B 2UW

020 7911 5000 (enquiries)
course-enquiries@
 westminster.ac.uk
www.westminster.ac.uk
www.uwsu.com

The Times Rankings
Overall Ranking: **100**

Student satisfaction:	=105	(69%)
Research quality:	=69	(0.5)
Entry standards:	78	(267)
Student–staff ratio:	=47	(16.3)
Services & facilities/student:	97	(£1,032)
Expected completion rate:	=87	(79.3%)
Good honours:	89	(52.7%)
Graduate prospects:	108	(53.2%)

courses in complementary medicine, including a BSc in acupuncture. There are degrees in herbal medicine, naturopathy and nutritional therapy, and a diploma in the traditional Chinese massage technique of Qigong.

The university weaves work-related skills into its degree programmes and the dropout rate is now below 17 per cent – and better than average for the university's subjects and entry standards. But scores in the 2009 National Student Survey were among the lowest in the country for the third successive year, featuring in the bottom 10 universities. Only anatomy, physiology and pathology, politics, sociology and some biological sciences had satisfaction rates of more than 85 per cent among final-year undergraduates.

More than four out of ten undergraduates are from working-class homes – a much higher proportion than the national average for the subjects offered. The university also exceeds its benchmark for the admission of students from state schools and colleges. However, those from lower participation neighbourhoods are under-represented. The scholarship programme is the largest of its kind, with three As at A level securing a "gold level" award of £4,000 a year in tuition fees and cash, while three Bs merit a "silver level" of £2,000 a year fee remission. Other scholarships are available to both home and overseas students, while all those receiving a maintenance grant qualify for a £400 bursary.

Westminster's students, like those at all the London universities, complain of the high cost of living, particularly for accommodation. The university has added considerably to its residential stock in recent years, with the opening of a £6-million block of halls in Harrow and the refurbishment of its Marylebone halls, but there is no way round the capital's inflated housing market at some stage. The Harrow campus is lively socially, but those based on the other sites tend to be spread around the capital. Sports facilities are also dispersed, with playing fields and a boathouse in Chiswick, west London.

Undergraduate Fees and Bursaries

- » Fees for UK/EU students: £3,290
- » International student fees: £10,125
- » Bursary on full grant: household income up to £25K: £400
- » Bursary on partial grant: £400
- » Scholarships based on circumstances or by competition.
- » For full details see the university's website: www.westminster.ac.uk/study/fees-and-funding

Students

Undergraduates:	**11,340**	**(5,090)**
Postgraduates:	**3,010**	**(3,720)**
Mature students:	**28.5%**	
Overseas students:	**17.1%**	
Applications per place:	**3.9**	
From state-sector schools:	**95.5%**	
From working-class homes:	**43.9%**	

For detailed information about fees, grants and bursaries and how they work, see chapter 7.

Accommodation

Number of places and costs refer to 2010–11
University-provided places: 1,350
Percentage catered: 0%
Self-catered costs: £77 – £168 a week.
First-year students have priority. Residential restrictions apply.
International students: as above.
Contact: studentaccommodation@westminster.ac.uk
www.westminster.ac.uk/study/student-accommodation

University of Winchester

Winchester stresses its "human scale", with fewer than 6,000 students and an emphasis on providing a supportive community for students to unlock their potential. There were successive finishes around the top 30 in the National Student Survey and while the university dropped to around 50th in the latest survey, it would still appear that the approach has struck a chord. History achieved a 100 per cent satisfaction rating in 2009, while American and Australasian studies, academic studies in education, and sports science also did well. Applications were up by 27 per cent at the start of 2010, well above the national average increase.

The university traces its history as an Anglican foundation back to 1840 and has occupied its King Alfred campus since 1862. The compact site is on a wooded hillside overlooking the cathedral city, ten-minutes walk away, with views of the surrounding countryside. A second centre, which opened in 2003, occupies a large 18th-century rectory in nearby Basingstoke and concentrates on lifelong learning. It offers Foundation degrees in community and creative industries, cultural studies, education and social sciences.

Known as King Alfred's College until 2004, the university is still best-known for teacher training, which accounts for about a third of the places. It is one of the largest providers of primary school training in England, but courses on the main campus also span business, arts, humanities, health and social care, and social sciences. Degrees range from choreography and dance, through social work, business, accounting, law, media and teacher training to ethics and spirituality. Street arts, global tourism, sustainable development management, philosophy, and health and wellbeing were added in 2009. Ancient, classical and medieval studies, modern liberal arts, sociology and vocal and choral studies were added in 2010. Global history and politics, criminology, and a range of new psychology programmes are among the innovations planned for 2011.

Winchester improved on already respectable grades in the 2008 Research Assessment Exercise, when it was ranked second among the new universities in history, with over half of its submission considered world-leading or internationally excellent. Overall, more than a third of the university's work reached the top two categories and there was some world-leading research in four of the six subject areas.

The university is particularly proud of its low dropout rate. At just over 12 per cent, the last official projection was below the national average for the subjects and entry grades, although the university puts the true figure lower still. Over 95 per cent of the British students are state-educated and about a third

---

Winchester
Hampshire SO22 4NR

01962 827234
course.enquiries@winchester.ac.uk
www.winchester.ac.uk
www.winchester
students.co.uk

The Times Rankings
Overall Ranking: **=74**

Student satisfaction:	=46	(77%)
Research quality:	=69	(0.5)
Entry standards:	=73	(270)
Student–staff ratio:	55	(17.4)
Services & facilities/student:	104	(£936)
Expected completion rate:	48	(85.4%)
Good honours:	68	(57.5%)
Graduate prospects:	110	(51.6%)

are from working-class homes. Male undergraduates are heavily outnumbered and there are about 150 overseas students from a range of countries. Winchester students can take advantage of exchange schemes with American universities in Maine, Oregon and Wisconsin, as well as with Beppu University in Japan.

The main campus is well equipped, with its theatrical performance spaces, sports hall and fitness suite now supplemented by the £3.5-million Winchester Sports Stadium, which opened in 2008. Open to local people as well as students, the stadium has an Olympic standard 400-metre eight-lane athletics track with supporting facilities for field events and also a floodlit all-weather pitch. There are six performing arts studios in a new building that opened in the spring of 2010 on the King Alfred campus. The two-storey building offers the latest technology for student productions.

An award-winning University Centre opened in September 2007, transforming the students' union, adding a nightclub, cinema, catering facilities, a bookshop and a supermarket at a cost of £9 million. A "learning café" creates an informal working space with networked PCs and wireless internet access. An award-winning extension to the library made room for 200,000 books, 450 study spaces and 150 computers.

A £12-million student village provides nearly 1,000 residential places – enough to guarantee accommodation for all first years, as well as those from overseas. Another hall of residence, with en-suite rooms arranged in cluster flats with shared kitchen facilities, is under construction and will be ready in time for the new September 2010 intake. Students value the close-knit atmosphere and find the city is livelier than its staid image might suggest, with a number of bars catering to their tastes. Southampton is not far for those who hanker after the attractions of a bigger city, and London is only an hour away by train.

Undergraduate Fees and Bursaries
» Fees for UK/EU students: £3,290
» International student fees: £8,370
» Bursary on full grant: household income up to £25K: £820
» Bursary on partial grant: household income up to £39.3K: £410.
» Scholarships based on circumstances or by competition.
» For full details see the university's website: www.winchester.ac.uk/?page=6891

Students
Undergraduates:	**3,870**	(800)
Postgraduates:	**150**	(1,085)
Mature students:	**18.8%**	
Overseas students:	**4.3%**	
Applications per place:	**4.3**	
From state-sector schools:	**95.2%**	
From working-class homes:	**34.5%**	

For detailed information about fees, grants and bursaries and how they work, see chapter 7.

Accommodation
Number of places and costs refer to 2009–10
University-provided places: 956 on campus; 320 off campus
Percentage catered: 15%
Catered costs: £3,658.20 (term-time only).
Self-catered costs: £3,458–£3,892 (40 weeks).
First years are guaranteed accommodation if conditions are met.
International students: non EU, as above.
Contact: housing@winchester.ac.uk

University of Wolverhampton

Wolverhampton has joined the small group of universities that have refused to release information on their performance after finishing towards the bottom of league tables. The university was just outside the top 100 last year, although its student satisfaction and dropout rates had improved and it might have finished higher in this edition. A statement on the university's website says that tables such as ours disadvantage universities like Wolverhampton and do not represent a fair picture of their strengths. As a result, it is missing from both the main ranking and all the subject tables.

Wolverhampton's success in widening participation in higher education is such that it is the only British university where a majority of students come from working-class homes. Almost all the students are from state schools and almost one in five comes from an area of low participation in higher education. The university draws two thirds of its 21,000 students from the West Midlands, although it has an international outlook, with a growing contingent from overseas. A third of the places are filled by mature students and its four campuses have a cosmopolitan feel, with about the same proportion coming from the region's ethnic minorities.

Wolverhampton pioneered the high street "higher education shop" and more recently, a dedicated Student Finance Support Unit and Student Gateway Service, bringing all student support together in one convenient location. Big outreach programmes take courses into the workplace. The four campuses each have their own learning centres and are linked by a free bus service. Two are in the city, while sport and performance, education and part of the School of Health are based in Walsall. The original site is in the heart of the city centre. A purpose-built campus at Telford in Shropshire focuses on business and engineering in a county with no higher education institution of its own.

The university has been investing millions of pounds in an infrastructure programme known as "New Horizons", which is almost complete. The project has seen £26 million spent on the City Campus, notably on the flagship Millennium City Building, and a teaching and administration building. A 350-bed student village has opened on the Walsall campus, together with a Lottery-supported sports hall offering elite training facilities for judo and a Sports Science and Medicine Centre that are being used to train Olympic contenders. A £12-million building for the School of Education and the Institute for Learning Enhancement opened in 2008. At Telford the £7-million e-Innovation Centre has already won awards for the

**Wulfruna Street
Wolverhampton WV1 1LY**

01902 321000 (enquiries)
enquiries@wlv.ac.uk
www.wlv.ac.uk
www.wolvesunion.org.uk

The Times Rankings
Wolverhampton blocked the release of data from the Higher Education Statistics Agency and so we cannot give any ranking information.

support it offers to e-businesses. There are also plans for a new performing arts centre on the Walsall campus.

The projected dropout rate is now just below the benchmark for a university with Wolverhampton's entry grades and subjects, at less than 17 per cent. The university runs a national teaching centre focusing on retention, progression and achievement. Teacher-training courses are rated in the top four in the country by Ofsted, and Wolverhampton academics have been awarded six National Teaching Fellowships by the Higher Education Academy. The university improved its scores in the 2009 National Student Survey, but still featured inside the bottom 30. History, archaeology and accounting were the only subjects that satisfied 90 per cent or more of the students.

The university claims a number of firsts for its academic programmes, pioneering interactive multimedia communication degrees, as well as offering one of the first degrees in British sign language and one of the first in virtual reality design and manufacturing. It was the first university to be registered under the British Standard for the quality of its all-round provision. The university stresses innovation and enterprise in its work with students and businesses, encouraging student "start up" companies and leading a project to develop student placements in their own companies for those who wish to become entrepreneurs. The Flying Start Programme for Sports Business is the first of its kind in the UK, providing a series of specialist workshops.

Research is mainly applied, serving the needs of business and industry, as well as underpinning teaching at all levels. The main strengths are in applications of computing and biomedical science, including groundbreaking work on brain tumours. The university was ranked fourth in the UK for statistical cybermetrics (the analysis of web content and traffic) and sixth for computational linguistics in the 2008 Research Assessment Exercise. A relatively low proportion of the academics were entered for assessment, but 30 per cent of their research was considered world-leading or internationally excellent.

Social facilities vary between sites. Wolverhampton has a growing nightlife and the university has been voted the friendliest in the West Midlands. The cost of living is reasonable and the attractions of Birmingham are now only a metro tramride away.

Undergraduate Fees and Bursaries
» Fees for UK/EU students: £3,290
» International student fees: £9,150
» Bursary on full grant: household income up to £25K: £500
» Bursary on partial grant: household income up to £35K: £300.
» Scholarships based on circumstances or by competition.
» For full details see the university's website: www.wlv.ac.uk/default.aspx?page=20893

Students
From state-sector schools:	**99.5%**
From working-class homes:	**53.1%**

For detailed information about fees, grants and bursaries and how they work, see chapter 7.

Accommodation
Number of places and costs refer to 2010-11
University-provided places: 2,048
Percentage catered: 0%
Self-catered costs: £2,394–£3,541 (37 weeks).
First-year students are offered accommodation provided requirements are met. Residential restrictions apply.
International students: same as above.
Contact: residences@wlv.ac.uk

University of Worcester

Worcester has the most ambitious development plans of all the new universities created in 2005. It is spending £120 million on a second campus in the city centre and another £60 million on a unique library and history centre that will be the first joint public and university library in Britain. Work is already under way on the second campus to cater for an additional 4,000 students over the next five years. Some 200 student residences opened in September 2009 in restored Georgian buildings, and the project is due for completion by 2011.

At the start of 2010, applications were up by much more than the national average, at 38 per cent, following healthy increases in the previous years. The demand for places even grew in each of the last five years before university status arrived. Business courses have been particularly popular and there have been big increases, too, in physical education, sports studies, forensic science, marketing, pre-hospital and emergency care, journalism, social work and advertising.

First as a post-war emergency teacher training college and later as a university college, the institution has always been the only provider of higher education in Hereford and Worcester. The university remains strong in education and also in nursing and midwifery – a mix that explains an overwhelmingly female student population. Former Home Secretary, Jacqui Smith, trained as a teacher there. But the six academic departments also cover applied sciences, geography and archaeology, a business school and arts, humanities and social sciences. Degrees range from animal biology to sports coaching and computing.

The 23 academics entered for the 2008 Research Assessment Exercise represented the smallest contingent from any university in England. Only English had any world-leading research, although there are pockets of excellence such as the National Pollen and Aerobiology Research Unit, which produces all Britain's pollen forecasts. Results in the first four National Student Surveys were more positive, placing Worcester in the top 40, but results in 2009 declined, leaving the university just outside the bottom 40. The most satisfied students were in teaching and sports science.

Almost 40 per cent of the undergraduates come from working-class homes. The projected dropout rate has declined and, at nearly 19 per cent, is above average for the university's subjects and entry grades. As well as the normal range of bursaries, the university offers £1,000 scholarships for academic achievement in the first year of a course and extra-curricular activities such as voluntary work.

The existing campus occupies a parkland site 15-minutes walk from the city centre.

Henwick Grove
Worcester WR2 6AJ

01905 855111 (admissions)
admissions@worc.ac.uk
www.worc.ac.uk
www.worcsu.com

The Times Rankings
Overall Ranking: **=90**

Student satisfaction:	=59	(76%)
Research quality:	=107	(0.1)
Entry standards:	=85	(260)
Student–staff ratio:	98	(20.7)
Services & facilities/student:	107	(£930)
Expected completion rate:	79	(79.9%)
Good honours:	93	(52.1%)
Graduate prospects:	68	(62.4%)

Recent improvements have included a £7-million science facility which houses state of the art teaching laboratories and the new National Pollen and Aerobiology Research Unit. A £1-million digital arts centre and drama studio, and another 182 residential places were added in a £10-million development that opened in September 2009. Sport plays an important part in university life: a well-appointed sports centre also provides employment opportunities for students, while competitive teams are successful and the facilities for casual participants extensive. A mobile 3-D motion analysis laboratory has been used by the England Cricket Board. Modest sports scholarships are offered in partnership with Worcestershire County Cricket Club, Worcester Wolves Basketball Club and Worcester Hockey Club. The basketball team have been national champions for three years in succession.

The new campus, which is being developed with the aid of regional and central Government grants, will occupy the site of the old Worcester Royal Infirmary. It will include teaching, residential and conference facilities, as well as the new library and learning centre is due to open in September 2010. It will also be home to the Business School. The university has undertaken to continue improving the existing St John's campus, which will still be the place of study for two thirds of the university when the new development is completed. It contains three halls of residence with a total of 589 rooms, most of which are allocated to first years. There will be shuttle buses and a cycle route between the two sites. The university also has a number of partner colleges around the region offering Worcester courses.

Social life revolves around the students' union, which also has a "job pod" to help members find work experience and part-time jobs. The cathedral city is not large, but is safer than many university locations, and has its share of pubs and clubs that cater for a growing student clientele.

Undergraduate Fees and Bursaries
» Fees for UK/EU students: £3,290
» International student fees: £8,500
» Bursary on full grant: household income up to £25K: £750
» Bursary on partial grant: £625; if not eligible for maintenance grant: £500.
» Scholarships based on circumstances or by competition.
» For full details see the university's website: http://www.worc.ac.uk/student/finance

Students
Undergraduates:	**4,745**	(1,920)
Postgraduates:	**460**	(1,195)
Mature students:	**29.6%**	
Overseas students:	**4.1%**	
Applications per place:	**3.8**	
From state-sector schools:	**96.8%**	
From working-class homes:	**39.6%**	

For detailed information about fees, grants and bursaries and how they work, see chapter 7.

Accommodation
Number of places and costs refer to 2010–11
University-provided places: 970 university-owned; 260 university-managed
Percentage catered: 0%
Self-catered costs: £73–£121 a week.
First-year students are guaranteed accommodation, on a first come, first served basis, if they have accepted an offer by 1 May. International students are accommodated provided requirements are met.
Contact: accommodation@worc.ac.uk

University of York

York has regained its accustomed place in the top 10 in *The Times* league table this year and is also moving up the world rankings, finishing in the top 70 in the latest QS comparisons. But the university has decided that, with just over 12,000 students, it is too small to maintain that standing, play a leading role in the economy of the region and satisfy the growing demand for its places. In an audacious move for a highly selective university, York is developing a second campus to accommodate an increase of up to 50 per cent in student numbers and strengthen its research capability.

The first building on the campus expansion – a new residential college for 600 new students – is now complete. New buildings for computer science, law, management and theatre, film and television are under construction. They will be ready before the start of the 2010–11 academic year, but the development will take 10 to 15 years to complete. Eventually, the expanded campus will contain housing for an additional 3,300 students, as well as more academic buildings, sports facilities and a performing arts and community complex.

Expansion into new subjects has already started. The first intake of undergraduates in law and in writing, directing and performance in theatre, film and television arrived in 2008. The university believes that, with eight applicants for every place, other departments can grow at the same time as retaining or achieving a place in the top 10 for their subject. The new subjects helped York achieve 17 per cent growth in applications in 2009, a feat that it practically repeated at the start of 2010.

Medicine was introduced in 2003 in partnership with Hull University. York also runs its own nursing and midwifery programmes. The university has also done well in the National Student Survey, finishing in the top 30 in all five years of polling. History received a 100 per cent satisfaction rating, whilst theology and religious studies, biology, electronic and electrical engineering, archaeology and chemistry also produced particularly high levels of satisfaction in the 2009 results. Around 20 per cent of the current student population are international, and around 25 per cent are postgraduates.

Entrance requirements are high and the dropout rate of only 4.5 per cent is among the lowest in the country. Eight out of ten undergraduates are state educated and nearly 22 per cent come from working-class homes, just less than the national average for York's subjects and entry qualifications. Every student has a supervisor responsible for their academic and personal welfare. Extra-curricular courses include language and computer literacy training, as well as courses on personal effectiveness, financial

Heslington
York YO10 5DD

01904 433539 (admissions)
admissions@york.ac.uk
www.york.ac.uk
hyms.ac.uk
www.yusu.org

The Times Rankings
Overall Ranking: **9**

Student satisfaction:	=11	(81%)
Research quality:	9	(2.9)
Entry standards:	12	(423)
Student–staff ratio:	19	(13.7)
Services & facilities/student:	14	(£1,920)
Expected completion rate:	=9	(94.9%)
Good honours:	13	(75.3%)
Graduate prospects:	33	(71.5%)

management, active citizenship and an introduction to accounting. The business community is involved at every level. Undergraduates can also take the "York Award", comprising a range of courses, work placements and voluntary activities which aim to prepare students for the world of work. Over 600 students work as volunteer teaching assistants in local schools through the award winning York Students in Schools programme.

York was among the top 10 institutions in the 2008 Research Assessment Exercise, when more than 60 per cent of the work submitted was judged to be world-leading or internationally excellent. The university was ranked top in the UK for English and health services research, joint top for sociology, and among the leaders for linguistics, and nursing and midwifery.

The current campus occupies 200 acres of landscaped parkland, a mile outside the historic, picturesque city centre. Students join one of eight colleges, which mix academic and social roles. Most departments have their headquarters in one of the colleges, but the student community is a deliberate mixture of disciplines, years and sexes. Nursing apart, only archaeology and medieval studies are located off campus, sharing a medieval building in the centre of the city.

Social life on campus is lively. There are television and radio stations, as well as several newspapers and magazines, to keep students abreast of campus issues. Sports facilities are good, and include a 50-station fitness suite, four sports halls, and dance studio. Extensive playing fields are on campus and the River Ouse fosters a strong rowing tradition. Cultural events abound in the city, which is also famous for a high concentration of pubs. The club scene has improved, but students still head for Leeds for the top names.

Undergraduate Fees and Bursaries

» Fees for UK/EU students: £3,290
» International student fees: £11,300–£14,850
  £22,700 (medicine)
» Bursary on full grant: household income up to £25K: £1,436
» Bursary on partial grant: household income up to £35.9K: £718; household income up to £41K: £360.
» Scholarships based on circumstances or by competition.
» For full details see the university's website: www.york.ac.uk/studentmoney

---

Students

Undergraduates:	8,350	(1,050)
Postgraduates:	3,145	(940)
Mature students:	6.7%	
Overseas students:	11.1%	
Applications per place:	6.1	
From state-sector schools:	80.2%	
From working-class homes:	21.6%	

For detailed information about fees, grants and bursaries and how they work, see chapter 7.

Accommodation

Number of places and costs refer to 2010–11
University-provided places: 4,540
Percentage catered: 9%
Self-catered costs: £81.76–112.42 a week.
Catered costs: £99.82 a week.
First-year single undergraduates are provided with accommodation if terms and conditions are met.
International students: as above.
Contact: accommodation@york.ac.uk
www.york.ac.uk/admin/accom

York St John University

One of the four universities designated in 2006, York St John is a Church of England foundation that dates back almost 170 years. The eight-acre site faces York Minster across the city walls and is a five-minute walk from the city centre. Now serving over 6,000 students, the campus has seen £60 million of development in recent years and more is planned. The Fountains Learning Centre, which has 500 computer workstations, an internet café and lecture theatre, provides a striking entrance to the university. Another new teaching development, mainly for health and life sciences, opened at the end of 2008 and is intended to be a signature building linking the university quarter with the city centre. De Gray Court, which cost £15.5 million, won a prize at the Royal Institute of British Architects Awards in 2009.

York Diocesan Training School opened in 1841 with one pupil on the register, in whose honour the current students' union is named. Divided between York and Ripon for most of its existence, the institution diversified beyond teacher training in the 1980s and decided at the start of this decade to concentrate all its teaching on York. Almost three quarters of the students are female and only about half come straight from school.

Education and theology remains the biggest faculty, with 1,700 students taking programmes in teacher education, education studies, theology and religious studies. Health and life sciences are not far behind in terms of size, with 1,600 full-time students and 200 part-timers studying health courses such as physiotherapy and occupational therapy, as well as psychology and sport. The Faculty of Arts, which was established in 2001, is expanding, particularly in media subjects such as film and television production, one of the university's most popular degrees. The York St John Business School, launched in May 2008, engages with a range of local and regional small- to medium-sized enterprises, as well as offering the normal range of undergraduate and postgraduate courses.

The university was awarded a national centre for excellence in creativity, based on its work in English and theatre studies, which is providing an enriched curriculum in the creative arts. The C4C Centre, based in a renovated Victorian Gothic chapel situated on campus, provides facilities for students, staff, and creative partners to work together. Another music technology suite has been added, and a refurbishment programme has begun in the design and technology block.

Satisfaction levels varied widely in the National Student Survey published in 2009. More than 90 per cent of final-year undergraduates in theology and religious studies and initial teacher training were satisfied with their courses, while history

New Mayor's Walk
York YO31 7EX

01904 876598 (enquiries)
admissions@yorksj.ac.uk
www.yorksj.ac.uk
www.ysjsu.com

The Times Rankings
Overall Ranking: **=81**

Student satisfaction:	=59	(76%)
Research quality:	=95	(0.2)
Entry standards:	=60	(280)
Student–staff ratio:	90	(19.9)
Services & facilities/student:	64	(£1,259)
Expected completion rate:	=45	(85.6%)
Good honours:	=74	(56.2%)
Graduate prospects:	96	(57.1%)

polled an impressive 100 per cent. However, the proportion was under 50 per cent for design studies, and only 56 per cent in cinematics and photography. Drama, dance and performing arts was the most successful field in the 2008 Research Assessment Exercise and the only one to contain world-leading research.

Applications were up by more than 10 per cent at the official deadline for entry in 2009, following a run of good figures since university status was announced and in a successful year for nearly all universities, applications increased by a further 30 per cent in 2010. More than 94 per cent of students attended state schools or colleges, while almost a third are from working-class homes. The projected dropout rate had improved considerably in the latest survey and, at less than 9 per cent, is significantly below the national average for the university's courses and entry qualifications.

The university was one of a handful that set undergraduate charges below the £3,000 maximum when top-up fees were introduced, but it has since joined all other universities on the top level of fees, £3,290 a year. Charges for Foundation degrees have been set at the standard level of £1,310 a year in 2010–11.

Relatively high numbers of locally based mature students ease the pressure on residential accommodation. As a result, first years who want to live in university-owned accommodation are usually able to do so. More self-catering accommodation for 230 students, costing £10 million, opened in September 2008 and another 200 places are planned. Sports facilities are not extensive, but York is popular as a student city with a growing range of clubs as well as, supposedly, a pub for every day of the year.

Undergraduate Fees and Bursaries

» Fees for UK/EU students: £3,290
» International student fees: £8,250–£11,250
» Bursary on full grant: household income up to £25K: household income up to £18,360: £1,610; household income up to £20,970: £1,075.
» The university does not award bursaries for students on partial maintenance grants.
» Scholarships based on circumstances or by competition.
» For full details see the university's website: http://w3.yorksj.ac.uk/welfare/welfare-team/fees-and-funding.aspx

Students

Undergraduates:	4,375	(1,215)
Postgraduates:	235	(710)
Mature students:	18.1%	
Overseas students:	2.1%	
Applications per place:	4.5	
From state-sector schools:	94.4%	
From working-class homes:	32.0%	

For detailed information about fees, grants and bursaries and how they work, see chapter 7.

Accommodation

Number of places and costs refer to 2010–11
University-provided places: 1, 334
Percentage catered: 11%
Catered costs: £122 (semi-catered package) a week (33 weeks).
Self-catered costs: £74–£128 a week (44–48 weeks).
First years choosing university as first choice are guaranteed accommodation. Residential and age restrictions apply.
International students: guaranteed housing.
Contact: accommodation@yorksj.ac.uk

Colleges of Higher Education

This listing gives contact details for higher education institutions not mentioned elsewhere within the book. All the institutions listed below offer degree courses, some providing a wide range of courses while others are specialist colleges with a limited range of courses and a small intake. Those marked with a * are members of GuildHE (www.guildhe.ac.uk).

Arts University College, Bournemouth*
Wallisdown, Poole, Dorset BH12 5HH
01202 533011
www.aucb.ac.uk

Bishop Grosseteste University College*
Lincoln LN1 3DY
01522 527347
www.bishopg.ac.uk

Conservatoire for Dance and Drama
Tavistock House, Tavistock Square
London WC1H 9JJ
020 7387 5101
www.cdd.ac.uk
includes **Royal Academy of Dramatic Arts**
62–64 Gower Street, London WC1E 6ED
020 7636 7076
www.rada.org

Edinburgh College of Art
Lauriston Place, Edinburgh EH3 9DF
0131 221 6000
www.eca.ac.uk

Glasgow School of Art
167 Renfrew Street, Glasgow G3 6RQ
0141 353 4500
www.gsa.ac.uk

Harper Adams University College*
Newport, Shropshire TF10 8NB
01952 820280
www.harper-adams.ac.uk

Leeds Trinity University College*
Brownberrie Lane, Horsforth,
Leeds LS18 5HD
0113 283 7100
www.leedstrinity.ac.uk

Liverpool Institute for Performing Arts*
Mount Street, Liverpool L1 9HF
0151 330 3000
www.lipa.ac.uk

Newman University College*
Genners Lane, Bartley Green,
Birmingham B32 3NT
0121 476 1181
www.newman.ac.uk

Norwich University College of the Arts*
Francis House, 3–7 Redwell Street
Norwich, Norfolk NR2 4SN
01603 610561
www.nuca.ac.uk

Ravensbourne*
(from 30 September 2010)
6 Penrose Way, London SE10 0EW
020 3040 3500
www.rave.ac.uk

Rose Bruford College*
Burnt Oak Lane, Sidcup, Kent DA15 9DF
020 8308 2600
www.bruford.ac.uk

Royal Agricultural College*
Stroud Road, Cirencester
Gloucestershire GL7 6JS
01285 652531
www.rac.ac.uk

Royal College of Art
Kensington Gore, London SW7 2EU
020 7590 4444
www.rca.ac.uk

Royal College of Music
Prince Consort Road, London SW7 2BS
020 7589 3643
www.rcm.ac.uk

Royal Northern College of Music
124 Oxford Road, Manchester M13 9RD
0161 907 5200
www.rncm.ac.uk

Royal Scottish Academy of Music and Drama
100 Renfrew Street, Glasgow G2 3DB
0141 332 4101
www.rsamd.ac.uk

Royal Welsh College of Music and Drama
Castle Grounds, Cathays Park
Cardiff CF10 3ER
029 2034 2854
www.rwcmd.ac.uk

St Mary's University College*
Waldegrave Road, Strawberry Hill
Twickenham TW1 4SX
020 8240 4000
www.smuc.ac.uk

St Mary's University College
191 Falls Road, Belfast BT12 6FE
028 9032 7678
www.stmarys-belfast.ac.uk

Stranmillis University College
Stranmillis Road, Belfast BT9 5DY
028 9038 1271
www.stran.ac.uk

Trinity Laban Conservatoire of Music and Dance
King Charles Court
Old Royal Naval College,
Greenwich, London SE10 9JF
020 8305 4300
www.trinitylaban.ac.uk

Trinity University College*
College Road, Carmarthen
Wales SA31 3EP
01267 676767
www.trinity-cm.ac.uk
Note: from autumn 2010, it will merge with Lampeter to form University of Wales, Trinity Saint David. However, applications for 2011 through UCAS will remain direct to Trinity University College and Lampeter. See profile for Trinity Saint David on page 508.

University Campus Suffolk
St Edmund House, Rope Walk
Ipswich IP4 1NF
01473 338000
www.ucs.ac.uk

University College Birmingham*
Summer Row, Birmingham B3 1JB
0121 604 1000
www.ucb.ac.uk

University College Falmouth*
incorporating **Dartington College of Arts**
Woodlane, Falmouth, Cornwall TR11 4RH
01326 211077
www.falmouth.ac.uk

University College Plymouth St Mark and St John* (Marjon)
Derriford Road, Plymouth, Devon PL6 8BH
01752 636700
www.marjon.ac.uk

University of the Highlands and Islands
UHI Millennium Institute
Ness Walk, Inverness IV3 5SQ
01463 279000
www.uhi.ac.uk

Writtle College*
Chelmsford, Essex CM1 3RR
01245 424200
www.writtle.ac.uk

Index

1994 Group 28
A levels
   choosing 17–19
   those not accepted 19
   and UCAS tariff 18
Aberdeen, University of 296–7
Abertay, University of 298–9
Aberystwyth University 300–301
academic subjects 22
Academic World Ranking of Universities 43–5
access courses 24
Access to Learning Fund 206
accommodation 220–30
   choices 221–2
   costs 29, 220–21, 223
   after first year 225
   private sector 223–4, 226–9
   university 223–5
   useful websites 230
accommodation agreements, university 225
accounting and finance 61–3, 255
Adjustment period 188, 195, 246
admissions tests 19, 20
adult dependent's grant 207
Advanced Highers, and UCAS tariff 17, 18
aeronautical and manufacturing engineering 63–5
African studies 150–51
agriculture and forestry 65–6
American studies 67–8
anatomy and physiology 68–9
Anglia Ruskin University 302–3
anthropology 69–71
application process 187–97
   international students 252
   parental involvement 245–6
application timetable 192
applications
   deadlines 189, 191, 192
   decisions on 191, 192, 193–4
   increases in 26, 39
   most popular universities 27
   useful websites 198
Apply 188–91
archaeology 71–3
architecture 73–5, 258
architecture, history of 129–30
art and design 75–7, 255
   end of UCAS Route B 187
   Foundation courses 24
art, history of 129–30
Arts, University of, London 512–13
ARWU World Ranking 43–5

Assembly Learning Grant, Wales 203
assured shorthold tenancy 228
Aston University 304–5
astronomy 162–4
Athletic Union 236
audiology 156–8
Australia, studying in 42
Balliol, Oxford 265
Bangor University 306–7
banks, and student accounts 209
Bath, University of 308–9
Bath Spa University 310–11
Bedfordshire, University of 312–13
biological sciences 77–80, 256
BioMedical Admissions Test (BMAT) 20
Birkbeck College 295, 424
Birmingham, University of 314–15
Birmingham City University 316–17
Bishop Grosseteste University College 112
Bolton, University of 318–19
Bournemouth University 320–21
Bradford, University of 322–3
Brasenose, Oxford 265
Brighton, University of 324–5
Bristol, University of 326–7
British Council 249
British University and College Sport (BUCS) 233–4, 237
Brunel University 328–9
Buckingham, University of 24, 330–31
Buckinghamshire New University 332–3
budget, student 210
building 80–82
bursaries 29, 204–5
   by university 211–19
business studies 82–5, 255
Cambridge, University of 334–5
   A levels not fully accepted 19
   application and acceptance by subject 264
   application process 189, 259–65
   choosing a college 260–63
   college fees 28
   college profiles 279–93
   state-school applicants 259, 260
   and subject tables 58
   Tompkins Table 260
campus universities 26
Canterbury Christ Church University 336–7
Cardiff University 338–9
Cardiff, University of Wales Institute 340–41
career planning 39
catered accommodation, university 224–5
Celtic studies 85–6
Central Lancashire, University of 342–3

Central School of Speech and Drama 425
Certificate of Acceptance for Study 253
chemical engineering 86–7
chemistry 88–9
Chester, University of 344–5
Chichester, University of 346–7
Child Tax Credits 201
childcare grant 207
China, studying in 42
choice of university courses 15–24, 27
　checklist 30
　number of 27, 189
　and UCAS Apply 189
　useful websites 30–31
Christ Church, Oxford 266
Christ's, Cambridge 279
Churchill, Cambridge 279–80
cinematics 100–103
Citizen's Advice Bureau 228
city universities 26
City University London 348–9
civil engineering 90–91, 257
Clare, Cambridge 280
classics and ancient history 91–3
Clearing 27, 194, 195–6
Combined Honours 22
communication and media studies 93–6, 257
Community Service Volunteers 198
complementary therapies 156–8
completion measure 51
computer facilities, and league table 50–51
computer science 96–9, 255
conditional offer 193
Conservatoires UK Admissions Service 187
Corpus Christi, Cambridge 280–81
Corpus Christi, Oxford 266
Council Tax 229
counselling 156–8
courses
　choosing 15–24
　distance learning 23
　full-time 23
　modular 22–3
　part-time 15, 23, 39
　and professional qualifications 21–2
Courtauld Institute of Art 425
Coventry University 350–51
Cranfield 295
Creative Arts, University for the 516–17
Cumbria, University of 352–3
dance 100–103
De Montfort University 354–5
deadline for applications 189, 191, 192
deferred place 189, 197
degree results, and league table 51
dentistry 99–100

deposit, accommodation 228
Derby, University of 356–7
design 75–7, 255
design, history of 129–30
destinations, graduate 32
disabled student allowance 207
distance learning 23
Downing, Cambridge 281
drama, dance and cinematics 100–103
Dundee, University of 358–9
Durham University 360–61
East and South Asian studies 103–4
East Anglia, University of 362–3
East European languages 170–71
East London, University of 364–5
economics 104–6, 255
Edge Hill University 366–7
Edinburgh, University of 368–9
Edinburgh Napier University 370–71
education 59, 107–9
Education and Library Board, Northern Ireland 202
Education UK 249
electrical and electronic engineering 109–11, 256
Emmanuel, Cambridge 281–2
employability 32–9
　enhancing 33
　and league table 51
　schemes 15
employers, most favoured universities 33
employment agencies, student 207
employment regulations, international students 242
England, financial support 202–3, 205
England, tuition fees 199–200
English 111–14, 258
English language requirements, international students 252
English Literature Admissions Test (ELAT) 20
entry regulations, international students 241–2
entry standards 24–5
　and league table 50
　and subject tables 59
environmental sciences 120–22
Erasmus 24, 41
Essex, University of 372–3
EU students
　fees 250
　financial support 206
Europe, studying in 40–41, 42
exam grades, lower than offer 195
exchange programmes 24, 41
Exeter Award 38

Exeter, Oxford 266–7
Exeter, University of 59, 374–5
expenditure, student 208–10
facilities, and university choice 29
facilities spend *see* services and facilities spend measure
fee remission 205
fees, by university 211–19
finance 61–3, 255
Financial Contingency Fund, Wales 206
financial support
    between different UK countries 205–6
    England 202–3
    EU students 206
    Northern Ireland 203
    Scotland 204
    timetable 203
    Wales 203–4
    websites 210–11
firm acceptance 194
Fitzwilliam, Cambridge 282
flat sharing 226–7
flats, renting 226–8
food science 115–16
forestry 65–6
Foundation degree 23–4
French 116–18
Fresh Talent scheme, Scotland 253
full maintenance grant 211
full-time course 23
gap year 198, 206
gas safety certificate 229
general engineering 118–20
geography and environmental sciences 120–22
geology 122–4
German 124–5
Girton, Cambridge 282–3
Glamorgan, University of 376–7
Glasgow, University of 378–9
Glasgow Caledonian University 380–81
Gloucestershire, University of 382–3
Glyndŵr University 384–5
Goldsmiths, University of London 386–7
Gonville and Caius, Cambridge 283
good honours measure 51
graduate employment 32–9
graduate endowment, Scotland, abolition of 200
Graduate Medical School Admissions Test (GAMSAT) 20
graduate prospects 28, 51, 59
graduate recruitment, and course choice 22
Graduate Teacher Training Registry 187
grants 202–4
Greenwich, University of 388–9

guild of students 29
Guild HE 28
hall of residence 224
Hardship Fund, Scotland 206
Harper Adams University College 65
Harris Manchester, Oxford 267
Health Professions Admissions Test (HPAT) 20
health sciences 156–8
health services management 156–8
helicopter parent 244–5, 247
Heriot-Watt University 390–91
Hertford, Oxford 267–8
Hertfordshire, University of 392–3
HESA 32, 48, 51, 58
Heythrop College 425
Higher Education, Colleges of 536–7
Higher National Diploma 23
Highers, and UCAS tariff 17, 18
history 126–8
History Aptitude Test (HAT) 20
history of art, architecture and design 129–30
home, living at 26, 222–3
Homerton, Cambridge 284
honours, good, measure 51
hospitality, leisure, recreation and tourism 130–32, 257
hostel accommodation 225
household income 202, 211
Houses in Multiple Occupation (HMO) 227
Housing Act 2004 227
Huddersfield, University of 394–5
Hughes Hall, Cambridge 284
Hull, University of 396–7
Iberian languages 132–4
Imperial College of Science, Technology and Medicine 58, 398–9
income support, from Government 206–7
industry sponsors 38
information management 140
Institute of Education 425
insurance 210, 229–30
insurance choice 27, 194
International Baccalaureate 17, 18
international fees, by university 211–19
International Graduate Scheme 253
international students 248–58
    application process 252
    employment regulations 242
    English language requirements 252
    entry regulations 253
    family members 254
    university support 254
    what to study 251–2, 255–8
    where coming from 249

where to study 250–51
internet, reliability of information on 29
interviews 193
intramural sport 232–3
inventory 228–9
Italian 134–5
Japan, studying in 42
Jesus, Cambridge 284–5
Jesus, Oxford 268
job prospects 32–9
Joint Honours 22
Keble, Oxford 268–9
Keele, University of 400–401
Kent, University of 402–3
King's, Cambridge 285
King's College London 404–5
Kingston University 406–7
Lady Margaret Hall, Oxford 269
Lampeter, University of Wales 508–9
Lancaster University 408–9
land and property management 136
landscape 183–4
law 21–2, 137–9, 255
Law Advice Centre 228
league table 37, 47–57
   changes in measures used 47
   value of 47
   universities not in 57
   weighting in 48
lease 227–8
Leeds, University of 410–11
Leeds Metropolitan University 412–13
Leicester, University of 414–15
leisure 130–32, 257
librarianship and information management 140
library facilities, and league table 50–51
Lincoln, Oxford 269–70
Lincoln, University of 416–17
linguistics 141–2
Liverpool, University of 418–19
Liverpool Hope University 420–21
Liverpool John Moores University 422–3
living at home 26, 222–3
living costs 208–10
LJMU 422–3
loans, student 200–202
   interest on 214
   maintenance 201
   repayment of 202, 214
   tuition fees 200–201
location, university 25–6
lodging accommodation 225
London, cost of 28–9, 221
London, University of 424–5
London Business School 295, 425

London Metropolitan University 426–7
London School of Economics and Political Science 58, 428–9
A levels not accepted 19
London School of Hygiene and Tropical Medicine 425
London South Bank University 430–31
Loughborough University 59, 432–3
Lucy Cavendish, Cambridge 285–6
Magdalen, Oxford 270
Magdalene, Cambridge 286
maintenance grant 202–4
maintenance loan 201
Manchester, University of 434–5
Manchester Business School 295
Manchester Metropolitan University 436–7
Mansfield, Oxford 270–71
manufacturing engineering 63–5
Marjon 161
materials technology 142–3
mathematics 143–6, 256
mature students, loan support 201
measures
   league table 47–51
   subject tables 59
mechanical engineering 146–8, 256
media studies 93–6, 257
medicine 21–2, 148–50, 256
medicine, other subjects allied to 156–8, 257
Merton, Oxford 271
Middle Eastern and African studies 150–51
Middlesex University 438–9
Million Plus Group 28
Modern and Medieval Languages Test (MML) 20
modular degrees 22–3
Murray Edwards, Cambridge 286–7
music 151–3
National Admissions Test for Law (LNAT) 20
National Recognition Centre 42
National Student Survey 16, 23, 26, 47–9, 58–9
National Tenancy Deposit Scheme 228
New College, Oxford 271–2
Newcastle University 440–41
Newman University College 179
Newnham, Cambridge 287
Newport, University of Wales 442–3
Norrington Table, Oxford 261
Northampton, University of 444–5
Northern Ireland
   financial support 203
   tuition fees 199–200
Northumbria University 446–7
Nottingham, University of 59, 448–9

INDEX   **541**

Nottingham Trent University 450–51
nursing 153–5
nutrition 156–8
occupational therapy 156–8
offers 193–4
Office for Fair Access 204
Ofsted 59
Olympic Games 2012 231, 234
online application, UCAS 188
open days 27, 246
Open University 23, 295
ophthalmology 156–8
optometry 156–8
Oriel, Oxford 272
orthoptics 156–8
osteopathy 156–8
other subjects allied to medicine 156–8, 257
overseas degrees, recognition of 42–3
Oxbridge 259–93
Oxford, University of 452–3
   application and acceptance by subject 262–3
   application process 189, 259–65
   choosing a college 260–63
   college fees 28
   college profiles 265–78
   Norrington Table 261
   state school applicants 259, 260
   and subject tables 58
Oxford Brookes University 454–5
parents, their role 244–7
Parents' Learning Allowance 201
partial maintenance grant 211
part-time course 23, 39, 196–7
part-time work 207–8
Pembroke, Cambridge 287–8
Pembroke, Oxford 272
performance indicators 48
personal statement 189–91
Peterhouse, Cambridge 288
pharmacology 158–60, 257
pharmacy 158–60, 257
philosophy 160–62
physics 162–4
physiology 68–9
physiotherapy 156–8
planning 183–4
Plymouth, University of 456–7
podiatry 156–8
politics 164–7, 256
polytechnic 28
Portsmouth, University of 458–9
positive destinations 33
   and subject tables 58
Post-Study Work, overseas students 253
private accommodation 223–4, 226–9

private sector, renting 226–9
Professional and Career Development Loan 207
professional qualifications 21–2
property management 136
prospectus 29
psychology 167–70, 257
QS World Ranking 43–5
Queen Margaret University 460–61
Queen Mary, University of London 462–3
Queen's University, Belfast 59, 464–5
Queen's, Oxford 273
Queens', Cambridge 288–9
radiography 156–8
RAE *see* Research Assessment Exercise
Reading, University of 59, 466–7
recreational facilities, and choice 29
reference, UCAS 191
rejection 193
religious studies 181–3
rental agreement 227–8
rents, average student 220
repayment of loans 214
Research Assessment Exercise 49–50, 51, 58
   and staff numbers involved 49–50, 51
   research quality measure 48, 49–50, 51
   and subject tables 59
residence, hall of 224
resits 196
results day 194–5
   and parents 246–7
   Scotland 195
Robert Gordon University 468–9
Robinson, Cambridge 289
Roehampton University 470–71
Route B, UCAS, end of 187
Royal Academy of Music 151, 425
Royal and Ancient scholarships 235–6
Royal College of Art 295
Royal College of Music, London 151, 472
Royal Holloway, University of London 472–3
Royal Veterinary College 425
Russell Group 28
Russian 170–71
safety, student 229
Salford, University of 476–7
sandwich course 22
scholarships 204–5
School of Oriental and African Studies, London 478–9
School of Pharmacy 425
Scotland
   financial support 204
   and National Student Survey 48, 58
   tuition fees 200

universities in 25
Scottish qualifications, and UCAS tariff 17, 18
Scottish students studying outside Scotland 205
security, student 229
self-catering accommodation, university 224
Selwyn, Cambridge 291
services and facility spend measure 50–51
Shanghai Jiao Tong University, and world ranking 43–5
Sheffield, University of 480–81
Sheffield Hallam University 482–3
Sidney Sussex, Cambridge 291–2
Sixth Term Examination Papers (STEP) 20
SOAS 478–9
social policy 171–3
social work 173–5
sociology 176–8
Somerville, Oxford 276
South Asian studies 103–4
Southampton, University of 484–5
Southampton Solent University 486–7
Special Support Grant, Northern Ireland 203
speech therapy 156–8
sport 231–43
  cost of 234–5
  for first years 232
  increasing importance in university choice 231
  intramural 322–3
  opportunities for 231–3
  scholarships 235–6
  websites 236, 239, 241, 243
sports courses 235
sports facilities 234, 237–43
  location of 235
  and part-time jobs 236
sports science 178–81
St Andrews, University of 474–5
St Anne's, Oxford 273
St Catharine's, Cambridge 289–90
St Catherine's, Oxford 273–4
St Edmund Hall, Oxford 274
St Edmund's College, Cambridge 290
St George's, University of London 295, 425
St Hilda's, Oxford 274–5
St Hugh's, Oxford 275
St John's, Cambridge 290–91
St John's, Oxford 275
St Mary's University College, Twickenham 126, 176, 182, 204
St Peter's, Oxford 275–6
Staffordshire University 488–9
standard offers 25

Stanford Test 22
Stirling, University of 490–91
Strathclyde, University of 492–3
student accommodation accreditation schemes 227
Student Awards Agency for Scotland 200, 202
student budget 210
student credit card 209–10
student debt 198
student expenditure 208–10
student facilities, and league table 50–51
Student Finance England 201, 202
Student Finance NI 202
Student Finance Wales 202
student finance, and parents 244
student loans 200–202
  interest on 214
Student Loans Company 198, 202, 214
student overdraft 209–10
student satisfaction measure 28, 48, 49, 59
student–staff ratio measure 50
Student Visitor entry route 253
students' union 17, 29
studying abroad 40–46
  costs 40–41
  as part of UK degree 43, 46
studying costs 28–9, 209
subject selection 15–24
  earnings prospects 33, 36–7
  employment prospects 32–3, 34–5
  most applications 21
  most popular 21
  studied by international students 251–2, 255–8
Sunderland, University of 494–5
Supplementary Application Questionnaire, Cambridge 263
Support Funds, Northern Ireland 206
Surrey, University of 496–7
Sussex, University of 498–9
Swansea Metropolitan University 502–3
Swansea, University of 500–501
Talented Athletes Training Scheme 236
tariff, UCAS 17, 18
teaching quality 47, 59
Teesside, University of 504–5
Thames Valley University 506–7
theology and religious studies 181–3
Thinking Skills Assessment (TSA) 20
third semester 24
Tier 4 approved institutions 253
timetable
  application 192
  financial support 203
Tompkins Table, Cambridge 260

top-up fees 28–9, 244
tourism 130–32, 257
town and country planning and landscape 183–4
Track 193, 194
travel time to university 222
Trinity, Cambridge 292
Trinity, Oxford 276–7
Trinity Hall, Cambridge 292–3
Trinity Saint David, University of Wales 508–9
Trinity University College, Carmarthen 508–9
tuition fee grant, Wales, withdrawal of 200
tuition fees 199–200
  review 199
tuition fees loan 200–201
two-year degrees 24
UCAS
  application process 187–97
  Apply 188–91
  course code 189
  Extra 27, 194
  form, importance of 187
  personal statement 189–91
  reference 191
  Route B, end of 187
  tariff 17, 18, 50
  Track 193, 194
  website 17, 30, 196
UCL 514–15
UCLan 342–3
UK Clinical Aptitude Test (UKCAT) 20
Ulster, University of 510–11
unconditional offer 193
unemployment, and graduates 32, 33, 34–5
universities
  accommodation provided by 223–5
  best in world 43–5
  fees and bursaries 211–19
  league table 47–57
  most favoured by employers 33
  most popular with international students 250
  support for international students 254
  top for applications 27
University Alliance 28
university choice 15–16, 24–9
  and cost 28–9, 198–219

and the countries of the UK 25
and facilities 29
and location 25–6
non-academic factors 25
and tuition fees 199–200
and reputation of 28
schemes to enhance employability 33, 37–8
University College London 514–15
University College, Oxford 277
University for the Creative Arts 516–17
University of the Arts, London 512–13
University of Wales, Newport 442–3
university profiles, definitions 294–5
USA, studying in 41, 42
UWE, Bristol 520–21
UWIC 340–41
vacation work 207–8
veterinary medicine 185–6
visa regulations 253–4
vocational diplomas 18, 19
vocational subjects 19, 21–2
voluntary work 38, 206
Wadham, Oxford 277–8
Wales
  financial support 203–4
  tuition fee grant 212
  tuition fees 200
Wales, University of 295
Warwick, University of 59, 518–19
Welsh Bursary 203
Welsh students studying outside Wales 205
West of England, Bristol, University of 520–21
West of Scotland, University of 522–3
Westminster, University of 524–5
Winchester, University of 526–7
Wolfson, Cambridge 293
Wolverhampton, University of 528–9
Worcester, Oxford 278
Worcester, University of 530–31
work experience 38
work placement 38, 206
World of Work, Liverpool John Moores 37
York, University of 59, 532–3
York Award 38
York St John University 534–5
Young People's Learning Agency 207
Young Students' Bursary, Scotland 204
Z-scores 48